A Wild Perfection

A Wild Perfection

The Selected Letters of James Wright

Edited by Anne Wright and Saundra Rose Maley,

with Jonathan Blunk

Farrar • Straus • Giroux / New York

Farrar, Straus and Giroux
19 Union Square West, New York 10003

Portions of this book previously appeared in *The American Poetry Review*, *The Georgia Review*, *The Literary Review*, *New England Review*, and *The Virginia Quarterly Review*.

Owing to limitations of space, acknowledgments for permission to reprint previously published and unpublished material appear on page 633.

Library of Congress Cataloging-in-Publication Data
Wright, James Arlington, 1927–
    A wild perfection : the selected letters of James Wright / edited by Anne Wright and Saundra Rose Maley.— 1st ed.
      p. cm.
    Includes index.
    ISBN-13: 978-0-374-18506-0
    ISBN-10: 0-374-18506-9 (hardcover : alk. paper)
    1. Wright, James Arlington, 1927—Correspondence. 2. Poets, American—
20th century—Correspondence. I. Wright, Anne (Edith Anne). II. Maley,
Saundra Rose. III. Title.

PS3573.R5358Z48 2005
811´.54—dc22

                                     2004017488

Designed by Jonathan D. Lippincott

www.fsgbooks.com

10 9 8 7 6 5 4 3 2 1

To the Memory of Elizabeth Lyons, James's Beloved
Grandmother

To the Memory of W. Milne Holton

To the Happy Family

Do you happen to know Stanley Kunitz's poems? He hasn't had a wide reputation, but I like him tremendously. I'm going to review his newly published *Selected Poems* for *Sewanee*. I really think you would like his poems, and I think I'll type a couple of them for you on a separate sheet of paper, so that you can see what he's like. For a long time, virtually unnoticed and yet enduring, he's been writing poems of real agony and love in a kind of lost and transient underground of the American jungle of academies and businesses. I think that the appearance of his *Selected Poems* is inspiring. It shows that defeat, though imminent for all of us, is not inevitable. He wrote to me recently, since I know him slightly—and you might like his concluding words: ". . . it would be sweet, I'll grant, after all these years to pop up from underground. America, it's true, either spoils you with success or withers you with neglect. What other morality has the artist but to endure? The only ones who survive, I think, beyond the equally destructive temptations of self-praise and self-pity, are those whose ultimate discontent is with themselves. The fiercest hearts are in love with a wild perfection." Those words mean much to me. Please write.

Yours,
Jim

—from a letter to James Dickey
August 12, 1958

Contents

Foreword *by Anne Wright* / xi

Acknowledgments / xvii

Introduction: The Great Conversation *by Saundra Rose Maley* / xxi

Chronology *by Jonathan Blunk* / xxvii

Beginning (1946–1953) / 1

Be Glad of the Green Wall (1954–1958) / 53

The Fire of the Daemon (1958) / 101

Descent (1959–1962) / 195

A Time of Wandering (1964–1966) / 279

New York City (1966–1974) / 343

Roots and Wings (1975–1977) / 413

The Last Journey (1978–1979) / 485

Appendix / 553

Correspondents / 603

Index / 613

Foreword

When we were married in April of 1967, James brought over a small suitcase of clothes and a huge suitcase of books, papers, and letters from his room at the Regent Hotel to my railroad apartment on East Eighty-fifth Street. Once we were settled in what became "our" apartment, we bought a filing cabinet for our combined papers, most of which were James's. I organized all correspondence, drafts of poems, and various notes for our teaching jobs and tried to keep up with the rapid growth of additions.

Then, in the spring of 1973, Robert Bly sent thirty-four boxes of James's papers, which had been stashed away on the Bly farm for a good ten years. First we put the boxes in our storage unit, a former coal bin, and later, after a move across the street, on the fire stairs of our new apartment. James had full intentions to examine and sort the contents of each and every box, but never did.

James worked at my old desk in the screened-off portion of our bedroom in the railroad flat. When we moved, he finally had a study of his own, as well as a large, old-fashioned office desk left behind by former tenants. We even bought a second filing cabinet.

Mail was very important to James. I would come home from work to find the dining room table covered with opened letters. Often there would be penciled messages for me on the envelopes, such as "A good letter from our niece Karin," or "What can I do about this student? He breaks my heart," or "It'll be a cold day in hell before I read at this place!"

James made a great, if spasmodic, effort to keep in touch with good friends as well as young writers who sent their poems to him and asked for advice. He was particularly moved by a letter from seventeen-year-old Janice Thurn, who, in April of 1975, struck by his Minneapolis poems—that was the city where she lived—sent him copies of her work. They were to exchange many letters over the next four years.

However, there were still tall piles of unanswered letters in both his in- and out-boxes. To think of answering all the demands contained in such a voluminous amount of mail was impossible. It would have been an overwhelming task. James did what he could; he felt guilty when he couldn't reply to all the letters and happy when he did.

I was usually at my teaching job when James tackled work at his desk, so I did not have an opportunity to observe the ritual involved in the writing of poems and letters until we traveled to Europe. During those trips he would spend several hours after breakfast at the desk in our hotel room while I did some sightseeing. Then we'd meet at a café, have a cappuccino, and plan the rest of the day. Usually he'd arrive carrying a sheaf of answered letters in his hand, which he waved in the air to show me what he'd accomplished.

We traveled with a portable Olivetti, carried in a small blue suitcase nicknamed "the traveling desk." Beside the typewriter were small notebooks used as journals, carbon and typing paper, and a big brown envelope of mail. James kept a special notebook for carbon copies of all letters he wrote. I couldn't imagine why he wanted to keep copies, but now I know. Thank goodness he did!

After James's death in 1980 I had to go through the contents of all the boxes we'd stored on the fire stairs and the top of the study closet. I was fortunate to have the incomparable help of two graduate students, Keelin Curran and Nicholas Gattuccio. They loved James's work and respected each and every scrap of paper scattered across the floor of my living room. There seemed to be a million pieces of paper; most were drafts of poems, but many were letters. As I assimilated the contents of all the boxes, I discovered a different side of James from the man I had been married to for thirteen years. I learned new facts about his childhood and family and gained further insight into the important years at Kenyon College and the University of Washington in Seattle as well as his close friendships with fellow students and poets. I was exposed to both familiar and brand-new thoughts and ideas of James's on life, poetry, teaching, and politics, not to mention his own particular brand of witty and bawdy humor.

We filed all the letters to him in appropriate folders and examined several notebooks filled with carbon copies of his own letters. Apparently, James did keep a careful record of his correspondence from time to time, despite his inconsistency in answering mail.

For the last two years of his life, however, James was steadfast in his exchange of letters with the Native American writer Leslie Marmon Silko. Their correspondence is rich with discussions of the problems and pleasures of writing, family relationships, and reflections from the past. "A poem is a very odd duck," he explained to Leslie. "It goes through changes—in form and color—when you leave it alone patiently, just as surely as a plant does, or an animal, or any other creature." Leslie was a splendid storyteller, James an attentive listener who gave advice and encouragement.

In a letter from Bruges, Belgium, James described the small city and enclosed a lace-edged handkerchief, with these words:

> Sometimes I wonder about things like lace, things that human beings make with their own hands, things that aren't much help as shelter from the elements or against war and other kinds of brutality . . . Nevertheless the art continues to survive.

The Wright-Silko letters were published by Graywolf Press. The title, *The Delicacy and Strength of Lace*, reflects the above passage.

Once *The Delicacy and Strength of Lace* was published, I decided to compile a more extensive collection of letters with another book in mind. I was greatly inspired by a gift from Susan Lamb Graham, a friend and classmate from Martins Ferry High School, of James's early letters. The letters date from 1946, when he joined the peacetime army and served in Japan, until 1950, when he was a student at Kenyon College. The letters themselves were as touching as the fact that Ms. Graham had saved them all those years.

At first I was overwhelmed by the gigantic amount of work it would take to edit such a book. Fortunately, Saundra Rose Maley, an English professor from the Washington, D.C., area, was also interested in such a project, and we decided to become co-editors. I first knew Saundra when she was writing her Ph.D. thesis, *Solitary Apprenticeship*, on James's German translations. Ours was a wise and happy decision, for we work very well together. My respect and admiration for her written work, her constant enthusiasm, and her dedication to and love for James's work have continued to grow.

We had notebooks of carbon copies, the Wright-Silko letters, and those from Susan Lamb Graham for an excellent start. A number of friends and family members sent us copies of their letters from James. Among those who made this contribution are Sheri Akamine, Nicholas Crome, Liz Esterly, Roland Flint, Jack Furniss, Edward Harvey, Eugene Pugatch, Gibbons Ruark, Ann Sanfedele, Debra Thomas, Janice Thurn, and Helen Wright. James's letters to Theodore Roethke are part of the Roethke collection in the University of Washington Manuscript Department, while his letters to Wayne Burns, his friend and thesis adviser from that university, had already been published as *In Defense Against This Exile: Letters to Wayne Burns*, edited by John Doheny and published by Genitron Press in 1985.

A majority of the letters came from the Manuscript Division of the Elmer L. Andersen Library at the University of Minnesota in Minneapolis, where James's papers are housed. We will forever be indebted to Alan Lathrop, curator of manuscripts at the Andersen Library, for his interest and support. Barbara Bezat, his assistant, gave us invaluable help in searching out innumerable letters and was responsible for having them copied and sent to me in New York, always with great cheer and enthusiasm.

Wherever they came from, each batch of letters brought surprises similar to the ones I experienced when examining the long-stored collection of James's papers back in 1980. Most important was the story of James's life, which threaded its way through so many of the letters. Now I had a better understanding of dark times from the past and was reassured when reading of the pleasure he took in our travels, particularly through Italy. There were many examples of his raucous humor and irreverent comments for comic relief.

The highlight of our work on this volume came with the arrival of letters to Robert Bly, James Dickey, and Donald Hall. Mr. Chatham Ewing, curator of the modern literature collection in the Department of Special Collections at Washington University in St. Louis, supplied us with copies of James's letters to James Dickey. Donald Hall requested Mr. Roland Goodbody, curator of special collections at the University of New Hampshire Library, to send him his copies of James's letters, which, in turn, he sent to us. There are well over two hundred of these letters. Such a magnanimous gift reflects both

Mr. Hall's valuing of their close friendship and his great interest and generosity.

In the summer of 2002, after a trip to Minnesota, Jonathan Blunk brought back three dozen letters from James to Robert Bly. Then, in time for Christmas, Robert himself discovered a box of more than sixty letters from James tucked under the eaves in his attic. We all celebrated.

This was a high point of our work, and, together with the letters written to James Dickey and Donald Hall, these splendid and amazing documents make up the bulk of the section titled "The Fire of the Daemon." I doubt if there is another body of correspondence comparable to that of the four poets, who wrote to one another long before they actually met. The use of a typewriter and the postal system was common in the late fifties and early sixties, for it was an era long before E-mail and fax, when one still hesitated to call long-distance.

"I have never, thank God, regarded a poem as an absolutely finished thing," wrote James to Robert Bly. "I think critics who think a poem is absolutely finished once it appears in print are morticians."

In a letter to James Dickey, James pays tribute to the first meeting he had with Robert Bly and James Dickey in 1959: "I can't really describe what it meant to feel free to emerge into that tremendous, ample sunlight of noble and heroic men with whom I spent those three days, drinking the great green waters of the first and last seas."

Years later, in 1970, on our first of many visits to Paris, James sent a card to Donald Hall bearing this message: "Here I am—sitting in a café in Paris, happily writing to a beloved friend, just as I need and want to do."

"I'm a lousy correspondent," James once complained to Robert Mezey. "Write and stimulate me into prose." It was true. There were still stretches of time when James didn't answer letters but let mail pile up and spill over his desk. Then he'd experience a burst of renewed strength and enthusiasm, and I would hear the typewriter clatter away for several hours until he emerged from the study, pleased and relieved by all he had accomplished. He might even quote his father, Dudley Wright, with the comment "blessed work." For to him, too, work was a blessing.

"There is something about the form and occasion of a letter," he wrote to a friend, "—the possibility it offers, the chance to be as open and tentative and uncertain as one likes and also the chance to formulate certain ideas, very precisely—if one is lucky in one's thoughts." I feel James was usually very lucky in his thoughts, both spoken and written, and I am well aware how lucky I was to read and hear these thoughts for thirteen years. My life certainly changed when I met him and continues to change in abundant and wonderful ways as I do what I can to help his work go on. As we were rarely apart, I have only a few letters from James but many, many little notes. One such note was written to me after James finished reading a new book from our close friend Gibbons Ruark. He described how shaken he was by the work: "This man is real. So he's a real poet. There is no other kind."

The note ended with what might be construed as a poem:

>Poets pass on a chill spring
>and a dying fire to one another,
>but poetry is not a cheap trick.
>It is the true voice. It isn't an
>ornament flung random on life. It's
>the flowering of life, as Guillén said.

James Wright was a real poet who wrote real letters. He took the opportunity to be "open and tentative and uncertain" and to "formulate certain ideas, very precisely." We are all very, very lucky he did.

Anne Wright
Westerly, Rhode Island
Summer 2004

Acknowledgments

First and foremost, we shall always be eternally grateful to James Wright for making carbon copies of so many letters. Thank you! Thank you! Thank you!

We give very special thanks to Robert Bly, Nicholas Crome, Susan Lamb Graham, Donald Hall, Gibbons Ruark, and Janice Thurn for their generous contributions, as well as their enthusiastic and devoted interest.

Other contributors were Ted Wright's widow, Helen Wright; the biographer Diane Middlebrook; Kenyon and University of Washington classmates Jack Furniss, Lloyd and Gege Parks, and Eugene Pugatch; Kenyon College professor Edward Harvey; and two former students from the University of Hawaii, Sheri Akamine and Debra Thomas. Liz Esterly, daughter of Henry Esterly, supplied us with letters to both Henry and Elizabeth Willerton Esterly. Additional contributions came from friends George Allan Cate, George Lynes, Ann Sanfedele, and Betsy Fogelman Tighe, as well as from fellow poets Madeline DeFrees, Roland Flint, Merrill Leffler, Philip Levine, Robert Mezey, Leslie Marmon Silko, and Sander Zulauf.

Credit and grateful acknowledgment are also given to those who first published the following letters: Bobbs-Merrill Press, for a letter written to Robert Mezey in 1967, appearing in *Naked Poetry*, edited by Stephen Berg and Robert Mezey (1969); the publishers of *American Poets in 1976*, edited by William Heyen (1976), for letters to Donald Hall (September 25, 1973), Laura Lee (September 30, 1973), Karin East (November 9, 1973), and Franz Wright (November 27 and December 17, 1973); the publishers of *Ironwood* 15 (Spring 1980), edited by Michael Cuddihy, for a letter on H. R. Hays to Michael Cuddihy (September 16, 1979); Genitron Press, for letters to Wayne Burns (November 30, 1957; February 1, 1958; Spring 1958; June 19, 1958; and August 13, 1958) appearing in *In Defense Against This Exile*, edited by John Doheny (1985); Graywolf Press, for letters to Leslie Marmon Silko (October 12, 1978; March 14, 1979; June 15, 1979; and July 29, 1979) appearing in *The Delicacy and Strength of Lace* (1986); Logbridge-Rhodes Press, for letters to Betsy Fogelman (February 25, 1979), Donald Hall (March 7, 1979), Roger Hecht (March 7, 1979), Hayden Carruth (April 3, 1979), Franz Wright (April 6, 1979), Elizabeth Esterly (April 27, 1979), Richard Hugo (April 27, 1979), Franz Wright (May 4, 1979), Kay and Gibbons Ruark (June 6, 1979), and Janice Thurn (June 8, 1979), appearing in *James Wright: A Profile*, edited by Frank Graziano and Peter Stitt (1988); *Great River Review*, 1999–2000 (No. 31), from "Dear Jim: A Friendship in Correspondence" by Janice Thurn, for letters to her (May 4, 1976; September 25, 1976; February 26, 1977; June 7, 1978; and June 8, 1979); and W. W. Norton, for a letter to Henry Rago (November 25, 1959), appearing in *Dear Editor: A History of* Poetry *in Letters, The First Fifty Years, 1912–1962*, edited by Joseph Parisi and Stephen Young (2002).

In addition to our friends at the Andersen Library at the University of Minnesota, the University of New Hampshire Library (who include Alison Carrick), and the Department of Special Collections at Washington University in St. Louis, we also received gracious care and attention to our requests from Dr. Michael Basinski, curator of the poetry collections of the university libraries at SUNY Buffalo; L. Rebecca Johnson Melvin, associate librarian and coordinator of the Manuscript Unit, Special Collections Department, at the University of Delaware; Saundra Taylor, manuscripts curator in the Rare Books and Manuscripts Department of the Lilly Library at Indiana University, Bloomington; Tara Wenger, research librarian at the Harry Ransom Humanities Research Center at the University of Texas at Austin; and various members of the library staff at Kenyon College. We thank them very much. We also extend warm thanks to former Kenyon College librarian William Dameron, who took extremely good care of the James Wright Papers when they were on loan to Kenyon.

We also thank the following individuals who have supplied the photographs that grace the part-title pages: Carol Bly, Liberty Kovacs, Richard Pflum, Peter Simpson, and John Unterecker.

We have been the recipients of gracious hospitality from Ann Slayton and Merrill Leffler in Takoma Park, Maryland, and from Brother Rick Wilson, TOR, at St. Jerome Friary in Alexandria, Virginia.

Jonathan Blunk, the authorized biographer of James Wright, blazed a trail from Seattle to Minneapolis in pursuit of letters. He has expended much time and energy to proofread the manuscript again and again. In his position as consultant for Farrar, Straus and Giroux, he has given us support, enthusiasm, and wise advice. In his position as a friend, he has added humor and good spirits to our sessions of hard work.

Elizabeth Hoover spent the summer of 2003 preparing the manuscript in fair copy—a gargantuan task! Trudy Gerovske took up where she left off and helped immensely with many additions and revisions.

Our editor at Farrar, Straus and Giroux, Jonathan Galassi, has been a paragon of encouragement and support. He accepted the book in just four days, after reading a sample manuscript based on twenty-eight letters. His insight and great enthusiasm have kept us going. The good cheer and thoughtful input of his assistant, Annie Wedekind, have been most helpful, too.

Loving thanks go to friends who have been bastions of support, interest, and enthusiasm as they followed each and every turn of our adventure, from search to final selection. Saundra is especially grateful to George Allan Cate, Judith Serlin Cochran, and Gail Lowke. I thank my many involved friends from Wheelock College, the American Overseas School of Rome, and the Para-Educator Center, as well as those in New York City and Rhode Island; also the DeCinque family and James's many friends, in and out of poetry, who became my friends, too. We are both blessed. It's as if we had a crowd of supporters so numerous they could fill the arena in Verona many times over.

Anne Wright

Introduction: The Great Conversation

In a man's letters, his soul lies naked.
          —Samuel Johnson

James Wright was an immensely influential poet—he was also an omnivorous reader with a photographic memory. He loved discussing and quoting the writers he was devouring. Plato, Aristophanes, Dostoevsky, the author of *Beowulf*, Thomas Wolfe, Tolstoy, Nietzsche, Sterne, Dickens, Ortega y Gasset, Cather, and Orwell appear in these letters, as do poets from across the ages: Catullus, Horace, Sappho, Herrick, Heine, Edward Thomas, Rilke, Goethe, Whitman, Robinson, Hardy, Georg Trakl, César Vallejo, Jorge Guillén, Roethke, Louise Bogan—the list goes on. Wright read and wrote poetry for his very sustenance. That need had its origins before he entered Kenyon College and began his formal study of poetry in the late 1940s. Nick Crome, a classmate and lifelong friend, described the atmosphere at Kenyon, where Wright, who was several years older than most of his fellow undergraduates, was at the center of the Great Conversation, in which stories and poems and those who love them talk eternally with one another.

While the letters here give details of James Wright's life, they also tell the story of a deep thinker. Some letters read like crafted essays and reveal a side of Wright that he brought to the classroom, both as a student and later as a teacher. On his college entrance application, Wright wrote that he wanted to be a philosopher. Readers of his poems are aware of their startling images and idiosyncrasies, especially in *The Branch Will Not Break* and *Shall We Gather at the River*—the most frequently anthologized poems are taken from these books. Some may know the uneven power of the clipped and angry poems of *Two*

Citizens, or the gentler, more narrative turn his poems took in *To a Blossoming Pear Tree, Moments of the Italian Summer*, and *This Journey*, his final volume. These letters give us a vivid picture of the craftsman behind those poems who both agonized and reveled in his work.

Jorge Luis Borges once said that his idea of heaven was an enormous library full of books. In Wright's heaven, too, there are books, but there are also comfortable chairs for him and his friends to sit in as they converse. I am sure there are roomy armchairs for the writers already mentioned, and special places for his high school teachers Helen McNeely Sheriff and Elizabeth Willerton Esterly; his Kenyon teachers John Crowe Ransom, Philip Timberlake, Andre Hanfman, Philip Blair Rice, and Charles Coffin; his colleagues and friends at the University of Washington, Theodore Roethke and Wayne Burns; and those he knew and loved at the University of Minnesota, and later at Hunter College.

In my earlier study of Wright's work, I discovered the expanse of his intellect and craft; in these letters, I am most touched by his generosity of spirit. While working with Anne Wright to select from the hundreds we had collected, I had the opportunity to meet Wright in more intimate and startling ways. Keats wrote that he was "certain of nothing but of the holiness of the Heart's affections and the truth of Imagination." Wright's letters brim with these qualities.

James Wright may be among the last generation of poets whose letters we will have. In these years of the Internet, E-mail has fast become the common mode of writing. Once read, these communications are lost forever with a click of the Delete key. Fortunately for us, we have many of Wright's letters—full, expressive, and exploratory letters that document his part in the Great Conversation—what he calls in one letter to Miss Willerton "an open argument" that includes all poets, living and dead. Wright had this to say to Miss Willerton of his own letter writing:

> I suppose this letter, before it really gets finished, will run to many pages, and be typed on odd kinds of paper, all different. Some of it may be done on this lined stuff, some on typing paper, with various kinds of type, or composed in long hand with varying colors of ink or lead. On the other hand, the letter may end after a mere page or so. But you know the inconsis-

tency of form to be found in my correspondence. I like to write spontaneously. Letters can be very close to conversation; and hence they can be valuable.

As we read these letters, we pull our chairs into the circle and listen to both Wright's serious and comedic discussions of the relationships and rivalries of one of the great generations of American poets—with Wright at its center, where he belongs.

* * *

James Wright's initiation as a letter writer came naturally, as it did to many young men of his generation, when he joined the armed forces. When Wright enlisted in the army right out of high school and left the Ohio valley for the first time, World War II had just ended. During his training, he was selected for engineers' school and was stationed at various posts around the country until he eventually became part of the occupation forces in Japan. His letters home to family, friends, and teachers show a young man determined to continue the education he began at Martins Ferry High School. He read widely and wrote daily, mostly sonnets, while enduring the rigors of army life. In December 1946, a letter to Susan Lamb, a high school friend, suggests the breadth of his reading, while at the same time it gives us an example of his humor and his ability to blend the mundane and the majestic: "Will you be patient with the brevity of my letter? I am in the latrine, only a few moments ago having beaten the last line of Ovid to the floor."

In the course of working on this collection, Anne and I read hundreds of letters that came to us from various sources. We met several times a year, most often in Anne's light-filled living room in Manhattan or at her cottage in Rhode Island, where we worked our way through the letters chronologically. We would sit together, each with our own copies, stopping at predetermined points to discuss selections. More often than not, we agreed; when we didn't, we discussed a letter's merits or lack thereof.

Our criteria for selection were simple. We chose letters of literary and biographical importance, for their intrinsic interest, and, as our editor Jonathan Galassi counseled, for their readability as part of a narrative. We also wanted to include representative letters to as many correspondents as we could from Wright's wide circle of friends and acquaintances. The underrepresentation or absence of letters to some close friends—John Logan and David Ignatow come to mind—is not an oversight; owing to the fact that they lived in New York, Wright saw them frequently. Wright's letters demonstrate the care and concern he had for the work of his fellow poets. When friends, and even strangers, sent him their poems, he would respond with detailed and meticulous comments and critiques of their work, and when he closed a letter with the words "send poems," as he often did, he meant it.

Anne writes in her Foreword of our excitement at the arrival of more than sixty letters that Robert Bly found in his attic in the fall of 2003, including the first letter Wright had written to him in July 1958. I had wanted to see that letter since I met with Bly in 1987 to discuss his and Wright's collaborative work in translation. I had learned of the letter from an interview in which Wright mentioned writing to Bly out of sheer exhilaration at having seen the name of Georg Trakl in the first issue of Bly's magazine, *The Fifties*. Wright described his letter as "sixteen pages long and single spaced." I asked Bly then if he still had the letter, and he said he would look for it when he returned to Minnesota. It was not until 2003 that Bly finally found the box after being spurred to the nether reaches of his attic by a visit from Jonathan Blunk. After many years I had the opportunity to read that feverish first letter to Bly—"the one that almost got away." It was not as long as Wright remembered, but it was worth the wait. Anne and I had many such surprises. Another splendid moment came when we read a letter to Bly in which Wright mentions that Anne had come up with the title *To a Blossoming Pear Tree*—she had completely forgotten about that!

Wright's letters pull us into the heart of American poetry in the decades following World War II and show us his and his generation's struggles with the formalism of the New Critics, the great shadow cast by the Moderns, and their own desire to break new ground. Like many of his contemporaries, Wright knew his forms. He defends the iambic to Bly and talks of his attempts to bring the image into the iambic line. Writing to Donald Hall, he characterizes his vacillations between artistic poles in a prose that is intense and passionate, not to say hyperbolic:

> The two American poets who mean the most to me as an individual human being are, for God's sake, Whitman and Robinson! Now, stylistically they are as far apart as two men could be

and still write in the same language. I have never known how to fuse them; and so, as you are undoubtedly aware, having endured the very genuine hysterias of my correspondence for some years, I have helplessly and nauseously swung back and forth terrified by great space on the pendulum from the one to the other. Now, there was nothing wrong with this, and there was a time for me—as there was, inevitably, for every young poet writing in America right now—to commit himself to the traditional syntax and the traditional meters of English verse; for many of the writers who preceded us were so sloppy, that we had to begin not by revolting against competence and restriction, because except for a few writers there was no competence, but rather to begin by creating *our own* competence. Thus, the next step—the really terrifying one, the appalling one, the one that drags the blood, the real red blood, out of one's veins, is to move through and beyond that necessary competence into individual creation.

Wright also wrote tender, philosophical, and instructive letters that are often at their most revealing when he was traveling. The distance gave him the quiet space he needed to express deep feelings. Early letters to Susan Lamb, for instance, read like love letters; they included poems he had written to her. But Susan told Anne that on one visit to her house when he was on leave from the army, Wright sat in her living room without speaking a word.

So we have the letters to fill the silent spaces. When I first read Wright's poems, I was drawn to their searing rightness and simplicity by a magnetic force. Over the years, and in these letters, I have come to know and appreciate the magnitude of the mind and spirit behind that force. The letters collected here reflect a fraction of what James Wright wrote. Though some have been lost or destroyed and others may surface in the future, we are confident that this collection offers a well-rounded picture of Wright's life and his thoughts on poetry, friendship, his country, and literature.

* * *

I have dedicated my part in this work to the late W. Milne Holton, professor of English at the University of Maryland. It is to him that I ultimately owe the privilege of co-editing these letters. Nearly twenty years ago I waltzed into his office to discuss my choice for a dissertation topic. I had scribbled three names on a scrap of paper. Professor Holton quickly dismissed them. Then I timidly suggested James Wright, whose poems I had been introduced to in the late sixties in a course on poetics with Rod Jellema. Holton, who had the most expressive eyebrows I've ever seen, sat forward in his chair, eyebrows lifted nearly to his bald pate, and said excitedly, "Yes, James Wright! Get out there and see what you can find and come back to see me next week!" Well, the weeks turned into years and I kept going back. Though I cursed him many times over, Holton held my feet to the fire, and I'm grateful that he did. Although the work on the dissertation took much longer than I expected, the journey led me into the heart of James Wright's poetry, and fortunately, too, it led me to Anne Wright. Thank you, Professor Holton!

Saundra Rose Maley
Washington, D.C.
Fall 2004

Chronology

1927 Born James Arlington Wright, December 13, on Union Street in the Aetnaville section of Martins Ferry, Ohio, an industrial town on the western shore of the Ohio River, five miles north of Wheeling, West Virginia. Father, Dudley Wright (born 1893), labored as a die-cutter at the Hazel-Atlas Glass Company in Wheeling his entire working life. Mother, Jessie Lyons Wright (born 1897), came from a large, poor farming family in West Virginia. Siblings include adopted sister Marge (born 1918), older brother Ted (born 1925), and younger brother Jack (born 1934).

1932–41 Attends public schools in Martins Ferry; family moves frequently within the town during the Depression and early World War II period. Wright is eight years old at the time of the historic flood in March 1936. Around the age of twelve, he is introduced to the poetry of Byron.

1942–45 In 1942, death of maternal grandmother, Elizabeth Lyons, with whom he was close. Misses a year of school due to nervous breakdown. Returns to his sophomore year in high school in September 1943, determined to attend college. Encouraged by his Latin teacher, Helen McNeely Sheriff, and his English teacher, Elizabeth Willerton Esterly, with whom he maintains lifelong friendships. Wright's translations from Latin poets lead to his writing his own original first poems.

1946–47 Enlists in the U.S. Army immediately upon graduating high school in June 1946, recognizing the opportunity presented by the GI Bill. Travels around the country for the first time, to training camps in Washington State and Virginia, before deployment in the occupation army in Zama, Japan. Continues rigorous course of independent study, reading widely in philosophy and world literature and writing constantly. Discharged in the fall of 1947, he returns to his family's new home, a small subsistence farm fifteen miles west of Martins Ferry in Warnock, Ohio.

1948–51 Enrolls in Kenyon College in Gambier, Ohio, in January 1948 at the suggestion of a fellow soldier, Jack Furniss. Teachers include John Crowe Ransom, Philip Timberlake, Charles Coffin, and Philip Blair Rice; Roger Hecht, Robert Mezey, E. L. Doctorow, and Eugene Pugatch are among his close friends. Becomes fluent in German and begins translations of Goethe, Heine, Hesse, Rilke, and others. Poems (including "Father") accepted by Ransom for publication in *The Kenyon Review* (Autumn 1951). Awarded the Robert Frost Poetry Prize.

1952 Graduates magna cum laude, with high honors in English, from Kenyon in January, having written a thesis on Thomas Hardy. Marries high school classmate Liberty Kardules in Martins Ferry in February and teaches the spring semester at the Tenney School in Center Point, Texas. Receives a Fulbright Scholarship and sails for Europe in September to study German literature at the University of Vienna.

1953 Continues translating the work of Theodor Storm and encounters the poetry of Georg Trakl. A son, Franz, is born in Vienna in March; the family returns to America in June. Wright enrolls in graduate school at the University of Washington in Seattle in September.

1954–56 Begins study with Theodore Roethke and, later, Stanley Kunitz. Other teachers include Robert Heilman and Wayne Burns, who becomes his adviser for his doctoral dissertation. The poets Carolyn Kizer, Richard Hugo, and David Wagoner are among his friends and classmates. Begins lifelong correspondence and friendship with Donald Hall; publishes poetry widely in national journals and periodicals. Also publishes the critical essay "Meditations on René Char." Receives his M.A. in poetry and continues work toward his doctorate, studying the English novel. W. H. Auden selects Wright's manuscript *The Green Wall* as recipient of the Yale Series of Younger Poets award.

1957 *The Green Wall* is published by Yale University Press. Begins teaching at University of Minnesota in Minneapolis in September, with classes in both the English and humanities departments. Colleagues include Allen Tate, John Berryman, and Sarah Youngblood, with whom he continues to work on translations of Rilke.

1958 A Kenyon fellowship grant affords him a break from teaching to complete his dissertation. Begins brief career as a "hack-reviewer" to supplement his family's income, initiating an important correspondence and friendship with James Dickey. Second son, Marshall, is born in July. Meets Robert Bly and his wife, Carol, and begins frequent visits to their farm in western Minnesota on weekends; works on translations of Trakl with Bly. In fall, travels on a reading tour across the Northeast.

1959 Receives Ph.D. from the University of Washington with dissertation titled "The Comic Imagination of the Young Dickens." Marital problems lead to first separation from his wife. Hospitalized for a nervous breakdown in summer; heavy drinking first recognized as a problem by friends and associates. Second collection of poems, *Saint Judas*, published by Wesleyan University Press. Receives National Institute of Arts and Letters award. Continues immersion in Spanish and Latin American poetry and extensive work in translation.

1960–61 Withdraws new manuscript, *Amenities of Stone*, after it was accepted for publication by Wesleyan. *Twenty Poems of Georg Trakl*, translated with Robert Bly, published by Bly's Sixties Press in 1961. Begins summer teaching appointments at Moorhead State, outside Fargo, North Dakota.

1962 Divorce finalized; in August Liberty moves to San Francisco with Franz and Marshall. *The Lion's Tail and Eyes*, including ten new poems (together with work by Robert Bly and William Duffy), and *Twenty Poems of César Vallejo* (translations by Wright, Bly, and John Knoepfle), both published by Sixties Press. Louis Simpson, Donald Hall, Fred Manfred, and John Logan are among the visitors to the Bly farm and become good friends of Wright's.

1963–64 *The Branch Will Not Break* published by Wesleyan. Receives notice from University of Minnesota in May that he has been denied tenure; begins teaching at Macalester College in Saint Paul in September. New American Library (under the editorship of E. L. Doctorow) publishes *The Rider on the White Horse*, a translation of selected novellas and short stories by Theodor Storm. Wright later acknowledges that this work sustained him through a period of intense depression; friendships with Roland Flint, Isabella Gardner, and C. W. Truesdale also important.

1965 Postpones a Guggenheim Fellowship until June to honor his teaching commitments at Macalester; travels to California to visit his sons and to stay with Elizabeth Esterly and her husband. Visits with his parents in Ohio before settling in New York City at the suggestion of his close friend Roger Hecht; works steadily on a new collection of poems.

1966 Participates in the Poets Against the Vietnam War readings organized by Robert Bly and David Ray around the country. Through the sponsorship of Alan Mandelbaum, begins teaching at Hunter College in the fall, where he becomes a tenured professor with classes in both English literature and humanities. Meets Galway Kinnell and Edith Anne Runk, a schoolteacher with whom he begins a courtship.

1967 Marries Anne in April; teaches a summer session in Milwaukee, Wisconsin, before traveling to Minnesota, Ohio, and California. Couple begins tradition of retreats to Lake Minnewaska outside of New Paltz, New York, before resuming their teaching in September.

1968–69 *Shall We Gather at the River* published by Wesleyan; Sixties Press publishes *Twenty Poems of Pablo Neruda*, translated with Robert Bly. Returns to Milwaukee to teach summer session in 1968; the following summer, teaches at the State University of New York at Buffalo; continues reading tours around the country.

1970 A Rockefeller Foundation grant and an Ingram Merrill Foundation grant release him from a semester of teaching; travels with Anne for ten weeks to Italy, France, Austria, and Yugoslavia. Translation of *Poems* by Hermann Hesse published by Farrar, Straus and Giroux.

1971–72 *Collected Poems* published by Wesleyan; elected a fellow of the Academy of American Poets. Awarded the Pulitzer Prize in poetry for *Collected Poems*; invited to join the American Academy of

Arts and Letters; translations of poems and prose by Hermann Hesse with son Franz published as *Wandering* by Farrar, Straus and Giroux. Meets Pablo Neruda in New York City. Returns to Seattle to give the Theodore Roethke Memorial Poetry Reading in May. Receives the Melville Cane Award from the Poetry Society of America.

1973 Father dies in August; Farrar, Straus and Giroux publishes *Two Citizens*; travels for seven months in England, France, Italy, and Austria; begins to write prose pieces that become central to his work.

1974 Mother dies in March; Kenyon awards him an honorary Doctor of Humane Letters degree in May; first appearances of prose pieces in periodicals. Teaches another summer session in Buffalo, but is hospitalized in September due to mental stress and exhaustion. Upon release, begins attending AA meetings.

1975 Interview and new poems published in *The Paris Review* as "The Art of Poetry XIX." Hospitalized in November for acute gastritis.

1976 Dryad Press publishes *Moments of the Italian Summer*. Contributes to *American Poets in 1976*, edited by William Heyen; travels to University of Hawaii in Honolulu to teach in the summer, visiting with John Logan and W. S. Merwin.

1977 *Ironwood* 10, edited by Michael Cuddihy, is devoted entirely to the work of James Wright. Participates in a seminar on Chinese poetry in New York City in April organized by Betty Kray; travels in France and Italy throughout the summer. Farrar, Straus and Giroux publishes *To a Blossoming Pear Tree*.

1978 Distinguished Guest Professor at the University of Delaware in Newark for the fall semester; his good friend Gibbons Ruark also teaches there. Begins correspondence with Leslie Marmon Silko (published posthumously as *The Delicacy and Strength of Lace*). Receives a second Guggenheim Fellowship. Wrights attend Christmas Eve services at Chartres Cathedral, beginning nine months of travel in Europe.

1979 After visiting with Galway Kinnell and his family, Wrights continue leisurely travels throughout France and Italy, with extended stays in Verona, Venice, Fano, and Sirmione. Spends month of

August in Paris. Returns to New York to teach at Hunter in September; gives final public reading at Harvard in October. In December, chronic sore throat diagnosed as cancer of the tongue.

1980   In January, attends White House tribute to American poets and poetry hosted by President Jimmy Carter and First Lady Rosalynn Carter. Completes manuscript for his final collection of poems. Enters Mount Sinai Hospital in Manhattan, where he decides on the title *This Journey* and requests that the manuscript be shown to Galway Kinnell, Robert Bly, Donald Hall, Robert Mezey, and Hayden Carruth. Dies on March 25 at Calvary Hospital; buried in Woodlawn Cemetery in the Bronx.

—Compiled by Jonathan Blunk

Beginning

1946–1953

James Wright, circa 1946

I began in Ohio.
I still dream of home.
—from "Stages on a Journey Westward"

At Fort Lewis, Washington,
Twelve years ago, when I was eighteen,
We fired all day long at practice targets
And wounded one of our own men.
When I ran to help him,
I saw a whole gray earth
Opening in a vein of his cry:
From full green to emptiness,
A mile's field of dead fir stumps
High as the level of adolescent waists,
Low as a man's knees.
We had mown a grove down.
I was one of the State's gardeners.
—from "The Trees in Minnesota"

As far as the school proper is concerned, Jack and I both are supremely satisfied. The caliber of the teachers is evidently very excellent, and consequently the requirements are stiff. We shall be expected to wrestle with the books often and with energy if we want to retain our feeling of intelligence.
—from a letter to the parents of Jack Furniss
February 29, 1948

The earliest of James Wright's letters to be found were written in the spring of 1946. One is to his high school English teacher, Elizabeth Willerton, and the other is to her friend Professor James L. McCreight. In each letter James discussed plans to enlist in the service and presented personal views on Latin poetry, his great love.

James enlisted in the army that summer. After completing basic training, he served with the peacetime army in Japan. He continued to read, study, translate the works of Catullus, and admire not only Latin poetry but poetry in general. He also wrote to his parents, Jessie and Dudley Wright; Susan Lamb; and Elizabeth Willerton.

Susan Lamb, later Graham, was a classmate from Martins Ferry High School. She and James had worked together on the yearbook staff of the 1946 *Ferrian*, he as editor and she as assistant editor. He often included a sonnet or translation in his letters to her. Elizabeth Willerton, later Esterly, was portrayed by James as a teacher who "introduced her high school students to literature with a clarity and intelligence, a kind of summons to enter whatever nobility there is in the human race, with something very like genius."

After he was discharged from the army, James returned to his family, who had moved from Martins Ferry to a farm at nearby Warnock. "As for home," he wrote Susan Lamb, "I am situated on a farm, plopped down in the wilderness about fifteen miles out of Bellaire. The atmosphere suits me famously. I have music for passivity, books for activity and a free-thinking mother for conversation."

James met Jack Furniss, a young man from Ohio, while in the army. Furniss recommended Kenyon College in Gambier, Ohio, to James, and they both were accepted, enrolling as freshmen in January 1948. James formed close friendships with many fellow classmates, including Albert Herzing, E. L. Doctorow, Roger Hecht, Robert Mezey, and Eugene Pugatch. Equally strong bonds were formed with his teachers John Crowe Ransom, Philip Timberlake, and Andre Hanfman. Most of these friendships were to last throughout his life.

The letters written during his four years at Kenyon reveal James's scholarship, growing interest in music, and broadened exposure to literature. After graduating from Kenyon in January of 1952, James married Liberty Kardules, a fellow student at Martins Ferry High School. The young couple went to Center Point, Texas, where James taught for a semester at the Tenney School, and then sailed for Europe that fall, as James had been accepted at the University of Vienna in Austria as a Fulbright Scholar. Their son Franz was born there on March 18, 1953.

In the spring of 1953 James sent a highly detailed six-page letter to Robert Mezey. It was handwritten in the cramped but neat style that James would employ throughout his life. The first four pages contain extensive comments on a group of Mezey's poems, including one very long one. The last two pages, which are included here, offer both advice and encouragement to Mezey. The end of the letter divulges James's own thoughts on Vienna and America as seen from a new and distant perspective. The letter closes with loving words about his new son.

To James L. McCreight

Martins Ferry, Ohio
Spring 1946

Dear Professor McCreight:

Of course, by this time, you have forgotten our discussion of Latin and English poetry. Still, ponder a moment and recall me as the rather wild-eyed young man whose conception of the Muses stirred you to send him a volume of Catullus.

As I told you, I discovered Catullus in a Caesar book during my second year of Latin, and the white gush of nobility in his lines ate at me considerably. Perhaps his ability to create poetical images could not approach that of Virgil, or even that of the more sensible Horace, but his cries, such as:

> —*nam tui Catulli;*
> *plenus sacculus est aranearum.*

—charged me with a weird hunger, such as that created by Chopin or Poe.

I have included with this letter a few translations, or paraphrases. They do not cling to his purity; no translation, however perfect, can do that, for a poet's balancing of his native tongue is shocked by a translation, and can scarcely be reconstructed.

Your kindness in sending me the books has given me the courage to include, also, a work which I consider my most mature. The defects in my "Elegies" are very apparent. I am conscious, in my re-reading of them, of a clumsy straining after effect. But in no other attempt have I so utterly succeeded in speaking for myself, and I am convinced that any originality which exists in them is valuable enough to overshadow their weaknesses. As you read them, you will be conscious of the absence of a syllable here and there, and even of the discarding of iambics altogether. I would rather sacrifice technical skill than sincerity. And I have let the rhythm of emotion govern many of the lines rather than the rhythm of Milton.

Within a few days I shall undergo a physical examination for the Navy. If I pass, I shall be two years removed from a formal education. However, I hope to become well situated, so that I may work more with Catullus, and thus keep Latin alive within me.

If you will pardon the colloquialism, I don't understand why I continue my writing of these damned verses. I tell myself that I care little or nothing for people's opinions, but my vanity prods me toward attempts at publication.

Most likely, I shall starve, a degenerate.

Thank you again for your consideration in sending the poems of Catullus. His songs are pure gold, and he will live forever.

Thank you,
Jim Wright
Kuckuck Lane, Stop 4
Martins Ferry, Ohio

To Elizabeth Willerton

Martins Ferry, Ohio
Spring 1946

Dear Miss Willerton:

Having nearly lost count of time and space, I have no idea when this letter may reach you. Yet, the thing must be written, and the boil must be squeezed.

John Harrison and I have been barred from the Navy, because of our eyesight. Whether or not we shall pursue the Army, I cannot say. For God's sake! I don't know where to turn. If I attempt to attend school, the draft will surely suck me up. Still, I am almost certain that I can scrabble through one year on what I have saved. My longing for Latin is deeper than ever now, since I have assembled a vocabulary large enough to read the beautiful volume of Catullus not only with pleasure, but with a great deal of fire.

Among his lyrics I discovered a sweet little song which weighs the merits of a lovely Gallic maiden with the beauty of Lesbia. His hendecasyllables are without blemish, and so I used the same meter in my translation. The spondee, the dactyl, and the three sparkling trochees ripple quickly but in a loosely hung rhythm, like a flicker of light. Also I have paraphrased his "spring song" into iambics, which hardly do justice to its purity. O for a tongue like Latin, full of thunder, each word being supported by its separate classical marble column!

You will be interested to hear that I have only recently completed the reading of Thomas Wolfe's novel, *Look Homeward, Angel*. I have nothing to say. Only I would give my tongue for a chance to review it with you. It confirms a wild idea of mine: that Tom Wolfe and William Saroyan are two of America's greatest poets, although their genius ran, and is flowing, through the medium of prose.

I found Wordsworth's "Idiot Boy" as nauseating as you declared, but I turned thereupon to his sonnets, and again I found him to be what a low and ancient whisper had long before claimed: that, regardless of any allusion to degeneracy, William Wordsworth was a noble poetic spirit, and his sonnets rank with any cry in their weird simplicity of effervescence. Damn the disillusion after the French Revolution! Damn the reversion to the Tories! Damn the "Idiot Boy"!

Wordsworth is alive.

Finally, I acknowledged Professor McCreight's gracious act in sending me the Catullus volume. In response to his invitation I sent him my nine "Elegies," together with a few translations from Catullus.

Forgive me for being so damnably self-centered in this letter, but this siege of walking the streets, cursing through teeth, browsing nervously through the library, and speaking Latin into the wind while riding in an automobile will wreck me thoroughly unless I speak.

I still have two of your books in my possession, and somehow I must return them. Speaking of books, I have obtained a copy of Housman's posthumous poems. Among them is included a review of Housman by Christopher Morley.

Please, O please be patient with the two or three sonnets I send. They are weak, but I cannot escape writing them.

And please write to me. Touch me with your beauty, the longed-for, the sought-for, the found beauty; for it is an ancient beauty, such as a man, being a diluted poet, may scarcely come upon in a world like the one into which I have fallen.

Your warm friend,
Jim Wright

To Jessie Lyons Wright

Fort Lewis, Washington
July 28, 1946

Dear Mother,

Since this is the weekend, and since I passed yesterday's inspection all right, I'll write again today. I just returned from church, and I am enclosing the bulletin. The chapel here is a beautiful building, built just like any simply constructed church. The men fill it for every Sunday morning service.

Weariness and fatigue are rapidly losing their grip on me, and only the quick, heavily striking tiredness remains. But this tiredness comes only in spasms. We go to sleep after a rough day, thinking that in the morning we shall be so damned stiff that we won't be able to make reveille, and yet, when the CQ charges and gallops through the barracks at 5:30 a.m., beating his gums and blaring his varied screams, we leap from bed, dress, wash up, sweep, mop, make beds, and fly out to formation and to chow in such a crazy hurry that we forget that yesterday we were tired. By that time, it is too late. After healthy exertion, sleep seems to charge a man's battery.

I hope things are fine at home. My mail is beginning to seep through a little, but I could use more. You must understand how much even one flimsy letter means, after hearing the soft purrings of the drill corporal.

I'll write again later. I just wanted to let you know that everything is fine.

Love to everyone,
Jim

P.S. Get Jack and Pop to write.
P.P.S. Don't forget to tell Marge to write, too.
P.P.P.S. And, most important, *you* write!!

Fort Lewis, Washington
August 5, 1946

Dear Mother,

I received letters from you and Pop today, and in yours you told me to ask for anything I wanted. My wishes are still for the same things: Miss Willerton's address and the poems of Gerard Manley Hopkins. Don't forget that, if you cannot find that particular poet, I want you to send my copy of *Sonnets from the Portuguese* by Elizabeth Barrett Browning. These would certainly make me feel much better.

Don't misunderstand. Physically and mentally I am in fine condition. I can toss the heavy rifle around now like a toothpick. But, being my mother, you know that I am a little off balance, and that I require vast chunks of fuel to sate my imagination, which very often rushes hot as a furnace.

I see Sebastian about every night, and we surely have enjoyable talks.

I must hit the sack now. Please write soon, and tell the others to do the same. I would write to each of them, but my minutes are jammed completely full.

I am sending Sunday's Chapel bulletin.

Love,
Jim

To Susan Lamb

Fort Lewis, Washington
August 7, 1946

Dear Susan,

Finally I have torn away from the company area, for the sake of writing in peace. To sit in the Service Club Library is a relief, because my bones still ache from today's detail. The First Sergeant caught a few of us who had hung up our trousers without buttoning them, and he had us scrub-down the outside of the barracks. Next time I'll remember.

Susan, have you ever read the poems of Thomas Chatterton? He lived just before the time of Keats, and he wrote some lyrics that are marvelous. But the fact that shocked me sharply was that he was only *seventeen* years of age at his death! John Keats was devoted to his writing, and dedicated an exquisite sonnet to him.

This afternoon I sat alone in the barracks behind my bed near the wall, and I was just weary enough to permit remembrances of beauty [to] flood over me. I was so lonely and lost, and so desperate for love of Something unknown, misunderstood, that I thought of Keats—not of the poet of sensuous color, but of John Keats, the confused little boy who loved his life, but was more passionately devoted to his death.

He said:

> Verse, fame, and beauty are intense indeed,
> But Death intenser; Death is Life's high meed.

And suddenly I wanted to see him, to talk the whole mess over with him, for he would understand. But I called, and he was dead.

Susan, will you please read my sonnet?* I am conceited and self-centered with no justification, but please hear my outpouring.

And will you write soon?

Jim

Fort Lewis, Washington
September 3, 1946

Dear Susan,

For several weeks now I have pummeled my head bluntly against a wall. There were a hundred million words in me, each one separately raising its singular hell, but finding no medium of effluence. Now it seems that, since I have released from myself the puerile foolishness, the uncontrollable impossibility of which I wrote in two or three letters, the words are flooding outward like venous blood. Indeed, this afternoon I felt so fluidly facile that I dipped into a rhythmic form which I had come to consider not only lost to me, but irrevocable. This is the hendecasyllabic line, the peculiarly marvelous hippety-hop cadence which Catullus popularized in his love lyrics. I have not forgotten much of the dear purity of Catullus. Just before I came to the Army, I wres-

*See Appendix, p. 555, for the poem "To Keats."

tled with many translations which I had already completed, and with a few that somehow I had missed, endeavoring to retain in English a larger share of Catullus' spirit by utilizing his own favorite metre.

The poem which I enclose is not a translation, nor is it even a paraphrase. It is merely more outpouring of guts on paper, concerning which I received your permission several weeks ago.

It is not a poem, nor a lyric of any sort, but only a release. I hope you will not receive it as more of the silliness which you have probably already laughed off. Just read it, aloud or silently, hide it in an old dictionary, burn it, sell it to one of the 10¢ pulp magazines, or whatever you like. At least it is out of me, and through it I can more clearly recall Catullus. I must surely not be akin to him, because, although he most deliciously soared upon his physical and spiritual consciousness, he never was the brutal sensualist which my corruption of his form has shown me to be.

> Yours, apologizing for this interpolation of boredom,
>
> Jim

> Washington, D.C.
> October 5, 1946

Dear Susan,

The whole weekend is mine, and at the moment I am in the United Nations Service Center in Wash., D.C. This afternoon my two friends, from Missouri and California, and I floated around the city, and we are very tired. I feel as though I must write now to someone, not concerning anything in particular, but only for the sake of pouring, pouring, pouring.

I wonder if ever, in my whole idea of things, I can trade with someone, this whipped-up agony of love of life. Now, in music I have found in you a deeply gratified passion. In poetry for poetry's sake I have sent echoes down the entire universe through Miss Willerton. Believe me, if I hadn't been able to write to you, I would have died. But there is something else, and I don't even understand how to describe it. I shall try.

I love to be alive. For me it was ever a rare holiness to lie down at night, and to draw into my breast a long deep breath, just before I went to sleep. There was an open sidewalk, laid bare to wind, along the streetcar line parallel to Wheeling Steel in Martins Ferry, and in the rain I used to walk straight against the wind, and lashed into a shakiness by its breath, I sang and prayed and cried to myself a hundred thousand times. It was because I love the earth and my chance to live on it that I used to lay my rifle down in the Washington forests, and stroke my fingers through the needles and dirt. Lines of poetry from Thomas Wolfe, mighty, burly cries by Caesar, a fiery scream by Byron or Brooke—all used to set me pacing the floor.

Flooding my tired feet with hot water—tasting buttermilk after awaking from sleep—listening to "Claire de Lune"—smelling newly-ground coffee—singing as I washed my face—touching a dog's fur—seeing hair blow in the wind, glittering in the sun—these describe the undescribable for me. I love them, but such is common. The miracle is that often I hate them, too, only to run back blindly, falling at their feet with a more fierce love than ever.

Do you see? Do you understand? I love it, the whole wild, senseless, confused, dying mess of my life, and I don't even know why.

Please answer—O, please, Susan. Answer often, if you can, because I need you, more deeply than I can write or you can realize.

Is my reasoning so blasphemous?

Jim

Fort Belvoir, Virginia
October 13, 1946

Dear Susan,

Yesterday afternoon my two friends and I crossed the long bridge beyond the Lincoln Memorial, and wandered silently through the stillness of Arlington Cemetery. As we stepped up the marble shelter encircling the amphitheatre the autumn heaven throttled the air with a gloom, and we only slid past the columns when the rain began. Even with the gnarled groves bent down by the sheets of wind and water, and the yellow leaves shot like bullets beneath the huge marble panel, whereon is carved the thoughtful remark of Horace:

Dulce et decorum est pro patria mori.

—we beheld it: the bed of that nameless young man who is asleep, and cannot very well enjoy his honor.

We watched the guard change, and in a few moments we charged wildly down through the torrent to the bus stop.

Susan, a little earlier I had stood beneath a column at the rear of the Lincoln Memorial, and gazed across the Potomac at the wooded area wherein is enclosed the monument to Sheridan. And a wind was blowing, and over the bridge a bird was fighting it, and I heard music that I had believed dead in me.

Because I was moved yesterday, and because I thought more clearly than usual, this morning I wrote something for you. It seems that all the beauty and nobility which I have seen have given me a little conviction. Finally, I have a solidness on which to stand [. . .]

Goodbye for the moment.

Love,
Jim

Fort Belvoir, Virginia
December 2, 1946

Dear Susan,

Will you be patient with the brevity of my letter? I am in the latrine, only a few moments ago having beaten the last line of Ovid to the floor.

This afternoon I received your letter of Nov. 30. Thank you, Susan. I was damned sure that the absence of your letters was due only to the fact that you were busy. Did you enjoy Thanksgiving? I believe you must have done so, for you have a splendid capacity for enjoying your life. Please continue to write to me, and always tell me of your love of life. You have no idea how it keeps me at ease.

I intend to write again the first chance I get.

I have enclosed my little tale from Ovid.* I want you to read it first, for I have discovered your warmth in the same manner as Pygmalion found his—in the soundless depth of beauty, in the singular echo of understanding.

Please write.

Love,
Jim

*See Appendix, p. 556, for the poem "Sonnet—Peace."

To Elizabeth Willerton

Zama, Japan
January 6, 1947

Dear Elizabeth,

Tonight I felt lousy. Therefore I turned to Catullus for a sea in which to drown. This lyric (other side), an ode by a very sensitive and young poet to Lesbia's pet sparrow, is the first paraphrase I have attempted in weeks.* I tell you, Catullus is as dear to me as are sleep and music.

Please look for neither ecstasy nor a moral in my paraphrase. It is only a softly mournful remark, and the Latin is unspeakably gorgeous. Catullus therein created a line which sings thus:

Et solaciolum sui doloris.

Elizabeth, read this line aloud. The relationship between the "l's" and "o's" is a miracle of liquid floating ecstasy.

Forgive me. I told you my mood was crazy again.

The lights are going out.

I shall not sleep well. Catullus and I are pacing the floor.

Love,
Jim

To Susan Lamb

Zama, Japan
March 24, 1947

Dear Susan,

There is nothing this evening except the usual thrum of silence. Honestly I have endeavored to quell the spasm of my writing for the sake of reading the darker realisms which I have so long evaded for more explosive thoughts. Susan, I have plunged deeper into Dostoyevsky; I have tried to absorb some of the brutal richness of the Negro, Richard Wright; I have undertaken an analysis of the style of John O'Hara; and tonight I intend to begin a churning dive toward reading and studying Thomas Wolfe's last novel, *You Can't Go Home Again.* If my

*See Appendix, p. 557, for the poem "Ode to Lesbia's Pet Sparrow—Catullus, 15."

14

letters savor of any undue unhappiness, it is surely a reflection of my reading and of my struggle against the romanticism toward which I tend. How I long for realism! On the other side of realism, somewhere, lies the Nirvana.

Please do not think me aimless. I fully realize that there is no door for my writing. So desperately I need to be alive that somehow I believe my whole life to be only a long heavy period of studying and writing and drowning in the sensualism which is the surest pivot for the piercing dream.

You must know that I shall need to attend school when I leave the army. Of course, I shall not remain for long; but nowhere else will I ever find a single chance of sleeping beneath the controlled brilliance of Catullus, for whom I own an honest and a genuine love.

I am lost, Susan. I feel that I am pretty far gone by now. But I want to be sure that you know and understand this: In my dreaming, in my reading, in my writing—in my every concept of the undissolved ghost which must be the answer and the hope to my life, and thus to the life of everyone who lives, and has lived, on the earth—you are the warm body of a girl, the comfortable face, the sleep, and the smoothing pool into whom I have been sure that I can pour unrefined all of my longings, my physical passions (of which the spiritual are only projections), my frustrations, and the unhappy, strange explosions of beauty and truth which through your letters have quickened these quavering days of my early manhood. For these reasons, I love you, Susan. If you do not desire to have me love you to such a length, please write of it to me. There it is, as clearly as I can say it.

Will you write to me?

Love,
Jim

To Elizabeth Willerton Esterly

Gambier, Ohio
May 10, 1949

Dear Elizabeth,

After a long period of silence, I have here only a short note to accompany the three large envelopes of typescript which I want to ask you to take. A word or two of explanation is not even necessary, I know. It never has been, with you. You always understand the weirdest actions—probably (certainly) because a human being is likely to do anything at all. However, here are a few stage directions for my action:

I began these, as a series of apprentice compositions, about the middle of last July. In them, I tried, more than anything else, to maintain the rude energy, the directness. In the early pieces, I had to sacrifice form altogether; but, as Mann pointed out, man's life (even in America) is, among many eruptions of brutality, an almost instinctive search for form, for order, or—as you always say—for the Answers, whatever they are. Therefore, at present, I am working steadily toward a synthesis of form and energy. I'm afraid the only things I'm learning now are technical—but I am 21, and I am going to live until I die. You are going to find many bad poems here, Elizabeth—bad, as such—if you should want to read any of them; but remember that in America, in Ohio (please don't think me a nationalist—I'd rather be a human being than anything else) the truest expression (Emerson called it fully half of our being—I agree) has always been sprawling, and full of mistakes and tremendous, compassionate insights—Whitman, Wolfe— Sherwood Anderson—and thus easily criticized. Forgive me—I'm not trying to rationalize away my mistakes. God knows, I'm a bad enough poet—I only want you to recall that anything I ever write will be sprawling, screaming, and enormous in size. This is not an intention but a basic element. I am not a sculptor of cameos, but an idiot monster licking the world with a fire tongue. My problem is to let myself find the right form. These things here are, as Ransom said, full of a certain crude energy. For this reason, I often irritate and offend my fellow versifiers here at Kenyon (there are several—a couple of Eliot boys, a classicist, a metaphysical agrarian, and one fellow who is a poetic genius in my opinion—his name is Robert Nugent—more of him later, with one of his splendid poems, if I can get one). But I'm not afraid.

I only ask that you take these experimental compositions and hide them from me. Read a couple if you like. Forgive me for not writing. Lost in work, as you must be this time of year. Please give my regards to your folks and to Henry.

I don't yet have a job lined up for the summer. If I don't find some way to make money, I may not even get back to school. If that should happen, I don't know what I'd do. Army again, I suppose.

Please—if you can find a time—a note? I'll have a small surprise for you before commencement, I think.

Thank you, Elizabeth.

—Jim

To Susan Lamb

sometime in August.
I don't know what
the hell the date is
Warnock, Ohio
[August 9, 1949]

My dear Susan,

I threw away my cigarette, and began to make little mystic symbols in the sand with the rubber toe of my left combat boot. Two early fireflies left the limb of a willow, and drifted past my face in two trailing arcs of yellow that remained marked in the twilit air in afterimages of green and blue. It was the first time in my life that I had left the world as it was, and had become but nothing. There was meager consolation in the remembrance that the western world was not breaking into fits of weeping because I had left it to sit near a riverside at Sagami, smoke an American cigarette as if it belonged to me, watching the amorous airdances of two lightning bugs, and hear the musical raindrums thudding in pagan cadences up out of Atsugi five miles down the river.

Sand had piled itself into little silver dunes of astonishing regularity, that reminded one of the backs of minnows that run away from fingers at the edges of a creek back in Ohio. But these creatures were arrested in their escape, and seemed frozen. The ambiguity of visual imagination that turned them from dunes to tiny fish to dunes again was the very element which forced me into a musing about two other things at once. I thought of the friends I had almost had in the west— almost had, and lost in the most profound sense, because of my failure to control the great winds which tended to come up unexpectedly out of my solar plexus. Other people seemed frightened to death at me. I could not convince those of my sincerity face to face, and had resorted finally to the composition of a journal, in which at least I could practice the releasing of my full powers. And yet even this was almost never successful; because writing is not only music. It is also architecture, demanding the technique, mastered only after months and years of the bitterest labor, which that art possesses—if the architect is to construct a cathedral of merit instead of a mere group of disordered, flimsy outhouses. At this particular period of which I speak, I was somewhere around the eightieth page of the new journal folio, and already had begun to realize that I had been too musical—that there was a certain want of body on my pages—that I was drowning, as Shelley almost did, in pale lemon jelly. I suppose a young man gets a green sickness at times, certainly; and mine was particularly bad that late afternoon. The second thing, beyond my own shifting and fading friendships back west and my own fundamental technical collapses in the journal, I had further meditations. The wind rose a bit, and brought with it the first scents of October which, so far as I have been able to tell, are identical the world over—at least over half of it which I have traversed during my service career. And, as I looked over the few cherry skeletons over the river, near the rice paddies which rise up a gradual slope into the heights which eventually gather into the tremendous blue peak of the Oyama mountain, I suddenly realized, as for the first time, that I had spent almost a year in Japan. I remembered the dollface of my friend who had lost her lover in the Chinese campaigns, and who, at forty-two, retained a youthfulness which I should be the merest romanticist to describe. I thought of how my section commander had given me hell (laughing, as I learned, afterwards) when he had caught me wasting working hours by listening to her as she translated for me a small poem which she had written for a children's magazine. Recollection of that single charming incident brought back a horde of others. There was Nakano, my thirty-eight year old clerk who had a small daughter whose picture he never tired of showing me; and who had spent, I know, laborious evenings in translating in English several of the haiku (little seventeen-syllable verses) of the poet Basho, of whom I had requested information. I saw their faces come floating out to me from the bare cherry scrubs on the other side of the river; literally hundreds of faces, some whom I knew by acquaintance, some whom I know well, and many whom I could not even name, but nevertheless recalled vividly. Like evening birdsongs, their names: Nakano, Gloria, Tada, Kazuko, Tomiko, Kazoe, Inoue, Akira, Yokomizo, Hashida, Yuriko, Kodame, Matsumoto, Iko. Honey bucket collectors, painters, old begging ladies, poets, and gentlemen who row boats over the Sagami rivers. I wondered if they would ever arrange themselves in order—the kind of order which I know of, as a young man reared in the west. And then I wondered if they might not be more cosmic in their present arrangement, gathering together with their own inscape like the patterns in a Japanese painting which are never repeated, and yet which retain a thread of community.

The raindrums were quiet now, but the wind was still rising easily. A cicada blew a flute over the water, and was answered by a dryad in the locusts to my left. Now it was all dark, and the whole air was heavy with firefly comets burning over the river like a disturbed and microcosmic firmament. I had my hair combed, and my hat off at my side. It seemed that, no matter how much the wind rose, my hair lay perfectly parted except for one tiny lock which I couldn't make go up with the rest; so I let it hang over the right side of my forehead. Far and away across and down the river, on the other side, I could see two figures in shadowy kimonos moving down near the shore, evidently to look over the water, and then move back up a path between the two forest clumps, disappearing at once past the little rise which lay between the river and the first of many rice fields. These two people did not make me feel any more akin to my own world; and, if anything, their presence, distant as it was, only accentuated my isolation. One feels kindly toward the people who come in sight. Between myself and these two there was only a single shallow river. Between myself and America there was a huge ocean. And between myself and the people whom I used to know, and even those with whom I had somewhat corresponded, there were great gaps of water and space, and walls of an invisible but evidently impenetrable structure. Being set off like that, I spent perhaps whole hours in wondering how I was ever to gain any real contact with my own environment, wherever it happened to be at the moment. The early verses had clearly faded quite away on the notes of a music applied to the wrong medium. At that time, of course, I had never even heard of LaFountaine, and Parks, and Ransom, with their tremendously vital and incisive criticism. I had no intellectual tools with which to go back to my own journal and begin an unfeeling onslaught against myself for my own good. The cold but necessary implements of logic were not my forte, and without even recognizing their existence I was sorely missing them—missing them to the extent that I felt practically dissociated from my own body. So self-centered, and therefore so lost, I think it was a good thing that most folks kept clear of me. I probably would have hurt them pretty badly. But this confession was not on my mind at the time of which I write. At the end of that evening, I simply sat on the edge of the Sagami on the sand in the light of fireflies, and using in my own mind the two disappearing people on the other side as symbols of the disappearing world which went away warily along with the note of a dying cicada that I was sure was singing itself utterly away. I threw away my cigarette and made a few more mystic symbols on the sand with the rubber toe of my left combat boot, before rising, putting on my hat, and starting back up through Zama in order to make it inside the post before ten o'clock.

Sitting by this window at Warnock during these evenings, remembering how much bitter work has gone into the journal, how repetitions and experiments in both German and English have swollen it to upwards of seven hundred pages in the past year, and remembering also how I have gone into print a couple of times and not seen the sky subsequently fall, I feel often more able to reach forth to the other people in the world as they exist in flesh and blood, to probe a little with their dreams as well as my own, to love and respect the humor and irony of the existence of any young man, in America or anywhere else! Believe me, dear Susan my friend, this slow transmogrification has been horridly difficult for me, selfish as I am by nature. That's why I feel that a long correspondence is such a medicine for myself. True, this also is selfish; and yet only my best friends will endure it. That's why you endure it. Of course, you don't have time to answer at much length; but this simply means you're busy with creation. I feel good over the whole correspondence.

By now it is entirely dark here. A rain has begun to blow up; and— [. . .] all the lights in the damned house have gone out. Some electrical disturbance outside, I guess. Now they're on again, and you see that I made a typing mistake a few lines above which makes the whole

damned paragraph look like a freshman theme introduction. I shall begin again, now.

* * *

If I slip into dramatics in this or my other letters, remember that I
have a hideous time in expressing myself clearly. I mean it. Perhaps the
ability to write a single sentence from beginning to end and the same
time make clear sense out of the words is one of the rarest of human
achievements. And yet, I still need to write, and extensively. I can't tell
you how much better I feel if I can only write a long letter to someone
who, I feel convinced, will read it—even though writing takes all the
guts out of me. It always exhausts me, and yet I can't help writing like
a fire hose. Perhaps the great fury is caused by the essential loneliness
inherent in any creative activity, whether profitable or not. I am sure
that often you must need terribly to talk to someone—just talk and talk,
without sticking to any particular subject—and yet find yourself at a
loss as to the method and idiom which you can use as an easing outlet.
This has been, in one sense, a kind of damnation for me; for I recall
one occasion a few years back when I must have made something of an
idiot of myself by pouring out my uncertainty of passion for the world
in the form of a group of alleged "love-letters"; and have since often
regretted the action for many reasons. Probably the most important
reason is that what I said in my earlier, and younger, letters was not at
all what I was trying to say, to get out of my system in a creative manner. It is the previously mentioned problem of trying to apply impres-
sionistic music to the wrong medium—language. Language is as much
architectural as musical—possibly more the former. Therefore it is not
a matter of singing straight off and irresponsibly the surface feelings of
one's consciousness. It is a matter of patiently constructing and re-
building. One ought, in writing a composition in words, to build the
cathedral first, and support it with buttresses of meditation and reason.
The music comes later, with emotional maturity. The music is the understanding which might be symbolized by the insertion of an organ
into that very cathedral—not during the cathedral's construction, but
after the architect has made sure that the granite stones will not fall
down about the heads of both himself and the person to whom he is
trying to sing. But I was very young at eighteen years of age—younger
than my years, I guess—and I very nearly lost a precious friendship by

shooting off my mouth, so to speak, through the mails. I ought to have devoted *all* of my diffuse emotions to the discipline which came later. That I did not lose that friendship of which I write—and I hope there are indications that I have not lost it entirely—seems to me somewhat miraculous, when I consider the reactions of most folks to such explosions of irresponsibility. The young person to whom those early letters were directed happened to be one of unusual kindness and understanding for one of her years—she was just my age, or a little younger. I look back on the situation with some amazement now, astonishment that I was not told in no uncertain terms to go to hell with my childish blubberings. In a sense, possibly this would have been a wise action on the part of the young lady who was the target. And yet it is not out of the way of the argument here to remember also that I was an extremely nervous, lonely, and confused young man. I am bound to be prejudiced in my appreciations, and therefore I say without stint that the young lady displayed great wisdom by easing me back to my disturbed senses courteously and lightly.

It is most enlightening, and somehow (I don't know why) rather ghostly curious that only recently, by sheer accident, I began to correspond with that young lady again. At the present juncture she has already finished attending the school inhabited by her during our last correspondence; and is studying and working at her chosen profession at a hospital in Columbus. The opportunity for writing letters to her arose quite naturally and easily—so easily that I half-suspect the operation of some old law of compensation that demands old ruins be reconstructed on the principles of reason and emotional maturity, with a minimum, even absence, of the old and irresponsible impressionism. It is difficult to describe in this short space the importance and value which can accrue to me through writing to that friend again, under the newer and better controlled conditions. I ought to point out that the present period of my life has to be devoted to a reemphasis of the intellectual tools with which I want to try to understand and appreciate the environment in which I live, and am going to live in the future, in the world. Now, the most precise way for expansion of a person's faculties is his speaking to his friends. If one is social, or is a smooth conversationalist, he can seek his friends' minds by talk. I possess neither of these qualities; and, besides, only a few friends will allow a person to write to them extensively. I have a few such, and they live a considerable distance from my home, all of them. Thus, the immense intrinsic value to me of my correspondence. Every letter is a voyage of discovery into my friends' personalities; and the voyage is carried on, at least from my end, by my language alone, without the distracting and possibly disgusting influence of my physical person. My corresponding friends have been so few and so far away, that they have not begrudged me the satisfaction of writing to them at length. I reckon there must be, at the present time, five persons with whom I exchange letters of some length. Two of them are poets (who possess excellent senses of criticism which they enjoy operating); a playwright from San Francisco; a young lady, just graduated from Bryn Mawr in Philadelphia, and now working in biochemistry; and the other young lady, upon whose consciousness I have again recently begun to make inroads with letters. It may be objected that long letters are boring and disturbing and distracting. I answer by saying that, such is my friendship that my friends will tell me at once if I write at too great a length. I would not be embarrassed by such a statement of a fact. Exchange of courtesies, and even objections, by means of words is an excellent procedure, and eliminates embarrassments which naturally arise with physical presence.

* * *

You'd enjoy seeing this farm, Susan. It had lain fallow for the most part during some fifteen years before my folks obtained it a couple of years ago. I returned from overseas just about in time to join the general struggle against a wilderness of weeds and other disorganization. A little noticeable progress has been made. Of course, I am away from home for more than eight months out of every year; but my father and brother get home every evening, while my mother is here to keep her hands on the reins, milk the cows, and prevent the six pigs from escaping from that devil's island of a pen. Circumstances have allowed me to remain here during this whole summer; and my brother and I have just this week brought in a fair load of hay, the first crop we've yet had. This hay situation is just one indication of the whole process. We attack everything at once and systematically, and little by little signs of progress become visible. It will take some length of time, though, before we can call the place truly productive and self-sufficient. The rudiments are here. We have two cows and a new calf, several pigs and chickens, a fairly decent garden of corn, potatoes, tomatoes, peas, beans, and a creditable pasture. Our set of animals, both wild and domestic, is a fine one—kind and intelligent. The bull frog who lives with his wife and kids down the creek near the pasture spring is a superior singer, one of the most gifted of minstrels. Sometime you must be sure to come and visit me.

My home, as I hope I have implied, is in no way upper, or even middle, class. It is simply and plainly a small Ohioan farm, still trying to find its way out of fifteen years' fallowness. There are two types of confusion in the house proper: my younger brother has half the house covered with scientific apparatus; and I have snarls of books, records, and notebooks covering the other half. We have our own ideas of order, and do not expect others to understand them. We are the Nietzschean farmers in the best degree and sense. We will yield to the prejudices of others, even visitors, even rich ones, if there are any (and there never are); we will salute the flag, vote, and pray when the occasion arises; we will acquiesce with the prevailing social mores and folkways, whatever they happen to be at the moment, whenever we step beyond the rusty barbed wire fence; but by God our conceptions of confusion owe nothing to the French, our ideas of harmonium owe nothing to Plato; we have concepts of confusion floating about the premises, and these are of private manufacture. Thus, if you ever visit us, you may have to undergo a deal of orientation, in order to pick your way among the crags, fens, hills, bogs, dens, fogs, rocks, and caves of the Wright homestead. However, the invitation stands. Give me a ring sometime when you're free.

Yesterday I was visited by my friend Ethelwyn Clark, a former student of Bryn Mawr. She drove here from Philadelphia to spend a few hours before returning to help her mother move to a new place in New Jersey. The high point of the brief visit is the fact that Eff left her gorgeous St. Bernard, Melly, to stay with me for three weeks. Melly has not yet attained her full growth, but she is still monstrous in size. After she gets more used to the rural company she is going to have to keep, she won't be any trouble at all; and she has a sweet nature. Susan, I don't know what it is—but there is a marvelous luxuriance about a St. Bernard. It makes a person feel rich to have one around. I don't mean rich in the superficial sense, but deeply wealthy in spirit. I suppose it's the very hugeness of the dog that does this for a person. Melly is large in body, face, everything; and her affection is so pure and innocent, that one could ask nothing beyond having her sit at his feet, and the universe is temporarily satisfactory. My older brother will be down this coming weekend, and if he gets any creditable photographs of her I'll send you one.

Pete Lannum will leave at the end of this week for Chicago, where he will attend a television school.

I spent a little time during the past week with Liberty Kardules (you remember her). She has just finished her first year of nurse training at Martins Ferry hospital, and, I suppose, will go to Cleveland to study before long. Speaking of nurses, perhaps you know that both Mary Margeret Hughes and Sarah Davies finished their training this spring. I spoke with Mary Margeret briefly last week; and found her to be slightly disillusioned. Perhaps this was merely an inadequate surface impression. I haven't seen her for months.

Your letter, dear Susan, was another concise and thoughtful one. My lack of comment on it and its controversial material has a reason. Tomorrow I am due to leave for Lancaster, where I will spend the next few days with a friend from the army and school. For this reason, I wanted to dash off the present note, in order to make sure I had your letter answered before I get involved in other activities. However, I shall continue to write to you in the present free style—retaining your thoughts as well as I can, ruminating over them, and letting the responses come to you as they form themselves. After I get home, I shall probably have time to answer the problem you pose more directly from my opinions on the subject—and I have several on the topic of organized religion, although they may sound a little grotesque, and even absurd.

In the meanwhile, thank you very much for your letter. It is always a pleasure to hear from you and about your activities and thoughts. Don't be in any hurry, but please answer when you have time. Meantime, always think of me as your friend,

Love,
Jim

To Jack Furniss's Parents

Dear Friends,

My last few days have been spent in setting my affairs in order, and for this reason my letter of acknowledgment and appreciation is coming a bit late. Late though it be, I want to state right from the beginning that my few days' visit at your home were most pleasant, and I shall not ever forget my being treated with the greatest courtesy and friendliness. The trait which I have appreciated most in Jack is his unfailing talent for making himself old friends with diverse personalities in a very few moments, and then always treating those friendships as precious. Believe me when I say that now, having spent a few days in Jack's domestic environment, I understand the kind of splendid family training which is behind his immediate warmth and sincerity.

As Jack has possibly told you, my visit to Lancaster was my first to that part of the state. I still do not know my native part of the country nearly as well as I should, and an acquaintance with Lancaster, the Lake, and so on, will certainly influence my wanting to see it again sometime.

But, as I say, the moments at the Furniss home were best, and warmest. I thoroughly enjoyed the discussions there, as well as the interesting people I met—especially the Eymans. I have a particular desire to renew acquaintance with Hubie sometime; for he strikes me as being one of the most sensitive, intelligent, and sincere young men I have met in a very long time.

Please tell Jack that I am almost finished with his book *The Naked and the Dead*, and I shall send it back to him very soon. When he reads Tolstoy's *War and Peace*, I am certain he will find many interesting parallels between that noblest of novels and Mailer's considerable work. The exploration of each character's background, right down to his spiritual beliefs, is a huge device, and only the greatest talent possesses the imagination and insight to use it to correct advantage. Although *The Brothers Karamazov* is the deepest novel I know, *War and Peace* has a greater and more significant setting—the Napoleonic invasion of Russia—and is bound to present more acute difficulties, of the dramatic sort especially, to the omniscient novelist. Tolstoy used his magnificent material—an examination of all kinds of men, from ruler down to peasant—to great and perhaps unsurpassable advantage; but I am convinced that even

Tolstoy's preeminent position as a war novelist is a little shaken by the explosion caused by this young man, Norman Mailer. As a reader I am only a layman; but, between you and me, I predict great things for the latter. We have had novelists of great talent in America. There is no sense in despairing over the literary achievements of a nation that has fathered Ernest Hemingway, Thomas Wolfe, Sinclair Lewis at his best, Herman Melville, and some others; I merely wish to point out, by way of passing, that the appearance of *The Naked and the Dead* is a definite, undeniable indication that the drive of the great vision of democracy is not dead by any means. Regardless of my frequent criticisms, I still believe passionately in my country. I still believe that we have come closer in actuality to the great social dreams of thinkers of the past than any other group. It is not necessary for me to point out to you, who know and understand American history more thoroughly than I do, that any nation thrives on self-criticism, self-examination; and that, as long as it can attempt to understand itself in a healthy manner, it remains young. Such a self-evaluation is *The Naked and the Dead*, and it deserves to be read as such. This is my opinion.

Again allow me to thank you all for a splendid few days at your home. I hope to see you again during the next semester at Kenyon.

Sincerely,
James Wright

To Elizabeth Willerton Esterly

Warnock, Ohio
January 1, 1950

Dear Elizabeth,

Just a few minutes ago I talked to you on the phone. Let me tell you immediately, before I forget, that I very nearly phoned you again. I want to remind you that Liberty Kardules is now in training at a hospital in Cleveland, and that I promised her I would give you her address.

Here it is: Miss Liberty Kardules
1803 Valentine Ave.
Cleveland 9, Ohio

Please let me urge you to write to her very soon, even if you can find time only for a short note. For months now she has wanted very intensely to see you or hear from you; and circumstances of one sort or another have always managed to get in the way. I imagine her being so far away from home so suddenly will bewilder her for a little while. This is not to say that the sky will fall if you don't write to her, of course. It's just that your writing to her would also give her access to your own address and situation; would allow her to write back; and thus afford both of you a distinct pleasure. She is a whole person, as you are; probably one of the most real people I know. I like to think that the three-dimensional people of my acquaintance are in contact with one another. I mean, of course, that there are so few whose total dimensions I personally am able to see; and the mutual forces operating among them somehow gives me further drive to find the depth in the others whom I don't yet know.

Elizabeth, I spoke for a couple of minutes tonight about Rilke, who is in my opinion the greatest poet of this century. (I have no true right to say this, for I can't read French, which is as may be.) Perhaps the only book through which to begin an acquaintance with him—his literary work, his philosophical concepts which have influenced more Europeans than most crisis-mongers would admit, and his personality—is a small volume entitled *Letters to a Young Poet*. It is available now in an excellent translation, but I can't remember the publisher. I can find out easily enough, and would like to send you the information; so that perhaps you can find it. You and Henry should both read the thing. When Rilke was still an adolescent, he was sent by his family to serve in a certain Prussian military academy. This was toward the close of the 19th century. He had a hell of a time, and never forgave the operators of the place, even though they wrote to him on the publication of his third or fourth book. The point is that a little later another young German fellow, named Franz Kappus, at the age of 19 was attending the same school. He had written a few verses, and suffered under the routine of the academy. Wondering whether to give up his own identity and really be a soldier, or to pursue the course of creation, he wrote to Rilke (this was about 1905), sent a few poems of his own, and asked for advice. Rilke, who was 28 at the time, answered at once, and the two maintained a correspondence for roughly a decade. It is Rilke's half of the correspondence which is printed in the little book I mentioned. The letters are fresh, and yet profound. You will discover therein one of the most vital intellectual and spiritual currents of our century, one that is not spent because so many other young men, even though isolated, have recognized it and examined themselves in its light. Rilke was a personal friend of the French sculptor Rodin (*The Thinker, The Kiss, The Hand of God,* etc.), and discusses him at length. He also knew, and was intensely influenced by, Tolstoy. It is not ivory-tower stuff. It is an important influence by a genius, an influence which has been neglected in its true significance by all save a few poets and philosophers; but which is enormously important for the shape of the future. There is a Dutch student at my school who told me that many of his European friends, both Dutch and Belgian, literally worship Rilke's poetry. Jim Clark (you recall Miss Charlotte Lane) corresponded with a German who frequently mentioned Rilke as an extremely popular Lyriker. Can we say the same for Walt Whitman on this continent? I don't know. We should be able to. The true poet is not secluded. He is a man of enormous vitality and vision, a man, as Wordsworth said, speaking to men. They are our eyes. Nothing manmade ever existed in actuality unless it existed first in somebody's imagination. If this were true only in the artistic realm, then we could take Beethoven or leave him, depending on personal taste, and continue to listen to hillbilly music if it pleased us. But it is not true only in the artistic realm. It is also true of Karl Marx, Sigmund Freud (consider the insane asylums of the not-too-distant past, the Bedlams and so on), and whatever socialistically-minded thinker who conceived and worked out the plan to educate decently the veterans of the recent war. Get this Rilke book, please. Beethoven says more than music. Rilke says more than poetry. He has much to say about three fundamental facts in his letters: sex, death, and God.

Perhaps it will give a decent idea of his approach to the world, his world, the God in it, the objects and the harmony in which they can be seen, the Gestalt (a wonderful German word which you can translate as something like "the general configurations which objects joined together can assume, almost spontaneously, before your senses") appearing in diverse objects, if I quote a little verse, very famous among Europeans, which is simple enough to be analysed briefly. It is called "Herbst," or "Autumn":

> *Die Blätter fallen, fallen wie von weit,*
> *Als welkten in den Himmeln ferne Gärten,*

Sie fallen mit verneinender Gebärde.
Und in den Nächten fällt die schwere Erde
Aus allen Sternen in die Einsamkeit.

Wir alle fallen. Diese Hand da fällt.
Und sieh die andre an: es ist in allen.

Und doch ist Einer, welcher dieses Fallen
Unendlich sanft in seinen Händen hält.

The leaves fall, fall as from a great distance,
as though withered in the far gardens of heaven;
they fall and their gestures are those of surrender,
and in the nights falls the heavy earth
out of all the stars into loneliness.
We all fall: this hand falls there,
and behold the others: this falling is in all,
and still is one, which this Fall
eternally, tenderly gathers into its hands.

It is difficult to transfer to English, which has its own kind of humor, the subtle pun darting back and forth between the verb "fallen," the change from this verb, which of course means to fall, into a neuter noun Fallen, meaning not only the gerund "falling" but also the Fall of the year, as in English. Consider the progression of images. Leaves fall not only from trees, but out of far gardens in heaven; then a shift to the earth as it falls through space (friends tell me that this is a legitimate astronomical view—will you please ask Henry about it?); and, before this sense of great spaciousness and significance fades, a cornering of the central image, the idea of falling and blending with the world, the universe even, and applying it to us all. It is death perhaps, but not the view of death held by most men. It is a surrender to the temporary ruin out of which humus is formed—the humus of dead leaves from which living plants appear; and the broader humus of the human spirit, through which emerges the tragic sense of human life on this planet. (The true tragic sense is optimistic—you taught me that, in your discussion of Sophocles, in your paper on Dostoyevsky, and elsewhere—remember?) The one thing which is really missing from this discussion, the thing which is indispensable, is the chance to read the "Herbst" poem aloud. Rilke is as musical in German as Keats is in English, and you know what that means. Music and meaning run very closely parallel, and enrich each other without confusion. Swinburne confuses, because he sacrifices meaning for music. Keats is enormous because he never, at his best, sacrifices either, but makes them reflect each other and enlarge each other; so that, if you are paying attention, you never come to the end of the poem. It is a living, breathing entity, ever enlarging itself and the reader of it, reaching further and opening new doors of apprehension and consequent appreciation of things which are perhaps not even directly related to the poem. Do I make myself clear? When you hear "To be or not to be, that is the question" you do not shed tears over poor Hamlet's sex problems. You try to answer the question "to be or not to be"; and in trying to do so you find that the question involves more than Hamlet, more than the whole Elizabethan theatre, even more than Shakespeare himself. This is why I regret that we can't discuss the Rilke lyric without the inherent music. If you know any German people down there, and there are bound to be either a couple of Germans or a few students of German, please ask one of them to read you this Rilke aloud. If I am being vague now, you will know what I mean when you hear those long euphonious assonances, almost a phenomenon in German poetry until this century. Of course, some scattered few (I speak from the *Oxford Book of German Verse*) made wide variations on the old folk-stanza, but none with the genius with which Rilke adapted the language to the long, spread out cadences which seemed made only for more inherently soft languages, and made it sound as if a man can't write his thoughts in any other way.

You both would enjoy my German professor, and his wife, a Lithuanian who is most vivacious. His name is Dr. Andre Hanfman, and as far as I know he was born in Russia. They have made me welcome at their house, and I visit them often when there is a slow evening.

You asked about my own work. I told you that it is different from anything of mine you have ever seen before. I am glad to be partly free of myself. Perhaps the most acute of artistic problems is the emergence from one's self. T. S. Eliot observed that, for the artist, art seeks to escape from personality. He meant that an audience is more interested in your insight into the nature of truth among men and objects, and your most objective creations, than in your allergy to headcolds, your taste for green neckties, or your liking for beer. Of course, it is a just view as well as an accurate statement. My problem has always been how to get out of myself—perhaps how to most effectively project myself beyond the limits of my many pettinesses. You remember Browning's last poem in the Men and Women series, "One Word More," in which he undertook an explanation to Mrs. Browning, that he was like the moon, never revolving; he shone to the world through his poems, but kept the other side, the undiscovered one, for more private revelations. He was right. At least I believe he was right. Perhaps I state it with conceit, but I mean to get to the central problems of the century, the ones that flow in all our veins, and not in mine alone.

However that may be, if you really want to see something of mine, and I believe you do, let me offer you one of a series on which I have worked intermittently for some months. Perhaps it will be of interest, since we spoke on the phone tonight about what had happened to God during the past half-century. The poem speaks of him, or them, if you prefer. One or two explanatory points can be made for your convenience. The poem is in the form of the verse epistle. It is presumably written by Tityrus, a farmer and poet, to his friend Hirpinus Snodgrass, with whom he has been corresponding for years. The names are probably familiar. Virgil's *Eclogues* are written about several characters, and the first begins with a reference to the shepherd Tityrus. The name Hirpinus comes out of one of Horace's odes in the second book. Over toward the end of the poem you will find the lines:

> . . . I should still remember . . .
> one poet whose magnificence of insight . . .

The poet is, of course, Hart Crane; and the reference is to his phrase in "White Buildings," "They say that Venus shot through foam to light."

Forgive a long and single-tracked letter. Give my regards to Henry.

Jim Wright

To Susan Lamb

Gambier, Ohio
January 4, 1950

Dear Susan,

We have here another quick note, absolutely limited to fifteen minutes, which may not last out the present page.

If I remember correctly (and I am not sure I do), I answered your welcome card; but the letter, if there was one, probably was pretty confused, since I had to do so damned many other things during the vacation. I read a German novel, wrote four pages of my imperishable German prose, read a biography of August Strindberg, read another novel, *The Fountainhead*, translated six more verses by the poet Rilke,* wrote 20 more pages for my journal, saw our excellent friend Pete Lannum (who, for my part, is one of the greatest men of the twentieth century), ate about 50 lbs. of a recently butchered hog, fired a rifle at a dead branch of an oak tree on my place, missed, translated 200 more lines from *Beowulf* in Anglo-Saxon, and got so drunk last Saturday night at a joint just past Stop 7 in Martins Ferry that I couldn't even open my eyes, at one point, for about fifteen minutes running; and got the dates of days mixed, so that I came back to school a day early.

I'm very sorry you had only a day at home. You will be interested to hear that I spoke to the former Miss Willerton over the phone for a little while. She says she and Henry and his (their) little girl are fine; but that she misses teaching. I can see why, of course, after her spending so many years in the profession. In case you don't have it, here's the address [. . .]

Damn it, before I forget: please, for God's sake, give me your phone number in Columbus. Everytime I get down there, I think of calling you, and never never never never never have the number.

I must go now and eat. Buy Bonds.

Love,
Jim

---

*See Appendix, p. 558, for the poem "The Ghost with the Silver Lyre," after Rainer Maria Rilke.

To Albert Herzing

Warnock, Ohio
[July 1950]
Saturday

Dear Al,

Congratulations on this Martha Foley affair. Her collection is widely known, and it will mean that you will hear from any number of publishers. I've only read one of your stories and, as you may remember, I enjoyed it very much. Even Timberlake liked it immensely. His antipathy toward modern literature is very great, you know, and he seldom admits enjoyment of anything in *Hika*. This may seem like a small thing to say, but I thought you might be interested.

I had a letter from Edgar Doctorow two days ago. He spent the summer taking care of kids at a camp. I also heard from Willie Hass who did the same. Both seem concerned over this Korea thing, as everyone is, I guess. The entire affair, of course, is without sense and meaning, and all one can do is try to stay away from it as long as possible. I suppose we all shall have to go in time, and there is nothing whatever to be gained by the venture. I cannot imagine anybody with a spark of mentality being taken in by the hysterical propaganda which is being exerted in order to justify the war. The tactics of the Gestapo have crept even to some degree into official circles; so all one can do is try to keep his mouth shut and his conscience assuaged by self-inflicted lies. To me, Truman sounds like the most stupid, cliché-ridden figure in the entire history of western politics. It is just our luck to lose the advantage of Roosevelt's imagination and vision at the present terrible moment; but I suppose we can't expect to be guided by genius every moment of our history. But I didn't mean to get sidetracked so on politics. Several friends have written me their candid opinions on the present international situation, and then asked me to burn the letters. This is a dangerous attitude, and it is time that every thinking man take a stand on his right to opinion. I served my country in the army, and I still believe in its destiny. This, I believe, is not incompatible with a desire to help improve it. In our businessman culture, the business man has taken upon himself the odious job of self-appointed guardian of public morals and patriotism. If the army wants me, I am entirely willing to serve again and again, if necessary. I am not willing to grant to the Rotary clubs the right to form my opinions for me, with the alternative of being damned as a left-winger and either disgraced or jailed. During the history of our troubled race, countless thousands of men, most of them greater than I, have been faced with a choice between spiritual death and social discomfort. I don't know whether or not I have the courage to follow their positive choices; but I do know that I feel something fundamentally wrong with the government of my country, and I think a sound change is needed in the direction of the country's life. Perhaps a change from the Dems to the Reps would be sufficient to revitalize our policies both at home and abroad. I hope this is the extent of the difficulty. Regardless of the flexibility of any system, any government is only as strong as the men who happen to compose its positions at any given moment. Truman, like Andrew Johnson in relation to Lincoln, has neither the physical force nor the imagination required to continue the work of his great predecessor.

But enough of that. I might point out that you need not burn this letter.

Along with an increased interest in politics this summer, I have worked hard at verses and have written three stories. These are the first tales I have ever tried to compose, and I'm not sure whether they're successful or not. I may wish to offer one to *Hika* if the editors think them worthy.

Thanks for [Richard] Gibson's address. I shall write him directly.
Please write.

Yours,
Jim

To Jack Furniss

Warnock, Ohio
[August 1950]

Dear Harry,*

Although I am no surer of my motives now than I generally am, I have been engaged through the whole summer in some kind of consid-

---

*Jack was sometimes addressed as Harry, while Wright often referred to himself as Adam, a nickname given to him by Furniss. When they first met, Wright was sitting naked on his footlocker, reading James Joyce's *Ulysses*.

eration of the country I live in—in the traditions from which it came originally, in the men who founded it, in the present situation of its people, and their meaning on this lonely continent. I think you must agree that one of the grandeurs of America is its loneliness. Of course, this is not to say that often, mostly in our small towns, we possess remarkable capacities for warmth and intimacy of relationship. That also is one of our grandeurs, and it is the more precious because of the loneliness of the stage on which it is played. For the loneliness I speak of is related directly to the very hugeness of the land, the fabulous range of its plains and mountains, and the brooding sense of the great spaces which fills us all who were born here and possess in our blood the sense of largeness. Perhaps this may account for our being in large part a nervous and restless people, anxious sometimes, but always energetic, continuously experimenting with ourselves and the manners in which man has engaged himself in order to find the harmonious relationship with the universe and with his fellows. I think I was extremely fortunate in my army travels, because I got to travel across these states four times—twice across the north, once across the south, and once across the center. The things I saw and was reminded of were equally multitudinous. This latter word is huge; but such words in terms of America are singularly appropriate. I say this because, as I suggested above, I think there is a peculiar relationship between the lay of the land here—its physical character—and the specific problems of existence which beset us the inhabitants. You know that in America we are dealing with a phenomenon; the marvel of men trying, and in a remarkable degree succeeding, to be free. The fact that we have clung so tenaciously to this notion, that the individual man is mostly capable of governing himself and of directing the interests of his own life has been the root of our national paradox. It makes us weak and, in turn, this very weakness is our strength. There is a vital point here, one which, in my consideration, cannot be dispensed with, if you or I or anybody is to understand America. I say, then: being weak, we are strong. I speak of weakness in terms of immediacy, such as that of national preparedness in time of war. This will make a workable example. Consider with me, then: almost invariably America, at the beginning of any conflict in which it is involved, is caught unprepared. Why? I think it is because the very great majority of us are not interested in joining the service and thus being always on our toes against war. Now, I do not deny that people in other nations, great or small, may feel the same. They do not want to die either. Agreed. But their governments may think otherwise, and, if so, they can compel the citizens to be ready for war whether they like it or not. This is a strength, the strength of immediacy. That is, when somebody (e.g., North Korea) wants to strike a blow, they can be entirely ready. Why? Because in more normal circumstances they have their feet on the necks of their people; and this characteristic, as far as living as a human being is concerned, is a weakness. I hope I am making myself clear. I hope this, because the paradox which I have tried to state may well be one important key to the other idea at hand; namely, that in time the Americans generally turn out to be enormously strong. The catch is that this strength takes time. It takes time for people who are normally engaged in the pursuits of peace to shift their power into the channels of war. However, we can point to history (very recent history, even; that of World War II) and indicate that, long though it may take, this strength, when it has arrived, is huge. The American capacity for teamwork and efficient cooperation, despite the cynical remarks of many muddle-headed, "bright" young men, is factually speaking one of the more remarkable phenomena in the history of western civilization. I am almost sure that the fact of its taking so long to organize and direct is a direct outcome of that diffuse scattering of talents and energies which I mentioned above. You have only to reflect for a moment on the infinite variety to be found in any single human being. Then remember the some 160 billion human beings we have, restless and energetically moving about on this continent, and on top of this, doing pretty much what their interests direct them to do. It is enormously complex, and it is always shifting. You may object that many, a great many, of our people have to stay situated in one place in order to take care of their families. I answer that you should consider the situation of similar men in countries of older cultures. A very important consideration in this instance is offered by Laski, Wolfe, and other commentators on the American scene. This consideration is in the sense of possibility which we still possess, and, God willing, always shall. Even if a fellow, for example, spends his life in a coal mine, this does not mean that his sons and daughters must do the same. I agree that many of our new citizens, who came from other countries, still possess old views, and therefore may feel that their children ought, ethically and traditionally speaking, to follow the same line of work which has been pursued by the family for generations. But also I ask you to remember that these new citizens are living and working in another historical and social context. The American spirit (by which I mean the general attitude of the people toward the ideas which have shaped, and still shape, the way of life here. An excellent example may be found in the sport of baseball, where teamwork combines, and not incompatibly, with an opportunity for brilliant individual experimentation) constantly insists that, despite the temporary and transient opinions of local folks and Sinclair Lewises and Babbitts alike, the individual is to be commended proportionately as he realizes, or attempts to realize, his individuality. That is the general feeling in this country, whether it is vocally expressed or not. It is operative. Finally, I hope you will not be offended at my using you yourself as an example which ought to drive home my point. Your father is in the insurance business; and, if you were a European or an Asiatic, there is little doubt in its being assumed that you would be in the insurance business also. Needless to say, you and your neighbors would exert enormous force of social opinion that your son should follow the same course; and so on, as long as possible. Now, consider the actual situation, and the two conditions are eliminated. I do not know what you eventually will be in your society. You may be an insurance man. On the other hand, I am not aware of any kind of pressure, on the part of your parents or of society in general, to make you be an insurance man. You will be distinguished, I have no doubt, sincerely speaking. But there is a power in the very air, rooted in the ideas of our progenitors and in many of our contemporaries, which will give you great leeway in your choice of the field in which you wish to be distinguished. Now, there is another thing to think about: there *are* in America families who would like to see their sons hang on to mamma's breast for their entire lifetimes. But we have no business considering these anomalies in any general survey of America. They are the business of the mental doctors. I am trying here to speak of the folks who have, in my opinion, attained to that freedom, not only of individual accomplishment, but of spirit, which permits a fellow to follow his bent without injuring his conscience. The point of all this is to remind you that this freedom is going inevitably to mean a certain wildness in the complexion of the whole nation. If everybody is given much freedom of choice and selection, we are going to be much more restless and energetic in our pursuit of lives. We are also going to be lonely. Not lonely, perhaps, in the sense of our relations with our immediate families; but rather in relation to those two great corresponding facts: the hugeness of the country and the hugeness, the space, of the ideas and traditions which accompany it.

As in any group of free men, there is some confusion. Also, there is, and has always been here, the search for order. Here I can make use of two accurate terms by the German poet Nietzsche, who suggested that there are two great forces in the world. One of them is the force of pure animality and physical energy, called the Dionysian. The other he called the Apollonian, which represents the desire to bring order out of chaos. America is fascinating to watch when one considers it according to these forces which are in operation without ceasing. There is a strain between the confusion and the search for order. This strain is our life, our national vitality. It may be compared to a sculptor (the sense and desire for order) working with a huge mass of pure white marble (the shapeless confusion) which resists the sculptor's hand, but which often responds to his sensitivity and his skill, and yields forms of great strength and loveliness. I think more and more, as I grow and mature a little, that the strain, the power of directing and unifying our mass originality together with our sense of order and organization, is one of the most vital motivations in our lives as individuals and in the life of our nation as a whole.

Undoubtedly you will find in these previous remarks many things which do not concur with logic or with the facts available. However, I hope they stimulate further discussion.

There is an author with whom, to my knowledge, you have not become acquainted. However, I want you to know him, because, knowing him, you receive many interesting and valuable insights into that America which we have been discussing and which commands both our affection and our awe. This author is Thomas Wolfe. He has been recently attacked by certain critics because his books do not meet their rules as they think novels should be written. This is absurd, of course, because Wolfe was not a novelist at all. He was a poet, and his books are full of gorgeous paeans and lamentations over the enormous and heroic beauties of America. In order to illustrate his insights, and perhaps to draw you into reading an author whom I am sure you would enjoy with great intensity, I want to quote a passage taken from his huge book (1,000 pages) called *Of Time and the River*. This is one of Wolfe's most notable descriptions of life as he sees it in this country, and I want you to read it for pleasure. The passage really may make a poem; and it may be called "America." Read it, and look into your own memories:

> America has a thousand lights and weathers and we walk the streets, we walk the streets forever, we walk the streets of life alone . . .

[Wright goes on to type out a full five pages from *Of Time and the River*, Book II ("Young Faustus"), Chapter XIV.]

* * *

You are no doubt wondering by this time the reason for running on so, this long attempt to say something single and clear. It is this: I have been trying to give some conception, together with a reinforcement through quoting the man whom I consider one of modern America's leading interpreters, of the manifold variety of the country in which you and I are young men. I am simply trying to remind you that in any free country such variety must exist. The fact that it does exist—the fact that we can possess and consider the ideas and opinions of sincere liberals—means that we are still operating under a principle of freedom. It is a fact. Think it over: if we were under a totalitarian system, we would have no liberals, nor conservatives either. We should all be goading it to the self-awareness which is the primary condition of improvement.

Meanwhile, my position on the present war situation is clear. We are endangered, there is no doubt. And I stand ready to answer when I am needed. America is precious to me, and not least among its virtues is the right of free discussion and criticism.

Jack, believe me, you do not need to be apprehensive about the willingness of the liberals to support this nation. Nowhere else could any man attempt to speak his mind so freely. The whole point is this: there is a temporary confusion arising from the fact that we are free, and that therefore every man is talking at once. But a common danger from without will unite us to the immediacy of the common defense.

Of course, it is a moment of crisis, and that is what prompted your letter. It is also what prompted my quick and sincere answer. I hope I have succeeded in explaining what I mean by America's temporary weakness and this weakness (i.e., the right of every man to mind his own business) as its strength in the long run. Only free men are strong. A bully may punch Joe Louis in the back, and it may take Joe fully five minutes to turn around and face him. But when that turning is accomplished, Joe only needs one punch. This is exactly what I think is the situation in America. The Korean situation arose, as did Pearl Harbor, when we here were minding our own business. At the moment we are turning around. When our power is mobilized (and the Americans are widely known for their power of cooperation in crisis), it will require but one punch.

In the meanwhile, let us retain our mutual sense of discussion. It is this discussion which gives us the strength to respond to aggression. Without it we should be as weak as is any country under totalitarianism.

I hope I have made myself clear.

Sincerely,
Adam

To Elizabeth Willerton Esterly

Warnock, Ohio
January 6, 1951

Dear Elizabeth,

I suppose this letter, before it really gets finished, will run to many pages, and be typed on odd kinds of paper, all different. Some of it may be done on this lined stuff, some on typing paper, with various kinds of type, or composed in long hand with varying colors of ink or lead. On the other hand, the letter may end after a mere page or so. But you know the inconsistency of form to be found in my correspondence. I like to write spontaneously. Letters can be very close to conversation; and hence they can be valuable. In an honest and vigorous conversation, a man is always open to attack; and through attack he is instructed.

That is the kind of thing which frightens me about Henry. As you yourself pointed out very excitedly, he often closes his arguments with excellent figures of speech. The catch is that a discussion ought never be closed, by a figure of speech or anything else. I think I very well understand your statement: that a perfect solution to any human problem makes you want to tear it to pieces.

This is all leading up to Ivan Karamazov. It is close to midnight now, and I shall be up all night with Dostoyevsky. You know, of course, that I read the book with your essay on it back at Martins Ferry in the early days. I read it again in Japan. Now I am reading it again. I am afraid it is not a work which one can read for fictional pleasure. I don't mean to deny the coherence of the structure of the book. I only mean that reading, say, the perfect and lovely poems of Robert Herrick is quite a distinct experience from reading *The Brothers*. For, regardless of aesthetic considerations, Dostoyevsky has this in common with Shakespeare: his characters are, above all, human. Hence, all pleasant possibilities of perfect consistency are removed, and one has to face a train of very violent and frequently unexplained contradictions. You remember that often, very often in fact, D. declines to explain his characters' confusions. He, again, is not being precious or "artistic"; but there is only one way to expose his great themes, and that is to show them in operation among people projected, as far and as clearly as possible for a writer, as they actually are. One of the great themes, for example, is D.'s insistence that social justice is an element which must figure in any metaphysical "Weltanschauung" or that "world-view" is too limited to be of value to the serious thinker. Nobody can escape, indeed nobody ought to escape, the touch of mortality, the sense of guilt and responsibility toward his fellows. Not even Alyosha escapes. Does not Ivan point out to him that even he (Alyosha) is a Karamazov and therefore has a devil seated in his heart? Now, in this connection, let me suggest that you look at Goethe, in case you ever look into *The Brothers* again. Goethe defines the doctrine of the devil and man as traveling hand in hand. Briefly, dreadfully oversimplified, I should present Goethe's definition thus: man is innocent and virtuous without the devil, but he is not able to account for the problem of evil, which problem is always with us, and must therefore be understood if it is to be dealt with; now, only the devil can stimulate man. Once man is stimulated by the devil, or the challenge of evil, he begins to get restless, he begins to move about and search, he begins to realize that his separate branches of knowledge and achievement (science, poetry, sex, architecture, music, jurisprudence, etc.) are as nothing unless he can find the principle which reveals their interrelation. Here comes the Goethe paradox of principle as action, for only in action can man find the underlying principle of harmony. The principle is love. Towards the end of *Faust*, Part II, Goethe has this famous line:

> *Die Tat ist alles, nichts der Ruhm . . .*
> The deed is everything, fame is nothing . . .

Principle as action, action as principle. The best example of the conception I can think of is the life of Christ. Look up the 9th chapter of the gospel according to St. John, and ask yourself: who has the more powerful understanding of the universe, Christ or the public critics; in other words, who possesses the keenest insight into an underlying principle (love) which is able to bind the situation of the blind beggar into a coherent metaphysical whole, in which all elements, even the hypocrisy of the Pharisees, are set in order?

But the way of getting at these ideas is a devious one, even more so in Dostoyevsky and Shakespeare than in Goethe, because the latter is too willing sometimes to give up his people, characters in preference for the clarity of the idea; while, as we say, the other two authors are always and everywhere concerned primarily with the place of the living, frequently self-contradictory human being in the metaphysical system of justification for God or order or whatever you want to call it, according to your religion or atheism etc.

This is my reason for thinking suspiciously about Henry's stopping the discussion with a good figure of speech about boundaries. I think the function of a figure of speech, in a discussion, of course, quite literally, is to be attacked or broken. We establish certain points in our analyses, clarify and illustrate them through simile or metaphor, and then proceed, as humbly as may be, to tear holes in them and look through them to a deeper understanding. For no matter what Henry says about masochism or your alleged "enjoyment of your dissatisfaction" the problem of evil remains a Gothic one, one which I still feel is not an ultimate problem but rather a developing one.* Hence the need

---

*In the margin: "That is, it is real and pertinent for us as for, say, an ancient like Socrates, or for a future thinker."

for reinterpretation of it, for the double need of trying to understand and fit things together even while, as you and Henry so justly say, one must try to get to know as many fellows personally as possible. For my part, I may insert the parenthetical remark that I am beginning to think my only salvation in the present and future crises will be in my fighting my own native reserve, and in compelling myself to do all sorts of things like hitch-hiking, in order to find the human being. I do not believe the human being can be given Utopia. He is too tough to understand. The very depth and toughness of understanding required for any humble student of his human brothers is perhaps the keenest thing I am getting out of my third reading of the Dostoyevsky novel. If Henry doesn't know the book you certainly ought to introduce him to it. For you yourself only *tell* Henry that perfect solutions to the human problem are suspect. Dostoyevsky has the valuable and useful (for us) ability to portray this suspicion in dramatic form. We can refuse ideas dissociated from life for the sake of hypothetical discussions, but it is simply out of the question to refuse life itself, and that is what D. is trying to indicate to us.

I hope I am making myself clear. I am not finally secure in my ideas on the subject, and hence the supreme value of personal discussions. We can check and recheck one another as we proceed.

Monday night the religion class meets and discussion of Dostoyevsky will begin. Dr. Andre Hanfman, the [German professor] and linguist will be with us, I think. He is also a student of Russian and general European history. Another fellow here, Dr. Richard Solomon, is a very brilliant historian trained in one of the old school German academies. If we can get him in on the talk, we should really have something. His knowledge of European history is prodigious; and, to top it all off, he also knows Russian.

I'll let you know about the class. I expect, frankly, most of the divinity students to be rather smugly resentful about Dostoyevsky and the latter's relentless probing into the human being; but the discussion is the important thing, and the problems are too real to deny. Hence, it is my intention to keep my ears open, my mouth shut—at least until some of our authorities speak their pieces.

If you're interested, I've written two poems in German. If we ever solve our periodical's financial troubles, I think I'll print one, just for the hell of it.

I wish you would find time to write Liberty a note. She needs some such thing, and would appreciate it so much.

This will have to do temporarily. When I see Dr. Sutcliffe again, I'll procure some stuff for you to look over.

Write me when you have time.

My best to Henry,
Jim

Warnock, Ohio
December 29, 1951

Dear Elizabeth,

It's too bad I missed you. I was down in Martins Ferry, wrangling with Liberty's father, when your card arrived. Then I phoned the farm on Thursday night, but you had already gone [. . .]

I must return to Gambier about next Wednesday; and a short time after my return I must take the comprehensive examination in English. I am not especially confident of my ability to remember the intense intellectual and emotional experiences of the past four years in my study of literature at Kenyon. However, I suppose I'll manage to pass. I am a candidate for a degree with honors, you know; and one of the horrors of my life is the prospect of re-writing, within about one week, the honors essay which I turned in to the English department just before the Christmas vacation began. The paper is entitled "The Will in the Thought and Art of Thomas Hardy," and is 245 pages long, with notes and bibliography. It is rather a lurching, sprawling thing, with extensive discussion of many nineteenth-century European trends of thought; and the head of the English dept. has already expressed disapproval of some of my methods. (It isn't Sutcliffe, who is teaching at Harvard this year; but Dr. Coffin, considerably more conservative and, though a generous man, less brilliant.) The work on the paper became something of a monster to me at the last; and I am not sure I can take much work on it in terms of revision—since I have made three copies of the third and (I thought) final draft. The life of the scholar can drive a person nuts, as you must certainly know. I say this especially because, during the writing of the other thing, I have been struggling terribly on a new poem, a very long one; and I must confess that I've not even finished the first scene. It will be the fourth long poem I've done. The last one, called "The Earth: a True Romance," is the most successful; but if I ever get the time for the present piece it can be even better. I am going to enter "The Earth" in a contest.

Since I last saw you people I have had a few more publications. The most important were two verses in the autumn issue of the *Kenyon Review*. But the most fun were a series of five imitations from the German of Heinrich Heine, which appeared in the most recent issue of *Hika*—the Kenyon undergraduate literary magazine. Incidentally, because of political difficulties, *Hika* is being printed this year by an independent group of students. Reactionary forces of athletes, fraternities, and other *Putsch* groups (rampant at Kenyon as at most other colleges in America, I suppose) put the finger on the radicals in the most fascistic student assembly I have ever seen outside of the movies. The only missing elements were mugs of Bavarian beer and a rank of blackshirts chanting the Horst Wessel song. This year I emerged, incidentally, from the ivory tower, and have taken to writing articles for the school newspaper, all of which articles have been intended to reform the morals and manners of Kenyon students (who are becoming absolutely weird, a completely new race of monsters oriented to the current war propaganda). My last "letter to the editor" literally instigated a small riot. I was not molested, however; two successful fistfights earlier in the semester have informed my political enemies of my position with regard to certain techniques of personal slander.

The muckrakers among American undergraduates are eternally unpopular anyway. Unpopularity is one of their social functions. Van Wyck Brooks, in his earlier and more astute moments, pointed out that the poet would be against the government even in Utopia (this would be good for Utopia, because it would save it from ossification). These young men had better realize what the hell is going on: the exploitation of the people's weariness of world war for the sake of establishing a new fascism—to get us right back where we started from, namely, dying for nothing. Lost causes are the only enduring ones, said Matthew Arnold. Perhaps he meant that we will never really overcome those two-fisted authoritarians who are at present performing in the guise of red-blooded American boys. Do you know George Orwell's perfect picture of horror and degradation? Imagine, says he, a boot, forever being pushed in your face. Not for me, by God. Before long, anybody with the smallest sense of morality is going to have to take a stand. The communists and fascists are both still loose; and free men are still snagged between them. What do we mean when we say life is worth living? I wonder . . . please write . . .

Jim

To Albert Herzing

Warnock, Ohio
February 3, 1952

Dear Al,

Will you please subject these verses to the mercies of your editorial staff out there?

* * *

I have not been writing because, as you know, I have been completing my term at Kenyon. I passed, incidentally; and affairs are beginning to pile up on me. No sooner had I taken the oral examination, than I was offered a job at a prep school in Texas, of all places. Still drunk from a rough test, I accepted. Next Sunday afternoon (Feb. 10th) Liberty and I will be married; and on the morning of the 11th we will leave by train for Center Point, Texas, fifty miles or so from San Antonio. Though various friends of mine have insisted that Texas is hell, I have few misgivings. I don't intend to stay longer than the spring semester. Also, I had no other job, and must do something now that I will have a wife to take care of. Besides, I was in Texas only once—passed through on a troop train—and I expect we'll have a rather engaging time, finding out about southerners and so on. We'll be only about 150 miles from Mexico, and may even get over to see a bull fight, or buy some pornography and send it to Lorrie Bright by pony express. Whatever happens, I'll keep in touch with you. As soon as we get more or less settled down there, I'll write you again.

I have a couple of tentative plans for next fall. But I am so relieved to get out from underneath academic pressure, that I may spend another year teaching or working elsewhere before I try to enter a graduate school. Also, there is a possibility still that I may get the Fulbright to Austria. The latter would solve problems for a year.

But at present I am simply relaxing after those gruelling last weeks at Kenyon. I am convinced that the whole damned educational system in the United States is falsely conceived and inadequately executed. We never have time for thinking—there are always too many footnotes to be made. If the deal in Texas works out the way I expect it to do, I ought to have a reasonably pleasant spring. But the prospect of an eventual two or three years in almost any graduate school I can think of is not too attractive to me. I have a very long poem boiling on the stove, and I am having one sweet leaping hell of a time with it. I hope to get time for it during the next few months.

Meanwhile, as I say, I'll keep in touch with you. Incidentally, Roger Hecht says he heard from you, and that you will appear directly in *Poetry*. I'll look for the poems with pleasure. They're devoting an issue to the Poetry Workshop of Iowa, aren't they?

Please write to me at Warnock, unless you hear from me at Texas. Anything sent here will be forwarded to me at once.

Yours,
Jim

Center Point, Texas
March 17, 1952

(Ah-bah! San Antone!)
Dear Al,

You must excuse a hurried note. In a few minutes I must dash over and help to direct a rehearsal for the spring play.

Liberty and I were thoroughly pleased to hear from you, and now that contact is established we must maintain it. What are you going to do this summer? We are trying to find something in Philadelphia. Just before we left Ohio for Texas, Liberty was notified that she passed the state board exam for nurses, and is now R.N. However, since the nearest hospital here is 12 miles off, and transportation is difficult, she is resting from nursing, and is serving as the school's secretary and nurse. But, as I say, we are trying to find something in Philly. Our contact is Bob Mezey (you met him) who, incidentally, is coming down here with Tom Tenney to spend Kenyon's spring vacation. They will arrive either tonight or sometime tomorrow morning.

I wonder if you would tell me the number (month, etc.) of the *Poetry* issue in which your stuff appeared, so that I can order a copy.

I have been told that *Coraddi* this year is printing pieces by Mezey, Roger Hecht, Jay Gellens, Nick Crome, and myself. Also, this year Kenyon established a prize for poetry—the Robert Frost Poetry Prize. It isn't much really, only an autographed copy of Frost; but since much interest was shown, and many manuscripts submitted, the prize is bound to increase in value. At least it will be maintained at Kenyon, and perhaps some sort of public social recognition will give the poet some acceptance there; even some prestige. I won the prize this year, I have been told, with a long poem called "The Earth." I don't think you've seen it. I am gratified mostly because it *was* a *long* poem (about 35 pages) and the prize indicates that the judges (Ransom, Coffin, Chalmers' wife, Babb, Timberlake) read it.

Listen, I'm late—had an interruption. Please write again soon, and let us know what you're doing this summer. The enclosed things are left entirely to you. I hope you like them.

Yours,
Jim

Martins Ferry, Ohio
August 3, 1952

Dear Al,

[. . .] Liberty and I had been living and working in Philadelphia for the summer, but were called home by the illness of her mother. I'm helping my folks who are moving to a large new farm near Zanesville, Ohio—and Lib is in Cleveland at the moment, seeing about a specialist for her mother.

I forgot to tell you that my Fulbright was granted, and we are scheduled to sail from New York on September 10. I'm to study for about a year at the University of Vienna.

It's good to hear that [Richard] Gibson's novel is on the way, and bad to hear that he will be drafted. Is he still in Europe? How the hell long did his fellowship last, anyhow?

Liberty and I, as I said, spent much of the summer in Philadelphia, a very strange and interesting place. We associated there with a Kenyon undergraduate named Robert Mezey, whom you met during your visit to Kenyon at last fall's dance weekend. Mezey is a bright boy and a pretty promising writer of verses. He was successful with a paper or two in Ransom's classes, and, you may recall, was printed in *Coraddi* in the spring. He would like very much to write you, and I promised him that I would tell you about him. He will also send you some poems, some of them pretty nice.

Please write to me at the Martins Ferry address on the envelope. Also, if you have extra copies of anything you've written recently, may I see them?

Sincerely,
Jim

To Robert Mezey

Vienna, Austria
April/May 1953

Dear Bob,

[. . .] You have labored strenuously this year, and I hope you are assured, in your own mind, that your work has meaning. All I can do here is confirm what you must already realize: that, beyond merely technical considerations, you have achieved a greater and finer depth of emotion in the poems of the past year. Of course you know how important emotional maturity is. You no longer are satisfied with phonetically perfect hysterical outbursts on the sexual theme (here I assume you are not satisfied with "The Dream of a Sleeping Serpent"). With "The Ape," "In the Environs of the Funeral Home," "A Post Mortem Speech," "Texas," "The Salesman," you have deepened appreciably in short forms. There is nothing to say about the long poem but that it is beautiful as it stands; and that I am especially glad because it testifies to a belief in life, a celebration, a promise of many more wonderful poems, songs, and humanity. I told you once that I dislike references to poetic genius in your case. You are still young for that kind of thing—and there are fires of agony to come. Yet it is equally important, at this period after difficult labor, that you should not hurt yourself by denying the great value of this year's production. Probably another publication would do much for you now. But you must be ready for long and bitter waiting. Publishing procedures are as complex and frustrating as most other institutions in the modern world. Seek always the divine simplicity of poetry. Poetry like this wonderful piece, and yet better.

No use sending you anything else of mine now. I am just midway in making a selection of forty or forty-five poems to show you in a group. I should say I have utterly and thoroughly revised the poem about waiting for Franz, and it is now called "A Legend of My Child's Awakening," with an epigraph in Low German by Storm. I hope you aren't shocked to hear that it now has about 11 stanzas instead of the 8 of the previous version. But nearly everything is changed. I threw out everything as you advised, and wrestled long and deeply with the experience. I think it is the most effective piece I have done this year. You will see.

I hope you see [Eugene] Pugatch. I will write him directly. Instead of getting him the beer stein which he requested (they are hideously expensive, and quite beyond our means), I think I am going to bring him a book. I also will have a small gift for you. I hope you realize that its slight price does not reflect the great affection which prompts it.

Presumably you will have seen Pugatch, and made precise arrangements about our going from N.Y. to Boston and back again. I have something to add: in N.Y. we may conceivably be forced to stay overnight again, and I wonder if it would be possible (and cricket) to exploit the Goldhurst brothers [Richard and William] once more. Of course we want to see Wilbur, Rutledge, and Edgar Doctorow. I would like at least to phone Sy Weissman in Brooklyn—and what a marvel it would be if we could get in touch with Harvey Robbin.

Furthermore, presumably you will have seen John Schmitt at Kenyon during commencement. Please bring me news of him. When we all get rich, you and John and I must return to Vienna and write an opera together. We saw *Wozzeck*! It was the greatest piece of drama I ever saw. Also fine was Wagner's "Meistersinger," a fine positive snort of bawdiness, and an orgy of ecstatic song.

But now I am sick of Vienna and Europe. It is too heavy, too slow, too arty. I long for some of that glorious barbarism, that gratifying bleakness and loneliness which is so much of America to me. There is no denying that country America is crude and strange and frightening, but man I love it with my whole person. Beethoven was lonely in this town. What his contemporaries liked was pretty tunes. Now his statue broods very gray in the Zentralfriedhof, bleak as ever, grand and lonely and fulfilling. God damn it! I want to hear the people on the street spitting and snarling my own language. You will never know how much I anticipate our hitchhiking from Chandlersville to Gambier to see Timberlake, Coffin and Pappy. And you will be crazy about Franz. He grows rounder and rosier and plumper every day, and now he can laugh aloud and try to imitate the vowel sounds. Please write from Philadelphia.

Love, and a letter soon, from Lib.

Jim

Be Glad of the Green Wall

1954–1958

James and Franz Wright, Washington State, April 1954

Seattle seems like some impossible Eden. It is certainly the only town that I ever really cared to live in . . . I can survive in Minneapolis. The students are wonderful. Allen Tate is friendly. It's not a town to commit suicide in, at any rate (the waterways are always frozen over).

—from a letter to Theodore Roethke
February 11, 1958

I just don't like the Midwest very much. Minneapolis is okay, but I just don't like it. I think I served my time in such towns when I was a kid . . . and I was happy with the air and everything else up there near the Pacific Ocean. It is, for one thing, very lonesome here . . . I always loved the west, and I would like to live and teach there again.

—from a letter to Theodore Roethke
March 27, 1959

James, Liberty, and infant Franz returned to the United States from Vienna after a pilgrimage to Thomas Hardy country in Dorset, England. James had been accepted into the graduate program at the University of Washington, and the family settled in Seattle that fall. They lived there until 1957, when James completed everything but the written thesis for a Ph.D. in English literature. In the late summer of 1957 the family moved again, this time to Minneapolis, when James accepted a position in the Department of English at the University of Minnesota.

From Minneapolis, James kept in touch with two teachers at the University of Washington who had become important friends: Theodore Roethke and Wayne Burns. Letters to Burns, his thesis adviser, were mostly concerned with his dissertation, *The Comic Imagination of the Young Dickens*. He wrote to both men of his difficulty in adjusting to the Midwest after Seattle, though his letters concentrated mainly on discussions of poetry. During this time, James also began an important and lifelong correspondence with the poet and editor Donald Hall.

To Donald Hall

Dear Mr. Hall:

Thank you very much for your extremely kind letter. Your invitation gives me a chance to send you some things which are pretty rough, but which I genuinely care about. There are three pieces. The theme of each one is very violent, and so I tried to write them as smoothly as I could. However, you will undoubtedly find all kind of groping rough places. So whether or not you're interested in them enough to accept them, I'd deeply appreciate hearing how you feel about them. On the other hand, if you're as busy these days as I am, you might feel numb about commenting on the thousands of verses you must get every month. But you will judge.

Sincerely,
James Wright

Seattle
February 1, 1955

Dear Mr. Hall:

You undoubtedly know the kind of cold letter one can often get from an editor; so you can see how surprised and delighted I was to get your friendly note.

You're right about the mistyping in the George Doty poem. The lines ought to read:

> He stopped his car and found
> A girl on the . . . etc.

As for the title, do whatever you like. I called it "A Poem About . . . etc." only because somebody told me that the fellow's name alone would make it seem that the prisoner himself was either talking or meditating, at least in the first few lines. Of course, the piece is *about* the prisoner, and is a speculation by a person who stands outside the prison and thinks about the person within. It might be called "A Complaint for George Doty in the Death House" or something like that. But if you think the introductory words aren't necessary, then by all means leave them out.

And thank you very much for your extended comments on the poem about the girl's dream. Your letter contained what is probably the most incredible rejection slip ever seen—the kind of editorial justification which everyone desires, and almost no one gets.

Yes, I went to Kenyon. I'm still trying to resist the influence of that wonderful place. And I was in *Coraddi* a couple of times, so we were probably printed side by side. I don't know Mr. Matchett very well, but I'll tell him you asked about him.

As for biographical material: I've gone to Kenyon and the University of Vienna, I'm studying in the graduate school here at the University of Washington, and sometimes feel like a fool (but don't put that in a contributor's note). I've had a lot of stuff printed in the *Kenyon*, *The Sewanee*, *Poetry*, *The Western*, and the *Avon Book of Modern Writing*. Other things are to appear sooner or later, but that is neither here nor there. I just turned twenty-seven, and I have a wife and child.

We consider that we have escaped from the East as from a mad and furious master. But if you ever get to Seattle, our house is certainly open to you and yours. Thanks a lot for writing; and I hope we can keep in touch.

Sincerely,
Jim Wright

Seattle
June 15, 1955

Dear Don,

My father is a little older than yours, but it took me many, many years to come to an understanding of what he is, of what he means in my life. He is not very well educated, you see. He went to school as far as the eighth grade, and then became a laborer. For something more than fifty years he has been a machinist at a glass factory in Wheeling, West Virginia. What with one thing and another, he and I never had anything to say to each other till, one day at Kenyon, I threw off the atmosphere and hitchhiked to our farm, which is located in southeastern Ohio, about 120 miles from Kenyon. No one was home in that barren, ugly place, a perfect hell of twisted little farms and slag piles and taverns, except my father, who sat looking out a cracked window. It was very strange to me. I felt as though I had suddenly materialized out of the air. For about three hours we talked, and read together, out of the Bible, the only real book, I suppose, he has ever known anything about. The meeting was not spectacular, but it shook me very deeply. I had not known of the man's existence before. It was like falling in love. Somewhat later I wrote a little poem called "Father" and Mr. Ransom printed it, in *The Kenyon Review*.

The poem, and the experience of writing it, was curious. Now, although I went through a period in which I produced a great bulk of verses, the actual writing of anything rhythmic has tended to be agonizingly hard for me. Different minds work different ways, and my mode of thinking is slow and laborious. But this particular poem came out with a slightly startling speed and wholeness. I couldn't understand it after it was done, and showed it diffidently to Mr. Ransom, who genuinely frightened me when he said he wanted to print it. It was the first thing I ever had published in an important magazine, and I sincerely thought it was gibberish. I guess I had seen that business about water and birth, and so on, but I'm sure I hadn't paid any attention.

Anyway, I'm just leading up to typing out the poem for you. Perhaps this will seem impertinent; but, really, I was terribly moved by the anguish of your letter's beginning, and I wanted to answer in the best, most dignified way I could find. So here is the poem "Father" which is, I think, a kind of love poem to him, if there are things like that:

In paradise I placed my foot into the boat and said:
Who prayed for me?
                    But only the dip of an oar
In water sounded. Slowly fog from some cold shore
Circled in wreathes around my head.

But who is waiting?
                    And the wind began,
Transfiguring my face from nothingness
To tiny weeping eyes. And when my voice
Grew real, there was a place
Far, far below on earth. There was a tiny man:

It was my father wandering round the waters at the wharf.
Irritably he circled and he called
Out to the marine currents up and down;
But heard only a cold unmeaning cough,
And saw the oarsman, shawled in mist and ether,
Drifting out of the great forgiving deep.

He drew me from the boat. I was asleep.
And we went home together.

* * *

Perhaps it's like that. We get the fog apart for a moment, and we rush through the opening, and find them. And then we look around us, and the whole country is strange and new, and we are men. The whole affair seems to last so short a time.

I'm delighted that your book will be out next year. It will certainly be one of the three or four books a year I can afford to buy. I've been thinking a good deal about the style of your poems, and I've concluded that you must be one of the few civilized men left in the world—that is, you must take as much delight in great poets like Dryden as a very few other young men can do. Perhaps it is the next swing our language must take. We must realize that the metaphysical lyric, though gloriously demonstrated in the age just past, cannot be re-written a thousand times. Imitators of Donne generally turn into Cowleys and Clevelands. On the other hand, our alternative is not necessarily to reestablish the more rationalistic grace of the heroic couplet—though, as Eliot said in writing of Samuel Johnson (one of my gods, incidentally), that form is far from worn out. Ages do not repeat themselves so closely. We have a chance to do a million things Rilke and the rest couldn't do. We can be funny and gross and graceful, all of these; but

we can get deeper than the lyric itself. We can bring back into our poetry the rich stuff of drama—not the form of the stage, though that is
possible and I am unqualified to write of it or speak of it, but the devices of drama which toughen and deepen poetry through its exploration of point-of-view, personality, and so on. I have written about ten
dramatic monologues, and I expect to go on trying. By the way, nobody will publish a damned one of them. The old mossbacks say that
we can never equal the lyrics of the first half of this century, and yet
they are squeamish about publishing the other tries we make. But this,
of course, is just an excited squeak about some of the many thoughts
which your pamphlet of verses set going in my head.

I have a very young friend named Robert Mezey who was a good
associate of mine back at Kenyon a while ago. He has just been discharged from the army, is twenty years old, and is wandering around
Philadelphia lamenting the fact that he has already written himself
out. The idea of a twenty-year-old's saying such a thing was so funny
to me, that I thought I'd mention him. He is really one of the most
gifted people I know, and has written two or three very beautiful poems. One of them in particular is striking. While he was in the army he
had some nervous ailment, and was in a mental hospital for a while.
One afternoon he heard a woman weeping in one of the wards; and
that so set him off, that after a good deal of labor he wrote a poem
called "Dusk Near a Mental Hospital" which is one of the finest and
most touching poems I have seen in a long, long time. I don't know exactly what he'll do next. He's thinking of going to Iowa. But whatever
he does, he certainly ought to be a brilliant poet. You ought to like
him—he is a likeable person, and can write epigrams. (As I told you
once, I have an obsessive admiration for writers of epigrams. I'm one
of those people who can never think what to say till the party is over.)

I hope the opening of this letter doesn't offend you. I wanted, and
needed, to say something; and almost everything I could think of
sounded stupid. There is a time when prose absolutely breaks down.

Yours,
Jim Wright

Dear Don,

Your letter was splendid, as always. Let me depart from my own usual procedure, and try to answer directly some of your questions and remarks.

Yes, I've seen [W. S.] Merwin's new poems all over hell's half-acre. If I've ever mentioned his work to you, it was probably with a kind of half-amused despair. For a long time it was a joke between my wife and me that every time I got a poem printed it would be either preceded or followed by a poem of Merwin's. The joke was based on the fact that his stuff has got so good it is astonishing. To speak straight, I think his talent is ripening remarkably, and that he will be a great poet. Some objections to his earlier pieces had to do with his concern for technique over deeper emotional effects; but I think he always must have been a man of feeling, for even in the early pieces you find "The Ballad of John Cable and Three Gentlemen," one of the most beautiful poems I know (and, by God, it appeared in *The Kenyon Review* right smack dab in front of the first poem I ever had printed!). His range of learning and wit and meter always fills me with admirations, and I should be very pleased to meet him sometime.

I heard from Yale (simply that they received the ms.). Of course, Don, I realize that the field is crowded, and that my book doesn't have the chance of a snowball in hell. I have pretty well satisfied myself with the expectation of running into a publisher some years hence. I don't know but what this situation satisfies me best. I have so many things coming out in periodicals; and I write sometimes at such hectic speed (I have to, I have so much else to do), that I want to get time one of these days to go over everything again. As for Auden, he is no doubt one of the best writers of our day, etc.; but I wonder if it has ever occurred to you how much power he has over our generation, as a reviewer, as a contest judge, and as a direct influence. Sometimes I don't like it. He has many noble things to say about poetry, and many noble poems of his own; but there is also a streak of smart-aleck in him which is easy to imitate, and which, I think, is sometimes too easy for him to exercise. Maybe this is just a rambling restlessness. To tell the truth, I have a great deal more faith in somebody like Louise Bogan, who is certainly not without wit of the most acute kind, but who also possesses a deeper sympathy for younger people. Both she and Auden spoke here. Auden was entertaining all right; but Bogan was something else. She was a radiant presence. Chatting with Auden, I felt like a punk, which is no doubt what I really am; but talking with Bogan, I felt like an acknowledged human being with something important to do.

Roger [Hecht] had mentioned [Louis] Simpson many times in letters, and has done everything possible (as you have done) to get me to read his poems (which I have done, in complete agreement with both you and Roger). I hope, incidentally, that you can meet Roger sometime. You will enjoy him. I never met his brother, though I have admired him for a long time.

I'm very glad that Thom Gunn took those two poems, particularly "Unborn Child," which is one of your best. I wonder if Merwin is going to be in that group. Gunn may as well throw the book at those English.

In April and May and June I'm going to have a little spate of poems popping up all over hell's half-acre. Gunn says the *London* will be out in about May. In April I'm having a spring song in *New World Writing*. In the April issue of *Poetry* I have four new poems. There's one to appear in the *University of Kansas City Review* sometime in the spring. And I just heard from Jackson Mathews that he's going to use three of my translations from the contemporary French poet René Char in a book (called *Hypnos Waking*) which Random House is supposed to publish on June 4.

Incidentally, you ought to know Jackson Mathews, if you haven't met him already. He was a great teacher here at Washington, and he's just gone to Paris on a Bollingen fellowship to work on a new edition of Valery's works. He is a friend of Char (one of the great masters of our time, I think) and is constantly preoccupied with the problem of translating him. Mathews and his wife edited the New Directions edition of Baudelaire that just came out last year. Most of Jack's poems and translations come out in *Botteghe Oscure*; but his articles elsewhere, chiefly in the *Sewanee Review*. I think it was in the *Sewanee* of Fall 1953 that he had his review of Roy Campbell's *Baudelaire*, and in it he set forth his theory of translation, which you would find extremely interesting. (Briefly, it would require an almost inconceivable biological accident for a poet in one language to have exactly the same temperament and technical equipment to translate a great poet like Baudelaire;

hence, the idea is to translate him by parceling out his works to a good number of poets in English who can give single poems sufficient study. This notion might sound fragmentary and odd; but I think it produced a tremendous translation of Baudelaire, probably the definitive one in English.) Well, Jack Mathews works and produces with great energy—criticism, translation, stories, poems—but his productions are nothing compared with the man himself. You ought to know him [. . .]

About Bob Mezey: to tell the truth, I'm starting to worry about him. A while ago he wrote and said he and his wife were going to jaunt around the country, and then come to Seattle in March. Well, I answered his letter, but I haven't heard anything; and now that you say your letter was returned from both Raleigh and Seattle (by me), I'm wondering if the two Mezeys haven't got stuck somewhere. It's been snowing like hell all over the country, even in Seattle; and they might well be holed up in Butte, Montana, or someplace like that. Have you heard anything?

J. V. Cunningham is coming out here to give a Shakespeare course this summer. It will be fine to have him around. We need some intellect in this community, now that Mathews and Roethke are gone. Among the active writers, [Charles] Gullans is the only effective defender of the classical mind in the whole town. Incidentally, he showed me some new things which are quite fine.

I know I haven't sent you anything new for a while. To tell the truth, I haven't even typed much, though I've been writing like hell, mostly stuff that isn't coming off. I can't say that I feel barren—far from it. But I'm going through some odd stage in which changes, which I don't understand, are taking place. I don't want to sound like *Letters to a Young Poet*; but it's the truth.

Well, I'll enclose one brand new piece, of which I am not at all sure. It lies at the moment in my notebook in a final (?) longhand version. I guess this fumbling and searching around is symptomatic. People are ready for books at different times, and I guess I just ain't ready; because I don't yet know just what the hell I'm doing.

Please write.

Yours, Jim

Seattle
May 17, 1956

Dear Don,

I've won the Yale prize! Dear Don, I don't know what to say to you, I am so happy.

Jim

To Philip Timberlake

Seattle
August 25, 1956

Dear Dr. Timberlake:

It was very good to have your letter. I'll be glad if we can keep in touch now and then, not only on the matter of the possible Kenyon instructorship, but also for friendship's sake.

You spoke of the rising tide of freshmen. I should tell you that whatever college teaching I've done (three years of it, with the fourth coming up) has been with freshmen. I've taught the greenhorns in the daytime and the adults in the evening. I've taught rather basic courses in the composition of essays; others in logic and slightly more complicated problems in rhetoric—for example, we try to explain to the Freshmen just what kinds of meaning are involved when, say, Mc-Carthy refers to *Alger* Stevenson; and I've taught also the third course in our three-quarter sequence—a kind of introduction to the study of literature. Finally, I've had a little experience in teaching a remedial course in grammar and sentence structure, and I'll probably teach another such course in the coming year. It might be useful for me to tell you that I enjoy teaching freshmen very much. Nothing in teaching can give me so much satisfaction as showing students that it is illogical as well as immoral to use the personalities and writings of other men simply as crude material for their own undeveloped sensations. I think freshmen respond more directly and honestly to a teacher in these matters than do the slightly older literary "sophisticates," who, these days, are often well on the way to corruption. But I see that I'm beginning a pedantic sermon here, instead of clearly telling you what I've done and what I like to do.

All I meant by saying I was a little apprehensive about your judgment of my book was that you were the hardest reader to impress with undergraduate tricks back in my old days at Kenyon. We used to feel—Roger Hecht, Jay Gellens, and the rest—that you read not only as a contemporary but with some of the great and Johnsonian past which insisted that poetry was a serious matter and should not be fiddled away in nonsense. Yet undergraduates are full of nonsense, and nonsense always quakes under the searchlight of the Johnsonian reading. I must say that, what with the intervening years of intense writing and disillusionment with editors, I would rather be called a minor versifier by Johnson than praised as a new Shakespeare by Stanley Edgar Hyman (who, I believe, is a catastrophe in the English language comparable to the bombing of Hiroshima). What I am trying to say can be expressed in words which have been used often but which cannot be worn out: "The irregular combinations of fanciful invention may delight a-while, by that novelty of which the common satiety of life sends us all in quest; but the pleasures of sudden wonder are soon exhausted, and the mind can only repose on the stability of truth." All that is not to say that I dislike fooling around with language—far from it. But the fooling has sooner or later got to expose itself to the judgment of that larger and more generous common humanity which is more important than poetry, and in vital relation to which the final importance of poetry is, or ought to be, defined.

Speaking of Roger Hecht, he spent a week with us recently. He is working in New York, and seemed in good physical condition—he hadn't had a fainting spell in about two years. We had a perfectly splendid reunion, with lots of beer and music and conversation. I think he will be writing you soon, if he hasn't done so already.

I've waited till the end of the letter to mention the enclosed poem.* It isn't necessary to talk about it, except to say that I had the dream a few nights ago, and couldn't think of anything to do but work the thing out—I wrote the first version very fast, and the second and final one very slowly. If you think the poem is worth anything, I wish you would offer it to the *Kenyon Alumni Bulletin*. I don't know what you thought objectively about Dr. Coffin's voice in the reading of poetry—I know that it carried a certain twang—but a voice in poetry is not the same as a

*See Appendix, p. 560, for the poem "A Dream of Charles Coffin's Voice."

voice singing Mozart; and, even if the voice were bad, I should still remember it as beautiful, because it was the first voice I ever heard reading Milton aloud. It had the freshness of the early world; it had the
dew upon it.

Please write a note when you get around to it—it needn't be
long—just something by way of keeping in touch.

Yours,
Jim

To Donald Hall

Seattle
March 31, 1957

Dear Don,

I guess you've occasionally wondered what the hell, but you'll remember that I had that Ph.D. general exam to face. Well, I faced it,
and I passed. Now it can be told: next year I'll be an instructor in humanities at the University of Minnesota in Minneapolis. From what I
hear, and keep hearing all the time, it's a good place—scholarly as well
as vitally creative. Arnold Stein went there (you know him), and there
are people like Monk, Unger, Tate, and John Berryman.

Speaking of Berryman, what do you think of "Homage to Mistress
Bradstreet"? Just the other day John Haislip (who, it seems, is a good
friend of Berryman's from way back) lent me the poem in its newly
published form, and I must say that I was often overwhelmed by it—
although two or three times I lost the point of view, and couldn't even
straighten it out with reference to the notes. Perhaps further reading
will clarify the argument. In any case, it is in many ways a great poem,
I believe. What do you think?

Robert Lowell spoke here last week, and, though he is probably the
world's worst public performer, he certainly is an appealing man. His
poems are magnificent.

Philip Booth sent me a copy of his book, and I like it fine—though
the frequent compound adjectives in the first part of the book are
sprinkled a bit too thick. The political poem (I think it's "Easter, 1954")
is one of his best, and a fierce and beautiful poem. He has a good deal

of stuff in him, and is going to produce a great poem one of these days, if I am not mistaken. There is a certain uncluttered honesty about his mind, which certainly reminds one of his hero Thoreau.

As for me, my book isn't out yet. It's got me terribly skittish waiting for it. It's worse than waiting for the god damned Ph.D. oral. To make matters worse—much worse—is the fact that, as far as I can tell, I've got another book done. Now, I can't just sit and stare at it. Yet it would be ludicrous to send it to Yale (they have the option on the second book) even before the first one is in print and on the stands. I might hand it over to the tender mercies of Bill Matchett (he gave me a fine reading at one stage of *The Green Wall*) or Arnold Stein (who has promised me to go over it, and he will certainly cut it to ribbons), but I don't know what else to do. It's extremely nerve-racking to me to have the thing lying around inert. The prospect of sending it to Yale in a little while is very frustrating; because it's obvious that they're going to reject it, and I'll have to go through the whole business of finding a publisher all over again. I swear to God one of these days I'm going to give up poetry and go directly in for a life of crime.

As a matter of fact, I've written one new poem in a while, and it's a political poem of a sort.* Well, what the hell, I'll enclose it. It's got its prison scene, and a sort of submerged surrealistic hymn in the second part.

You haven't written for a while, and I don't blame you, but I hope to God you are well, and that your family is well, and that you are getting your work straightened out the way you want it.

Please write soon.

Yours,
Jim

To Theodore Roethke

Minneapolis
September 13, 1957

Dear Ted,

We've been here about three weeks now. I might say that we're reasonably settled, though there are still a few things to do. The neighbor-

---

*See Appendix, p. 562, for the poem "American Twilights, 1957."

hood is comparatively quiet. There are several kids of Franz's age; so we'll live.

Mr. Hornberger, the head of the English dept., greeted me pretty hospitably, and I met William Van O'Connor, who was quite cordial. For the rest, the building that houses the English dept. is in a hell of a mess, because of redecoration or painting or something. At any rate, I now have an office, and there I have occasion to write a poem:

> My office-mate
> Will be Allen Tate,
> And if I get on his nerves
> It will be no more than Hornberger deserves.

We've made friends with some cordial people from the humanities dept., but, for the most part, the town looks as socially bleak as it is physically attractive. I expect that my chief resources through a cold winter will be Dickens, footnotes, teaching, and whiskey—the last of which is moderately priced and easily available, thank God.

I hope you don't mind my mentioning this, but it has been on my mind: I remember our talking one time about your new book, and the problem of reviewing it for *Poetry*. I don't know for sure that you would take to the idea of my writing a review, or whether Rago would agree, or how I should go about writing him, or what. If you have any thoughts on the subject, would you tell them to me? I think I could do a good job on it. At least, I would do my homework. However, it's up to you, of course.

Lib has a turkey in the oven, and it is about ready to emerge. I guess there are compensations for leaving Seattle. We could have had turkey there, however, and I'm not sure whether I like this place or not. I think I don't. But that's neither here nor there.

We hope that Beatrice is better, and that you are feeling well.

I don't know what sort of correspondent you are, but I'll soon find out.

Yours,

Jim

Minneapolis
October 24, 1957

Dear Ted,

I see by the return address that you're hospitalized. Well, you sound good in your letter. Get a good rest; and, if there's anything you want sent to you, or anything you want done, don't hesitate to give Lib and me the word. I can't think of any use for our phone number at the moment, but in case you want it for anything, it's FEDERAL 6-9829.

Just as soon as I got your note, I wrote an explanatory letter to John Palmer at *Yale Review* about your new book. He hasn't had time to answer yet, but as soon as he does I'll tell you what happened. The same evening, I wrote to your publisher in London, and ordered a copy of the book. I asked them to send it to me pronto, because I want to see it soon. I have my copy of "The Waking," but I need to see the entire book in one piece, since one of my main points would have to do with the recognizable coherence of development from the early pieces to the most recent ones.

By the way, in your earlier letter you said you were going to send me the new piece you had been working on. From your description, it sounded pretty exciting. May I still see it?

There's a fellow here—named Morgan Blum—a smart man and really a sweet guy—who is thoroughly familiar with your poetry, and who has a really sensitive knowledge of poetry in general.

In your note, you asked if Minnesota wants you to read here when you come east. Here is exactly what I did: I broached the matter to Theodore Hornberger (head of Eng. dept.), who said that such a reading on short notice was probably out of the question, because lectures for this year had already been arranged last summer; and that any break in this routine schedule would have to be made through the chairman of lectures and concerts (whoever he is), and that this chairman is difficult to persuade. HOWEVER—note well—Hornberger asked me to get Allen Tate's advice. Today Allen told me that, though there probably isn't any chance for a reading here *at the university itself*, he may be able to arrange something at the Walker Art Gallery. He said that, of course, a reading at the Gallery—where he has arranged readings for Spender, Viereck (I think he said), and others in the past— would not be able to pay two hundred dollars. Finally, he told me to hold my pants on while he found out what could be done. This is the extent of my information. I will write you immediately as soon as I see Allen again, if he has learned anything.

As for myself, I am laboring my nuts off teaching, roaring and raging like Billy Sunday at my humanities class. I'm teaching Rousseau, whom I hate—I think him sentimental, cold, cruel, dishonest, a fucking fascist, and a shit in the lowest sense. However, I have also been teaching Hobbes, who is such a magnificent writer that the students like him, and I love him. If he is a totalitarian, then he at least is honest about it. And that prose! "The life of man is solitary, poor, nasty, brutish, and short." I can hear the old son of a bitch snorting with laughter and gusto as he wrote that sentence, certainly among the most beautiful I have ever read. It never fails to send a shiver up my back.

I wish I had some new jokes to send you, but life among my colleagues has been singularly humorless. It's a hell of a note when a man has to make up his own jests and smirk at them in empty rooms at the humiliation of no audience.

Excuse the obscenity, Ted, and please get a good rest. Lib says that whether or not a reading works out here, she hopes you can stop to see us, and I hope so too.

Love,

Jim

To Wayne Burns

Minneapolis

November 30, 1957

Dear Wayne,

Do you think that poetry is some kind of a disease? It is very early on Saturday morning, and I have just got a thing done after wrestling with it, in the worst way (with headaches) for many months. This time, I found that I had wasted a full page on something that I could have said in a single little phrase of three words. So this morning, I said it in a single little phrase of three words, and rebuilt the whole thing around them. This paragraph is just to illustrate what has happened to me and words during this whole quarter. It seems that the only thing I can actually write down on paper is verse. I rise early and read like hell—all kinds of nutty, sinful stuff: Shaw, Tolstoy, George Gissing, Shakespeare, Sterne: and these are my Dickens critics!

What I mean is that I've been through the Dickens shelves in the Univ. of Minn. library (my God, you ought to see them, they would startle Dickens himself), and I've even looked through the whole *Dickensian*, and yet the only useful critics I can find are all of them utterly strange and unlikely. I know you won't mind unorthodox critics on Dickens in my essays (and when, Oh for Christ's sake, when will those essays be written?), but—well, reading such stuff in line with my own obsession about Dickens is not going to make me a very good Victorian scholar.

Look, I have an important (to me) question to ask: as far as I can find, there is no standard critical edition of Dickens' novels. Do you think it will be all right if I identify my quotations from Dickens simply by noting the chapter number (of the appropriate novel) just after the quotation right in my text itself? In the first place, there is, as far as I know, no *textual* problem in Dickens, as there might be, say, in *The Vision of Piers Plowman*. Second, I see more and more that my little book on Dickens (I'm starting to think of that little book with affection, even though it has no physical body yet) as a real *critical* job, as distinguished from the kind of genuinely scholarly work that John Butt and Kathleen Tillotson are doing. Third, in order to substantiate my pitch about the nature and operation of Dickens' imagination, I will probably have to quote extensively, and I hate the clutter of footnotes. Well, to repeat, can I just quote a passage, and then refer to the chapter number?

I also found the perfect image of the Dickensian imagination in *Don Quixote*. I don't know why it never occurred to me before, but do you remember that comic passage where Sancho tells the story of the man ferrying the hundred goats across the stream one by one (with full detailed description of each goat and each ferrying trip) and is interrupted by Don Quixote with the demand that he say simply that all hundred goats were ferried across? The joke is that a story-teller ought to get to the point. But Dickens is backwards from this. If we conceive his plots as the "point," then he never gets to it; and, in the process of evading it, he forgets, and makes us forget, the other side of the stream, and he forgets what he wanted to do there; he is so delighted with his goats—the brown goats, the green goats, the old goats without beards, the young female goats that need shaves, the ferryman's plastic leg, and, perhaps most exciting of all, with the ferryman's second cousin's sister-in-law's goiter. Anyway, I have conceived the grand strategy of retelling the story as I found it in *Don Quixote* and using it as a critical metaphor. What do you think?

Herbert Read was here and I got to talk to him again, though, of course, this time I was more considerate. There was a real honest-to-God reason for being considerate this time. You won't believe it, but I swear it's the truth: Herbert Read and Billy Graham arrived at the Minneapolis Municipal Airport at the same time on separate planes. Having been informed that a famous Englishman had also arrived, Billy Graham strode (you know, *strode*, like Eisenhower in *Time* Mag.) over, smacked Read on the shoulder blades, and welcomed him to the Twin Cities.

So I simply told Sir Read (this is what Billy Graham called him: well, I told you you would think I was lying) that I was engaged in preliminary work for an essay in defense of Little Nell. He smirked (I don't blame him; wouldn't *you* smirk? I would). Read and Allen Tate are old friends. By the way, Tate (who is my office mate—I can't keep it from rhyming) has turned out to be an extremely nice guy. I've always liked his poetry, and he himself is a good man.

I feel in an idiotic position. In *Epoch* magazine, a guy favorably reviewed my book (which is okay), but he used it to flog the San Francisco writers. Now, some of the San Francisco stuff I like (Ginsberg's "A Supermarket in California" is a very beautiful poem), and some I don't like. However that may be, I don't want to be used as a polemical weapon either for or against anybody. Can you imagine a more farcical position to be in?

I just remembered another wonderful Dickens thing (disguised) which I found: in one of his essays on art (I'll look it up later), Tolstoy tells us how to read a great book. The whole passage is striking and true. No wonder Tolstoy liked Dickens so much. Incidentally, your seminar method of finding the true Dickens criticism is working (I hope). I just read the great novels, and the great novelists on one another (like Gorky's *Reminiscences of Tolstoy*, a book by God that would *make your hair stand up on end and dance Dixie*), and, if those writers are post-Dickens, they make some comment on him sooner or later. Sometimes, as in the case of Sterne and Cervantes, they comment on Dickens even before he was born. Has anyone ever studied *Tristram Shandy* as a work of literary criticism? It's loaded.

I've exchanged a couple of letters with Larry Lawrence. He was depressed the first time, and I tried to comfort him, but you know how that sort of thing goes. Larry has a morose streak which is all but indistinguishable from his humor, and one never knows what the epigram will amount to. I would like to tell him, of course, that the one forty-page chapter out of his novel is the best fiction written in America in the past ten years; but you know that he would just think I was trying to make him feel good; and the inhibition makes things impossible.

I was interrupted for a moment, and lo and behold it was Glenn Leggett on the phone. It was good to hear his voice. I told him, of course, the very thing I would report to you: the people in this town have been nice to me, and I hate the town like death. I am so unutterably miserable in the midwest that I am numb for all of every day except in the very early morning hours, when I read and write. I'm afraid to speak of this, yet I must. I'm afraid, because I can't seem to make anyone understand the dreadful, practically subconscious, effect that the landscape of a town makes on me. I was so happy in Seattle that I almost felt sinful about it—a sure sign of happiness. I think often how I would like to ask Leggett or Heilman to let me come back to Washington; but I can't write the appropriate letter, because I realize that they would say no, that they would say I am just suffering from the graduate student's lonely neurosis during the first year away from the womb of his native graduate school. So it seems impossible to escape. Will you please keep this in mind, Wayne? I've not said this to anyone, because it sounds so silly in words: but—everything I write in this town seems a fight against Nature, and I'm sick of fighting Nature. I fought it till I escaped from the Ohio Valley, and I was in harmony with it in Seattle. I achieved a great amount of work there, and I could do it again. I've written some verses here; but I always have the feeling that I'm trying in despair to nourish myself from within in defense against this exile. During my years of study at Washington, I labored with joy, and I produced, I got my work done. I did well, and in addition to graduate work I wrote a book. Yet it seems that my simply having attended Washington was a crime for which I have to be punished by exile. Please don't laugh at my melodramatic tone. These are the terms in which my life presents itself to me all the time.

But I'm afraid there's little point in talking about this. I go on lamenting to myself about it continuously. There have been a couple of times in my life when I found my surroundings unendurable, and I revolted against them. But in every case I planned for a long time. Up to my fifteenth year I abominated the Ohio Valley, and at that time I hated it so that I had a nervous breakdown. In the hospital I decided that I would not die for any thing or any place, not even for love, not even for guilt. But I didn't run away when the hospital released me. No. I returned to school, studied Latin and mathematics very hard for two years, and then went to the Army which, I knew, would pay me for going to school. The GI bill paid for school till my last year, but according to my correct calculations I had done well enough in school to receive a full scholarship just at the time when the GI bill ran out. And now I find, after half a lifetime of labor, that I've got to go through a similar process. I'm not sure of the strategy yet: but I'm going to work like hell and produce everything I can, and then I'm going to apply at Washington again. If I'm rejected, I'm thinking of getting out of the academic world altogether, and coming back to Seattle to work at Boeing or something.

Please forgive me for running on like this. But the subject is an obsession with me. It twists and turns grimly at the center of my brain, like the axis of the planet Earth. And I am getting sick of spinning on an ellipse through the dark. The hell of it is that I've now got a whole set of new poems on this subject of exile and revolt, and that I'm pleased with them, and that I don't know who the hell would publish them. They're really Romantic, you know. I read just one of them aloud to Lib, and she was so shocked that I've just kept the others in my notebook. If she finds them intolerable, I don't know what the hell the editors would think. I am getting absolutely furious at the state of things. Here I am, almost 30 years old, half-dead, with language roaring around like mad in my skull, and I ought to be doing the work of joy, but here I am, writing attacks and angers and laments. The ghost-theme, or attitude, has taken hold of me two more times, and I've got appalling poems on it.

I think I'd better control myself, before I go haywire. Even now I don't know how you're going to make coherent sense out of this letter.

To get to something perhaps amusing, I've been corresponding with my best student at Washington, a talented young person (God, I feel about a thousand years old) named Miss Sonjia Urseth. I sent her a copy of the new poem called "All the Beautiful Are Blameless," and asked her to give it to you. I also wanted her to meet you. It develops that she has tried about fifteen times to get an appointment with you, and that she hasn't been successful. I hope she succeeds pretty soon. I think she needs to talk very much with someone like you. You don't mind, do you?

Please write soon, and let me know about the question on quotations from Dickens.

Season's greetings.

Yours,
Jim

To Theodore and Beatrice Roethke

Minneapolis
December 15, 1957

Dear Beatrice and Ted,

We've heard through the inevitable scuttlebutt that you're both well, and this makes us happier than we can say. I'm getting ready to send you two or three new poems. You don't have to feel that you need to comment on them, but I want you to see them nevertheless. I have some news which will make you proud, I hope: Ransom strictly enjoined me to keep it secret till the *Kenyon Review* appears in early January: I've been awarded the *Kenyon Review* Poetry Fellowship for next year. I'm going to spend six months of it in Seattle (Fall and Winter quarters of next year) . . . I trust by this time that Mr. Stange from the English dept. here has written you about a possible reading in the Spring. From the way he talks, the university would be prepared to make you extremely welcome. I hope this was the sort of thing you had in mind when you dropped the remark (in a note to me) wondering whether or not they would like you to read here. I think I've told you that Allen Tate has been very kind to us. He certainly seems to think you're the Heavyweight Champion of contemporary American poetry.

This is the 15th. On the 18th we're driving to Ohio to visit parents for the vacation. Among other things, we're going to visit Pappy Ransom at Kenyon. He seems awfully lonesome there, and no wonder.

Ted, with the poem that you sent, you mentioned a long letter you had written me; but I haven't received it yet.

I'm still plugging at the proposed essay which we've discussed, but I haven't come up with anything yet. I just had a new idea, but I'll let it simmer till I have something real to offer. Meanwhile, to defeat the inescapable human tears of things, let us all turn to Julia A. Moore:

> The winter will soon be over,
>> With its cold and chilly winds.
> It is sad and dreary ever,
>> Yet it's dying, free from sin.
> Now the springtime is coming,
>> Ah, yes, will soon be here.
> We will welcome in its coming
>> In this glad new year.

> Love, and laughter too, from all four of us
> (we have a monstrous black dog),
> Jim, Lib, Franz, and Duncan

To Gege and Lloyd Parks

Minneapolis
December 17, 1957

Dear Gege and Lloyd,

Here we are at the University of Minnesota, drawn back to the midwest as by some evil spell. The town is unspeakable; but the people are okay. I teach English (advanced composition) and Humanities (damned near everything from Alexander Pope to Ray B. West Jr.). Tomorrow morning (Dec. 18) we're driving to Ohio to visit families and revisit the idyllic scenes of childhood. I feel as if I had swallowed ratpoison, and were irresistibly seeking to quench my thirst at the fount of nectar, the Ohio River . . . Anyway, now that we've learned what cities are like, I intend to go back to Seattle after the war . . . We hope you are well, and that your child is strong and happy. We're just about sure now that Lib is again pregnant, which is one natural joy in the midst of

Minneapolis. We've got a dog, a great black monstrous puppy which is driving Lib nuts, but which is actually quite charming. Lloyd, I wish that one of these days you'd send me your brother Howard's address. I'd like to correspond with him again . . . And please write.

Yours,

Jim, Lib, Franz, Duncan, and (potentially) Marcella

To Wayne Burns

Minneapolis

February 1, 1958

Dear Wayne,

How marvelous that you should have sent those 2 books at once, without any question! I hereby take the Pickwickian oath that I will guard them with everything except my life. I will even guard them with my honor. (My God!—"guard" and "honor" in the same sentence, even as a joke—I read and liked Cozzens's *Guard of Honor* in almost exactly the same way that I read and liked Wilkie Collins's *The Woman in White*. They were both entertaining yarns (I use the word "yarns" deliberately—sometimes you can see a good "yarn" on TV. Some science-fiction writers write good "yarns." etc.) written by extraordinarily clever and almost totally unimaginative prose-stylists. The best example of the TV yarn-type thing is the Alfred Hitchcock program on Sunday evenings. Do you remember the protagonist in *Invisible Man* eating the candied Carolina yams in the cold winter morning, and suddenly, in the snow and the bleakness, swearing that never again will he be ashamed of things that he likes? Well, he liked yams, and he ate them; I like yarns, and I read them or watch them on TV. Wilkie Collins wrote yarns; James Gould Cozzens wrote yarns. I read one of them, and I liked it. But I won't read *By Love Possessed*. The sociological controversy over it makes it probably impossible to read *it*. I mean *it*, not *Time*'s review of it (the greatest detail in this superbly written review was the one about Cozzens preparing to write by sitting alone and picking his nose—this is supposed to show that he is not one of those horrible escapist, maladjusted experimenters, but a classical realist)— not even Irving Howe's. Both reviewers agree that in this book Cozzens has gone "all out" and tried to produce a "major work." It's exactly as though the scriptwriter of the TV show *Wyatt Earp* had, with a straight face, announced between the commercial and the first scene that in tonight's show he had labored carefully to present the public with his masterpiece, and concluded his announcement with "Yr. most obedient, humble servant."

If and when you get time to write me a note (and it need be only a note), will you tell me, just for convenience, exactly when you are going to need the 2 books you sent me? If you're teaching Dickens next quarter, I of course don't want to deprive you of two crucial books. This is my plan: though I am halfway through a rereading of *Pickwick*, and have taken exactly thirty pages of notes, I will suspend that job and immediately begin a careful and thorough rereading of Forster. On most week-days I work at least 3 hours in the morning on Dickens, and I find that I can read, reflect, brood, and jot my way through about 50 pages in 2 hours. The Forster will not take as long as you might think; because I'm making careful notes only on the early part of the book, the part that is immediately related to the first six novels, *Pickwick* through *Chuzzlewit*. Absolutely as soon as I finish, I'll insure the book and send it back to you. Then I will go through the Ford in the same way. Meanwhile, I've decided to order Ford from the publisher, and will pay for it somehow. Every time I get a check of any significant size from an editor (poesy rears its ugly phiz), we buy a washing machine. (The basement of this house now contains about ten washing machines.) If I ever again, however, have an appreciably large clutch of pomes [*sic*]* accepted and paid for, I am about decided to use the money on Dickens alone. It is time I started my own Dickens library by seriously securing the basic works. I need things like the Ley edition of Forster, Ford, Surtees, Egan, the new Butt and Tillotson (which I've ordered), a file of the *Dickensian* (God knows where I'll get one, or why), and (perhaps on the Judgment Day) a complete Nonesuch (I'm afraid I'd have to knock over a bank in order to get the money for that).

As you can see, I'm moving steadily, but I hope you don't mind my moving slowly. Everything depends on my arrogant confidence that I can write like hell once I get actually started. My having mentioned, both to Hornberger and to you, my hope of finishing the dissertation during the time of the poetry fellowship is beginning to frighten the

*Wright's own addition.

hell out of me. What if I *don't* finish it? And, even more troublesome, I wonder why I'm anxious. I shouldn't care. Have I got job anxiety? No, by God, I can still say I don't really care whether I keep a job here or not (though I like the place pretty well). It must be this God damned catathymic compulsion I suffer from. (Yes, I found out its name. I used to think it was the Muse.)

There is a beautiful new poem by Allen Ginsberg in the current issue of the *Partisan*. The only thing wrong with it that I can see (it's a catalogue of the attractions of Mexico, and they deliberately invert the typical tourist attractions listed on travel pamphlets) is the line "Here's a hard brown cock for a quarter!" That's just a straight commercial.

Speaking of Ginsberg, there was a curious affair: in the mag. *Epoch*, my book of poems was reviewed by a man named William Dickey. He liked my book, and I was flattered, of course. However, I soon noted that he wasn't reading my book at all. He used it as a weapon to clout the writers of San Francisco. You know the pitch: the SF men are irresponsible, ill-adjusted, immature, romantic, paranoid, technically inefficient, etc. Now here, he says (you can see him taking it dramatically out of his pocket) is a poet who is "responsible." Me, for Christ's sake. Now, look, I don't give a damn what a critic does, but, man, a book is a *book*. Even a bad book is a book. It's not a pick-handle with which to thwack the enemies of the Lord of Hosts. Anyway, recently I heard from Jerry Enscoe, who read Dickey's review, became furious, and wrote Dickey a harsh letter. The two are now corresponding, and neither will yield an inch. Jerry asked me what I thought, and this is what I think: I believe that gangs are evil, and that they endanger art. Gangs as such are bad, even if one gang happens to be headed by Kenneth Rexroth. The insane irony of the affair is that both sides are victims of the essential evil which each applies to the other and neither can see for himself. J. Donald Adams is the paid whore of advertising, but it is not money which makes him bad, it is his losing his identity in a gang. Kenneth Rexroth is nobody's paid anything, unfortunately; and his fury and anguish are understandable. But as a critic he is useless; he doesn't read the work, he distracts you from it. From the viewpoint of either Adams or Rexroth, it is impossible to see what really matters: things like the fact that, in "A Supermarket in California" Ginsberg has written a musical lyric of great delicacy and tenderness. Now, who the hell would associate delicacy and tenderness with Ginsberg? And from the viewpoint of either Adams or Rexroth, it is impossible to see that, say, Anthony Hecht (who is supposed to be a perfect counterfeit, the very self and voice of the poet-in-the-gray-flannel-suit piddling with words) has written, in a poem called "Christmas is Coming" (in his book *A Summoning of Stones*), an anti-war poem of really dreadful depth and power.

I ramble. Please write a note. The mimeographed type on this sheet (which you can see, inverted, above) is a list of what I have published since our arrival here. I thought you might want to see it. Thanks again, very much, for the use of those 2 indispensable books. Love to Joan.

Jim

To Theodore Roethke

Minneapolis
February 11, 1958

Dear Ted,

How horrible that I should have waited so long to answer! But I've been running and bleeding like a Dickensian criminal with his head pulled off. I work like a son of a bitch for at least three hours every morning before daylight—on my thesis. It is absorbing. And my teaching schedule this quarter is such an exciting one, that I get wildly lost in it almost every day. Do you remember Falstaff's description of Justice Shallow, when that old fart had ranted and danced in the brothels near Lincoln's Inn Fields fifty years previously? "And when 'a was naked, 'a looked for all the world like a forked radish, with a head fantastically carved upon it with a knife." I jot down things like that all day and all night.

You know, it must have been two months ago, at least, that I wrote to Secker & Warburg *with the address that you gave me*, in order to get a copy of *Words for the Wind*. It hasn't arrived yet; and, since English publishers are always prompt, I can only figure that you gave me the wrong address. Can you give me the right one? The notion of writing an essay on it still quivers in the thin air of possibility, and I imagine you're pretty disgusted with me by this time—all that bragging, and still no essay. But maybe one will come up soon. Please don't be cross.

I've corresponded a bit with Mr. Heilman in London. He seems well—having a good time. Like a fool, however, I mentioned to him my hope of returning to Seattle some time; and he answered, directly and clearly, that as far as he was concerned graduate students should never return to the scene of their crime (the place where they took the work and the degree), and that I absolutely could *not* go back to Washington. This was really a sharp shoe in the gut; but there is nothing I can do about it. Seattle seems like some impossible Eden. It is certainly the only town that I ever really cared to live in. Apparently, this is just what Mr. Heilman thinks is wrong with my living there. As I get it, the idea is that you are not supposed to like the place where you live too much, because your liking it will somehow destroy you. It sounds almost like Jeremy Bentham's viciously sarcastic definition of the principle of asceticism: an action is to be judged morally good in so far as it causes the greatest amount of misery among the greatest number of people. But argument is vain. Mr. Heilman will not be moved.

And I can survive in Minneapolis. The students are wonderful. Allen Tate is friendly. It's not a town to commit suicide in, at any rate (the waterways are always frozen over).

I should mention (unofficially—I am the most unofficial man in town) that Bob Stange seems to have given up arrangements for your reading here, because of confusion. I haven't talked with him at length, but he said in passing something about your agent's writing to different places also, and his (Stange's) not knowing how to make arrangements. Allen Tate, however, keeps telling me that the Walker Art Gallery here would probably like very much to have you; and, since you're going to be in this part of the country in March anyway, it is my opinion (which nobody asked for) that the Walker would be a good arrangement. At any rate, I hope things work out. It would be magnificent to see you again. I myself feel that I've screwed things up more than I've clarified them; but I always feel that way.

I've got what amounts to an invitation to Yaddo for this coming summer; but I'm not going to take it this time. (There may never be another chance, but I can't help it.) I plan to sweat over Dickens here in Minneapolis and, unless unforeseen difficulties arise, come to Seattle in the Fall . . . Also, an extremely crazy and improbable thing just happened: I got, by God, a very cordial "fan" letter from Randall Jarrell at the Library of Congress. He said some nice things, and he said them very graciously. He also asked about my recording some stuff for them, which I will do when I get the time.

My second book is "done" though it hasn't yet received the proper stripping away of punk poems and junk (it contains about fifty pieces, and I want just thirty, and this time By God I'm going to have just what I want or else I won't publish it). The University of Minnesota Press is reading it at the moment. Yale University Press rejected it, as I knew they would do (though they just told me that *The Green Wall* is having a second printing). I would like to have some nice publisher do a nice pretty plain job on it, and I want it to contain exactly thirty tough, stripped, cold, furious pieces. As usual, I'm having a hell of a time (or I've *had* a hell of a time,—I haven't even looked at the damn manuscript for about two months) deciding just exactly which poems to cut out. I need help. Maybe the editor here at University of Minnesota Press can help me, if they want the book; or maybe a couple of other people would help. The tentative (and permanent, unless the prospective publisher—maybe I'll find him in heaven—objects) title is *The Lamentation of Saint Judas*.

We're buying a house, and Lib is getting fat. With child.

Please write, and please send me the right address of Secker & Warburg.

Love to you and Beatrice,
Jim

Minneapolis
February 14, 1958

Dear Ted,

Heaven knows you have enough verses to read; but I thought you might care to see the enclosed. It's about the fifteenth version of an elegy for Philip Timberlake.* Perhaps you remember last year my wanting to talk to you one late afternoon, and your driving me over to a joint near Green Lake for some whiskey. I had just heard of Timber-

---

*Wright's elegy, "A Winter Day in Ohio," appears in *Saint Judas* (1959). Intermediate drafts of this poem appear in letters over the next few months.

lake's death in rather a startling manner (I had just received a letter from the Kenyon people, asking me to write an obituary for him; and I hadn't even known he was ill).

I've got to hurry to my Shakespeare class soon. Please write.

Yours,

Jim

Minneapolis

March 12, 1958

Dear Ted,

You mustn't feel bad about having to cancel your tour. Certainly everybody in Minneapolis who had anything to do with the series of readings expressed only concern that you should follow your doctor's orders very closely. Chas. Gullans once told me that the people in this city are very civilized, and he was right—they are real human beings. Of course, many people were looking forward to hearing you, and I'm very sure that they will lose no opportunity to hear you in the future, wherever and however they can. The main thing, everyone agrees, is for you to take it easy right now.

I have this little suggestion—or rather request—to make. You know, the series of readings here is supposed to feature about four internationally known poets like you and Tate and Berryman, and then the last reading will "feature" two young punks—Reed Whittemore and myself. (Of course, Whittemore is not a punk, but you know what I mean.) I wonder if you would object to my reading a couple of your things—and would you have any preference? As a matter of fact, it's ironic that I should grow suddenly pious enough to ask your permission, because I've already given a small reading here (to the undergraduate English club, you know the sort of thing), and I read two of your poems to them. Beforehand, Bill O'Connor (really a sweet man, with a perfectly adorable wife with whom I am madly in love) pointed out that, though the undergraduates here (they are extraordinarily bright) know about your stuff, they are not really very familiar with it; and so he agreed that their education demanded a bit of Roethke. I said "Elegy for Jane" to them (with single poems by Yeats, Hardy, and W. H. Davies) at the beginning. After a coffee intermission, I gave a little snotty discourse on the epigram, and I couldn't resist saying "Academic." The audience at the Walker Art Center will be a good deal larger and more widely read; so may I read something of yours? And, if so, what? I have favorites, as you know, but since you won't be able to come here I thought you might have planned something special. What do you think of my reading a short poem from *Open House* (I still think that whole book ought to be reprinted), one from *The Waking*, and then a new one? If you think this would be all right, would you please send me a copy of one of the new ones? One that you especially like? Please don't hesitate to say if you think I shouldn't read anything at all. I really want to do this for the sake of the citizens of Minneapolis, who, as I say, are very civilized, and who, I am certain, would be delighted at the chance to become more familiar with your poems. Please let me know what you think, how you feel, etc. I have to give my reading on May 7.

I know how terribly hard you labored a few years ago—working at four jobs, and so on—but you say "look what it got me." Surely you must be aware of the irony in that statement! But I won't go on. I've never directly told you what I think of you, because I'm afraid you would think I am turning you into a father. I swear I never have thought of you as a father. Will you be insulted if I tell you that I and all my friends who are knocking and thumping around, trying to write true poems that are well-made, regard your work as an absolutely solid achievement, the indestructible evidence that in the nineteen-fifties and sixties there was at least some lyric poetry written in America that was great enough to nudge aside the Englishmen of the seventeenth century? I don't have a single intelligent friend who doubts this. I myself feel funny about writing it down on paper. It's as though I were reminding myself that I am breathing, or that I am happy, or that I just won a fist-fight. But to love the work of a great lyric poet is not the same as making a papa out of him. Do you know what I mean when I say that I always think of Ben Jonson, Thomas Hardy, and Catullus as my *contemporaries*? If they are "dated," then man is also dated, and I happen to be a man. Well, I am running on and on.

One day soon I'm going to send you a new poem, which has caused me furious work for about six months. It began as a little piece in heroic couplets—about ten lines long. Then it grew a bit—still in heroic couplets. Then it grew still more—and I shortened some of the lines. That version is the one which Allen Tate is going to discuss with me this afternoon (it's the first time I've asked him to go over a poem with me). But last evening, I got to fooling around, and I, so to speak, *fell into* the middle section of the poem, and thrashed around and broke it all up and threw pieces out the window, and I wrote a sketch, appallingly Biblical and wild, for that middle section. Either I've written my first good poem, or else I've produced a piece of pompous balderdash. I honest to God don't know. I'll send it soon. Love to Beatrice and to you. Please let me know about the reading.

Love from Lib,
Jim

To Russell Lynes, Harper & Brothers

Minneapolis
April 3, 1958

Dear Mr. Lynes:

Your note of March 27 filled me with pleasure and gratitude, and I know you'll excuse my waiting for a few days to answer. As I told you in my previous letter—which contained the notes for your P & O column—I had just reached the point of retyping and retouching the whole manuscript of my new book; and I wanted to be sure that I could finish the job fairly soon. I now know that I can do so; and I'm almost certain that I'll be able to mail the manuscript of *The Lamentation of Saint Judas* to you on Monday, April 7.

I think I should like to send the book directly to you, if you wouldn't mind passing it on to Miss Elizabeth Lawrence. It was especially kind of you to mention my request to her, for I know that you are very busy in your own right. As soon as I send the manuscript, I should like to write a note to Miss Lawrence. I want to explain, as briefly and clearly as possible, what I have in mind by the arrangement of the various parts. Furthermore, there are four or five very detailed and specific questions I want to ask her. I hope she doesn't mind. The questions have to do with the title of the whole collection, and with a few final revisions of phrase and punctuation.

And, as I said before, I am quite aware of the special problems which the most noteworthy American publishing houses have to face, as far as poetry is concerned. A nation produces its literature first of all through its individual workmen; but this distinction is chronological at best. The whole literature—which I should understand as that strange and unique fusion of the individual's eccentric contribution and a deeply vital tradition—is, in the highest sense, a creation whose achievement and meaning are shared among people who write and people who read and listen and people who provide occasions for the writing, the reading, and the listening. This is one sense in which all great art seems dramatic. I think it is the plain sense of Whitman's remark—so much deeper and more complex than perhaps he himself understood—that to have great poets there must be great audiences too. Maybe Americans aren't writing "great" poetry at the moment; but, in any case, it won't be written without the human civilization which gives its occasion and defines its meaning. That kind of civilization—simply a free tradition—is the problem of everybody who cares about life at all. So your difficulty is mine too. As you can see, I've been reading Edmund Burke. Please excuse my long-winded garbling of his style. I'm grateful for your willingness simply to read the manuscript, and I'll send it soon.

Sincerely,
James Wright

To Elizabeth Lawrence, Harper & Brothers

Minneapolis
April 7, 1958

Dear Miss Lawrence:

Mr. Russell Lynes has written me a note about his telling you of a manuscript which I have completed. It is a second book of poems, and its tentative title is *The Lamentation of Saint Judas*. My first book was *The Green Wall*, winner of the Yale Series of Younger Poets for 1956 and published by the Yale University Press in March 1957. That was just a year ago; but I had been working on *Saint Judas* for about a year before *The Green Wall* was published. The present version of the new book is the result of a series of ruthless excisions and changes which seem to me fantastic. In any case, it is stripped as bare and direct as I can make it, I think.

My request to Mr. Lynes—that he tell me whether or not I might send the book to Harper's—was not quite so naive as it might have sounded. I know that even the most solidly established and distinguished publishers in the United States cannot afford to publish much poetry. I guess this fact is just part of the general democratic struggle toward civilization that we all share, whether we like it or not (I happen to like it—after a year of study in Europe, I got miserably homesick). On the other hand, I was aware that publishers like Harper's are consciously—more acutely than I am, certainly—trying to solve the problem of making poetry available. That awareness gave me the courage at least to ask if I could send the manuscript. I have no illusions about its easy acceptance. (As a matter of fact, I think I should be really shocked by surprise.) But your very willingness to read the manuscript is marvelous, and I am more grateful than I can say. This morning I am sending it by parcel post to Mr. Lynes, who has promised to hand it on to you.

I hope you won't mind if I make a few remarks about the manuscript. They might possibly be helpful:

I've sent you the fair copy. Please excuse the fact that the type on some pages differs from that on others. I had to prepare the final version of the manuscript at different places and different times. It's probably silly to mention this, and yet it's just the kind of thing that, personally, I would find very nerve-racking. Anyway, the whole fair copy is perfectly legible.

At the beginning of the book I've placed a page of acknowledgments. Almost all of the poems contained in the manuscript have been either published or accepted for publication very soon. (For example, Mr. Ransom writes me that four of the poems in the fifth section— "Girls Walking into Shadows"—are going to appear in the Summer issue of the *Kenyon Review*.) I don't yet have letters of permission from the editors of the various magazines and books in which the poems have appeared, but they are almost all of them people with whom I have friendly correspondence of one kind or another. I'm sure there would be no difficulty whatever in securing permission; so I felt free to include a page of copy in the manuscript, just to suggest what it would look like.

On the page which introduces section VI ("The Lean Ones"), I've written a passage, very brief, from René Char's poem "The Rampart of Twigs." A friendly correspondence with M. Char convinces me that there would be no trouble getting his permission, and that of his publishers (Gallimard, Paris) to quote the line. It is rather an important epigraph for the section of poems: "Dear beings, whom the dawn seems to wash clean of their torments, whom it seems to restore with a new health and a new innocence, beings who will nevertheless shatter and vanish after a couple of hours . . . Dear beings, whose hands I can feel."

The book is constructed in 6 sections. The whole book begins with a prayer to the Muse, and it is both a description of my farm life in Ohio and also an implication of that horrifying old Greek story about the lazy brother's being the blessed one. It is a poem about being loved without deserving it. And the final poem in the whole book—"Saint Judas"—is both a dramatic monologue (though very short, a sonnet in fact) and a statement about the significance of a loving action (i.e., such an action can have moral meaning only if it is performed without hope of reward—and Judas, who was in the perfect position to perform an action without hope of reward, by his performance of hopeless and despairing love attains what I would hope to regard as sanctity). The book is designed to unfold its theme between these two brief poems: the theme of human love as a kind of miraculous agony. One does everything possible in order to escape it, and yet it is everything.

The first section is called "Lunar Changes." It contains seven poems. Each of them deals with some sort of miraculous change, and all have to do with the love that this painful change embodies. Even the comparatively "light" poem about Andrew Marvell's housekeeper—in addition to being a serious parody of Marvell's style, which I admire and envy as much as any English style I know—places the speaker Marvell in a position (that of ghostly death) from which he cannot possibly hope to gain any reward for the poems which, after all, he wrote because he loved them. Incidentally, his housekeeper, Mary Palmer, actually claimed to be his widow after his death, and actually did publish his verses with an introduction signed "Mary Marvell." She wanted to get some of the back rent money, or an equivalent. Think of it! To smirk at her would be blasphemous. Marvell—even Shakespeare himself—would have adored her. What better way to *use* Marvell's beautiful poems in the world than by selling them in order to pay the back rent after his death—dunned by creditors and evading debtors' prison? And so Marvell's ghost loves her, even if they weren't married after all (he was very young, and I imagine she was a sour old hag—if so, so much the better). Each of the poems in the first section uses some device of transfiguration or other, and most often it is the moon, the sudden emergence of the moon, at once coldly impartial and warmly illuminating.

The second section is called "Midnight Sassafras." The title of the section comes from the penultimate line of the first poem "Complaint," an elegy for my grandmother. This poem, and those that follow it in the section, combines the theme of the defeated and the unrecognized with a further development of the theme of love, the love that I am trying to celebrate in this book—the highest love I can think of, which is given without reserve, whether the beloved "deserve" it or not. I might observe of the poem called "A Note Left in Jimmy Leonard's Shack" that it is to be considered a note written by a little boy to the brother of the town drunk—fearful and disturbed at the possibility of the wicked old bastard's drowning drunk in the river; and it is also an attempt to see if I could get away with making the kid hysterically call the frightening older brother a "son of a bitch" without making the reader snicker. American profanities are beautiful, but they have a diminishing effect, they cancel each other out. One curious result of this effect is that, in the Army, where everybody swears as a matter of course, it is almost impossible to create a genuinely original and felt curse; so that soldiers are always being driven, by the exhaustion of their own formal poetic diction, to the invention of new curses. Somebody must study this matter some day.

The third section is called "Fire." The religious theme, I suppose I can call it, rises in this section. The desire for the love (as previously presented) is shocked by the evil and violence of nature, and by the fact that many of the miraculous transfigurations in the natural world seem to have nothing to do with man. I suppose the climax of this section is the last stanza of "At the Slackening of the Tide," in which, after the beautiful and peaceful afternoon at the beach has suddenly been transformed into lamentation and hell by the drowning, the futile drowning, of the small child, the speaker in the poem looks to see if the waters will mourn for man, and hears only the sea itself, far away, innocently washing its hands of man, like Pilate.

The fourth section is called "Surrender." It tries partially to answer the terrified question asked in section three: where does a man find his place in a natural world where the significance of life—life itself—can quite possibly be transfigured into nothingness in a single unpremeditated moment? The answer given in section four is perhaps corny, but it is the only one I know of. The section consists of three love poems to my wife and—I was about to say "children," but I must explain a strange detail. In dedicating the section, I mention "Marcella"; but my wife won't have her second baby till July. If by some off chance you should find the manuscript acceptable, and if by some off chance my own anticipations should be frustrated and the baby should not be "Marcella," then the manuscript would have to be changed. (Can you imagine any arrogance—the arrogance of a cocky young man— greater than that, more profoundly infuriating? It's like commanding the grass to bloom.)

The fifth section is called "Girls Walking into Shadows." All I can say is that these poems are all about the pitiful young. Since I am thirty years old now, I must sound like a prematurely old man, as I have no doubt I am, in some ways. The final poem in this fifth section, "On Minding One's Own Business," was completed very recently, and has just been accepted by *Harper's Magazine*. It occurs to me that it summarized the whole theme of the section very well, so I placed it just yesterday at the very end. All the poems deal with the virtue of our letting one another alone. Thoreau, I guess.

The last section is called "The Lean Ones." The title is a paraphrase of Isaiah, who cried out his leanness in the midst of the world's self-satisfied and ostensible plenty. The poems in this section are religious, I hope; they are certainly not "social," in any recent connotation of that term. The poem called "At the Executed Murderer's Grave," for example, is not an *attack* on capital punishment. It's simply a lament for a human being. I just don't believe that people ought to kill one another, for any reason whatever. This poem is the real "lamentation of Saint Judas," if there is indeed any at all.

Finally, if and when I get this new book published, I would like to add a page for a general dedication; but this is so personally sacred to me, that I would prefer to omit the page for the time being.

Please forgive this verbal explosion. And thank you so much for consenting to read my manuscript.

Sincerely,
James Wright

To John Crowe Ransom

Minneapolis
May 25, 1958

Dear John,

It was a pleasure to hear from you, as always. Thank you very much for arranging to pay us the full stipend of $4,000 in July. It will ease matters considerably—though, as I told you, my being a financial moron hasn't diminished Lib's talent for balancing figures and budgets. I was a bit hysterical at first, you remember; but you also remember my habit of over-reacting to problems of one kind or another. If I could curb my personal hysterias, then perhaps by the same token I could purge my verses of their violence. Violence is weakness; it is precision and grace that are strength. I wish I could practice what I preach to myself.

At any rate, please print my four poems whenever it is convenient to do so. I wouldn't mind at all having them appear in the Autumn issue rather than the Summer.

Speaking of practicing certain virtues, I have taken it on myself to become—temporarily, at least—a hack-book-reviewer. I have a review of six new books coming out in, I believe, the summer issue of *The Yale Review*; I've just sent the ms. of a review of four others to *Poetry* (Chicago); and just recently Mr. Spears at *Sewanee* assigned five new books to me, for a review which is supposed to be done by Aug. 1 for the Fall issue of *The Sewanee Review*. I blush (somewhat ironically) to admit that I am doing this job primarily for money. With that confession out of the way, however, I have to admit also that I am having a good deal of fun with the reviews. Moreover, I am learning something in the way of what is coming out just now, and I am forced in the writing of prose to limit my long-windedness and to state (for myself, if for no other) just what poetry, in its various manifestations, seems to be.

I wonder if you would care to turn over to me any new books of verse for review? I told Murray Krieger (whom we have got to know here—he is a fine fellow) the other day that my book-reviews will revolutionize the whole practice of reviewing in America—because they will introduce the prose style of Theodore Dreiser into American literary criticism. Actually, my prose—though too flippant and "young"— isn't as clumsy as one might suppose, and I am learning, bit by bit, to cut the cackle and make the point. I have some favorite reviewers—

Reed Whittemore, who is very funny and engaging; John Peale Bishop, whose poetry grows deeper and more important to me every day, and whose book-reviews seemed to me to contain point and grace of style as well as depth of critical vision; and Allen Tate, whose ponderous seriousness can relieve itself by sudden savage epigrammatic turns of phrase and mind, as when he ends his praise of Emily Dickinson by saying, suddenly and shockingly, that her personal explorations of the Puritan decay are "almost obscene," that she is so startling because she employed for dramatic effect a theology in which she could not wholly believe, and that—marvelous, marvelous!—"Cotton Mather would have burned her for a witch." It is the last sentence of his essay, and it is magnificent, Hardyesque in its honesty, Swiftean in its intense comedy that becomes almost tragic. But Bishop and Tate are masters of a kind. I am just trying to learn from them one comparatively simple rhetorical skill: to write book-reviews that are genuine essays. Do you happen to have any loose reviewing jobs lying around?

A few weeks ago I gave a reading of poems at Wayne State University in Detroit, and there I had the pleasure—finally, after many years of admiration and interest—of meeting and making the acquaintance of Tony Hecht. As you well know, his humanity is as considerable as his poetic gift, and we had a delightful time. Mr. Elder Olson was also there—he's a visiting professor at Wayne during the Spring Quarter— and we philosophized far into the night. I like Mr. Olson very much too, and he had many stimulating things to say, though I agreed with only about half of them. Incidentally, he protests that he is being misrepresented by Prof. R. S. Crane, and that he is really, way down deep inside, a Platonist. Well, his grandfather's mustache. He even looks like Aristotle (whatever Aristotle looked like, he must have looked like Mr. Olson).

Then, a couple of weeks ago, I gave a reading and a couple of lectures in Iowa City, where Bob Mezey and I had—for the most part—a good reunion. However, I'm sorry to say that we parted in quite painful argument. It seemed to me that he was growing unprofitably bitter about things—the slowness of publication, the difficulty of writing, and the struggle of marriage (though his wife and child are beautiful). At the moment, our relations are extremely cold. They will thaw, however. I realize that I worry too much about him; but he is one of the finest and most talented friends I have—I only wish I possessed half of his native ability—and to see him scatter it is profoundly disturbing to me. Better men than he or myself have perished because they haven't faced the concrete realities of the world. But—well, I don't know. I really don't know.

But speaking of the realities of the world, I've just read—at the instigation of Morgan Blum, one of the fine men here—Robert Penn Warren's new book of poems. It is a gorgeous book, highly significant at this state of American poetry. One of the best poems in it is called "Court Martial"—and its concluding line—a line that comes right at the climax of as powerful an evocation of ghosts as even Hardy can show—its concluding line is "The world is real. It is there." This poem, and several others in the book, excited me, not only because they seem to me the best poetry that Warren has published yet—including the parts of "Brother to Dragons" that were grand—but also because of their solution to certain technical problems that are driving younger American poets out of their heads. In "Court Martial," for instance, Warren has the trimeter; but, for heaven's sake, it doesn't sound like Yeats. The enormousness of this achievement can be grasped, I believe, if one were to imagine an eighteenth-century poet writing blank-verse that didn't sound like Milton. I'm sure of Warren's achievement, and I have a pretty good idea of how he did it. The subject would make an essay on prosody—though not on prosody alone, but on the relation of prosody to diction and traditional external-forms (by which term I mean simply the trimeter, the sonnet, the pentameter, etc., that anyone can get from a handbook of poetic forms). As a matter of fact, I have thought so often of this subject since I've read Warren's book, especially the poem "Court Martial," that I've more than once thought of undertaking a genuine essay on it.* I feel a little hesitant, however. After all, the business of setting up as a critic is frightening. On the other hand, maybe it wouldn't hurt to be frightened. The poets of my generation have not found their way out of the *solutions* they have attained. Do I make myself clear? I mean that there must come a time when, after a man has mastered the essentials of the craft, he must then crack and break and snarl his own smoothness, so that he can let

---

*In the margin of the letter, Ransom indicates his intention to request this essay for *The Kenyon Review* (see "The Stiff Smile of Mr. Warren" in Wright's *Collected Prose* [Ann Arbor: University of Michigan Press, 1983], p. 239).

his own voice come through his poems; but he must accomplish this breakage without letting his language degenerate into gibberish, into mere animalistic grunts; and he must escape that terrifying threat by doing the bold and lonely things, by inventing his own form, of which traditional prosody and external forms provide just one essential part. Without them, he is nothing; but with them *alone*, he is still unidentified. Warren's use of the trimeter in "Court Martial" seems to me a perfect example of the success I mean, and even in the writing of this present letter I feel the temptation to spell out my meaning become even stronger and yet stronger.

But perhaps this is another pipe dream. I have plenty of jobs to perform. On the other hand, I always work best when I am doing about four separate things at once. Who knows? I might even write a real essay.

Please excuse the verbosity. Thanks again for the promise to send the whole $4,000 on July 1. Please print my four poems whenever and however it is handiest. And please give our best wishes—and especially my little boy's—to Mrs. Ransom.

Yours,
Jim W.

To Wayne Burns

Minneapolis
[June 1958]

Dear Wayne;

We're still alive and well. Excuse a short note.

What sex child did Lawrences have? Boy? Girl?

Lib is due in July. She's healthy, great.

I think I told you that, for the sake of supporting my old Aunt Money, I've become a hack-reviewer. There's one coming soon in the *Yale Review*, one in *Poetry* (Chicago), one in the *Sewanee Review* (in the Fall issue), and I'm dickering again with the *Western Review* for a hack-job. Hence, Dickens has taken a rest.

However, all the research I needed is finished (I think). I hope to Christ you are going to be in Seattle during the Summer vacation; because chapter by chapter I am going to send my dissertation. I've got to: in late November and first half of December I'm giving a series of poesy-readings and lectures in the East (Univ. of Connecticut, Tufts Univ., probably at the Poetry Center at the YMHA, etc.); and it's very important that I try to come to Seattle sometime after January in order to defend my dissertation (if this meets with your approval). Here is my plan:

The various chapters are outlined. I will read the six novels again, and then spend about 6 hrs. per day at my desk. I write prose very fast, even though it sounds like hell. The faster I write prose, the more likely I am to write something sensible. Anyway, I'll write each chapter, revise it, and keep a carbon copy of the revision. Then I'll send the chapter to you, and ask you to read it and criticize it and—as soon as you possibly can—ask Mr. Fowler and Malcolm Brown for their own criticisms, and then send all of these criticisms and suggestions for further revision to me, so that I can get on with the work. Is this an acceptable procedure? Please forgive me for sounding as if I were pushing you. I certainly don't mean to sound that way. It's just that I am bursting, literally bursting, with ideas and projects again—and I go nuts when I can't keep up the rhythm of labor in writing, once I let it get started. Can I go on with the plan that I've outlined here? Please say yes. (My God! How arrogant I am!)

You may like to know that a magnificent and complete new edition of Swift's poems—those gorgeous and neglected things—has been published in England by the Muse's Library. The editor is Joseph Horrell who, in addition to a clear and illuminating introduction (*e.g.*, consider his comment, "Nobody ever linked poetry with life more mercilessly than Swift."), [gives] a full set of explanatory notes at the end of each of the two volumes; and there are footnotes to explain the topical references and the meanings of the magnificently obscene and genuine, raunchy words that Swift uses in his poetry. The two volumes cost me nine bucks in a bookstore here in Minneapolis; but that was just because I couldn't stand to live another day after seeing the books in the window of the store. Even before I raked (practically stole, that is) together the money to buy them, I saw in Blackwell's new catalogue that the 2 volumes together are available at Blackwell's for 18 shillings ($4.90). So you can see the real saving. But I'm glad I paid nine dollars for them anyway. It was an act of devotion to the curious, tragically passionate and funny Muse who moved Swift. I know of no other poet just like him. I think there is no one at all like him. His poems are white elephants in the history of literature. They are not only odd things to appear in the Augustan age. They would not quite fit *any* age. I take such joy in them, that the volumes are a treasure to me. Listen to this little thing, which he apparently wrote after hearing old women selling fruit outside his window in Dublin:

APPLES
Come buy my fine wares,
Plums, Apples and Pears.
A hundred a penny,
In Conscience too many,
Come, will you have any;
My Children are seven,
I wish them in Heaven,
My Husband's a Sot,
With his Pipe and his Pot,
Not a Farthing will gain 'em,
And I must maintain 'em.

* * *

Wayne: there's a whole set of these wonderful, human, audacious, irreverent verses . . . Please try to write quick.

Love from Lib,
Jim

Minneapolis
June 19, 1958

Dear Wayne,

I gratefully received your note. Please forgive the nagging tone of my letter about criticizing my chapters as I send them. You know my catathymic hysterias when I work on something, and—though I try constantly—sometimes I can't spare even my very best and closest friends from the flying debris. In a saner mood, I quite realize that you can't very easily receive a chapter from me, immediately hit the telephone, and order Fowler and Brown to get the hell over to your office and write out their criticisms and send them to me by return mail OR ELSE! Your own remarks are the best: when I am satisfied (temporarily) with a section of the dissertation, I'll just send it to you, and then proceed with others, revising when I need to. Then, when it's all done, I'll be sure that it's in your hands; and, if the passages that I've already sent you have been subsequently revised, I'll send you a careful and clear list of such further revisions, with clearly-marked page-references to the copies that I've sent you (in order to keep this plan straight, I'm keeping a carbon copy of every single page of manuscript that I send to you, so that all you need do is refer me to the number of a page or pages). Okay?

Believe it or not, the first chapter is damn near done, though I started writing it only this week. I spent months studying over it and brooding about it (I go through such hell when I work on something, that my writing tends to be somewhat excessive simply because of the physical relief it provides), and, as I warned you, I do the actual work of writing at a terrifying rate of speed. Anyway, and I hope you don't mind, the first chapter is going to be at least fifty typed pages long, and probably a little bit longer (with footnotes). It is the hardest chapter of all to write, because it indicates not only the direction I am taking in the more specific analyses to follow but also what I think is a workable theory about "how to read Dickens' early novels." You'll find it laden with my usual screaming and horseshit, but I am praying that it will make sense. Please don't laugh—or, if you laugh, tell me that you wept—when I say that Dickens has shaken me to the very bottom of myself. I chose him to work on mainly because I liked him, but liking a writer and finding him to be one's own imaginative resource—one of those really terrifying people like Cervantes—are two different things. I've had so many poems begin after reading Dickens that I ought to send part of the payment to his Estate. (By the way, one called "At the Executed Murderer's Grave," a long one, will soon appear in *Poetry* magazine in Chicago.* I was going to send you a copy, but it will be in print soon anyway. The poem, I fearfully believe, is a son of a bitch on wheels. If I haven't done it this time, then I quit. Perhaps worse, if I *have* done it—i.e., made my meaning clear, I'm liable to be investigated the next time we have a war. The poem begins as a meditation at the real grave of a murderer, suddenly goes into a wildly surrealistic scene

*See Appendix, p. 564, for the poem "At the Executed Murderer's Grave."

derived from Amos and Nahum and Revelation in the Bible, and turns out to be a lament—a *cursing* lament, the only real kind, the kind Heathcliff speaks to Cathy Linton on her deathbed—for the real murderer, which is of course society and—since I belong to society, since I didn't defend the human being in the grave—a cursing lament for myself. It's a crazy poem, horrified, anarchistically religious, murderous, and—I have to face it, though God almighty knows what was going on in the dungeon of my own mind—suicidal. But then—the theme of the poem is suicidal too, isn't it? I mean that every man who kills another man kills himself too, and every man who lets another man be murdered kills another man, and has actually let himself be killed—for nothing, nothing, nothing.)

The letter I wrote you about Swift's poems got me so riled and excited about him, that I wrote the enclosed.* Do you mind the title?

Chapter One of the Dickens will be sent soon.

Yours,
Jim

To Elizabeth Lawrence

Minneapolis
June 19, 1958

Dear Miss Lawrence:

I shudder to realize that you might well think I am pestering you about my manuscript of poems, which is now in your hands. Please believe that I am letting you alone.

I just want to ask you to address any further communications to me at the address given in the heading of this letter. The spring quarter at the University of Minnesota has ended; since my family and I will be living on the *Kenyon Review* Poetry Fellowship till next Spring, my headquarters (at least my mailing address) will be here at home.

Of course, in spite of the first paragraph above, I wouldn't want to

---

*See Appendix, p. 567, for the poem "To Wayne Burns: On the Appearance of a New Edition of Swift's Poems."

imply that I'm at all indifferent to hearing from you. But I've been in this game at least long enough to develop the external numbness required for continuous work. And work, I guess, is the only thing that matters anyway, in the end—a kind of savage and hopeless work, a matter of pouring it all out on the pages and then spending two years hacking it into shape with every brutal principle of self-criticism you've ever heard of or dreamed up.

Anyway, here I am at home.

Thank you.

Sincerely,

James Wright

The Fire of the Daemon

1958

With Marshall and Franz Wright, Minneapolis, 1959

So you can see that this summer has given me my baptism of fire: he's [Bly] hit me from one side, you've hit me from another, and I've scurried around like a man caught in an open field by the cross-fire of machine guns. But the summer is over, and *I am not dead*! This joyful thought fills my mind each morning when I waken. I have a new son, and I am in touch with poetry again—not metrical tricks, but the fire of the daemon!

—from a letter to James Dickey
August 25, 1958

Nineteen fifty-eight was a most important year for James. First, another son, Marshall John, was born on July 30. Second, James began a brilliant correspondence with Robert Bly and James Dickey in addition to continuing a fine exchange of letters with Donald Hall. James visited Hall in Michigan and Bly on his farm in Madison, Minnesota, where he would spend many weekends over the following years. There he was to meet William Duffy, John Knoepfle, John Logan, and Louis Simpson, among many others.

To James Dickey

Minneapolis
July 6, 1958

Dear Mr. Dickey:

I have just completed a book review for *Sewanee*, and tomorrow morning I will send it off. Mr. Spears wants it by August 1, so I assume it will appear in the fall issue. Having read your essays with interest and attention for some time (I realize that you will consider this statement a lie), I have added a discussion of your criticism to my review. I am going to tell Mr. Spears that, if the discussion is too long, he can either cut it or remove it altogether. In any case, you have a right to read it beforehand, whether or not you think it is worth answering in print. I wish to say that I realize there are several of its points which are inadequately stated and, more often, inadequately developed. For example, I refer to my discussion of your remarks on Eberhart and Bridges. The issue is a major one, but I was cramped for space, having already exceeded the generous limits suggested by the editor. If you care to bother answering, I will try to elucidate the discussion further.

Before I quote the section of the review: I understand perfectly well that, as far as you are concerned, I am a bad poet, probably not a poet at all in any sense that you would care about or believe in. My reason for writing you this note—in addition to my recognizing your right to see a discussion of your ideas *before* it appears in print, so that you can answer it as you see fit—is that, unless I utterly misunderstand your writings, the sense in which you care about poetry and believe in it is very similar to the sense in which I care about it and believe in it myself. This is another statement which you will probably consider a lie. However that may be, I would not argue against your adverse judgment of my own work even if it were possible to do so. Since you both think and feel that my verses stink, it is your responsibility as well as your privilege to say so in print. But even if my poems are bad, and even if you do not believe that I care about poetry in the same way that you do, I am asking you to believe, purely on faith, that I do indeed care about it in *some* sense. There is something else that I want to say: in my discussion of your writings, I refer to Mr. Philip Booth. Perhaps you will immediately conclude that I am merely being protective about one of my friends. I have never met Mr. Booth. I have had a brief correspondence with him about editorial and other business matters; I told him that I enjoyed his book, especially the poem "First Lesson"; and I wrote him a note to thank him for his review of my book, a review which, though sober and courteous, was hardly drunken with enthusiasm. As a matter of fact, I am friends with very, very few current poets, and most of them are students who have never had anything published. I think, however, that generosity is not only a moral virtue. I think that it is also an act of intelligence. Sometimes students have cautiously and tentatively brought verses to me, under that somewhat silly impression of very young people that my having had something in print made me a valid judge; when their verses were sentimental and inept, I believe that I have criticized them honestly and severely; however, I have never greeted a student by telling her to go fuck herself and shove her hideous poems up her ass because they have blotched my soul and insulted the names of Homer, Dante, and Shakespeare. I believe your attack on Mr. Booth's verses amounted to something similar. I did not like it. It was destructive not only to Booth, but to you, and indeed to everybody who gives a damn about poetry, and who realizes that its best ally right now would be a courteous and judicious criticism. I think the relation of hatred to criticism is the same relation that exists between life and poetry. A good man will not necessarily thereby become a good poet; a good poet, on the other hand, is, I believe, by definition a good man. Sometimes a man tries to write poems and fails. I think the critic has fulfilled his responsibility when he says so and explains what he means. Sometimes good critics explain the standard by which they judge (I said *explain*, not merely *state*), and sometimes they go so far as to admit that there may possibly be, somewhere in the universe and in human history, standards different from their own. But if the versifier (like myself, as you well know) fails to achieve a poem, I don't see why the critic has to kick him in the balls.

Nothing that I've said about hatred can in the slightest way disqualify what I've said about my belief in the importance of your writings in *Sewanee*, but of course this is just one more belief in which you will not believe. The relevant section of my review is enclosed.

Yours,
James Wright

Minneapolis
July 20, 1958

Dear Mr. Dickey:

It is difficult to know how to begin. Perhaps it is best simply to start by asking if you will be kind enough to read my letter, without just throwing it in the waste basket at once, as you would be justified in doing.

I received your letter just a little while ago. Its firm courtesy startled me into an inexcusably belated realization of the extraordinarily ugly thing I had done in writing you, a person who had done me no harm except to tell the truth about me, a letter which—to put the kindest interpretation upon it—was stupid. Just before beginning the present note to you, I wrote air mail to Mr. Spears at *Sewanee*.

Instead of including my discussion of your criticism in my book-review proper, he had decided, upon receiving it, to print it as a "letter to the editor." I have just written to request—as urgently as possible—that he print the passage in neither place. If he complies with my request, it will, of course, be a favor to me and not to you. I am sure you cannot, and would not, be affected one way or another by being attacked in print. Indeed, it is almost a kind of compliment to be attacked by a fool.

It would afford me some personal relief if you would now permit me to comment on many of the points contained in your letter to me:

1. "Under the influence of God knows what powerful, self-protective compulsion, you have evidently invented a dreadful, irresponsible,

arrogant fellow named James Dickey who thinks of you as a person congenitally unable to tell the truth . . . etc." It is true that my letter to you was both paranoid and hysterical, both inaccurate and vicious. As I sit here, I think I know why I was hurt. You simply said that I was not a poet. This remark of yours only confirmed what—obviously enough—is a central fear of mine, and which I have been deeply struggling to face for some time. It is now plain that I am not man enough to face it. I know that an attempt to apologize would only compound an insult which I have already, to put it mildly, carried far enough—too far indeed. But you surely deserve an explanation of the letter itself, and of its genuinely sick-minded tone. My explanation will sound so childish and silly that it is painful to write it down, but somehow I have got to face it: I have always wanted I think as much as I could want anything in the world, to be a poet, because I felt that poets, especially the real poets of the modern world, were great and admirable men. When my first book was published, in spite of the fact that it was reviewed with what I can best describe as intemperate politeness, I looked into it and knew at once that it contained merely competence, and that competence alone is death. This is a bitter truth to face.

2. The passage about the *Handbook for Boys** was such an obvious smirk that to recollect it shames and humiliates me beyond description.

3. ". . . absurd formulations like: 'a good poet is, I believe, by definition a good man . . .' " The formulation is admittedly absurd and confused. You ask, "By *what* definition? Not by that of literary history, I hope, or reference to real poets." In the phrase "by definition" I wanted to suggest that—well, take the poets whom you mention—men like Baudelaire, Villon, Dylan Thomas simply by the act of writing good poems became good men. I am sure, for example, that my own life is a good deal more regularly ordered, law-abiding, and even sanitary than Villon's life was; and yet, as a great artist he demonstrated something of genuine human goodness and greatness; whereas, as a counterfeit, I demonstrate nothing except the too obvious fact that I have learned, through imitating real artists, how to ape mechanically some of the devices, like meter and rhyme,

---

*From Wright's "A Note on Mr. James Dickey," withdrawn from publication in *The Sewanee Review* but included in draft with Wright's previous letter.

which they subdued to their own creative, imaginative purposes—a purpose which involves not merely imitating somebody else, but rather illuminating some of the meanings of human life.

4. Your refusal to honor my "ridiculous challenge" is justified, of course, for it was not a challenge at all but rather a squeak of terror from a person frantically incapable of facing his lack of talent.

5. I most nearly approach a state of flinching self-horror when I come to your next remark, and yet somehow I have got to face it: "If you ever have occasion to address any further correspondence to me, do me the courtesy of leaving obscenity out. Childish as your references are, they nevertheless constitute a considered insult to me and to my family. As such, they effectively remove you and me from the plane of literary controversy." I can think of only one single thing to write you that would not make matters worse, and even that one thing exposes itself as a sniveling, whining plea. Nevertheless, I proceed with it, and ask you—out of a kindness which I distinctly do not deserve but of which I stand in terrible need at this moment, to convey my respect and my apology to your wife. Also, in this particular matter of my hysterical and brutal obscenity, I would like to offer my apology to you also, sir. I would consider it a considerable sign of kindness if you would accept the apology.

For in just two days my own wife is due to bear her second child. Perhaps one thing which partly accounts for my going so weirdly haywire (I have had some nervous illness, a fact which I feel sure will not surprise you) is that, in my talentless and therefore quixotic struggle to support my adored family, I have sometimes sustained myself with the illusion that my gifts might after all be genuine, though minor. In any case, my closeness to my own family, sir, makes it possible for me—at this belated moment—to appreciate the honest feeling of revulsion with which you and your family must have received my letter. I flatter myself that I have at least enough human decency to imagine your disgust, and for the sake of my feelings concerning my wife and children—feelings to which I cling with some desperation—I would be grateful if you regarded my request with a sense of forgiveness.

6. You observe, in your concluding paragraph, that "such language addressed to the home of a total stranger must be taken either as the doing of a hopeless crank (which I do not believe you are, quite),

or of someone who realizes the implications of his actions, and is prepared to be held responsible for them: i.e. to resolve the differences in personal action, rather than in print."

To confess that I did *not* realize the implications of my actions would be stupid, even beyond the stupidity of my previous letter to you. I ask you to believe that I am not again groping for the effect of heavy-handed irony which characterized my letter, when I say that it *was* the letter of a crank. That, indeed, is just what frightens me. To win my personal struggle against becoming a *hopeless* crank is the secondary reason for my writing you the present letter; the primary reason is to beg your pardon for my unprovoked and hostile letter to you, and for exposing both you and your family to a neurotic display which is indecent and distressing, to say the least. If I understand your reference to "personal action" as the suggestion of physical violence, please let me assure you that such would not be necessary. Feeling as horrified by myself as I do just now, I would certainly just sit on the ground and look at you, and I would not know what to say.

May I add two notes? First, if I win the struggle to know myself as a versifier lacking in any talent, it may be possible for me to be a good teacher and an honest man; so that some kind of human self-regard is possibly available to me. Second, I would like to say that, in spite of the cowardly hysteria to which I so unfortunately exposed you, I have at least not taken out my frustration in hatred of the good poets themselves. It's an idiotically small thing to cling to, but it's all I have. Mr. Dickey, I am ashamed and humiliated. Even *this* letter is one long adolescent whine. I would take it as a very great, though of course undeserved, personal kindness if you were to accept my apology for insulting your family and you.

Sincerely,
James Wright

To Robert Bly

Minneapolis
July 22, 1958

Dear Mr. Bly:

This afternoon I walked over to the University for something or other—I forget just what—and picked up from my mailbox the copy of *The Fifties* which you were kind enough to send me. I am writing you now to thank you.

But the phrase "thank you" is too conventionally cold.

Let me start again: I looked at the line on the inside of the front cover,* and was absolutely fixed with concentration for more than an hour, reading and reading the magazine, wondering at the weirdness of it all.

I don't mean in the previous sentence that the magazine is weird (as a matter of fact, the magazine *is* weird, but not in the previous sentence). The weirdness I mean grows out of the fact that I had just about decided to stop publishing any verses—to force myself to stop publishing, really—for at least a year or two, and maybe even to stop writing altogether. The reasons for this decision are hard to state—that is why the issue of your magazine meant so much to me. Recent reviews and discussions of American poetry have been filled with a niggling and carping despair. It was the niggling and the carping that depressed me—I already had plenty of despair of my own, without being reminded that, at a time when—as sometimes unpredictably and inexplicably happens—the very atmosphere seems shaking with poetic imagination and, more than that, poetic *possibility*, almost every young American poet known to me was just *tired*. Of course, I refer to others only in order transparently to cover up the fact that I am referring to myself.

I will now offer what will sound like the most idiotic compliment-fishing since Uriah Heep announced "Me and my mother is very 'umble." But I really was in despair because, in spite of several reviews that were filled—some of them dripped, I should say—with well-intended courtesy (and I *was* grateful for the courtesy, which is a great human virtue—I am not trying to be heavily ironic), my book of verses, except

---

*"The editors of this magazine think that most of the poetry published in America today is too old-fashioned."

for about three experiments that practically no one paid any attention to whatever, stank.

It's true that my stuff contains 'umble, "sincere" displays of all the current cute tricks in meter and rhyme. But what I am trying to say is that—still with the exception of two or three breaths of vision, just breaths and not *poems*—*The Green Wall* might very easily have been written by any normally educated Englishman of, say, the eighteenth century, if he ever took time off from his work as Master of the Fox Hounds in order to play around with a little polite versifying. If it is nothing else, my book may well be the most insipidly polite book of verses in the past twenty years. If you will consider the record for a moment, you will see that this is not a light statement. My book was dead. It could have been written by a dead man, if they have Corona-Corona typewriters in the grave. For all I know, it *was* written by a dead man.

It is conceivable that you might wonder why the fact should matter enough to me to make me decide to quit—just quit, cut the God damned cackle, stop committing the blasphemy of pretending—or of letting others think, in their good will and their courtesy—that there was any essential relation between myself and any genuine poet at all, other than the fact that we both belong to the erstwhile human race.

Well, maybe I can explain by saying that, when I was young, I wanted to be a poet like Walt Whitman, and I hated the God damned place where I was born (Ohio) enough to try it at least. To be like Whitman meant to try to be original. I had no illusion that this was not difficult, but I had nothing to lose, and I didn't give a damn about that unspeakable rat-hole where I grew up. I went to the army when I was 18, and wrote wild things, all of them bad. But after college I got a Fulbright to the University of Vienna. My whole so-called project as a scholar was a laughingly complete failure; but I blundered (I actually *blundered*, I stumbled in by mistake, and I didn't even know where I was for about three lectures) into a classroom at Vienna where a little Italian scholar named Susini was softly lecturing. The audience consisted of five very small and withered old men—anyone would have taken them for hoboes in America, but everybody's a hobo in Austria—and myself. And every afternoon at 3 o'clock, I think it was four days a week, I walked through that terrible cold and unheated winter city, to hear Susini whisper in his beautiful, gentle, liquid voice the poems of an Austrian of whom I had never even heard, but who had the grasp and shape of what you in your article called the new imagination. I tried to catch it. I didn't understand how to *do* it. I wrote four hundred pages that year, and saved three of them.

But back in America I have had an impossible time even trying to get anyone to admit that Whitman existed, to find anyone at all—*anyone at all*—who has even heard Trakl's name.

So I used to get hideously drunk at parties of academic intellectuals, and after the point of no return I would stand and bellow Trakl, and Carossa, and Rilke, and Hölderlin, because nobody knew what the hell I was saying, and because I only slightly *felt*, rather than *understood*, what in the name of God was crying in the miracles of those images that were sane to the depths of their being and which yet followed no rules that anyone else had ever dreamed of, and in the tide-suck of that music that sounded like the sea burying its birds or a jellyfish crying out in pain.

But my friends made fun of me, and I can't stand it, so I quit drinking so much.

And in the face of mockery I deserted Whitman, whose book was a holy book to me so long. I deserted him in order to learn to write little tetrameter couplets.

What I mean in the above rant (I apologize, by the way, for my wordiness—I can't seem to help it) is that I have simply quit. I deserted poetry a good while ago, and there's little sense in plugging couplets into the socket and shooting General Electricity into the dry-cell battery of a stiff.

This caused me a difficult struggle, as I am sure you can easily imagine. I was really and truly in one hell of a shape—I had made up my mind not even to *write* anything that did not dig coldly and murderously into what I knew (how nothing's that!) and then fling it out, by God even if *The New Yorker couldn't* understand it. I had just this morning, in the first pain of the old bitching snarling of muscles in the head for about five years—done the honorable thing, the thing that Robert Herrick tried to do (Herrick failed, because by some accident he couldn't possibly succeed—in other words, he actually *was* a poet, and it was a wonderful joke on him, I think): that is, I wrote my own "Farewell to Poetry." Plodding through the images of the slag heaps and the black trees and the stool-washed river and the chemicals from the factories of Wheeling Steel, Blaw Knox, the Hanna Coal Co. which—God damn fate, this is too much, it's comic when you come to think of it—are the only images of childhood I can ever have, I begged pardon (I really did, I mean it, and I meant it) of the Mother of Roots or whoever the hell she is who gets into Whitman, Trakl, Neruda, Lorca, Char, Michaux—into almost everybody, in fact, except me. And I said—as obscurely and gibberingly as I *felt* like saying—that the hell with it, I was getting *out*. And I got out.

And that is really why your magazine meant so much to me. It's really extremely strange that I should receive it today, just after I quit. For it confirms everything that I feared, and yet the facing of the fear—that is, about my own third-rate identity—a facing really made possible by your arguments—is a relief so deep that I'm beginning to think, this evening, that I must have been really *suffering* with this sense of failure, of betraying what within me I genuinely *knew*, though I denied it on the surface, what poetry was.

Mr. Bly, I've looked over the previous two pages, and I see how hysterical and profane I've been—and of course I have absolutely no right to send you this letter. However, I am going to risk it, in the hope that perhaps its very tone of nervous instability might convey to you the gratitude with which I read the first issue of your magazine. There is surely nothing objectionable about writing you a completely unsolicited letter. But you would be justified if you felt that such a letter, filled with profanity and personal hysteria, constituted a rudeness, perhaps even an outright insult, to you, especially in view of your graciousness in sending me a copy of *The Fifties*, of which I had not heard. Let me, therefore, try to state, with an attempt at normal human decency of tone, what I think about the magazine:

It is, to my mind, the finest little magazine to be started during this whole decade. It is funny, honest, deeply compassionate and intelligent, and intolerant of the second- and third-rate which some American poets of genuine gifts are letting themselves be tricked into regarding as the real poetry of our time. Moreover, you state with unmistakable clarity the fact—so oddly compounded of painful shock and painful joy—that our own age, the brief time we have on the earth, is all we've got, and that the imaginative men in other countries today, as well as the unborn, are not going to have time to care anything in particular about the fact that, during the fifties in America, there were a great many competent punks and, unfortunately, two or three real poets who comforted themselves by scratching one another's tweedy backs while poetry in America went gurgling, once more and yet once more, down the drain without even the benefit of the ease provided by the liberal use of Old Dutch Cleanser. In the part of this letter which preceded the present paragraph, I spoke again and again and again of despair, and I hope you will excuse me for the self-indulgence. Actually, your magazine's editorial policy offers the only kind of hope there is for po-etry, in my belief (which, after all these years, I have dared to state to myself, in the hope that, as usual, I am either drunk or inattentive). I sincerely thank you for sending it to me. To be included on the mailing list of the first issue was a great human honor. As for my own depres-sion, I am sure it will pass (well, reasonably sure, anyway). I remember, long ago when I was young and fiery and stupid, I read in the lovely book Rilke's *Letters to a Young Poet* that one ought first to journey into himself, and determine whether or not he is a poet. It sounds like a cruel thing to suggest, said Rilke in his very great sympathy and ten-derness to Kappus and to all men as young as I myself was young, and yet, even if one finds that he is *not* a poet, he has discovered something which is miraculously worth living for—that is, a true vision of his true self and what he might be able to do with it. Well, perhaps Rilke was a little naive, for it is harder to journey into one's self in youth. I had to wait till now in order to bear the journey. Now I have made it. It gives me a kind of odd happiness to have looked into the face of the Gor-gon, and yet to find that I have not turned utterly to stone. Now I can paraphrase that fine author James Baldwin, and say that I would like to be a good teacher and an honest man.

I will have to wait till about the end of the month—perhaps a bit longer—before I can afford to subscribe to *The Fifties*. I apologize. I will certainly subscribe at the earliest possible moment. All the poems were genuine, and the one by Donald Hall was, by God, an absolute knock-out. He has come a thousand miles beyond his first book.

Please accept my very highest personal regards, if I may offer them, and also my deepest and best wishes for the continuance of your splendid magazine. As I brought it deliriously home to my wife this evening, and read practically all of it to her (I swear this is not an exaggeration), a bell rang in my skull, and I looked up Bernard Shaw's 1907 Preface to his booklet *The Sanity of Art*. Maybe this salutary quotation will interest you, even thrill you as it thrilled me:

> The writer who aims at producing the platitudes which are "not for an age, but for all time" has his reward in being unreadable in all ages; whilst Plato and Aristophanes trying to knock some sense into the Athens of their day, Shakespeare peopling that same Athens with Elizabethan mechanics and Warwickshire hunts, Ibsen photographing the local doctors and vestrymen of a Norwegian parish, Carpaccio painting the life of St. Ursula exactly as if she were a lady living in the next street to him, are still alive and at home everywhere among the dust and ashes of many thousands of academic, punctilious, most archaeologically correct men of letters and art who spent their lives haughtily avoiding the journalist's vulgar obsession with the ephemeral.

Thank you again, very much. The magazine was a personal kindness to me.

Sincerely,
James Wright

P.S. This is the morning after (July 23). I've just looked over the magazine again; and, since I've run on so long about nothing really except myself, I thought it would be all right to make a couple of other comments:

W. D. Snodgrass: I have long thought of him as probably the most gifted of all American young poets now alive; and these two poems of his, especially "The Men's Room in the College Chapel," absolutely prove, as far as I am concerned, that I was right. No one else could have written that poem. It follows nobody's imagery and nobody's rhythm but its own. Do you know what I mean when I say that there is something deeply *restoring* about such a poem—that the exposure of the cyst or the cancer is more lovely, more reviving, more human, because more alive, than all the cosmetic devices of Helena Rubenstein?

Gary Snyder: Kenneth Rexroth is a personal friend of mine (another of my dirty little secrets)—I swear to God that if I even mention this fact among my academic friends, a really dreadful and powerfully oppressive hush suffocates the whole room—it is exactly as though I had grinned, slapped somebody's grandmother on the back, and shouted, "Well, Granny, I buggered another stray dog last night! Haugh! Haugh! Haugh! Haaaaaargh!"

I mention Rexroth, because of the two poems by Gary Snyder (guilt by association?). Now, I never met Mr. Snyder, but in Seattle two or three years ago, before *Time* magazine discovered the fact that in San Francisco (and perhaps elsewhere, even on the campuses of our colleges where these men are being paid good money to defile Our Children?) a few obvious lunatics announced that, no thank you, they would just as soon stay alive, if it's all the same to you Mr. Luce,—before, in short, the advertising wave buried Ginsberg, Ginsberg and Snyder gave a poetry reading at the Univ. of Washington. Ginsberg said bad words (!), and no one ever heard of Snyder again. Now, all I wish to say is that "Milton by Firelight" (*The Fifties*, pp. 32–3) is a very beautiful poem—the real thing.

And Snyder reminds me of a friend, a good friend of mine, named Richard F. Hugo. He lives in Seattle. He works in Boeing Aircraft Co. His address is:

Richard F. Hugo
6809 8th Avenue N.E.
Seattle 15, Washington

The point of mentioning Hugo is that his stuff has a good deal in common with Snyder's—that is (and excuse me for appropriating the phrase, which I like, I think it is really a *liberating* phrase), Hugo's poems have the new imagination. Now, for several years, he has labored truly and deeply on words—imagery, the new imagery, is his devotion. Unless I am really a complete imbecile after all, as my wife tells me in fights, then his poem "A Troubadour Removed," which is about $1\frac{1}{2}$ pages single-spaced and which is unpublished and which is magnificent, would convince you completely—or almost completely, anyway. Since I've gone this far, and since—if you haven't passed out from exhaustion in reading my letter already—you might feel too numb to mind my further verbosity, I want to quote a bit of Hugo in a moment. First I want to say that he has been pretty depressed sometimes; but the difference between his depression and mine is that he has a right to his—that is, he can't get decently published because he is a real poet, and I get published everywhere because I'm *not*. Please, I don't mean to imply that he has any jealousy whatever, because he doesn't. He's had stuff in little mags in the west, and in *Botteghe Oscure* through the good offices of Jack Mathews (incidentally, Mathews is the one who edited, and partly translated, *Hypnos Waking*, Random House, 1957, selected poetry and prose by René Char—Jack is in the states again after working in Paris on the edition of Valery's translated complete works, and I know very well that he would be deeply interested in *The Fifties*. Far be it from me to try to influence your editorial policy—but Mathews knows an enormous amount about exactly the great new poetry that you celebrate, and he is also a personal friend of both Char and Michaux—if you care to, you can reach him at: Mr. Jackson Mathews, The Bollingen Series, 140 East 62nd Street, NY 21). But Hugo's book ought to be published by now, and he does not have the chance of a snowball in an incinerator. I myself have submitted his ms. to Univ. of Minn. Press, but they've had it forever, and no word yet. Why have I tried to help him? Personal friendship and admiration, of course; but the main reason—it should be obvious—is guilt, old-fashioned GUILT (my God! even my sins are old-fashioned) that a tremendous poet, who is doing something to catch his time and place *alive*, nevertheless perishes because the magazines, the books, and heaven knows what else are in control, not of people who *hate* poetry (there's no point in being sentimental), but of something far more destructive and suffocating— that is, of people who, like myself, are *afraid* of it.

Now for quotation. Please don't mind. The following stanzas are from "A Troubadour Removed" by Richard F. Hugo. It describes a man journeying alone into an exotic jungle, where he witnesses and participates in some mysterious ceremony (it is really the Jungian night-journey, though Hugo didn't theorize, he just *wrote*), but then, attempting to return, takes one wrong trail after another till he is lost in the growth. What is really nutty and beautiful is Hugo's vague remark (when, like the usual paraphraser—i.e., killer, of poetry, I asked him what the poem "meant") that he was thinking of the poets like Lorca and Thomas, who came to America and discovered the jungle. Here are a couple of quotations from his poem:

He planned his course on Orinoco charts.
Past Barrancas snoring, odors of the journey
Named the flowers native in his bones
And fed by ivory mandolins and wine
Copper wives were peeling by the shore.
He had been here like a bird before.

At night, he navigated by the toucan's blare.
Day was blinding but a dragonfly
Hung steady in his octant like a star
And riprap nudged his boat around the turns.
Where waterfalls denied a water course
A wild brown girl was waiting with a horse . . .

He climbed above the fading of his guide
And castles came with a golden roar through clouds . . .

Against the walls a lemon wing was beating
And then the walls were gone. Above the steam
Of primitive meat he strung on poles to dry
A dead bird turned black wings
To silver in the sun and flew away
And had no lime or luck for pilot aid . . .

                  . . . He took wrong trails
To waterfalls and horses, tame and tan.
A drum defined the rolling of his eyes.
(Sing with effort what he sang was easy,
Spinning songs to rock the seagulls dizzy.) . . .

Rice and idols foxtrot in the distant towns
And monster flies are chanting on their knees . . .

And so on. I've quoted you these lines without his permission, but I know he won't mind, and I hope you like them. He is a good, decent friend of mine; but I have the additional pleasure of knowing a real poet personally.

Vassar Miller: she lives in Houston, Texas. Her work has appeared in *The New Orleans Poetry Journal*, Box 12038, New Orleans 24, La. Of all the formalists whom you recognize as gifted but who, in your view, are injuring themselves by writing in the old way, I think she is one of the best. Do you know her book? If not, you can get it for one dollar from the *New Orleans Poetry Journal*.* It is certainly worth looking at. A fair sample of her style is in the anthology by Pack, Simpson, and Hall. Her work is richly dense with imagery, almost all of it originally and powerfully imagined. I again apologize for presumptuousness, but having gone this far, will suggest that she deserves study by the estimable CRUNK. (My God! Why hasn't somebody created CRUNK before this? This essay on Simpson was one of the most profoundly searching works of literary criticism—of really *living* literary criticism, the kind that Simpson himself called for in his essay-review "Poets in Isolation," *Hudson Review*, Autumn, 1957, an essay highly worth looking up—that I have read or even heard of. It reminded me—humor and all—of Sainte-Beuve's review of Taine's *History of English Literature*: a passionate devotion to the living and gifted author, and the honorable compliment of true and sympathetic description of that author's problems—it is a kind of loyalty to the human imagination that is either present or not, with no possibility for compromise in between: it simply cannot be faked.

I must turn myself off. But your magazine, and your vision of poetry, and your dream of hope and life in the human imagination—these things I can summarize by saying that they were all of them as far distant from being "fake" as, in my mind, it is possible for anything whatever to be.

Please pardon the volcano of bad prose and the embarrassing, unsolicited confessions of my assorted self-betrayals. And thank you.

Sincerely,
James Wright

---

*In the margin: "This sentence is rude. I wish I could *afford* to send you Vassar Miller's book myself. I'm *certain* that Richard Ashman, editor of the *NOPJ*, would send it to you free, if you're *editorially* interested. I'm reviewing Vassar Miller in the coming Fall issue of *Sewanee Review*. If it isn't too presumptuous, I'd be very happy to write a CRUNK essay on Miller, subject to any editorial approval or disapproval you wish to apply to it. Shall I try?" Crunk was a pen name used by Robert Bly and other writers for their critical essays on contemporary poets in Bly's magazines *The Fifties* and *The Sixties*.

Dear Mr. Bly:

Please don't be annoyed. I promise not to flail you with another 6-page crank note.

But, looking again through your essay "Five Decades of Modern American Poetry," I am troubled by something; and, though my previous letter was obviously one of those unavoidable perils of editorship that you will probably be receiving from nuts all over the country, I would appreciate it very much if you would clarify a point for me:

Now, as I understand it, the new imagination is "modern in the profound sense, in which ugliness is grasped as ugliness, and the terror the ugliness inspires is left in the work, and not explained away," and that what this "content" requires—and there can be no doubt whatever that this quotation from your essay irrefutably *does* describe the truth of modern American life—a "new style." Then, at the bottom of page 37 and over almost through page 38, you describe—again excellently—the "new style" in terms of *imagery*. So far, I'm sure I understand, and of course I think you are right again. Then you face the immediate and practical problem of what to do in order to get rid of the old style: you face, and I think solve, the problem by saying that

1. Poets do not write today about the only truth available to them (things like "business experience, despair, or the Second World War," or—in the case of W. D. Snodgrass, the academic world—my God! how magnificently he reveals a terrible and profound poetry *even there*, in "The Men's Room in the College Chapel"—talk about proving that absolutely all reality of experience is legitimate material for a first-rate poetic imagination!). That there are a few exceptions does not weaken your general position, a position which is true.

2. Poets do not write about the only available truth of experience, because they need an imagery that can only be created in that experience itself, and that therefore cannot possibly be created in terms of a style which was forged long ago in order to deal with the experience of an age which is dead. (Am I paraphrasing you correctly? As I say, I'm not only paraphrasing, but also agreeing.) Now old style is—what? This is the point at which I get befuddled, and the befud-

dlement is the occasion of my present note. My confusion is based on what you say on page 37 about *iambic* meters. Is the use of iambic rhythm *as such necessarily* a sign that American poetry is "moving backward"?

Consider, please, your statement: "some poets, such as Robert Lowell, even going so far as to go back to the iambic couplet, and the iamb came back into poetry and settled itself with a vengeance, like an occupying army returning on a people that had temporarily evicted it." Then you say (rightly) that Karl Shapiro's poems, though contemporary, are not modern in the profound sense, because—

Now, look, are Shapiro's poems written in the old style *because* he uses iambs, or because of his *imagery*? In the fine Wax Museum, you, or your associate Mr. Duffy, say that the most real, the deepest threat to the "new imagination" is what you call "dying language—that is, totally without images." Now, I am certain that I know what you mean by *imagery*, and I am completely convinced that your definition of *dying* language is clear and true. Would it be possible, in your opinion, to say that Shapiro's poems fail to be "modern in the profound sense" for the following reasons?

1. His language is dying, in your sense—for *imagery* is not simply the prosaic photographing of the surfaces of *things*, but the verbal complexity created by the passionately committed imagination—a complexity which thus *contains* both the "imagination and terror" and also the poet's creative *revelation* of what this terror means. Please note that I don't say the poet's *statement* or *gloss* on the terror, but his revelation of its meaning: like Lorca's lines at the end of the "Ode to Walt Whitman," where he cries that he wants to call down all the large warm air to announce the arrival of a black boy who will reveal to the gold-worshipping whites the arrival of the reign of an ear of corn (I've screwed it up, I haven't got the poem handy—excuse me).

2. But is it Shapiro's use of *iambic* per se, or his failure to build a genuine personal rhythm out of iambic, that makes his poetry weak, a poetry in which "the imagination and terror are dimmed by the *con-*

ventional iambic line"? Is it your word "conventional" [. . .] or your word *iambic* which explains the failure of the "old style"?

I didn't mean to carry on so long again. I have this strange compulsion to discover the truth about my failure—ever since I received your magazine yesterday.

Every rhythm must be new and original, if it is to contain genuine *imagery*. Right? Or am I missing the point? But if this *is* the point about rhythm, then I want to ask if you do or do not think it is possible to build a new and original rhythm *on the basis of* the iambic measure.

If you don't have the time or inclination to go into the question, it's perfectly understandable. If you regard my two letters to you as merely obsessive things, profitless to your discussion and interest and therefore merely annoying to you, I promise not to bother you again. But I really *care* about what you are doing. You've blasted open in me an abandoned cavern where the sacred mysteries used to be clumsily but reverently celebrated, before I found it was, upon the whole, somewhat more comfortable to be dead.

Here is Crane in a passage which I have always thought magnificent in its imagery (that is, when I used to read Crane—I just dug out the book, the first time I've opened it in about six years, really):

> The phonographs of hades in the brain
> Are tunnels that re-wind themselves, and love
> A burnt match skating in a urinal . . .

But the passage is *iambic*—isn't it? Somehow the great image helps to build a new rhythm *on* the iambic measure? Or doesn't it? I don't know. If you would care to answer, I would be grateful.

Thank you,
James Wright

P.S. In view of this letter—which lengthens my "thank you note" to 8 pages in a single day, I bet you'll think twice hereafter about distributing *free* a new magazine that actually contains ideas!

To James Dickey

Dear Jim,

This is the way you signed your letter, and I know you won't mind my using your first name.

A bit later I should like to try to explain in greater detail why it was that I blew up at your merely mentioning my name in a phrase of three words. The general reason—at least now—is obvious enough: at the very end of your review (*Sewanee*, Spring, 1958), you wrote the following: "The belief in the value of one's personality has all but disappeared from our verse. Yet the inexhaustible vitality and importance of writing are there, and nowhere else. Berryman and Roethke show us this, and so do Warren, Durrell, Muir, May Sarton, William Smith, and Richard Eberhart. Let the poets of my generation ask as much of themselves." Well, I did *ask* myself; the directness of the question made the answer inescapable. It was a question, and it evoked an answer, that I believe in; and it was not the answer itself that I dreaded, but rather the ghastly and fierce reminder that a truer answer would exact awful labor from me. For the true answer is that to create a real poem is just as difficult a task as to discover, and *face*, "the value of one's personality." It was getting so easy for me to publish just about anything I wrote, that I didn't *want* to be told the truth; and yet I am not a phony, and I knew that I *did* want to be told the truth; and, between the fear and the devotion, between the money I get for the three or four pieces of easy and competent junk I publish on the one hand and the exhaustion and relief I get for the one very occasional piece which—again to use a phrase of yours—"comes close to what I want," I got stretched on the old American rack, and I screamed hysterically. My letter makes me shudder, because the shock of truth evoked from my personality a real strain of hateful paranoia. I accused you of every sin, I think, that I have ever committed or dreaded to commit.

As for your most recent letter: let me say, first, that, if there is anyone on earth whose honesty I can regard with absolute and unquestioning confidence, it is my wife Lib (that's a nickname for Eleutheria—you pronounce the "u" as though it were an "f," roughly—she's a Greek, sort of); now, she had listened to part of the original crazy note I sent you, and had grown profoundly uncomfortable about it, and yet, because when I am normal she can trust my judgment too, she hesitated to tell me the truth, viz. that I was irresponsibly flinging painful curses at a person who had never in the slightest way intended to harm me. She saw me suffer under the stern dignity of your letter; but what I want to tell you is that, frighteningly honest as she is, she warmly and yet savagely agreed with me that your letter was distinguished by courtesy, human decency, and unquestionably justifiable annoyance. You say that you are "simply appalled" at the "dreadful condescending" sound of your letter to me. That you should feel this way is, as far as I am concerned, just another sign of your decency. However, since you yourself say "I had better do some apologizing myself, lest I be shamed out of existence," you may be sure that any apology you think you need to offer me is completely and unconditionally accepted. There is a decorum in a growing friendship that I believe in, because genuine friendship, like genuine anything (genuine poetry, for example) is often startling and disturbing—i.e., reviving and restoring to one's spirit; so the decorum is not a dull and trite form, but a necessity. Nevertheless, I can't help feeling an irony (one out of many ironies, as I'll try to explain later) in your apologizing for a dignified defense of your intelligence and integrity against a hostile and unprovoked letter from a stranger who—there is no evading the fact—actually *blamed you* (when actually, I suppose, God alone is responsible) for the fact that there is, after all, a difference, to put it mildly, between Lorca's "Ode to Walt Whitman" and the typical *New Yorker* verse that is written to order (by people like myself, my God!) for the purpose of filling left-over space between the perfume-ads.

Well, a good many people in my life have treated me with kindness and generosity which I did not deserve; and sometimes people have stung me with truth and honesty the shock of which I *did* deserve; but I assure you that very few people in my experience have been either willing or able to be so unyieldingly honest and yet so warmly generous to me as you have been in *both* of your letters to me; and, if those letters weren't acts of rare friendship, then I don't have the slightest idea what the word "friendship" means. It is a friendship which I welcome with relief, and with a gratitude—especially in the light of my initial action—which, I am sure, I do not need to belabor.

You mention that there will be a new long poem of yours in the August *Poetry*. As far as I can tell, I am going to have a couple of new ones in the same issue; and, if this is so, then the coincidence will be really marvelous. I am honored by your request that I look at your poem and tell you what I think. If (as was certainly not the case) every other sentence in your second letter had been shaking with cold fury, that one request would have demonstrated the genuineness of your kindness as nothing else could do. I promise to study and enjoy* the poem, and to write you everything that occurs to me about it. And I would be glad if you would look at mine, if they are indeed in the same issue. I have more faith in two of them than I had in my whole book. It took me as long to write one of those as it took me to write at least one-third of the poems in the book, and for once I refused to send it out before I had asked a couple of very sharp, courteous, but critically ruthless people (one of them was Allen Tate, whom I don't pester much because he is busy, though he is always generous with his time and criticism, if a writer has the nerve to *endure* such criticism) to apply the blow-torch to it.

Since you say that you intend to read more of my work, I am going to take the liberty of sending you a copy of my book. I know you will read it and say exactly what you think; but there is one detail in which I beg leave to defend myself: on the dust-jacket it says that I say: "I've tried very hard to write in the mode of Robert Frost and Edwin Arlington Robinson. I've wanted to make the poems say something humanly important instead of just showing off with language." Now, I am subject, as you know, to many kinds of humorless foolishness; but before you cringe at that quotation, please remember that it makes me snicker also. I wrote it in a very fast note to the production manager of the Yale University Press, and I had no idea they would print it on the dust-jacket. It makes me feel like the exposed Uriah Heep (Oh, Master Davie, me and my Mother is very 'umble). The only response a person not an utter imbecile could have to the quotation is derision; or perhaps the civil and salutary derision of Mr. Howard Nemerov (whose writings I admire very much), who commented that it "sounded like being against sin." The rest of the book will just have to take its bumps—it was very poorly reviewed. Maybe that's what weakened me

*In the margin: "This strange phrase ('I'll enjoy it if it kills me, etc.') merely means that there are others of yours I've enjoyed. I'll mention them later, if you like."

so much—most reviewers praised it lightly, and I think my pleasure in their mostly valueless (and even dangerous) praises tricked me into the position of a man who tries to live on skim-milk and nothing else. The first poem in the book tried to announce an *anti*-Georgian tone; but, of course, the tone came back and suffocated much of the book. The poems in it that I dislike, am ashamed of, and would like to bury under the sea are the ones that have in them nothing whatever except the very weakness and glibness which you've spotted: "On the Skeleton of a Hound" (what a brazen thing, after Eberhart and Baudelaire!); "Autumnal"; "The Three Husbands" (one reviewer, Mr. John Simon in *Audience*, made the extremely cutting, really funny, and yet unexpectedly accurate comment that this poem sounds like Sara Teasdale's "Colin kissed me in the spring . . ." (ugh!) rewritten by Edgar A. Guest); and others which you will spot for yourself, all of them tyrannized by iambic thumpings. The poems I believe in, if not for their actual accomplishment then for their honesty in attempting to be *poetry* as distinguished from competent *New Yorker* cunning and trickery, are the following: "A Fit Against the Country"; "Lament for My Brother on a Hayrake"; and "Morning Hymn to a Dark Girl."* These poems have, or at least come closer than any of the others to having, *imagery* (as distinguished from mere illustrations of simile-and-metaphor that one can mechanically adapt from any predigested popular handbook of "verse"—like, say, Robert Hillyer's).

Well, you would do me an honor by accepting the book, and by making any comment you may have time to make (of course, I know you have your own work to do and your family's living to make—Lib and I have the *Kenyon* Poetry fellowship this year, and it's nice, though skimpy—as you well know, having had the *Sewanee*'s).

Good heavens, I could go on writing forever—so I had better spare you and get back to my dissertation. It is on Dickens, who is, as everyone knows, sentimental, non-intellectual, clumsy, arch, stupid, murky, and frightened. But I adore him. Devoted as I am to his work, and to what it means, I have taken strength from my remembering—in the midst of guilt-inspiring easy publication (something I swear I am finished with forever, come what may!), I turn to two little quotations

*In the margin: "And the one called 'Eleutheria' also."

which for some time have had great meaning for me, precisely because, in the midst of a time in which I have been in danger of destruction by *slickness*, they have given me the healthy flinch of great truth:

> The errors of a great man make your rule,
> Rather than the perfections of a fool. (Blake)

And this, the last stanza of "The Guilty Man" by Stanley Kunitz (I think he has changed the last line to something different—and, I think, inferior—in his *Selected Poems*, which have just appeared, and which I am reviewing for *Sewanee*):

> Teach me my reasons, I would know their names,
> Cry scandal, drive my secrets out, because
> I hate the good-enough that spoils the world.
> Depart from me, therefore, you virtuous men
> Whose treason is to turn the conscience kind.
> None may forgive us for the ancient wrongs.

But let me at least *try* to be brief, and write down a few more things which I thought might interest you:

In view of your critical essays, and especially your lonely attack on "the good enough that spoils the world" (by the way, the "hatred" I spoke of in that weird review was really my own self-hatred, but that is obvious), you would surely be interested in the appearance of a new magazine called *The Fifties*. The editor, Mr. Robert Bly, whom I have never met but some of whose poems appeared in the Meridian anthology,* sent me a copy. Perhaps he's sent you one also. In any case, you ought to know of it; inside the front cover is this stark and rather startling line: "The editors of this magazine think that most of the poetry published in America today is too old-fashioned." The magazine is good. Your review in the Spring, the appearance of this magazine which is nothing if not self-critical, the explosion of self-dissatisfaction inside others—like, for example, Donald Hall and yourself as well as in me—these could be haunting signs. Do you remember your phrase, in

---

New Poets of England and America, edited by Donald Hall, Robert Pack, and Louis Simpson (Meridian Books, 1957).

an earlier review, about self-dissatisfaction being "not the wildness, but the practicality of hope"? Well, you may or may not agree with many of the ideas presented by the editors in *The Fifties*; but you will, I know, be glad to see that at long last younger American writers are getting jagged, in one way or another, out of that hideous cloud of smugness that has been absolutely eating away the bones of so many of us, into the realization—or the admission—that poetry is a terrifyingly difficult and magnificent thing, not an alternative to chess, checkers, and croquet. To suggest to you the tone of *The Fifties* (which has humor, even mockery, in it as well as seriousness), let me say that they have, among other things, a section called "Madame Tussaud's Wax Museum." In this section, they say, first off, the following: "Many very young poets have written us, while we were collecting poems for this issue, asking our advice on specific poems or on poetry in general, and we decided the best thing would be to include a small group of lines showing what, in our opinion, to avoid. We write poems today in the dying language—that is, totally without images." (Note: they explain what they mean by *images*, or at least try to explain, with fair success, in an essay by Bly in the same issue called "Five Decades of Modern American Poetry.") "In order to achieve its intensity, such poetry is forced sooner or later to depend on (1) four-letter words, or (2) classical references. It is possible to rhyme in such language, even to state ideas, but not to achieve poetry. Language without images is abstract, and poetry cannot be created out of abstract parts." (Another note: I don't think they had enough space to give the subject the discussion it has *got* to have; however, if you happen to own a copy of *Poetry* (January 1957), and would look over an essay by Thom Gunn—by the way, do you remember—this is horrible and unkind, but I can't get it out of my mind, so I may as well say it—do you remember *Ben* Gunn in *Treasure Island*? "I've dreamed of cheese, Jim—toasted, mostly!"—my God! My digressions are starting to sound like *Tristram Shandy!**—anyway, Thom Gunn, in praising and therefore threatening a talented poet—in praising Edgar Bowers, argues in favor of abstract language with such deadly thoroughness, that all you need do is read his essay, turn his argument ex-

---

*In the margin: "This is really inexcusable—I don't know what's happening to me—I've got to stop this stupid and irrelevant maliciousness. I don't know Gunn, and very little of his work. I disagree with his ideas, but that's no reason to make fun of his name."

actly upside down, and you have the argument of Robert Bly etc. in *The Fifties*. I think the magazine would be important and interesting to you. It costs fifty cents a copy. I never even heard of it till they sent me a free copy last week (everything exploded at once); but here is its address:

The Fifties
Briarwood Hill
Pine Island, Minnesota

Oh, yes: I forgot to say that the "small group of lines" listed in their "Wax Museum," designed to illustrate what they meant by "the dying language," included brief quotations from the following: Yvor Winters,* Allen Ginsberg, and Henry Wadsworth Longfellow. Now, this represents a real attempt (not smug, either) to get at an *idea*. Moreover, the passage from Winters is the one that contains the four-letter words!—two of them in a very brief quotation, in fact.

One more bit: considering the fact that you've been fighting for the sake of unqualified resistance against "the dying language" without any help from any of the moral cowards and self-betrayers (like myself—and this is not compliment-fishing, this is a truth for which I have bitterly fought) who ought to have been fighting on the same side from the beginning, it may give you some pleasure to hear a remark from John Berryman. We rarely see him—I'm told he's writing a good deal again—but at a picnic in the end of Spring we chatted a moment; and Berryman, who is almost insanely incorruptible, and who I am told, and believe, *never* reads anything about himself in print if he can possibly avoid it, commented on my intention of writing some book reviews by saying that he had read your review in the Spring *Sewanee*, considered it a genuine *essay* with a leading and developed *idea* rather than a mere hodge-podge-review of the usual sort which is becoming a literary stock-convention as rigidly repressive of feeling and thought as a late 18th-century Georgic in heroic couplets, and felt that you were one of the most brilliant and serious writers on poetry to appear in a long, long time. Now, he had no way of knowing that you were going to mention his name in the review, for the books listed did not include

*In the margin: "By the way, there are *some* poems of Winters that I like."

him. It disturbed me, I admit; for I knew he was right, and I dreaded to face the truth of what he said. Please excuse length, and write soon.

Yrs,
Jim Wright

To Donald Hall

Minneapolis
July 25, 1958

Dear Don,

According to the schedule you sent me earlier, you're in Ann Arbor now. I hope so. An extremely weird thing has happened, and it has left me as shaken as anything that has happened to me since I started trying to write verses some years ago. Forgive me for having wept on your shoulder sometimes—it's not really what my present subject deals with. It's rather something that crystalizes and clarifies many uncertainties that have been haunting me, not only about myself but also about poetry in These States at the present time. You recall that I mentioned some dissatisfaction concerning the Meridian anthology when we were in Detroit, and that you were interested in hearing my thoughts about it. When I actually came to write my thoughts down, I found myself in a confusion that was not only intellectual—it was deeply and emotionally painful to me to discover that at the very depth of my consciousness I was divided—really divided, as on the blade of a sword—between my loyalty to those of my contemporaries who were trying to write with intellectual grace and to those, far more disturbing and ruthless, who were raising hell and demanding greatness. It is really impossible to describe all of my feelings about this division, but they go so deep as to be almost psychotic. Let me try to suggest what I mean by saying—what is perfectly true—that the two American poets who mean the most to me as an individual human being are, for God's sake, Whitman and Robinson! Now, stylistically they are as far apart as two men could be and still write in the same language. I have never known how to fuse them; and so, as you are undoubtedly aware, having endured the very genuine hysterias of my correspondence for some years, I have helplessly and nauseously swung back and forth terrified by great space on the pendulum from the one to the other. Now, there was nothing wrong with this, and there was a time for me—as there was, inevitably, for every young poet writing in America right now—to commit himself to the traditional syntax and the traditional meters of English verse; for many of the writers who preceded us were so sloppy, that we had to begin not by revolting against competence and restriction, because except for a few writers there was no competence, but rather to begin by creating *our own* competence. Thus, the next step— the really terrifying one, the appalling one, the one that drags the blood, the real red blood, out of one's veins, is to move through and beyond that necessary competence into individual creation. But I never went through the first step of this process with any really conscious intelligence; for, as I said, I already felt within myself the secret guilt at my denying the darker and wilder side of myself for the sake of subsisting on mere comfort—both academic and poetic. May I use your own work as an example? I said at first, and I say again, that I loved your first book because it was packed with a masterly competence. The key word is "packed," for the size, the variety of subject, and perhaps most of all the humor (gutty humor like Falstaff, not wit like Oscar Wilde) promised powerfully that the competence which you had striven to master, and *which is absolutely necessary if the individual breakthrough is to reveal a newly created, coherent and yet uniquely painful and thrillingly beautiful poetry*—the unmistakable voice of a man singing to men about the terrible truth of our age—these things revealed, I say, that the very extent of your formal mastery would be one of the powerful forces that would break through it and create the new thing, the unique and yet coherent and illuminating work.

Well, I just read the issue of Robert Bly's *The Fifties*. You and W. D. Snodgrass are the two young American poets who have broken through in order to create instead of breaking through in order to destroy. I'll come to your poem in a moment: first I want to say how significant it is that Snodgrass, in a very brief poem which is far more original, dense, and forcefully clear in its imagery, far more deeply personal and individual in its rhythm, and almost hilariously more *radical* (in the real political and social sense) than Ginsberg is even capable of imagining, should thwack the hipsters on the skull, thwack them from the magnificent height of a perfect *demonstration* of the very vital and original art which, in their ads in *The New York Times Book Review*, they have been claiming for themselves.

But your own poem: "The Foundations of American Industry." It could not have been written unless two conditions had been fulfilled: 1. the mastery first of a formal technique; 2. a lament, a grief so deeply agonized that I can only call it Greek. Forgive me—this is as delicate a subject as I could possibly mention to you, but I will mention it because I can speak out of the center of my grateful spirit—your poem "The Way to Death," whether or not you yourself are *technically satisfied* with it, was the most important experience, I believe, that you have ever had as an artist. What makes this fact relevant is that the task of spiritual courage which you set for yourself in the actual subject of the poem was Greek and terrible in the old sense, instead of decadently Christian. Refusing, in your own sense of dignity as a man, to translate your father's pain into a Billy Graham–type commercial, you faced death itself, in the only way in which it can ever be meaningfully faced at all—i.e., in the hurt body of a beloved. Facing this truth made it possible for you to break through the formal competence of your accomplished first book, and in the poem "The Foundations of American Industry" your *new style* and your unflinching vision of the *truth* are absolutely inextricable from each other. You know how well I've liked some of your poems. Well, in *both* technique and vision, "The Foundations" is about ten thousand miles beyond anything in your first book. If you want me to argue this point further, just drop the word, and I stand ready to do so. It is very important to me personally, as I'll try to explain directly. But do I make myself clear about the two necessary steps of creation of a great and original poetry? 1. Mastery of formal competence in one's tradition (there is *always* tradition, and it is as ruthlessly inescapable as breathing, hunger, and death. Those who deny the existence of the past, said Santayana in a line which makes me shudder with fear, are doomed endlessly to repeat its mistakes). 2. Then the *breaking through* this formal competence, in order to *create* a poetry which is unique and all one's own: the truly shaped voice of one's self. Let me try further to clarify this notion by giving two examples which will be, I trust, sufficiently vivid. If a writer leaves out the first step in the process, then he cannot possibly even *take* the second, for the second consists partly in breaking through the effect of the first. If a writer leaves out the first step, in other words, we get Allen Ginsberg, who does not move from mastery of formal competence to the creation of original art, but rather moves from chaos and sloppiness to their counterparts of commercialism and advertising and back again. On the other hand, if a writer follows both steps in terms of his own intelligence and experience, and if his personal vision and spiritual courage are strong enough to sustain him—especially in an age like ours, when the *truths* of public irresponsibility and powerful nihilistic sophism among the manipulators of the public language are so hideous—then you get Pablo Neruda.

As we're starting to get Don Hall.

What was wrong with the Meridian anthology, I think, was simply that it appeared too soon. Even the most talented writers in the book were more or less in the first stage described above. I think there are perhaps three or four people in that book who could, if they have the guts to fight for it, for the vision, become great poets, and in this sentence I am not using the word "great" lightly at all. But still, the book gave an overall impression of competence alone. Competence is essential; but when it appears alone, we get critical discussion—maddening, endless, smug, mealy-mouthed—of "mere" competence. The sneer conveyed by the word "mere" actually makes me physically ill.

James Dickey, however, was not sneering. This brings me to "The Follies of Young Worthless: a Farce in two acts," starring James Wright.

I need not repeat the extremely trivial and mean-spirited complaint about Dickey that I wrote to you earlier. The less said about my "epigrams," the better; for they were nothing but pettiness cast in extraordinarily bad verse. The truth is that I was obsessed, raving, reacting against something in myself with such horror, that Dickey, by merely mentioning my name in print, became accidentally the target of a quite terrible hatred. It was self-hatred, I am sure; and, since I could not simultaneously admit that I hated myself and sustain the illusion that I was a poet, I seized the occasion of Dickey's review in order to relieve the unbearable pressure of hate in myself, and, I'm afraid, for myself. Finally I went haywire—literally went haywire. To a book review which I was doing for the Fall issue of *Sewanee*, I added a section in which I dishonestly, and with all kinds of false modesty and Uriah-Heepish phony humility, attacked Dickey with a viciousness that was embarrassingly self-revelatory rather than intelligently critical, and obscene rather than satiric. I sent off the review to *Sewanee*, and immediately sent a copy of the relevant section of it to Dickey himself. And I enclosed a letter to him which—this is going to sound like an exaggeration, and yet, having seen me bubble up toward hysteria, real hysteria, during our whole correspondence, you must believe that I am describing what I wrote restrainedly rather than otherwise—I can only describe as very nearly outright psychotic.

His answer, which arrived soon thereafter, was, of course, an angry one. But his anger was stated in sternly dignified words, and he not only insisted upon his integrity as a man and as a critic, but also said (what was perfectly true and unarguable) that my letter—which, as I say, was not criticism but really blatant, aimless, wild hatred, in which I even exploded once into outright obscenity—constituted a considered insult to him and to his family; and that, if I was not willing to consider myself a crank, I would have to see that I was responsible for my action—i.e., a wholly unprovoked and hostile attack on a total stranger. He concluded by assuring me that, if I persisted in distressing him and his family by writing such things to him, he would certainly take steps to see that I was made to desist.

It's useless to describe how I was crushed—not by Dickey, for—whatever you may think of his ideas, Don—imagine how you would feel if you had mentioned some writer's name (he wrote three words about me—*three words*, one of which was my name)* and then suddenly received from him a letter such as mine, which I have accurately described. No, Dickey had a right as a man to defend himself and his own. But *I* was the one who had crushed myself. I read his letter, and realized finally that my own message had been written to myself, to that part of myself which had betrayed poetry by complacency. For it seems to me that what he said in his review, harsh as he may have been, was nothing but the undeniable truth without the facing of which no man will be a poet. I looked at this truth, and I knew that I was too weak and cowardly to bear it; and, as a result, I completely lost control of myself, and gave a great wail of terror. I was not, and am not, man enough to behold naked my own emptiness.

In any case, his letter shocked me back into control of myself, and in a mood of self-loathing which it is useless to talk about, I wrote an apology to him and to his wife. I granted the justice of his words (I am

---

*In a review of *New Poets of England and America*, Dickey had used Wright's work as an example of one of the ways the poems included "fulfill many of our notions of what poems should be . . . ploddingly 'sincere' (Wright)."

not exaggerating—they were indeed just words), and I tried, in a muddled way but as well as I was able, to make some sense out of the reason for my attacking him.

This was on Monday. On about Wednesday (this past week), I received Robert Bly's *The Fifties*. Now, in spite of certain confusions in terminology and argument, I am sure that Bly is right. And what he said was only what Dickey has been saying for some time, except that Bly is consciously courteous and Dickey is rather unapologetically cold. But these were only theoretical evidences of my own failure and incapacity. The absolute clincher came with your new poem, and with the poems by Snodgrass. So I quit. I have been betraying whatever was true and courageous (how nothing's that!) in myself and in everyone else for so long, that I am still fairly convinced that I have killed it. So I quit. In what I suppose may be the dullest and most numb anguish of which my physical body is capable, I took a day off from working at my book on Dickens, and wrote "His Farewell to Poetry," which is a terrible poem and, as far as I can honestly tell, my last.

I would not like you to think I am depressed about this. As a matter of fact, I am more relieved at facing the truth than I have been for years. Moreover, my one justification for my own existence as a literary operator (and one of the slickest, cleverest, most "charming" concocters of the do-it-yourself *New Yorker* verse among all current failures) is that I have not reacted, even during what I can honestly call my weeks of insane fear, by hating poetry. Not at all—on the contrary, my love for the art deepens by my recognition that it is, after all, a wholly different kind of experience from that in which I have been flattering myself. Moreover, I continue in prose. I would like to get in on some critical movement in which I can believe. There are not many poets, after all, and most of us must get used to the fact that we are somewhat like Walter Bagehot in relation to Dickens. Bagehot read Dickens sensitively and appreciatively; and yet, of course, for all his intelligence and cleverness, he would not have been capable of imagining even the meanest of Dickens' creations, not if he had studied rule-books about novel-writing for the next ten million years.

What has happened, I think, is that, since there is a natural selection among artists as among sea creatures, I am one of the dripping and daydreaming serpents who roared at his tidal death.

To get on with it: on Thursday of this week, Dickey wrote me a letter which was remarkably generous, full of a fine and manly spirit of pardon which I did not deserve, and which made me grateful. We are going to correspond. He pointed out, among other things, that he is as hard on himself as he has been on me, Booth, Wilbur, Hecht, etc., and I believe him. The authenticity of his feeling was perfectly proved, as far as I am concerned, by his saying that he would "consider it a kindness" if I would look at a new poem he will have in the August *Poetry* and let him know what I think of it.

What is the meaning of all this? I don't know. For the time being, and quite possibly forever, I am through as a writer of verse. Whatever it was in me that got poems started looks and feels like a large, defenseless, blanket-bombed city. The sewer-rats march with tubas and bass drums through the soccer-field, and the cathedrals are pitched headfirst, like unfrocked saints dizzy with bay rum and canned heat, into the garbage dumps, and the devaluated coins of finance darken the gutters of the black market of my self, and heave like a rain of artificial blood.

People are, by and large, pretty good to me, but I am not a good man. I fought the devils to win that truth. I want to be an honest man. That's all. For me to try to write poetry is in bad taste.

Somebody ought to write something like the argument of this letter to Phil Booth,* but I'm awfully tired. Will you try to write me soon? I would appreciate it.

Love to you and yours,
Jim

To Theodore and Beatrice Roethke

Minneapolis
August 5, 1958

Dear Ted and Beatrice;

I haven't much time, what with this thesis and all, but I wanted to tell you both the news that Lib had her baby last Wednesday morning, July 30. Only this morning have I gotten around to writing notes to

*In the margin: "I don't, for heaven's sake, mean that he ought to quit, but that he ought to be sustained in his struggle."

people. It's a boy; 8 lbs. 2 oz. at birth; named Marshall John; and Lib and the child, who came home from the hospital yesterday afternoon to rescue Franz and me from the lollocks, are well and happy. Please don't think I'm being insensitive and stupid when I say that Lib and I think of both of you very often in the hope that you are well and happy too.

Ted, I can't tell you what pleasure it gave me to receive your off-print of "Her Becoming." One of these days I'll write you at greater length about it—but it creates the clearest form of any of the old lady's poems yet. Lib and I remember your reading us one sketch for it. It's gorgeous, George.

My career (aaaargh!) as a reviewer and essayist (when a reviewer calls himself an "essayist," he somehow sounds like George F. Babbitt during the latter's campaign in Gopher Prairie to get clients to speak of "realtors" instead of "real-estate men") continues. I'm reviewing a bunch of stuff, some of it good, in the Fall *Sewanee*. I'm having an essay on R. P. Warren's new verse (very rough but daring and interesting) in the Fall *Kenyon*. And I've arranged with Spears to review Stanley Kunitz's *Selected Poems* in the *Sewanee*, probably for the Winter issue.

And what about the famously proposed essay on Winterset Rothberg? Well, I've decided that John Palmer at *Yale Review* was right. He said to wait till the book *Words for the Wind* came out in America. Then I can probably have it. I still wish to Christ Allen Tate or somebody would write an essay about Roethke. It's different with Stanley who has, I think, touched greatness two or three times, but who has been neglected. But nobody with any sense in America or Italy or South America or Mexico or France or Germany has any doubt that there are three or four indisputably great poets living and writing in the world now—Neruda, Vallejo, Char, Ekelof, Roethke—and discussion of these men is not a matter of "book-reviewing," for Christ's sake. (As far as Neruda is concerned, for example, I think that writing a book review about him would be something like writing a book review about the Bible.)

I have been depressed as hell. My stuff stinks, and you know it. It stinks because it is *competent*. The irony is that, beginning with nothing but absolutely unbearable clumsiness when I was about nineteen years old, I deliberately set out to learn the craft. Well, I seem to have learned it. Good God! If you want to see what I think of that anthology *The New Poets of England and America* (and, if you haven't read it, for God's sake spare yourself and use your energy next Winter in reading W. D. Snodgrass's book, which, I see, is going to be published by Knopf; and which, along with Dave Wagoner's new book, and with a few things by John Woods and Robert Huff, probably represents the whole God damned genuinely *poetic* impulse of the whole American generation under forty. Now, this is more than a literary vacuum—this is a catastrophe for human civilization. I've been cracking my own facility, my competence, my dead and dull iambs, to pieces. What makes this so ironically depressing, as I say, is that I am trapped by the very thing—the traditional technique—which I labored so hard to attain. Not till this year did I *really* understand the heroism of your advancing through various stages of style—for style in your work has not been *only* a technical matter, but rather primarily self-discovery, self-conquest, self-revelation. When I consider how appalled at myself I am right now, and how terribly often you have gone through much worse self-overcomings than this (self-overcoming! How right Nietzsche was!), I see the limits of the mere human physique, and consider that the incredible *energy* of both rhythm and imagery in "Her Becoming" must come from some divine indefinable thing like genius after all, and I feel like lying around drunk, waiting for the Muse to strike. (But I don't do this. I work like hell, chipping away perhaps one tiny pebble per day from the ten-mile-thick granite wall of formal and facile "technique" which I myself erected, and which now stands ominously between me and whatever poetry may be in me, and that's probably damned little if any . . . Ted, don't let me get you down. I'm just trying to say, without being mawkish in the least that I think you are not only a great poet but also something even more important—a heroic human being. This is not flattery: this is the statement of something of whose existence I need to know right now, need like food and drink and blood in my heart. Please write.

Love from Lib,
Jim

To Robert Bly

Dear Mr. Bly:

I'm sure you understand me when I say that I could regard your letter as a good deal more than mere courteous editorial clarification. On my side, let me say what should be obvious—that the long, groping letter which I wrote you was one which I had to write—your own phrase about "rising from the dead" connotes some of the shock of self-recognition which has got to take place among us, not only among people who are trying to write poetry, but who, simply as human beings, are sane. The relation between poetry and human experience is one which has got to be urgently established among us. It is, of course, always a matter of life and death—it always has been—but in our own time this becomes a *literal* matter.

Do you know Orwell's "Politics and the English Language" and "Looking Back on the Spanish War"? The bit in the latter about his being utterly unable to shoot an enemy simply because the man was running along the top of a trench as the dawn broke, and the man was holding up his trousers with one hand. Such a man in such a position is not a "Fascist," but a fellow-creature. Taken with the essay on politics and the language, I'm sure that what Orwell says is related to your own concern with imagery and rhythm.

Anyway, let me say that I'm sure I've got your point now. We could argue on and on forever, of course, about the theoretical possibility of "building a personal rhythm" on iambic. The real point is that such a rhythm is preventing many American poets right now from fully realizing their gifts in the material which is actually, *but not stylistically*, available to them. To come down to cases, I wrote you this long lamenting harangue about "quitting," etc.; but I know that you recognized my lament as inevitable. As a matter of fact, I don't think I have been playing it as safe as my first book does—and the really powerful essay in *The Fifties* on *Louis Simpson*, whom I have never met but whom I admire, ought to note—or, rather, CRUNK ought to note—the fact that Simpson (with many others) had been feeling disturbed and restless already, and that therefore *The Fifties* itself will survive and prevail for a long time—it answers a genuine need for the voice of and urgent and *instinctive* recognition of the necessity of *breaking through the old style*, a style in which nearly all of the American poets in the Pack, Simpson, Hall anthology had achieved a certain competence. I think that this competence will hurt no one—it can even be an advantage, for to attain it means that one has succeeded at least in identifying the very thing that has to be breached and surpassed. Now, what is happening—something which *The Fifties* instinctively recognized and rose to discuss—is that each poet in the Meridian anthology must effect a whole revolution in himself, and take upon himself a terrifying burden of accomplishing a task which society itself is not yet capable of accomplishing: the revolution of style from the old to the new. This is one implication I derive from your writings so far, and unless I am mistaken in my interpretation of your words, then you can see what I mean when I call the *competence*—competence in the old style (iambic)—which characterized "most of the poets being published in America today" need not be an insurmountable obstacle, but, on the contrary, can be for those who have or can develop the spiritual strength, a distinct *advantage*. Why? Well, there are some enlightening remarks—at least I find them so at this point—in Valery. Maybe he was a formalist, but there is, as you bloody well know, far more to Valery sentence by sentence than one would guess from the way he is regularly and tritely characterized in the little magazines. In his essay "Problems of Poetry," he speaks of "the amazing richness of lyric invention" which appeared in France in the last quarter of the nineteenth century—and he was referring, in part anyway, to the explosion of the "new imagination" which you justly locate as a world-wide phenomenon in the 10's (of course, exact dating of the thing is not to the point). Let me quote this whole absorbing passage of Valery:

> But, in this very nation which sings so little, an amazing richness of lyric invention appeared during the last quarter of the past century. Around 1875, when Victor Hugo was still living, and Leconte de Lisle and his followers were reaching fame, the names of Verlaine, Stephane (I'm going to leave out the accents for convenience—I want to get this letter off to you—Jim) Mallarme, and Arthur Rimbaud arose, those three Magi of modern poetics, bearers of such costly gifts and such rare spices that even the time that has elapsed since then has altered neither the glory nor the power of these extraordinary gifts (by the way, Valery is writing this in 1936).

The extreme diversity of their works, added to the variety of models offered by the poets of the preceding generation, has conduced, and conduces, to the conception, understanding, and practice of poetry in an admirable number of very different ways. There are some today, no doubt, who still follow Lamartine (N.B. just as "some today" write the iambic— okay?); others continue the work of Rimbaud. (Note again, Mr. Bly: I'm going to continue with Valery's very next sentence, but I wanted to emphasize the fact that the subsequent passage is the one that clarifies my point about the *advantage* of gaining *competence* in the *old style* first. Valery continues:) The same man may change his tastes and his style, burn at twenty what he adored at sixteen; *some kind of inner transmutation* (my italics) shifts the power of seduction from one master to another. The lover of Musset becomes more *mature* and leaves him for Verlaine. Another, after being first nourished by Hugo, devotes himself completely to Mallarme.

These spiritual changes generally operate in one particular *direction* (Valery's italics) rather than in the other, which is much less probable: it must be extremely rare for *Le Bateau ivre* to lead eventually to *Le Lac*. On the other hand, by loving the pure and hard *Herodiade* one does not lose one's taste for the *Priere d'Esther*.

(He starts to lose me in works I haven't read, but, if I follow him, I would paraphrase the idea by saying that it is generally more profitable to move from a love of Bridges to a love of Lorca, than the other way around, because the first strategy (1) clearly *defines* the old style which exists to be broken and (2) *dramatizes* one's liberation from it.)

(Then Valery concludes the passage:) These defections, these sudden accesses of love or of grace, these conversions and substitutions, this possibility of being successively *sensitized* to the work of incompatible poets, are literary phenomena of the first importance. *Therefore no one ever mentions them.* (My italics.)

I find it interesting that Valery should have used the word *sensitized*, because the word also occurred to you in your intense and, I might add, entirely convincing argument (in your recent letter to me) about the ascending vicious circles: "We construct, but the great poets are merely sensitive—." Nothing could be finer than that formulation of yours. But let me get on.

Louis Simpson provides a good example of the master of the old style who feels from within himself (see Valery's phrase above—"some kind of inner transmutation") the stirring of need for the new style to deal with the *new imagination*. (By the way, that is a magnificent phrase—I wonder if you were conscious of the profoundly vital parody through which it rebukes things like the *new criticism*, etc.) In the *Hudson Review* (Autumn, 1957, in an essay called "Poets in Isolation," p. 463), Simpson is discussing Amis' anti-romanticism: "The anti-Romantic vision too often sounds like a Holiday at the East Peebles Latin Grammar School. The trouble with Amis' verse, *as with so much verse nowadays*, is that while it is in good taste, intelligent, humorous, sensitive, et cetera, it lacks the right kind of disorder. Intelligence can be dull. A little of the conviction held by Socrates and by Coleridge and his peers, that poetry is a kind of insanity, wouldn't harm our boys at all. Of course, the Romantics wrote a lot of windy stuff, but they also wrote the 'Ancient Mariner,' 'The Ode on a Grecian Urn,' and 'The Triumph of Life.' I'm afraid that with our virtues of good taste we throw out the Mariner as well as the Idiot Boy."

Now, Mr. Bly, Simpson is not here taking the same tack that you have taken (though I suspect he must inevitably do so), but the point is that his passage reflects a profound and unconscious dissatisfaction— and you are perfectly aware, as only James Dickey has been aware, that the dissatisfaction results from the terrible and windy gap between Simpson's *mastery* of the old style and his *need* for the new style. Speaking of Dickey, did I mention him in my last letter? His essay "In the Presence of Anthologies," *Sewanee Review* (Spring, 1958), is a brilliant and appallingly fierce *reductio* of the American section of *The New Poets of England and America* to its essential *absurdum*, though he does not, as you *do* (in your essay "Five Decades of American Poetry"), trace the reason for his dissatisfaction. He lashed me into the earth with a single brilliant satirical phrase. I wrote him an angry letter. He answered with anger. He is now, I suppose, one of the best friends I have ever made in my life—honest, brilliant, outraged, deeply passionate and original, and absolutely incorruptible.

(Speaking of Dickey, I'm enclosing two bucks: could you do me a favor? Please send a copy of the first issue of *The Fifties* to:

Mr. James L. Dickey
2930 Westminster Circle, N.W.
Atlanta, Georgia

And would you be so kind as to write on the first page of the magazine something like "with the compliments of James Wright" or something of the sort. Then, for the other $1.50, would you send me the next three issues of *The Fifties* as they appear? I admit that this is a hell of an irresponsible way to subscribe to a magazine, and I swear to heaven that as soon as I get my mitts on some ready coin I'll ask you to send copies to some other people who ought to read *The Fifties*. They would support it.)

Perhaps this would be the place to say something really important: Mr. Bly, whenever I make some suggestion or other, please accept my assurance that I am *not* trying to butt in on your magazine, which you and Mr. Duffy, I am sure, are brilliantly capable of handling on your own. I want you to understand that I am personally involved very deeply in your poetic concerns, and that, for such reasons, you should know that my assistance is immediately available to you *if you should ever happen to need it or want it.*

I spoke in my letter to you of having quit. What I meant, let me repeat, is that I was responding to the shock of getting my bumps. I described earlier ineptitude, and the hopelessness of writing anything at all that didn't just squidgle off the sheet like a sick jellyfish. Then I sought the classical discipline. Writing to you, I was afraid that I had got it so well that it had got me. Whether it did or not I don't know. I do know that I'm not quitting.

I certainly don't expect you to answer my letters at great length. My leisure, such as it is, is explained by the ironic fact of my living right now, with my wife and 2 kids (the new boy came last Wed. morning) on the *Kenyon Review* Poetry fellowship. Writing to you this way is in part a matter of sheer interest and involvement; but it is also more instructive—that's the wrong word, I mean *illuminating*—to read your letters than I can easily describe.

I'm going to ask if you will be kind enough to look at the enclosed poem. I mentioned having written a "Farewell to Poetry" even before I saw *The Fifties*. It grew out of my shock at having attacked Jim Dickey for having written the painful (and yet, really, magnificent) truth about all of us. The difference between what Dickey saw and said in *Sewanee* (Spring, 1958) and what you saw and said, and what Simpson saw and said, and what Hall and Snodgrass have seen and done, is superficial. It is that we have learned the tricks too well, and that having arrived at a point of beginning, we have assumed that we were completed. All that happened to me is that I was stung awake, by Dickey who was cold and furious, and by you who were friendly and polite but equally uncompromising. Now, it may turn out that I do indeed have nothing in the way of vision and imagination. But I am stuck now; if I have nothing, I am convinced that I can face the fact without bitterness; the *new imagination* is so important, to all living human beings and not just to literati, that I am going to continue to search for it—and if I cannot find it in myself (though I believe I can), then I will identify and fight for it in others. And this is not mock-humility—I see blood in this matter, I really do. The enclosed poem is the revision of what began as "His Farewell to Poetry." I honest to God don't know whether it is worth a penny or not. It might be. It more probably isn't. But I have got to learn how to open myself more and more to the imagery which is ours and only ours, and to crack the iambic shell which used to be—and usefully, I believe—a *mold*. It is as though a man who had broken his neck had asked a doctor to prop his head with a plaster cast, and had strengthened the muscles of his throat till he was sure he could hold his head up and look at the world in front of him, and then had discovered that his doctor, whether mistakenly or not, had made the cast out of cement. I could have cracked the plaster with a blow of the hand; but now I must chip and claw the cement away with the few fingernails I have left. Maybe I'll die first. All I say is that I'm not going to die in the act of writing the poems of Robert Bridges over again (since he already wrote them so beautifully, in a world that is gone, with a style that is, alas, still here). But no matter how bad my enclosed poem is, it is at least not written in the old style. Mr. Bly, please understand that I'm not trying to burden you with a poem for detailed criticism. However, if you care to bother, I would attend very closely to whatever comment, general or other, which you might make about it.

Now, before I spare you, I want to conclude by asking some questions and making some points:

1. In p. 39 of yr. mag., you say: "There is an imagination which assembles the three kingdoms within one poem: the dark figures of politics, the world of streetcars, and the ocean world."

   a. Will you please explain, however generally, what you mean by "the ocean world"?

   b. I don't know Jung at all. I know Freud too little. Will you please tell me what to read and study from the works of these two writers?

2. You probably know this already, but if not it will be useful and interesting: Ben Belitt's translation of Lorca's *The Poet in New York* (An Evergreen Press Book. New York: Grove Press, 1955. $1.45), a really thrilling translation by a poet who *does* know what the new imagination is, contains Lorca's lecture-essay, "The Poetic Image in Don Luis de Gongora," and I wonder if Lorca's words seem to you (I mean it, I am really groping in things I never dug out before) a fair indication of your own notions of *imagery* as conceived by the new imagination.

3. Do you mind if I write as often and as long as the spirit moves me? I am conscious that this is a *hell* of an imposition.

4. What do you think of the two British (Scotch, in the latter's case) Jon Silkin and W. S. Graham. Have you read Graham's *The Night-fishing*? It seems to me a great book, a truly great one.

5. Hardy is not a victim of iambic—it does not come natural to him. What do you think of him as a modern?

6. *Please note*: Do you own, or have you access to, Random House publication *Hypnos Waking: Poetry and Prose of René Char*? Edited by Jackson Mathews. If not, please look at it. I wish I could afford to send you a copy, but it costs five bucks. I did three of the translations—as a matter of fact, I did seven but Jack could use only three (he had assigned others).

   Also: do you happen to have a copy of a little European paperback book called *René Char's Poetry*: Studies by Maurice Blanchot, Gabriel Bounoure, Albert Camus, Georges Mounin, Gaetan Picon, René Ménard, and—by God, I'm proud of it;* Mrs. Caetani asked

*Wright's essay, "Meditations on René Char," is included in his *Collected Prose*, p. 63.

for it at such an awkward time that I didn't have time to consider whether I was being academically "correct" or not among all my neo-classic associates, and I came out like a nut in favor of Whitman, Kafka, Rilke, etc.—*James Wright (My italics)* (My italics of "my italics"). *If you don't* have a copy of this second booklet, please let me know, and I'll send you two or three. One thing of which I am honestly and legitimately proud is a letter from Char about my essay, and a little painting which he sent me and copies of his new books as they have appeared, and a letter (appalling in its pity and generosity) about my own book, and God knows what else from him— he has the kindness of St. Francis, the physical strength—according to Theodore Roethke—of an actual giant in a circus, and the true *new imagination*, with the endlessly happy and startled productive power and inventiveness of Dickens. A great man, and a very great poet.

7. I want to write something about Neruda. Do you know the Neruda and Vallejo translations by H. R. Hays? They are superb in English, but a little hard to find. If you're not familiar with them, please mention the fact when you write, and I'll send you a little bibliography which I have painfully but carefully assembled during the past three weeks or so.

Thank you immensely for everything, *everything*. I, too, feel as if I had risen from the dead. Please write again. I have so much to say that I could not even begin to get it all into this note, this mere note.

Thank you,
Jim Wright

To James Dickey

Minneapolis
August 12, 1958

Dear Jim,

Please excuse my slight delay in answering. My wife and new child are now home from the hospital, you know, and, enjoyable as the occasion has been, it's of course involved the usual interesting adjustments. I am so pleased with my new son! His health is excellent, and it always delights me to imagine that I can actually see small waves and shapes of a baby's own identity forming. The expressions of severe anger, the voluptuous chuckles, and even the sneers of an old, high mockery are wonderful. I had never thought of myself as a father, and so I had no defenses at all against my children—they've both invaded and conquered me completely.

Your own most recent letter was a pleasure and a relief to read. The mood of explosive outrage and personal impatience in which you wrote your earlier attack on your job and on what you have actually achieved so far in your own writing (that is, on *your own conception* of your achievement, and this is a powerfully necessary conception to you) is one that I ought to have recognized. It is the very mood of impatience and dissatisfaction with what one has already achieved that I was in terrible danger of losing, when our correspondence and friendship had its *unfortunate* beginning.* However, anyone who can reach that deeply and honestly into himself and into his work is bound to have the moral and artistic strength that made "Dover: Believing in Kings" inevitable. I was afraid, when I wrote to you, that you were being too hard on yourself. Your answer, and the new poem in *Poetry*, simply demonstrate that you were being just hard enough.

Speaking of that issue of *Poetry*, has it occurred to you that the two of us must surely have submitted our respective pieces to the editor long before I wrote you that idiotic letter of mine? I think it was inevitable that we should bump heads sooner or later—the only thing that I really regret so much is that our meeting should have resulted from the side of myself which is the worst—the most mean and petty and dishonest. And yet I'm sure I was right when I wrote that our poetic ideals are something that we can honest-to-God *share*. My brief note to you concerning your long poem may have sounded a bit flighty and silly, but actually what I was trying to say was to describe my *real* visceral reaction: I was swept up by the imaginative vision of the poem, by the belief in *reality* (you remember your saying in that long critical dialogue on Jarrell that one of Lorca's most dense and strange images was closer to real life than Jarrell's listing of mere items as from a phone book? Well, that's the reality I'm talking about in your poem), the marvelous way in which the imagination can grandly sweep over

*In the margin: "And I mean the *beginning* was unfortunate, *not* the friendship."

great spaces of meaning and music and then quickly alight on a concrete and affectionate detail—the girl sleeping on the bed, the putting on of the blue-jeans, the shadow from within which is indistinguishably both literal shadow and shadowy father, and the blaze of light on the waves that is both literal blaze and the blaze of the discovered and newly created Self, "big-footed with glory" (that phrase is matchless—I swear that when I read it, I was not jealous—I simply wanted to take off my hat and salute you), and among many other things the complex lucidity, the really *original* subtlety of the rhythm and *sound* of the language. I mentioned W. S. Graham, but this matter of rhythm and imagery is one where the only connection between the two of you as poets is your ability to dazzle me. If this praise sounds silly, you must simply keep in mind what you have plenty of evidence for noting—my own tendency toward hysteria. I am clearly an unstable person emotionally, and this is simply a description of me—not, please understand, a request for compliment, but rather an attempt to qualify the terms in which I talk about poems that I really *like*, that make me know once again—as in the old days when I was an honest man, merely because I had no opportunity to be *dis*honest—that poetry, the real stuff, is not a substitute for or a mere comment on *something else*, but a great force of creation, one of our glories. The word "glory" is out of fashion, of course. Thank God. How could there be a fashion in glory? Do you know Herbert Read's phrase "the sense of glory"? It's haunted me (partly with guilt for denying its importance and scoffing at the men who achieved it—Lawrence, Whitman, Neruda, and others) for some time.

I said that a correspondence and a friendship too was probably inevitable between us, precisely because—particular performances as artists aside nevertheless we both believe poetry ought to strain its guts out rather than settle for anything less than grandeur—Longinus's old bolt of lightning. Well, take a look at the two poems we had (side by side, surely no coincidence, and yet wholly unplanned—there's a mystery in things like that, I believe, I really do) in *Poetry*: I think yours is sublimely effective—I really have nothing to say about it beyond reporting the fact that it makes me grateful for my ability to read the English language, and that I will read it fifty more times, in addition to the twenty or so that I've already read it. I think that mine *partly* works and partly doesn't work. But that's not the immediate point. What matters here is that we both have tried the big thing, to undertake a poetry commensurate with the magnificence of our human lives. I know very well that I've written many verses that are technically far more adroit than the big ode, and I also know that there must be at least a hundred "technicians" (not, assuredly, poets) in America right now who could have written them, and would have been *satisfied* to write them. Well, at least I claim that I was *not* satisfied to be competent, and I *tried* the ode "At the Executed Murderer's Grave." Whether the attempt was successful or not is, at this point, less important than that I tried it, and that *I know it matters*. Don't misunderstand: I realize very well that I may be, and most likely will be, second rate and "adequate" in my actual writings for a long time to come, and quite possibly as long as I live. But I will never be smug enough again to think that second-rate adequacy is anything other than itself. So I've got a *chance*; and before we started writing, I didn't even have that.

The news about your book was exciting, and it was a pleasure to hear you talk about it. I was especially pleased at the news in view of "Dover: Believing in Kings," which I had just read. That poem alone will make the book a beautiful one; and a book that can add to it "The Work of Art" (which was, I think, my favorite among your poems before the "Dover" arrived), "The First Morning of Cancer," "The Child in Armor," and "The Red Bow" is going to be an important event.

By the way, let me note before I forget that your general comments about the flaws in my work are extremely useful to me, especially at this time when I am undergoing the terrible effort of looking at them critically on my own, and I want to say that I appreciate everything of this sort that you have time to write to me. As you know, I suffer from a rather Tennysonian (Tennyson at his worst, not his greatest, unfortunately) and soporific ear. A good ear for poetry is not one that puts you to sleep, nor one that merely keeps you awake (No-Doze will do, and doesn't cost as much as the average modern book of verse), but it is one which wakens you into dreams that include and surpass the data of your experience. At least this is the general conclusion that I've been reaching recently in my going to poets who have the great sorceries, the magic that *reveals* and doesn't merely *reassure*.

Do you happen to know Stanley Kunitz's poems? He hasn't had a wide reputation, but I like him tremendously. I'm going to review his newly published *Selected Poems* for *Sewanee*. I really think you would like his poems, and I think I'll type a couple of them for you on a separate sheet of paper, so that you can see what he's like. For a long time, virtually unnoticed and yet enduring, he's been writing poems of real agony and love in a kind of lost and transient underground of the American jungle of academies and businesses. I think that the appearance of his *Selected Poems* is inspiring. It shows that defeat, though imminent for all of us, is not inevitable. He wrote to me recently, since I know him slightly—and you might like his concluding words: ". . . it would be sweet, I'll grant, after all these years to pop up from underground. America, it's true, either spoils you with success or withers you with neglect. What other morality has the artist but to endure? The only ones who survive, I think, beyond the equally destructive temptations of self-praise and self-pity, are those whose ultimate discontent is with themselves. The fiercest hearts are in love with a wild perfection." Those words mean much to me. Please write.

Yours,
Jim [Wright]*

To Wayne Burns

Minneapolis
August 13, 1958

Dear Wayne,

I hate to pester you again, but I wish you could find time to write me a note. The trouble is that I seem to have run out of juice. Perhaps it's the emotional drag of the arrival of the child (he's really a wonderful new boy). But, more seriously, the trouble is that this summer—of all the god damned times for it to happen—I've suddenly fallen into another internal explosion over poetry. To write verses is most of the time a pleasure and a relief; but there are certain times when it becomes a real anguish that I honest to god wish I could avoid. You see, I am following something like this process: I begin at a certain period trying to say something human, and to say this thing with clarity and truth. But I immediately find that I have no *way* of saying it. So I begin to explore the ways—that is, learning a technique. And after a long,

---

*Wright's brackets.

long, long, long, endlessly long labor of search and self-discipline, I master a way of holding the language, of moving it, of molding it from the inside out until it will both embody and become whatever skinny and minor "difference" or "vision" I may possess. But then the ironic thing happens: whatever advance I've made in technique, instead of giving me a very long rest, pretty soon—too *damned* soon! it's not fair!— won't fit whatever new things I have to express. So what must I do? I must deliberately set about smashing, obliterating if possible, all the techniques that I took so long to learn, and then start all over again. Now, this inner blasting doesn't happen too terribly often—my God, it completely kills me, it exhausts me, it makes me curse the day I became a neurotic poet, it makes me want to have a pre-frontal lobotomy, and I want to quit, quit, quit, I am so god damned sick of it. Well, I finished *Saint Judas*, and I *know* that it is a hell of a lot truer and clearer—i.e., better—than *The Green Wall*. But, look here: the hideous fact, which I wish to holy Christ I could forget, gouge out of my mind, smash in my skull, is that even my second book is *still* second-rate. Oh, yes indeedy, it is technically proficient, it is capable, it is adequate, it is smooth—in short, it makes me sick. You'll read "At the Executed Murderer's Grave" in the *Poetry* I sent you. Now, I got hold of a *great* theme. But does it make you weep, does it make you want to strip off your clothes and run out into the street and gash your own skin to bleeding with your finger-nails? Does it, in Lorca's words about that great book, possibly the greatest human book of the twentieth century, *Poet in New York*, does it "lash your eyes open"?

No, it doesn't. At best, it makes you think that it's rather academically interesting that a second-rate punk American poet in a grey flannel suit should try to write an ode to dejection so many years after Coleridge's "France: An Ode." Wayne, this feeling is hell, it's like *dying*. I read my competent stuff, and then I look at any of the poems of, say, Pablo Neruda (ten times the stature of any other living poet), and I want to quit.

That's the real reason for the snag in the Dickens.

Look, I want to explain why I've spent so much space on *Pickwick*. The dissertation, aside from the first chapter, really consists of three strategic steps in my attempt to say something about the Dickensian imagination: first (with *Pickwick*), show that to describe the imagination alone is critically *not enough*, that one must *show* with analysis just how

Dickens succeeded in fusing it with certain technical strategies into *art*. Second, to show more briefly the imagination at work on other things (that is, things and institutions). Finally, to bring the whole argument to bear on *Chuzzlewit*, in order to show how the imagination in Dickens, working at its full powers of self-discovery and illumination, undertakes a great modern theme and gives that theme (the nature of social tyranny in democracy) perhaps its highest treatment in literature. *Please, before I flip my lid entirely and irrecoverably*, write and tell me whether or not this strategy is okay. What it amounts to is that *Oliver Twist, Barnaby Rudge*, and *The Old Curiosity Shop* are not going to receive so full a treatment as *Pickwick, Nickleby* (which I am going to machine-gun), and *Chuzzlewit*. I am directing things toward *Chuzzlewit*, because I still think that, if one has to choose a masterpiece, here we have Dickens working in the Shakespearian vein. Please tell me if this sounds okay.

I'm not tired. Just confused. But, as Alun Lewis once wrote, my insides are haggard.

My new poems are terrible, but they're not merely smooth. To tell the truth, they sound like the ravings of a madman.

Wayne, old man, if you want the artistic shock of years, go down to the bookstore, and buy the following (paperbound): Federico García Lorca, *Poet in New York*, translated with notes by Ben Belitt, Evergreen Press, 1955. Lorca is a very great genius. His "Ode to Walt Whitman" makes me want to tear my hair with terror and joy. I don't know what to do.

> Please write me soon, and give me a little
> reassurance, if you possibly can. I sure as
> hell *need* it. Love to Joan from us,
> Jim

To Donald Hall

Minneapolis
Friday—August 14 or 15 or something, 1958

Dear Don,

Your letter of comfort, so full of kindness to me when I needed it most, came just after Lib had the child, a boy—Wed. morning, July 30. His name is Marshall John. Both he and Lib are fine, and home now

. . . My correspondence with Dickey has turned out to be part of a larger rhythm of jolts and enlightenments this summer, and such rebirths are full of pain, as you know better than I. What I regret is that the correspondence between James Dickey and me had to begin with my presenting on a greasy platter, without being asked, the very worst sides of myself—the dishonesty, the smirking pseudo-intellectuality (when actually I am nothing but a big slob of hulking instinct, and my appearing before students as a professor is a pose and a fraud), and the tastelessness, the obscenity . . . But let me get on to a couple of important points.

First Jerry Enscoe showed me some new poems of his, and, since they are so well done, it occurred to me that you might just possibly want to consider them in your editorial capacity. If I can find another stamp upstairs (I work in the basement, with the furnace, the moths, the skeletons of mice and the necklaces of twilight) I'll enclose them (three of them) now; if not, I'll send them Monday. I hope you like them.

Second, let me broach a subject, a request, fraught with conditions, but please, not intentionally selfish and rude: you see, this summer (since the first day of July) I have written some 180 pages of prose on my dissertation, and when I get the present chapter done I've *got* to get away from it for a while. Moreover, I've had two terrible shocks (growth or defeat?) about poetry, and I need like death to talk with somebody who is a really close and understanding friend. And I still feel cheated as *hell* about not getting an adequate conversation with you in Detroit. I could go on and on—Lib's divorced sister and her five-year-old son are visiting us temporarily (haugh!) in our very small house; etc. etc. etc. The point is this: *if* you and yours are going to stay in Ann Arbor for the rest of the summer, do you think it would be all right for me to visit you for a bit? I would give one of my two heads for the chance to talk with you at length, drink beer, rant in three languages (all of them English), review our correspondence of the past four years or so, and generally take advantage of you, of your friendship, your hospitality, your patience, your sympathy. Be warned that anyone who would have the Midwestern gall to recommend that you invite him to your home will (or would be) an offensive guest, to say the best for him. Would you answer me about possibilities post haste, and include every conceivable objection? I have the vague impression that you and your family are going East for the rest of the Summer. However, if you're going to stay in Michigan, I suggest that this would be an excellent time for us to have a conversation longer than fifteen minutes.

But, look, speak as harshly and bluntly about this request as you possibly can. If it is out of the question, I perfectly understand. But if it is okay, please let me know when it would be best to come, how long I should stay, whether or not you could put me up, etc. This is probably another, ah yet once more, cracked-brain scheme, but as a daydream it is truly wonderful. I would be enormously grateful.

In any case, will you please write out for me the formal rules for the composition of syllabic verse. I've been engaged in cracking the egg of my skull, and my enemies are the strict meter and the Tennysonian sonority. I need hacks, cackles, writhing high-tension wires, rocks, and soda pop.

Actually, Don, I feel fine—the summer has purged me, though I swear to God I think I would have perished without two or three instances of friendship—one of them the correspondence of Robert Bly, whom I am going to visit next week. I take it you know him. He is *first-rate*. His letters are honeycombs of ideas. As for me, I'm not tired—just stripped clean and pure, and I need to talk about so many things that correspondence just won't hold them.

Please write.

Love to yrs. fr. us,
Jim

To Robert Bly

Minneapolis
Friday Evening
[August 15, 1958]

Dear Robert,

Your invitation is marvelous, I accept with real deep gratitude for reasons which I'll explain in conversation, and I will now explain why I'll have a slight delay: you see, I am thrust deep into a problem of finishing a chapter in my dissertation (on Dickens), and already it's been put off and put off because of the new birth, the visit of my wife's divorced sister and child who will now live in Minneapolis but who aren't yet ready to find a place of their own. I think I can get it done over this weekend, for if I get the chance I write prose fast (too fast as you know already, to the grief of your poor retinae). But this has been a crucial summer, and I am, in one sense, exhausted—in another sense, exploding with strange new wild movements of idea and feeling . . . I'm sure (having talked with her on getting your letter) that my wife and children can't come with me this time. She's too weary yet to drive (I am the American slob who can't drive yet), and the new kid's too small. But I was hunting last night for a place to ride a bus or something; and, since I have about five hundred more questions to ask you about everything in the universe except your opinion of the heroic couplet (which I think I can infer), I would like very much to come.

Since I don't know exactly about bus schedules, or about my work on the Dickens, etc., and since you suggest that I come out "next week or so," I think I will phone you some time—perhaps Monday or Tuesday. You never have any return address other than RFD—I take it this means that you live in the boondocks. If and when I can make it, would you object to picking me up? I mean at the bus station. And would you send me your phone number?

I'll bring the Char, the Valery, the Hugo manuscript, and whatever else—oh, yes, the poems of Vassar Miller and Stanley Kunitz (I'm reviewing the Kunitz for *Sewanee*,* and have already done the Miller).

Come to think of it, I think that, before phoning you, I'll wait for your brief answer to this brief note.

Pardon me if I sound rude, but I just didn't quite understand: when you write "we have plenty of room," do you mean that you could put me up overnight or over two nights?

It would really be a great pleasure to meet you and talk. I have so many questions, arguments, comments, jeremiads, etc., that my letters are monstrous—I do you an injustice by throwing so many half-formed and not clearly thought out questions at you. I must say, however, that your answering letters have suggested to me things that I never before even began to understand.

Your cutting of the poem was superb. Whether or not the way it stands is much good is beside the point. What matters is that I see your principles of cutting, and that you are certainly right.

---

*"The Terrible Threshold," a review of Stanley Kunitz's *Selected Poems*, is included in Wright's *Collected Prose*, p. 249.

As a matter of fact, so many fundamentally earthquaking things have happened to me this summer, that I'm not so much tired as dying of thirst to talk with someone. I don't have many friends here—when we meet, you'll see that I am a hick, and it takes me about five years of living in a town before I get to know many people—and the few that we know are either busy on other things, not writing at all, or satisfied with the current facelessness of so much poetry in America.

Please, won't you write me a postcard at once, and let me know:

1. If you can pick me up at the bus station with your car.
2. Your phone number.
3. Whether or not you can put me up overnight (or perhaps if I can find a cheap room).

I can't tell you how I appreciate the kindness of your invitation. It really came at a moment when I needed it. I wish to heaven my wife Lib could come (she's a Greek), but I'm sure we can all meet later.

Thanks.

Yours,
Jim

To Theodore Roethke

Minneapolis
August 18, 1958

Dear Ted,

There's only time for a note, and I'll write at length later; but I want to write you at once about your letter.

It was—what's the use belaboring and embarrassing you. Let me merely say that I have always been aware of making a "papa" out of a teacher and writer whom one admires, even reveres—and I have never made a papa out of you, I am sure. You're just a poet and a man—both enormous, as far as I'm concerned.

Your concern about my health was not only moving, but sharply perceptive. First let me say that I decided at once (and Lib agreed) to take your advice. Since I've got this poetry fellowship, and have *some* money (we're all right financially, by the way) whether I work or not, I simply bow to the wisdom of your advice: that is, I intend to take about 2 weeks off at once. I've met a guy who lives in Madison, Minnesota, way on the other side of the state from Minneapolis, and he's twice invited me to visit him and his wife for some time in the country. He invited me, by the way, just when Lib had been telling me, a few days ago, exactly what you said in the letter about easing up.

But look: I didn't tell you earlier, because I didn't want to worry you. But I already *have* seen a doctor—a psychiatrist. The trouble was that I was getting mildly depressed, and snapping Lib's head off for no reason. This doctor is at the university health service. I talked with him weekly for about 4 months, beginning last January or so. Here's the upshot of his remarks: I am a very mild catathymic, which is a kind of nervousness characterized by "perseveration"—this means that, once I get started on any kind of work—*any* kind—I get compelled to keep my fangs sunk into it till it's done. A few conversations with the doctor made clear that I do need occasionally to slow down. The mild depressions I had been feeling were completely knocked out by a pill called dexamyl (I think that's how you spell it—it's got dexadrine [*sic*] in it, but the difference is that my pill keeps me from getting depressed and yet doesn't make me high or jittery).

Ted, I'm really okay. The doctor was delighted with the way things turned out. He's a specialist in this sort of thing, and says that such depressions are extremely common among people of my physiological structure (i.e., slobs).

As I say, I never wrote you this because, though it wasn't serious, I was afraid that it might have worried you unduly. But in view of your letter, I can tell you everything—and I hope to God that what I am saying is as reassuring to you as it was to Lib.

But your advice referred less to medical matters than to the purely physical fact of my beating myself by working too hard. That is why I hereby swear to you, honest to God or whatever, that day after tomorrow I take off for the country. By the way, another thing was getting me down a bit: Lib's sister, who is pretty but—well, not bright—has been divorced, and she and her five-year-old son are staying with us. Our house isn't too big, and we have a new baby, and 2 kids 5-years-old running around, and—well, you know. This is not the sort of atmosphere in which one challenges Shakespeare.

I do hope you're reassured. I announced at the beginning of this note that I would not get maudlin about your concern, but—it's simply beyond expression. Please have a good rest. And please be sure that the man who writes "Her Becoming" is not played out—he is merely a master.

Lib and I both hope Beatrice is well also. How did you like the picture of the kid? He's charming.

When I write again, I'll try to explain more clearly what I meant by saying that so many American "poets" under 40 are simply self-satisfied. Have you seen the Meridian anthology *The New Poets of England and America*? The whole gang of Americans were pretty tired and dismal, you must admit. But I still think Snodgrass is marvelous. And I don't think *everything* I've written is "nothing." That was just a mood. On the other hand (cheek?) I can't just sit on *The Green Wall*'s dead ass forever. You never mentioned the pile of Swift poems I sent you. I hope you liked them.

More soon. Thank you—thank you.

Love,

Jim (Lib, Franz, Marsh)

To James Dickey

Minneapolis
August 25, 1958

Dear Jim,

Please excuse the formality of the enclosed. I'm sending a carbon of it to Spears at once. The point is that, if you agree (and *only* then), I want my letter to appear in *Sewanee*. At the beginning of this summer I was in the hell of loneliness and despair. I had written a great deal of verse, and sometimes it had promised to become poetry, but it hadn't succeeded, and I had lost touch with hope, and then came the traumatic beginning of my correspondence with you: your moral support gave me the courage to try self-honesty, and also to admit how deeply and dangerously I *cared* about poetry. At this very moment, I believe that it would be valuable for us to air *some* of our discussion on the pages of *Sewanee*—not *all* of our discussion, of course (we would take up the whole magazine!). Think of the advantages: first, we have become really *good* friends who listen to each other with attention and respect; second, we agree that unless a poem can plainly and simply knock the reader out, smite him with Longinus' lightning-bolt, then all discussion of technique is "nit-picking" (I can't get over that phrase, that so perfectly describes something that simply drives me *mad* with frustration). Well, we agree so closely on so many things, that I think there will be special force in our discussion of our disagreements. One disagreement here is about Philip Booth. Now, Booth himself, at this stage, may very well not be important enough to justify a printed correspondence (more about Booth later, by the way). However, note in my letter to *Sewanee* my reference to your sentence about Eberhart and Bridges. Your sentence, and my loose and semi-obscure comment on it, seems to me a perfect opening for you to engage a deeply important critical problem (and, for me, a "deeply important" criticism is one which illuminates the miracle of creation in art. If it doesn't effect this illumination, or isn't interested in creation, then I would frankly much sooner read Mickey Spillane). Out of your sentence, perhaps we could argue (in the Socratic sense of arguing in order to learn, instead of in the James Wright sense of arguing in order to keep one's ego comfortable) about what I take to be a very important disagreement between you and me: namely, the poetry of Yvor Winters.

We haven't discussed Winters yet. I just said that "I like some of Winters," and you answered by saying that you couldn't understand why he, or anyone, should write a poem about "The Opening of the Wm. Dinsmore Briggs Reading Room." Well, the fact is that, when you are smitten dumb by the lightning-bolt of Richard Eberhart's perfect poem "To Evan," my own response is the same; *and yet*, I feel the same about Winters' poem "To My Infant Daughter." I believe that something important is going on here. Perhaps it is simply that I am muddled and fence-straddling, but I am not yet convinced. In any case, whether Winters is a real and thrilling poet or a mere dull academic illustrator of handbook-terms, the fact is that his influence is at work right smack dab in the midst of our generation: and a debate about him would be valuable to you, to me, and to all of us. You yourself said, "Let the poets of my generation ask as much of themselves." You were referring to the achievement of certain Americans slightly older (Berryman, Roethke, etc.). Well, what I propose is one practical way in which you and I can responsibly and *usefully* begin to ask exactly what you want us to ask.

I hope very much that you are convinced. Now let me note a couple of painful things. Spears is sending you a galley of the letter, and you can cringe in solitude over it. All I can do is to assure you that I myself cringe far worse; after all, I am the author of the idiotic passages as well as of the reasonably intelligent ones.

However, I note in the body of my book review itself several sarcastic and completely paranoid references to you. You will note them, if you read the review. It is now too late to recall them. I will say this, however: I am deeply sorry for having written them. When I wrote them, I was not in my right mind—that is, I was disturbed with the hope that I might get to know you and be helped by you in my lonely concern for the romantic impulse in modern poetry. Finally, if you would care to write *Sewanee* (as I suggest above) and refer to these sarcastic remarks in my review, I am willing to acknowledge their stupidity and inhumanity in print.

Now for a few more personal notes: thanks very much for the sketch of you! I'm putting it on the wall downstairs in my study (I work in the basement most of the time). I have a sketch (not a portrait—just a sketch of flowers) which I am proud to say was sent me by René Char, whom I helped translate into English. I'll put the sketch of you along with Char's sketch. Your face is striking, as I knew it would be.

I'll send you the booklet of seven essays about Char immediately. I think I mentioned the general section from his writings published by Random House and entitled *Hypnos Waking*, edited by Jack Mathews. I was one of six translators who helped in the job. The book costs five bucks, and is too expensive for me to send you. I wonder if you will accept, in lieu of the book itself, the shadow of a genuine desire to send it, a wish that I could afford to do so. In any case, I recommend it strongly. I think Char is a very great poet and also a great man. I've never had the honor of meeting him; but, if I ever get to Europe again, I intend to make a bee-line for Paris or Provence, where he alternately resides. My God! Listen to this single line—rather, a single poem in itself—from one of his long prose-poems: "Within the swallow's loop, a storm searches, a garden grows." Talk about coming into the presence of God!

Now for another matter: having wronged you by the strange (and yet, how transparent) expedient of pretending to defend Philip Booth, I considered it a point of honor to write Booth and tell him, first, that

I had used his name and his poems in a letter to *Sewanee* and, second, to tell him how I myself had found your criticism and your letters to be among the most fertilizing and creative forces I've ever had the luck, almost the grace, to encounter. I told him that he was bound to be hurt by your criticism in the *Sewanee* of last spring, but that your criticism represented that indispensable shock of reality without which none of us can even know what poetry is, much less write any of it. Well, Booth answered. His letter was long and appreciative, and it showed what I have felt before: that he has a human depth which his poems themselves do not yet reveal. Perhaps his poems will never reveal it. I don't know. I just don't know. *But* he is capable of taking the creative shock of genuine criticism, and this is what matters at the moment. I know he won't mind my quoting the single sentence of his answer which summarizes the whole thing: "I'll write another hundred poems or three more if I have to; only maybe because of Dickey's caring and wanting I'll match his need with my own and take strength from him and make it five. And be thankful."

I've mentioned Booth, and quote him, simply as objective proof that your review last Spring has sent a tidal wave of reawakening over a good number of the writers whom you discussed. If that [is not] *the* major function of literary criticism, then I give up and confess that I don't know what criticism is and don't care to know or be bothered by it.

It was magnificent of you to take on, completely alone, a whole damned generation of writers. Perhaps you didn't have any doubts about the creative effect of your review. But in case you did have such doubts, the reaction from both Booth and myself ought to dispel them.

One of these days I'll show you the verses I've been writing. You'll faint. They're so different from everything I've ever done before, that I can't get over it. I don't know whether or not I should try to publish any—not yet, anyway. For one thing, I think that, valuable as they may be *to me* in my attempt to overcome my private demon of facility, they are, objectively considered, a little *too* much like James Dickey—at least, so far. However, I've been genuinely helped in this exciting search for my true self—such as it may turn out to be—by Robert Bly, editor of *The Fifties*. I asked him—in a letter of thanks—to send you a copy of his magazine. He delighted me by answering that he had already done so. Now, I think the essential thing to say about Bly is *not* theoretical.

That is, he may be right *or* wrong about iambics. But I think that when, on the inside of the cover of his magazine, he says that "most of the poems being published today in this country are too old-fashioned," he is saying exactly what you yourself said in your sentence about most of the faceless ones in *The New Poets of England and America*: i.e., you liked a few, but "the rest seem mostly each other."* Now, this is a bitter truth; but the point is that it is the *truth*. If "the rest" don't grasp it, then we will be worse than mere bad poets (a distinction we have already achieved): we won't even know what poetry is, and *this is horrible*. Both you and Bly grasp this truth. Now, Robert Bly lives in Madison, Minnesota, on the other side of the state from Minneapolis. So you can see that this summer has given me my baptism of fire: he's hit me from one side, you've hit me from another, and I've scurried around like a man caught in an open field by the cross-fire of machine guns. But the summer is over, and *I am not dead*! This joyful thought fills my mind each morning when I waken. I have a new son, and I am in touch with poetry again—not metrical tricks, but the fire of the daemon! It is "the gift beyond price," indeed, and your phrase describes my feelings flawlessly . . . Let me conclude by once more greeting your wife, and hoping that your child is now well born and happy, with your wife and you.

Love to you all!

Jim (Wright)

To Robert Bly

Minneapolis
August 26, 1958

Dear Robert,

This is just a note to tell you that, if we don't hear from you by Friday, we won't come this weekend. However, if we *are* invited for this weekend, we would like to take the bus from Minneapolis in time to reach Madison around 10 or 10:30 p.m. Then we would want to leave on Monday, in order to get the 5-yr.-old to school on Tuesday. But please consult your own convenience in this matter. I apologize for misleading you about my visit this week. I would have postponed my visit

---

*"The rest all seem to be each other."

to Don Hall; but his wife's parents were arriving so soon that they wanted me there and out as soon as possible. So I left immediately. Since Kirby's folks came on Sunday morning, I was able to spend part of Thursday, all of Friday, and all of Saturday with the Halls. So many things happened to me—I think that Don must have performed the final blasting operation—that my letters to you will probably hereafter be much shorter. In other words, I am back in my notebook, working for four hours or so at a stretch, and coming up with a mess out of which maybe a phrase emerges. As you saw clearly, I'm sure, I had suddenly shrieked with suffocation in the iambic dungeon, and, not knowing what else to do, and being determined in any case not to die, I simply knocked at the man-hole lid with my skull. James Dickey was helping me from the dark, from beneath—the energy spent in our correspondence is simply fantastic, and he needs friends like no one I've ever seen or heard of, since he is a man of enormous devotion, courage, and humility who fears to starve his soul by writing advertising copy in Atlanta. By the way, he doesn't write iambics. He kept out of it by instinct; but somehow I have the feeling—which I don't understand—that his present poems would be better, more powerfully rhythmical, if he *had* written a good deal of iambic verse. This is one question I would like to ask you when we come out. But to get back to the man-hole: evidently you had already blasted a way up and out (Don just reminded me of your poem in the new *Paris Review*; I hadn't read it yet; I want to ask about it, but I would like to say for the moment that, like Don's "Foundations" in relation to *Exiles and Marriages*, "The Fire of Despair"* is about ten thousand miles beyond anything else of yours I have ever seen; and, even if you had not convinced me through your letters, that single poem would have done so. When I first wrote you I think perhaps the fire of despair was burning me, too. But, as I left the Halls, I said that I felt as if I were eighteen years old again—vicious, arrogant, shaking with impatience to work—but the difference is that, this time, I have an idea of what to do . . . The earlier poem I sent you—"His Prayer to the True Muse"—I have shortened by about ten more lines, and stripped and stripped ruthlessly. Ordinarily I wouldn't have sent it to you in its monstrous shape.

---

*A revised version of Robert Bly's poem "The Fire of Despair Has Been Our Saviour" appears in his second collection, *The Light Around the Body* (1967).

My first drafts are almost always downright imbecilic; but this time I couldn't really get *past* a first draft, and I think I sent you the poem to reveal just what kind of a mess I was in. But right now it is about one-tenth as long as the original; and I have a bit of another done. I'll send both soon, once again praying the descent of your pickaxe. When we come, I'll bring stuff. Do you have the new *Poetry*? I'm working furiously (i.e., about four or five lines a day) on short (i.e., ten lines or so) poems by Trakl, Benn, and others; I'm sending copies of *The Fifties* to M. Char and to the Italian poet and editor Alfredo Rizzardi and others. Finally, I have a Polish friend here, and he and I are going to spend time in about 2 weeks, working over some Polish poets in the current renascence over there. I feel born again. All I want is to work. I thought I was finished, I really did, but I'm not finished. But this will take a long, long time. Please write a *note* soon about our visit, and save longer letters right now for bare periods. I'm descending into another hole now; not a man-hole this time, but rather into Neruda's eustachian tube . . . I'll send you the Valery reference tomorrow.

Yours,

Jim

To Robert and Carol Bly

Minneapolis

September 4, 1958

Dear Carol and Robert,

Please forgive the slight delay in our acknowledging your hospitality to us. We all retain sensations of luminous space and kindness. I myself feel as the ripening orchard must have felt in the moonlight of late summer.

Trakl: I enclose this time 3 poems that you will want to see. I've marked out others to send, up to the number of ten or twelve; but I want to get these off to you. Others deal remarkably with cities. Each time I write, I'll send a couple—2 copies of each, so both of you can have a text to read. I'm still keeping back "Der Schlaf"—it is such a great lyric, only 13 lines; and I am mining it like a vein. I'll send the original and my translation soon.

My enclosed poems: I've made a final (?) version of the first poem

I sent you.* The poem *is* an oath; and thus the last 3 lines, which I've added. I worked about 12 more hours on the very end of the poem, and suddenly I remembered a terrible thing I saw at Fort Lewis, Washington, in 1946: behind the rifle-range in the basic training area, in the middle of a rich forest of evergreens and birches, one saw almost clear off to the horizon a line of stumps about the height of a human being: a couple of generations of young trainees had mown down the birches and spruces and so on. I wanted to dedicate myself to those executed trees. I wanted to look and look. However, if you think the last 3 lines are wrong, please hack them out as usual. I feel strongly that they belong there, but of course I am still fumbling around.

I enclose also another version of "My Father's Lullabies."† It needs no comment from me. I would be grateful, as always, for the instructive editorial blue pencil.

Before I forget, you will want to consult sometime the following: Michael Hamburger, *Reason and Energy: Studies in German Literature* (Grove Press, Inc., 1957). Paperback. $1.75. Essays on Hölderlin, Novalis, Kleist, Heine, Büchner, the crucial year 1912 (with discussions of expressionists like Georg Heym and of Rilke's poem "Wendung"), Trakl, and Benn. This is an excellent book.

Directly I will have, I think, 2 other very short poems to send. By the way, I hope you don't mind my heaping on your back the additional burden of teaching me how to cut. It goes without saying I realize your own work—this goes for both of you—comes absolutely first. It's just that I'm still trying to find my way in this strange new world—after living in it all my life like a blind man stunned by formaldehyde, or like a chloroformed geek; and any comments are a help for which I am enormously, unspeakably, grateful—the harsher and more merciless the comments the better. There's a small poem in Pound's *Personae* which I have often quoted to myself. I never knew what it meant till now, and I wish we might let it stand as a motto for your critical comments to me:

Go, my songs, seek your praise from the young and from the intolerant,
Move among the lovers of perfection alone.

*See Appendix, p. 569, for the poem, "The Trees in Minnesota."
†See Appendix, p. 571, for the poem "My Father's Lullabies to Me in 1932."

Seek ever to stand in the hard Sophoclean light
And take your wounds from it gladly.*

That says it.

The very best to you both
from all of us,
Jim

To Donald Hall

Minneapolis
September 17, 1958

Dear Don,

I have time for only a note. And I'm looking forward to your longer letter. But it seems important for me to say something that is plainly bothering you, and that has caused me a bit of concern also:

As far as your book is concerned, you must understand about Bob Bly (and how strange it is that I, who am admittedly very unperceptive about people, and who have talked to him only once while you have known him for years, should be in a clearer position than you to say this): he is a genuine and natural-born *editor, critic* (do you remember Housman's remark in "The Name and Nature of Poetry" that a *real* critic is almost a miracle, far rarer than a real poet), and *propagandist of new ideas*. In short, he is a genuine *fanatic*. You used the word jestingly; and yet, after talking with him for a few hours, I told him to his face that he was indeed a *fanatic*. Now, the value of a fanatic depends wholly upon the goal toward which he directs his fantastic and apparently inexhaustible energy. A militarist fanatic, like Hitler, is hideous. On the other hand, an editor and critic and propagandist of new ideas *in art*—some one, say, like *T. S. Eliot*—must of necessity suspend in his mind every technique of the past which can possibly distract his own and his disciples' attention from the pressing work at hand—that is, the formation of a *new* style. Eliot is highly unusual, in that, while admitting that Milton was a great poet, he was still able to toss him out, *not for the sake of any eternal critical condemnation*, but for the sake of making Milton shut up while us young people learned to write in our own language. Now,

*"Ité," from Ezra Pound's *Lustra* (1916).

Bly is like this, though he doesn't have Eliot's learning or skill in polemics. On the other hand, he has something just as significant: he has *force*. Now, look: just to needle him, I had him read Kunitz—the whole book. He admitted that there was *one* "good" poem in Kunitz's *Selected Poems*. Don't you understand? Bly is not a fool by any means. Quite the contrary. He has an enormous intelligence, and moreover he has the weird talent for suspending everything in this intelligence from its characteristic catholicity in order that he might direct *all* of its extraordinary power along one channel—the channel of the new style. So you are not justified in saying that his remark about your book is "bitter." It's nothing of the sort. It's just that some of your book doesn't at the moment fit his current (and, I may say, enormously creative and important) project of exploration. I'm sure this is true, Don . . . As for Wagoner, I also finally got a copy of his book. I can't tell you how pleased I am that you two have made some sort of contact. I always thought you would like his poetry, and I know he will like your new book. The same is true of Roethke—I'm glad, not only that he wrote you (what did he say about the book, by the way?), but that he was *able to write at all*—you see, I hadn't heard from him for a while. It's good to know he is still improving . . . What do you think of my latest table of contents for *St. J.*? Send other poems, I'll send back notes on them, raw and harsh as possible, within the week. I heard from Rago, who says you also had requested G. Hill's book to review, and that he wants to read it himself first. Well, I'll try someone else. I haven't had time to write Hill yet, but I will soon. Listen, Don, am I blind or something? I mean that Ch. Tomlinson is *superb*. I wish to God I could afford to buy *Seeing Is Believing*, but I can't, and they ain't got it at library, and I'm *going* blind reading it poem by poem as I stand at a shelf in the bookstore. God damn this being poor! God damn it!

Love,
Jim

To Robert and Carol Bly

Dear Carol & Bob,

Excuse the brief delay. I finished another chapter on Dickens, have another loosely sketched. Also, I've been spending some time with Arthur Waley, Soame Jenyns, Freud, Jung, and—I just bought a simple cheap little Spanish grammar, to which I apply myself regularly (the will, the sheer force of *will*, has *some* use, you know, even though, as I am finally starting to grasp, it has been wrecking my own poetry). I used to be able to read Spanish, and the realization of what is available to us made that vague, muddled, half-comprehending gaze at Neruda etc. on book-shelves simply and physically unbearable. I'm not getting much written—perhaps this is an illusion, perhaps the writing of a single genuinely true phrase in a space of two months is a more genuine fertility than the writing of ten "poems." But for the most part I can see that this is going to be a year of meditation and self-exploration through the way of the Chinese, the poems of Denise Levertov (whose poems I am copying into a little notebook, wherever I can find them), and through effort at translation.

Speaking of that, let me say how valuable your long letter has been, and will continue to be, to me. The major point is, out of fear and evasion, I have been driving the poet's (Trakl's) imagination down out of sight—in effect, repressing it—*not* with my own imagination, as you said, but with my *will*. (I know these terms are vague and scientifically imprecise; but I'm also sure you know what they mean, since they are your own terms; understanding them is my own struggle, and will take a long time.) Anyway, I've made extensive penciled notes on your letter and kept it in my notebook. I study it regularly—you know, I haven't truly *meditated* literally for years, not in the real sense, which is quite distinct from daydreaming—and it applies, as I say, not only to problems of translating, but to the sickness in myself, a sickness of hysteria, evasion, brutality. You spoke of arrogance, but an even stronger term is needed, like brutality; for the impulse is, and has been, actually destructive, actually an aggression against whatever imagination I may have. It's curious that this fact should emerge so clearly, at this time, in the midst of translation, rather than even in your discussion of my own verses. Hence, another value in translating, this time a value for me—a kind of personal aid in the attempt to learn how, if at all, I can heal myself of the hatreds and murders I have imperceptibly been absorbing into myself for so long . . . Sorry for the egotistical self-analysis in public. The point is that I wish to say once more, it is so important to me at this time, how expertly and courteously valuable your quick, direct, epigrammatic criticisms have been. They can be likened to confident strokes of a surgeon, i.e., warmth and excessive tenderness in the surgeon would be fatal. Precisely in proportion as he is cold, direct, and true, he is also kindest . . . I've tried a few other lines, and I'll send them later. However, I think it is about time for me to try to exercise whatever I have learned about cutting *on my own* . . . I have another curious request: please understand it, and the motive: since I am still fighting myself *and* the whole iambic tradition so hard, would you mind *not* sending me any of your own poems yet? When my mind is wildly open like this—it's really rather frightening—it absorbs things like an amoeba having lunch; and, judging from "The Fire of Despair," your own work, Bob, whatever will happen to it in future, is nevertheless already discovering its own form. That is why it's quite safe, I believe, for you to criticize my own pieces—in addition to any considerations about comparative depth of native imaginations, etc., which has nothing to do with it. I am, in fact, trying to *free* myself from urges of competition. They are mere delusions, I think. They seem to be mere "literary" or, better, academic formulations of our old curse, the desire to get on the "rising curve of success" in order to attain "the American dream." But I would like some day to discover truly what I am, and then to be it—without anger or hatred, but with a clear eye for the images inside, outside, and above. To achieve this clarity of sight, I need meditation, I must read good poets outside iambics, etc.; and yet I feel I must not read *you* yet, because you are helping me so much with myself. Am I making this all clear? . . . I will send a version of Trakl's "Klage" soon, and will study out "Der Schlaf" again. It is magnificent, isn't it? And your remarks are all of them so close to the center that I would rather study them further, before I try it again . . . Your answer to my request for information on possible visitors when you stay with us is exactly what I wanted to know. I know exactly how you feel, and you can depend on complete freedom from social or any other commitment when you are both here. However, please answer this: would you like to *say hello* to Phil and Ellen Siegelman? They live 2 blocks from us, and Ellen says she knows Carol. Also, would you like to talk with Berryman? He liked *The Fifties*, I hear, and might have suggestions. Please let me know, and keep us posted on your plans. We leave to visit Ann Arbor on Oct. 22; perhaps you'll be there at that time also.

Best to both,
Jim

To James Dickey

Minneapolis
September 28, 1958

Dear Jim,

It's just a little past noon on Sunday. My entire brood (which includes my wife, my two children, my sister-in-law, and her 5-yr.-old son) has gone to church. They are all Greeks you know; and I am invariably taken aback by their beauty which, under some circumstances of my own life and background, seems exotic still. One gets used to his wife in the daily affairs. But these Greeks possess the appalling gift of ceremony. Suddenly out of the commonplace they emerge, and the women are more than merely disturbing in a physical sense. They are almost frightening. They give one the feeling of being in the presence of a severity and intensity which knows all about the confusion of the usual five-thumbed human beings, and they are neither untouched nor pitiless about this confusion; and yet they look at it out of purity of form. They seem to have known all about it forever. This feeling (maybe I'm just being paranoid again, but I doubt it) is not depressing. Far from it—it is, in a way, both exhilarating and reviving. It is like what Henry Miller wrote at the very end of *The Colossus of Maroussi* when he stood at the tomb of Agamemnon: "Peace to all men, I say, and life more abundant!"

By the way, you mentioned a certain admiration for Miller once, and I've never said that I share your pleasure in him. In case you haven't seen it, his marvelous book on Greece (*Maroussi*) is now available for about a buck and a half in a New Directions paperback. Whatever critics may say for or against Miller's other books may or may not be justified. I am not interested in them.* But this particular book is a great one—a masterpiece beyond dispute, as far as I am concerned. Do you happen to know of the poems of Georgios Seferis, Miller's friend whom he mentions in his book?

And, speaking of modern poets, I was typing out a translation by H. R. Hays of a poem by the Chilean Pablo Neruda,† and I thought of you. That is, it's been a little while since you answered my last letter; and, since you're obviously too busy to write at the moment, I thought that it might be nice to send you the Neruda poem by way of sustaining the correspondence. I have a little notebook in which I am finally collecting a group of treasured poems. It is a good exercise for me, simply because it is the physical embodiment of a treasure-house, a beautiful place, in my own mind which—in the midst of so many corruptions and dishonesties mainly committed against myself—I have never really betrayed. From time to time, if you have no objection, I would like to send you some poem or other from my private anthology, to show you what I have in mind and in heart when I use the word "poetry" in the highest sense which I am capable of giving it. It may well be (it probably is, in fact) that you are familiar with the Neruda already. If so, no harm done. But if you aren't familiar with this poem, and with his other work, I think he will give you some sense of the high joy which is all that matters, the joy without which—I finally confess, having learned that I will not shrivel up like a moth at the confession— poetry is considerably less interesting than boxing.

Speaking of sports, Jim, it just occurred to me that you and I ought to be able to exchange some views and feelings about the coming football season. I myself have never been very skillful at athletics, though I have boxed and wrestled a little, and I used to be a delighted fourth-rate track man. However, I enjoy some sports very intensely, and football best of all. Nothing—but nothing—can describe my pleasure in the fact that yesterday afternoon the U. of Washington (Seattle, where I used to live) defeated this ridiculous, snobbish, arrogant team of ludicrous punks from Minnesota. I like Minneapolis quite well, but I think that football is a matter of high skill. It is truly one of the few areas left

---

*In the margin: "The critics, not the books, I mean."
†H. R. Hays's translation of "Walking Around," from the Spanish of Pablo Neruda, is included in the Appendix, p. 572.

in American life where—in spite of the usual vermiculate phonies—it is simply taken for granted that what matters is excellence of imagination. This may sound silly, but I don't think it is. For example, if you were to compare the two activities—poetry and football—in America for, say, the past twenty years, which do you think would reveal the larger proportion of hollow technicians, of really empty human beings? Furthermore, I think that someone like Jim Thorpe had a life and career which without straining the word could be called genuinely tragic . . . I mention all this in the hope that you like to write about such things.

Let me say that I hope you are well now, that your children are growing in charm and humanity, and that your wife is well and happy. (And I may be ready to send you a couple of poems soon, but I'm not sure. My way of writing has so utterly changed, that I just don't yet know what to make of it all.) And let me know what you plan to do with your book. I may have an idea or two, but it's best to wait a bit, till Grove gets a chance to act.

Yours,
Jim

To Donald and Kirby Hall

Minneapolis
October 11, 1958

Dear Don & Kirby,

Don, are you home (yes, you should answer, "No, I am in Moscow.")?

I have, of course, that telegram from Mr. Lockwood*—one never really gets jaded, and the telegram was terrifying. Lib got to read it to me over the phone, just like the last time—a deeply moving ceremony for the both of us. We've been extraordinarily happy, by the way. Marsh is going into his greatest period—discovering that there are sounds in him beyond those of lamentation and anger. The moment in about the third month when the kid discovers the reality of joy is one

*Willard Lockwood, editorial director of Wesleyan University Press, accepting the manuscript of *Saint Judas* for publication.

of the true genuine glories, and that Lib and I should be so terribly in love—My God, as we never have been, depths on depths opening within us, whole continents of music and pain we never even suspected—and that Marsh and Franz should both be well, and that with all this we should be visiting you and Kirby (who will be in Lib's wave length immediately, without a word exchanged—you'll see—that's one of the many realizations that made me happy at your home)—well, these are glories. I would feel sinful to deny their proper celebration.

Monday I get 3 teeth pulled, but I don't give a damn. I've given teeth their due. Now let the moon be served.

Yours with belief and devotion,

Jim

To Robert and Carol Bly

Minneapolis
October 16, 1958

Dear Carol and Bob,

Quite soon I will write at greater length, for some other things have occurred to me—even some things that don't deal directly with your beautiful letter which just arrived a few minutes ago. At the moment I want to try to answer the immediate thoughts of your letter, and to reaffirm what I believed in, and to qualify the undoubtedly irritated tone of the words I wrote you over the weekend.

I will begin at once to compose a little paragraph about the Valery quotation—in so far as I recall it; and it is clear in my mind, as far as its main point goes. However, if there is time—oh, I was going to ask you to send me the quotation, and I just realized—as if I had awakened to the fact of being in the world after all—that I can surely find a copy, in the library perhaps. It would, of course, be better to check Valery's exact words, in the context of his whole essay. I must say that he is a far greater man than I had been led to believe by the critics who refer to him in the little magazines. He is discussed as if he were the classic exponent of external, mechanical, classic "form" which is to be imposed on experiences. And this is nonsense. The whole book *The Art of Poetry* is a series of explorations—that is why I found them so exciting: they seemed to have the power of breaking through the appalling clutter of clichés in my own head. Having tried so hard for so many years to learn a technique that was actually obstructing whatever I needed to see and say, I felt very self-betrayed at the beginning of the summer—and when Jack Mathews had the Valery sent to me, I read it as though it contained some hint of salvation. I believe it does—but the entire book must be pondered. These are just reflections, and they do not diminish the power and the value of the quotation I sent you. I'll write more on this subject soon.

By the way, have you generally agreed with Carol and Mr. Duffy on—I can't avoid the word—a "deadline," at least a tentative one? I don't mean that I expect you to say that you should receive all relevant material by November 5th *or else*. I would just like to know generally when you intend to send the stuff to the printer.

You didn't do me an injustice. But, through sheer good will and inadvertence, you did happen to strike a sore spot. You are perfectly right in saying that my "refusal"—how childishly huffy it was!—to let my poem be printed was absurd! But I ask you to recall the context in which I thought of that poem. It gave me such joy to work on it! the real old joy that I had when I was about eighteen, and knew only that I knew nothing, and didn't think about anything except the struggle to make the words true. But by the beginning of last summer, I had reached the stage at which I could just about print anything I sent off. In short, I had begun by wanting to be a poet, and I had, in some insane way, got sidetracked on the old rising curve of success, the American Dream. For weeks I could think of nothing except that somehow I had got to get off it, out of it, away from it—to be naked and alone again, somehow, somehow, even if I had to refuse myself the chance to send a poem to any editor whatever. There seemed a kind of hope in that refusal—there could hardly be anything dishonest in my love of the words and the images, if I didn't even send the work of a month or two to let an editor look at it. I think—though I'm not sure—that I was hurt by your suggesting I publish only one poem per month for at least a year. It sounds strange, and yet I had determined not even to submit anything in verse for publication till God knows what distant date in the future. It was brutally unkind and unfair of me to howl at you in that way, after the devotion you had taught me—you must try to remember hereafter that I really and truly *am* a genuine neurotic, and that such people sometimes can be set off by kindness as well as by shock.

I think that the real solution for me is simply to continue to send poems, or parts of poems, to you and to Don, in the hope of your making comments that I can study. I can say this with hope, because in a comparatively short time you have shown me a good deal about *cutting*—and cutting is perhaps the central problem of poetic composition, if I am not mistaken. The main reason for my not sending things so often is that I have been trying to see if I could do some of the job myself—eventually I must do all of it, of course. Do you remember the little piece which I sent you recently, called "In Fear of Harvests"? I find that, when I speak to myself the few lines that you think ought to be retained, they almost make a whole poem in themselves. It is not a very big poem, but I am starting to learn that the smaller a poem *can* be—in length of lines, in number of lines, in number of images, etc.— the more power it can have. I don't know just how to handle this poem yet, but I look at it, and say it to myself, and I now have a path struck through its wilderness. You know very well what I must learn to do—to wait, wait, wait, and to wait without despairing. It is hard. It is hard for everyone in a different way.

I've received the Rilke translations, and they are so beautiful that I want to keep them long enough to type out several into a little notebook I'm keeping. Would you have any objection to my reading any of them aloud on this lecture tour?*

On the poem, "Farewell to the Old Moon" seems to me to make more sense in the scene of the poem than "It Will All Be Forgotten." Perhaps Carol is right in objecting that it is too romantic. On the other hand, the second title which you suggest is awfully obscure. Don't you think? The first at least makes it clear that the moon is being addressed, and the word *moon* does something to illuminate all those scarped crowns and laurelled seas and so forth. I can't quite come to a decision. Please choose the title which you think is clearest. As you know, I have trouble with obscurity—and I know very well that this trouble means that I am still often afraid of coming out and revealing whatever it is that I see. And that, in turn, is the longing for the old iambic womb. I have a terrible fear of pain, and loneliness, and regret.

---

*Two notes in the margin: " 'Out of Childhood' is simply magnificent" and "I'm typing 2 copies of M. Hamburger's chapter on Trakl for you and Carol, by the way. If you have any of Rilke's letters, you might look for his comments on Trakl. I've got a lead."

Perhaps this is another reason why I've spoken so unjustifiably and harshly about not wanting to publish anything at all. I'm afraid it will be so nice to see my name in print, that the shock of the early summer will turn out to have been just one more trick of self-delusion. Again, I hope you and Carol are not embarrassed at my saying personal things —but I trust your judgment, the judgment of both of you, completely. The new country is so strange! I can't go back to the cities! And yet I'm so easily frightened. The result is a confusion of motive and search which will, which *must*, solve itself through a spiritual struggle of weeks, months, years! I've got to learn whether or not I have the stamina. I can't go back, I can't go back.

By all means send any stuff you like, and I will study it at length. As I said before, I've run into two published essays on Trakl by an old friend of mine with whom I went to school in Vienna—one deals with the way to read Trakl's images, and the other deals with the influence of Rimbaud on Trakl. The friend was Herbert Lindenberger, whom I mentioned to you. I still haven't written him, but I will do so soon, and ask if he has any offprints of his essays (I'm sure he must have some). But there's no hurry about this. I love to study Trakl, to read him aloud—somehow I feel that if we could really catch his voice we could catch a good deal more besides!

Your comments on the future of imagery reminded me of Ben Belitt's translation of Lorca's lecture "The Poetic Image of Gongora," which is one appendix to Belitt's translation of *Poet in New York*. Lorca's remarks are tremendous. You have a copy of the Belitt, don't you?

I seem to have done nothing lately except get three huge back teeth pulled (a hellish experience), and brood endlessly over *Civilization and Its Discontents*, that great and noble book, so savage and Hebraic and scornful in its pity.

More soon. Meanwhile, please consider whatever irritation you found in my last letter to be a part of that in myself—the arrogance, the cruelty, the dishonesty—which, at long last, I am trying to face down and overcome.

Have you seen the October *Poetry*? It contains a beautiful poem by Denise Levertov. Called "To the Snake."

Lately I've had the curious experience of looking at 3 hack-reviews of mine that have all come out at once—in *Kenyon, Sewanee,* and *Poetry*.

They seem strange, alien—I have the sense that I wrote them in the grave, and I can't quite decipher their language. I feel somewhat the same way about my second book of verses, though it is not a dishonest book, and I am not ashamed of it. There is one poem in it which allowed me to see what I saw and say what I needed to say—the rest of it seems exercise. I really hurt Lib's feelings when she read me the telegram over the phone and I responded in a dull, bored voice. This is a curious time of life. You remember Arnold's "Drifting between two worlds, one dead / The other powerless to be born." I don't think the other is "powerless," but it is having a difficult birth—a breach, a caesarian, a cry of outrage. In the Freud, there's a beautiful sentence in which he admits with sorrow how pleasant it would be to go back to the womb. The only trouble is that we can't! All I want is not to want to.

Yours,
Jim

To Jerome Mazzaro

Minneapolis
November 9, 1958

Dear Jerry,

I not only remember very well the small chance we had to talk together, but I've also wished many times that my visit to Detroit had been longer for the sake of such talk. As a matter of fact, a couple of weeks ago my wife and I, with Don Hall, were able to visit Jerry Enscoe in Detroit again—but we only stayed a short time.

Anyway, it was very nice of you to write—I certainly hope the correspondence can be kept going from time to time, though I imagine we're both about to go nuts with one busy project or another—and to invite me to submit something to *Fresco*. I'm enclosing three pieces. You may very well find them inadequate—if so, please don't feel embarrassed about rejecting them. I realize how important it is that you print good stuff in your first issue especially, in order to make the university pay attention.

I've been working so hard in the attempt to break out of certain stylistic devices that were trapping me into what you very accurately diagnosed as a lack of range, that I have had very few finished pieces at hand. The three that I enclose will entirely clean me out. I felt it would be best if I didn't voluntarily submit anything to editors for a long, long time; but it's different to be asked by someone whom I respect and whose editorial ideas I can believe in. Whether or not the enclosed are suitable, I nevertheless consider it an honor to be invited. The group of writers whom you mention include some people like John Woods who are not nearly well enough known. I think he is one of the most tremendous poets alive in America—William Stafford (who is, I think, in the English Department at Portland State University, Portland, Oregon) is another. I've just discovered Stafford and his poems give me great pleasure. I used to think his rhythmical sense was just slack; but I'm finding that that isn't the case at all. He has a very eccentric but subtle ear, and he is able to convey a quiet humor which I find very pleasing. I wish somebody would give him a break—like Woods—and like Richard F. Hugo in Seattle, another fine writer—he is a man with a genuinely personal style—he may or may not be able to change it, and yet it conveys so many fine things that there's little reason why he should.

Beyond the generosity, for which I am grateful, I think you said many perceptive things in your review, and I appreciate your sending me a copy.

I hope to see you again.

Yours,
Jim

To Robert Bly

Minneapolis
November 11, 1958

Dear Bob,

It is evening, and tomorrow I am going to send you your essay on the faults of iambic meter. Reading it over again I saw that I had rudely made a few notes on your manuscript; and, as I read, I made others. I had intended to type out another copy for you; and yet I think I would like to send you your own copy, to let you see some of the observations I made, and some of the doubts I had. If you like, I'll certainly type the whole thing over for you. I really ought to have recorded my thoughts on another sheet of paper, but I didn't want to lose track of them while I was hunting for something to write on. As you'll see, I was often confused enough as it was.

Let me say one word about the tone of the notes. If I ever sound discourteous, please understand that I don't intend to. It's just that, reading the essay, I found certain difficulties in my own thoughts and feelings becoming clear enough at least to write down, and I wrote rather rapidly.

There is one thing that I feel I must say—it is entirely personal to me, and it may be that I will seem to betray something. I wish it were possible for me to make these feelings clear, but I have no capacity whatever for theoretical discourse, especially about poetry. Perhaps it's best simply to tell you what I think and feel at this point about what I take to be the direction of your theories: the utter rejection of the iambic tradition, and the absolute insistence on a "new style" to express the "new imagination" (both of them pretty well suggested to me in letters, but neither of them precisely defined—the suggestions, when short and concrete, have been practically instructive, but the definitions have tended toward absolutism, unless I am greatly mistaken, and theoretically meaningless). First, it is my feeling, so far, that your attack on iambics is pretty futile. The selection of a bad line out of one of Shakespeare's sonnets, for example, to show that the English language is unsuited to iambic meter seems to me a terrible waste of time and energy. I could go on about this—and, as you may be noting, I am not getting your point—but, anyway, your most lucid and helpful—I should say inspiring, for that is what I mean—discussions, as far as I am concerned, have been those that have shown your exploration of the possibilities of non-iambic verse. The trouble is that even the non-iambic verse is not clearly enough defined or delineated, and so I find myself getting mindlessly lost in amorphous sound—the very thing I was trying to cure in myself. I know that one has to be afraid of closing himself off from what you justly call "the most important experiences of our time." But one can close himself off from these things in non-iambics as well as in iambics. Perhaps this is theoretically false; but, in terms of actual writers, it seems plain that Louis Simpson with his iambics is far closer to the major experiences of our time than any non-iambic writer in America known to me. Please understand that I think your essay on Simpson can be enormously helpful to him, for it could make him question his own style. But whether he discards it or not will have to depend on personal considerations of his own—won't it?

A strange thing has just happened to me. Before I can describe it, I must say something about what the writing of verse has always proceeded from in my own experience. I was always embattled, fighting my own environment part of the time and an unrecognized illness in myself for the rest of the time. I think that in order to survive—merely to survive, without having more than one nervous breakdown, one being quite enough to last me for a long time—I learned a discipline of classical verse—of iambics. That was obviously a mere defense against the hell I grew up in, and, if it is not poetry, then it's not poetry. But I needed some kind of release from the painful pressure of this neurosis also, and that came out in the devotion to Whitman, and Trakl, and others who sought technical freedom. And yet—at least I'm sure of this, whatever else may confuse me—the question of technique, or style, has never meant anything at all to me in itself. I realize that such an admission probably exposes me to the charge of not being a poet at all, merely a neurotic versifier. Actually, before last spring and early summer, when a couple of things happened to me* that just about finished off my nervous system for good, I had always thought of myself as a neurotic versifier. Anyway, poetry was always necessary for me personally, and both aspects of it were necessary: I always let them symbolize themselves in my mind as Whitman and Robinson. You remember how horrified I was at myself at my going completely haywire when one single critic dared to imply in a single phrase that I wasn't the equal of Shakespeare after all. Since it seemed the iambic aspect of poetry that was to blame—this was wholly irrational—I dug down to the other—the Whitmanesque. The most amazing development of this is the way you have been able to show me some of the precisions and restraints that can exist within the new style you have been trying to teach me, that while it has a great and necessary freedom it can also have direction and clarity and discipline. But—and here's the rub—I've just swung into the other direction again, and remembered how much force and grandeur the iambics can have also.

*In the margin: "They weren't book reviews, by the way."

What happened was my leafing through some old notes, and I found a version of a little poem in iambics which I had written about a close friend of mine who, last year, suddenly died two weeks after he had written me a beautiful letter. The poem had never jelled, it was too wordy, too overstated, and so on. But, without really meaning to do so, I got to fooling around, cutting and cutting and cutting again, and suddenly it went "click" for me. I had finished it. Now, I am not going to enclose it, because I know you would not like it. Perhaps you would think of it as a betrayal of American poetry. And all I can say is what I was always able to say before that damn asinine book of mine was so idiotically over-reviewed by a bunch of punks who wanted to impress W. H. Auden: that is, I can say the truth. I know that in my very short iambic elegy I said something that it was personally necessary for me to say. I know I can be easily persuaded that it isn't poetry. All right. It isn't poetry.

Bob, I'm trying to say that your insistence on the utter rejection of iambics is, I believe, an expression of fanatical absolutism. I say this as a man who is your friend—and who has read enough of your poems in the new style to receive real joy from their beauty. What this will mean in your own mind I don't know. (Please don't be humorless and simply give me up as a bad job—I didn't say that you were wrong. I said that the most fruitful part of your work so far has been, not your attack on the iambic style, but your discussion and practice of the new style; and that I have found I simply am not strong enough, or original enough, or something, to break so brutally out of the classical need without ripening for a longer time.)

I have been swinging on a pendulum. What I was escaping was the really terrible and difficult fact about myself as writer of verses: I need the commitments of both E. A. Robinson and Pablo Neruda. I recall that you don't think anything of Robinson. I can only say that he means a great deal to me. For several days I have been horribly depressed. But as I write this note, I feel better, because I have been trying, very hard, to tell you the truth about whatever impulses in myself seem to make me want to write poetry. My God, it's really terrible: no matter which impulse I reject, I feel sick with betrayal; the only thing I can possibly do, unless I am to be torn in half, is to continue the search for a new synthesis. I know I will never find it. Then I will just have to write to relieve nervous pain. Bob, please understand. And have you ever read *The Green Wall*—I mean all of it? If not, would you do so? I can send you a copy. And please let me know about your poems. Best to Carol.

Yours,
Jim

To Donald Hall

Minneapolis
November 12, 1958

Dear Don,

Wonderful to get your note—though we're both sorry that you and Kirb were ill. Is Andrew okay? You know, it was miraculous that we took Marsh across the Lake (I didn't know it would sound like that, so help me God!) twice and yet he didn't even get sick. Our entire trip, in fact, was magnificent in every way—except the entirely unexpected crack-up on the last evening. I'm sure you and Kirby realize that I wrote of it at such length in concern for the both of you, simply because Lib knew of it, and had seen it before, and had seen it as a much worse thing. As a matter of fact, I'm much improved. But it came as a surprise to you both, and I don't wonder you were hurt.

Thanks for sending the clipping. I read your letter—and clipping—before I looked at the *Times Book Review*, which arrived at the same time. It really is very encouraging, you know, since the sonnet is the last piece in *Saint Judas*. Anyway, now I can say that I made at least a small dent on English literature. That Guinness anthology was a nice thing, though it could have been much better.

For the past several days I have been severely depressed, morose, unaccountably miserable. Then yesterday a strange—a really weird and unplanned—thing happened. As you know, I hadn't written anything in iambics all summer.* As a matter of fact, I hadn't written much of anything at all. I knew I was morose because the first great sense of *liberation*, which came to me when I first wrote to Bob Bly and came over to see you, was seeping away, and I had no idea where it was

---

*In the margin: "Good God! I just looked at the date. 'The summer is past, the harvest is ended, and we are not saved.' "

going or why. I got to leafing through some old poems which I had never been able to finish; and among them was a short—or reasonably short—blank verse elegy for an old Kenyon teacher of mine, who had written me a gorgeous and moving and proud letter about *The Green Wall*—and then, two weeks later, just two miserable weeks—the editor of the *Alumni Bulletin* wrote without warning and asked if I could care to write Dr. Timberlake's obituary. You've been through all this, and far worse; and you also wrote short poems about it, compulsively. Moreover, you declined to put those poems in *The Dark Houses*. (I still have them, incidentally, and study them, hoping one of these days to make some kind of usable suggestion, however brief.) Well, to try for once to come to the point, I looked at my fragment of elegy, and felt fresh pain for that great old man who hated the suffocation that had come over modern poetry in the form of arty criticism, who had taught me Chaucer and Shakespeare and Anglo-Saxon, who had been shell-shocked in World War I and suffered from insomnia, and who had driven with Roger Hecht and a couple others and me all over the hell's half-acre of Ohio in the middle of many nights (we once gave him a book for Christmas, and wrote in the front of it ". . . for we have heard the bells at midnight . . ."),* and who had told us again and again that nothing in a writer was worth a damn except his attempt to tell the truth to himself and to everybody else. As I say, I had felt low even when I looked at the poem; but I just couldn't take any more—I gave up commitments to every damned program of a literary or any other kind, and I cut this little elegy to bits and built it up again, as bare and brief and terrible as I could make it . . . And after it was done, I suddenly knew part of what was depressing me. The sense of liberation was departing because I had turned it over to Robert Bly. You know, Don, how I have tried to explain to you, to make you feel with me, how it would be impossible for me to give up my deep devotion to Whitman. I don't know why I feel this way, but I do. And I've told you how impossibly it confuses me that Winters, whose poetry is also deeply important to me, thinks Whitman a fool and literally a madman. With Robert I had just tried to escape the nearly intolerable pressure of a kind of loneliness.

Anyway, just after I finished the elegy in iambics, I found myself

*In the margin: "You remember—it's Falstaff addressing Justice Shallow."

184

writing to Bob and actually *confessing* that I had done so. When I realized what I was doing, I tried to assure him of my respect and friendship for him, and of my deep belief in what he is writing in verse and prose; but I still insisted that I—as well as every man—had to find his *own* truth and then find his *own* way of dealing with it stylistically. My criticism of Bob is that he wastes about fifty per cent of his time and intellect on attacking iambics, whereas he ought to devote himself wholly to expounding the virtues of non-iambic *possibilities*. God damn it, the trouble with the man is that he won't *let* himself talk about possibilities—only *necessities*.*

In short, I had hoped to evade my own personal curse, my equal love of Whitman and Winters. I held first to the Winters and then to the Whitman. As far as I personally am concerned, to give up either impulse is to repress at least half of my own personality. I can't be somebody that I'm not. If I'm nuts, then I'm nuts. The hell with it. I have been called two-faced, stupid, schizophrenic, everything—and I got so sick of it, that I tried to get a rest by committing myself to this entire viewpoint or that entire viewpoint. But there is no rest. The only entire viewpoint that can mean anything to me is the one that realizes the real possibility of American poetry for greatness: that is, it contains *not only* a language that could surpass Neruda's (given the genius to dare the style), *but also* a language that can write like Robinson (given the genius to dare the style).

I have no idea what Bob will answer. He might do any one of the following: 1) simply give me up as a traitor and a bad job, a fool, a neurotic, etc.; 2) call me a coward for turning back; 3) be terribly upset. Now, the first two will be okay, because, like you, I really believe in the man, and I want him to believe in himself even if he has to call me an idiot in order to do so. However, I'm hoping dreadfully that he won't be upset. Anyway, I told him about the poem, that I absolutely had to write it, that if it is phony then it's phony, and that I wouldn't send it to him because I knew he would hate it. Please write me about this when you get a moment. All I know is that I've got to find my own way, and there's no escape. I can't wholly hand over whatever skimpy imagina-

*In the margin: "I wish you would write me about this. I am really devoted to Bob and Carol, and yet my impulse to do the Timberlake elegy was *true*, even if the poem is bad. God damn it, can't I make Bob realize that I want gratefully to *learn* from him, not be his *disciple*, for Christ's sake."

tion I may own to *anyone*, not even to a real liberator. Sometimes Bob reminds me of the Red orator in the Yiddish comedian Willie Howard's joke: "Comes the revolution, you *will* eat strawberries and cream."

Here's the poem, and the devil take the hindmost. If it's bad, I honest to God don't give a double-damn. I am a victim of Tolstoy. I believe that men are more important than art.

WHAT A MAN CAN BEAR

—*P. W. T., died Summer 1957*

The evil of winter proves my death of cold.
Philip, good man, below your classic grave
Christ and the gentle Plato whom you dreamed,
Furious at death, cry forth their savagery.
Vanquished and daunted by the bitter ground,
They flee, blind motes that quiver in God's eye.
Clever, defensive, seasoned animals,
Plato and Christ desert you where you lie,
Philip. Only a man can bear to die.
Between the woodchuck and the cross I mourn
Your philosophic hands, your laborer's brow.
But I, too, flee; I cannot stand the sight
Nor sound of snow sifted above your face.

* * *

Whatever a poet has been in the past, right now he is defined, to me, as a man who has both the power and the courage to see, and then, to show, the truth through words. If I'm a bad poet, that means a liar; and I'm not going to get out of that by imitating Pablo Neruda.

Love,
Jim

P.S. Lib and I heard Sir John Gielgud. Iambics? Nonsense! Imagery and honesty! It was so beautiful. We felt like crying. God, man is greater than poetry—but only a great poet can make you feel it.
Final P.S.: Listen, man, I *found* Robinson's poem in praise of Whitman!

F. O. Mathiessen's *Oxford Book of American Verse*. I'll send it to you soon. (I love Mathiessen, flaws be damned!)

Another P.S.: Reed Whittemore just had a review of *Green Wall* and Phil Booth's book in *The New Orleans Poetry Journal*. It's a great and true essay, far and away the best comment on either book—and a fine piece in its own right [. . .]

Minneapolis
November 19, 1958

Dear Don,

Your letter was so important, so true, so moving! Damn it, I wish I didn't write prose so melodramatically. I've clearly given you the impression that I was mad at Bob Bly! You used the word "furious"—and that was all right. But you still thought I was angry, and it's not the same thing. Anyway, this is what I think has happened: you and I were telling each other, ostensibly in a joking way but *actually, underneath the joke,* in a hurt and confused way, that we would have to write iambics without Bob's knowing it. Now, this is not only silly; it is destructive—to Bob's ideas, to ourselves, and to poetry. Poetry as a created thing has got to have a form; but it is equally necessary that the poet be allowed to begin his creation with a sense of utter freedom. Otherwise, he can't even discover what his meaning is, let alone shape it into something beautiful and comprehensible. I wrote Bob two very long letters in which I tried to explain what I mean. (Furthermore, I am so sure that my arguments were *clear*—as well as true and respectful—that I am going to ask Bob to let me shorten one of them and submit it to *The Fifties*—it deals with the nature of expanding style.) Now, Don, man, you speak of his writing you a fine letter in response to your criticism of the J. P. Morgan poems. But talk of angelic! You should see the letter he wrote me in response to my defense of the occasionally necessary iambics. His letter was, quite simply and flatly, magnificent—in its imaginative understanding of the ways of growth, in its profound grasp of what was disturbing me personally, in its further evidence of his greatness. (For I really do think he is a great man.) You said "it's not his fault that you believe in him." This is true. But I don't think it's a question of "fault." It's a fact that he *is* an innovator—you get one in a generation, if you're fabulously lucky. I really believe it's the duty of anyone who recognizes the original man to believe in him; and this belief consists, I have finally realized, not in discipleship, but in searching and serious questions, in *criticism* . . . This coming Sunday we're visiting the Duffys in Pine Island, and the Blys will be there. I'm going to ask him if he minds my sending you the letter he wrote me about iambics—it's not only beautiful, but enormously fruitful in its ideas, as I said before. Here's what has happened: something in Bob's tone or emphasis has very strongly implied an utter condemnation of iambics *per se*. Yet in his letter he can't see how we got that impression! I outright told him that it was personally necessary for me to write the elegy in iambics (the new version is enclosed, by the way—thanks for your terrific criticism!), and that I wouldn't send it to him because I knew he would hate it. He wrote back that he, also, wrote sometimes in iambics, that "one can't do everything at once," and he promised that, for every poem in iambics that I sent to him he would send one in iambics to me! I immediately wrote him a note of thanks—of real gratitude. Don, I think it's not the tone of Bob's prose that's in itself at fault—I rather like his serenity and force—but it's a tone which actually distorts his meaning. We stopped to see John Woods (marvelous) at Kalamazoo on the way back to Minneapolis, and he had read *The Fifties* and received the same impression: an utter and violent uprooting of iambics. If this is not Bob's whole meaning, then I still believe it is worthwhile to tell him how and why that whole meaning is not being clearly conveyed . . . I must close. But, really, I'm so pleased. What fantastically fine friends I have! . . . On 2 readings, and maybe I'm wrong, your poem on the Hungarians is superb. I think Bob will faint with joy when he reads it. Talk about imagery! Listen, man, I think things are going great, I have tremendous hope! I leave for the East soon. Love from Lib et al to Kirb and Andrew. We're glad you liked the cheese.

Jim

Minneapolis
December 15, 1958

Dear Don,

I was just invited to be the poesy consultant at the writers' conference at Portland next August, on your recommendation. I accepted. Thank you very much. My God, I love it out there.

* * *

In a few days I'll give you a full account of my reading tour, which was fantastic, almost dadaistic. Dick Wilbur's wife was just waiting to have a baby when I arrived, and they had had four false alarms, and I had the shakes from speaking every day (sometimes twice a day) for about a week, and Dick and I had a therapeutic drunk, and it was lovely, and I was remorseless; and earlier in Boston I spent five beautiful hours with Robert Lowell, and taught his seminar; and Philip Booth is a tremendous person, and everybody was beautiful to me; etc.

* * *

Right now, however: God, what a great letter of details on the "Winter Day"! Now, I feel wonderful about all this. I feel like a bulldog clinging to someone's calf. Anyway, I have this version in straight blank verse now:

HOWEVER: it strikes me that this poem is changing. There is something unnatural (perhaps I'm wrong here) about setting it arbitrarily in blank verse. Why not let the cadences, which are chiefly iambic, set themselves on the page according to the natural syntactical pauses? Then there is still a short poem, with one spare image, as Robert argues for an image, and yet there is nothing fruity about it. Thus:

> Clever, defensive, seasoned animals,
> Plato and Christ deny your grave.
> But a man,
> Who slept for years alone,
> Will turn his face to the common wall,
> Always before his time.
>
> Between the woodchuck and the cross,
> Alone all afternoon,
> I take my time to mourn.
> I am too cold to cry against the snow
> Of roots and stars,
> Drifting above your face.

* * *

What do you think? My God! Think of it! Me! Writing short poems at last! Anyway, if you think it is worth it, I would like to put this one in the book in place of some softer one. Please write. I'll write soon. Do you know where Robert is? I ran into all sorts of interesting reactions to the first *Fifties*, and when you or he or Duffy can let me know where he is, I think I'll write a very long letter to him (he can have the master copy, carbons give him the shakes, part of his revulsion at the stink of the classroom) and send you and perhaps Duffy carbons. Do you mind? I mean (man, what I mean), I'd tell the both of you the same anyway, and I may as well keep it straight. I met Ralph Maud at Buffalo, and like him a lot. We had dinner. He liked the *Fifties*, wants to submit poems. We talked a good deal about your idea, "The Margins of the *Hudson Review*," and he has the real itch to help or start a magazine—I think his own *Audience* was in many ways superior to the present luxury product. And Philip Booth was excited by the mag, because he has a couple of new poems that are really good, full of genuine imagery. Wait and see.

I have a marvelous letter from Geoffrey Hill. I finally wrote to him when I was howling drunk late at night, and dreaded to look at my face in the mirror after I was ass enough to send it. Yet the first thing he said in his reply was that he was delighted (he used that word) that I had decided to send the letter the next morning. His God damned publisher, as you know, has put off the book till the Spring. Why the hell doesn't he come to America where there is literary adventurousness as well as brains? The young English poets are good, but they have a simply impossible task in trying to crack the publishers.

Please write, and let me know about Robert. Love to Kirby and Andrew, that magnificent wit and graceful friend of my son.

Send poems, for you say you're writing. I'm writing prose. (Dickens.)

Love,
Jim

P.S. I just counted the numerous "My God!s" in this letter. Excuse me for sounding like (ah!) G. M. Hopkins.

To Elizabeth Lawrence

Minneapolis
December 16, 1958

Dear Miss Lawrence:

I was both surprised and delighted to get your friendly greeting card. It was especially nice of you to send it at this time. I had just returned from a "tour" of the East, where I read poetry at a variety of places—Tufts, Wellesley, Brandeis, Boston U., Connecticut, Bennington, Wesleyan, the Poetry Center, etc. Being a genuine hick from Ohio, I was glad to get back to the Bible Belt, where one can be alone and write.

I can't get over the kindness of your reminder that "Harper's door remains open." I suppose I'll never really escape that old midwestern fear of big publishers. And I certainly wish I could have sent the new mss. to you, for one of your objections dealt with its size. It is to be published next Fall by the Wesleyan Univ. Press; and it will be cut to no more than 30 poems, many of them severely cut and revised from the mss. which I sent to you. Its title is still undecided.

Thank you again—and, of course, if you pass through Minneapolis, you are to consider that you have a standing invitation at our house for refreshment.

Yours,
James Wright

To Jerome Mazzaro

Minneapolis
December 16, 1958

Dear Jerry,

Thanks for the card. I just got back from a reading-tour in the East. Everybody, of course, goes off his nut this time of year, especially those who are already nutty enough to write poems. Anyway, I'm delighted you liked the 2 poems enough to use them.

There is one thing that bothers me, however. I hasten to say that you should proceed with the poems (by this time they must be printed) as you choose. But—and this is curious—I've revised the poem "What a Man Can Stand" so extensively that you will scarcely recognize it. I've suddenly learned a little patience; so that I am waiting, with most things anyway, for them to "ripen" somewhat before sending them out. I think the "Animals" is all right as it stands; and I think "What a Man Can Stand" is at least an acceptable version of the other piece. But it is now changed—having corresponded at length—feverishly, I might say, for he and Robert Bly are finally trying to teach me how to revise (so much in my first book was just inexcusably sloppy)—with Don Hall, I have cut the poem to the bone. I thought you might be interested in seeing what it looks like right now. Here it is:

A WINTER DAY IN OHIO
—*P. W. T., died in the Spring, 1957*

Clever, defensive, seasoned animals,
Plato and Christ deny your grave.
But a man,
Who slept for years alone,
Will turn his face to the common wall,
Always before his time.

Between the woodchuck and the cross,
Alone all afternoon,
I take my time to mourn.
I am too cold to cry against the snow
Of roots and stars,
Drifting above your face.

* * *

One official point here is that I would like to put this poem into my new book (next September is publication date), and, since it is really the poem "What a Man Can Stand," though fiercely cut and changed, I wonder if you would write me an official note, giving me permission to reprint it. Then I can include *Fresco* on the list of acknowledgements, and feel like an honest man. Also, would you include permission for "The Animals"? It won't be in the book (as yet untitled), but I'll probably want to do something with it later.

* * *

By the way, just between you and me, the book is being published by Wesleyan Univ. Press, Middletown, Conn. They're starting a program of poesy, though they want to shy away from most public announcements till next Spring. Also, the general editor (Willard Lockwood), whom I saw at Middletown about a week ago, told me that they're asking prospective authors to withhold manuscripts till Spring. You see, they have a poetry board that can meet only occasionally, since they're scattered all over hell's half acre. Nevertheless, this sounds like a real step forward in publication of poetry in this country. Everyone realizes you can't make money at it, and it's the responsibility of the Univ. Presses to take it on. They've long realized this, but at Wesleyan they're doing it in an intelligent way. I offer this information for what it's worth to you. I don't know whether or not you have a book ms. ready, or, if so, what you're doing with it. Perhaps it's accepted already—and if it is, fine! The whole point here is that, having mooned and wailed limply for years over the inability of American publishers to make their poetry programs more coherent and realistic, it is now time for the poets themselves to step in. Why not? They've always done so in Europe.

Good luck with *Fresco*. The issue which I received I enjoyed. I take it you saw Bly's *The Fifties*. Nutty, but nice. What the hell? It's about time somebody had nerve enough to take the chance of falling on his face, especially in view of the many fine ideas buried in the occasional sophomoric, campus-humor-magazinish jokes.

Keep in touch.

Best,
Jim

Descent

1959–1962

On the Bly farm, Madison, Minnesota, circa 1960

Be patient. I am coming in a glad
       Descent, rapidly as my eyes can close.
       Move over; refuse me not my peace in the earth.
                                        —from "Sonnet—Peace"

Love to Joan and you, and,
   my God, I'm so happy and
     relieved! I really believe
        in this thesis, and I pray
          for it, and for all of
            us: Lib, and Franz, and
              Marsh, and me. We can't
                starve now! Not with
                  this great family
                    finding itself at
                      home at last, and me
                        writing books like
                          a cement-mixer!
                            Jim
                              —from a letter to Wayne Burns, January 7, 1959

       My personal life is indescribable hell.
                              —from a letter to Donald Hall
                                        June 1, 1961

The exhilaration of 1958 continued for James, especially when he, Bly, and Dickey met in New York City in November of 1959. James celebrated the occasion in a letter to Dickey written on November 19:

> I can't really describe what it meant to feel free to emerge into that tremendous, ample sunlight of noble and heroic men with whom I spent those three days, drinking the great green waters of the first and last seas.

However, as the late fifties gave way to the early sixties, many good things in James Wright's life were greatly threatened by severe problems. Although he wrote Donald Hall this whimsical depiction of how he worked—"in the basement, with the furnace, the moths, the skeletons of mice and the necklaces of twilight"—his marriage, his job, and his health, because of emotional and alcohol problems, were in jeopardy.

To James Dickey

Minneapolis
January 2, 1959

Dear Jim,

Here comes, I'm afraid, another snippet of a note in this irresponsible correspondence of mine. I think of you very often, mainly because there are about five thousand questions I'd like to ask you about everything under the sun. Also, I've been reading Spanish like crazy— you know, it's quite easy, even after you've had the little French I've had; and then, like you, I had a bit of Spanish in high school. I've found out all sorts of nutty things, mainly about a place where one can get great books cheap. I'll write you about this soon.

Right now, I want to ask a big favor. You see, I'm going to have a book next year published by Wesleyan. (You know about this deal, and, when I get a moment, I'll send you everything I've found out, just for your own information, since you write that Hall asked to see your mss. At the moment, you are wise to make them ask you. However, it doesn't hurt to have a little data at hand—I'll write you within a week. Mainly, Wesleyan sounds like a good deal.) Anyway, I am working like fury to get certain poems revised adequately (?) for the book; and, although a couple of the editors are a bit preciously horrified at my longer poem "At the Executed Murderer's Grave," I am insisting that it be in the book. I've already written you my reason—that it, whether or not successfully, is *not* a safe poem. In your first friendly letter to me, you made a series of comments about my work that you may have forgotten, though they have been helping me more than I have time to describe right now. For example, you said "there is a real danger in facility." That's why I was so happy that my murderer poem came out in *Poetry* right beside your "Dover." For I hoped it would show you that I understood what you meant about the danger, and that I had started to understand even before I made my abortive (and, now, somewhat comical) self-introduction to you. Well, in discussing the executed murderer poem, you said you liked it, but that you had some objections here and there. You hesitated to discuss them, and you were right to hesitate for the reason you have given: namely, that critical nit-picking quickly becomes absurd.

However, Jim, just such "nit-picking" would be enormously helpful to me right now. Will you do the following? Look in your copy of the August *Poetry*, number the lines of my poem (by fives or tens, as I did with yours), and then write me your objections. I really want to make this poem stand as an attempt to do something real. And, as you've also observed, it's after the imaginative leap that the drudgery properly can begin—and not *before*, which produces only the current school of dry pedantry, which I would do almost anything to break out of. I would tremendously appreciate your help.

Of course, I understand if you are too busy. It's just that this poem needs the kind of warmly ruthless and terrifyingly honest criticism that comes to those with sense enough to pay attention from James L. Dickey the Southern Antagonist.

I saw Clemson on TV damn near beat LSU! A great game—thought of you then, too.

More later. Please write. I've got to have this mss. done by February—I only wish there were more time—I would ask you to look at the whole thing—but even your comments on the one poem would be great.

Yours,
Jim

P.S. I'll send some new bits in the next letter. I want to get this one in the mail. By the way, I had a fine note from Geoffrey Hill. More on him later.

To Donald Hall

Dear Don,

I'm here to defend my thesis, now complete. Still loaded with work: 2 abstracts to be completed by Jan. 21—one six–eight pages, the other 1 page. Hence, accept thanks for great carbonated letter to me and Lockwood, and even greater uncarboned note to me. First, and most important, as you know, I love [William] Meredith's poetry, and I have faith in his judgment. All I meant (in addition to the paranoia, and we need not go into *that*) was that I was taken aback by his shyness. In this, he is exactly like Stanley Kunitz. And you know how I've come to care for Kunitz. I realize that only a superb, warm human being could have written the sonnet "The Illiterate." Enough.

On your recommendations: I agree with all—except one. I don't want to put "Under a Streetlight" in. I'm fooling around with it. I will add "The Farmer." I am also adding a revised and much cleaner version of "Girl Walking into a Shadow." Now, I got your note last night, with Lib's first letter; and I wrote her just a minute ago (it is very early, and Dickens is howling at me from the door-knocker), asking her to send the *St. J.* mss. to me the moment it arrives. Okay, now please do this, and forgive the inconvenience:

I will get all revisions straightened out, and then send the thing on. *But* (please forgive me this really unforgivable boo-boo) I left Minneapolis without the Sept. 14 version of the table of contents—and the carbon of *St. J.* which I brought is all screwed up. Now, there is still time, since Lockwood said to me the first half of February would be all right. So—now please—will you send me a copy of the table of contents (Sept. 14) to which you were referring in your letter? I am wholly convinced by your argument that the order ought to change, that the "Midnight Sassafras" poems ought to be first, etc. I'm all a-tremble. (God damn it, Dickens, shut up! The whiskey is in the third drawer!) If you can possibly send me that Sept. 14 table of contents, and do so immediately, then everything is fine. But if you haven't got the copy with you, I don't know what the bleeding hell. I've got one in Minneapolis, but I hesitate fiercely to send Lib into my study—it's like inviting visitors to an open house in the middle of your eyeball.

If you happen *not* to have that Sept. 14 table in your possession, I am going to do this: I will send the mss. to *you*, man, directly (and don't shoot me—I know you too are busy, I'm not trying to pull a Stephen Potter!), and ask you to arrange it, or else ask you to send it on to Lockwood (assuming that he will have the Sept. 14 table of cont.), and let him put the poems in the order which you suggest. I'm hoping to God this doesn't annoy you. As you know, I'm getting too old to care about anything but truth: and I would rather have the book gain your respect than anyone's. There is just one thing about the arrangement of the table of cont. which is simply and flatly of crucial importance to me— and that is the following:

No matter what happens to the rest of the book, I want a single section of the poems to be called "Into a Shadow." This section is to include the following poems in the order in which I type them here:

A Girl Walking into a Shadow
The Alarm
In Shame and Humiliation
The Ghost
But Only Mine (title changed from The Dream)

I hope, again, that this section pleases you. At any rate, I know you understand wholly when I say that I must have the section. As I recall, there are at least 3 of the poems in it that you didn't like much. But the whole story is too morbid.

Would you, man, by the way, mind writing a note to Alfredo Rizzardi, via Mengoli 5, Bologna, Italy, and tell him that he can feel relieved about printing those poems of yours without paying you? And would you—could you—ask Mr. Simpson, and anyone else you happen to be seeing or writing who was in Rizzardi's Italian anthology, to do the same? He's dreadfully upset about copyright dangers. I realize that, in one important sense, he should have been aware of such difficulties in the beginning. But in a far deeper and more important sense, he did a work of devotion, and he produced what is to my mind a startling, a magnificent book of good poems, gorgeously printed (and he had to bully the publisher into it), and, I am told, well translated. He and I have corresponded, and my heart really goes out to him. Can you help him?

I'm reading Jiménez like hell! Do it, man! You know French, so

Spanish is about twice as easy to read. Just learn the pronounciation, also easy, and read some, I beg. My God, my God, my God! but Jiménez is lovely, lovely, lovely. I'm reading *Diario de Poeta y Mar* (*The Journal of Poet and Sea*), and here is one:

ROSEBUSHES

(written on a train, 21st of January, 1916)

It is the sea, in the earth.
The colors of the earth, in the winter sun,
contain the loud shiftings
of the sea and of the coasts . . .
Oh tomorrow in the sea!—I say, in the earth,
that is moving now into the sea.*

Love and joy to you, great friend (I sound like a bad translation from a tribal ritual). Love to Kirb, with affection and sympathy for her getting sick. What a hell of a note! But she and Andrew will come back all golden from the sun. How lonely I am, and how laden with work. Oh, I don't give a damn for anything but love.

Love,
Jim

To Robert Lowell

Minneapolis
February 20, 1959

Dear Mr. Lowell:

I feel awkward in apologizing for taking such a horribly long time to write you—not because an apology isn't called for, but because my failure to write is really a piece of genuine rudeness.

But I am sure you will understand the delay. You see, I returned to Minneapolis from my poetry-reading tour on Dec. 13, worked till Christmas on my dissertation for the doctorate (Dickens' early novels), resumed work on Dec. 26, and finished just in time to travel to Seattle

---

*In the margin: "Do you think Robert would advise Jiménez to cut everything but the first line? Oh, let an old man rest."

and defend myself against the questioning committee. I am now a Ph.D., which provides—or, rather, I hope will provide—some economic relief to my family, at least. And while I was spending three hard-working weeks in Seattle, I was also working in the evenings in order to revise, rather thoroughly, seven of the poems in my new book, *Saint Judas*, which the Wesleyan Univ. Press will publish next fall, as I told you in Boston. Another parenthesis: though I may have seemed somewhat quiet during your seminar at Boston U. on Dec. 2* (a time I shall always remember with very deep pleasure at your kindness and the fresh intelligence and talent of your students, and with the certainty that simply being invited was something that I can regard without hesitation as one of the few genuine honors I have ever been given—and not just with regard to poetry), I was listening closely. Many of the revisions of poems in my book had to do with making their *locality* clearer, more specific. I've even tried the Ben Jonson device of using my own name in one of the poems—though I think it works, I can't be absolutely sure.

I had seen several of your new poems—in *Partisan*, the *New Republic*, *The Nation*, and *Audience*—most of which were exploring new areas of rhythm; I was not sure how I felt about them; but, having been at least partly cured of the vice of trusting my own stock responses to poems by having talked with Mr. Ransom and Mr. [Philip Blair] Rice—and they really taught students something of the art of intelligently regarding one's own emotions, did they not?—I bided my time. And I was right to do this, for the four new poems that just appeared in the current issue of *Partisan* came through to me completely. I could *hear* them, and they seemed to me, all four of them, not only very beautiful but also new and original poems—for you and for modern poetry as such. My pleasure in reading these four makes me eager to re-read the others, which I had seen and been unsure of, when they appear in your forthcoming book. I'm not quite sure why, but the new poems—with their superficially apparent "looseness" and yet their very delicate precision of rhythm when one takes a look, or when one finally tunes his ears to their wave-length—evoked very strongly in my feelings the tradition of Hardy himself. And that is very exciting to me, because, as far

*It was at this class that James Wright first met Anne Sexton, who wrote to him for the first time on February 10, 1959.

as I know, Mr. Ransom is the only considerable poet who seems to have *used* this eminently usable tradition in modern verse that has any claim to excellence. Perhaps this is just a mnemonic irrelevance, as they say they say at Harvard.

Please give my regards to your wife and child, and tell them what a pleasant thing it was to meet them.

And thank you, once again, for the great honor you did me by inviting me to your seminar.

Yours sincerely,
Jim Wright

To James Dickey

Minneapolis
March 2, 1959

Dear Jim,

How marvelous it was that you phoned! Did I really sound as calm and "easy-going" as all that? For I was genuinely shaken, you know. I understood at once that you had called purely for the sake of greeting, and it was a noble act. And I am sure I will not ever be able to say what your response to the Doty poem means to me. By the way, on your telephoned advice, I've had the title changed back to "At the Executed Murderer's Grave."

A couple of things occurred to me about your phone call. You said, "do I sound like a madman?" Now, I often use *Gulliver's Travels* as a text in a course of advanced prose writing which I give; and, of course, sooner or later some student, naturally enough wishing to defend himself and his self-satisfied universe against the poetic imagination of Swift, asks if I don't *really* think that Swift was just insane. My answer is invariably this (and it is uncalculated—the first time the question was posed to me, the answer popped out furiously by itself): of all the authors whose books I have ever read since kindergarten, there are, I suppose, two or three whom I would call, without qualification or apology, healthy-minded and sane; and Swift is the sanest of all. You, James Dickey, are a madman in this sense.

You asked a question which contained your characteristic directness of tone: how far would I be willing to stand by your book? I said, with some equivocation which was the result of my slight phobia of telephones, that I would deal with what I believed in. Actually, I saw later that my statement had been pompous. Let me say this: I have seen a few poems of yours that are considerably less fine than your best. I am coming moreover to realize that it is a sleazy and dishonest thing to praise a greatly gifted writer when he has not lived up to his own search, his own vision. Thus, if any of those less adequate poems were in your book, I would 1) damn them; 2) explain the vision (as far as possible) in terms of which the weaker pieces are to be judged; and 3) proceed to the major works like "Dover," like the three in the *Quarterly Review of Literature* (all of them real knockouts, like absolutely nobody in America today), and like "The Work of Art" (in the Fall '57 *Hudson*), all of which are profoundly important poems, and all of which I am getting to understand, I believe, quite well. In other words, I think I may say without boasting *too* much, that I am in a pretty good position to examine your book, because I have studied your poems—your biggest ones so far. I have made notes on "Dover," for example, which are very detailed and careful. (So did Bly, by the way.)

Sorry this note is shorter than usual, but I've got to go over to the university and see about some plans for teaching again in March. On the matter of teaching *without* a Ph.D., I've got a couple of ideas which may or may not interest you; but I'll mention them later. The situation is not so completely dominated by pedantry and academicism as you seem to think, though God knows it is bad enough.

Meanwhile, I am enclosing a copy of a poem by R. F. Hugo, a man in Seattle, exactly your age (unless I'm wrong in thinking you are 35), who also works outside academia (he's at the Boeing Aircraft Plant), who also served in the air force in WW II, and who, interestingly, is an admirer of yours. When I mentioned corresponding with you, he was astonished that anybody had paid any attention to your poems (he calls you a *unique* poet, and this is a word of considerable meaning) precisely *because* you are good. He's a little bitter, you see, at the predominance of grey-flannel-suit poets etc. Well, I am proud of the fact that I am a friend of both Dickey and Hugo, for this friendship demonstrates that I am at least capable of distinguishing between, say, Robert Pack and Hart Crane. Hugo's poem is wonderful, I think: it is an elegy for Dylan Thomas! Consider the idea—what a stroke of genuine imagination!—of an explorer going into a kind of Incan, Peruvian landscape—this is the United States—and losing his way. And no room for the sentimental drivel that so many fifteenth-raters wrote on Thomas.

There are other, and better, poems by Hugo which I will send later. But I send this one for your pleasure.

Please write. Good luck with the book, which will be a fine one. If I get a chance to review it, I will lash the hell out of it, because I know that it contains great rocks against which the sharpest of critical instruments can only have the effect of revealing the fine vein of the stone, the dazzle and polish of the imagination itself.

My own plans are so insane that they may shock even you. I will write about them when they are clearer.

Yours,

Jim

To Theodore Roethke

Minneapolis
March 27, 1959

Dear Ted,

I'm afraid you must be about ready to send me an old sock stuffed with rancid iguana-livers by this time. I was never so negligent before, and I guess it's been getting that damned thesis out of the way (though I shouldn't curse it, because I really enjoyed it—I hope that some day soon you and Dave and I can read some Dickens aloud—he's really a hell of a lot of fun).

I was certainly delighted to see your essay (or was it that speech to MLA you gave a little while ago? I remember your talking about it) in the *Yale Review*. I have a hell of a time convincing anybody that there is a fundamental difference between imitation in the great, living, traditional sense and, on the other hand, mere aping of stylistic mannerisms. I remember at Reed College a couple of years ago (do you remember that mildly silly weekend there, a weekend redeemed by your reading—the greatest reading of poetry I have ever heard anywhere?), I read to the students a poem that sounded like a lurid, juicy bit of personal experience, and, when someone asked how I came to write the poem, I answered that I had been trying to imitate the tetrameter couplets of Andrew Marvell. They all laughed knowingly. Or, as Ring Lardner has one of his characters say, "They laughed hardly." But nevertheless, the passion of living tradition is greater and deeper than the passion of quirks. And it doesn't constrict—it liberates. Your essay gives the most daring statement of that truth.

I've written to Dave Wagoner once since I got back here to Minnesota, but he hasn't answered yet. I was kind of tired at first, and I must confess that I did work awfully hard for a while. But, please believe me, Ted, I took your advice about tapering off. That is, I didn't stop immediately. And I'm going to be okay.

I know it's no use asking Heilman for a job up there, so I am going to dicker for something else in the Northwest, if possible. The plain fact of the matter is that I just don't like the Midwest very much. Minneapolis is okay, but I just don't like it. I think I served my time in such towns when I was a kid (though Minneapolis is cleaner than most), and I was happy with the air and everything else up there near the Pacific Ocean. It is, for one thing, very lonesome here. I miss the stimulation of you and Dave and others. Of course, one can get used to missing such things—my God, a man isn't going to run into many such people very often in *any* town. But I always loved the west, and I would like to live and teach there again.

One thing I've been doing is studying Spanish—just to taper off, as I mentioned above. It goes pretty easily and pleasantly, and I've made a few translations of lovely little poems by Juan Ramón Jiménez which I think you would enjoy. (I don't have them with me at the moment—I'm at the Humanities office, and it's Good Friday—but I'll send them to you quite soon, and I promise never to let crucial correspondence slip again as long as I live.)

Speaking of my Dickens thesis, there is one chapter of which I am proud. It is about the "absorbing eye" of childhood, and deals with *Oliver Twist*. Come to think of it, I think it would interest you (at least I hope it would—though it's hard to imagine anyone being very interested in a Ph.D. thesis). I'm going to work it over slowly, and maybe try to get it published. When it's done, and if you'd like, I'll send it to you.

I told Lib I was writing you this afternoon, and she sends her love.

Please don't be too cross with my neglect. I'll write again soon.

Love,

Jim

To James Dickey

Dear Jim,

I know you must be terribly annoyed with me for my failing to write for so long, and I know such annoyance is justified. For I feel as you do—I have very, very few friends, and as I grow older and older I become less patient with the light use of the word "friend."

But you will understand at once, when I tell you that I have been, and still am, quite gravely ill. The illness is strange—I tried to describe it to you in one of my earliest letters to you. It is that catathymic depression again, but this time it has come very close to crippling me to the point of really blocking off any ability to function at all. Under new medication, however, I am very slowly coming out of it. I have somehow been able to teach for the past week, and I expect to continue. But for several weeks—ever since I returned from Seattle, in fact—I have been getting the shuddering horrors, indescribably so, and frequently going to pieces, sometimes in really mad and violent ways. I am better, but it is still very difficult and painful to write anything at all, especially those few letters which have any absolute meaning for me.

Dick Hugo wrote that he had received some splendid letters from you, and I am delighted. The two of you have a great deal in common: utter honesty, rich humor, and unmistakable talent—not to mention the more depressing fact that neither has received one fiftieth of the recognition that any sane literary climate would afford you.

Please write when you can, and I know you'll excuse my temporary silence.

Yours,
Jim

Dear Jim,

Your letter was splendid, touching even. My illness is called catathymic depression. When I am in the midst of a fit of it, I go through what used to be called, in healthier times, the dark night of the soul. Worst of it is that it hits me as pure egoism. Thus, the slightest mention of my name, or even reference to it, is sometimes enough to set me off into the terrible swinging pendulum of self-destructiveness and, as an inverted form of this, destructiveness against others—and the really ghastly feature of the latter is that I get destructive, not toward my enemies, but toward my friends—or else toward people whom I admire. I think I told you once that one thing about your mentioning me in print that upset me was that I had read your essays for some time in *Sewanee*, had increasingly looked on them as the sort of thing that had to be done if poetry in America were ever again to be anything beyond a kind of prissy chess-game, and had indeed intended to write and tell you so. And then, suddenly, I got sick with this ridiculous depression, and you know the rest. Enough of that episode, which was silly enough, and now, thank God, is dead. Back to the depression, it sounds like paranoia, but the difference is that this catathymic business is a physical matter. It has to do with my physiology, etc., and I don't understand it myself.

There is, however, good news to the effect that my doctor seems finally to have found the right kind of medicine to control the thing; and, physically speaking, I feel far better than I have felt in months.

And there is bad news to the effect that my wife and I have separated—a week ago. But the affair, though it was painful in the beginning, is not so anguished as you might imagine. What it amounts to is that we simply couldn't live together. I don't know what happens next.

I do know that for the past two weeks, heaven knows why, I have started writing again. And I am getting adroit as hell in reading Spanish. I have discovered the Peruvian poet César Vallejo, and, man, he is one of the great ones. Here is one of ten poems that I have translated:

OUR DAILY BREAD

Breakfast is drunk down . . . Damp earth
of the cemetery freezes the precious blood.
City of winter . . . the biting crusade
of a wheelbarrow appears, hauling
an emotion of fastings in chains.

I wish I could beat on all the doors,
and ask for somebody; and then,
look at the poor, and, while they wept softly,

give bits of fresh bread to all of them.
And plunder the rich of their vineyards
with my two blessed hands
which, with one blow of light,
could blast nails from the Cross!

Eyelash of morning, Thou wilt not rise!
Give us our daily bread,
Lord . . . !

Every bone in me belongs to others
and maybe I robbed them.
I came to take something for myself that by chance
was meant for another;
and I think that, if I had not been born,
another poor man might have drunk this coffee!
I feel like a dirty sneak-thief . . . Wherever I go!

And in this cold hour, when the earth
transcends human dust and is so sorrowful,
I wish I could beat on all the doors,
and beg pardon from someone,
and make bits of fresh bread with it
here, in the oven of my heart . . . !

How about that?

Speaking of our recent separation (i.e., between my wife and me), I would not be able to offer you any decent Northern hospitality if you were to come up here on your vacation, though, of course, I can't imagine any visit that would give me more pleasure (and that would lift my morale more). There are two main reasons for my not being able to offer you much: first, I am broke, really broke this time, for I really must give my whole paycheck, small enough as it is, to my wife so she can take care of the two kids, and I live on little; and second, I am living only in a small sleeping room. If things had worked out well in my now defunct attempt to create and maintain a family, I could, or rather Lib and I could have put you up at the house.

I mention these difficulties, however, only in order that you might know what would be required: you could easily find a room somewhere nearby, and we could spend time together at or near the university. It would be okay, if you could finance yourself. I really feel bad about having to say that to you, for normally I could have been hospitable enough. Yet I know you will understand. Let me say, also, that there is no enmity between my wife and me, and she would herself like very much to meet you. It sounds strange, but she and I get along amicably enough—when we are not living together.

Keep me informed about your plans.

On May 20 I'm supposed to get an award from the National Institute of Arts and Letters. That is nice.

It was, I take it, a good omen today that your letter arrived with one from Geoffrey Hill. He has good news, and I quote him: "It's almost completely certain that I come to Ann Arbor in the Fall of this year on an exchange lectureship. Donald Hall will be in England then, I believe. I'm almost speechless with the irony of it all (note: he means that Hall, who ordinarily teaches at the U. of Michigan at Ann Arbor, will be away). My luck being what it is, you also will doubtless be in Hawaii or New Mexico, or London!!! And Jim Dickey on a world cruise! I shall spend an instructive year with Anglo-Saxon scholars and college footballers. Damn Damn Damn!!!!!!" Jim D., don't be offended at that last remark about footballers; remember that Hill is a benighted Englishman, a mere Johnny-bull as my grandmother used to call them, and doesn't know any better.

Anyway, it's great news. Geoffrey sent a few new poems, and said that his book will be out in June. My God, it should be a great book. None of the current fast-talking balloons in Britain seem to pay any attention to Hill; but, if I could write with the grandeur and clarity of an electrical storm at sea the way he can, I wouldn't give a damn. If God gave me a choice between being Geoffrey Hill and being Thom Gunn, I wouldn't even choose. I think I would probably snicker or something.

Please write and let me know your plans. But let me assure you that I have no more troubles, really, than other people have, that it's time I got used to this fact and went on with my work, and that the latter is just what I'm doing.

Yours,
Jim W.

To Robert Bly

Minneapolis
April 26, 1959

Dear Robert,

I received your letter on Friday, and, having just simply and flatly dropped every "busy" job I had to do as if I were a snake shedding its old skin (the Spring is gorgeous!), I took Neruda, and two dictionaries, and a scratch-pad, and then walked all over the place: along the river, all over the campus, up and down this street and that alleyway and so on; and here is the translation. I think it is done. I had two very intelligent friends go over the English with me. I know I've got the Spanish correct. Well, anyway, all I can say is that I think it's done [. . .]

Let me say that, if you find any places in the enclosed version of the poem to be inadequate, or unclear, or too violent, etc., please make the necessary revisions on your own, so that you can finish your short essay and get the stuff off to the printer. The idea is superb, and it seems to me that it ought to be served forth while it is still steaming with the very audacity, that sauce without which it will be hard to digest.

In any case, whatever you decide to do, working on Neruda's masterful poem gave me a wonderful weekend of joy; and I needed that, as you can imagine. I feel like a green thing, growing.

Best to Carol,
Jim

P.S. I almost forgot—last night Ray Livingston, a philosopher who teaches in St. Paul, gave me the following line, and suggested that it might do as an epigraph for the audacious rejecting of Shakespeare and championing of Neruda:

"Omne verum a quocumque dicatur, est a spiritu sancto." ("The truth, by whomever it is spoken, is from the Holy Spirit."—Saint Ambrose.)

While I'm at it, here's an extremely beautiful statement which Ray found in Gerhard Hauptmann: "Dichten heisst, hinter Worten das Urwort erklingen lassen."* Isn't that fine?

Jim

*"The aim of writing is to get the primal word to chime behind one's own."

To Donald Hall

Dear Don,

Thanks for your note and for the new poems, all of which seem to me astonishingly effective and, most interesting of all, masterful in their ability to absorb the images of the real world. They have a fine, delicate and precise strength—very like the great Chinese poems. The one about snow is the one I think I like best, though it wouldn't mean much to say whether or not it is the most effective poem of the group. What matters is that your labors are beginning to produce concrete results, as you learn the new style.

You are right that there's little point in discussing my domestic troubles. There's been too much talking already. All I really know is that I am in complete confusion, and that I simultaneously wish life were not the way it is and stand aghast at the absurdity of my own wish. The only thing possible is to shut up and wait till my mind clears, if ever; and this is just what I am struggling to do, though it is difficult.

I had a nice, if somewhat forlorn, letter from Vassar Miller, who said that her new book ms. had been finally rejected by Macmillan and that she had several new poems, none of which she seemed able to get published. Knowing that you like her work, and remembering the pleasure we shared in reading some of it at Detroit that time, I just wrote and suggested that she send you something. I know you won't mind. She really is a fine poet. I once wrote Robert Bly a big letter about her, in order to argue that the current poetasters who are writing flatly and limply in iambics would undoubtedly write the same way in any other style, and that the problem is to learn how to adapt the solutions of form to the truth and honesty of one's impulses, and that it was silly to reject iambics categorically, since sure as hell some genius would set iambics afire just to spite *The Fifties*, etc. etc. etc. He wouldn't listen, of course. I now realize what he is doing: as a polemicist, he needs to take an extreme position. And he is, of course, the very opposite of a blind fool.

How did you like his second issue? I thought it a great improvement over the first, and your "Abednego" piece went well.* Though

---

*"A Note on Syllabics," published in *The Fifties*, Second Issue, 1959.

somebody—you or Robert—cut it down from the version I saw, it is still clear and therefore immediately useful.

For the most part, I've been just translating and thinking. I keep a journal again, and it is certainly a confused document. But I don't care. Don't let me get started on that damned self-analysis again.

Here is one poem of mine that Robert is going to print in his next issue:

THE DREAM OF THE AMERICAN FRONTIER
            On First Avenue,
            Seattle,
            The wharf slowly fills its dawn
            With Asian sailors.

            Old men
            Have been shipped out of Chicago
            In the dark.

            Deacons and janitors are drowning
            Sweetly, on the last beaches
            Of bay rum and salvation,
            A flop of graves.

            I wish I were the owner
            Of the sea.

* * *

I have several others, but I'm still picking at them. In a few days I'll type out several and send them to you. Perhaps you could make a few marginal comments and give me a few helpful remarks. This style is terribly difficult. For the most part, I've been trying free verse—though I still try, try, try to discipline myself in syllabics. And I will continue to do so. Of course, I'm a very long way from making them work. They are horribly difficult, thank God.

I'm glad you liked Carolyn [Kizer]'s book, not only for the book's sake, but for the fact that I knew she and you would like each other very much, now that that idiotic misunderstanding is cleared away. And I'm sorry you didn't like Hugo's so well, but that's the way it goes. I still believe very strongly in him, it goes without saying.

Please give my best to your family. Now I'm going to read Meister Eckhart, about two pages an hour. Please keep writing, however briefly.

Love,

Jim

Glenwood Hills Hospital
Minneapolis
[June 1959]

Dear Don,

Well, here I am.

Just as I was finishing my work for the Spring Quarter, and getting ready to begin the first Summer Session on the following Tuesday, I had a mild crack-up. You know, when Dave Wagoner took me to visit Ted Roethke at his rest home in Washington last January, lo and behold! Theodore the Bear, squatting among the other accursed Huns in the violent ward, surveyed my middle fingers—for both hands were stained with nicotine—and quite sanely predicted my collapse. And here I am.

I can't say it's really crucial. On the other hand, it's quite serious enough to knock me out of commission for a month at the very least (according to my doctor, who is by all odds one of the two or three most remarkably civilized men I have ever met in my life). In any case, no matter how long I remain at this excellent hospital, I am certain to undergo an entire summer of rest. You know, last January, when Lib herself—bless her long-suffering heart—had a somewhat milder nervous collapse and had to undergo a brief sequence of electric shock treatments, we received—out of a clear blue sky—three hundred dollars from the Longview Foundation (Harold Rosenberg, Chairman), which enabled us to get Libby straightened out without our having to go into debt. And now that it's my turn, we have the fifteen hundred dollars from the National Institute of Arts and Letters. Of course, there's Blue Cross also, as far as the hospital is concerned; but I was thinking briefly of supporting Lib and the boys. She was immediately willing to go to work again. But to hell with that noise. It is an endless source of wonder to me that her patience survives—but, then, she understood, even better than I, that I was ill, and so she didn't raise any fuss about my taking a separate room until the Spring Quarter ended. She's a jewel, like Kirby—very much like Kirb, in fact. How in heaven's name do the women endure us? You know, I would like to get well, and to be a good man—I really would. (You'll say—justly—that it's about time I got started.) Don, I wish you'd write me as often as you can, here at the hospital. Would you also write Carolyn Kizer? It would mean much to her. And do you think Kirb would write a note to Lib, who's awfully lonely?

Love,

Jim

To Elizabeth Willerton Esterly

Minneapolis

July 7, 1959

Dear Elizabeth,

Yes . . . it's been a couple of months since your great letter came. So what have I been waiting for? Well, there are plenty of answers that might do: I was busy teaching (that answer is phony), I was having the usual troubles (that is phony also), I wanted you to find enough time to read the copy of *The Green Wall* that I sent you (and that answer is fairly true, although it is false to imply that time is inadequate . . . time is adequate, alright . . . I don't know why, but it is). I think the real reason for my delay is in the last parenthesis: there really is plenty of time. You remember how, among my hysterias, the fear of passing time used to figure largely. Well, I fear time less, and grow to love warmth more.

At any rate, your letter was miraculously true in tone, and it showed me at once that this was the simple resumption of a correspondence in a friendship which has always been a source of pleasure and strength. So, without more ado: would you like to correspond? I certainly would. And there are so many things to say, that it is best to relax and take them, simply, one at a time.

Our phone number at home is FRANKLIN 1-7594, in case you ever wish to call.

How is your whole family? What is Henry doing? And why don't you work harder on the chance to teach? And Good God Almighty! I have so many things to say about teaching, that I'm almost afraid to begin. But I love it, and Minnesota is a magnificent place for the likes of me . . . as far as teaching, and many other things, are concerned.

You said, "If it were possible, I would share with you in person" the receipt of the grant. Well, I didn't go to NYC . . . I think I could have afforded it, but there were other things to do, and I didn't want to bother. During the past year I have traveled so far, and done so much work, that I was almost worn out (in fact, I just last Friday returned home from a three-week rest at a hospital . . . please don't worry, I'm already feeling fine, it was just a matter of making myself stop long enough to look around me). But the real point about your sentence is the evidence it gives of your having, somehow in a way which it would be frivolous to analyze, shared the whole thing with me in person. I could hear your voice in the letter.

And that is why I wrote the Koestler line on the flyleaf of the book I sent you. Do you remember where *you* wrote that very line?* It was on the flyleaf of Joyce's *Ulysses*, which you sent to me 12 or thirteen years ago when I was in Japan. You had been feeling kind of worn out and low, and suddenly I sent you a note, by some kind of instinct, which made you feel better. And that was something of the way your beautiful letter affected me. I'm sure you understand.

My new book will be published in September by the Wesleyan University Press (Middletown, Conn.). It is to be called *Saint Judas* (and *that* title will take too much explanation for this letter . . . I'd rather have you read the book first . . . it is very different from *The Green Wall*, far more severe and lyrical, or subjective, in style, and far darker in spirit . . . I regard it as a religious book . . . but those phrases mean little without your having seen the book itself . . . anyway, you'll be sure to receive a copy just as soon as Lockwood, my publisher, sends me the first ones). *St. J.* will be published in hardback and paperback, the latter costing $1.65, thank heaven.

I am sending you, today, a copy of a new magazine called *The Fifties*. You spoke of being irritated at Yvor Winters. Well, I respect Winters enormously, and I love his poetry; but I'm afraid that the word "irritated" will do little to describe the probable reaction of Winters and

*" 'My pain? How do you know?'

" 'Pain vibrates. If you close your eyes and listen, you can feel the radiation of any being in pain . . .' —Koestler" his students to *The Fifties*. The editor of the latter, Robert Bly, is a wild man, a great man I think, who returned from Norway a couple of years back with the idea that Americans had been writing too many iambic poems. Bly knows Scandinavian, German, French, Spanish, Italian. He loves Whitman (that's enough to get him shot). Well, anyway, when I saw the *first* issue of his magazine, all the old Whitmanism exploded in me . . . and also my reading of the modern Germans . . . all the God damned provincial graduate students at Washington used to regard me as a mildly amusing drunk when I railed at them for their ignorance of the gigantic modern poets Georg Trakl, Gottfried Benn, René Char, Pablo Neruda, etc. And now . . . well, I wrote Bly a letter 16 pp. long, single-spaced typed. I tried to write in free verse. And My God! What a teacher Bly is! One of the few honest to God editors living and working in America today, besides Ransom. In the issue of *Fifties* which I'm sending you, there are 2 new poems of mine. I send them because you wondered, in your letter, "what is your great concern." Well, the first of the new poems of mine in *Fifties*, called "In the Hard Sun," took me three months to write, with Bly's hacking and laughing and railing editorial instruction. And I've gone as far as I want to go, for the time being, with iambics in *Saint Judas*. So now I am a writer of free verse, a surrealist, and, most deeply in absorption and interest, a translator. Bly, H. R. Hays of Columbia, and I are doing a book of about 23 poems by the indescribably great poet from Peru, César Vallejo, whom I think I love beyond all others. I am having 10 translations of poems by the 1958 Spanish Nobel Prize winner, Juan Ramón Jiménez, in a book of translations edited by one Willis Barnstone. I am helping N. T. di Giovanni of Boston translate the difficult but rich Spanish poet Jorge Guillén, who has lived practically unnoticed in the US for the past 20 years. And Bly and I are translating 20 poems of Trakl, the Austrian, to be published in a book. I am in on all kinds of exciting, experimental projects . . . But I'd better slow down. I can't say everything at once. Let me know what you think of *The Fifties*.

As for my plans: God knows. In some ways, things are tangled up; but the hell with it, things are tangled up no matter what anybody does. I took the Ph.D. (on Dickens) at Washington last January. I'll be teaching here at Minn. for some time, I hope. Allen Tate is returning this Fall, and he is a terrific man, though he'll be annoyed with me about *Fifties*. That's okay.

You may not be aware of it, because most of them are small, but there are new magazines springing up right now all over hell's half-acre in this over-ripe, benighted, and daydreaming Eisenhooverian country. Please let's keep in touch. My literary associates become more and more radical, and my reactionary acquaintances begin to cringe away in horror . . . I'm not being sarcastic when I say that I find this cringing very funny . . . I have some ignorant acquaintances, who are so-called literary people in universities, who are appalled at the free-verse surrealism of, say, the poet Guillén. And yet he is about twice as sophisticated as, say, Wallace Stevens and J. C. Ransom combined. In America we are barbarous. And the embarrassed look on the face of a barbarian when confronted with something gentle and deeply warm and civilized like Guillén is . . . well, it is comic.

Please write.

Love,
Jim (for Lib and the kids, too)

P.S. On the other hand, I don't *wholly* agree with Bly either. Whitman and E. A. Robinson are not opposites—not by a damned sight. The problem is deeper than the merely metrical one. It is a matter of spirit—don't you think?

To James Dickey

Minneapolis
September 11, 1959

Dear Jim,

I just received your letter this afternoon. I think it's true that you did owe me a letter, but it's silly to talk in those terms, since I had been intending to write you pretty soon anyway. And, though your letter (that came today) raises other topics of interest, none of them is so important as what I wanted to ask you: would you mind going ahead and sending me copies of some of your newest poems?

You see, since I last wrote you, I've spent some time with the Blys on their farm in western Minnesota. We really had a splendid time—putting in fenceposts, visiting local farmers and businessmen in the nearby small town of Madison, getting mildly drunk late in the beautiful summer evenings, and talking, talking, talking. We also did some riding on Robert's beautiful new horse, which was delivered during my visit. Robert and his wife Carol are both very much countryfied people, though they spend about half of each year in New York . . . Anyway, during one of the many conversations, Robert showed me a new poem of yours which made my hair stand on end. I can't remember the title, or even if it had a title; but it was in stanzas of three lines each, and it began with a dog barking, and, before the poem was through, the dog had the moon in its voice. I don't know what Robert intends to do with the poem; but it seemed to me almost wholly successful ("almost" means that, as I recall, there was one word, somewhere or other, that didn't strike me as right . . . I don't have a copy of the poem right here). If it isn't too much bother, could you send me some of the others that you mention?

Robert and I spent some time working on a group of translations, from the German of Georg Trakl, whom I think I've mentioned to you. Something about your own poem, the one with the moon in the dog's voice, felt like Trakl's poems, though his are most often darker than yours, pretty morose in fact. We intend to have about eighteen translations published in the form of a pamphlet.

On the matter of our reading in New York: Robert appeared not to have his schedule completely worked out. However, he did say that we would probably be lined up for some time next Spring. One difficulty may be financial—at least, as far as I am concerned. That is, he said he could pay us something between thirty-five and fifty dollars, and I doubt if that would pay my round-trip fare between Minneapolis and New York. And, the way things are going in my private life (what a hell of a thing to call it!), I will be skimping, perhaps hoboing, by next Spring. In any case, I suggest that you keep in touch with Bly, who ought to know before long exactly what he intends to do.

As far as I know, Don Hall will be going to England soon. Maybe he's gone already. I haven't heard from him all summer. You can well understand that, during my weeks in the hospital, I lost touch with a good many people. By the way, let me step in here to thank you for calling me at the hospital, even though I wasn't there. The very thought of the call did something to lift my morale, just as your letter itself did today.

On Geoffrey Hill: now, as I get it, he is supposed to be at the University of Michigan this year, taking Hall's place. In fact, I have been intending to get in touch with him as soon as classes start. Since Allen Tate (a great admirer of Geoffrey's) will be back here this year, I have been thinking that we might be able to get him to come over to Minnesota to give a reading or something. Are you in touch with him now? Some months ago, I exchanged two or three letters with him; but my own personal troubles, as I say, pretty much cut me off from the world at large.

I am delighted that Hugo has written you, and that you like his poems, for he is one of the finest men I know, and one of the most honest and original writers. A couple of years ago I put him in touch with the Minnesota press people, and they are interested in his book; but their lack of money would make it necessary for them to put off publishing him for a couple more years, even if they decided to accept his book. And it will be a damned good book, too, with one long war poem—called "Mission to Linz"—that is magnificent. If I'm not mistaken, Bly is going to publish part of that poem in *The Fifties*. Dick Hugo has been a very close and highly valued friend of mine for a long time . . . since I first went to Seattle in 1953. He *is* a charming man, with an equally charming wife (a truly delightful person), and he is as thoroughly unacademic in his life as he is in his writing. He has worked for several years at the Boeing Aircraft plant up there. He has had some difficulty in getting his poems published as widely as they deserve. And one trouble with his getting a book published is that his way of writing is so different from what I might call the "period-style" of this decade. Of course, when all is said and done, when all the fashions have passed, that is what will save his poems. However, I too think (as I have thought for a long time) that Hugo's fine book ought to be in print. It was rejected by Wesleyan, and I am pretty sure that their editorial board didn't understand it. It would be an excellent idea for you to ask [John Hall] Wheelock to look at it for the Scribner's series . . . perhaps that series can be rescued yet.

As for me, I try sometimes to write, but it doesn't work very well. The new style is terribly difficult; and, besides, as I've said so often already, things are pretty snarled up here; and, though I'm not physically exhausted, something seems to be blocking me off from poetry itself.

Either tomorrow or Monday I'll send you a copy of *St. Judas*, now that Wesleyan has sent me several more copies. I hope you like it, though it still sounds to me as if the strictly classical iambic style were inhibiting the book somewhat. Maybe I just worked too hard at it to be a competent judge.

Please keep in touch more frequently, as I intend to do.

Yours,

Jim W.

To Robert and Carol Bly

Minneapolis
November 18, 1959

Dear Robert and Carol,

Please excuse me for not writing sooner, to thank you so very much for one of the most fantastic experiences of my life, and to let you know that I got back all right. There was a good deal of work to do, even on Sunday evening; and, true to form, Lib and I had difficulties, terrible ones. However, for some strange reason, things between us have since gone beautifully. Who knows? We may have struck rock bottom, and begun to ascend. Certainly there was no other direction to move in.

I will write Jim Dickey as soon as possible. Your description of him on Sunday was kind of an unhappy one, and it made me feel very sad. Whatever his own struggles may be, he is a good and generous man, as well as a true poet. By God, I don't blame him for desiring to live within some sort of reasonable financial arrangement. I feel the pinch more and more all the time. It seems tragic, that if Jim Dickey lost his pain, the loss would mean that he had become well adjusted to a deathly world. God Christ, what a hell of a "civilization"!

I just today received a note from Willard Lockwood at the Wesleyan Press. It was a little confusing, but, as I get it, the "Poetry Society of America" (whatever that is) wants to award me a citation and some money (damned little—$250), *if* I am willing to attend their 50th anniversary dinner in NYC on Thursday evening, January 21. And they seem unwilling to pay expenses. However, I just wrote to Lockwood and asked him to tell them that I will accept. I have two reasons: since the affair is on Thursday, I'll be able to get someone to teach my classes on Friday, and will stay till Saturday night. That will give me a couple of days in NYC, which is a wonderful prospect. I hate to impose, but could you put me up? The other reason is that, even after expenses, I'll probably have a little money left, and we need everything we can get.

I haven't yet thought, in practical terms, about a job, because so much time has been consumed by teaching and reading. It may be that teaching itself will continue to be a full-time job. Sooner or later I may just give up teaching entirely. If I could find another job that wouldn't be exhausting, I think I would take it, at least for a while . . . a couple of years or so. In any case, my mind seems to be operating again. I just can't possibly tell you how much those few days with you in NYC did for me. The argument at NYU cleared my own mind considerably, about the relation between one's love for the past and his need to speak of the present in his own language, his own voice. In other words, I think I clearly rid myself of a dark guilt as far as iambics are concerned. I mean the sort of thing involved when somebody tries to make you admit that your desire to write in the new style is, in some obscure way, a betrayal of all that you love. But that destructive misinterpretation of things is not the issue, and I think we clearly eliminated it on Friday night . . . Well, onward and upward. Carol, you were, and are, magnificent. I hope you're getting settled now. Please give my best to Mary. And keep in touch. Best from Lib.

Love,
Jim

To James Dickey

Minneapolis
November 19, 1959

Dear Jim,

My God, here it is Thursday already, and I haven't yet written to tell you—or rather, to suggest to you, since I could never really tell it in a thousand years—how much it meant to me to be with you and Bly last week. Again and again I see you, saying so magnificently, with such enormous faith and strength in the face of all the absurd pain of things: "No, we're not going to die tonight." I wonder if you've thought much about that statement, or if you just tossed it off. In either case, it contains just about everything poetry has to say, as far as I'm concerned.

I want to say also how sorry I am to have missed you on Sunday. The Blys told me (in a note) that you did indeed come over to their place, and were also sorry not to have seen me off, etc. We didn't try to disturb you, because we thought you would be sleeping in. I myself would certainly have slept longer, but I had to catch the plane at noon. Well, no matter. I have deep inside me (God! it's been so long since I had any such feelings of deep faith!) the certainty—not just the hope, but the *certainty*—that we will meet again, and soon, and be able to talk once more at great length, in utter imaginative freedom, about what simply matters. Here's a possibility, though a vague one: this week Wesleyan informed me that, on the evening of January 21, the so-called "Poetry Society of America" wants to award me some sort of citation at a dinner in New York City. They're only giving me $250, and no expenses, and, since I'll have to fly both ways, this means that damn near all the money will be eaten up by the trip. But I figured, what the hell, I'll go anyway. Now, when are you to be in NYC again? I don't exactly remember when you said you would be, but I faintly recollect it would be some time in January.

I'm very glad you brought Dave Johnson over. He is a wonderful man, one of the most uniquely human and naturally generous men I ever met. For one reason or another—I suppose I should have said for one horribly entangling reason or another—I have to spend just about all of my inner, imaginative life in cautious solitude. So—to get back to my former inarticulateness—I can't really describe what it meant to feel free to emerge into that tremendous, ample sunlight of noble and heroic men with whom I spent those three days, drinking the great green waters of the first and last seas. Maybe now I can just face the fact of my own alienation, maybe I can realize—in such a way as to be able to work—that you have your own alienations and yet are able to fulfill your humanity, your (I can't withhold the word, and I hope it doesn't embarrass you) greatness, in those poems that you read, poems that, in the face of all the hostility and blindness and deafness and absurdity around us, make sense in some kind of ultimate and tragic and triumphant way.

What I mean to say is that I feel changed—perhaps restored, saved. I think I can go on now.

Let's keep in touch when we can. And hang on. Because, by God, we're not going to die. Not tonight, anyway.

Yours, in entire and grateful friendship,

Jim

To Henry Rago, Editor of *Poetry*

Minneapolis
November 25, 1959

Dear Mr. Rago:

Of course your suggestions for revisions in my review were reasonable; and all your points are well taken—with the possible exception of the phrase "classic comics" on page 4, line 3. The fact is that I don't know whether the word is "classic" or "classic*s*." I always use the latter word when I mention these comics in conversation. (I guess I should buy some . . . long ago I read *Hamlet* in classics comics, and it is marvelous. Hamlet's dying speech: "I, too, must go to join my dead father. Aaaaaaaaaaaaagh!") [. . .]

To Robert and Carol Bly

Minneapolis
December 13, 1959

Dear Robert and Carol,

Today is my birthday. It is also Heinrich Heine's.

Here are versions of two prose poems by Trakl:

WINTER NIGHT (*Dichtungen*, pg. 149)

Snow has fallen. After midnight, drunk on purple wine, you leave the dark areas of men, the red flame of their hearth. Oh the night's darkness.

Black frost. The ground is hard, a bitter taste in the air. Your stars lock themselves up at those evil symptoms.

With stony footsteps you trample along the embankment, with wide eyes,* like a soldier storming a trench. Avanti!

*In the margin: "your eyes wide open?"

Bitter snow, moon!

A red wolf, that an angel is strangling. Your skeleton clatters, striding, like blue ice, and a smile full of grief and arrogance has turned your face into stone, and your forehead, faced by the sensual frost, is white;

or else it bows silently over the drowsing night watchman, sunk down in his wooden shack.

Frost and smoke. A white jacket of stars burns on your laboring shoulders, and the hawk of God strips flesh out of your metal heart.

Oh the stony hill. Silently melting away and forgotten, the cool body has fallen in the silver snow.

Sleep is black. For a long time, the ear follows the path of stars in the ice.

When you woke, bells were ringing in the village. Out of the gate in the east, the silver day walked, opening like a rose.

* * *

(Note: I took liberties with the very end. The rest of it is close to literal, I think.)

Here's the other one:

. . . (LAST PART OF "OFFENBARUNG UND UNTERGANG,"
p. 194)

I came on silver soles down the thorny stairs, and I walked into the whitewashed room. A light burned silently in there, and, without making any noise, I wrapped my head in purple linen; and the earth cast up a child's body, an image of the moon that slowly stepped out of my shadow; and with broken arms the stone cover-lid sank down, filaments of snow.

* * *

I think the second is interesting, and I think I've got it right *except* for the phrase "with broken arms" all the way to the end. The images are marvelous, but I haven't got their connection clear. Will you please check the original? Yes, I know that it would be easier, and more sensible, to ask some authority on the German language hereabouts; but somehow I can't get rid of the stubborn idea that it is better for us to grope our own way through these poems. The farther we keep from mere paraphrase, the better. Does that make sense? I wish there were a clear way to state it. I'm haunted by what that lady asked me at NYU: "how much Spanish do you know?" Very little. I am trying to *discover* it, the way an explorer discovers a new continent.

Having spoken thus smugly, I feel silly asking for further help on Vallejo. Anyway, will you all do me a favor? Please ask some Spanish or Puerto Rican friend there to explain the literal meaning of Vallejo's poem called "Espergesia" (by the way, what does the title mean? I can't find it in the dictionary). I would like to make sure I have the whole poem right (it is on p. 113 of that monograph on Vallejo published in 1952 by the Hispanic Institute), but the passage that especially bothers me is the following (in the fifth stanza):

> . . . *Y que no me vaya*
> *sin llevar diciembres,*
> *sin dejar eneros.*

I can do the rest. And I want very much to finish the translation of this poem, which thrills me as nothing has done for ages. I think it is really sublime.

Thank you, Carol, for the beautiful invitation to sleep on the poet's pad, and for the offer to meet me at the airport. I will let you know the time and place in plenty of time. And thank you both, also, for having NYU send me that check. I don't know exactly when I'll come to New York. The dinner (at the Waldorf Astoria, wherever that is) of the PSA is on Thursday evening, January 21, at 7 p.m. Do you belong to the PSA? What is it, anyway? They sent me a report on the minutes of some meeting they had in October, and it sounded like a meeting of the Junior Order of the United American Mechanics. But they are giving some kind of citation to Robert Frost, and Robert Graves, and W. D. Snodgrass . . . by the way, it just occurred to me that it might be nice to get hold of Snodgrass that evening (I've never met him, but I take it that you know him), after the PSA gathering, so that we could talk about *The Fifties* etc. What do you think? . . . Things have been comparatively quiet around this place, but this afternoon we have to go to a cocktail party (hi Terry, hi Shakespeare, g'night Lil, good night ladies, good night sweet ladies, good night, good night. Ta ta!), and Lib has taken to giving me hell for outraging and insulting people, so that we never, or but rarely, get invited anyways anywheres. But I don't try to. I'm not trying to act like a school-marm's idea of a "poet." All I can say is: I do my best.

I've made some notes on rhythm which I'll send one of these days, when I expand them to include some other ideas. For the rest, I'm reading a lot of fiction: *Crime and Punishment* again! What a tremendous thing that is! Please keep in touch often.

Yours,

Jim

Minneapolis

January 31, 1960

Dear Robert and Carol,

You know, I have recently reread two reviews written by Louis Simpson and published in the *Hudson Review*. I now understand better his remarks, in the letters you read to me, about academicism. I wonder if they are putting direct pressure on him out there. Anyway, just after I got back from NYC, an ironic thing happened—ironic, because I had just come to feel that I was getting better and, one way or another, could go on living. Morgan Blum (I don't know whether you know Morgan or not) came to visit us briefly one evening, and with the usual circumlocution made it clear that my job here is in danger. That is, it develops that this mania for publication is a complex one. It's true that I've published many poems and essays. However, as far as some people in this department are concerned, the publication of these things has actually worked to my disadvantage. That is, they feel that, as Morgan puts it, "the department has enough poets already, like Berryman and Tate, and they feel that I could do better elsewhere." Well, having sweat my guts out over a Ph.D. dissertation on Dickens, I visited Clark the other day, and reminded him that I was not, and did not intend to be, a teacher of poetry, or "creative writing," as it is called. He was sympathetic—really. But he put the same question that Morgan did. If I want to teach 19th century fiction, then why don't I publish essays about it? That is, where is the evidence that I know something about it. Well, I had thought—naively, it appears—that my having written a dissertation on the subject should constitute some evidence. But apparently not. So they don't mean that they want evidence of my knowledge of the subject. Publication seems to signify something else. But what? I don't get it.

Another pickle I have got myself in is this: it seems, according again to Morgan B., who has the sweetness of Mephistopheles, that my getting sick last summer actually jeopardizes my position as a teacher. I would have been promoted otherwise. What do you make of that? Well, I am already assured that I can stay here at least another year as an instructor. Whether I'm to be promoted or not (and given a living wage with which to support my family) depends on what they decide in the Spring.

What a mess.

If they decide not to give me a decent raise, I don't know what I'll do. Oh, yes, I know that I'll probably grin at massa and smile like a spaniel. What I would like to do is quit teaching, get the hell out of here, and just set off blindly away from this life which, no matter how I try to compromise with it, is nothing but futility and despair.

Lib doesn't have the faintest idea what I'm talking about. This isn't her fault. And I know that I am responsible for this family, and can't desert it.

I see less and less reason for bothering with anything. Anything at all. I know I am too tangled in the wrong kind of life ever to get out of it. I just wish I could forget the despair.

The other night, while I was in bed, the phone rang; but it stopped ringing before I could get to it. It was probably Bill Duffy. If he doesn't call again soon, I'll call him. I was reading his poems again, and they are truly extraordinary. When I talk with him, I am going to persuade him, if possible, to let me send a bunch of them to Rago. God, I shudder to think of what is happening to him. God damn it to hell, how does anybody go on breathing through this snarl of a life?

Carol, Franz wants me to thank you for the postcards. And thank you, again, for your hospitality and patience with me.

If I am going to teach at all, I may as well stay at Minnesota. It is almost certain to be even worse in other places.

I'm awfully glad that you got to visit with the Mathews again, and to introduce M. Bonnefoy to them.

Will you please send me Tony Hecht's address? I want to correspond with him.

Well, I've got to snap out of this self-destructiveness. By God, by God: soon I'll send you some new things. There are some blessed hours of solitude that I spend with them very early each morning.

You know, I sometimes try to escape the thought, but it returns and returns and returns: that some day I shall rise at morning and simply walk outside and away, leaving everything behind, like Buddha. Yes, I shall be killed by a runaway checkbook or an insane life-insurance policy by the time I get two blocks from home.

Home. Home.

Please write, and send the Trakl when you can. I'll send you the two prose poems as soon as I type them.

Yours,
Jim

To James Dickey

Minneapolis
February 13, 1960

Dear Jim,

The recent trip to NYC went off okay, but I wish to God you had been there. The dinner of the Poetry Society of America was in many ways quite strange. I suppose I would describe it as a long, long, long evening composed of weirdness and boredom. I had to wear a tuxedo—the first one I've ever worn—and, between the various people at the long table on the dais who were being cited for one thing or another, there were many ladies with names like Gertrude Crumlett Sturdley who were also given awards for having written the best-double-sestina-on-the-joys-of-mowing-the-lawn-in-Connecticut etc. Robert Graves spoke extemporaneously and ramblingly, but I found him to be tremendously impressive in appearance. Most impressive of all was Marianne Moore, who was given a gold medal, and who is truly a magnificent human being. W. D. Snodgrass was also there: we didn't get any chance to talk, and even when he showed up at Bly's apartment the next afternoon I was already drunk and talking at length with Richard Gibson the novelist and with the marvelous Yves Bonnefoy, a French poet who had just got in town and looked up Bly at once. Bonnefoy especially was really something; and for his sake and yours, I just wish to God you had been there, Jim. Ah, God damn it, we have got to work out another trip to NYC! My publisher from Wesleyan was in Minneapolis a couple of days ago, and he said I might be invited to read at Wesleyan sometime in the Spring. If this works, we might possibly see each other, since you'll be at the YMHA in the Spring. Anyway, let's keep plans coordinated . . . Perhaps most exciting of all on the recent trip was the visit we paid on Saturday to Dr. and Mrs. W. C. Williams in Rutherford. I don't know if you've met them; but, if you haven't, then I despair of describing them. They are not quite like any other people I have ever met. Williams himself is an honest to God great man. What Norman di Giovanni recently wrote me about the old Spanish poet Jorge Guillén could be applied perfectly to Williams: he looks young men right in the eye as an equal. It was tremendously heartening to see him.

I came home and exploded into a lot of writing; and I thought you might like to see what has been happening.* What I enclose is just a selection, because, with whatever time I could find, I've been working even further on the translation of Vallejo. Speaking of Vallejo, here's a short passage of his poem "Pilgrimage" which I just finished translating. The poet is walking through a cemetery with a woman:

> Beloved, we walk on the fragile edge
> of a heap of earth.
>
> A wing goes by, anointed with oil,
> with purity. But a blow,
> falling somewhere I don't know of,
> grinds a hostile fang
> out of every tear.

---

*See Appendix, pp. 574–583, for the poems "A Bus Ride," "The Doors," "Morning Song," "Bells," "At the Great Northern," "The Empty Mill Field at Aetnaville, Ohio," "The Night Clerk in Pennsylvania," "The Vain Season," "Year Changes in the City," and "Prayer for Several Kind Women." See also p. 572 for "Walking Around," by Pablo Neruda, translated by H. R. Hays. The selection of poems in draft enclosed with this letter also included six poems subsequently published in slightly revised form: "Confession to J. Edgar Hoover," "Rain," "Snow Storm in the Mid-West," "Miners," "Spring Images," and "Twilights."

And a soldier, a huge soldier
comes back to life in the heroic evening,
with his wounds buckled to his shoulders,
and he laughs, and holds at his feet
the brain of life, like the hideous
reins of a horse . . .

Isn't that something?

Speaking of something, that poem of yours in the *Wormwood Review*
(what a glorious title for a magazine!) was one of your most deeply
moving. I'm looking forward to your book with a feeling of real joy . . .
my God, just when I was on the edge of the pit, you and a few others
have led me into a strange forest, a great green ocean of trees, and,
and, well, please write soon. I hope you are well. Please give my love to
your family.

Yours,

Jim

To Robert Bly

Minneapolis
February 18, 1960

Dear Robert,

Excuse me for waiting till today to get the enclosed three short poems of Lorca into the mail.* I got the big collected poems from the Library on Monday, as I planned to do, and I copied the poems a day
later, and then one thing after another happened, and here it is Thursday. Two different people during the past couple of weeks have asked
me to lecture their classes on Dickens, and one of these lectures had to
be given last night. I had only one day's notice. It went all right, and I
enjoyed it; but the preparation pressed me somewhat.

Dickens is a lot of fun. I can't get over the great novel *Martin Chuzzlewit*. During Martin's visit to America, he remarks to one American
that another American (chewing tobacco, spitting, flashing his bowie-

*See Appendix, p. 586, for the poem "Afternoon," translated from the Spanish of Federico Gar-
cía Lorca.

knife) is behaving like a slob. The American justifies the other American in these words:

> He is a true born child of this free hemisphere; bright and flowing as our mineral drinks; unspoiled by withering conventionalities as are our broad and boundless Perearers! Rough he may be. So are our Barrs. Wild he may be. So are our Buffaloes. But he is a child of nature, and a child of freedom, and his boastful answer to the Despot and the Tyrant is, that his bright home is in the Settin' Sun.*

Did you happen to see Tony Hecht's long book review in the Winter *Hudson*? I think it was pretty intelligent. He may have been excessively generous; on the other hand, he certainly read everything closely. I am especially pleased with the close criticism he gave my book. He gave it hell, but he *read* it. There was a very depressing stock-review of it that just came out in the *Kenyon Review*, and so Tony's article was a particular relief. The best thing in his review was the deserved praise he gave to Louis Simpson's book. I often hear Simpson mentioned by people who seem either not to have read his poems at all or to have read them with no intelligence. The trouble with my own book, as Hecht so clearly shows, is that it is deeply torn by personal confusions; and maybe I will never resolve them. Simpson, I think, is much more of a poet; that is, he is not so agonized by guilt and the bitter, really desperate anger at the absence of happiness in his human life—perhaps he has found such happiness. In any case, he has been able to accept the fact that he is human in this horrible world without for a moment letting such acceptance degenerate into self-satisfaction. On the contrary, his mind is amazingly alert, and his imagination very rich and inventive. His strong stance as a man is something that you always can feel, and it is a stance that lets him make his poems one at a time, and you can read them one at a time. They always give me a wonderful sense of liberation. I don't know quite why, but it is a feeling that the best poetry can give. I may as well admit that I am still very deeply torn by things: by different views of poetry—rather, by different feelings about it—and of life. I must say, Robert, that your own letters and

*See *Martin Chuzzlewit*, chapter 34.

234

other writings have given me a good deal of hope; and yet there re-mains what I am coming to regard as a kind of error in your psycho-logical strategy. It is true that there is something wrong in American poetry, and that a change is needed. However, changes are taking place everywhere, and they seem to occur individually, so that, in some mys-terious way, they suddenly may accumulate into a movement. You yourself very vigorously recognize the need for change, and your men-tion of the possibilities available to us in other literatures is a great, a major statement—or it would be, if you offered it as a possibility (the opening of a door) rather than as what you still too often seem to make it: a despotic command. Do you see anything in what I say? Let me try again, for I'm not being very clear: I am finding that, for me, any ab-solute position in the discussion of poetry is a position that something deep inside me instinctively rejects. Somehow, every absolute com-mand that my imagination hears is almost immediately turned into an insistence on its opposite—and this takes place not only as an assertion of the imagination's freedom; but also as a desire to subversively over-throw all the critical absolutes. Let me go further: in my own work, the iambics started to stiffen and then wither. I needed the green waters to flow into what I tried to write. But I think I need the green waters of possibility, and not the glacier of command. If Yvor Winters argues ab-solutely that Whitman is wrong and insane, my imagination instinc-tively moves to the side of Whitman; but when you argue that Winters is absolutely wrong, then my imagination—very subversively—reacts against your absolute statement also, and reveals to me all sorts of true poetry in Winters (and it is indeed there, just as it is in Whitman).

This is a problem that I will have to think about. But I have other thoughts about *The Fifties*, and the position that you take, or seem to take. But the growth of one's imagination requires not only the courage to break away but also the patience to let the green roots of the water find their own channels. Robert, am I making sense? Yvor Winters can certainly kill the plant by denying it water. And yet you can't *force* the flower to grow, you can't *command* it to grow. Even when someone floods it with water, it can die. And then it sometimes comes to life again when no one is looking. Well, please write me. Best to Carol.

Yours,
Jim

P.S. I'm to ask Princess Caetani if she can put our poems in the Spring *B.O.* [*Botteghe Oscure*] side by side. Then maybe she could give us some offprints. That would be nice. Or do you think so?

To Robert and Carol Bly

Minneapolis
March 3, 1960

Dear Carol and Robert,

I want to write at this moment and say how I too am delighted—that isn't the word for it—over the Trakl translations. Just a little while ago I went over them, and to do this after leaving them alone for a few days is to see how they really do sound—and look, and feel—like Trakl's own poems. It was a good idea of yours, Robert, to include the "Abendländisches Lied" . . . you received the version that I sent, didn't you? My God, I hope you did, because Bill Duffy was here last Saturday night, and I gave my copy of that version to him, so he could read and study it, and write suggestions on it.

I received the translations today when I felt terribly depressed, and they lifted my spirits. I am really living a very curious kind of life: I think I understand Lib's grievances against me much better now, and I certainly can say that I'm not angry at her as I was, and I can understand—without lying to myself—that she is a very fine good person, capable of great devotion; and yet it remains true that I can't wander off in imagination or meditation (to think about something I'm trying to work on) without first of all *realizing* that Lib disapproves (i.e., I am simply loafing when I should be working) and then definitely and distinctly *defying* her, so that I can go on meditating. In other words, Lib approves of poeg(no, I'm not going to write "poetry," I'm going to write "poegry," just as the typewriter wanted me to do)ry, but the only part of the writing of poems that she acknowledges is the actual slaving away at the desk. Worst of all is the fact that—I must face this—the fact that I have absolutely failed to explain to her. And I give up. And yet, as I said, her grievances are real. I really hurt her. I have no real grievance. I am just alien, that's all. My relation to everyday life, in short, is incredibly tortured. The only thing I can think of doing is to gather up whatever strength I can find, perform the inner gesture of defiance (it is hopeless to expect her to understand any explicit gesture), and then go on working.

At the moment, I am awfully pushed by affairs at school. So much work to be done continually. But somehow—God, literally, God knows how—I am going to hang on, to the translations at the moment and to other poems when they return. It is really very much like a man fallen overboard, clinging hopelessly and yet by pure subconscious instinct to a rope whose other end is held by somebody he can't even see, on the other side of a cloud of fog.

I enclose, once more, stages of Vallejo. They speak for themselves. Please go over them when you can. It occurred to me this morning again that Vallejo has poems of different kinds—different kinds of images, and different kinds of situations—and we might consider arranging them in that way. For example, he has several love-poems written about prostitutes. In this kind of poem, he is almost always walking alone in the rain in some city, Paris or Lima, and remembering the girl. I've been working recently on one poem of this kind. It's called "Poema para ser leído y cantado," and I made the following entry into my journal: "There are about 5 whore-poems of this kind—the thing is that V. is always deeply involved, as a male and as a human being, with the professional lovers whom he picks up—and he seems to carry the smallest details about them—their slight, unconscious and yet uniquely *characteristic* gestures of hands or feet—in his imagination, wherever he goes . . . It is crucially important to translate these strange love-poems *without* any tough-talk, any slang of the kind that some recent idiotic translators of Catullus have used, in short without any implicit denial of tenderness. I.e., the diction in V's poems to and about whores is delicate and respectful to them, as women and as human beings. Vallejo says *Thou* to prostitutes. Society considers whores inhuman. Even the whores themselves agree, and so they talk tough. What V's diction reflects is his tacit assumption that whores are women. It is really a very revolutionary idea. This ripple of male tenderness is what we must capture in English." And so on. Anyway, I enclose some more Vallejo material.

Thank you so much for the Trakl. It meant more to me than I can describe, especially today. In a moment I must go upstairs to the evening meal. Do you remember Sisyphus in hell, forever pushing the enormous boulder up the slope, getting to the top, slipping, and having it fall down again, again and again and again, forever? In a moment I must go upstairs to the evening meal.

Happy new year.

Yours,

Jim

To W. D. Snodgrass

Minneapolis

March 31, 1960

Dear Mr. Snodgrass:

I know that sounds pompous, and I would like to address you by your first name—do you mind?—but I don't know how to spell it.

It is very early in the morning, and I am writing this note, at long last, to tell you how glad I was to meet you last January in New York—and how honored also, in view of your extraordinarily beautiful poems.

I don't know if any reviewer has noticed, or mentioned, how very comely (I like that old-fashioned word) *Heart's Needle* is in its wholeness, its shape as a book. Somewhere, and a long time ago, Robert Frost remarked that a book of, say, 24 poems ought really to be 25 poems—the 25th being the shape of the book itself. That is the really true classical idea of comeliness, seemliness—a form of things that unobtrusively shapes a reader's whole self, imagination, soul. I suspect that's why so many readers have gone beyond mere admiration and praise of your book, and talked about it as they would talk—astonished—about an unexpected personal favor from a good man whom they didn't even know they knew.

Well, excuse that ramble (rumble?). On second thought, *don't* excuse it. By God, it's true. Why can't I write that directly and truly when I'm writing a book review? All hack reviewers will spend eternity in hell, writing magnificent vital critical essays which will be perpetually rejected.

Will you please give my very best to Jerry Enscoe and his family if you see them? Ask him to write me. I'll be in touch with him soon.

Again—it was very good to meet you. I'm sorry we didn't get much chance to talk. I hope we will get the chance sometime.

Damn it, this note sounds as stuffy as I had dreaded a letter might sound. Anyway—

Yours,
Jim Wright

To Carol Bly

Minneapolis
April 3, 1960

Dear Carol,

Thanks for your note. Yes, I promise not to give your phone number to any Talented Young Person. What I want to do with your phone number would not even bring a blush to the cheek of any Talented Young Person. I just want to put it into my little address book in case I get lost in New York. I have many kinds of neurosis, but some are more neurotic than others. For example, since I am nearsighted and all that, I still keep expecting to walk into a movie theater, blind, and sit on somebody's lap. In the same way, I keep expecting to arrive in NYC without having informed you of my coming, and not knowing how to phone you. It would be nice to get lost that way; but I still thought I should phone you and at least say goodbye.

It's true that Mrs. Sexton's poems sound like Lowell's new poems, except that I think they are better. But that is neither here nor there. The hell with it, and all that. As for her looking beautiful and intelligent, I never saw a picture of her. When I was in the east a year ago last fall, I briefly met her, but I remember only vaguely what she looked like. She was tall, and very thin, and jumpy. Her poems struck me as being really about something, not just empty fake imitations of Lowell's worst mannerisms. But, as Tristram Shandy says, "I will not argue the matter. Time wastes too fast." Or, more truly I guess, I take my stand with H. Allen Smith: I don't believe in anything, and therefore I am perfectly safe; and when I die I am not even going to be buried; I am going to be cremated by special arrangement with a friend, and then be shot out of the guns that they used to shoot puffed-wheat out of on that old late-afternoon radio program, Hop Harrigan. Do you remember that great commercial about puffed-what (I was going to write "puffed-wheat," but look what this wonderful typewriter did!: "puffed-what!")? The announcer would say: "It's Shot from GUNS!" His voice would give about four accent-marks to the word "guns," and then there would come the sound-effect, the sound of a Big Bertha cannon exploding and reexploding, with many echoes, BLAT-BLAT-BlAt-*blat*-blat-OOOO-sigh-spasm-fadeout.

Please tell Robert that I have arranged to go over the Trakl (the last time, for I've already checked the syntax myself with the various other printed translations I mentioned earlier) with Frank Wood sometime this coming week. Then I'll be coming to NYC on Friday. I'll let you know what time I arrive. If there is any hitch at the last minute, you can phone me at CH 2-6624.

I've seen, for the past month, an ad in the back of the *Nation*, to the effect that Kenneth Rexroth is trying to rent a room from somebody "either in Chelsea or the Village" for the month of April. Do you think we could find out where he is? Yes, I know, we'd be Talented-Middle-Aged Women, trying to Get Kenneth To Help Us With Our Work. Still, he is a good and true man, and it would be interesting to hear what he thinks of the magazine. What do you think? I swear to God, Carol, that this time I won't bring anybody up to your apartment: no more Talented Yung Poisons. The only thing I plan is to phone Oscar Williams, and I will go see him alone.

And I haven't heard from Betty Kray. So I don't know what's up, about other readings.

I have got a couple new poems. One is called "Poem to Commemorate General Eisenhower's Visit to Generalissimo Franco in December, 1959." It still creaks somewhat, and, as a Talented Young Person, I would like to discuss it with Robert. I want to give it to David Ignatow, who wrote me again about his Fall issue of the *Chelsea Review*.

Oh, I almost forgot: There is a bookstore and magazine store in downtown Minneapolis called Schinder's (628 Hennepin Ave.), and the owner asked me to ask you to send him 10 (ten) more copies of the third issue of the *Fifties*. He's sold out, and everybody is asking for it.

I'm sure to forget this: if you remember, will you remind me to buy that Hispanic Institute monograph on Miguel Hernández? I've got a couple poems of his in the works, and I want more.

That's all I can think of right now. I've got to get back to my study of the Old Bolsheviks, for my wonderful Humanities class, the advanced one where we're reading a lot of good stuff.

Right now Lib is at church with the kids. She is pretty well, and I know she sends her very best.

Yours,

Jim

To Ben Belitt

Minneapolis

April 6, 1960

Dear Mr. Belitt:

It is very early in the morning, and I have been sitting here reading, as I do so often, in *Wilderness Stair*. I just remembered that it has been a long time since I wrote you even a note. In fact, I never properly thanked you for sending me your beautiful book. So I thank you now. I am sure you know already how grateful I am for it. It's not only the fineness of the poems themselves that means so much to me, but also the patience, the truest virtue, with which the whole book was put together. Perhaps that's not clear: I mean that I have so far ruined so many poems through haste, that to know of the faith in the language itself that your book shows is both a comfort and a sustaining power.

I have also seen various occasional translations of yours, of which I especially admire the really astonishing "Springtime Salvation" of Jorge Guillén that appeared some months ago in the *Virginia Quarterly*. I don't know whether or not Norman di Giovanni has mentioned to you that I have also been contributing to the labor of translating Guillén. My Spanish isn't exactly masterful; but I wanted to read the poems in the original, and translation is a good way to learn how. I feel a little hesitant about bothering you, but . . . do you happen to have had any offprints made by the *Virginia Quarterly*, offprints of "Springtime Salvation"? If so, and if you have a couple of them to spare, I would dearly love to have them. I just want to give them to a couple of friends.

I've seen other translations—like the fine "Snow" of Quasimodo in the March 12 issue of *The Nation*. Seeing it, I grew curious about the progress of your work on the most recent poems of Neruda. And I also wondered whether or not you have ever thought of publishing a little book of translations—poems from various poets in Spanish and Italian. This is just an idle thought of mine . . . but I know it would be a book worth having.

I've met a young Colombian named Carlos de Francisco Zea. He studies at the University of Chicago. Soon he will publish a booklet of about forty poems of Jiménez. His translations are lovely, much better than any others I've seen. When the book appears, I would like to send you a copy.

I hope you are well, and that your teaching is as fruitful as your writing. That reminds me. I also saw your longish poem in *Poetry* a few months ago, and admired it very much [. . .]

Yours,
James Wright

To Robert and Carol Bly

Minneapolis
May 11, 1960

Dear Carol and Robert,

It was wonderful to see you today. Carol seemed somewhat less harried, but, even so, I'll bet it'll be a blessing to get back on the farm. After a while—after all the phone calls, the people, the almost insane assault on your life, on your very self—you feel like breaking out with hives or something. A good friend of mine who teaches over at Macalester in St. Paul was asked, by the Dean or someone, to state what was, in his opinion, "the greatest threat to academic freedom of our time"; and he answered, "Faculty committees."

I've been thinking of the two of you since you left. You seemed so sure, so relaxed somehow; and I think it was the very prospect of getting home. It's been beautiful in Minneapolis for the past couple of weeks; a perfect Spring. The farm must be miraculous. Right now it's getting dark outside; and I think of the farm, how spacious and kind it must seem. My God, how I wish Lib and the kids and I could get into the country for a day or so; but we won't be coming out till long after you've had the chance to shake the New York City out of your hair, and after we've finished this and that task.

I'm enclosing those 2 little poems, 2 versions of the one and the finished version of the other. I am really astonished at the Hernández poem—how it emerged. I have been trying to get at it—reach the poem, I mean, the poem still hiding, rather frightened, behind the rhetoric. I think that, in these new poems, I am still afraid myself, and all those little animals sense my fear, and all they do is wait for a long, long time, with their eyes every once in a while looking out between the leaves to see if I've grown patient and trusting enough to let them come out without my putting them into a cage and sending them immediately to *The Partisan Review*.

Things have gone better for us here at home than they have gone for years.

I'll close for now. I like to think of both of you, right this moment, sitting outside on the porch, or maybe walking toward the barn. I wish I could hear an owl tonight.

Love,
Jim

To Willis Barnstone

Minneapolis
May 12, 1960

Dear Willis,

I've been wanting to write you and thank you for sending me your book of poems, which I've read through several times. It is a beautiful book. The single poems that I like best are "Mexico: Avenue of San Juan"; "A Blind Beggar-Musician of Anatolia"; "Disappearance." I would like to remark also on the startling power and clarity of the dedicatory poem.

It certainly was a pleasure to meet you; and I wish there had been more time to talk about the Spanish poets. Robert Bly, as I told you I think, gave me a copy of your translation of Machado, and I have circulated it as much as possible. Perhaps the most wonderful thing that happened to me during my whole trip to the east in April was your writing down those two lines by Hernández on that little slip of paper and giving the poem to me. It was a very deep and magical thing to do, and it made the poem somehow more solemn and solid than merely quoting it would have done. I have been reading the book of Hernández containing his poems written in prisons, and it certainly is a great book, a really great one, not only as the document of a great man but also as the terrifyingly original creation of a great poet.

Please give my best regards to everybody there at Wesleyan.

Yours,
Jim Wright

To Robert Bly

Minneapolis
June 20, 1960

Dear Robert,

Here is the Trakl introduction. If you think it is basically all right, then please edit it as you see fit, in order to save time. My effort was this: to drop the whole academic pose of a "critique," and simply to describe that day in Vienna when I first heard Trakl, in that classroom that was so strangely like a grave . . . a grave from which, right before my eyes, everyone rose from the dead and began looking astonished into one another's faces. In short, the discovery was and is part of Trakl, for me.

If you feel, however, that the whole conception of this piece is wrong—i.e., irrelevant to the book—please write me a note at once, and I'll do another one. But this experience will probably force itself to the surface again.

I'm sorry I've been so long in getting this piece to you. Do you feel the poems are all finished now? We never did work together on "Dark mouth / Inside me," but I have the impression that you've gone through it again yourself. If there are still final problems, can we arrange to get together somehow? We could banish sloth, go through the entire manuscript, and type the final versions just as we finish them (I can type fast), and then send the book right off to the printer, if you like. What do you suggest? Anything you say: if you drive here, it should be a Saturday or Sunday, so I can be with you to work all day. If I come there, the same.

One word about us: we got home all right, after our visit with you, and we were, and are, all right. Robert, I know I distressed you terribly, and I must explain many things: chiefly, Lib and I are both terrifically intense; and we were dreadfully tired . . . the quarter had just ended, and I had to teach again on Tuesday . . . Let me say this: Robert, you were afraid that children would get unbearably on your nerves. I will simply comment for myself: Lib and I have always noted how hard it is with kids to visit even the closest of friends who themselves have no kids; the reason is strange—you can't really catch the fantastic, the downright incredible *rhythm* of children unless you have a couple of your own. I know my kids are hell-raisers; but they seem beautiful to me. They are among the most trustworthy listeners to poetry I have ever met. And you know how nervous *I* am. I think of my family as dark earth, and my roots go there. Well, try to forgive us if we seemed to bring agony to you. There have been great depths and silent places in Lib and me. Our love to Carol,

Jim

Minneapolis
June 20, 1960

Dear Robert,

I just saw the following error in my copy of the Trakl piece: p. 1 (3 lines fr. bottom): "in a world where seeing *and hearing* are . . ." etc. I think that's the only mistake . . . Tell me if you've received a copy of the *Chelsea* # 7, which has 3 of my translations of Vallejo* (the 2 surrealistic ones don't work at all), and a really startling poem of Hernández, translated by Willis Barnstone. He is very devoted to Hernández, you know, and is especially engaged with the poems written during those last 4 years in prison . . . Once more, I would not trade that moment of Barnstone's handing me the 2 lines of Hernández for all that I myself have ever written. It is an immortal, great moment to me, and I cling to it; it has already formed into a poem, but it changes and changes, and I won't write it down till it is satisfied to relax in the sunlight on the beach. If I have to I will wait for it until after I die. How beautiful that moment is, like Guillén's line, "Oh absolute present!"

Love,
Jim

*One of these three translations, "I Am Freed," is included in *Above the River* (1990), p. 100, in a revised version.

To Anne Sexton*

Minneapolis
July 26, 1960

Dear Blessing,

Well! Today is July 26, 1960. Ten years ago I secretly bought and hid this book and another copy which is identical to it in every respect. I have carried the other copy through 10 years, sometimes alive, mostly desolate. I also had an old, very personal copy of Whitman. But once about a year ago, in despair, I tore the Whitman to pieces and thrust it down into the rankest mucky bottom sludge of an old garbage can near a dirty railroad track in Minneapolis; then I burned my manuscripts. Years of them. A symbolic suicide, if there ever was one.

And yet—even when I planned, as I often did, to ignore "symbols" and just get the job over and done with, I never even thought of destroying this book of Edward Thomas. It was always the book I loved best, and I read it only when I was true and real. And I guess that it has preserved my best self when nothing else was preserved by anyone, in any way, anywhere. I am cruel, weak, and corrupted by fear and confusion. That is the most of me, I guess,—I may as well admit it. I am sick of lies.

But whatever in me has been worthy of life, for 10 years, clings to each page of this book. I always (even in the worst times) hoped to be worthy of giving this book to somebody. Oh, I knew you would come. But it was a long time. Thank you for being alive and for letting me give you this book. Because, in letting me give the gift, you give me at the same time a gift in return: myself. I never before knew my self was precious, but I know now.

I just flipped through the pages of the book; and I noticed certain sentences in the introduction by de la Mare which I underlined 10 whole years ago. (It sounds phony, but it's plain truth.)

And . . . and . . . well, read the sentences I underlined!

How? How? How could you have known? I think that, 10 years ago, you must have known.

I can't explain.

*This letter was inscribed on the flyleaf of a copy of Edward Thomas's *Collected Poems*, with a foreword by Walter de la Mare (London: Faber and Faber Limited, 1949). On the facing flyleaf page was written: "J. A. Wright / Old Kenyon 407 / Gambier Ohio 1950."

246

Well, here is one thing de la Mare wrote about Edward Thomas, and I marked it long ago, 10 years ago, for you:

"What he gave to a friend in his company was not only himself, but that friend's self made infinitely less clumsy and shallow than usual, and at ease." To quote another poet I love, "You seem like that." If I were to pray at this moment, I don't think I would say anything at all. I would just get down and lightly kiss the earth. That's the least I can do.

—J.

To Liberty Wright*

Minneapolis
August 12, 1960

My dear Libby,

Sitting down here today, listening to Sibelius in order to keep from going out of my mind, struggling to face at last my own responsibility for my sorry response to your love, sick of my corruptions and betrayals of myself and of everyone who ever cared for me, and clutching about desperately for something that might keep me coherent until I can get to the doctor this afternoon—in this mood,

I suddenly remembered the poem in this issue of the old *New Orleans Poetry Journal* (July, 1956). That used to be a secret we had—I mean that I could always get us fifteen or 20 bucks within 10 days, because old Dr. Ashman, the retired heart specialist who now writes political letters to *The Nation*, took pride in always answering contributors quickly and in paying on acceptance. In those days we really needed quick cash sometimes—nothing serious, just a few bucks for a movie, a record, a silliness that was somehow more profoundly alive and precious than all the longfaced "problems" of life ever could be. In those days, I remember, you sometimes stood and looked over my shoulder as I wrote, and once I was so delighted because you were right there, sweeping, and I called you to see a whole stanza take shape (later it was printed just as it came out that moment: "Witches Waken the Natural World in Spring," I think, that was in the *Gr. Wall . . .*). And, thinking a

*This letter was found in James Wright's copy of the *New Orleans Poetry Journal*; it may never have been sent.

few moments ago about those times, I suddenly remembered something that I had really forgotten, but which I had (honest to God) been unconsciously searching for. Since I want my new book to repudiate the suicidal despair of *Saint Judas* (in the only way it can be repudiated: with some laughter, and happiness, and love—the real love that can absorb anything), I have needed a poem as a cornerstone of the entire book, which is to be called *Now I Am Wakened*. And then I remembered the poem called "To a Girl Heavy with Child."*

I have only one copy of the magazine, so I am sure that I gave you a copy of it as soon as it was published. I never told you, at least I think I never did, that, on the day when I read it aloud in Ted Roethke's class, the comments. First everyone was quiet for a long, long time. Then Roethke said: "Blinked. Jesus Christ!" Carolyn Kizer said: "It's beautiful, and I think you're being very unfair to us, writing something that good." And, after class, some older woman whose name I've forgotten (if I ever knew it, which I probably didn't), stopped me in the door, and said: "If my husband could have felt that—never mind the writing itself—we wouldn't have got divorced."

I am not arrogant in quoting these remarks. I am simply corroborating my own feeling about the poem. I have always considered it the best poem I ever wrote. Whatever else I do or fail to do, for at least once in my life all I had to give in love, sharing of pain, and poetry, all of these, came together in one single and whole moment of life. I am glad I remembered this poem, especially right now. You know, I never published it—not because I thought it wasn't good enough for the book, but for the opposite reason: it was too good for either book, and I used to rationalize my leaving it out of *The Green Wall* and *Saint Judas* by saying to myself that I could use it as the cornerstone of the growth I would have to undertake sooner or later, if I were ever to achieve real manhood and real poetry.

That's true enough; and yet there is a deeper reason. I never put it in a book because it was private and (don't misunderstand my use of the word) sacred to me. I looked at the poem, and I was able to say: whatever I have to give—as man, as poet, as living creature on this earth—is here, and it is good. Here is the blossom which came from the true relation of love and poetry: their mutual fertilization.

*See Appendix, p. 584, for the poem "To a Girl Heavy with Child."

Am I being sentimental? I don't know.

I do know that I was glad I remembered this poem, and I wonder if you would care to glance at it again. I don't want to upset you, and if you would rather not, I will understand. As I sit here, I have no way of knowing myself at all: for all I know, I am a hired liar who has already gone insane and is convinced that his lies are truth; so this old poem is a kind of reassurance, like a compass in the hand of a man lost in a strange forest, or like a signpost in the midst of the desert. The bad things that I do and am are all of them clear, except for the very worst, which leave me with the feeling of being full of spiders and rats. But in any case, I wrote this poem, and therefore maybe I can hang on.

But even if I *can't* hang on, even if I go utterly to pieces, I wish you would look at the poem again anyway, because I wrote it once and it was as near to secure truth as I ever came or maybe ever will come again before I die.

Love,
Jim

To James Dickey

Minneapolis
August 19, 1960

Dear Jim,

In about five or ten minutes, maybe less, I have got to go somewhere. So this may be the shortest note I've ever written you. However, I am writing it to express the sheer delight at your letter that I felt, to ask you to send me some new poems (if you make carbons—Bly hates carbon copies—he says it's too academic, but it sounds neurotic to me), to assure you of a much longer letter as soon as I can get to it (probably tomorrow morning), and, finally, to take advantage of one of those mysterious secrets I found in William James years ago—namely, the importance of making actual *physical* gestures, of maintaining the actual rhythm of a living thing—friendship, poetry, love, boxing, or whatever. I write this note literally for the same reason Dempsey trained regularly: to keep in good shape.

It so happens that I have finally clicked with writing again—God knows where or how it will end, but I have been at it for days; and that is (egotistically, I suppose) one reason I'm even more than usual interested in seeing what you've been writing. I haven't your last letter handy, but you told me of a new poem of yours about looking for Civil War relics somewhere.* Would you send me that one, at least? I've been pondering recently a subject which goes very deep into my life and that of my parents. You see, I was born and raised in southern Ohio, just across the river from West Virginia. Both grandparents and their own forebears are southerners. Since I like my own relatives, and some of them very deeply, I feel very profoundly involved in the Civil War in a peculiarly terrible way. You see, my great-grandparents were in West Virginia about the time it seceded from Virginia, after Virginia seceded from the Union, and yet my great-grandparents had many relatives—close relatives, or *blood* relatives (in that old fashioned phrase, a great phrase that tells the brutal and direct truth about things) in the south proper. Now, I have never got this straight, perhaps because my family has deliberately kept hush about it (if so, who can blame them?): but it is just possible, and in fact I have often suspected, that many of my forebears on both sides of the family, and not too long ago when you think of it, fought on *both* sides in the War between the States: this is not merely a melodramatic fantasy of mine, either, because I have not merely seen (in my childhood) but *lived* and *felt*, in my childhood experience with relatives and *inside myself* during the last few years, this sense of murderous and despairing violence between *immediate close kin*, that lies underneath the Civil War, close to the surface, and somehow gives it its really *tragic* horror. By "tragic" I mean more than sad; I mean tragic in the old formal way, the way that all the giants like Sophocles and Shakespeare undertook to see the most horrible things men have to contend with: and all their tragedies are about violence within families. And so on. I still don't know what I think of all this, but it haunts me, and I want very much to see your poem. Could you send it?

Look, it's now time to take off. More tomorrow. But your letter is splendid. I look forward to your Fall review in *Sewanee*. I hope your gags about Gunn are as spirited in the review as they've been in your letters. First "I shot down Thom Gunn again," and now you speak of "the final ritual slaying of Thom Gunn." Those phrases have the kind

---

*"Hunting Civil War Relics at Nimblewill Creek," published in James Dickey's collection *Drowning with Others* (1962).

of gusto Swift had when he went to work on William Wood the Iron-monger in *The Drapier's Letters*, or (even more wonderfully, *masterfully!*) when he wrote the *Bickerstaff Papers*, which are probably as funny as the human physique can stand.

No word from Bly this week. More soon. Please send the poem. I'll deal with the other details (fine things) in your letter tomorrow.

Yours,

Jim

P.S. If I forget, please remind me to send you a translation I've just done, Vallejo's "Verdict."* Jesus Christ!

To Robert Bly

Minneapolis
September 7, 1960

Dear Robert,

Thanks for your note, and for Louis [Simpson]'s beautiful poem. You know, I had a thought . . . about your words on "that Moloch, *The New Yorker*." I.e., if they should ever ask me to send them every new egg I lay, so they could candle it before I have permission to send it to the farmers' cooperative, etc., I think I would say no—not because I have anything against money (on the contrary), but just because it would be too annoying to have to wait for them to make up their minds about every single thing I would write. You know, it turns the *NYkr* into a kind of Superego. I mean, if you know you have to send *everything* to them, you might be thinking of their "standards" (even if you opposed them) even before you started to write. I am neurotic enough.

But I'm being silly. It certainly didn't bother Louis. This is a beautiful poem. May I keep this copy?

I spent a lot of time this afternoon on the epigraph of Lorca's "Tarde" poem:†

---

*César Vallejo's poem "Espergesia"—translated by Wright with the title "Have You Anything to Say in Your Defense?"—appears in Robert Bly, ed., *Neruda and Vallejo: Selected Poems* (Boston: Beacon Press, 1971).

†See Appendix, p. 586, for the poem "Afternoon," translated from the Spanish of Federico García Lorca.

> *(Estaba mi Lucia*
> *con los pies en el arroyo?)*

I think I can translate it . . . but my translation sounds so absurd, that I'm afraid we've got hung up on something very idiomatic. Anyway, this is what I make of it:

> Was my Lucia
> standing (or walking) in the stream?

or

> Was that my Lucia,
> with her feet dangling in the water?

or

> Was my Lucia
> dangling her feet in the stream?

An *arroyo* is a stream-bed. But the dictionary doesn't help much.

Frankly, I'm afraid of the thing. Why not just omit the epigraph, both Spanish and English? I don't think it would show any disrespect to Lorca to do so, and besides, your point as I get it is to show how he could just write a little poem about "Afternoon" by waiting patiently for it to fill up with little images, like that "gauze painted with little green moons." The epigraph sounds awfully personal and obscure.

This is just my usual long-winded way of saying that I am not able to help very much.

If I can get any help at the university, I will. But tomorrow Lib flies to Cleveland, and will be gone till Sunday. I'm with the kids; so it will be hard to get away. And I know you want to get the 4th issue out of the way. I therefore suggest strongly that you just omit the epigraph. I think it would be perfectly justified.

I also think the Trakl translations look fine.* I look forward to your

---

*See Appendix, p. 587, for Georg Trakl's "Grodek," translated from the German by James Wright and Robert Bly.

introduction; as soon as it arrives, I'll finish mine, and speed it back to you. I think the 20 poems will make an extremely beautiful book. And I'm convinced we were right in waiting so long over these poems. They ripened into meaning for us. If prospective subscribers have complained, we ought to be aware of them, of course; but I think that our translation has profited a great deal by our doing it slowly. Because we had no model to go by . . . that's just the point. We were like Lewis and Clark, tracing out the delicate strange dark places inside Trakl, all alone, without anything from the *past* to guide us. His poems are there, and our translations are like encampments from which we make excursions in among the trees and sudden clearings, and make notes while we interview those odd beautiful little animals in there. So the delay was a ripening. There is a sentence in Meister Eckhart which comes to mind: "God will make up for all the time lost for His sake."

I've been going over the Ohio poems, and they get shorter, and I think better. I also wrote one about Pine Island, which I'll send soon. I think it would be a good idea to have Louis's poem, with the Harding poem, and one of yours, and maybe one of Bill Duffy's, etc., in an issue: "Poems about American History," or something like that . . . Another thought occurred to me: do you think it would be worthwhile to quote D. MacDonald's short passage about Whitman, Baudelaire, etc., "turning their faces away from the market-place"? For, you know, poets in America get hypnotized into fearing that, if they turn away from the market, they won't be poets anymore. It is stupid, but very powerful, and has got to be shaken off, among all the other soporifics . . . I also found a magnificent passage in Ortega's "The Self and the Other," which I'll send soon. It is really tremendous, the best thing of his I've ever read.

Love to Carol,

Jim

To Eugene Pugatch

Minneapolis

September 30, 1960

Dear Gene, old man,

This will be a short note. For, in writing to my oldest and most beloved friend, I will dispense with all rhetoric.

Dan Knudsen came hurriedly to Johnston Hall on Wednesday, and told me you were ill and despairing. It was just before my class. Immediately I responded by asking him to check cablegram and nightletter arrangements between America and England, and made a date for coffee with him (Dan) one hour later (that is, just after my lecture in Humanities). We had coffee, and planned to wire you (as I did, direct) and Dan was to write a nightletter.

I will not enter your own loneliness with smug moralisms and pieties. The ability to face and endure and—most of all—to acknowledge such suffering in its reality is what makes you a great man, a man of greater and fuller character than any I have ever known. You have never failed to sustain me in my own crises of suffering. Time and again you have told me that you were not "advising" me at all, but rather showing concern that I should survive—and not only survive, but prevail, endure. To be one's true self, and yet endure. That is everything. Out of the poverty of heart, the willing poverty that comes from putting off vanity, comes what Shaw calls "life with a blessing." We know that such life matters, and therefore we are among the happiest men of our time. Not the most comfortable. But the happiest. I want to tell you that I am absolutely concerned about you. If you were to summon me to your side at this instant, I would come. If I could not find the money, I would steal it. You know this. I send you every shred of courage and devotion and faith that I may have access to in my whole life, intellectual or physical or spiritual.

Take heart, my friend.

It is a piece of good luck that Geoffrey Hill, whom I consider a genius and the greatest living English poet except T. S. Eliot (greater than Auden), is now back in England. This weekend I am writing and asking him if he will contact you. Now, he is about 27 years old. Here is his address: [. . .] If he can't be reached there, he can certainly be reached in the dept. of English at the University of Leeds. Here are the advantages: Geoffrey is a *good, kind,* earthy man. He is snubbed by the other English "poets" because he is a giant among pygmies. He is strong physically, a solitary, powerful in spirit, a master of English style who recalls Yeats, a real poet. He snarls at arrogant authority of all kinds, is kindly and gentle and humorous and a bit unsure of himself, wholly a splendid person. He is a graduate of Oxford, and knows the place. I met him in the flesh just once, and loved him and his wife immediately. I have corresponded with him at length. Allen Tate thinks him the greatest of the new poets, in America or England, and I wholly agree.

Now, I am writing Geoffrey this weekend (this is Friday afternoon), and asking him if he can contact you. He is the kind of man who will do so, and will not be put off by minor problems. I know what some of your loneliness is about. It is just that: being alone in a place you do not know. You need the contact of the humane and the spiritual. Damn, I wish I knew somebody at Oxford itself, who could come to you.

But you must hold on. Soon music and poetry and laughter and humanity will be on the way. Hold the spiritual stronghold of loneliness and greatness and self-knowledge. Of all the men I know, you have the greatest courage and humanity. I depend on you more than you realize—and in the true, good way, the way which liberates me and makes me a freer and better man.

I will write again soon, and send you some new poems. My own life is going better than I had hoped. All problems are not solved, but I am going to them one step at a time. Remember: our life does not turn on trivialities, but on the stars.

Bless you in every way, my dear friend,
with devotion,
Jim

Minneapolis
October 7, 1960

Dear Gene,

I just received your magnificent letter. And at this moment it strikes me, with an absolute blaze of light, that the rhythm of answers is everything. You are there, and taking heart again: Good! And here I am, in God's name! In twenty minutes I have to go to teach, and I am not wholly prepared. And yet—this is fantastic, but perhaps it is the whole secret—*and yet* I will have plenty to say to the students, precisely because I am being true to my best self in answering your letter immediately, with this note. Length of letters, or of life itself, doesn't matter. Some of us dies anyway. What does matter is that we should keep faith—that means, precisely, that we should live life, in the very teeth of the devil's subtlest despairs and degradations.

So I have to go now. I will write at length as soon as possible. But what shall I send you now? Let's see . . . ah! Here is the final version of my new translation of Rilke's little-known masterpiece, "Christi Höllenfahrt."* It is legible, I think.

I haven't had time to write G. Hill yet. Could you drop him a card? I will do the same.

Love and faith,

Jim

To Carol Bly

Minneapolis

November 7, 1960

Dear Carol,

This is just a note to thank you again for that extraordinarily true and beautiful weekend. Last night, when I reached my solitary room, I remembered the sandwiches you packed for me. I took out one, and ate it (delicious)—but first I just looked at it for a while, and realized how much thoughtfulness and natural generosity the sandwich represented. I never go to the farm but what I feel a little less afraid of life; and the less afraid I am, the more marvelous I find things. I hope you and Robert realize how grateful I am for the chance to come out there. It is always, literally, a healing experience.

Robert's book *is* heartstoppingly beautiful, as you said. It occurs to me that perhaps I didn't make clear to him how thrilled I was by the book—we talked mainly about one of the poems that, in my opinion, needed a small bit of clarification. But the book is thrilling, and the title he's chosen is magnificent.

I had a note, a kind note, this morning from David Ignatow.

I'm afraid I won't be able to come out this weekend. This next weekend, I mean. But we must keep in touch. I keep thinking of that red-tailed squirrel. He absolutely charmed me!

Love to both,

Jim

---

*See Appendix, p. 588, for the poem "Christ's Descent into Hell," translated from the German of Rainer Maria Rilke.

To Madeline DeFrees

Dear Sister Mary Gilbert,

I wonder if I am addressing you correctly? Excuse my ignorance. I was so touched by your kind letter, and by your thoughtfulness in sending me the beautiful book *Springs of Silence*. I too hope that some day we might meet, though at the moment I don't know how I would come to Spokane. However, one never knows about these matters. They work out very strangely sometimes.

I recently had a letter from John Logan, that splendid man. He spoke of you. I think he is unquestionably a great poet, and I do not use the word "great" lightly. It occurs to me that Franz Schneider mentioned your being a little bothered by some of my own new poems, for their breaking with a previous way; and I have the impression (really, just a guess) that you may be dissatisfied with the magazine *The Fifties* (now called *The Sixties*) . . . if you have seen it. Anyway, I beg you to suspend critical judgment until the editor, Robert Bly, has had a chance to publish his article on the work of John Logan. However Bly may have erred on the side of inept attacks and sophomoric humor, the article on Logan's work—so curiously neglected—is an extremely important and valuable piece of criticism, and it is, in my opinion, enough to justify the whole existence of the magazine . . . John Logan and I met only once . . . last Spring in New York City . . . but we have corresponded for some time. Once, when I was ill and in the hospital, he wrote me a long letter, enclosing a new poem of his; and yet we had never even met! He is a noble man, and the mere thought of him always heartens me.

As you know, I think your own work very fine, and I am delighted that you will have some new things in Jerome Mazzaro's *Fresco*, a good and growing magazine.

Devotedly,
James Wright

To W. D. Snodgrass

Minneapolis
November 17, 1960

Dear De,

In about 20 minutes I have to go deliver a 2-hour lecture to an evening class in humanities. But I want to get this letter started, at least [. . .]

Our correspondence is starting to sound, in part, like a macabre game of lifemanship. Let me tell you, briefly and mildly, what is happening to me right now: the dentist has twice postponed pulling my six teeth, and is supposed to do it on Monday morning. Of course, I am tangled in the midst of work at the end of the quarter here. Today is Thursday. Tomorrow afternoon, my wife (with whom I am not living now; that is, I am dying alone) is going to talk with her priest (she is a Greek, you see; I am a democrat) about a divorce. For approximately 2 years we have been carefully and expertly castrating, disemboweling, and otherwise entertaining each other in the perpetual dentist's-waiting-room of our marriage. We have two sons, one 7 and one 3. The older boy is perhaps the only human being in God's more-or-less world (as Eisenhoover calls it) whom I really honest to God love. Do you remember the line in *Miss Lonelyhearts*, when the hero is being seduced by that "ugly woman loud in public"? West says something like this. "He felt like a bottle being slowly filled with warm dirty water." Life imitates art.

Twice now you've asked about my translations and new poems. Forgive (no, the hell with that corrupt and sadistic word "forgive") . . . excuse me (perhaps I should say "drive some bamboo slivers under my fingernails") for not mentioning this yet. When I get back from that class tonight (10 p.m.) I'll type out a couple translations and a couple new poems. I'm working late tonight.

The new poems are sometimes crazier than hell. What else? They are still not good enough. What else?

* * *

Well, it is now 11 p.m. I got back a little bit ago, and typed up three things: one translation from César Vallejo of Peru, and 2 new poems of my own. There are a bunch of shorter, weird ones, but I haven't got that notebook with me here. I don't know about these things. They may be imprecise and too vaguely wild; but, God damn it, they don't have to be. Vallejo isn't. And I don't think we have yet had a poet in These States who can even come near the clarity and precision of Machado and Jiménez. Well, that's hysterical, but you know what I mean. You don't have to say anything about these if you don't want to . . . you know, how things can be a damned psychic burden when somebody sends them to you, and you feel that you've got to either write back a 20 page critique with footnotes and bibliography, or else turn yourself into the sheriff. (I was going to write "in to" . . . but "into" is so nutty!) Anyway, say what you feel like saying . . . and if you feel like saying "Thanks," that's fine. You know what I mean.

* * *

De, on the previous page I started to tell you all my troubles. Frankly, does that bother you? I can see where it might . . . Look, maybe I can speak on this matter by reaffirming my own position about getting analyzed. Now, God damn us every one (as Tiny Tim said), anybody who criticizes or needles me for going to a doctor when I'm sick can go to hell. Think for a moment: it's like saying "I wish you were dead." No, I don't believe it's "wrong" or "inartistic" to go to a doctor; and I don't think anybody is a good writer *because* he needs to go to a mental hospital, whether it's every other year or forever. My own life happens to be a mess right now, but God damn it to Hell, I refuse to die . . . at least, I refuse to give my consent to my death. I made horrible mistakes, I have caused ghastly pain to people I love, and I agree with my wife's damnation of me, and yet I am not going to perish, I am going to take my medicine and live!

Please try to keep in touch.

Yours,
Jim

Minneapolis
December 14, 1960

Dear De,

Thanks very much for your letter, and the poem, which I like. I am relieved that you were relieved (etc.) about not needing to comment. I don't know why, but when I am allowed to read somebody's poetry without having to give a "critique," I feel as if I had been released from prison, or as if I had just wakened from a nightmare in which my father was trying to cut my balls off, or as if . . . you know what I mean. I like the arrangement of no-comment. On the other hand, whenever you see something of mine (that I send you, or that you see in print somewhere), please (I mean it, *please!*) feel equally free, anarchistically and irresponsibly and immaturely free to make any comment whatever, all the way from "Thank you, God" to "By the way, have you ever read *Diseases of the Skin* or *Bob, Son of Battle*, that masterpiece?"

I somehow felt that you wouldn't mind my jeremiad about domestic trouble; but I didn't want to push it too far. In fact, it stings hideously, and yet it is better to go in after it and face it. I feel better, though the problem itself is insoluble. John Berryman has a short poem which kills me, in which he says to his small son, under the same circumstances, "I can only offer you this world like a knife."

I have already cut one of those poems I sent you ("A Whisper to the Ghost") to about half its previous length.* I myself am not quite sure what I'm doing. I have a couple friends out West who mutter to one another that I am getting corrupted by associating with Bly, but that is absurd. I don't even agree with Bly (who is constitutionally incapable of reading an American poem that is iambic), God damn it a poem is a poem. But Bly is not afraid to leap into the dark and wrestle with strange animals. I myself started to feel glib, so I said, the hell with it, and leaped into another part of the forest. I do not know how things are working out *as poems*. But I will say this: I feel alive with them, and I am *seeing* (even though I'm not conveying, communicating) things that I never saw before. And, though it sounds (and probably is) immoral, I am having a hell of a good time with poetry. I had lost that, and to get it back is worth everything.

In your new poem there is a tremendous reserve of energy. Unless I am mistaken, you didn't put "A Flat One" in *Heart's Needle*, did you? That is a great poem. It absolutely knocked me flat myself; reading it, I was sure, absolutely certain, that you had claimed for the human imagination something (that vicious old son of a bitch dying) that nobody had so fully claimed in America before, except maybe Robinson . . . and I can't remember that even he is so honest in his revulsion and

*See Appendix, p. 589, for the poem "A Whisper to the Ghost Who Woke Me."

therefore so tragically true in his weeping. Well, I have many such things to say, and I hope you will keep in touch. I've got to go on reading: "The Kreuzer Sonata" by Tolstoy (Jesus H. Christ!).

But, before I close, let me say that I'll have some news for you soon about a reading over here. And please, for heaven's sake, if you are in touch with Betty Kray, tell her I'm willing to read all the way from New York to Afghanistan, because I need money very badly.

Are you getting your (financial) affairs straightened out? Fight it, God damn it! You know, when I was a kid I used to be fearless in fighting off all threats to my own identity and health . . . and I was right, and so are you. And as for the grief: well, we have got to hang on. Keep in touch when you can.

Yours,
Jim

To James Dickey

Bly Farm, Madison, Minnesota
Sunday afternoon
December 18, 1960
the sunset is beginning, there
are blades of gold outside the
window of this warm chickenhouse,

Jimbo, old man,

This will just be a note. I am on the Blys' farm, and they have gone to church this afternoon, to attend a Christmas program given by local children. This strange, wide, open, mysterious, delicate Minnesota plain, near the South Dakota border, is full of the graves of taciturn Norwegians and daydreaming taciturn children and (to use a beautiful phrase of Robert's) dreams of animals. I stayed here alone to meditate and, possibly, work. Robert and Carol will be home soon. Then maybe they will add a note to this note of mine, which I send to you without news of any practical kind, but simply for the sake of friendship. Last night we spoke of the possibility of phoning someone, some deep good friend, to greet for Christmas with love. Perhaps we'll phone you this evening. I don't know. Even if we don't, here is the greeting, no less warm for being slower than a phone call!

The fact is that I am drunker than hell. I sneaked my way into the wine over at the farmhouse after the Blys left, and I sat here for about an hour reading that rare, delicate, magnificent, kind spirit, Gerard de Nerval! And I was so utterly delighted, I felt "big-footed with glory" (Good heavens! A week never passes but that profound, glorious phrase rises in my mind to sustain me . . . and I really need inner sustenance these days).

I was so amazed with love for Nerval, that I stepped outside and plucked a blade of winter grass (so luminous with gold in the beginning sunset) and brought it in here and marked a place in the Nerval book with it. And I wrote a poem about him.* You see, he has a poem called "Politics," written in 1832, when he was in prison; in the poem, he thinks only that winter is coming, and he fills his lines with adoration for green things . . . beautiful, beautiful, beautiful! You know, Jim, when I first wrote you . . . about 2 years ago . . . the rudeness of my letter was caused, in part, by physical illness, and also, in part, by my feeling that what your reviews were saying was true: that in America we had let ourselves get annihilated by surrender to clever technique alone; and I was desolate about that; well, this afternoon, I feel terribly happy about poetry. Sitting here alone in this warm chickenhouse, I have an indescribably fine sense of warmth and love, I am as it were basking in the golden blades of light, the imagination, the friendship, the truth to the spirit . . . those precious things I had forgotten to love; and now at the very least I love them, and I know my love is true; so I feel very happy. All this is by way of saying that, if you yourself ever have any doubts about the bold stands you take in your reviews in *Sewanee*, I wish to tell you that you have had at least one reader who recognizes those reviews as reassurances about the truth of the soul. (No . . . I should say "two" instead of one; for Bly simply went into a spasm when he read the recent "The Suspect in Poetry"; it struck him with such enthusiasm that he immediately started to shape (in his imagination, which is delightfully agile and fertile) a book of James Dickey's "Collected Reviews" entitled *The Suspect in Poetry*.)† Now, Jim, don't be annoyed; I told Robert this morning that you yourself might

*See Appendix, p. 591, for the poem, "In a Warm Chicken House."
†A collection of twenty-six of Dickey's reviews with this title was published by Bly's Sixties Press in 1964.

dislike the idea; because (1) you've told me that you want to give up that business of writing reviews; (2) you think of yourself as a poet primarily, and therefore might conceivably dislike having your name hung onto a book, even a booklet, of occasional criticism. May I give my own personal opinion, and get it out of the way? First, even if you ever decide not to write other reviews, I believe what you've already written makes (without calculation, in the fine phrase of Jiménez) a book in itself; and, second, nothing, not even the publication of a book of your reviews, could modify the effect on intelligent readers (I consider myself an intelligent reader of poetry, and I do not apologize . . . far from it!) of *Into the Stone*. Well, there are other things to say; Bly will write you soon on this matter of collecting your reviews into a book. I will just repeat my own feeling: I think it is a good idea, I think it would only substantiate your identity *as a poet* even further, and I myself would be personally pleased to have the reviews available in convenient form . . . for I have read and read them over the past few years, and, when one wishes to read something in any case, convenience is a great virtue.

As for your poems, I sent the final version of my review to [John Frederick] Nims last Wednesday.* I haven't heard from him yet . . . I expect I'll have a note from him when I get back to Minneapolis day after tomorrow. In the review, I had to do eight books, and he suggested (i.e., rather insisted) that I limit myself to 7 pages. Now, in fact, my review took 8½ pages; and I'm hoping that Nims (who has seemed, on the whole, quite as intelligent and hospitable as Rago, and I respect Rago a good deal) will take the review as it stands. However, if he wants to cut it, or if he wants *me* to cut it, then I intend to insist that he leave untouched the sections that deal with you, and with Vassar Miller. I don't know if you know of Miss Miller; I suspect you won't like her as well as I do. However, she is, to me, a writer of genuine, honest to God feeling . . . in short, she *cares* about something in love and life and the imagination. Well, whether or not you and I agree on our response to her work, I feel sure we will agree that it is genuine (yes, it is *narrow* . . . BUT, for God's sake, you yourself cherish just six lines of James Kirkup . . . I mean the lovely passage you quoted in the last *Sewanee* . . . over whole books by more severely cunning people,

*Wright's review, "A Shelf of New Poets," appeared in *Poetry* 99 (December 1961) and is included in *Collected Prose* (p. 261).

haters of life and feeling, like Gunn . . . and that is just the way I feel about Vassar Miller). Well, you will see what I've done, *if* Nims takes the review just as I sent it. I had 8 books to review, as I say; and I spent 8½ pages on them. I gave 3 full pages to your book; about 1½ pages to Vassar Miller; and the remainder to a bunch of stuff.

What all this amounts to is this: I think *Into the Stone* is an important occasion; and, if I do say so myself, I am quite proud of my review of it. I think that, with the one exception of my review of Kunitz (you remember that), my previous reviews have been badly written *because* I was afraid to distinguish clearly between the true and the false. In this review for *Poetry*, however, I think, I really do honestly and delightedly believe, that I did a good and clear and honest and true review of your book. Well, however that may be, perhaps the point of this note of mine is to say that I do love the book, and the realization of my friendship with you (out of its rude beginning) fills me with extraordinary joy. (By the way, Bly was so outraged at John Holmes's stupid, indiscriminate review of *Poets of Today VII* in the *NY Times*, that he wrote one of his best letters to Holmes. But Robert will write that to you.) No more paper, and here come the Blys. Joy to you, and gratitude, for *Into the Stone*!

Jim Wright

To Madeline DeFrees

Minneapolis
February 8, 1961

Dear Sister,

I'm writing this note on the one clean manuscript page in my big, clumsy, overstuffed mss. notebook. It is—hm, let's see—it is now twenty minutes after eight in the morning; and I've been at this solitary desk for a long long time. This morning I accomplished little. Suddenly, thinking of you and your beautiful, moving letter which has lain for weeks unanswered over at the University, I began to write you a note.

Excuses for not writing letters are somehow exhausting, and I suppose it's because there is something false, something irrelevantly formal, about them. So never mind excuses. I think of you, and your poems, and especially your letter, very often.

I'm pleased that you've sent poems to Jerome Mazzaro, and I hope you'll do so again. Among all editors of little magazines, he seems to me one of the most honest and intelligent. He knows what to do with good writing when he's lucky enough to receive it.

As for my own recent experiments, let me say only that they are at once more complex—and tentative—than they may seem. I realize that they are small and fragmentary. Because of many things—illness, difficulties in my personal life, and other terrors of the usual kind—I had come upon a wall of stone. So I blasted. Really, you must take such a magazine as Robert Bly's *The Sixties* with the humor that pervades your autobiography. There are many things wrong with American poetry right now, as usual; but surely one of them is humorlessness. Misapplied solemnity seems to go along with an absence of real respect, even reverence. For myself, I can say that my own short poems in *The Sixties* are certainly smaller than Robinson (I think every American poet is smaller than he), even smaller than Roethke (that marvelous poet and man). But my own poems are merely attempts to cure myself of glibness.

Glibness is the worst thing that can happen—and not only in the writing of verse. Well, it was happening to me. So I started to fight it—I did so by leaping outside of every technical trick I had learned.

Really, nothing is "lost." You know, sometimes I think that current American poets fear our own powers of destruction too much. We are not that strong.

But all this "rationale" of mine is not much. When I get to a typewriter, I'll send you a new poem, and see what you think.

Meanwhile, have you seen the latest (fourth) issue of *The Sixties*? It contains some things I believe you would like—especially seven translations from Antonio Machado. Here is one of them, which I've learned by heart:

> At the doorsill of a dream they called my name.
> It was the good voice, the one I loved so much.
> —Listen: will you go with me to visit the soul?—
> A soft stroke reached up to my heart.
>
> —With you always!—And in my dream I walked
> Down a long and solitary corridor,

Aware of the touching of the pure robe,
And the soft beating of blood in the hands that loved me.

* * *

Please give my best to the [Franz] Schneiders, if you see them. And please don't be impatient with me for delaying so long.

Yours,
James Wright

To Anne Sexton

Minneapolis
February 15, 1961

Dear Anne,

I have no excuses. In order to support my family both now and during the summer months when I don't have a regular pay check, I am writing one hack essay after another; and, at this moment, I have two deadlines pushing their ugly mugs right into my mug. In addition, I am teaching three different humanities courses at once, and preparing a new course for the spring quarter that I have never taught before and about which I know very little except some scattered and disorganized reading.

Sure, I don't see any point in not mentioning me to Louis Simpson. Simply tell him we met, and got to know each other. And when you see him, give him my very best regards. I think his earlier poems are excellent, and his new ones fantastically good. He is the most intelligent writer of this generation, and probably the most enduringly valuable. By the way, if his wife Dorothy is with him, please be sure to give her my warmest regards, and ask her to pass them on to the kids. Dorothy is a beautiful girl, charming and generous in every way, and extraordinarily acute. By the way again, you might tell Louis that Bly and I have just about finished the translations of César Vallejo. As far as that goes, it just occurred to me that the Blys are going to NYC this week, and will stay there about a month; so they will probably see Louis anyway.

I wish you would stop picking at yourself about "prizes." You know as well as I do that you want to win all sorts of prizes; and you know that you will win them; and you know that they do not mean a damned thing except temporary flattery. As far as the "marketplace" and its flattery is concerned, it is all a question of making up one's mind. For my part, I would not trade one single poem by Vallejo or Miguel Hernández for everything published in American poetry since Robinson died, with I suppose the single exceptions of *Lord Weary's Castle* and the three books of Louis Simpson and the 2 books of Gary Snyder. The rest is good sometimes, more or less, but I would rather shoot a game of pool . . . My little boy Franz and I visited the Blys' farm a few weeks ago . . . we spent an entire afternoon hunting, and he shot a rabbit! . . . He was beside himself with delight . . . we rooted through an old deserted and haunted farmhouse that the Norwegians and hoboes don't live in any more, on that enormous bare and dazzling Indian plain country . . . and then we shot a few times at the deserted, crazy weathervane, and drove into Madison and, by God, shot a game of pool in the back of a beer joint . . . I didn't read a book for two days . . . and then I read Gerard de Nerval, and translated a poem of his . . .

I will write when I can. But I am terrified by the stalking ghosts of work. I'm sorry to hear that you're having a hard time. Keep seeing, and paying attention to, the doctor. As for me, in my real self, I am way off in the darkness and sometimes the light, dazzled beyond vanity, at war with sloth . . .

Don't be angry, but I think your short poem is startlingly bad. Bad, mawkish prose. It is very hard to write that way; if there is anything the Spaniards learned from Whitman (and it is the thing that nobody in America seems to suspect) it is a certain delicate joyousness.

I have to go work now. I'll try to keep in touch.

Yours,
Jim

To Donald Hall

The Bly Farm
Madison, Minnesota
April 22, 1961

Dear Don,

It is still morning . . . a spring sunlight over everything, the stones outside and the straw scattered in every direction outside the Blys' chickenhouse . . . I am here for nothing in particular. I arrived on Thursday evening, very late, in order to do nothing and be nothing in particular. At the moment, Carol is over in a grove behind the farmhouse, sawing and chopping dead trees away. A family of flickers lives over there. I saw them this morning, and I drew quite close as they went about their labors in the sunlight. They are not frightened, even by my face that feels crusted over by the city of Minneapolis and its long winter. The flickers glanced down at me somewhat tolerantly because, as Carol says, they are like farmers: they themselves are the only living things who are really doing God's work.

It was a joy to hear about you and Kirby and the kids. I hope it will be possible for you to come to Minnesota sometime this summer. Robert says perhaps even Louis Simpson will come, and that would be a marvelous thing. The farm is a good place for long leisurely conversations and silences that have the chance to enrich themselves perpetually.

Time and again during the last long winter I have been allowed to come out here in order to gain a little necessary strength from the silence, the uncluttered solitude, the warmth of this chickenhouse, where I have sat through some long afternoons either writing or doing nothing or being drunk, blissfully and shamelessly drunk, partly on wine and partly on things I have read and partly on nothing except the chance to drop my defenses for a little while in a world which comes to seem to me increasingly desolate in those very places which I once considered the only meaningful things: the work for a living, the city I live in, my personal relations with other human beings outside my own skull and body, my marriage . . .

Speaking of that, Lib and I are not divorced. Our troubles are deep, but perhaps we shall solve them. I myself have been a sick savage, as you know; and perhaps my own efforts to get well can have a good effect on Lib. I will not belabor this painful trouble further, except to say that we are living apart. Well, you couldn't call it living, for it ain't.

Robert tells me that the two of you spoke at length about your new poems, and touched upon something that Robert and I had meditated upon. My own feeling—it is pure feeling and not a considered thought—about your new poems is that a marvelous delicacy and gentleness emerges sometimes and comes through most truly and directly in very short poems. There are a thousand things to say in this connection, but perhaps it would be most useful for me to say just one thing, that gets clearer in my mind the more I meditate on it: that is, to speak of your secret gift for the small poem is by no means to imply a small talent. On the contrary, an accumulation of small poems that are each of them wholly true and kind is perhaps the richest kind of greatness. I have been reading Spaniards like Jiménez, as you know; and his whole genius comes to us through poems that are small, sometimes tiny; but the marvelous thing is that each of his small poems suddenly becomes vast in its echoes and colors, and sweet with the kindness that he distills there, like a drop of fresh water. But perhaps the best and most authoritative example of a very great poet whose vision and feeling are preserved in very short poems is the Chinese master named Lu Yu. In the old "Wisdom of the East" series, there is a lovely book, a small book of Lu Yu, translated by Clara M. Candlin. I wish you would look it up in your library, if you don't know it; because I think it would make you happy.

I want to ask you if it is all right if I send my book to you now. It consists of three sections: academic (or, perhaps, formal or traditional) poems; some three or four monologues etc. which I call "fictitious voices"; and then a number of new poems, which perhaps I will call Explorations, or Experiments, or Open Poems, or something like that. The book has an idea behind it okay: it just begins in an unhappiness which is even worse than the end of that extremely morbid and sick and inadequate book *Saint Judas*, which I regard as the shedding of sickness into pages by an emotional cripple; but then the new book goes through its attempt to break out of all that neurotic darkness, and moves on finally, through a lot of short poems (including four that I am going to call "Poems Written upon Several Occasions When I Was Drunk," three of which are to be in the *Hudson Review* soon), to a set of little things at the end that pretend to be nothing except moments of happiness. Perhaps the idea of the book is the attempt to recognize and acknowledge vanity and then to shed it.

In any case, it is all typed and so on. Shall I send it to you? And, if so, will you send it on to Lockwood if you think it is all right? And, of course, you would not hesitate to reject it outright or say what is wrong with it in detail.

Recently I have had bunches of the new poems appearing in several places: *Poetry*, *Botteghe Oscure*, the *Quarterly Review*, and so on. For the most part, I feel less and less absorbed by the old drive for publication. I want the book to have a shape all right, but not such a bitter and severe one as in the past. In truth, my life, my whole past life, is a wreck. I want nothing but to let the wreckage drift away. I go on writing because it is like breathing. It is a relief to sit here and breathe without whooping-cough, asthma, or whatever. To breathe the Spring.

Are you in touch with Geoffrey Hill? If so, will you greet him for me? I read his book often, always with deeper admiration and gratitude. As for my own correspondence, it is amazing how it has dropped away, and this letter to you, today, is the first proper letter I have written for several months.

Carol says that your daughter also has flaming red hair. The thought gives me enormous pleasure as I sit here writing to you. It makes me think of Andrew, whispering to my son Franz on the last morning of our visit to you that they would utterly flabbergast the adults by being good, by declining to get into any orneriness; I can hear old red-haired Andrew whispering with a kind of awe at their astonishing ploy, "We'll just wander around."

Please give my best regards to Kirby and tell her it would be nice to see her again. I have been making some progress with the shrinker. Actually, I think it is making me long to throw off the terrible burden of ambition. That relief alone makes me somewhat less barbarous and cruel than I was when she last saw me.

Well, this is enough for a while. Shall I send you my manuscript? It is long enough, and I may as well submit, without getting melodramatic about it. It is, really, just a collection of some poems.

Well, here is a little poem by Lu Yu which I cherish, and which I hope, and suspect, that you will like:

I WISH TO GO OUT BUT ENCOUNTER RAIN
East winds
blow rain
to vex
excursionists.
All the road
is fluid mud
in lieu of

powdery dust.
Flowers slumber:
Willows sleep.
Spring itself
is indolent.
Who knows
that I am
lazier than Spring?

                                        Love to you and all yours,
                                                        Jim

To John F. Adams

                                                    Minneapolis
                                                    May 10, 1961

Dear John,

I was delighted to get your letter. And I have to begin by apologizing for the brevity of my own answer. At the moment, I have a good many problems to solve and tasks to perform, and they increase as the hours pass, as the sparks fly upward. I will therefore come to the point . . . or, rather, to three points.

First, I find the prospect of the University of Denver a very attractive one, for many reasons which I won't attempt to state just now. However, I do not think it would be possible for me to come next year.

Therefore, I want to ask if it would be possible for me to be considered there year after next (that is, the academic year 1962–3). I am genuinely serious about the possibility, and I would appreciate your answering this question as frankly as is necessary.

I have yet another question. If I should come to Denver to teach, do you think it would be possible for me to avoid teaching so-called "creative writing"? I am willing, even eager, to talk with people unofficially and individually about their efforts to write poems etc.; but there is something about an official class in "creative writing" (revolting phrase!) that makes my blood run cold. I took the Ph.D. for several reasons. One of them was my desire to be a real teacher with a real subject matter. My position in this matter has so far been something like this: I believe that teaching and writing are related, but they are not identical; and the pretense that they are identical can only confuse both. At least, it confuses both in my mind.

I just reread your letter, and I noticed that you wanted me to write directly to Prof. Harvey Gross, Acting Chairman. But now that my letter is written, would you be so good as to report it to him? I have a hideously large bibliography, I have just finished a new book, I have published a couple of essays this year on nineteenth century fiction, and next September I am being invited to present a paper to the English Institute at Columbia University. The paper is to be called "The Delicacy of Walt Whitman."*

Whatever happens, let me repeat how really pleased I am to hear from and about you, and about Stuart James and old Rod Connor. (That is marvelous about his fatherhood! The child has a fantastic life in store.)

I hope that, one way or another, we can keep in touch.

As always,
Jim

To James Dickey

Minneapolis
July 17, 1961

Dear Jim,

I spoke over the phone to Robert Bly about your letter. He had come to Minneapolis, by car, in order to bring Don Hall and his family, and Louis Simpson's wife, to the airport. They had all been visiting at the Blys' farm for a few days; and Louis, I take it, is still there, his wife having flown on to New York ahead of him and their children, in order to see her parents.

As for your letter itself, I have hesitated to comment on it for fear I should spoil what seems to me an occasion of great and unmistakable heroism, of genuine *character*, perhaps *virtue* in the real, old-fashioned sense. When I first received it, I read it through once. Then, later, after I read and pondered it again, I jotted down at the bottom of the page the following passage, which is from *Job*, the place where God tells Job

---

*Included in Wright's *Collected Prose* (p. 3).

what a fantastically magnificent universe he actually lives in. Job, appalled at this magnificence, says these lines, which I guess are my favorite lines:

> I know that Thou canst do every thing,
> And that no thought can be withholden from Thee.
> Who is he that hideth counsel without knowledge?
> Therefore have I uttered that I understood not,
> Things too wonderful for me, which I knew not.
> Here, I beseech Thee, and declare Thou unto me.
> I have heard Thee by the hearing of the ear,
> But now mine eye seeth Thee . . .

Anyway, the lines sprang whole into my mind, when I reread your great letter, and they seemed to me perfectly appropriate. I can only add that I have entire faith in the strength of your decision and the wholeness of your imagination.

* * *

I myself spent about three days at the farm when the Halls and Simpsons were there together with the Blys. I went in order to talk briefly about my own new book, which, I guess you know, Wesleyan is going to publish next January. I was worried about the title; but now I think I'm just going to call it *New Poems.** I also rearranged it. It is now almost done and ready to send. The first part will contain some short pieces in more or less traditional form, and two or three dramatic pieces. Then part two suddenly changes over to the new things, a good many of which you've seen. There is a single one which I'm still trying to get right. I think it will be called "In Search of South America," and it is, in any case, as far from the old style as it is possible for anything to be. God knows how they ever accepted it, the book I mean. But they did, and now, in revising it, I want the second part to be as bold as I can make it.

Bly says that our translation of Trakl, which we want you to see especially, is due to arrive at any moment. I wish that Irish printer would hurry.

---

*This manuscript, originally titled *Amenities of Stone*, then *New Poems*, was withdrawn from Wesleyan University Press.

I find myself somewhat exhausted, because I had to teach during the past five weeks, in the first session of summer school. I had to lecture twice each day, five days a week, in Shakespeare and the eighteenth-century English novel. Actually, I had a good time—I had the latter class read *Don Quixote*, which is a religion in itself; but I am tired. One thing which can briefly be mentioned, but which is everything, is that my wife Lib and I seem, without understanding just how it's happening, to be finding each other again. She really is a great person, and I have been in a hell of a shape. It hasn't been easy for her at all; but she has great strength and courage.

I'll close this note with the hope that your own family is well. A man who is in harmony with his wife and children has the full strength of the seasons flowing into his back.

I'll write again fairly soon. In a few days I'm supposed to visit the farm again, and perhaps we'll phone you. Love to your family,

and to you,
Jim

To Michael Hamburger

Minneapolis
August 22, 1961

Dear Mr. Hamburger:

As you probably know, my friend Mr. J. R. de la Torre Bueno (an editor of the Wesleyan University Press, publisher of my second book *Saint Judas* and of my next new book, when it is satisfactorily finished) has corresponded with Mr. Jocelyn Baines at Longmans, concerning the possible publication of a selection of my poems in England. Mr. Bueno sent a copy of *Saint Judas* to Longmans. Then he received a letter from a Miss Amos, written August 15, in which she expressed interest in the book, and also requested galleys of my new book, which Wesleyan had accepted and had been ready to publish in January, 1962. Now a confusion has arisen; and I would like to clear it away, and to make a further suggestion.

You see, I have decided to withdraw my new book (which was to be called *New Poems*) from publication, for the following reasons: First, the book was in two sections, and I realized finally that they were so different from each other in style and tone as to break the book in half. Second, I suddenly realized that the second section (which was much the longer, and which contained that group of poems in *Poetry* that occasioned your first letter to me) was actually the basis of a new book in itself. Seeing this, I also saw that in a few months I could certainly expand and strengthen those newer poems into a genuinely new book, one which would be more truly unified. My decision to withdraw the *New Poems*, even after Wesleyan had accepted it for publication, was enough to tax anyone's patience, I know; and I must say that Mr. Bueno and Mr. Lockwood (editorial director at Wesleyan) have been very considerate with what must seem like a silly whim on my part.

However, I have had an idea about another possible plan. It is my own suggestion, and it would certainly depend on the approval of Wesleyan, to whose editors I have personal as well as legal responsibilities. (I am therefore sending a copy of my present letter to Mr. Bueno.) Here is the plan that I suggest:

I will write to the Yale University Press (publisher of my first book, *The Green Wall*, 1957, still in print), mention your interest, and ask them to send you a copy of the book . . . assuming they would have no objection to your publishing any or all of it. Mr. Bueno of Wesleyan has already said that he was quite willing to cooperate with the Yale Press, in case you might wish to publish any or all of the poems in *The Green Wall* and *St. Judas*.

Now comes the most important part of my suggestion: as I said above, my new book for Wesleyan (the one I've withdrawn) was to have two sections. I have removed the *first* section entirely, simply because the poems in it were out of tone with the second. But I would like very much to publish the poems of the first section in book form. There are 12 to 15 poems in the group, some of which are brief narratives and dramatic monologues, and all of which are composed in a classical iambic style. *If* both you and Wesleyan should approve, then this is my suggestion: a book containing *The Green Wall* and *Saint Judas* (or a selection therefrom); and, in a third section, the few poems that were to have been the first section of my withdrawn new book. Will you please tell me what you think of this plan? I will write Wesleyan also.

Sincerely,
James A. Wright

To James Dickey

Minneapolis

August 24, 1961

Midnight

Dear old Jim,

I promised I would write you on Thursday—that is, the day after Robert and I phoned you.

But I suddenly couldn't bear to be away from my wife and kids for another day. So I rose very early on Thursday, and took a bus back to Minneapolis. At the moment, I am alone at *home*. Lib and my two sons have driven to Canada, to be with old mutual friends for a week. Furthermore, I *have* to fly to New York next week, on the very day they return home. I won't see them for two whole weeks.

It is hard to bear, but I am going to bear it. It's true I've been terribly ill. But I love that girl. I really do. Did you know she is a Greek? A real one. Her name in Greek is Eleutheria—it means *freedom*. So help me God!

Now look, Jimbo—about your question, that I might be trying to do something *noble* in withdrawing my book—and also, your statement that you "wouldn't want to take another man's leavings." Well, boy, I fretted terribly, in the attempt to answer you truly, and I talked it over at length with Robert, whom I asked to write you about it—and, as you know, he is probably as honest as any man alive. As for me, I got immediately tangled in rhetoric. But tonight—sitting alone, sick for my love and my sons, I just thought I would strip rhetoric away for a change, and—

Look: amid much illness and uncertainty, I have found hope in the discovery that, in our own generation, there actually exist on the earth, in this country which I know we both love, a few men who contain within their bodies and souls a goodness, a tragically determined courage, and a poetic genius—all together, which have given me cause to go on living. I *believe* in these things. I started to write in ignorance that there are *real* poets in this generation. Now I have met you, and Bly, and Geoff Hill, and Louis Simpson; and corresponded with David Ignatow—well, I want to be worthy of myself. (P.S. Snyder also, and Stafford and Hugo.)

I never had that conscious longing before. It explains why I withdrew my manuscript. You are one of the best men I know, and one of the truest poets in American history. I withdrew my book because I believe I can make it a true book of poetry—it is the first time I ever dreamed that being true to myself, and to my friends, and to poetry, are all one thing . . . In practical terms, Robert told me he understood that our books (yours and mine) were accepted together for January, and they were . . . oh, he'll explain . . . Jim, for God's sake, you are one of the great men. I beg you to give me my chance to find my way to the holy place we both love beyond ourselves. As for "taking another man's leavings"—I would as easily think such a thing of Shakespeare, or Dante, or W. S. Graham (I worship his poetry), as of you, or of myself. Please write—I'll explain my own new book soon.

Love,
Jim

A Time of Wandering

1964–1966

Robert Bly, James Wright, and Louis Simpson, Madison, Minnesota, circa 1964

I suddenly realized that I absolutely could not bear to live in the Twin Cities again. As you surely know, I care very deeply for Minnesota itself—its countryside, I mean; and I believe I am not exaggerating when I say that I love the Bly farm as truly and freely and fully as I love any place on earth. But Minneapolis is another matter. I have had so many failures there, failures of every kind imaginable, and so many wounds, and so many defeats, that I just came to realize that the city has become, to me, a city of horrors. If only I could find some other place to live, I think I could be well again.

—from a letter to Carol Bly
January 16, 1966

By 1962 James's marriage to Liberty had ended in divorce. She and the two boys moved to San Francisco. In the spring of 1963 James arranged to take a leave of absence from the University of Minnesota to serve as guest professor at Macalester College in St. Paul for the following term. Before the spring semester was over, however, he was denied tenure at the University of Minnesota.

The only respite in James's life was frequent visits to the Bly farm. The companionship, affection, and respect he received from both Carol and Robert gave him the strength and courage to survive the terrible experiences occurring in his personal life and created a lasting and important impact on his poetry.

"The farm is a beautiful, peaceful place," he wrote to Donald Hall. In a letter to Robert he said, "I think your farm is the first such place I have ever really liked—it is beautifully mysterious and very much its own secret place."

While teaching at Macalester, where he was devoted to his students, James moved to Saint Paul and lived in a series of rented rooms and small apartments. He worked extensively on both a new manuscript and *The Rider on the White Horse*, a translation of short stories by Theodor Storm, and carried on a voluminous correspondence with many people. James taught a second year at Macalester College, by which time he had received a Guggenheim Foundation Grant that would enable him to leave Minnesota after the spring term in 1965.

Before he left, James packed carton after carton of possessions: books, phonograph records, clothes, drafts of poems and translations, manuscript notes for courses, and letters. Thirty-four of these boxes were left at the Bly farm; half a dozen were stored with Bill Truesdale, a friend and colleague from Macalester; and others to one or more students. Only the boxes cared for by Bly and Truesdale were recovered, which may help explain the absence of any letters from the year 1963.

After leaving Minnesota in the late spring of 1965, James spent several months in Cupertino, California, with Elizabeth and Henry Esterly. In the autumn he stayed at the Bly farm and then went to his parents' home in New Concord, Ohio. He had planned to go to England, but a visit to his close friend Roger Hecht in New York City during the winter of 1966 convinced James that Manhattan might be a good place to live. He applied for a teaching position at various colleges in the area and was accepted by Hunter College.

To Franz Wright

St. Paul, Minnesota

March 4, 1964

My dear Franz,

Just now, it is almost midnight. Today the very air that we breathe in the twin cities is sagging heavily with a strange white snowfall. After I lectured three different classes today, and doing some other necessary work earlier this evening, I decided a little while to follow my custom of taking a solitary walk for a few blocks, to get a breath of fresh outdoors air, and generally to rest my eyes—and also rest my spirit—after the day's labor. Then, as I walked down Dale Street from Selby Avenue here in Saint Paul, I suddenly found that the very innermost, most secret part of my mind had become filled with a soft clear light—the light that is like the green radiance of the air at that beautiful moment in Spring or early Summer when the shower of rain, that sprang up suddenly and fell down just as suddenly, is instantly gone, and left behind it a few people—like you and me, who like rain—soaked to the skin but happy to be soaked to the skin, and to be standing on a street corner, and feeling as though we ourselves were slowly turning bright green. How strange it was to catch myself, this evening, in the act of having a daydream of that kind, when all the while I slogged pleasantly through deep lakes of slush by curbs, or carefully picked my way across the six-inch snowfall on unfrequented sidewalks, balancing myself like a tightrope walker, in order to take advantage of the few big footprints left in the deep new snow by some gone and forgotten mailman, or milkman, or adventurous Great Dane—(of course, what I had secretly hoped to discover was the enormous footprint of somebody's pet Elephant in the snow—but, I'm sorry to say, the last pet Elephant who lived in this neighborhood has moved away, to take a job writing books full of People-Jokes).

But my most secret and most honest spirit, my dear Franz, was filled with light anyway, in spite of the snow. Because I walked into the fresh garden that still, and always, goes on growing deep in my mind, regardless of the troubles I face, the loneliness I feel, or the snowfalls I explore in search of some lost and mostly forgotten Elephant-prints. I walked into my garden; and you were there, waiting for me beside a dripping bright green house that grew right up out of the ground like a wild bush of flowers, a house with roots of its own; and you too were green and fresh, and you too were growing. You looked up patiently to greet me, and said, "Hello. You're a little earlier than usual; but then, I suppose I'm early, too."

"Well," I answered, "I was just taking a walk outside in the snow, and suddenly I found myself wanting to come into the garden. I didn't know why, until I saw the light shining there; and I knew that Spring had come; and I knew you'd felt so strong and hopeful this year that you'd started to grow already; and I knew that the garden in my most secret heart was shining with happiness because it is time for your birthday; and so I just came in to see you."

"Thank you," you said, and smiled a bit vaguely, as if there were some question that you wanted very much to ask but still hesitated, out of politeness, to mention.

But I already knew the question, and had answered it even before you thought of asking it, or wanted to ask it.

"I want to tell you something special, something that should be made clear, Franzie. You see, this visit with you in the garden was just a single, sudden inspiration that I had this evening. It is a very happy inspiration; but it is nevertheless just a message to wish you joy of the Spring, and to wish you the happiest of all happy birthdays!"

"Yes, I see," you replied, still looking entirely puzzled.

"In plain English, my dearest friend and fine son whom I love completely and forever," I answered, "in plain English, what I'm doing now is just greeting you with words. But the *present* which I am arranging to send you for your birthday this year—well, now, that's a horse of a different color!"

"Are horses green this year, like houses and boys named Franz?" you asked, still not quite sure what I meant.

"Whether or not horses are green; whether or not my letters to you are too short and too rare; it remains a fact that, in addition to this evening's message—this letter to you—I am going to send you your present quite soon. It won't be a letter, although I'll write you a note about it. It will be a surprise, of course. Anyway, it will be a real, solid present which you'll receive in a package through the mail. Happy birthday, once again! And always!"

"Happy birthday—always!—to you, too," you answered, smiling. "Happy birthday, Daddy, no matter what the date of the year is, and in spite of the snow."

"Thank you, my beloved son and best friend," I replied with true love in my heart, "I know just what you mean. And now, if you'll excuse me, I'll just go back and get a night's sleep; so that, tomorrow, I can go ahead with plans for your present. Good night, my dear."

"Sweet dreams," you said.

And I said, "Yes."

Love, and more letters soon, I promise,

Dad

To Dr. Harvey Rice, President of Macalester College

St. Paul

March 13, 1964

Dear President Rice:

My brief talk after dinner at the meeting of Kappa Delta Pi last Monday evening led me through a door, one of those two or three doors that somehow simply open for him at those moments in his life that are, somehow, eternal. Such a door opened in a green hillside at an odd moment when Jacob Boehme, the great 16th-century German theologian and mystic, was still a youthful cobbler's apprentice taking a stroll through the countryside on his day off. Even before I received your magnificent letter, I had been filling my journal with wonder-struck ponderings on the strange, sudden beauty of last Monday evening. It was truly as though a door had suddenly been opened and for a moment (not a "mere" moment, but an eternal one) all of us seemed to step silently through the door and emerged into a green place, a meadow of renewal: all of us—the President and his lady, the members of the faculty, the students, and the evening's speaker.

We all stood there together in the green place, and we held one another's hands. I discover in myself a response to your letter that is as profoundly authentic a response as I have ever felt, a response to something in your letter which reveals you as a man. It would have been gracious enough, heaven knows, had you simply greeted me; and, heaven also knows, I am old-fashioned enough to love the old formal civilities. But your letter, beautiful in its form and dignity, expressed not only the form but also—radiantly, indeed—the very *meaning* of what is, to me, most beautiful in Christian civilization. Edmund Burke has a great phrase for this meaning. He calls it "the unbought grace of life."

My present note to you sounds somewhat awkward, as I read it over. I came to the meeting Monday evening feeling uncertain and lonesome. And yet, consider what happened! Suddenly I realized that I was living in a moment which included everything I ever cared about as a teacher, as a writer, and as a human being among my fellows; included, and surpassed. If my note sounds awkward, it does so because I have never been so moved for so many truly personal reasons as I am moved by your letter.

I would now like to say something which so far, as a new teacher at Macalester, I have hesitated to say. At the most recent faculty meeting, you mentioned to the faculty how barbarously certain students reacted to your explanation of the new cafeteria plan. You told us, with a dignity, a nobility which was a revelation to me of what a civilized leader truly is made of, you told us that, whatever the students might wish to do to Harvey Rice, you would not stand for their hissing the President of their college.

I want to say that I would not stand for their hissing Harvey Rice either. The beautiful graciousness of your letter to me displayed the same noble vitality which made your words to the faculty so admirable.

I trust you will forgive me for mentioning, even in passing, a problem which cannot help but be distressing in its complexity. But your words at the faculty meeting have haunted me for several days, and I trust that you will accept what I say here as a token of faith in you.

It made me happy to talk with Mrs. Rice also, and I hope you will convey to her my warmest friendship and gratitude, as well as my highest respect.

Sincerely,
James A. Wright

To Bernetta Quinn

St. Paul
March 13, 1964

My dear Sister Bernetta,

It is just about daybreak. After an entire night of work, and a dawning moment, I suddenly turned to write you a few words, in obedience to an impulse—no, it is a voice, not an "impulse"—from within.

The voice speaks very often, and it occurs to me just now that perhaps I need only try to follow the voice out of the many voices, the one that bids me stand and live.

Your pages from the European journal are very beautiful to read and ponder, as indeed I do again and again. I read them over and over during those long hours when—still unsuccessfully, I fear—I have been actually trying, trying, trying to do something which is strange to me: I have been trying to meditate. Oh, I have "killed time" before in my life, plenty of it; and I have loafed stupidly; and I have gazed in stupor at the waste, and heard nothing.

I have actually begun to learn at least the difference between the above modes of non-being and true meditation. I believe I can truly say that it is not identical with them.

I find a beautiful solace, a real joy, in speaking to you this way— answering you, almost.

As you well know, I will give each of the copies of *The Branch* my most loving attention; and, probably, send them to you just before Easter.

Bless you,
Jim

To E. L. Doctorow*

St. Paul
March 13, 1964

Dear Ed,

Thank you so very much for the check, which arrived today. May I begin this note by immediately mentioning one or two matters that you will need to know about the job which I've just finished?

*At that time an editor at the New American Library.

(1) Miss (?) Ines Delgado de Torres wrote me a very kind note, dated March 3. (May I ask you, Ed, to convey to her my gratitude for her nice words of encouragement?) She was concerned about ten pages which were missing from the manuscript of *The Rider on the White Horse*, by which title I'm referring to the last of the eight stories; and by this time you should have received the missing pages. I had devoted an entire day, literally from daybreak to twilight, working and completing those ten concluding pages, lavishing upon them all my attention and imagination. It is very, very strange, almost unearthly, to realize what happened: after I had labored on that final scene with what can only be called ferocity, I laid them aside in an envelope; and I guess I just forgot about them, even when I put the entire manuscript together to send you. Now, here is what is so strange—I quote Thomas Mann's account of Storm's *own* obsessive concentration on those same final ten pages: "Storm lived almost to one-and-seventy. His ailment was the local affliction that plays a fateful part in one of his most powerful tales: . . . cancer of the stomach. He rose grandly to the occasion and demanded that the doctor be frank with him as man to man. But taken at his word, he collapsed and gave himself over to gloom. It was clear to those about him that he would not finish the *White Horse*, the finest and boldest thing he had ever ventured on. 'Children, this won't do,' they said, and put their heads together to deceive the aged poet, who as an artist stood in a Tacitean-Germanic *sera inventus*, but as a man had overestimated his strength. His brother Emil, a physician, held a consultation with two colleagues; after which science pronounced that the verdict of cancer was all nonsense, the stomach ailment not malignant. Storm believed the tale at once. His spirits rebounded; he spent a capital summer, in the course of which he celebrated his seventieth birthday with the good Husumers in festive mirth. Also he brought the *White Horse* to a triumphant conclusion, thus elevating to a height never before reached his conception of the short story as the epic sister of the drama. I was bent on giving this little account as a conclusion to my tale (of Storm). The masterpiece with which Storm crowned his lifework was a product of merciful delusion. The capacity to let himself be deluded came to him out of the will to live and finish the extraordinary work of art."

Ed, both in the concentrating and in the temporary forgetfulness, I seemed almost to have succeeded in summoning up the great shadow of Storm himself, because I have loved him and his work for years, and needed his presence in the final stages of my work on him, as it were. After completing his story, he died; but I just forgot. I am not dead. (Believe me, Edgar, I am not.)

Miss Torres also noted that there was a poem in the story "A Green Leaf" that still needed translating. I am enclosing the translated poem with the present letter. PLEASE NOTE: the prose-translation of the poem should appear *in italics* in the printed version.

(2) After talking with you by phone and resuming work on my introduction, I unfortunately found that something more than occasional brief repairs were needed. Although I sincerely apologize for the additional slight delay, I am nevertheless certain, Edgar, that you would not want me to apologize for laboring to produce the best essay I was capable of, for all the time it required. In any case, the final revision of the introduction was mailed to you by airmail on Saturday, March 14, and by now you should have it. I myself feel about three times as secure about it as I felt about the previous and unsatisfactory version. I hope you like the new one all right, of course; but I want you to phone me (and leave a message, if I'm not there) in case there's any further question about either the introduction or the manuscript of the translation itself. For your own convenience, let me say in writing, here and now, that any editorial corrections or revisions that you yourself might wish to make are perfectly all right with me. Even in addition to the devoted trust of old friendship, I am certain beyond question that I can utterly rely on your own sense of fitness in editorial matters generally; and, more particularly, you already know how deeply I believe in your own beautiful gift for hearing—as well as creating—the harmonies of prose.

I've added the point at the end of the previous paragraph simply to spare you further time and inconvenience if you feel that further revision—which you yourself can handle—is desirable. On the other hand, it goes without saying that I am willing to go on personally rewriting the introduction till hell freezes over, if you want me to.

Let's see: I think I've covered all remaining practical problems.

Edgar, I am fairly bursting to continue this letter with several other considerations, at once personal and practical. For one thing, I feel dreadful in realizing what an absolutely indifferent and irresponsible slob your fellow editors must consider me, in view of the length of time I spent on the Storm translation. But it is not true! (I want to cry.)

While I was working on Storm, I had to deal with two or three matters that I honestly believe I can call catastrophic (and I am aware of the dangers of self-pity and exaggeration here). In fact, the chance to work on the Storm translation was, more than once, the chance to go on living, almost the one chance.

But we can talk about these things soon, Edgar. I want to thank you and the others for giving me the chance to work on this translation. Never once was it a burden. It was always, rather, a source of nourishment and refreshment; and the completion of the book is the fulfillment of an old dream of mine [. . .]

It is Spring, and . . . the leaves are falling upward!

Love to you and your family,

Jim

To a Reader

St. Paul
March 16, 1964

Dear Miss Richer:

I'm sure you need never fear that "it is seven kinds of insolence" to write a letter as charming as the one you recently wrote to me. In fact, it is one of the kindest things you could do, particularly in a country like America, which becomes the more huge and the more lonely the more we love it. But even if it were as small as one of its own river towns, and even if we all hated it, to write a friendly note to a person who is an utter stranger to you except for some of the verses he has written—that is a lovely thing to do. Thank you.

But I'm afraid I don't quite see how I can help very much with the poem called "Heritage."* I don't mean to be huffy and aloof about it. On the contrary. And I don't mean that I think it capable of providing a "total experience" (to quote your own excellent phrase) already, beyond the possibility of obscurity. Far from it. All I mean is simply that I don't quite understand just what you are asking me to clarify.

I will tell you all I know. It is a poem about my grandfather. He was a terribly violent man who constantly held his wife and children at bay

*See Appendix, p. 592, for the poem "Heritage."

by regularly frightening them witless through his indulgence in drunkenness so fantastic as seriously to call into question his capacity for any human feeling whatever. Moreover, he devoted his long life to the effort—apparently—to become the very opposite of what used to be called, in more gracious times, a "good provider." For some reason, which relatives have never been able to fathom, he hated, really hated people who said things like "good provider." He is not at all a victim of apathy. For all his obsessive negations of things, he was not to be merely identified with the farmer's horse in the old story. (The horse—as they said in Ohio—would sometimes amuse himself during the ploughing season by persistently straying off across the furrows to the edge of the field, where he butted his head against as many trees as he could manage before the farmer could catch him. One day a passing stranger called over to the farmer from the road, and asked what the hell use it was to try to plough with a blind horse. "Blind? Blind?" bellowed the horse's owner, astounded. "That horse ain't blind!" "Then why does he wander off from the line of furrows and bump into all them trees?" "Oh, that," said the farmer; "well, you see, some days he just don't give a damn.") But my grandfather gave a damn. He went in the other direction, awesomely. And yet, he couldn't be disposed of as a misanthrope. The mere mention of his dead brother Jim suddenly evoked from him such baffled and deeply affecting expressions of love that, at such moments, he puzzled his relatives far more completely than he did during his times of normal, predictable destructiveness.

When he was quite old, I was just a small kid. You can imagine how delighted he was at my name, and he told me so. I believe him. I love him, too.

He was struck down on a street in Bridgeport, Ohio, and died with his broken back inadequately tended to.

My family in Ohio have great powers of affection, but for some reason we are all unbelievably reserved with one another, not only in matters of feeling but even in matters of transmitting the plainest and most obvious bits of information. I didn't know completely how my grandfather had lived and died until about three years ago, when my older brother—after such a long time, such an impossibly long, long, endlessly long time—told me the story and its details.

Now, Miss Richer, I don't claim that this long-drawn-out explanation will make the poem any clearer. And that it ought to be made clearer seems to me beyond question.

I hope you'll forgive me for seeming to respond to your request for clarification with a letter which, in part at least, is less a helpful answer than a mere request for clarification of your request!

Again, thank you for your kindness in writing me. May I ask who you are? I would be delighted to know.

Sincerely,
James Wright

To Kenneth Rexroth

St. Paul
April 2, 1964

Dear Kenneth,

I believe you'll forgive me for such a long delay in replying to your splendid letter, which was dated February 24. The reason for the delay is a perfect revelation of the kind of idiotic inefficiency which possesses my mind almost in direct proportion to my desire to be helpful to a friend. In short, instead of following your simple directions and just writing down four or five names on the postcard which you enclosed. (For heaven's sake! Think of it! You did everything except phone me long-distance and then arrange for an answering-service to hold the line while you flew here to St. Paul by jet-plane to speak my answers into the phone, while I stood by grinning like an amiably maddening imbecile—a kind of civilian Good Soldier Schweik.)

[. . .] I sincerely hope that I'm not too late to be of some help to you, however small. I will proceed this evening to do two things: first, I'll complete this letter to you; second, I'll type out the names of young poets whom I mention in the letter, and send you both the postcard *and* the letter—I feel that the latter might serve as a kind of explanation of the names on the list—and also, of course, an occasion to greet you and wish you well.

First, the names of the poets under thirty-five whose work I know well enough to declare without hesitation that I really *like* it—whose poems move me in the same way, and for the same causes, that, say, the poems of a very great poet like Tu Fu move me. In other words, I want my selection of names to be guided by a spirit which moved you to write (in your prefatory note to the *One Hundred Poems from the Chinese*, which includes the thirty translations from Tu Fu, and which I can honestly describe as one of the most personally precious books that I have) something like this: "I make no claim for this book as a piece of oriental scholarship, by the way. Just some poems." Discovering your Tu Fu translations was like rising from the dead, as far as I'm concerned. And so, in the same way that they might be called "just some poems," I hereby offer some names of young persons who are "just some poets."

1. The first who comes to mind with full force, and seems to me an unmistakably beautiful, deeply fertile, unaffected, marvelous poet, is a young man of about 25 years of age who has the wonderfully un-poetick name of *Bill Knott* [. . .] His work has appeared in the latest issue of *Choice*, the Chicago magazine edited by John Logan. (It's the issue that contained Robert Bly's scarifying essay, "The Destructive Tradition in American Poetry.") Knott's poems appear under the pseudonym of "Saint Geraud" [. . .] If by chance you haven't seen the issue of *Choice* mentioned here, I'm sure Logan would be delighted to get a copy to you almost immediately, so you can read the fairly substantial group of Knott's poems published there.

2. Another young man, also about 25 years old, is named *Tim Reynolds*. He has had several poems published in *Poetry* (Chicago). I've never met him; but I've wanted for some time to write him a note of gratitude for the several beautiful, genuine poems that he has so far published in *Poetry* and one or two other places. I'll write him this very evening—just a note of thanks for his poems, and a brief request that he send a few of his poems (say, 5 or 10, but no more) directly to you. I trust you won't mind, or think me discourteous—I do realize that the task you've undertaken might easily threaten to snow you under with manuscripts from well-meaning but inefficient friends like myself. Still, I *do* admire the poems of Tim Reynolds; I believe you would like them, too, whether or not you have space to say much, or anything, about them in your projected essay.

3. Finally, a very, very quiet young man (a victim of one horrible streak of old-fashioned hard-luck after another . . . but never mind that, at the moment): a fellow named *Dick Shaw*. He is about 30 years old. He has been teaching, off and on, in Minneapolis for about

5 years. He holds neither the Ph.D. in Incomparative Cunnilinguistics (excuse the heavy-handed humor—I seem to be speaking in tongues this evening) nor a Teaching Certificate in Elementary Larkspur Lotion Selling-and-Distribution. He is just a quiet fellow who has been writing quiet and genuine poems, of real delicacy and unobtrusive strength, for the past few years. He's published a fair number, and I wouldn't mind seeing a selection of them in a book. Anyway, I think he is a good poet, and I would like to see him get some help. Even a word of encouragement can have enormous meaning for such a man, as you well know. Of course, the worth of his poetry is something conceivably quite distinct from his need for encouragement. (We all need it, for heaven's sake, even when we write bad poems—perhaps especially then.) [. . .]

There they are: 1. Bill Knott
2. Tim Reynolds
3. Dick Shaw

Thank you, Kenneth, for asking me to help. It is a true honor to be asked to help, however slightly, in a project conceived by one of the most generous and civilized men I have ever met. If I can be of any further help, I hope you will give me the chance to do so.

* * *

I was in New York City last week, where I spoke at the new Guggenheim Museum, and fooled around with a publisher for whom I've just translated eight Novellen from the German of Theodor Storm, etc. I hear that, to my regret, I had just barely missed seeing you again. Anyway, I *did* get a copy of *Natural Numbers*, which simply delights me—it contains almost all of the short poems of yours which I love best, and which still seem to me a new beginning, our true life.

Best,
as always,
Jim Wright

To Dr. Arnold Stein

St. Paul

April 8, 1964

Dear Arnold,

I am certain that I speak only with the restraint and gravity suitable to the occasion, when I tell you that your beautiful letter to me (dated 23 March) was incomparably the most important achievement I have ever made in my life as a man who loves the high literary art. I want somehow to assure you, Arnold, that I am fully aware of the honor which you've done me in inviting me to contribute a critical essay to the volume of studies on Roethke's poetry. The more I ponder your determination to "honor Roethke not by testimonials of praise" but rather by our best and truest efforts to see his work "in the hard, Sophoclean light" exactly as the young Pound asked to be seen, I am astonished at the splendor and nobility of your conception. For implicit in a gesture which ignores even a moment's possibility of flattery and promptly begins the essential labor of criticism—that true criticism which is so rare among men, and so instantly recognizable for its magnificent terror of confounding its tentatively outlined summaries of poems for the "secular sacrament" (in Mr. Ransom's dark and oracular phrase) that is moving and serene at once, and at once the ending and the beginning of the word when it is comely of vesture and countenance and then suddenly awesome in the bluntness of its unarguable deathlessness—implicit in the quiet, grave gesture toward seeing Roethke's poetry in the company of Landor and Donne and Ben Jonson is in itself, I do most reverently believe, the gesture which Roethke labored and fought for a lifetime to make. To cherish his work, his art, by demanding that it respond to our most severe and attentive questionings by revealing suddenly, as it were, the precious stones that vein it, and accordingly by daring it to sag or crumble or heave up geologic "flaws" or more crumbling sandstone and fool's gold, is to love the art as the poet himself loved it. I believe that, as time passes, and as factions perish and seas move and all the rest that dies and dies forever is forgotten, some of Roethke's poems will remain among all our priceless things. And it is only the true criticism, the honorable effort of our very best intellectual attention, that can clarify for us what there is of immortal and mountainously enduring in Roethke's art. I think of those cranky, somehow haunting lines of Mr. Winters: "Few men will come to this: / The poet's only bliss / Is in cold certitude, / Laurel, archaic . . ." Arnold, I've written a bit more than a mere grateful acceptance of your invitation would require, because I wanted to clarify for myself the deep meanings which I instantly sensed in your distinction between mere rote praise and the living praise of critical devotion; and I feel, even more deeply now than at the beginning of my letter, how very beautiful and noble your plan is. In addition to considerations which I've been so far touching upon lightly and unsystematically, there are perspectives and kinships and echoes that become clearer with each moment: there is the very great tradition of aristocratic friendship and the sense of loving duty, of Vergilian *pietas* that is its very inmost vital spirit, the love that tenderly asks the friend to please us by acting and living and working in aspiration toward the achievement of the high style, the deed that Sidney would instantly notice and know as precious, and the work of art in words, the evidence that the friend pleases us in studying to sing whatever is well-made. In such an eternity of friendship, such a garden of worthiness, perhaps Ben Jonson's phrase about Shakespeare's impatience with revision reveals how shallow its apparent curtness truly is, and how deep is its tenderness and affection; perhaps Jonson meant simply that he would not have his friend live, even forever, in any work in any sense inferior to his highest ability: the occasional work of classical achievement, the poem that does not really need our flattery, that in fact grandly ignores the chattering supererogatory bleatings and fawnings of the trivial and silly false critics who apparently live with the miraculously idiotic [. . .] that to praise what is itself nobly worthy of praise is a facile act that any fool and knave can lightly toss off, as they themselves were no doubt tossed off quite as lightly, and then got "twixt asleep and wake."

Oh, Arnold, I am deeply moved by the beauty of the plan you've asked me to help you to fulfill. I accept the invitation with all the pride I am capable of; and I pledge you my best powers of thought and feeling as I slowly seek to write truly and honestly of Roethke's work. I'll be in touch with you to ask your advice from time to time as the essay takes shape.

At this moment I know myself able to respond to what is noble, to recognize the true radiance when it appears at last, and to love my friends and masters because they are themselves the very embodiments of the nobility which they invite me to share in my best faith. I want to quote some lines which leaped this instant to the very center of my mind's stage out of their accustomed shadow in the wings from which for years they have whispered me counsel about words; I want to quote them because they are to my mind great and noble, certainly the kind of high poetry that Roethke aspired to be worthy of:

> It is not growing like a tree,
> In bulk, doth make man better be:
> Or standing long an oak, three hundred year,
> To lie at last a log, dry, bald, and sere.
> A lily of a day
> Is fairer far in May;
> Although it flower and die that night,
> It was the plant and flower of light.
> In small proportions we just beauties see,
> And in short measure life may perfect be.

"The greatest of all desire," Nietzsche remarked, "is the desire to be great." You and I have both many times heard Roethke quote with resonant and ferocious approval those lines in which Yeats asks (as his words seem carved on marble in the very air before our eyes) for himself, and for all true poets touched by the fire-coal in holy secret, to be praised or damned by his peers and in the presence of their own nobility:

> I know what wages beauty gives,
> How hard a life her servant lives,
> Yet praise the winters gone:
> There is not a fool can call me friend,
> And I may dine at journey's end
> With Landor and with Donne.

An inn for the high-hearted pilgrim, indeed! To fancy Roethke sitting down at table for supper is a fine dream. Joy to that sparse company or the rare ones who are both blessed and can forever bless.

As always,
James A. Wright

To Kenneth Rexroth

St. Paul
April 14, 1964

Dear Kenneth,

On April 2, I wrote a reply to your request for the names of a few young American poets whose work I enjoy and who might help you in your essay on American poets under 35. I'm sorry to be so long in securing a few poems by Dick Shaw, one of the three persons I mentioned and discussed. You see, I was invited to spend a couple of days last week at a Catholic girls' school named the College of St. Scholastica, up at Duluth—I spent the time well, I think, in strolling and chatting with the nuns or the girls in the classes, or with both, and also in lecturing on such matters as what I feel is the "underground" connection between such seemingly diverse Americans as E. A. Robinson and Whitman (a stream of agony and sympathy for bums and sixteen-year-old soldiers and all the others who, in the period of American manifest destiny, were getting pushed in front of sadistic surgeons or pre-Edward-Teller weapons, or else were getting shoved down manholes and behind roadside billboards), and the really very thrilling fact that Robinson was aware of himself as the end of something and of Whitman as the beginning; and I talked about Irish street-poetry of the 18th century; and also about the art of translation and its joys (I quoted your remark explaining why you give time to translating the great poets of Chinese and other languages: "You meet such a nice class of people"); and I generally kept busy with those rather fine, touching girls up there in Duluth.

Then I returned and got copies of five of Dick Shaw's poems from his sister-in-law, who'd secured and typed them in the meantime; and I hereby enclose them.

Again, please let me know if I can help any further.

Yours,
James Wright

To Marshall Wright

St. Paul
April 27, 1964

My dearest Marsh,

A few days ago, I received a letter from Momma. She told me that Franzie had received his birthday present all right, just as I sent it to him through the mail. But she told me that the record which I had sent to *you* through the mail . . . had arrived but, when you unwrapped it, it was broken!

I imagine some accident happened that nobody was really to be blamed for: maybe some nice, friendly pet Elephant was sitting in a post office one evening, feeling in need of some friendly conversation or perhaps a bit of excitement and games, to while away the time until the Postman-in-Charge-of-Elephants-Being-Sent-Across-America-By-Parcel-Post got him all wrapped up and put enough Postage Stamps on him to take by First-Class-Mail from Chicago to, maybe Mukilteo, Washington, or perhaps to Cucamonga, Southern California. Maybe that nice pet Elephant was just sitting all alone in the Chicago Post Office Parcel-Room and happened to look down and find that his cage-door had somehow come unfastened. Well, if I were a pet Elephant, and if I had a chance to sneak out of my cage for a few minutes of recreation before resuming my Postal Journey, and I snuck out and started snuffling and nuzzling around the other Packages, and if one of those packages happened to smell (or taste) like a record of *The Story of Sinbad the Sailor*, well . . . I don't think I could resist unrolling my elephant's trunk and just flipping the Record up on the turntable of Record Player, just to hear a teeny bit of *The Story of Sinbad* . . . Wouldn't you do the same thing, Marsh?

And so the record must have slipped and broken.

I believe you and I can understand how such things happen, my dear big boy Marshall.

So I patiently waited for the chance to get to a department store and find you another record.

I am happy to be able to tell you what I found: another, brand-new copy of exactly the same record: *Sinbad the Sailor*! I also found a nice little book called *The Friendly Tiger*. I've sent you another little package containing the record and also (just to keep an eye on the record so that *it* doesn't get broken in the mail like the other one) the little book with the friendly tiger in it.

Love,
Dad

To Louis and Dorothy Simpson

St. Paul
May 11, 1964

Dear Dorothy and Louis,

Several months ago, out at the Blys' farm, I read Robert's copy of *At the End of the Open Road* pretty nearly to a frazzle. I even have some of it by heart. Heaven knows how many letters of gratitude I wrote to you about it—only in my head, alas. But never mind (as night keeps whispering at the window). Resuming correspondence (and, in a very real sense, sanity, I think) at last, I'll try to describe the weird dumbness and paralysis of will and heart that lay on me like a black cloud for month after month after month during the past year. But that, as I say, is for later newsiness.

The occasion of the present moment is the only occasion when the past is worth a damn anyway; and the past has got to work its way into the present through proper channels. Take *this* present moment. Earlier today I had a note from my former wife, in the course of which she mentioned her own pleasure in the Pulitzer Prize for this year.

It is about time.

My own pleasure in the award, Louis, is rather more complicated than Lib's (though by no means any less sincere, for all that). I mean that I have what I would confidently describe as an unusually thorough experience of your work; for I have read *The Arrivistes*, and copied many of its verses into a little notebook of my own; and I've read, many times over, *Good News of Death*; and also *A Dream of Governors*. Now, I have pondered the poems in these four volumes. Several of them I have got by heart. I have a good sense of what they sound like, because I have read them aloud for my own secret sake, over and over, as a composer of serious intelligence will sometimes withdraw to some private place and play Mozart over and over—not, as some might think, for the sake of the instruction alone, but first of all for the joy of the music. Anything a man learns that doesn't come to him permanently by way of the joy that it gives him is, well, just not much worth learning—I suppose one might learn, from sitting on stoves, not to sit on matches; or learn, from listening to LBJ, for Chrystes sake, not to sit on radios or pull the ears of television tubes; or learn, from vanity, to learn the duty of misery; or . . . but never mind, never mind. The prize makes me happy, because the poems make me happy, for themselves and also for their tremendously original fulfillment of the earlier fulfillments in the other books. What I mean is that *The Open Road* is certainly not to be understood as the *only* fulfillment, the *only* finished achievement, among the four books . . . it's not Louis Simpson Makes Good By DISPENSING WITH IAMBIC VERSE (ah, me! you tell him, Louis, *you* try him for a while: there isn't enough strict iambic verse in the English language to bother resisting; anyway, Wyatt already resisted it, and everybody knows that Wyatt was nothing but a passing dago, a mere hyphenated Guinea, a kind of nightingale-among-the-Assistant Professors, as one might say; so never mind, Robert, NEVER MIND!) . . . No, *The Open Road* is a new and wholly distinct work, one of whose most powerfully moving features is the unmistakable life that flows from one end of the *whole* book to the other and back again, as though the single poems in it, like the organs of a man's body, are severally distinct and miraculously whole creations and, at the same time, the very fuels and engines of one another, as the ventricles can function alone only because the brain somehow remembers to imagine them alive and so grant them the shape of their own natural flowings and fallings. The book is overpoweringly *one* poem. One reads it—one is *compelled* to read it, all of it—from beginning to end, even if he merely thinks he is looking up a single poem for reference or renewed pleasure (I actually found this strange thing happening to me three different times, at the very least; I started out by trying to flip through the pages of *The Open Road* to find a single poem or line, and was almost irresistibly drawn to the beginning of the entire book, from which I simply found what I sought by reading my way toward it; and I loitered with it for a time; and then moved naturally and truly forward to the San Francisco lines and the end.) It is different in many other ways, also—different from the other books, a new shape of the book that has strangely loomed up almost of its own strength; it no more supersedes the great lyrics like "A Woman Too Well Remembered," say, or "The True Weather for Women," or "Carentan," or several others, than—oh, . . . than Africa can be said to "supersede" Asia or North America. Political regimes, stylistic fashions in poetry, be damned to them, we been there before; but a new continent uplifted from the sea only ennobles the Asias and Americas whose own forms are both new and old, and they return the nobility as the sea gave it. Nobody "owns" a true nobility, for God's sake. In the presence of the noble, he is ennobled.

I feel ennobled by *At the End of the Open Road*. (And I mean it: any obscurities in this letter are the consequences of clumsiness in my effort to write down on paper the thoughts and feelings about a body of work which I suddenly have realized to be deeply important to whatever is vital and growing in my own character.)

Please give Annie and Tony my fondest love, and please accept it, with all gratitude, from

Your friend,

Jim

To Liberty Wright

St. Paul

May 28, 1964

Dear Lib,

It's just past daybreak. A few minutes ago, starting to type a clean copy of a recent manuscript, I rather absent-mindedly recorded to-day's date in the upper lefthand corner, as I customarily do. Suddenly, within space of an instant, more than a decade of life vanished, and I recalled myself standing awkwardly in the presence of a weary, impatient, and yet amused police-clerk down on the other side of the Stiftskaserne in Vienna, which was (you'll remember) all the way around the corner and far down the street from Breitegasse 7/11. The police-clerk sagged behind his ancient, worn-out desk, and the amazingly brilliant autumn sunlight seemed to sag with him, till he finally took on the appearance of a tree from which the very last leaf had given up the ghost and fallen to earth very very slowly, just in time to avoid the un-familiar company of the very first flakes of snow. Do you remember? Surely you do; for I had to come and fetch you, in order to complete the process of registration (Anmeldung). In my own memory I stand there forever, as eternal and golden as the sunlight of that happy time: a poor, God-forsaken American horse's ass, incapable of remembering a crucially important date.

It was the date which I entered on my manuscript just a few minutes ago. Suddenly I felt the perfectly simple and spontaneous desire to write you: Happy birthday. I trust you not to be offended, for I meant no irony in writing that I hope you feel happy today. I realize that a decade of life isn't to be wiped out of existence, just like that. On the other hand, I so seldom experience any simple, direct feeling of any kind whatever, that I just thought I would follow it for its own sake. And now that I've started, I think I'll try to describe what's happened to me during the past year, and where I seem to stand at the moment. But first I want to thank you for the good will, the friendliness, which you offered me in your letter of a few weeks ago. I don't have it handy at the moment, I'm sorry to say. But I'm not going to let myself use that fact as an excuse not to finish this present note to you and send it. Instead of succumbing to such a paralysis of will (a truly horrifying experience, which I don't know how to begin to describe), I'll just mention one thing that I recall from your letter. You said something to the effect that you hoped I wouldn't decline any offer of a job on the west coast simply because you were there. No, I wouldn't decline any such offer for any such reason, Lib. But I've had no such offer. And next year I'm returning to teach at Macalester.

Let me say a word about Macalester. I began this past school year feeling as thoroughly defeated as I can imagine. The way I was treated at the university was utterly shocking. I will not at this time try to list all the details; but if you knew them—as I finally learned them only within the past couple of months—I believe you would clearly agree that they are offensive far beyond any personal failure of mine that might account for them. But to return to my earlier point about Macalester: I began classes last September with the conviction that everything in life, that I'd ever considered worth living for, was ruined almost beyond repair. Most terrible of all, my self-confidence as a schoolteacher was utterly shattered. As I vividly recall that time a year ago, only one connection with reality was left: that was Edgar Doctorow's miraculously heartening assurance that my big book of translation from German—the Theodor Storm stories—which I'd been totally unable to work on during the terrifying months of insanity in the spring (I'm not kidding: insanity), could still be completed and that the publisher would certainly accept it. I had nothing else to turn to; and I turned to that book again. I often wrote for two or three days over a weekend, indifferent to food and sleep, simply because the only alternative that occurred to me was literal death. Bit by bit I clutched a way back to the everyday world. When classes at Macalester actually started, I had regained enough hope to at least *want* to face the wreckage of reality, and to start to rebuild myself as a teacher, rebuild literally from scratch. Day after day after hellish day, I labored more intensely than I've done on scholarship since I studied Latin in high school. And day by day revealed no particular progress, no particular sign that my effort had any meaning; I just struggled blindly on. There's a place in E. A. Robinson that suggests how I felt for months: where he speaks of "some poor devil on a battlefield / Left undiscovered, and without the strength / To drag a maggot from his clotted mouth."

Then a startling thing happened. It was last March 13th. The student-officers of the Macalester Students' Honorary Society requested that I deliver an after-dinner speech at their monthly meeting. I consented, and prepared a lecture on "The Art of Translation." I arrived at the meeting totally surprised to find it a very formal, serious gathering, attended by every dignitary at Macalester, including the President and his wife. Be that as it may, I delivered my lecture, and went home. In a day or so I received an astounding, magnificent letter from President Rice. Moreover, he had caused copies of his letter of praise to be sent to the Dean of Students and to the Chairman of the English Department (Ray Livingston, of course). Actually, what had happened wasn't particularly spectacular: I had just been heard and judged as a teacher and scholar by someone who wasn't a hired spy or a company fink or a vicious fool. Anyway, I was indirectly asked how I would like to be invited to Macalester again. I said I would accept with relief.

At this point, I must introduce another element in the course of events, a very strange one which still strikes me as silly, at best, and perhaps even a bit unreal, a bit irrelevant to me and the way my life appears to be shaped. It turned out that Mrs. Elizabeth Kray (from the Poetry Center of the YMHA in New York, formerly, and now an official at the Solomon R. Guggenheim Museum—you met her once in Minneapolis, and she liked you a great deal) had been exploring the possibilities of my being granted a fellowship by the more famous branch of the same family: the John Simon Guggenheim Foundation. The entire affair is weird, ironic: I was sent application forms three times in personal notes from the chief director of that huge Foundation, and simply (so help me God, I speak the truth) simply forgot to answer his notes, much less fill out the forms. My private feeling then—and, to a large extent, even now—may be described as a plain refusal to believe that such things as fellowships, grants, etc. (that is, the very idea of an entire year of opportunity to work on my next book without at the same time being forced every moment to struggle with suffering and punishment and anxiety of an endless, hopeless kind) had anything to do with me. Now, let me return for a moment to the letter from the President of Macalester (mentioned in the previous paragraph): I clearly informed the Macalester authorities that, however ironic it sounded, a Guggenheim fellowship was being all but shoved down my throat; that I was unable to take it seriously enough even to reject it, in the improbable event that it might be offered me; and that, *regardless* of the Guggenheim's decision about me, I definitely was willing to return to Macalester next year. Then, if the Guggenheim was granted me, I would postpone it until at least the Autumn of 1965; and, if such postponement were not allowed, then I would simply reject it. Well, more briefly, I officially was offered the Guggenheim fellowship. I was also officially invited to return to Macalester next year. I intend to return, because they are short of faculty and need me; and also because I need them. I honestly can't imagine any other way of regaining the minimum of health, psychological health, absolutely necessary to go on living. As for the Guggenheim, it was at least a month-and-a-half ago that I received the official letter granting me the fellowship. I haven't even written a note of acknowledgement, though I've received *two* urgent special-delivery requests for such a note. Within the next couple of days, I'll try to write a request for postponement; but it will be pretty half-hearted. The plain truth is that I *still* don't much care to get emotionally entangled in what is sure to be an impossibility. My conviction is that hopeful things don't happen to me, and so to hell with them.

Incidentally, Robert Bly received a Guggenheim; he accepted it immediately, and combined it with some other award he'd just received. He and Carol and their two little girls (the younger is named Biddy; she is as bald as Yul Brynner, a nice baby) left their farm about a month ago. The last I heard, they were headed for the town of Thaxted in England, near London, to visit Donald and Kirby Hall; but I don't know what they plan thereafter: somewhere in Scandinavia, I imagine.

Oh, yes, Lib, I just recalled another item of news in your letter: about Louis Simpson and the Pulitzer Prize. I was pleased, and wrote him a note of congratulation. He has written well for many years, and he deserves the recognition. Do you ever see him and Dorothy? They're in Berkeley again. The address I have for them is 800 Spruce St., Berkeley 7, Calif. Dorothy always liked you, and you liked her too. You should call them . . . Right now, I'm exhausted, and I begin summer school soon.

Love to you & the boys (I'll write them soon.)

Jim

To Louis Simpson

St. Paul
May 29, 1964

Dear Louis,

I must say how delighted I am to have your letter. You sound marvelous, clear-headed and confident in your own decisions about the nature and depth of your strength. There was always an amazing toughness of independence in your work; and the more you come to accept it for what it is (simply the normal breathing rhythm of a man who is, in Keats's startlingly irreducible phrase, "among the poets"), the more fully you seem able to give clear expression to your very great resources of personal kindness and generosity . . . I seem to be getting lost in rhetoric already. Let me try again, because I think the point is important . . . One of the most characteristic of your poems (I think it's in *A Dream of Governors*) is a short one in which a man wakes at night, recalls some moment of his previous life as a combat soldier, hears a night-breeze blowing through the window and over himself and his sleeping wife and children, and just lies there awake and smiles to himself; and then comes the last line-and-a-half of the poem:*

> . . . His life is all he has,
> And that is given to the guards to keep.

The phrase "His life is all he has" trembles in every single word, every single letter, every pause even; and I choose the word "trembles" with some care; for I want to suggest how your phrase (indeed, the whole poem) suddenly and conclusively discovers a poetry of tenderness, and discovers it in the very act of creating a poetry which is true—to yourself in the present moment, and consequently to your personal past, and, again consequently, to our whole American history that truly does reveal itself when we wake at night and allow ourselves to feel that strange, strange tenderness toward our own lives and all other lives that are awake *or* asleep at that very moment; for the tenderness is somehow the very resource of strength that clears the mind and makes it attentive to our own nature in this country. Maybe I can describe what I mean a little more clearly still, by quoting an odd remark which I recently found in José Ortega y Gasset's book *History as a System* (now in a Norton paperback, and very worthwhile, by the way): "Man has no nature; he has only a history . . ."

It occurs to me that your power (practically unique just now) of evoking such splendid and dark poetry from the stream of American history is perhaps the simple consequence of your personal admission (again, just about unique) that such a thing as American history actually exists.

I don't mean to imply any scorn for the American writers, historians and others, who don't seem to realize, or admit, that our history exists. It takes some courage to admit that. And sometimes the moments of that history are so comic that they can make a person shiver with something like fright. For example, I read somewhere (I think it was in Frederick Lewis Allen's *Only Yesterday*) that a few enterprising newspapermen, apparently as cynical as the disillusioned reporters at the beginning of the chapter in *Miss Lonelyhearts* called "Miss Lonely-

*"Old Soldier," from *A Dream of Governors* (1959) by Louis Simpson.

hearts and the Clean Old Man," took a trip to Marion, Ohio, to interview the *father* of President W. G. Harding, before the Teapot Dome affair was publicly revealed. Now, these reporters asked old father Harding just how in hell the President could be so stupid as not to know that his bosom-friends of the Ohio Gang in Washington were ransacking the public till and laughing behind his back. Harding's father, according to Frederick Lewis Allen, meditatively continued chewing his plug of tobacco for a few moments, and then remarked, "Well, all I got to say is, it's a damn' good thang Warren warn't born a wawman. He'd always be in the family-way. Just can't say no."

I just thought of a recent "Peanuts" comic-strip which I found, and which in a way embodies something of the same sense of frightening assininity (sp?) that President Harding seems to suggest. I'll enclose the "Peanuts," but please return it to me after you've shown it to Dorothy. Charlie Brown is simultaneously heartbreaking and infuriating.

I can't say how grateful I am for the comments you made about the poems which I sent you. The comments provided just the right tone that I very much needed: without jumping into the poems blindly and blindly trampling underfoot both the weeds and the potential flowers alike, you stood patiently among them and thought about your own feelings, and then told me what you thought. I am so clearly in agreement with nearly everything you've said, that I'm writing the present letter during late afternoon, a kind of crest of a wave of revision and further writing which your intelligent, considerate comments helped to release.

However, let me remind you of a very important qualification of which you're already aware: please do *not* feel that I will be disgruntled, or resentful, or bitter,—or anything that would oppress you with guilt, however minor—if you should ever receive a batch of new poems from me and find yourself just too out-of-sorts, or too distracted, to comment on them specifically. It goes without saying that your comments are enormously welcome and helpful; but they are all the more helpful for having come freely and spontaneously. In exactly the same spirit, I am eager to receive your own new poems—the ones which you mentioned in your wonderful letter. I propose the following principle: let's both feel entirely free to send each other some poems; let's grant each other the widest possible latitude of criticism and comment—all the way from the kind of very careful and specific comment which your recent letter offered me, to a mere acknowledgment by one of us that he's received verses from the other. Do you agree? I make this suggestion because I believe it will provide the best atmosphere, the freedom to read a poem and merely say that you like it or don't like it. After all, we read things that leave us cold, and we don't know why, nor do we care; on the other hand, we read some things (Thomas Hardy wrote some of them) that Randall Jarrell, for example, could go on picking apart avidly in hell through all eternity, and yet we are entirely willing to just let Hardy write his own poem in his own way, because we know it is beautiful and noble and well-made, we don't really care how.

Agreed? I very much hope so. I am, as I say, really eager to see your new poems. I will respond to them, I know; and I'll write down my response as truly and clearly as I possibly can.

As a token of my enthusiasm, I enclose a couple other new pieces. My God, I feel something of what a grizzly-bear must feel a few minutes after he wakens from his hibernation.

* * *

I have a letter from Robert. It was written from England, just across the street from Donald and Kirby Hall in Thaxted, about 40 miles from London. The mere thought of Robert in England is odd, isn't it? But not really: the oddness is an illusion planted in my mind by Robert's performance of a role. It can be an entertaining and even useful role, nevertheless: I heard him tell the assembled English Departments of Carleton College and the Morris, Minn. branch of the U. of Minnesota that, compared with poetry in some other languages, "English poetry can scarcely be said to exist." Nonsense, yet it pleases me sometimes to think of it. (Louis, I sincerely hope you will find it in your heart to forgive me for the previous sentence. Sometimes I fall into ghastly bad taste.) Robert's letter begins characteristically: "Well, here I am in England! I feel like a whore in a police station! Etc."

By the way, speaking of people who have trouble respecting the English, I've just read all the way through the *Collected Poems* of Hugh MacDiarmid. He is a great poet. Sometimes he is sublime. I'm not exaggerating. Robert once told me you'd met MacDiarmid. I hope so. I wonder about him. It occurs to me that his poems often embody the same powers of independent courage and tenderness that I mentioned at the beginning of this letter.

This letter is long enough for this time. Before I conclude, however, I want to copy out some riddles which I've recently collected into a little notebook. I think that your little girl Annie might like them. As for me, I think that #1. (in the list below) is one of the most wonderful things I have ever encountered in the English language:

RIDDLES FOR ANNIE SIMPSON

1. What's purple, weighs about two million pounds, and lives at the bottom of the sea? (Answer: Moby Plum.)
2. What's black and yellow, and squeals when you turn it over? (Answer: A school-bus.)
3. What's black and lives in a tree and is very dangerous? (Answer: A crow with a submachinegun.)
4. What is covered with salt and has a twisted mind? (Answer: A thinking pretzel.)
5. What is soft and yellow and lethal? (Answer: A shark-infested custard.)
6. What's brown and has two humps and lives at the North Pole? (Answer: A lost camel.)
7. What's red and squishy and comes through the wall? (Answer: Casper, the friendly tomato.)

Love to all,
Jim

To Jack Wright

St. Paul
June 6, 1964

Dear Jack,

I've been up all night writing like hell (it's now—Jesus Christ!—it's now exactly 1:37 p.m.!) And I suppose I'm just hysterical enough—or perhaps outright drunk on words—to have one of my rare flashes of insight: viz., everytime I admonish myself to actually *answer* your incredibly beautiful and devoted letters to me, I start to punish myself with a separate guilt for each letter; and, since the letters number into

the hundreds, I always end up throttled once again with guilt. However, just a moment ago I realized that I was by this time so God
damned guilty that I had become almost innocent again. So I figured
I'd just give up the "plan" to *answer* your letters one at a time, and simply *write* to you.

Please be patient again, Jack old man: I'm going to mail this note
right now, so that I won't be able to leave it half-finished for the next
five years. It will be step number one. Number two will be a copy of
my latest book (which Roger Hecht assigned its prize-winning parody-
title in the regular competition among old Kenyon wags: viz., *The
Branch Bank That I Broke Last Year, and Other Revels*). It isn't really very
much of a book, but I hope it pleases you some.

What is gray, weighs six tons, and sings calypso? (Answer: Harry
Elephante.)

(I believe that one is the chief masterpiece in this major new *genre*.)

I'll be in touch sooner than you can possibly think. You write too.
Meanwhile, here goes this little letter, for once!

Love,
Jim

To Richard Eberhart

St. Paul
June 6, 1964

Dear Dick,

Your letter is such an important moment in my life on this earth,
that I have finally come to realize why I haven't been able (literally, I
haven't been able) to answer it. For how could one "answer" one of
those passages in which a good man's utterly selfless generosity and lov-
ingkindness suddenly, by authentic miracle, become perfectly identical,
body and soul, with the words in which he offers the entire abundance
of his spiritual life to another person? Are you acquainted with James
Dickey? In a thousand astonishing, unexpected, and yet inevitable
ways, he and I have become the most deeply steadfast and enduring of
friends; whenever we meet, either by accident or design, we invariably
devote at least a couple of hours of our visit to a slow stroll somewhere—last Spring he spent a whole weekend at Macalester, and he

and I picked our way down the steep eastern bank of the Mississippi and then walked on and on and on, now and then tossing a sand-dollar out over the slick, melting ice—Jim flung one so perfectly sharp and ferocious that it skipped clear out past the very frailest lace of dissolving ice and skated on and on and on, over the dark blue water itself, clean out to the middle of that wide river, almost—and, as always, we communed in silence a good deal of the time. He is a manly, tender, affectionate person of great physical strength, utter courage, pride, dignity—in one of his poems he speaks of his brother's "loved face," a phrase that would have occurred only to a genuinely strong man. He is also, in my opinion, a critic of almost frightening lucidity, depth, and force—I think he is the most intellectually brilliant literary mind of my generation. And his own poetry continues to move, volume after volume, toward the fulfillment of his unique radiance of imagination. (In a poem about one of his solo-combat-flights in the Pacific during the Second War, he writes of suddenly feeling someone peering over his shoulder, and turning instinctively and catching a glimpse of "a great ragged angel of sunlight." The radiance of the phrase is entirely characteristic of his great poetic gift) . . .

Well, during such strolls during visits together, Jim and I do occasionally speak aloud, mostly about the few poets and poems that are secret and indispensably precious to us both. I can distinctly remember at least three different occasions, including the stroll down to the Mississippi last Spring, when Jim Dickey and I quoted the poetry of Richard Eberhart to each other aloud, and then proceeded with the stroll in silence, so that we could listen to the echoes.

Your letter to me was a presence, as your poems have been for a long, long time—indeed, ever since I was an undergraduate at Kenyon College (1948–1952) and learned of your poetry through your (characteristic) generosity in giving a new poem of yours to the editor of our old literary magazine *Hika*. Ever since then, I have cared about your poems as I care about few others. More than that: I've studied them, fiercely, and tried to learn something of the inner craft of them (the greatest of them invariably convey an unmistakable sense of your own astonished and astonishing discovery of each poem's holy secret, its unrepeatable and eternal miraculousness) . . .

And so, when I finally—finally!—was blessed and honored by meeting you in New York, I had that strange feeling of confirmed faith, that comes to us a few times—I felt, truly, like a devoted friend of yours already; and now I earnestly hope that the friendship is formally sealed by the good clasping of hands.

I said (above) that I couldn't properly speaking "answer" your beautiful letter; and just before I began to write to you, something else that is precious to me came leaping like unannounced lightning into my mind. Without pretending to explain why, I feel that it's important to copy it out for you; it made me happy to remember it, and I hope it pleases you, too. It's simply a few scattered sentences from Thomas Hardy's gorgeous novel *The Woodlanders*. The parts I suddenly recalled with such overwhelming clarity a moment ago are concerned with Hardy's mysterious, green, unutterably beautiful character named Giles Winterbourne, the young man who lives and breathes in the intimate presence of the trees (mostly apple trees) which he raises in his own woodland tree-nursery, and who, each autumn, suddenly is transformed into Autumn itself, as he travels about with two horses and his home-made cider-press.

Here is Hardy's little account of Giles's appearance in the latter role, as he is seen by the girl Grace Melbury, at the very moment just after she has finished speaking with Fitzpiers the tree surgeon, now vanished. Grace stands musing about her pet horse:—

"Thus she had beheld the pet animal purchased for her own use, in pure love of her, by one who had always been true, impressed to convey her husband away from her to the side of a new-found idol. While she was musing on the vicissitudes of horses and wives, she discerned shapes moving up the valley towards her, quite near at hand, though till now hidden by the hedges. Surely they were Giles Winterbourne, with his two horses and cider-apparatus, conducted by Robert Creedle. Up, upward they crept, a stray beam of the sun alighting every now and then like a star on the blades of the pomace-shovels, which had been converted to steel mirrors by the action of the malic acid. She opened the gate when he came close, and the panting horses rested as they achieved the ascent . . . (Giles) looked and smelt like Autumn's very brother, his face being sunburnt to wheat-color, his eyes blue as corn-flowers, his boots and leggings dyed with fruit-stains, his hands clammy with the sweet juice of apples, his hat sprinkled with pips, and everywhere about him that atmosphere of cider which at its first return each season has such an indescribable fascination for those who have been born and bred among the orchards. Her heart rose from its late sadness like a released spring . . ."*

* * *

(Yet another passage, just a plain, simple, sort of homely description, and yet it is a miracle that must have occurred to Hardy's imagination as helplessly and overwhelmingly as a blossom occurs to a branch. It deals with one of Giles's visits to the town of Sherton Abbas, where he regularly takes orders from the townsfolk for saplings grown in his nursery. The apparition of good, green Giles Winterbourne from the country, standing confused on a town street-corner with his arm around an apple-tree that he's carrying along with him, must have made Hardy simply close his eyes in a moment of prayer, just before he recorded this vision):—

"It was his (Giles's) custom during the planting season to carry a specimen apple-tree to market with him as an advertisement of what he dealt in. This had been tied across the gig; and as it would be left behind in the town, it would cause no inconvenience to Miss Grace Melbury coming home.

"He drove away, the twigs nodding with each step of the horse† . . . (Next, the girl Marty South, who sometimes helps Giles in his nursery and who is also visiting town on the same day, catches sight of him, again and again, during her shopping):

"It was impossible to avoid rediscovering Winterbourne every time she passed that way, for standing, as he always did at this season of the year, with his specimen apple-tree in the midst, the boughs rose above the heads of the crowd, and brought a delightful suggestion of orchards among the crowded buildings there. When her eye fell upon him for the last time, he was standing somewhat apart, holding the tree like an ensign, and looking on the ground instead of pushing his produce as he ought to have been doing. He was, in fact, not a very successful seller either of his trees or of his cider, his habit of speaking his mind, when he spoke at all, militating against this branch of his business." (And, finally, Giles's keeping his appointment with Grace Mel-

---

*From chapter 20 of *The Woodlanders*, by Thomas Hardy. The parenthetical interpolations are Wright's.
†From chapter 4.

bury):—"His face became gloomy at her necessity for stepping into the road, and more still at the little look of embarrassment which appeared on hers at having to perform the meeting with him under an apple-tree ten feet high in the middle of the market-place . . . He gave away the tree to a bystander as soon as he could find one who would accept the gift . . ."*

* * *

Your letter was like the tree, I think, and I was the bystander; I accept the gift, indeed, with great happiness and gratitude. (I feel delighted endlessly by Hardy's words; may they refresh your spirit also!)

Yours,
Jim Wright

To Oscar Williams

St. Paul
June 8, 1964

Dear Oscar,

Your letter of June 3 sketches a *stunning* vision of the *New Anthology of the Great Poems in the English Language.*

I am honored and delighted by your invitation to contribute a brief critical note (1000–1,500 words) to this book, which may very possibly be your anthologistic masterpiece. (I mean what I say, and with my whole heart, Oscar; everybody who cares about poetry surely carries in his secret heart a spiritual anthology without which he could not live and breathe at all; and I would say, conservatively, that fully half of the poems I love best were poems that you revealed to me, magician that you are.)

Of the three poems which you offer for my critical note, may I work on Frost's "Stopping by Woods on a Snowy Evening"? I am instantly confident that I can write you something succinct, sound, and worthy.†

---

*From chapter 5.
†Included in Wright's *Collected Prose*, p. 91.

* * *

You will understand that I merely offer the following information to you as a loving suggestion, which of course you will use or ignore, entirely as you see best: Among the three poems which you offered for my critical contribution to your new anthology, you included Yeats's "A Dialogue of Self and Soul." I love this great masterpiece, but learning is required as well as love, in order to do it justice; moreover, it requires a scholarly gloss; and such a gloss must, I realize, be a model of sensitive taste and brevity. All these points lead me to inform you that my friend and former colleague, Dr. Sarah Youngblood, Dept. of English, Univ. of Minn., is on the threshold of publishing a Handbook on Yeats. Oscar, I would stake my mind, my feelings, and indeed my very life on the promise of her handbook's power and importance. It will be instantly recognized, by anyone with half a brain, as one of the curiously few necessary introductions to Yeats. Sarah is a genius. If I were Yeats, I would wobble her ouija-board. In short, she could do *the* masterful note on the Yeats poem. I'll mail this note now. More soon.

Jim

To Tomas Tranströmer

St. Paul
July 6, 1964

Dear Mr. Tranströmer:

I want to beg your pardon for seeming so ungracious and ungrateful in my long silence. More than four long months have passed since my friend the poet Robert Bly traveled from his farm in western Minnesota in order to visit me in St. Paul; and, of course, he brought with him, among other things not nearly so pleasing, your beautiful letter to me. May I assure you that, in spite of appearances to the contrary (in view of my long delay in replying), I was immediately and deeply grateful to you for your letter? In fact, I have read it over many times; and was prevented from promptly answering—prevented by a tangle of problems too obscure and, perhaps, too dull to describe at this time.

I suppose the best proof of my good faith in demonstrating my gratitude is the enclosed group of new poems. When I call them "new," I mean that they were written since the completion of my most recent book, *The Branch Will Not Break* (which you mentioned so kindly). Furthermore, some of the enclosed new poems are really quite recent. I do not know just what forces came together and wakened me (about a month ago) into a kind of fury of ecstatic writing (it lasted for about two weeks, and then paused). But I think that I felt quickened, in some mysterious and yet very definite way, by two events: one was your letter to me; and the other was a long article about *The Branch* which appeared in Japanese, and was sent to me by way of my publisher, the Wesleyan University Press. I am afraid that I am not expressing myself very clearly; but when I saw my own name printed *in Japanese*—and, even more deeply, when I saw the title of my little book printed *in English* (tiny, tiny little English script!) deep in the very center of a page of Japanese script, I suddenly felt astounded—and even overjoyed—I felt as if there were actually a great deal more of life, and perhaps of *kinds* of life, in my own soul (as God created it) than I had ever even thought about before. And your own letter, my dear Mr. Tranströmer, with your mention of the three translations of my verses into Swedish, made me feel exactly the same way.

For this reason, I want to ask a favor of you. Would you be so kind as to send me the Swedish versions of my poems that you have already made? It is sadly true that I do not speak nor read Swedish. But several of my friends can do both; and it would please (and nourish) me very much to hear someone read the translations to me aloud.

I just realized that my delay in replying to your letter has probably made it impossible for you to include any new translations of my verses in the American issue of *Ord & Bild*, which you mention in your letter. If that is the case, I beg you to excuse my delay, and not to distress yourself on my account. The poems which I enclose with this letter may or may not be translated, according to your own taste and convenience. If you do not have occasion to translate them, then I hope you will simply accept them from me personally as a gesture of gratitude and friendship. My friend Robert Bly has shown me only one of your own poems in his English translation; and I value it for its sensitivity to stillness, its patience, its very deep and clear powers of *reverence*. (I trust that my word "reverence" does not trouble you in this connection; at any rate, I tried to choose the word with some care.) May I ask if you are familiar with the poems of the Austrian poet Georg Trakl, who died in 1914, at the very beginning of the First World War? I believe he is a very great and true poet, and your own poem brought his distinct poetic presence to my mind.

You asked for "information" about me. There is little that matters. I was born in Martins Ferry, Ohio, in December, 1927. I have traveled a great deal—across America, and to Asia, and once to Europe—and I am a rather rootless, homeless, dull sort of person, presently a schoolteacher. My own three books of poems are *The Green Wall* (Yale, 1957); *Saint Judas* (Wesleyan, 1959); and *The Branch*. Please write to me again. Thank you.

In friendship,
James Wright

To Liberty Wright

St. Paul
July 7, 1964

Dear Lib,

I received your letter this morning, when I went to Macalester to do some odd jobs and then spend a couple of hours in the library, searching out the brief detailed "bibliography" to send to Edgar Doctorow as the absolutely final touch on the Storm book. I could have read your letter on the run, of course; but I didn't want to. Without pretending to "analyse" the feeling, I will simply say that it pleased me to carry the letter in my pocket all day. Now, back in my room, I've just read it.

In another moment I must rush off again, this time to Minneapolis, to tend to further matters having to do with my teaching at Moorhead. It's not that I feel any desire to evade (why did I choose that word "evade"? Why, indeed!) this answer of mine by cutting it short. On the contrary, I am actually eager to write to you at considerable length on a variety of topics, some of them serious and some lighthearted.

But I want time to think as I write. So I will write you again shortly after I'm settled at Moorhead.

Besides, all I really want to say to you at this very instant—since I've just finished reading your very true, beautiful, and encouraging

letter—is something quite simple. It leaped straight up into clear consciousness; and I want to state it simply, so as not to spoil it by my usual
longwinded pseudo-intellectualization.

It's simply this: Lib, your note to me was, beyond any question, the
friendliest thing you've ever written to me.

The thought does move me in deep old (surely not "old") emotions, and the source of the emotion is surely obvious. Before I identify
that source, I believe I'll just ask you, for the fun of it, if you recognize
what I mean . . . Please keep in touch. I needed and loved those two
weeks. Please hug the boys for me. More soon.

Always,
Jim

Moorhead, Minnesota
July 22, 1964

Dear Lib,

I'd just arrived here, and had just begun to make the necessary ex-
ertions to launch two new courses with two wholly new groups of students, when I received a perfectly charming little letter from Franz.
Though most of the letter dealt—rather excitedly—with his baseball
team, for which he so delightfully says, "I get to use a uniform," the
first two very brief sentences in the letter did more to lift my spirits
than I can say. Franz simply opened his letter thus: "How are you? I'm
fine." The two sentences don't seem like much; and yet, how much I
have to learn from them! Franz not only asked a sincere, concerned
question about my welfare; he also knew (by some instinctive delicacy,
some essential health of the spirit) that he could positively contribute to
my well-being by the simple and powerful expedient of affirming
his own, thereby conveying some of it to me. (Shall I be a bit more
pointed? Well, consider: every time I informed you, via telephone from
my office at the U. of Minn., that I felt bad or was outright sick, I conveyed just that much sickness to you. Now, I could multiply examples
of this strange and yet undeniable psychological phenomenon, but I
would rather just state it once and then drop it. I have to see it, grasp it,
and live it. One example is enough. Besides, I am just as sick of being
sick as you are (I'm sure) of being sicked. Maybe there's yet another

psychological principle, a more helpful one, to be discovered here: To be sick of being sick is to prefer to be well. Anyway, I feel good. Franz made me feel good by telling me that he is "fine." Fine.)

I want to send you this note at once, Lib, for the following reason: Franz said in his letter, "Just about every boy on my team has a pair of baseball spikes. I sure wish you would send me $5.00 so I could get a pair. They help you grip the ground when your running." Lib, my first impulse was to send the check direct to Franz, out of sheer pleasure in his pleasure. This was an impulse which I am certain that you fully understand and share. *But*: are *you* pressed for cash? *or*: is Franz perhaps straying beyond the bounds of his allowance in this case (without calculation, I'm sure)? In either case, if I sent the check for $5 direct to him, I would be undercutting your own admirable and delicate relations with him. Now, for here and now till death, such undercutting is just *out*. So I enclose the check to *you*. Please transmit it to Franz, or else put it in his savings account, or otherwise employ it according to your own best judgment in the matter. Then, would you please let me know (by return mail, if possible) what you've decided? Then, you see, I can write to Franz in response to his nice letter and his request.

One more thing: as far as I am personally concerned, I do hope that, in the present case, it is all right to make an exception and let Franz have the baseball spikes. On the one hand, the happiness I would thereby feel is (almost certainly) a rather shoddy relief from guilt (i.e., how nice, I am hereby allowed to betray and fail the persons who mean more to me than my own life does, and for a mere five bucks, etc.) . . . On the other hand, there *is* something special about little boys' sporting-gear. My father used to make me eternally happy, at the beginning of each autumn, by strolling some unpredictable afternoon from the Hazel-Atlas factory uptown to a sporting-goods store in Wheeling and, just for the sheer idiotic, extravagant hell of it, buying me a dazzlingly expensive new leather football, which he would proceed to hide on my chair so that I wouldn't even suspect its existence till I tried to sit down for supper. Well, I know that he is lonely and frightened nowadays; and I seem to say little to him; but, at least, in the old days when I was about Franz's age, I know that I was able to convey to him that I *understood* what he had done for me, and what it meant: he hadn't just bought me a new football—He'd given his utter and unquestioning, unhesitating approval to my own secret longings;

and I love him very much. Soon my mother will be dead, and my good father will die soon after (she's a bitch, mainly, but he didn't give a damn for that—he loved her without qualification for fifty years and more). I'm not sure what it means, but it almost certainly means exactly *nothing*: that my old man lived out his endless years of brute labor in silence. But I'm so glad he got me a new football each autumn when I was a kid; and, at least, I will say this much for human life: I loved and will always love my father, and furthermore I was (at least then) able to convey my love to him . . . Well, maybe I'm just exaggerating. Still, other things being equal, it would make me very happy to hear that it's okay to give Franz the five thrillingly extravagant and very special dollars, for those baseball spikes. My God!—"They help you / grip the ground when your running." Please write to me soon.

Love,

J.

To Marshall Wright

Moorhead, Minnesota
July 28, 1964

My dear Marshall,

Here is the poem which I've written to celebrate your birthday.*

I hope you like it.

If there is any of it that you don't quite understand, Momma will explain that to you.

Right under the title I've written what is called an epigraph. An epigraph is a quotation from some older book, or poem, or story, or anything that's written by some wise person. Poets sometimes copy epigraphs under the titles of their poems, so that the souls of the wise men, or the saints, will help them to make a good poem. An epigraph is like a prayer.

A good poem is a poem that says "I love you."

A saint is a person who (really) loves everybody he knows, whether he gets paid for it or not.

A great saint from India, named Shree Ramakrishna, got sick when somebody called him a saint.

*"For the Marsh's Birthday" is included in *Above the River*, p. 169.

All that means is that a saint is more interested in other people than he is in himself.

Ramakrishna said that we should love one another whether we are good or not. Then, we will all be good. If you love somebody, your love makes him good.

I know perfectly well that you are a good boy, because I know I love you. If I know anything on this earth, I know I love you.

I know you love your momma, and your brother Franz, and me.

That is why I feel so good. Thank you, my dear, dear Marsh. Happy Birthday.

Tell Momma that *The Bhagavad Gita* appears as *The Song of God*, translated by Swami Prabhavananda and Christopher Isherwood, with an introduction by Aldous Huxley, published by Mentor Books (New American Library: serial number MP466). It is one of the most beautiful books ever written, and I think Momma would like it very much.

I like her very much.

And you too.

I love you,
Dad

To Robert Mezey

St. Paul
November 17, 1964

Dear Bob,

Bless your good and steadfast heart. There really is such a thing as sin, by God; and mine are so many, and so fantastically crushing to me, that I am writing you this note simply out of gratitude, not only for your beautiful invitation to stay at your farm during my (postponed) visit to California, but also—and more deeply—out of my somewhat desperate realization that true friendship is really a holiness, strong enough even to forgive the loved friends who are unworthy. I am certainly unworthy; but your note to me reminded me that I am loved, as always. In the bowels of Chryste, I beg you to help me to sustain the lines of communication now that you've been compassionate and courageous enough to open them.

This would sound coarse and arrogant to others, but not to you, surely: I know I do not have to offer you a list of explanations for my long silence, even though on several occasions my failure to respond to your letters must surely have hurt you very much. I beg you to forgive me.

Too many things have happened to me, physically and professionally (I mean academically) and spiritually, for me to list them all at once. But I can assure you that I have been following your work more faithfully than you might suspect. I resort, in my few remaining solitudes that survive unwounded and unbroken, again and again to your magnificent defense of the noble art against the almost innumerable current American schools of literary know-nothingism; I think especially of your great, brave, entirely sound evocation of "Robert Burns of Ayreshire," who, I am always hearteningly reminded, took a turn or two of his own in the necessary labor of pronouncing maledictions upon

> A set o' dull, conceited hashes
> Confuse their brains in college classes;
> They gang in stirks, and come out asses,
>   Plain truth to speak;
> And syne they think to climb Parnassus
>   By dint o' Greek.

Your poem led me back to him, that great spirit, a craftsman, by God.

Jascha Kessler has some good poems of yours in his new anthology (just arrived today), but he should have included at least twice as many by you.

Bob, I can't put off telling you this, and I find myself doing so almost helplessly, without shame: I have but recently been released from a stretch of over six weeks in three different hospitals with a breakdown brought on by shock (an honest to God trauma, which I cannot yet bear to think about for more than about thirty seconds at a time) and consequent anxiety. It was day and night of authentic nightmare, by far the worst bout of nervous terror that I have ever had in my life—and, as you know, it wasn't the first of such hospitalizations. I am now returned to teaching, at least; and I have evidence to assure me that I have been performing, since my return, coherently, and sometimes even (my most intelligently judicious students have told me) with a kind of ferocious brilliance. The main trouble is that my students, marveling at what they can only interpret as the quick recovery of an essentially strong man, conclude that my most effective lectures are expressions of serenity and happiness; whereas, in almost inexpressible fact, I have lectured most clearly and even movingly at those very times when I felt I absolutely had to do something inventive in order to escape the unspeakable demons of agony and despair which I constantly (even at this moment, insane as it may seem) bear in the very pit of my breast like a snagged fragment of old shrapnel too twisted to be removed and too close to my heart and lungs to be relieved by sedation in any noticeable way.

Moreover, I cannot help feeling, overwhelmingly, that I live without hope of relief, ever. Neurotic or not, that is the feeling, not to be refuted by argument. Even my doctor—a good and highly intelligent man who has helped me sometimes in the past—appears (to my mind) to sit quite beyond the range of my fantastically frightened struggles to describe to him what I think is happening to me. It is, at this moment, exactly 5:37 a.m. in St. Paul; and I have been awake all night, trying to summon up my forces of language and clarity so I can talk with the doctor over in Minneapolis, a few hours hence. I am frightened by the prospect of frustration again; and I fear that, if I don't succeed in telling him what's still tearing me apart, I might quite possibly just throw my head back and howl like a stray dog whose ribs have just been fastidiously flogged by a raildick's pick-handle.

Forgive me, my beloved old friend, for pouring out so much of this pain at once; but I cannot help it.

* * *

[. . .] *Please* write me a note, Mez, and send me new poems. Next time I'll send you a sonnet (!) which I've just written . . . No, wait . . . I have absolutely got to keep this note going long enough to quote for you a beautiful epigram by John Wilmot, Earl of Rochester, which I found a few weeks ago and found some unaccustomed joy in. It is called "The Sole Arabian Bird":

> 'Tis the Arabian bird alone
> Lives chaste, because he is but one;
> But had kind Nature made them two,
> They would like doves and sparrows do.

Well, here's my sonnet. It may not be much (I can't tell . . . I am in a hell of a shape, really); but it gave me another touch of secret joy which I needed very badly; because I love the art of the sonnet very much. It is about itself . . . i.e., the attempt to write a sonnet after long having lost touch with this noble form:

TO BUILD A SONNET

I had not gone back there, because to go
Meant pouring moonlight of a skinny kind
On slag heap, that my mother used to know:
Slow smoldering hell, shrunken, and hard to find.
Now I have gone back there, it is no dream;
It is broad waking; I have leave to go,
But not of anybody's goodness now.
It is my native rocks I go back to,

And build a sonnet. Laboring as I hide
Behind the shadow of this great hinge flung wide
Where Clare, John Ransom, Robinson stepped forth,
I lift my slight wall, yawing to one side,
My spine a splinter between winds, yet worth
More than the losses of my life on earth.

* * *

Again, forgive my nebulous caterwauling. (You probably expect to discover that the objective correlative of all that was something like a mild case of buboes.)

Mez, I am so happy that you are settled and married. Tell me about your wife. I am, among other things, so wretchedly lonely and lost as a human being that when I look into the mirror on arising I see all kinds of hallucinatory faces staring back, for I cannot bear to see my own face. I see, oh, long submerged subconscious crustaceans like Joe Hall, and a thousand nameless other such. My God, think what Hell must be like! They'll probably all be there, only there we'll actually remember their names, as we sit in a grandstand and, through a soggy eternity of Kenyon fraternity-Tuesday-evenings, review them in their multitudes as they stride past out of step, whacking their tenderized doodles or, occasionally so as to charm us with the variety of our infernal destiny, pause and rest at the side of some wear-proof middle-path painted green, eating one another's corporation-mothers-in-law.

I've seen [Frank] LeFever once or twice in NYC. Please write me.

Love,
Jim

To Dudley Wright

St. Paul
December 5, 1964

Dear Pop,

Thank you very much for your letter of November 18. I'm sorry I haven't answered till now, but numerous complications have got in the way. I still do not have all of the exact information which you will need to know of, but I will send it to you when I have it.

First, I very definitely intend to come home to be with you and mother and the rest of the family on Christmas. But I am not yet able to tell you exactly when I will arrive. The reason is that I am not yet sure just when I will have completed all my teaching labors: —for example, I am scheduled to give one final examination to a class on the afternoon of Saturday, December 22. That means that I will have to work all Saturday night grading the students' papers, so that I can turn in their final grades to the college Registrar *before* I depart for Ohio. Roughly speaking, I think I can plan to arrive home some time on Monday, December 24, *if* I can secure a flight reservation for that day. If I can't, then the only thing I can do is take a train; and that would mean getting the train *from* St. Paul *to* Ohio on, say, late Sunday, certainly in the evening. I don't know exactly how many hours it takes by train to get from here to Ohio.

So you see that the details of my planned trip home are still uncertain.

Still, it's only the details that need to be settled. As for the trip itself, I repeat that I do definitely plan to be there. I'll write you again just as soon as I'm able to inform you definitely about the date and time-of-day of my arrival in Columbus.

I plan to phone Jack soon, probably tomorrow. You know he and I already conversed by phone a few weeks ago, and even then we agreed to go home for Christmas.

Pop, it was kind of you to mention my old girl Barbara; however, I should inform you that she has decided to marry somebody else. She's a good girl, and I hope she is happy . . . I also hope mother is well; as for you, you sound just splendid, and I'm eager to see you . . . Please keep in touch. I'll write again quite soon; but, even now you can definitely count on my coming home for Christmas.

Love,
Jim

To Franz Wright

St. Paul
December 5, 1964

My dear Franz,

I haven't forgotten the wonderful letter which you wrote to me a few weeks ago. At that time, I was in the hospital. I was sick with what I might call nervous exhaustion. Your letter meant a very great deal to me. I am writing now to tell you that, as far as I know, I am much better. I am now able to teach all the time.

Also, I have been able to leave the hospital. If you will look at the top of this page, you will see that I have a new address. I am now living in a little apartment, about three blocks away from Macalester, the college where I am a teacher. It is much more comfortable than the single room that I used to live in.

I want also to tell you that I will be traveling in California next spring. It will be at the end of March and the beginning of April. I am going to lecture and read poetry at about eleven different schools in California. I will soon be able to write to you and let you know exactly when I will be there, especially when I will be near enough to San Francisco so that I can come and see you and Momma and Marshall.

Are you still playing the trumpet? It was fun to see you and hear you play last summer in Spokane, when we all had such a nice time visiting with Barbara Schneider and her family . . . Please give my love to Marshall and to Momma. And tell Momma that I am much better now, and not to worry about me. I hope she is feeling and doing well in her teaching and other things too. Are you and Marshall enjoying school again? Please write.

Love,

Dad

To Susan Gardner

New Concord, Ohio

December 23, 1964

Dear Susan,

I am sitting in a very old gray frame house at the very eastern edge of New Concord, Ohio, where my parents live. It is already very deep into the late evening, which, in Ohio, always seems like a loitering twilight, just as the Ohioan twilight itself, falling as it does so early and so pitilessly beautiful and fierce, like a chicken-hawk, seems in winter to be a nervously eager midnight. When I was a child I knew a man who went to funerals. All the funerals, not just the incestuous ones, those nests that most of us never fly away from, we dawdle so. The man of my childhood was not an eccentric. Apparently he grieved for the dead. He always arrived too early, as some people habitually arrive early at parties; and he was often known to hang back, hang back, till the cars drove singly back down the steep road and there was only the sexton to chat with. It has always given me a curious sense of gladness to think of that man, who went forth to greet the darkness early, and then outlasted it by dint of courtesy, friendship, and concern for the laborer who did the holiest of services in smoothing and comforting the earth, that fine and private place. Outside, now, the night has arrived in full dark blossom of twilight. I can imagine the two of them standing together at the top of the hill behind this house: the sociable twilight, and the night with a spade on its shoulder. I still do not know why I should feel glad of their presence, but I do. A few months ago I was astounded—I mean it—to discover that the Hindu deity Siva, whom we in the West usually consider fearsome because we have been told he is called The Destroyer, is actually revered by the pious for the manifold abundance of his presences, the variety of his secret actions, the dependability as it were of his good faith. He dwells at times alone on a peak of the Himalayas, from whence he leaps into a form of a ruby of fire (according to an 11th century poet) and soars back down to us when the voice of the sea prays to him. Sometimes he can be found at crossroads when they are deserted by all save the loneliest of persons, who stand at their own crossroads, amazed, as if just that moment wakened while sleepwalking, wondering where to turn. I have myself wakened thus, a couple of times. Siva (the pious say) knows where to turn. That, you will agree, is a useful thing to know. He is the deity of regeneration.

I am glad that night has fallen and that it is still twilight in Ohio.

My brother Jack, who had planned to meet me at the airport in Columbus, is not yet here; so I have spent a while talking quietly with my parents, mainly with my strange mother, who has been ailing recently (rather seriously, I'm afraid), but who seems quite well at the moment. And now I am sitting alone. Having come home to this essential solitude, I thought suddenly of you, and felt an urge to share with you, for the moment, this solitude, this silence, this secret place [. . .]

Do you mind such long, rambling letters? I hope not. It has been a delight to write to you. Merry Christmas, again.

Yours,
Jim

To Ghazi Al-Gailani

St. Paul
March 14, 1965

My dear friend Ghazi,

I am ashamed for neglecting to write to you. But instead of writing out a long list of silly excuses, I think I will simply rely upon our steadfast friendship. That is, in the hope that you will forgive my neglect in the past, I will write to you in the present. And I enclose copies of several comparatively recent poems, as I promised to do.

The one entitled "Before the Cashier's Window in a Department Store" just yesterday appeared printed in the March 13 issue of *The New Yorker* magazine. Except for a few random verses in the Macalester College magazine *Chanter*, this poem in *The New Yorker* is the first one I've had printed in what seems a long, long time. I suppose I just stopped sending poems to editors, because—for the most part—I needed to make some strange voyages off somewhere in my own secret silences. But now I am beginning to print the poems—at least, a few of the poems—that I brought back with me from those silences. I hope you like this one, and the others also—they have not yet been printed anywhere.

I have thought about you constantly since you left—and I have been somewhat concerned for you because of the loneliness which you revealed in your notes to me. Of course, it is not enough merely to feel concern, and I promise to demonstrate this concern more frequently by writing to you. At the moment, I want only to assure you that I have indeed thought about you and your life in Tulsa. Rather often I have talked about you during occasional conversations with that lovely and intelligent and kindhearted girl, Sherry McClelland. Speaking of Sherry, by the way, she has loaned me several newspaper clippings written either by you or about you; and, as you will imagine, I have read them with the greatest interest. Ghazi, I hope very much that you will struggle to express yourself in some poems about your life (and I mean your real, your *inner* life) in American places like Tulsa, Minneapolis, St. Paul—and Mandan, South Dakota, too! I am enormously eager to have you meet my old friend the editor Robert Bly, who will certainly want to print translations from your work and the work of other Arabic poets in his internationally distributed magazine *The Sixties*.

While you are there in Tulsa, do you think you could have some of the translations of your poems reproduced (by zerox, or whatever they call that machine), perhaps at your newspaper office, and would you send them to me? I will gladly pay for all costs. Please write to me soon.

Yr. friend,
Jim

To Paul Carroll

St. Paul
[March or April] 1965

Dear Paul,

That was good of you to mention the *New Yorker* poem (my curse on one of the local department stores; God damn it, I hate money, I honest to God *hate* it, because of its undeniable power of transforming human beings into humanoids without our even being aware that anything unnatural is taking place. In this connection, I'm thinking of the two people—the cashier and the junior assistant life-guard, or whatever he was—whom I mentioned in the new poem. You see, I was at the time considerably behind in payments on my credit account at this place in Minneapolis; and I felt like hell for a multitude of other reasons quite distinct from my bill at the dept. store; and I was wearing a horrible (yet somehow magnificent!) ancient baggy overcoat that my father gave me years ago, a coat which (before I retired it formally some months ago) possessed that weird old-fashioned virtue of resisting all fraying of elbows, sleeves, collar, etc., while at the same time offering a spectacular repertory of other varieties of decline, decay, ruin, distension, etc., featuring sudden and unaccountable green humps that would appear on the side of the damned coat, or on its clavicle— humps that would heave up there mysteriously, like geologic flaws or the subcutaneous varicosities that loom up suddenly, alpine and pinnacled dim in the intense inane of flash-bulbs, when (as sometimes surely must happen) one of Elizabeth Taylor's flesh-tinted rubber-bands snap and her features begin instantly to subside back to the wild, like fields full of junked trolley-cars shared with obsolete and discredited stocks of whole "lines" of rupture-trusses once featured by assorted quacks during, say, the years when the advertising columns of the immortal magazine *Captain Billy's Whizz-Bang* were as widely effective as the comparable columns in today's *New Yorker*.

(As you can see, I've been rereading—rather, re-singing—*Finnegans Wake*, and last evening I just found a new recording of Siobhan McKenna (reading "Anna Livia Plurabelle") and Cyril Cusack (reading "Shem the Penman"—You remember: "Shem is as short for Shemus as Jem is joky for Jacob" . . . "Tell me a tale of Shem and Shawn! O Lor! Latten me that, me Trinity scholars, out of our Sankrate into your erse!")

Please excuse my little explosion of horseplay. Really, I am so happy to be in touch with you both again, and my weird response in this letter is simply a kicking-up-of-heels. Belle had talked to me about your both probably coming up to visit with the Tates "sometime in May" (your words). I want to note here something that is, to me, very important to be kept in mind, selfish as my motive may be: you see,

I'm going to be on one of Betty Kray's lecture-circuits in California—between Thursday, April 23, and Monday, May 9—that is, I'll be arriving back in Minneapolis–St. Paul in time to resume my classes on the Monday.

Of course, you have both got to consult your own plans and conveniences first of all—even so short a trip will require certain delicate arrangements about jobs, etc., however minor—and such arrangements may compel you to come for your visit during my two weeks out of town.

But I hope to God not! Because it would be absolutely *lovely* to see both of you, and particularly at that time—say, the middle of May—when, if ever in Minnesota, come perfect days.

Paul, you must particularly dance the beautiful Inara on your knee at my request, in order to inform her of my warmest respects and greetings at this time—and to mention my own memory of authentic delight at meeting her and seeing you both together, when the very existence of the two of you in the same room at the same moment created some new dimension of air that I—really ill as I certainly was—could breathe and breathe with a breath of love that I could entirely trust.

So the "delight" I speak of is something different from the ordinary formality however in itself graceful.

* * *

Do you hear anything from John [Logan]? I plan to send him about five new poems within the next 48-hrs. (I have taken to setting deadlines for myself, and so far the device is working). My God, I wish I could send him an eye, or something.

I'm enclosing one of the newer poems that—Paul, didn't I read it aloud to you and Inara and Saint Giraud at your apartment in Chicago last November? Anyway, I remember how I promised that I'd send it to you. And here it is at last. (I should say "them," not "it," maybe . . . this is the brown cricket who lives in Robt. Bly's chickenhouse; Robt. and I were once enchanted to discover that we had both written poems addressed to this nice cricket, and neither of us had mentioned his poem till an evening last March in NYC, when Robert and I both read verses at the Guggenheim Museum: just by coincidence, we both read our poems to the cricket. A very congenial cricket, indeed . . . Well, here are my poems to him.*

Please write me soon, even if only a line or two; and I'll respond in turn. Paul, I will be writing you again on the matter of what strange dark new thing is emerging from behind what you thought was going to be another half-humorous mock-epic. "You are the most bitterly brutal because your words are dead birds" is a great line: harrowing and unmistakable. I know what I'm saying. Well, the big dark poem will speak in its own way, so be patient, as it assuredly will not be with you, should it suddenly wish to come out all at once.

Love,
Jim

To Mary Oliver

Cupertino, California
July 10, 1965

Dear Miss Oliver:

I hardly expect that you will actually read this note, because the address on the envelope is incomplete. But I will go ahead and write it for my own sake. I have loved your poems for a long time, but until I found and read your book† I hadn't realized how much they had come to mean to me. It is an extraordinarily beautiful book that you've written, and it haunts me in some secretly desolated place in myself where I had not hoped to see anything green come alive ever again.

Am I correct in remembering that you once wrote to me? Or am I simply imagining things? I recall a dreadfully unhappy letter from you, which heartened me. At the time I was quite ill; and, before I could answer your letter, I lost it. I hope you will forgive me. I have lost so many things. So many.

Till the very end of this summer I will be staying with a couple of very old friends here in California. I don't know why I tell you this. Of course, I am a liar. I know perfectly well why. If you should receive this

*"Poems to a Brown Cricket," included in *Above the River*, p. 173.
†*No Voyage and Other Poems* (New York: Houghton Mifflin, 1965).

note, and if you should find a moment, and if you should feel patience, I would be truly grateful to hear from you. I have been laboring heavily from time to time on a new book of my own. It has been pretty jagged and difficult going, and the example of your book has given me some of the encouragement which I sorely need.

Wherever you are, and whether or not you even read my words, thank you for writing your book.

Sincerely,
James Wright

To Elizabeth Willerton Esterly

Madison, Minnesota
September 16, 1965

Dear Elizabeth,

When I arrived late Sunday evening at Montevideo, Minnesota, about twenty miles from here, I was greeted by Robert and another guest, Paul Zweig, a brilliant young philosopher and poet from Paris. Today is Thursday. I woke this morning at 6 o'clock, in order to bid a temporary farewell to Paul, who was catching a bus from Madison and plans to be back in Paris within a day or so. Between the Sunday evening greeting and the Thursday morning farewell, there were several days of discussion, disquisition, and intellectual exploration that can only be called blistering in its intensity, lavish in its excitement. Paul is going full blast on three projects: a new book of poems; an anthology to be called *The Poetry of Vision*; and a philosophical study called *Narcissus*, which is at once an extenuation and a refutation of Denis de Rougemont's exasperating classic, *Love in the Western World*.

I spoke above of bidding Paul a temporary farewell. What I mean is that he has invited me to contact him if and when I cross the channel in the winter. He is cordially eager to help me find my way around France, and even to find me a place to work in a beautiful countryside abbey which he knows about and where he has himself been able to accomplish a good deal of writing in an atmosphere most congenial. I have never had the opportunity to visit the French countryside, really. I went across it by train; and that is something in itself; but you know what I mean. One cannot get to know a place by observing it alone, though observation alone is beautiful. One needs to love the animals, to cut the grass, to spend long hours with the sundown and with the rhythms of friends. Isn't it so? You often spoke this summer of your "way of life." Yes, it is true. Life is not an observation nor a summary. Life is a way of life. So many ways, so many depths, so many hummingbirds and mountains.

I am just now getting settled. Just yesterday I wrote to St. Clairsville for a copy of my birth certificate, which I need for a new passport. And so on. I'm going to get this note off at once, in the hope that you will answer soon. Please give my love to Henry, Allison, Debby, Dinah, and all.

Love,
Jim

To James Dickey

Madison, Minnesota
September 16, 1965

Dear Jim,

It was just a week ago today that my brother Jack and I came up to visit with you and your family again. I am writing now to tell you what a beautiful visit it was for both Jack and me. I have no doubt at all that Jack cherishes the day of the visit as deeply and abidingly as I do. You see, the thing about both Jack and me is that we are lonely men who nevertheless carry within us an unchangeable need for family. Almost immediately after the trouble erupted at Watts this summer, I found myself—rather, placed myself—in what practically amounted to a three-way telephone conversation with both him and our parents back in Ohio. All of us in our family are perpetually haunted by our failure to keep in adequate touch; and yet, as soon as the faintest possibility of danger or joy seems to arise in the lives of any one of us, the others' voices suddenly come rushing across great spaces, speaking all at once in messages of desperate affection and relief. Perhaps I'm not succeeding in writing down my thoughts very clearly here. But I believe you will know what I mean anyway. Jack is my younger brother. He has always been one of my truest concerns. So it gave me very special joy to be in his company at the very time when I got to be all day with you and Maxine and your wonderful sons: people I care about as much as I care about anything in my life.

As you see above, I'm here on the Blys' farm. I expect to be here from about three weeks to a month. At the moment I'm in the midst of straightening out various problems in order to apply for a passport. Eventually, I guess I will go to England. I don't yet know how long I'll stay there; but in any case, the Blys will forward any mail which I receive at their address.

It occurs to me also to mention how personally grateful I was for the chance to visit your home at a time when I was more relaxed and human than I was during the previous visit. As you'll recall, I was terribly tense because of that reading-tour in the spring. This is all by way of telling you, really, how moved and delighted I was by that whole day of music. Please write soon.

Love to all,
Jim

To Mary Oliver

Madison, Minnesota
September 16, 1965

Dear Mary,

As you can see, your letter was forwarded to me from California. I had left Cupertino (near Palo Alto, Stanford, San Jose, etc.) roughly two weeks ago, and next spent a week with my beloved brother Jack in Venice, Calif. (part of Los Angeles). I had been terribly worried about him, as you can well imagine. Venice is one of the many ghetto-suburbs of Los Angeles. It is some twenty miles from the Watts area. Fair enough. But, as my mother said over the phone a few weeks ago, twenty miles is quite close enough to the kind of thing that was going on in Watts at the time. My parents, by the way, live in New Concord, Ohio. Muskingum College is there. It is a pleasant town, something like Clyde, or Fly, or Cadiz, or Gambier, or Belbrook (the home of none other than Jonathan Winters). Yes, I love Ohio, too, and hate it, too, and it haunts me. It always will, I guess. But that's all right. My father worked for fifty years at the Hazel-Atlas Glass Co. in Wheeling, West Virginia. Now he is retired, of course. I have the feeling that you would like my parents. They are sturdy, steadfast people, poorly educated and . . . especially my mother . . . very well read. My relatives are strangely unpredictable and rather wildly kind.

For the time being, I am staying with the Blys on their farm, which I love very much. As you can see, I do indeed know them. I am the godfather of their older daughter Mary.

I hope there will be an occasion (during coming correspondence) for discussion of Robert's ideas and poems. But that occasion is not yet. I mean that I would first like to hear what you mean by "image-crazy." I think I understand, but I'm not sure. But let that go, for the moment anyway. Right now I am so thoroughly enjoying the farm, that I would like to relax and tell you how happy it made me to receive your letter. I don't know quite how to explain, but what I felt more than anything else was plain old-fashioned relief when I heard from you. How shall I explain? So many things are involved, I suppose: Ohio, and poetry, and loneliness.

Will you tell me what you are doing now? What does your husband do? Do you have children? (I have two beautiful sons, whom I saw for two good weeks during my summer in Calif.; but I am more or less alone—more more than less, I think.) This year I am on a so-called Guggenheim. After a good deal of indecisive pondering, I have more or less decided to go to England. But that won't be for a couple of months yet. For one thing, I have a number of things to take care of here in Minnesota, and in Wisconsin, and in Iowa. For another, I like to be here in the autumn.

But you've been to England. I have the impression that you've spent a good deal of time there. Will you please tell me about it? All about it?

This note is too short. But, as you know, I sometimes neglect the very correspondence that I care most about; so I am going to send this at once, in the hope that you will answer soon. I hope very much that you are well. Thank you for saying "please be happy." Your letter made me so. I am not going to analyze that feeling. But it is there; and I hope my letter pleases you, too. Please write.

Yours,
Jim

To Donald Hall

Madison, Minnesota
September 29, 1965

Dear Don,

At the moment I'm sitting in that little one-room house just east of the Blys' farmhouse. I have a very nice old-fashioned wood stove, which has served well from time to time during the need of the last couple of weeks. But today the sunlight has broken the long drizzling and soaking rains; the stove has got too warm by half; so I've opened the door; and now I'm aware of a kind of golden breeze. Through the door to my left I can see part of an alley which Robert and Paul Zweig cut through all the way to the cornfield. Pretty soon a schoolhouse will be moved there, from a place about four miles away. Robert bought it from some auction or other. It's going to be a guest-house, I'm told.

I've been reading *A Roof of Tiger Lilies* with pleasure, especially the poems which you've arranged in the first section, and which I've always liked—ever since I first saw them. Robert and Carol both point out that you seemed rather downcast, partly because the book didn't appear to make much contact with readers in America. I'm sorry for that, and I am sure that this is a time when it is necessary for us all to be in fairly frequent touch with one another again. It goes without saying that such a remark comes with outrageously bad grace from me, after my almost endless failure to write. But bad grace or not, what I say is true. I have myself been having an extremely difficult time with writing. I wrote you earlier that I had a manuscript ready; but by now I've torn it all down again, with Robert's help. I think I have got at least a beginning again. My main trouble is not knowing quite how to work. One begins to understand something about the real labors undergone by the saints and the really great poets. My God, John Keats must have been stronger than Cassius Clay and Sonny Liston combined.

I dearly wish there were a chance to see you and your family. I have had a vague promise of a reading-date dangled in front of me: sometime in November, at Ripon College, Ripon, Wisconsin. But I haven't heard from the dean there, and I suppose they've forgotten it. So I suppose I'll go to St. Paul tomorrow—Saturday I mean—and return here to the farm on October 15. Then, on October 29, I go to Ogden, Iowa, to attend a wedding. After that, unless nothing else turns up, I more or less plan to go straight to New Concord, Ohio, and spend the month with my parents. If, by that time, I've secured my birth certificate, I'll get a passport and go to England. As you can see, this Guggenheim year has its grim aspects for me. I am sick of being so rootless and unsettled and alone. I feel like a hobo in the thirties.

Please write when you can. I'll send a few poems later—actually, I don't have very many of them.

Love,
Jim

To Isabella Gardner

New Concord, Ohio
December 12, 1965

Dear Belle,

I tried to phone you last night. You weren't at home. You see, your letter didn't arrive till yesterday, what with its double trip to Ohio. It was awfully strange to see what was stamped on the first envelope: "No such person here, return to sender," or something to that effect. The effect was ghostly: I haven't been back in Martins Ferry, Ohio, for some ten years. After my father retired from the factory in Wheeling, West Virginia, my parents moved to New Concord, this small and comparatively peaceful college town on Route 40, just a little to the west of Columbus. I've been here since the beginning of November. I hadn't been able to visit my parents for any reasonable length of time for some years; and, what with the Guggenheim and the general rootlessness that this year has brought about, here I am. My plans are more or less clear: during the first week of January, I want to go to New York, and live there till about the beginning of March. Then I'll probably go to England for a couple of months.

When I tried to phone you last night, I had only a couple of things to say: first, I wanted (and want) to tell you that I have been thinking of you often—I wasn't sure of your whereabouts, though I had heard that you were in Italy during the summer. Second, I want to tell you that I am thinking of you now, and that I will certainly keep in touch. Third, I want to remind you of what you already know—that if there is anything, absolutely anything at all, that I can do for you, you have only to say so.

If you had been home last night, I would have told you, however clumsily, that I promise not to ask you all sorts of silly and prying questions. I do realize that almost nothing on earth can be so tormenting as the enquiries of friends when you are in the midst of such anguish.* You mustn't mistake the rather pedestrian tone of this letter for evasiveness or indifference. God forbid. I rather trust you will know that I am simply waiting to hear—with all sympathy and willingness to respond—any details which you yourself feel able to express. Actually, your brief letter already has expressed the pain itself, and its occasion.

So, instead of stinging you with a lot of fool questions, I will keep in touch. Also, you asked me to send you some poems.

I enclose copies of three. They were actually finished during the summer, but you haven't seen them, at least in these versions.

In your letter you also mentioned your book. As a matter of fact, I happened to find two paperbound copies of *West of Childhood* in Ann Arbor, Michigan, last weekend (during a brief visit there). But I would be extremely pleased to have a copy of the book from you. For one thing, that would enable me to give my two copies as Christmas presents to a couple of other people who, in their own way, matter to me very much.

Belle, I send you my bafflement, my friendship, and my abiding love.

Always,
Jim

To Carol Bly

New Concord, Ohio
January 16, 1966

Dear Carol,

Thank you very much for your beautiful letter. I am so glad that you and the children liked the presents. For my part, I am happy to have the big book about the Indians. Did Robert show you what I gave him? (The book of Tu Fu.)

Carol, I am in a severe pickle. Really, it is very serious. I have a new

*Gardner was divorcing her husband, Allen Tate.

letter from the University of Minn. Library, and they sound ominous. They demand the return of several books which are still charged out to me. There are five books which Robert evidently still has on the farm. Here they are, with their call numbers:

824M92 OS	Munchausen	*The Surprising Adventures of Baron M.*
839.5Ek195 OU	Ekelof	*Tuflykter*
860.1 L373	Laurel	*Antología de la poesía moderna en lengua española*
868.01 P365	Pellicer	*Three Spanish American Poets*
895T159 JP	T'ao	*Poems of Tao Chien)* (or T'ao Yuan Ming)

I would be terribly grateful if you would ask Robert to return these books, just as soon as possible, to the following:

Mrs. Evelyn Furber, Assistant Head
Circulation Department, Walter Library
Univ. of Minnesota, Minneapolis, Minn.

* * *

This stationery from Michigan means that I spent last Monday up in Ann Arbor again, being interviewed for a job next year. I had a wonderful time, both with Don and Kirby and at the University itself, a place which struck me as being very congenial. And on the morning of Tues., Jan. 25, I'm supposed to visit the office of the President of Sarah Lawrence College, Bronxville, New York. I had a lovely letter from them, and there's at least a slight chance that I might be teaching there next year, if Michigan doesn't work out. In any event, I hope to God that at least one of the two works out, because I am definitely not going to return to Macalester. I suddenly realized that I absolutely could not bear to live in the Twin Cities again. As you surely know, I care very deeply for Minnesota itself—its countryside, I mean; and I believe I am not exaggerating when I say that I love the Bly farm as truly and freely and fully as I love any place on earth. But Minneapolis is another matter. I have had so many failures there, failures of every kind imaginable, and so many wounds, and so many defeats, that I just came to realize that the city has become, to me, a city of horrors. If only I could find some other place to live, I think I could be well again.

Your poem is beautiful, and I am going to carry it in my wallet, an herb of healing, a balsam, and a sign.

I think of all four of you all the time. Please write as soon as you can. And please impress on Robert the dreadful importance of returning those five books. (Forgive my sounding so neurotic about them, but I can't help it—I'm sure you understand.)

Love from my parents and me,

Jim

New York City

1966–1974

James and Anne Wright, New York City, 1971

. . . the melancholy ecstasy of New York City, which is more glorious because it cannot be captured save by experience.

—from an essay that accompanied Wright's application to Kenyon College
April 18, 1947

Now I am living in New York, teaching at Hunter, writing pretty well, and able, at last, to write to my best friends again. What I mean is, I found my true love, too, after all this time.

—from a letter to David Wagoner
February 9, 1972

James began teaching at what was then called "Hunter Uptown" in the fall of 1966. He lived at the Hotel Regent on Broadway and 104th Street, where he had a room, bath, and miniature galley-type kitchen, although he ate most of his meals out.

Elizabeth Kray, director of the Academy of American Poets and wife of composer Vladimir Ussachevsky, took him under her wing. He was often a guest in the Ussachevsky home and used Betty's office as a place where he could write.

When James had been in New York on job interviews he had met Anne Runk, a teacher and director of a nursery school. As Anne puts it, "two incurable romantics met each other." They married on April 29, 1967, exactly a year and a day after they met, and moved into Anne's old, forty-eight-dollars-a-month rent-controlled garden apartment.

From 1967 to 1969 James taught in various programs for the summer terms; twice at the University of Wisconsin in Milwaukee and, in 1969, at the State University of New York at Buffalo, where he renewed friendships with Jerome Mazzaro and John Knoepfle. In the summer of 1970 James and Anne took their first trip to Europe together. James was able to show Anne his Vienna, and she introduced him to her Italy.

James won a fellowship from the Academy of American Poets in 1971. The fellowship was not only a great honor but also provided the financial means for the Wrights to take time off from teaching and to travel. The first long journey began in June of 1973 in England, where they explored Hardy country in Dorset. After a leisurely visit to Paris, some of it with Marshall Wright, they drifted off to Italy for several months, spent October in Vienna, and returned to Italy. The journey ended with a six-week stay in Paris. Many of the poems and prose pieces eventually published in *To a Blossoming Pear Tree* and *Moments of the Italian Summer* evolved during this time.

They returned to New York in time for the 1974 spring term at Hunter. By now the railroad flat was no longer suitable, and a large, sunny apartment just across the street was found. The Wrights moved there in May, and James finally had his own study.

Despite this positive addition to his life, while teaching in the summer school program at SUNY Buffalo during the summer of 1974, James fell into a deep depression. Major causes were concern about his son Marshall and the loss of both parents, Dudley in July of 1973 and Jessie in March of 1974. He was hospitalized for a month in the fall; then he was able to return to his classes at Hunter in the spring of 1975.

To Robert and Carol Bly

Hotel Regent
W. 104th & Broadway
New York City
September 4, 1966

Dear Carol and Robert,

First of all, please note the above address. It's the same address I had last Spring. (The phone number here is MOnument 6-1000.)

I arrived here by plane on late Thursday afternoon. According to the plan, Nina Flannery had arranged for me to go to something called the Midtown Hotel, over on 70th St. on the east side. I was supposed to look the accommodations over and then decide whether or not I wanted to make my residence there for a while, perhaps the whole year. Well, sir, Nina was ill; so I did the investigating myself. You won't believe this, but the accommodations at the Midtown Hotel were dreadful, impossible. The clerk showed me a specimen room that made me feel like one of Nelson Algren's heroes. The room contained a sink and a bed, which was in itself a kind of sink (if I may turn literary for a moment). The weather still being ghastly warm and muggy, I phoned my old place here, the Hotel Regent. It turned out that they remembered me quite well, and, by what I still consider great good luck, were able to offer me the same room (with its quite nice bath and kitchenette) at the same rates. So I believe that I'll stay here till further notice.

Carol, that was a splendid time on the farm, during those three weeks or so! I received the two sets of photographs from you while I was in Ohio; and, as usual (+"#$%%*!), neglected to write to you about them. But I'm doing so now, with gratitude. You know, I'm amazed at how wonderful I looked to myself in the picture in which I have Mary and Biddy on my lap. I looked pretty bad on the others,

347

alas—I mean that I looked very unhealthy. Well, be that as it may, I did lose a little weight in Ohio. Anyway, Mary and Biddy have a distinctly healthy influence on me in every way. You must tell both of them that I lose ten years and twenty pounds whenever they and I tell stories, sing songs, and have our picture taken together.

By the way: I'm making a note to myself right at this instant to get you a copy of that book of Isaac Babel's letters and stories that I told you about. I looked for it in the Twin Cities, without success; but here I can either find it at once or else order it at once, because the publisher is here. I'm also eager, as I said, for you to meet Patricia Blake, a very nice person who is writing a biography of Babel. She is a sort of prim and proper girl, very pretty and attractively serious and dignified, one of the nicest people I've met in New York.

Robert: I've had an idea. I wonder if you would be so kind as to send me the complete manuscript of that translation of Lorca's "Ode to Whitman" which I made a while ago. I really feel rather urgent about this. I suddenly remembered the month or so which I spent on it, and how much it meant to me. The reason I want to have it with me is hard to explain, but it has something to do with a need to place before me a kind of manuscript of some kind—something that will strengthen my morale at this particular time, just before I begin to teach at Hunter. Am I making sense? Also, I want to ask what you think of the possibility of including this translation in a new book (whenever I get a new book put together). Because the Lorca translation is somewhat different (in my mind) from many of the other translations I've done. The translation is actually a kind of effort to absorb Whitman through Lorca, and so the translation feels closer to me than most other translations have felt. Do you see what I mean? Will you please send it to me? I want to look at it again, go over it again, and so on.

"Hatred of Men with Black Hair," in the recent *Nation*, looked very strong. Do you have any further news about your book?

It was marvelous to see you all and also Louis [Simpson] and Fred [Manfred]. (But that sounds awfully stuffy—I want to keep in touch, and I have great hopes of snapping out of my particular darkness this year.)

Give my love to everybody, and have it for yourselves.

Love,
Jim

P.S. Robert, by the way, my mother asked if you would return to her that book about poverty in the Cumberlands, in West Virginia. Do you remember?

P.S. How is the Hernández issue coming along?

To Donald Hall

New York City
November 25, 1966

Dear Don,

Here I am after forever, getting in touch. So many things have happened since last we saw each other. As you know, I'm teaching at Hunter. The job is all right. It's really kind of difficult, with its comparatively heavy schedule of class hours. But it's a living, and I like it pretty well. I commute to the Bronx every day, and I'm becoming a regular subway hound.

I do think that, all things considered, I'm getting along pretty well in New York. It's as lonely as any other place, but no lonelier. I can't say that I'm making any huge progress with writing. But, in part, that's a matter of secret natural growth anyway. I will say that I've just about got a manuscript ready. It consists partly of the one I showed you—when was it?—about a year and a half ago. It's curious how the thing has been written. I've gone for a long time in a kind of compromise with despair, not conscious of having written much, just conscious of several kinds of defeat. And yet, somehow, the poems have appeared now and then, accumulating in a darkness. Over a period of about three years they've accumulated, and a few weeks ago some forty-five of them seemed suddenly to organize themselves into a manuscript. I've shown it to two people, and both surprised me by liking it. (One of these was Robert Lowell, whom I've got to know somewhat. He is a wonderful person, as you know better than I.) The trouble, as usual, is that I can't think of a title.

I had Thanksgiving dinner at the Hechts yesterday, and Tony was there. He looks well. During conversation earlier in the day, Roger and I were expressing great admiration for the poems of Jane Cooper. Are you at all familiar with her work? Roger and I agreed that we would both separately remark to you about the beauty of her poems, and ask if it would be wise for her to submit her manuscript to *Harper's* [Harper and Row]. She really is quite fine. Please write, and give my love to Kirby and the kids.

Love,

Jim

To Edith Anne Runk

New York City

November 29, 1966

Dear Anne,

I just got home, and thought of something, and I want to share it with you. Rabindranath Tagore translated it from his own Bengali on shipboard to England in 1910. I think it is a love poem. And I think it is a prayer. I don't know.

> In the deep shadows of the rainy July,
> With secret steps thou watchest, silent as night,
> Eluding all watchers.
>
> Today, the morning has closed its eyes,
> Heedless of the insistent calls of the loud east wind,
> And a thick veil has been drawn over
> The ever-wakeful blue sky.
>
> The woodlands have hushed their songs,
> And the doors are all shut at every house.
> Thou art the solitary wayfarer in this deserted street.
>
> Oh my only friend, my best beloved,
> The gates are open at my house.
> Do not pass by,
> Like a dream.

I don't know. He won the Nobel Prize for his own translation out of which this poem came. It is called in English and Bengali *Gitanjali*

(Song-Offering). He lived a long time, and gave his last years to commitment to Gandhi, and to a school.

He remembered looking out the windows when he was a kid. So he started a school outside.

Well: he is one of the greatest poets and teachers who ever lived. And I remembered his poem, which means so much to me, so I thought I would send it to you.

Jim Wright

P.S. I don't have the text here, so I may have lied, here and there. But not all that much.

To Dudley and Jessie Lyons Wright

New York City
March 24, 1967

Dear Mother and Pop,

I hope you'll forgive a short note. In a few minutes I've got to fulfill an appointment on the other side of town. But I have some rather special news that I want to give you.

Within the next few weeks—perhaps in June, perhaps a bit earlier—I am going to be married to an elementary school teacher named Miss Edith Anne Runk. She is a splendid person, and I know we will have a good life.

This summer, between the middle of June and the middle of July, I am going to be a visiting professor at the University of Wisconsin in Milwaukee. After July 15, Anne and I intend to visit the Blys briefly in Minnesota. After that visit, we want to come to see you in Ohio. Will that be all right? I'm sure you will like Anne very much.

Please write and let me know how Ted is doing.

Love,
Jim

To Robert Mezey*

New York City
Spring 1967

I have only a few brief statements to make about my own practice. I have nothing to say about the theory of prosody. During the past few months I had occasion to read several of Dr. Williams's discussions of prosody pretty thoroughly, and I have yet to make any *usable* sense out of his phrase "the variable foot." He had a perfectly tuned ear; he could write in the "musical phrase" that Pound asked for, though his poems are capable of including many more different kinds of music than Pound; but the unity of his poetry is not to be found in his prosody alone. Perhaps that is why he has had so many bad imitators. In order to write as well as Dr. Williams wrote, one has to have a fine instinctive sense of music in the American language, the music of speech and the music of song; and one must have the character of a great man who loves women, children, the speech of his native place, and the luminous spirit that lurks frightened in the tortured bodies of the sick and the poor. Without these gifts, many new poets have devoted their attention to the art of typewriting; and their poems (to refer to another useful phrase by Pound) look and sound like bad prose hacked into arbitrary linelengths.

For myself, I have never written in syllabics, which sound to me even more tedious than the rhymed iambics which no fashionable poet would be caught dead writing these days. If any principle of structure can be disentangled from the poems that I have written in free verse, it is, I suppose, the principle of parallelism, a term which of course need not be limited to a strictly grammatical application. For the rest, I have been trying to grope my way toward something which I cannot yet describe, but whose interest, if any, is not limited to the concerns of prosody and form.

James Wright

---

*From a letter to Robert Mezey, editor (with Stephen Berg) of *Naked Poetry: Recent American Poetry in Open Forms* (Indianapolis: Bobbs-Merrill, 1969).

To William Claire

New York City
September 17, 1967

Dear Bill,

I hope I haven't impossibly annoyed you by taking so long to answer your note of the summer. The truth is that Annie and I have done so much traveling and working during the summer that it has been very difficult to keep up much correspondence beyond postcards. The course which I taught in Milwaukee lasted only a month, but it was very condensed and required a good deal of reading, researching, and lecturing. For the rest, we proceeded to Minneapolis, then to western Minnesota, then to Ohio, then to Rhode Island, and finally to upstate New York. We returned to the city just recently, and my classes at Hunter have just begun.

There hasn't been time or real opportunity to construct the kind of full-scale essay on the poetry of Roger Hecht that his work deserves. I don't know whether or not a more brief and general statement will be of any use to you in your magazine; but I will try to offer one as follows:

Roger Hecht has been working silently and devotedly at his poems for more than a decade. Last year he published his first book. These *Twenty-Seven Poems*, however, cannot be described simply as a selection made at large from the substantial body of work which he has so far produced. The selection was rather guided by this poet's preoccupation, through an unpopular style, with a painful and necessary set of themes, the latter largely having to do with the rupture of American national idealism, a rupture long ominously prefigured by the sentimentality of American private life and the hysteria of our public life. The most ambitious of these poems, and the one probably most splendid in its achievement, deals with the confrontation between President Wilson and what one must call something like the cracked old Adam of human reality in this world. Roger Hecht's style, which I call unpopular, is the great plain style in English, deriving its wide range of rhythms from three main sources: the author's familiarity with the English and American masters of prose; his mastery of lyrical verse; and his wonderfully fresh pleasure in the spoken rhythms of the American language. There is always something forbidding in the tone and measure of these poems, and this quality is the surest value of the style.

The author's integrity is such that he devotes all of his stylistic brilliance, all his linguistic spareness, all of his passionate intellect to his insistence on the irreducible difficulty of his subject matter. The poems are disturbingly beautiful, like the poems of Melville; beautiful because they are disturbing. Moreover, by their very existence they provide a relief to the mind of any reader who cares about a literary culture, for they are the basis of such culture: a steadfast devotion to language itself, and an abiding moral seriousness.

* * *

Will such a statement help you, Bill? I love Roger's poetry and have very specially valued it for a long time.

By the way, that was lovely of you to think of Annie and me in Washington on our wedding day. She sends you her best, as I send mine.

Yours,
Jim

To Miriam Black

New York City
December 13, 1967

Dear Miriam,

The sun is shining today in New York City, and a short while ago I took a walk out of the pure blessing. Yesterday I ploughed my way up to the Bronx through the worst downpour outside, and the grimiest subway inside, that I have ever known. The weather made me think of Minneapolis. Which needs no further comment. And yet, when I arrived at Hunter College in the Bronx, where I am teaching now, I ploughed further into my two classes, and after I had lectured for two solid hours on Alexander Pope, I emerged, and the rain had stopped, and I was happy.

I know how dumb that sounds, but it is true, and it contains a secret. As you know, back in the Twin Cities years ago my life collapsed into a lower level of darkness. In the midst of that dark, I got a Guggenheim Fellowship. Now, I had previously rejected several offers of such help, because I wanted to fight my life through at the very place where it confronted me. It did confront me, in the Twin Cities, and it defeated me. So I had to get out. And I got out.

After prowling around the United States for some months, I made up my mind to leave this country for good. I agreed with an old friend of mine, a man who had loved America and the art of poetry as I had when we were young. He wrote me an utterly terrifying letter, in which he said, "I hate this country, this big fat stupid whore that I used to love so much." To hate one's native place is more appalling than suicide, I thought, so I am getting out. But after I came to New York, I started to think that I might possibly rediscover the main current of my life. So I found a job teaching. Miriam, you will recall that much of the time I was a poor teacher. But you will also recall that sometimes—just sometimes—while lecturing I was able to waken a live nerve in the great tradition. And now, after about a year and a half of ploughing straight ahead, I have got a life going again. The pain of it is sometimes idiotically bad. I kick myself out of bed each morning. I know—I *know*, I have lived it some—that life is totally unfair, a hell of a mess. I look around me with what Ortega so precisely called a tragic and ruthless gesture, and I build. Somehow I have finished my new book. It will appear (Wesleyan University Press) next Fall.

Furthermore, groping for some significant thread in this city (which I do love, as you do love Jerusalem, and your love for it was unmistakable in your beautiful letter), I found my love. She is the director of something called the West Side Community Nursery School. It is a cooperative school for pre-school children, one third of whom are from poor families supported by the Head-Start Program. Her name is Annie. I don't know that people would look twice at her on the street. But she is a luminous person, a revelation. She embodies the living meaning of a remark made by Sri Ramakrishna: "God's wind will blow your boat across the sea. But you must hoist the sail." I think it is true. I think I now understand what Rilke meant in a poem which I read as long ago as 1950: "What will you do, God, when I die? . . . What will you do, God? I am afraid." I am still afraid. But it is all starting to make sense to me. Perhaps we are the instruments of creation in the midst of chaos. Yes, that is a hell to bear. But that is nothing new.

It makes sense. It is possible to create sense.

I'm afraid my letter must sound stuffy, especially after the marvelous free-wheeling letter you wrote to me. But I can assure you of this: at a time in my life when it was a matter of life and death for me to find my way back to the values that are enduring, you talked with me and made those values available to me again. As far as I am concerned, I care about your life absolutely. I have no idea what has happened to you personally to bring you to Israel with your maiden name. I will leave that to you. But I want to tell you that if you need any help that I can give I will give it [. . .]

Bless you, Miriam, and please keep in touch.

Love,

Jim

To John Crowe Ransom

New York City

January 15, 1968

Dear John,

A very few weeks ago, I was in Ohio. My younger brother Jack, whom you met once, was there also. And my older brother Ted, who lives near New Concord, was there with his wife and children. I wanted very much to phone you. And yet I didn't.

I think that I can now tell you why.

The last time I came to visit you, I was in very bad shape. Around 1963, my family broke up, and I myself went to pieces. My visit to you with my brother Jack was a visit of longing. A little later, my visit to you with Robert Bly was a visit of confusion.

But I want to tell you what happened after that visit. Because of my previous writings, I had received a Guggenheim fellowship. It was a blessing, because it enabled me to escape from Minneapolis–St. Paul and to go home to Ohio. Like it or not, I was homesick—the old-fashioned longing. After I brought Bly to see you, I thought I wanted to leave my country for good. I even went so far as to get all possible shots for all possible diseases in Europe and Asia. The nurses at the Licking County Health Center in Zanesville, Ohio, inoculated me against everything I can imagine.

Ready for all diseases, I came to New York. Then I came to feel that here I might find a job and come to terms with life in some sense.

So I didn't go back to Europe after all. I got my job at Hunter College, with your help, and with the especially striking help of Allen Tate.

And now for a year and a half I have been teaching, and teaching well. I suppose what I want most to say is that I have found a startlingly kind and lovely woman, Anne, who is the director of a nursery-school in New York. She and I were married last spring. She is good to me. She is a revelation. There is nothing special to say about her, except that she is very old-fashioned. My two sons came to visit us in New York during the Thanksgiving week, and she and they got along beautifully.

I think I was probably a little ashamed of myself, seeing that my life had had bad moments when I saw you last.

But I want to tell you that I have been trying my best to pull myself together. Although my new book of verses is to be published in Fall of 1968 by Wesleyan, I can't say that I am concentrating on the book right now. I am rather trying to teach well, for I care about teaching as passionately as I've cared about poetry. You undoubtedly know how I failed as a teacher at the University of Minnesota. True enough. But now I have shown myself to be a good teacher at Hunter. Next autumn I am going to be transferred from the Bronx campus to the campus downtown, and soon, I am assured, I will be allowed to give a course that I dream of, a graduate course: Dickens.

Actually, I have seen and talked with some intelligent men, and I have been getting some of my own work done. But my work is in essays. The main thing I am working on at present is a review of Hölderlin. The wonderful British scholar Michael Hamburger has spent twenty-five years in the attempt to render Hölderlin's German classical meters into English, and now I am trying to write a whole slow fastidious essay about the whole problem.

I wish I could tell you that I am all right now. The only way to show you is to show you Annie, who is a fine human being. Early during the coming summer, I am going to give a course at the University of Wisconsin in Milwaukee, and then we are going to Ohio. Would you mind if I phoned you from Ohio?

You must understand, John, that I am one of those men who get buffeted around for a bit before language starts to make sense to them.

Frankly, I am afraid to write to Allen, because in his eyes I am a terrible failure. There is no doubt that I have been, and a severe one at that.

But I don't think I am now.

I hope to hear from you. I am dying to send you some new thoughts about the metrics of our beautiful language.

Yours,
Jim Wright

To Fred Hein

Cupertino, California
July 28, 1968

Dear Fred,

You know, one evening in New York a few months ago, I phoned you on a sudden impulse. You weren't home, of course, and I spoke briefly with a young fellow. The conversation was a little uncertain, but he did tell me about Luie. I have to tell you that I wasn't really surprised, because I'd known about her illness. But I was grieved, and I still am. Maybe that was what moved me to call you. But not entirely.

I was somewhat worried about you. But I also wanted to tell you something of what had happened to me since we last met. You said in your recent letter that I wasn't in the best possible shape. Of course that was true, and, as you so well understand, that was why, by some sheer blind instinct for survival, I had to get the hell out of the Twin Cities.

It's curious, and yet significant, that you and I both went through about a year of wandering and searching. I left St. Paul early in the summer of 1965 and made a bee line for the very place in California where Annie (more on her in a moment) and I are spending about three weeks with old, old friends. I spent that summer here in the country. I don't know how familiar you are with California. Politically it is an insane asylum, and its cities are often tiresome but its countryside— the mountains, the coasts, the orchards—is a secret and healing place. After California, I went home to Ohio, where I visited for a couple of months with my parents. I was still a wreck of booze and nerves, but I did continue to struggle with my book, and I had a chance to read and think and walk. About that time I felt I ought to get out of the country for a while. It isn't that I don't love the place. In fact, when I am in decent health I feel rather as Mencken felt. In fact, it is almost a sign of health in me, this desire to remain standing on the wharf, wrapped in the flag, while the expatriates are shilling one another out of oysters and tiger piss in Paris and the sons of the Gold star Mothers are putting down sin in Asia by smiting the accursed hun. But, I felt—rather than thought—that I might possibly clear my head just by sailing to England and wandering for a while. You can see that I just wasn't sure what to do. But I did have a Guggenheim fellowship. So I went over to Zanesville, Ohio, and conned the ladies at the County Health Office to innoculate me against every disorder we could think of, from buboes to Montezuma's Revenge. And off I flew to New York City.

It was there that my mind cleared. I had visited the city many times before, and I had always loved its vastness, its impersonality, the charm of its many silences. It is a much quieter city than, say Minneapolis. And it soon became apparent in New York that there actually were people who held me in respect, not only as a writer but as a teacher. It occurred to me that it would be a good place in which to live and work. To my amazement, I was hired to teach at Hunter College, where I have now been teaching for two solid and effective years. I finished my book—called *Shall We Gather at the River*, it will be published by Wesleyan on Sept. 19—and now the writing is going so well and so strongly that Wesleyan will next undertake to publish my collected poems. I'm at work on some other things, too. When you reflect how scattered and self-destructive I was when you saw me last, you will see how New York has been a blessing. The best blessing is Annie. She is the director of the Westside Community Nursery School. We met through mutual friends at Hunter. Now we've been married a little more than a year, and I have never felt so happy and strong . . . And your own life sounds good and happy, too. I'm sure we'll keep in touch. True friendship is one of the few enduring things. The letter doesn't contain one-thousandth of what I have to say. Write if you can. We'll be here a couple of weeks yet.

Best always,
Jim

To Eugene Pugatch

Cupertino, California
July 28, 1968

Dear Gene,

I'm sorry to have waited so long to reply to your last card. My God, you sent it in May, and here it is almost the end of July. But apologies are silly compared with letters. So here is a letter. First, I want to tell you something of where we'll be the rest of the summer [. . .]

It goes without saying that we've thought and talked about you often. I seem to recall your once considering the possibility of settling in Manhattan. I can only say that such an arrangement would make me tremendously happy. So many things have happened during the past few years—so many struggles and searches, failures and false starts and defeats and new beginnings—and now I feel that I'm finding my way, that I'm once again capable of being the serious friend that I used to be, before my life began to fall to pieces. Annie has been so good to me. I have never been so happy with people and with my work. I believe that New York would be good to you, too. The place has so many splendors and advantages. One can do good work there, and it's comparatively easy to get away from town if you really need to.

I guess I'm being kind of selfish, but let me tell you just one out of many things that will be happening soon: Michael di Capua of Farrar, Straus and Giroux has asked me to go through the poems of Hermann Hesse, make a selection, and translate them with an introduction. You can imagine how exciting it would be to talk over this project with you! [. . .]

My new book, called *Shall We Gather at the River*, will be officially published by Wesleyan on September 19th. I'll be sure to send you a copy as soon as I learn more definitely about your plans and location. I also can tell you definitely that Wesleyan is next going to publish my collected poems. I haven't really got down to work on it yet, but I think, at this point, that it will include my four books, a selection of translations that I've done during the past few years, and a section of new poems.

Please do write when you can, Gene. Annie sends her love, as I send mine.

Jim

To Denise Levertov

New York City

December 5, 1968

Dear Denise,

I've been brooding about the letters which recently appeared in the *Atlantic*, in response to James Dickey's curious article about Roethke. I admire Beatrice Roethke's letter for its pride and dignity. But your letter remains the most penetratingly intelligent of the entire lot. What Dickey's motives were for writing such an essay I can't pretend to know. The essay itself seemed to me very troubling and murky.

You know already how deeply I cherish your own poetry, and I will not belabor that matter. But I also thoroughly admire and respect your opinions concerning literature and people, and for this reason I would like to say something to you in defense of Roethke as a man.

For four years in Seattle I knew him quite well, and then we corresponded while I was living in Minnesota. It is true that he sometimes became ill, but even then he retained his critical balance as far as literature was concerned. He certainly did not consider himself the "Greatest American Poet" (the phrase sounds like an advertisement for a professional wrestling match between The Crusher and Mad-Dog Vachon for the World Heavyweight Championship in the high school auditorium of Mt. Vernon, Ohio). He was not an outright idiot. He knew perfectly well who the masters were, and I believe it was this admirably acute critical understanding which partly made it possible for him to write, as you say, some wonderful poems. As his student and friend, I can assure you that Roethke understood Dr. Williams—that is, he knew, and was able to explain with lucidity and conviction that Dr. Williams was a great poet because he was a great man, and a great man because he was a great poet.

I'm sorry that I haven't seen you and Mitch for so long. I want to mention that I'm married now to a lovely woman who teaches in a head-start nursery school.

With love to you both,

Jim

To Allen Tate

Dear Allen,

I appreciate your note in response to the note which I wrote to you toward the end of the summer. Of course I do very much want to keep in touch, though it sounds rather lame to say so, after my neglecting to write for the past couple of months or so. Mainly I would say that for the past three years I've been trying to regain something of the sense of personal dignity and self-respect which I once had—and which I had certainly come close to destroying during my last years in the Twin Cities. I'm sure you see that the effort which I began to make some three years ago was of a kind that I couldn't, with any propriety, express to anyone, not even to my best friends—perhaps to such friends least of all, for I had worn their patiences pretty thin.

But now I can report, with fair confidence, that I've gone a long way toward regaining control of myself. I'm in my third year of teaching at Hunter, and I enjoy my work there. My attendance at my classes is no problem any longer, thank heaven. Some two years ago, I met, and subsequently married, a fine woman (Annie), who was the director of the West Side Community Nursery School. We live modestly and seriously in our small, comfortable apartment. And, without wishing to embarrass you by an outpouring of old personal problems, I believe it will mean something to you to hear that I am not drinking these days. Perhaps a glass of light wine when we have guests for dinner, but nothing beyond that. But no booze whatever, at any time. I am quite surprised, and pleased, at the improvement in my feelings about things in general. I don't mean that I feel euphoric. God knows, we are living in a very dark moment in the history of this country. I just mean that I feel generally healthier than I've felt in a long time. Perhaps for the first time in my life I am beginning to grasp what is meant by the life of private virtue, and to see why a man ought to try to lead such a life. It is an orderly life, for one thing. A disorderly life, such as I once fell into, is full of misery—not tragedy, but misery, and the misery is petty. G. B. Shaw scorned, and I believe justly, the "feverish selfish little clod of ailments and grievances complaining that the world will not devote itself to making (him) happy." Well! I don't mean to harangue. But my spirits have risen; and I feel like a man again.

My new book has finally appeared, and I am sending it to you under separate cover. I labored long and hard to form a unified book. But you will judge.

Annie sends her warm greetings. I hope you will convey our special respects to your wife Helen, of whom we have heard (from Cal Lowell and others) so many lovely things. We hope you have a good Christmas, and we'll be thinking of you. We're going to Ohio to visit my parents for the holiday, and I think I'll try to phone John Ransom, to say hello and extend the greetings of the season.

Love,

Jim

To Louise Bogan

New York City

December 8, 1968

Dear Miss Bogan:

I hope you won't mind receiving a note from a stranger.

Recently I acquired two books: *Andrew Marvell: Complete Poetry*, edited by George deF. Lord; and *The Blue Estuaries*.

I have read most of the poems in both of these volumes so many times for so many years, and with such devotion and attention, and I have committed so many of them to memory, that they have taken root in my very life, and grown there. Whatever of the meretricious and sterile I have ever encountered, or even sometimes been, I have always been able to turn to such poems as these and to know them for the true north. As far as I am able to judge and care, these poems are the true art. Humanity is in so many ways a botch, that I find it difficult to describe to you the consolation and encouragement that I have found in the plain evidence which these two volumes supply: that some few human beings, at any rate, have been able to create poems of surpassing excellence.

Perhaps everyone who cares about the art of poetry has his own personal fancies, which harm no one and even offer their own appropriate delight. One of my fancies has been to wonder what kind of letter I might have written to Andrew Marvell—or Thomas Campion, or Catullus—to thank him for writing the poems. But after reading *The*

Blue Estuaries, I was astounded to realize that my fancy was not vain after all; and that is why it makes me happy to write this letter to you.

With gratitude,
James Wright

To Diane Wakoski

New York City
December 23, 1968

Dear Miss Wakoski:

I was grateful to you for sending me your new book. It's been some weeks since I received it. To send it to me was a nice thing to do, simply as a mark of friendship.

But that is only a brief part of what I want to say. Today I was sitting in my office down at Hunter, feeling down in the mouth, and, what with one thing and another, sad and distracted and depressed.

I took up *Inside the Blood Factory* and began to browse. It's difficult to describe just what this beautiful book did for me. There is a freshness, an originality, a clarity—I suppose it is an unmistakable genius of human warmth signified by a brilliant intelligence—that lifted my spirits at a time when I needed your poetry. I have felt this kind of thing very few times. My experience with your new book this afternoon meant more to me—means more to me—than I can say.

Perhaps I can suggest what I mean by asking you, please, to look into your Whitman, and read once again the section of "Song of Myself" which begins "A child said, What is the grass? fetching it to me with full hands."

Sir Herbert Read wrote that the most important thing he knew of was what he called "the sense of glory." I want to thank you for being so kind a person as to send me your book. But, beyond that decency (precious in itself), I want to thank you for being the poet who wrote it.

I felt like hell this morning. But now I feel wonderful.

Thank you,
James Wright

To Anne Wright

New York City
January 8, 1969

Dear Mrs. Wright:

I don't wish to be an alarmist, but I really do feel you ought to know that I think you are the very best person I have ever known, and that I love you with all my heart.

Sincerely yours,
James
James A. Wright, Ph.D.

To Isabella Gardner

PROSPERO'S ISLE

They don't smoke pot
They bruise (booze?) a lot
They fight cocks
But the sound of the sea was so incessant
I just couldn't take it
They're every color of the rainbow
So they have no color problem
I got sick there flat on my back
For a whole week
I'm going to rest in Boston
And then
By God I'm going back
Come hell or high water
That damned place
I love it so

* * *

New York City
Tuesday, April 8, 1969

My dear Belle,

The above is exactly what you said to me on the phone last week. I'm attaching the longhand copy I made just as you spoke. I put "Prospero's Isle" at the top simply because you referred to the place that way.

What you do with it I won't venture to suggest. It is certainly beautiful as it stands. It is exactly what you said.

I'm going to phone you as soon as I mail this, because I still haven't heard anything from or about John.

Best love from Annie and me,

Jim

To Bernetta Quinn

New York City
February 10, 1970

Dear Sister Bernetta:

I just a moment ago received your letter, in which you acknowledged the books. Your quotation of the boy who thinks he is a panther is so beautiful, that I am thinking of asking his permission to use it as the epigraph of my (more or less temporary) collected poems, which I have to get to Wesleyan by the end of June.

But, now, look here: there was a time you remember well: I was in such black despair that I didn't even have the strength to commit suicide. You wrote me then. And, best of all, you gave me the chance to visit St. Theresa without being paid for it. For some reason, which, I guess, will always remain a mystery to me, your invitation, and, most of all, your acceptance of my conditions, brought me to life again. I am a cynic, a bad man, a hopeless, a brute. (A drunk no more, be that as it is.) But after I spoke to your students, one of them said to me, "God bless you."

I am pretty arrogant, as you well know, but not quite so arrogant as to reject the blessing of God.

Do you remember the little stray black and white dog? Mephistopheles in *Faust* arrives as a black poodle. Moby Dick is white. The cunning and the fury. But when they come together, a third is in the midst of them.

I've been invited to teach the Chicano children in Los Angeles for three days. Inspired by your courage, I am going.

My Hesse translation is done! My new book of poems is near done! And I enclose the poem I promised to send you. You told me in my grief that people needed me. They need you too. Take your own wisdom to heart, with

my abiding love,
Jim

To Richard Howard

New York City
November 30, 1970

Dear Richard,

Annie and I had a lovely time meeting Tom Victor. He is an extraordinarily fine and gifted man—very much like our favorite poet, Richard Howard.

I'm writing this note to tell you—re your anthology*—that my favorite poem is to be found in the King James version of the Book of Ecclesiastes, Ch. 9, 11–12.

For my own poem that I would want you to add? Personally, I would rather leave the choice to you. But that is a foolish escape. I know of no poem of mine that hasn't come out of the King James Bible. If I have to choose one that echoes the passage from Ecclesiastes, I guess I would ask for the poem called "To Flood Stage Again," which is in *Shall We Gather at the River*, page 31. That is fairly representative, I think.

We both send our

love,
Jim

To Jack Myers

New York City
March 23, 1971

Dear Mr. Myers:

Thanks for writing me about your collection of poems about Richard Hugo. Come to think of it, it is a haunting idea. I have the following suggestions:

---

*Richard Howard, ed., *Preferences* (New York: Viking, 1974). The collection featured photographs of the poets by Thomas Victor.

(1) My poem "On Minding One's Own Business," which appears in the book *Saint Judas* and in my forthcoming *Collected Poems*, is about Hugo. We were fishing. I think it was at Lake Kapowsin. Late in the afternoon, we drifted toward a far edge of the lake and saw a shack up the bank. With my customary gift for laziness and irrelevance, I suggested that we stop and explore the place. Dick said, "No, let them alone." He was standing at the prow of the skiff, looking like an illustration from *Field and Stream* magazine. He reached into his fishing kit, posed against the sunset, and tossed me a stubby of beer. That is Dick Hugo, all right: leave people alone, drink your beer, and mind your own business. If you want to use this poem, it's fine with me, but you'll have to get in touch with my publisher, Wesleyan Univ. Press [. . .]

(2) Some years ago, Dick Hugo, Ken Hanson, and I all wrote poems about a graveyard in Mukilteo, Washington. At the time, we had written the poems independently. When we found what we'd done, we had them published in *The New Orleans Poetry Journal*, edited by Richard Ashman. I don't have a copy of the issue now, but you could find it by writing to Mr. Felix Pollack, curator of the Marvin Sukov Little Magazine Collection, University of Wisconsin Library, Madison, Wisconsin.

(3) I wrote an introduction to a series of Dick Hugo's poems for a magazine called *Fresco* a few years ago. Again, I don't have a copy, but you can find one by writing *Fresco*'s editor, Dr. Jerome Mazzaro, Department of English, State University of New York, Buffalo, New York.

(4) Ed Bedford, of Goose Prairie, Washington (formerly, I trust), is, or was, a price-gouging, manipulative owner of the only tavern within miles of Goose Prairie. He charges, or used to charge, something like twice the money for beer that any normal, red-blooded American would expect to pay. I have always felt that the Feds ought to know about him, because he tried to undermine the capitalistic system. I suspect also that he is a very wicked man, and I would not be in the least surprised to learn that he is a vampire. His wife, Zetta, sounded like a 5 a.m. phone call from the ghost of the late John Foster Dulles. It's not that Dick Hugo and I were thirsty. There was water to drink. But beer is a food. Ed Bedford nearly starved us to death. Mr. Myers, if you can do anything about it, smite down this evil person.

Yours,
James Wright

To Freya Manfred

New York City
April 3, 1971

Dear Freya,

I am so glad you sent me the poems again. I have even more faith in them than I had before, and this time, I think, a better understanding. It may be that my note will arrive too late to be of any use to your publisher, but I want to make a comment anyway, and you can use it anywhere and any time you like.

> There is a secret and proficient music in these poems that sings to itself, like the lake in Minnesota which the French mistranslated Lac Qui Parle, the lake that speaks, after the Sioux for so long had been calling it, "the lake that whispers to itself." This poet goes farther. She listens to herself. She hears the earth itself. Her approach to the earth is so patient and true that, I believe, her response to it, and to herself, will go on blossoming and blossoming. I can hear in her poems something that will outblossom hell itself and help us all to turn it back into earth again. I welcome these poems as I welcome spring.

That is my comment. I don't think it's too flowery, but, if you do, please feel free to revise it. I'm so delighted to hear about your teaching, and I'm eager to see your new poems. As for publishing the book as it stands, I can only tell what I've learned: at a certain moment in your life, all you can do is bear your blossoms and fruits as well as you are able; you have to publish them, to complete them, so that you yourself can go on growing. I very much approve of your publishing this book. In some mysterious way I can't explain, it will help you with your further writing. Every good piece of work that we've had nerve enough to complete and to offer—to publish—will come back to help us when we try something new. Even if it's all done in a secret loneliness, the true work won't fail us. I know you'll know what I mean, and I am absolutely certain that your father will know too.

I can understand your being depressed. You'll have to find a way to be true to the depression, too, because it has a place in our lives, somewhere.

I hope you are in love and writing and staying close to living things.

Please write when you can.

Love to you and yours,
Jim

To Robert and Carol Bly

Montreal
August 5, 1971

Dear Robert and Carol,

Annie and I just received a note from Kathryn and Orrin [Bly]. They told us about Jim.* There's no need to tell you of the sorrow I feel. Perhaps the best thing to do, at this time, is to remind you of what you know already: that if there is anything at all that we can do to help, we certainly will. And please be sure to convey our sympathy to Lois and the children, and also to your parents.

We've been in Montreal for more than a month, and we'll stay here till August 27th. I've been teaching a course called "Comedy" to advanced students; and I must say that the students in this class are re-markable—intelligent, well-read, eager to speculate. I wish I could take them back to New York with me, where the students seem so apathetic these days.

Montreal is a lovely place, physically beautiful with its trees, hills, houses; very clean and yet rich with old markets, food from all over the earth, and kindly people. For a change, we're getting to live in a big, adequate house, which we rented from a friend here. For most of the summer we've had Annie's marvelous niece [Karin East] with us, and also my younger son, Marsh, now thirteen years old. He is splendid company—humorous, affectionate, adventurous, musical.

The older son, Franz, by great good luck, has gone to spend more than a year with a family in Belgium. The family seem charming and friendly. At the moment, they've taken Franz with them on a trip to Yu-goslavia. Then he's going to return to Belgium and go to school, mainly, I believe, to expand his knowledge of languages. His German

*Robert Bly's brother Jim had just recently died.

is already adequate, and he wants to work further on French and Dutch. From his letters, however, I think that the most important thing about his journey is the journey itself. It is really a voyage of the spirit that he's making. He can write beautiful prose about this voyage.

Annie is well, indeed. We're both finding this place and this summer to be good, though in a way we feel somewhat uneasy about returning in the Fall. America is so gloomy and exhausting these days.

Please write to us, and send some new poems. Robert, when is the Vallejo translation going to appear? And are you coming to New York this year? It certainly would be a relief to see you. I hope we'll be seeing Kathryn and Orrin in the Fall. We had some hopes that they might make it to Montreal, but there seems small likelihood now.

Love to you all from both of us,

Jim

To David Wagoner

New York City

February 9, 1972

Dear Dave,

Why has it been so difficult for me to write to you and perhaps four or five other friends who, through so many years now, have kept me alive. Once at the University of Minnesota you wrote to me and enclosed some beautiful new poems that you wanted to submit to the *Minnesota Review*. You also said, in that letter, that you had found your true love and were very happy.

Maybe that's what scared me. At that time I was so god damned miserable that the only thing I could do was translate Theodor Storm from German, have a bad love affair, get sick, go to a hospital, get visited by John Berryman (who went and taught my classes while I was sick), get habitually drunk, teach very well when I could bring myself to make a class, and, naturally, get fired.

Now I am living in New York, teaching at Hunter, writing pretty well, and able, at last, to write to my best friends again. What I mean is, I found my true love, too, after all this time.

Sometimes some of the best poets alive come to visit us, and, when they do, Annie doesn't go to sleep. You'll remember what I mean.

Your sending me translations of two poems of mine in Turkish was a peculiarly nutty expression of old friendship and love which I can understand without having to explain.

As for *Poetry Northwest*, I can say just this: there are precious few magazines of poetry that I read any more; but I never fail to read and cherish *Poetry Northwest* from beginning to end. The poetry magazine in America has fallen as usual on hard times, and the only ones I know that are keeping new poetry alive are *Poetry Northwest*, Jerome Mazzaro's *Modern Poetry Studies* (published at the State University of New York at Buffalo), and Theodore Weiss's *Quarterly Review of Literature*. C. W. Truesdale is beginning to do something important, I think, with the *Minnesota Review*, whose editorship he just assumed. There may be some few others I don't know about; but I do know, as well as you do, that there is no literature in America without the little magazine; and that without literature, for some reason, there is no country. A country which I still love.

Where Is My Wandering Boy Tonight? is not your best book. Your best book is the *New and Selected Poems*. But neither of these could exist without the other. I still think of you as primarily one of the first-rate poets we have, and your poems, even those lyrics that have the slight grace on the surface reverberate with the force that they have just because of the great and unsentimental and kindly novelistic imagination that is always there to buoy them up. Hardy, Warren, Pasternak, Emily Brontë. And Dave Wagoner. Who else? A precious few.

Yes, there is Goethe. He wrote a hell of a good novel called *Die Wahlverwandschaten*, and sometimes I think his poems, which I worship, wouldn't be worth anything—maybe wouldn't even exist—if it hadn't been for that big novel. Annie loved *Wandering Boy* so much that she gave it to my father for Christmas. He is now 79 years old, and he loves the book too.

There are so many things to tell you. But I'm going to be up there on May 25th, and please God we'll get a chance to talk. Give my love to the Matchetts and to your lovely Patt.

Love,
Jim

To Mark Strand

New York City
February 15, 1972

Dear Mark,

I have a secret with myself. I love the craft. The nihilists who damn delicacy and balance be damned. In a way, I flatter myself, but I think with good reason. Slithering technician, I know enough to know what craft is for.

When we talked the other evening, too briefly as always, I told you that *Darker* has meant so much to me. What I said was praise for your book *Darker*. But it meant something to me in yet another way.

I loved *Darker* for my own sake, and that is nobody's business but my own.

But I also care deeply about this book *Darker* because of the "Litanies" in it. They are lovely poems in themselves. Fair enough. But what matters most of all, to me, about them is that they taught you how to deal with something which is clearly terrible. If a human being is going to remain human, he is going to have to deal with his father's death. It so happens I have to tell you my own father, whom I love in ways that I will probably never understand, is still alive. Last Spring the best doctor in Zanesville, Ohio, opened his belly and cut something like one foot out of his colon. Over the recent Christmas vacation Annie and I went out to see my parents, and my father said he was okay, he just felt tired all the time. You know, he takes Annie into his arms, not just because he's glad somebody is nice to me at last (somebody is nice to me at last), but just because he likes her. And he likes her because she likes me.

I found the poems "Litanies" in *Darker* beautiful as lyric poems, and when I say this I return to myself as a very good craftsman. I guess in some half-awake part of myself I sensed that nobody could write those "Litanies" without following wherever they would lead.

By God, I was right. The craft of "Litanies" made it possible for you to come to the death of your strange father. My father is strange, too. Is that it? Is everybody's father strange? How should I know?

I know now. I am getting sick of putting on the act of humility. I know plenty about the craft of poetry. Gone through hell to learn it, it is mine. So now I think what I say is sound.

The function of careful craft is to contend with love and death.

The craft of "Litanies" led to your poem "Elegy for My Father." It is one of the greatest poems I have ever read. And I have read some others, and not sentimentally either.

Mark, please don't change a comma. If you revise the poem, I will attack your revisions in print.

When I read your "Elegy," I realized that my life means something, my life as a craftsman and my life as a human being. And I'll be damned if I'll give that up.

In your note to me, you worried about the rhetoric of your poem. How can I tell you? Your worry, your concern simultaneously about the precision of your diction and rhythm and your Vergilian grief and affection for your father—whose life is alive in your poem, precisely because his life and the life of your poem are so formally strange—is the exact difference between you and Rod Macuen (oh, for Christ's sake, I don't even care how he spells his name).

Never mind how muddled this letter is. The "Elegy" is a very great poem, because you have the exquisite craft to shape a heartbreakingly personal and inescapably human theme. I have nothing to brag about. But I love your poem, and I'm pretty sure I know why I love it.

Jim

To Helen McNeely Sheriff

New York City
June 11, 1972

Dear Miss Sheriff:

I'm sure I don't have to tell you that a letter from you means more to me than any prize could ever mean. Nevertheless, I may as well inform you that the Pulitzer was only one of four prizes won by the *Collected Poems* during the past year. The others were the Brandeis Award (directed, incidentally, by J. V. Cunningham, himself a beautiful spare poet and—significantly—one of the most brilliant scholars in medieval Latin alive); the Melville Cane citation from the Poetry Society of America; and a Fellowship from the Academy of American Poets. The Fellowship carried a stipend that will allow Annie and me to take good advantage of my sabbatical—an entire year, beginning in February, 1973.

You surely wonder who Annie is, and the name (beloved name) can serve as the occasion for me to account for the past years of silence. You may not be aware that Liberty and I were divorced in 1962. I hasten to add that she has remarried and is living quite well in California with her husband, a Hungarian named Miklos Kovacs, with our younger son Marshall, who is doing quite well in a private school out there, and with a new son of their own. My older son Franz, who was born in Vienna, is now nineteen years old and attending Oberlin College in Ohio. I should add that Franz has turned out to have a gift for languages, which he is pursuing at Oberlin, an excellent school. In fact, he and I collaborated on my most recent volume of translation. It is called *Wandering*, by Hermann Hesse, a strange and haunting work, a kind of metaphysical travel-book. Everything has turned out fairly enough, and for some curious reason, Lib and I have maintained a clearer and more serene friendship since our divorce than we ever had during the marriage.

However, for me personally, the years between 1962 and 1968 were riddled with a confusing and sometimes harrowing loneliness. I was teaching all the time, first at the University of Minnesota and then for two years at Macalester College in St. Paul, and I was sustained by the faith of my students and by the friendship of a few sympathetic people; but even so, I did a good deal of rootless prowling all around the United States whenever I got the chance. Some amusing things happened. For example, my publisher at Wesleyan got so exasperated in the attempt to locate my whereabouts that they came within an ace of hiring a private investigator to find me and make me sit still long enough for them to send me a royalty check. Then one year—I think it was the academic year 1964–65—a literary friend in New York urged me to apply for a Guggenheim Fellowship. I did so, somewhat diffidently, and to my astonishment I received the grant. At first I didn't know what to do with it. My health was none too good, so in May I accepted an invitation to spend the entire summer in Cupertino, California, with Henry and Elizabeth (Willerton) Esterly. During the years since 1962 up to then I had managed to hold myself together by writing a new book of my own and by collaborating with Robert Bly on his magazine and on two or three volumes of translation. Consequently, after leaving the Esterlys', I proceeded to the Blys' farm in western Minnesota right at the edge of the great western prairies where, even during the harsh years in Minneapolis I had been able to go and find some welcome and serenity. All this time, you must understand, I was slowly and tenaciously molding together a new volume of poems that proved painfully difficult to write. (The book eventually appeared, in 1968 I believe, as *Shall We Gather at the River.*) After spending a while at the Blys' farm, I suddenly found myself afflicted with homesickness, so I traveled on to New Concord, Ohio, to be with my parents, who, by the way, though well into their 70s, are still alive. I must have spent two or three months in that little Ohio town, reading, studying, and above all struggling with the book. During that period I also had a somewhat vague intention of traveling to Europe, perhaps to Vienna, where I had attended the University some years previously, or perhaps to England. I was so uncertain, however, that the nurses at the County Health Office in Zanesville inoculated me against what seemed like everything from beri-beri to bubonic plague.

Finally, sometime in February, I came to New York. After I got settled in a resident hotel, it occurred to me that, since I liked the city so much, and the Eastern United States in general, I might as well go and talk things over with several schools that had offered me a position. The word had got around, as it has a way of doing in academic circles, that I was pretty much decided not to return to the Midwest. I did visit several schools in upstate New York and even in Pennsylvania, particularly Franklin and Marshall in Lancaster, where I used to travel each Tuesday for seven weeks to teach an evening seminar for a friend of mine who had become ill. Then I suddenly received a call from Dr. Allen Mandelbaum, Hunter's great Dante and Virgil scholar. He urged me to visit the chairman of the English department on a given day. When I arrived, the chairman and the Personnel and Budget Committee were waiting for me; and, after a brief interview, they offered me an Associate Professorship on the spot. I accepted with pleasure and, I must say, with some relief. It meant that I had succeeded in establishing myself in the city, and that I could count on the stabilizing influence of teaching while I struggled to navigate this enormous, deeply troubled, and magnificent place. For the next two years I taught at the Uptown Branch of Hunter. It is now a separate school, Lehmann College. Those two years were a fantastic experience. I would rise quite early each morning, walk ten blocks, grab a quick breakfast at a hash-joint on Broadway called the Super-Duper (two fried eggs, a minute steak, fried potatoes, and what must surely be the best pickled cucumbers this side of the Hudson River), and then take the subway for something more than an hour way, way up in the Bronx. It was a splendid and, I daresay, restoring experience altogether. And during that time, sitting alone in my single room at the Hotel Regent just about fifteen blocks downtown from Columbia University, I finally completed *Shall We Gather at the River*. I pruned it to a little more than half of the previous version. What I had in mind, and what I would not abandon no matter what happened, was the idea of making the book spin with utter lucidity in its anguish from the very epigraph under the title to the final period of the final poem. Clarity and a classical rhetoric were everything. It is an unhappy book, and consequently I could not afford to submit to the temptation of the florid and extraneous. "Ars est celare artem," Horace observed, and he has always been the wisest of guides.

After the two years at uptown Hunter, the school became autonomous, and I came to teach undergraduate and graduate courses at Hunter downtown. I am happy to be teaching at Hunter, where I have now become a tenured Full Professor.

The central focus of this sketchy account is of course, my Annie. One evening while I was still teaching uptown, the distinguished Shakespearean scholar David Stevenson, with whom I had struck up a good friendship, invited me to a dinner party at his New York apartment. There were many friendly colleagues there, and also some people whom I did not know. Among these was a lady, somewhat slim and extraordinarily beautiful, who looked to me to be about twenty-five years old. I was sharply aware of her all evening, though we didn't exchange a single word. Some mutual friends, by happy chance, gave both of us a ride home. I stepped out of the car to see her to her door, and suddenly blurted out a request that she let me have her name and address. Miss Edith Anne Runk. Well. Shortly thereafter I returned to Western Minnesota to do some work during the summer. In the Fall, I returned, and a colleague* mentioned that she had casually asked about me. At about that time I was to read my verses at the auditorium of the 92nd Street Y, and I arranged for a ticket to be provided for her. Lo and behold! She appeared. Thereafter I began to court her, and that in the most old-fashioned manner imaginable. She gave the matter

*Allen Mandelbaum.

mature consideration, and eventually accepted me. We were married at the chapel of the Riverside Church on April 29, 1967.

It turns out that she graduated from Wheelock College in Boston some twenty years ago, had taught during those years at a school in Paris for a year and at another in Rome for two years. At the time we were married she was the Director of the West Side Community Nursery School. She is now the teacher and Director of an international nursery school in Brooklyn. Each summer during the five years of our marriage, we have left the city. Four times I was teaching summer school at such places as the University of Wisconsin at Milwaukee, the State University of New York at Buffalo, Sir George Williams University in Montreal. A couple of years ago we spent the summer mainly in France and Italy, which she knows so well and of which I was totally ignorant. We also had three weeks in Vienna and a week in south-central Yugoslavia where we'd been invited to an international conference of authors. (By the way, Miss Sheriff, could you believe—I scarcely can—that my verses have been translated into German, French, Italian, Spanish, Swedish, Turkish, Macedonian, and Japanese?)

I can truthfully say that I have never been closer and happier with another human being in my entire life. I have served as a substitute at Annie's nursery school, and she has often lectured my college students on the poetry and painting of children. She has also written some beautifully intelligent and sensitive stories and essays, one of which was a marvelous paper about the experiences of Hawthorne and Henry James in Rome, a paper which she presented to my Honors Seminar. Recently I fell ill because of overwork and other causes, and she was at my side in the hospital from morning till night. (My health is now improved.) If certain complications resolve themselves, we will be leaving for Paris, and then Rome, on June 19.

How in heaven's name did I, of all people, ever find such a person. Over the years I have certainly committed somewhat more than my share of peccadilloes and outright sins. The only rational answer that occurs to me is that I have been touched by some kind of grace. At any rate, that is the way I feel, morning and night [. . .]

Again, it was a delight to hear from you. Annie and I both send our love to you and Nancy.

With abiding devotion,

Jim

To Olive Faries

Dear Mrs. Faries:

Far from Ohio now, I am still far from forgetting the tremendous strength and delicacy of feeling and intelligence you always brought to our class back there in Martins Ferry. You know, Mrs. Faries, there is something that has been haunting me for years. In your class, where you labored so effectively to restore to us the great poets, and thereby some of the meaning of our lives, I acted like a snot. You were just out of college; you were just married, as I recall; you cared very deeply about life and about our quite terrible literary attempt in America to deal with life; and you wanted to be a good teacher.

I loved your classes, and I love them still. Through these many years of search among many languages and many books, I have come back again to the intelligence and kindness you had then and that you gave, and that you no doubt still give.

One sunny afternoon I was studying up in the old library at Martins Ferry High School, and Mrs. Wood the librarian asked me to come out and meet your husband. I remember him also, and Annie joins me in sending our best feelings to him.

And to you,
James Wright

To Gibbons and Kay Ruark

New York City
December 6, 1972

Dear Kay and Gib (and Jennifer and Emily),

In a couple of weeks, my younger boy Marshall will be with us here in New York. After a few days, the three of us will travel to Ohio, where we will spend the Christmas vacation with my aging parents. My older boy Franz, now studying at Oberlin, will join us.

Given the kind of strange glaze that I see all around me in the America which I still love, and taken out of my own homesickness for a little time this Christmas, I wanted to write you a note this evening. I don't think I have lived a very good life so far. But maybe I don't have to live all that good. I know I love you both and your family very much. Gib, your immortal poem about your father* brought finally to a focus my own wanderings about my own father, and that is what turned me to my Latin again, for some reason, my beautiful Horace, who is probably so great a poet because he understood and said we can probably live. My father in Ohio has white hair, and I will be surprised and hurt when he dies. But I got to live long enough to take long walks with him in New Concord, Ohio. We didn't go fishing together, as you two did; but we went swimming, back there, back down home. I've written a poem about the old WPA swimming pool in Martins Ferry, Ohio, that is going to be in *The New Republic* and then in my new book in February or March. I had some people in on that pool, and I swam in it when it first opened.

Given Christmas and our terrible Vergilian past, our south and our middle west, Annie (!) and I send you our abiding love, the only greeting of the season.

Emily is *not* a mess.

Love,
Annie & James

To A. R. Ammons

New York City
January 2, 1973

Dear Archie,

My grandmother† is eighty-eight years old. If I had not married my incomparable Annie, I would have done my best to marry the beautiful Grannie. Now I know why.

She gave me the *Collected Poems* for Christmas.

Back in St. Paul years ago, going to pieces as I usually go, I wrote to you because I discovered your poems in the *Hudson Review*, when someone had told me to look up something else. I don't even remember who something else was. I remember, as I have remembered for

---

*"Night Fishing," reprinted in Gibbons Ruark's *Passing Through Customs: New and Selected Poems* (Baton Rouge: Louisiana State University Press, 1999).
†Actually, Anne Wright's grandmother, Edith Hoyt Froment.

years, the way your beautiful poems rose right straight up out of the pages.

Since that time, groping here and groping there, I have always somehow depended on your work. Now I am justified.

The *Collected Poems* is even better than the *Selected*, which I found in Paris last summer. It is, in a bad time, one of the most beautiful books I have ever read.

I don't know if you think our time is a bad time, but I do, and I am specially happy to find something abidingly fine. The *Collected Poems* is, at any rate, a permanent joy. It is a work of courage, because it is happy, and nobody in my generation, not even Logan and Dickey, has had that much nerve.

Your book makes me happy.

Yours,

Jim

To Robert Bly

New York City
March 19, 1973

Dear Robert,

For many days now, I've been brooding about *Sleepers Joining Hands*, and I have held back again, because I did not want to write you a blurb. During the past few years it was necessary for me to take what strength I discovered in myself through you and your family and go try to find my own life. We have remained in touch from time to time, and surely there has never been any question about my perception of your strange powers, which to my mind have always included the western intellect and have gone beyond it. We haven't shown each other our new groping poems for years, because our friendship—the friendship of the imagination—sometimes provided fools with their delighted occasion to misunderstand. I came to your farm and your family because I needed to discover the life of solitude, and because I was simply unable to bear loneliness, which, as Bill Knott once said in a wonderful letter to me, rots the soul. I never cared all that much about the brevity of my life. What horrified me in those old lonelinesses was that my soul might rot. I'm pretty sure it won't rot now, because I've gone on so many of my own American wanderings, and now it is time for us to survey what has happened when we've left each other in his own solitude.

The relation between solitude and loneliness is a terrible and beautiful thing, maybe the problem we haven't yet solved in America. I still love this country, and yet I have to admit that I love [*sic*] it too. Robert, you are the most solitary human being I have ever met in my life, and yet I have never met any other human being who had such powers of giving. I am not going to pretend (I pretend about other things all the time) that I know what that solitude is, but it is no pretense to say that I have derived from it a good deal of the strength that I have. It would be easy enough prose to say that I derived that strength from the welcome I got every Friday evening, when I caught the bus from Minneapolis and arrived in Madison at twenty minutes before eleven with my cigar and my bottle of booze. What is more difficult to describe is the welcome I felt in the living creation itself.

I had never felt welcome on earth before.

Now I think I am beginning to understand what happened to me. The details are that Carol asked me to be my incomparable Mary's godfather, that I was given the chance to go out in the cold and give David (!) his corn and water at the middle of my night drunk, and that Annie and I arrived to be greeted for our honeymoon (it is the only one I ever had, and after six years it remains a crucial moment, and an eternal moment) in a schoolhouse that floated down the road. What happened to me in all those days was that I learned it was all right to be in solitude.

Your own solitude I will not violate. For these several years now, we have gone our own ways and written our own poems. We've kept in touch all right, but our correspondence has suffered, and not just because I don't like to write letters. I do like to write them. I think I was silent because in a way I was waiting for *Sleepers Joining Hands*, which is a golden book, your best, and consequently one of the best books we have. The prose essay in the middle of the book is all right with me, because it makes clearer than you have ever done before what poetry, the life of the imagination, has done in our lifetime, brief and damned though that may be, and our share in what matters, the attempt "to right our own spiritual balance."

What I came looking for in those days was not just the chance to be alone, but to learn a little bit about ways to be solitary.

What I've said in this letter is still sketchy. I don't know how to explain it. It seems to me that the poems in *Sleepers Joining Hands* are beyond explanation or attack or imitation. It is no good talking about political or natural or aesthetic "themes." One of these days I hope to be true enough to my own solitude to be able to offer forth a poem like that. I guess that is what I'm trying to say.

I want to tell Carol that the books arrived just fine, and we appreciate her handling the clutter so clearly. In June, Annie and I are going to Europe again, and in the meantime I have to speak at various places. Have you ever been down in Tucson, Arizona? Shortly I will write you about the beauty of that place.

Love,
James

New York City
March 22, 1973

Dear Robert,

The other day I started to read Dee Brown's book, *Bury My Heart at Wounded Knee*. I started to read even before the current trouble out there got started. What I had in mind was to read something documentary and entertaining, to divert myself while I'm not teaching.

Needless to say, I wanted to put the book aside, because it is not entertaining or diverting. But I made up my mind to read the whole disastrous record, which, as far as I can tell, is historically sound. At any rate, it is thoroughly documented, and the documents are available to anybody who cares to see them, like you and me, when I went with you to the old building (not that new thing) in Minneapolis to find contemporary accounts of the 1862–3 Sioux Rebellion.

Bury My Heart at Wounded Knee is quite enough to confirm any despairing person in his conviction that there is no hope for man on this earth. So I thought. And yet I found a paragraph that maybe calls that old neurotic assumption of mine into serious question. I don't know what to do with it, or really to think about it, but I quote it for you here:

> For a long time Crazy Horse had been waiting for a chance to
> test himself in battle with the Bluecoats. In all the years since
> the Fetterman fight at Fort Phil Kearney, he had studied the

soldiers and their ways of fighting. Each time he went into the Black Hills to seek visions, he had asked Wakantaka to give him secret powers so that he would know how to lead the Oglalas to victory if the white men ever came again to make war upon his people. Since the time of his youth, Crazy Horse had known that the world men lived in was only a shadow of the real world. To get into the real world, he had to dream, and when he was in the real world everything seemed to float or dance. In this real world his horse danced as if it were wild or crazy, and this was why he called himself Crazy Horse. He had learned that if he dreamed himself into the real world before going into a fight, he could endure anything.

Well, there is abundant evidence of the man's military genius, and his fierce despair so fierce in fact that, faced with the manacles and chains prepared for him at Fort Robinson he ran amuck and got bayoneted in the abdomen by a Federal guard (evidence comes proudly from the Union troops themselves), but what I want to know is, what did he mean by the real world?

And what is going on at Wounded Knee now? All I've been able to find out is that, as usual, the Indians have been trying to muck one another up and manipulate the news media. Those are probably lies, but they are all I can find. What does Fred Manfred think about the mess out there? Have you been in touch with him?

I can assure you that the worst damned place on earth to find out what is going on in America is New York City.

What do you think of Crazy Horse's ideas? What would he have done with those ideas if his country hadn't been assaulted? Wasn't he driven by the physical world into paranoia? No. He found his fears (I share them) justified by the Federal troops.

No wonder this country is sick. I am afraid of many things, but I am not afraid of all things, and maybe it would be good to live where I can trust the things I am not afraid of. But where are they?

I don't have an inkling of the answers to any of these questions, but I wanted especially to send you the paragraph about Crazy Horse. Please write me a good long letter.

Love,
James

To Mary Philo

New York City
March 31, 1973

Dear Miss Philo:

Your letter of March 9 gave me and my wife Annie great pleasure, and I can assure you that I am not about to forget Martins Ferry. Over the years I have been in touch with my teachers there, Miss Helen M. Sheriff, who now lives in Cadiz, and Mrs. Elizabeth Esterly (the former Miss Elizabeth Willerton), who meant so much to me when I was a boy.

You mention the poem "In Response to a Rumor, etc." Some years ago my brother Jack, who is now a mathematician in California, told me that he heard (hence, the rumor) that an old building at 23rd and Water Streets, Wheeling, once reputed to be a house of ill fame, had been torn down to make way for a supermarket. That is all I know, and I don't know which to deplore.

It is interesting that you remember the Doty case. It was, and remains, morally upsetting. I too remember the monstrous action that Doty committed, and I agree with you that he received what he deserved. Your letter sent me back to the two poems that I wrote about him, and I can now see that I placed more emphasis on Doty than on the girl he killed. Believe me, Miss Philo, I too mourn for Miss Alma Montag, night and day. No doubt my poem about Doty is morally confusing. I would try to summarize its theme as follows: I don't believe in rape and murder either; I believe in mercy. It is a hard religious problem, and I still like to think of my poem about Doty as a religious poem, even though it isn't clear.

I hope you will convey my affection and respect to Miss Annie Tanks, one of the great Americans of my lifetime.

Thank you,
James Wright

To Theodore Wright

Dear Ted,

You know how much I've admired you ever since we were kids. It occurs to me that I am in a good position to understand how much your photographic prize means, because I know something about the years of hard work and imagination that have gone into it. I am very proud to be your brother.

What a fine meeting we all had together in Arizona! I don't have to tell you, of all people, to achieve a decent life in this world is damned hard work. But that work has its appropriate rewards, and maybe the most important of them is to find the chance, in our huge wonderful country, to share your best work with the people you love best. You know, how many years it had been since you and Jack and I could be together, just to talk together, and tell each other what we've been doing, what we hope to do, and all the rest.

You also know what beautiful women we've all three been lucky enough to marry, and how kind they are to us.

I have my own dark solitary ways of worrying, but I've begun to realize that, after all, Mother and Pop were a hard depression couple; they've stuck together for something more than half a century; and their kids have done all right.

I've written three poems about the Arizona desert, which I'll send you when they're printed. In the meantime, how about sending the scenic shot you made down there? Our house is full of paintings and photographs that we love, and we would certainly be happy to have a copy of your prize-winner.

Ted and Dianna [Ted Wright Jr. and his wife] seemed wonderful to me. They are capable people, with strong roots [. . .] Ted has to decide about his next career, I know; but I have no doubt he'll make the right and clear decision. As for my boy Franz, he's doing fine there at Oberlin, and will be working there this summer [. . .]

I'm terribly proud of you, Ted.

Love,
Jim

To Marshall Wright

Dear Marsh,

The time of year is coming round again, and we are looking forward with great pleasure to being with you in Europe. Your Mom hasn't yet written to Annie, and I'm sure she'll do so when she has a moment. In the meantime, I want to write you a note to let you [know] something of what to expect in Europe this time.

We'll leave New York on June 18, and spend about two weeks traveling in and around the area of London. I haven't been there for some twenty years, but I remember it as a splendid place. According to the arrangements made between your Mom and Annie, we are hoping to meet you at the airport in London about July 10 or 11. That will give us a week in the south of England. I don't yet know whether or not Cat Stevens will be playing in London at that time, but I can assure you that I will know by the time you arrive. If he is, of course, we'll all go hear him together.

After that week in England, we plan to take the so-called Boat Train to Dover, and ride over the English Channel to Cherbourg, France, from whence we will proceed to Paris. We have made reservations at the Hotel Lenox, on the Left Bank, and we expect to have two gorgeous weeks with you in and around the greatest city in the world. By this time, we have Paris very well cased, and also the areas immediately around it and immediately to the south. In Paris, we want to take you to our favorite places: the Tour Eiffel, the great church of Sacre Coeur on the immense mountain Montmartre, and, most beautiful of all to me, the little tea shop along the great Seine River, after which we'll go downstream and take the boat tour that will show you why people for so many centuries have loved Paris so much. As for traveling outside of Paris, we have two schemes in mind, and have already made reservations for them. We want to take you to the little town of Chartres, where the most fantastic cathedral on earth stands on a little hill; and we want to take you down to Orleans, on the Loire, and show you the place where Joan of Arc inspired the farmers from all over the French boondocks; and then we will take the bus out to our beloved Saint Benoit-sur-Loire, an authentic French hick-town where we have made so many lovely friends.

Thence we'll return to Paris, and get you home. All told, you will be with us for three weeks. It sounds very full, and I hope it will be. We have learned how to travel with some real skill, and I have no doubt that you'll be delighted, especially with France, a place where nearly everybody is graceful and funny and musical.

Speaking of music, I wonder whether or not you'll want to bring your guitar. Personally, I would advise against it, because we are going to be moving around so often. I think you would be more comfortable by traveling as we travel: simply, with as few things to carry as possible. In Paris, we'll be staying at the Hotel Lenox, as I told you. On a typical day, we rise about 8 o'clock, have the continental breakfast of coffee and bread, and then strike out to see the city. We always spend a little part of the morning visiting one of the open markets, and we have our lunch as a picnic (the open markets of France are among the wonders of the world). There are so many beautiful things to see, and so many fine people to meet, that it is always well to move about in France as lightly as possible. When I suggest that you leave your guitar behind, I don't mean that we'll have no music. On the contrary, we want you to hear the magnificent mass at Notre Dame, and the organ mass at Saint Sulpice; and I'll certainly take you to one of the *correspondences* in the metro, where we can hear occasionally the great minstrels, who also play sometimes along Boulevard Saint Germain-des-Prés.

It makes me happy to think of being with you again, Marsh. I'm going to turn this note over to Annie now, for she wants to add something.

Love,
Dad

To Donald Hall

Dorchester, Dorset
June 26, 1973

Dear Don,

It's terribly good of you to write so soon, especially since I've been such a lousy correspondent. What I wanted mainly was just to get in touch again. It would have been good and reassuring to hear your voice, but letters are even better, in a way. Annie and I will be in Europe till the middle of January—I have a sabbatical, thank God, and some money from the Academy of American Poets. I love to be in Europe, but seven months is a long time.

A few weeks before we left for England, Robert was in town and stayed with us overnight. He spoke of you often. I feel kind of stupid in admitting that I hadn't even known you'd got married. Anyway, Robert spoke glowingly of both you and Jane [Kenyon], and Annie and I send our belated congratulations.

At the moment, I can't send you a full copy of our itinerary. I'll send it a bit later. In the meantime, the best address for you to use in reply is the one I've put on the outside of this envelope: c/o Hotel Lenox, rue de l'Université, 9, Paris.

As you can see from the above, we've been spending a few days in Dorchester. You've been here, surely? It's Hardy's town, of course, and both yesterday and today we've walked way out to Higher Bockhampton (Lower B. is Melstock) and to the church at Stinsford, where his heart is buried. (A few graves away, C. Day Lewis is buried, too. Is this chutzpah?) We'll travel on to Bridgeport and Eype tomorrow, and thence to Fowey in Cornwall; back to London for a couple of days to meet my son Marshall; then the boat train to Paris.

We haven't been in touch for a very long time, Don, not really. I've been realizing lately that this is a hell of a note, because the truth is that I seem to be losing touch with myself, if you follow me. I don't mean I'm boozing (I'm not), or that I'm ill in any other way (the doc at home says I'm in good shape). I just seem to have lost touch with poetry and don't know quite where to turn. I feel low about it. I just published a new book, which like an ass I didn't send you. I gave a copy to Robert, and I'm pretty sure he won't like it. My *Collected Poems* just got machine-gunned by somebody in *The Southern Review*—you know, one of those snotty jobs that sometimes make one suspect he may have just been making a fool of himself for the past 20 years . . . That's the kind of mood I've been in. Louis Simpson just got home, and I saw him once, not long enough to talk to. I really do hope you'll write. Next time I won't sound so gloomy, I hope, but I did feel a need to tell you what's bothering me . . . As for baseball, both the Mets and the Yankees, I see by the papers, are still committing suicide. Is America going nuts at last?

Please write to me soon.

Love,
Jim

Paris
August 5, 1973

Dear Don,

Well, sir, you may uncork the bung-starter from the back of my skull, but if you call questions into the orifice the only answer you'll probably get is something like "Hey you!" or "To the best of my recollection at that point in time," because I don't remember reading Jane's poems for the *Hopwood* a couple of years ago. It's true there were a great many manuscripts. I'm a lousy judge of such things anyway. I'd rather read poems one at a time. Or in one group at a time.

Like in the *APR*—which, by the way, is becoming a good magazine, don't you think? At first I thought it excessive, but now I see that it has real richness. I wish they could publish more often, and I hope they have enough money to carry through. I saw Serge Fauchereau, the critic, the other day and told him about *APR*. It rather resembles some of the journals poets have had in France from time to time.

Ah, yes—it is lovely to live with a woman with whom one can talk, and also with whom one *shares silences*. Annie and I have been married for six years now, and I still feel astonished. I had earlier reached the point of giving up, of resigning myself to a bleak life. I'd certainly done enough to destroy myself. And yet here I am—sitting in a café in Paris, happily writing to a beloved friend, just as I need and want to do. As for the public response in America that you mentioned, I am sick of that whole business. I don't give readings any more, and I was happy to decline an invitation to be a judge for the National Book Awards. (I'd accept, if it had been the *real* NBA.)

This is a short letter. We're going on to Italy in a couple of days. I've written our address in Venice on the outside of this envelope—that would be the best place to write to me. I'm sending this now because it is such a pleasure to be writing with you again . . . Just above me as I write, Apollinaire spent the last years of his life.

> Our flies know all the tunes.
> They learned them from the flies in Norway
> That are the divinities of the snow.

Love,
Jim

Venice
August 27, 1973

Dear Don,

I don't know anything about hagiography. Is there a saint who safely guides letters through the mountain passes, pizzerias, and puce bathing trunks of Italy to the outside world? The reason I ask is, we mailed a letter in Milan and it arrived here in Venice more than two weeks later. The two cities are just about three hours apart by train.

God knows when you'll receive this letter. I'm hoping that Annie will be back here at the hotel before I finish writing, so she can tell me what kind of return address to give you. If she hasn't been waylaid by a gondolier. (Here now, just a minute. Strike that last sentence from the record. I didn't mean that the way it sounded. Er. Uh. Oink.)

The poem "The Toy Bone," I think, is one of your most beautiful. It has all the clarified bulk of reality that your work has always had, and in this poem there is an incredible lightness of movement, as if something had been rescued for good and all. It is the utter naturalness that I like, the ease and affection with which the words first clasp and then entirely embody the life of the feeling. And it is good, clear, strong, true feeling.

By the time you receive this letter, you will have returned from New Hampshire. Annie and I are hoping that you and Jane will manage to buy the farm. So much that is beautiful and true in your life is associated with that place, and I can't help but feel that returning to it is, for you, a return to a clear source. By the way, can you possibly tell me where I can find copies of both *String Too Short to Be Saved** and the book on Henry Moore?† I don't have copies of either, and yet I want them both for Annie. She has taught me so much, about art and about Moore especially. We walked all the way across Florence one day last summer and explored the magnificent Moore exhibit on the hilltop across the river, at Forte Belvedere. It took us a long time to get there—we got lost for a little while—but after climbing up a long long stair way and walking down a long long street we came out on this place

*String Too Short to Be Saved: Recollections of Summers on a New England Farm (Boston: David R. Godine, 1992).
†Henry Moore: The Life and Work of a Great Sculptor (New York: Harper, 1966).

on the hilltop and spent the whole afternoon in simple awe. Moore's presence (I don't mean just his sculptures and drawings, I mean his presence) was everywhere. It was like spending an afternoon with Beethoven—you know, nobody asking stupid questions, no screaming at landladies, just an afternoon, walking from room to room, from hill to hill, listening to Beethoven playing the piano.

We have been having a divine summer of travelling and often loafing. For some reason, partly weariness and partly something else, I haven't been writing many poems. I do have a notebook which I keep pretty faithfully, and I found myself realizing the other day that I was having fun with it. It's been a long time since I regarded writing as much fun, so the notebook may mean something, even if I don't know what [. . .]

I'll probably write again even before we leave Venice. Right now we're going to take the vaporetto over to Giudecca, the seaward island across the canal from the place where we're living. Venice is exquisitely lovely, a little decay in the air and a great melancholy, but it is always my great delight to be with this marvelous Annie, drifting past houses on waters. And if you like seafood, Jesus Christ!

Love,
Jim

To John Logan

Venice
August 30, 1973

Dear John,

As I begin this letter to you, the boats keep appearing and disappearing outside on the big canal where we have been staying. Just across it I can make out many buildings on the Giudecca, the large long island that lies between us and the Lida. Annie just this moment stepped in the door. She's been walking for a while—you can walk in Venice, if you take your time—through what she calls the milk. For a strange haze is over everything today. The city is even more mysterious than usual.

And it is enchanting. D. H. Lawrence called it a slippery city, and some have felt this word to suggest his dislike. But perhaps he meant only to indicate how it constantly changes shape and even direction. It is very easy to get lost here, but we don't care. We're sure to find our way back to the water sooner or later.

We've been thinking of you often here, partly because you would surely love the great series of frescoes by Tintoretto at the Scuola of San Rocco. His *Annunciation*, in particular, is an astounding thing. It has the force of real shock. The divine enters the human world without warning or explanation, and you can almost feel the walls shake.

Your prose poem is a beautiful, strange piece. Have you finished the one about Florida that you mentioned? We have very few books with us, but one we centrally cherish is *The Anonymous Lover*, which I consider your finest single collection. I can well see why you wanted it to appear separately, because it is thoroughly unified.

We've been to many places: Milan, Lake Garda, Verona (a surprise and a great delight) in Italy alone. Next we'll stop at a couple more towns in Italy and travel on to Vienna. Meanwhile, we want to linger in Venice, which keeps dying and dying, everybody tells us, and yet becomes daily and nightly more fabulous. I suspect it will go on dying when most of us are dead.

Please write to us here, and our mail will be forwarded. We have almost two weeks to stay here, but the mail in Italy is kind of slow.

I've been writing a good deal of prose in a notebook, but not much else.

Love,
Jim

To Michael di Capua

Venice
September 4, 1973

Dear Michael,

At the moment I'm sitting practically in a balcony, looking out across the Giudecca Canal. Far up at the tip of the island on my left, San Giorgio stands in that peculiar rosy blue of late afternoon Venetian sunlight. Almost directly across from me I can see straight down one small canal, past one little bridge and yet another, to a place, largely invisible from here, where the members of the Che Guevara society meet in the evening, and play cards, and generally raise Italian hell, which is pleasant enough, at least before death. Far down Zattere on my right, I don't want to look. It's getting on toward 6:30, early evening already, and if I'm not mistaken, thousands of persons are still standing in line down there for their cholera shots. Annie and a friend and I are going to join that line very early tomorrow morning. No, I doubt if we're going to contract the plague in Venice. That would be too corny: a trite episode imitating a book made out of a movie. All we'll have is a long ordinary wait, perhaps made extraordinary by the long Venetian morning light, changing and changing.

Excuse me for getting carried away for a few moments. This place is so lovely.

In fact, our entire journey so far has been a rich one. We thought of you particularly in Verona, where, among other things, we spent a magnificent evening at the opera, performed in the huge ancient arena.

Did you ever get the letter I sent you from England? I certainly ought to have written to you since then, but I haven't been writing much except in my journal, a rather queer mass of pages that I don't know what to do with except continue to fill. You have our itinerary, don't you? If not, will you just write to us here? Our mail will be forwarded. Annie sends her love.

Love,

Jim

To Donald Hall

Vienna

September 25, 1973

Dear Don,

I'm hoping this note will reach you while you're still in England. We just arrived in Vienna a couple of days ago, and we'll be here also till about October 8. Mails in Italy have been erratic, as I think I told you, and I'm not yet sure where to suggest that you write next. I suspect Annie will be back here at the hotel before I finish the letter, and she'll have some idea of an address.

For we do indeed want to return to Italy. This summer I found myself becoming more and more attached to the place, and of course Annie has loved it for years. Early in November we're meeting her sister Jane (that sounds nice, doesn't it?) in Rome and we'll be with her for a while, but first we want to travel back there more or less slowly, so that among other things I can return to Verona, which may or may not be the most ravishingly beautiful city in Italy but will do for me until the second coming of Christ.

I hope very much that you will be able to buy the farm. The conditions you describe remind me of the same kind of problem that Galway Kinnell faces up in Vermont. The last I heard, he had determined to undertake the place before the developers do, so to speak.

While you're in England I don't know if you'll get the chance to see Geoffrey Hill. But if you do, will you please give him my fondest regards? And tell him of my admiration for the *Mercian Hymns*. I found the book in London last summer, and by this time I must have read it at least twenty times. I wrote a good many notes on it in my notebook, and one of these days I may even try to write an essay about it. It is wonderfully original, and it also suggests further lines of development, the first polysemous book of that kind that I've seen in a good while.

It's pleasant to be back in Vienna, where I was a student so many years ago. My German is rusty but adequate. In a way, it surprises me to find that I can speak more easily in German now than I could when I was actually studying here. I was so young then, with horse manure sticking out of my ears. Still, the city is apparently thriving, and I am glad to see this, because the Viennese, like the Italians, have a strong conservative feeling for the old places in their cities and are making every effort to preserve them among necessary new construction.

Sunday was a perfect Viennese day, early September and the beginning of the peculiar gold that a bright autumn gives here. We took a bus clear up to Kahlenberg, the last little hill of the Alps before you reach the Danube plain, and walked through the beech groves all the way down to the villages of Nussdorf and Grinzing, where we found, as always, many little inns quite generous with the great Heuriger wine. But today is melancholy, heavy with a soaking rain that seems to belong especially to Vienna. All the nineteenth century heaviness and darkness seem to emerge and become part of the weather itself, and in spite of the pathos of the fallacy, one feels a certain neurosis even in the rain, as though Dr. Freud had shrunk the buildings halfway and then the patients had run out of money. Or nerve. But I cheer myself with certain irreducible memories. One morning some twenty years ago, I was plodding lightheartedly through the sunlit snow across the huge Mariatheresianplats, and I found a real two-schilling piece in the snow. I don't know why, but the memory still delights me. I suppose it's because in those days two schillings was, after all, two schillings.

I appreciate your mentioning the *String* and the *Moore*. And I will surely remind you about them when we get back to America next January. Annie is about to return, and I want to get this letter off to you. Look where she comes! (Enter Annie): please write to us c/o American Express in Rome. We won't be there till Nov. 1, but intermediate plans are uncertain. I'll certainly write you before then. Love to Jane.

Love,
Jim

To Laura Lee

Vienna
September 30, 1973

My dearest Laura,

I have been thinking of you time and again in this beautiful city. I am sure it would belong to your heart once you visited it. Paris is of course the capital of the world, and it is an abiding pleasure to remember you there. I will always carry with me, as a secret treasure, the memory of walking with you along the Boulevard Saint-Germain-des-Prés. But what makes me think of you here in Vienna is the inner life of this city, the silences, the melancholy that can become quite dark at times, on rainy days in particular, but a melancholy peculiarly responsive to the occasional and very special sunlight. It is a city whose sunlight is preserved and sustained by the faces of beautiful girls who love music. In other words, my dear Laura, Vienna is your city. Just a street away from the great University, which I attended somewhat blunderingly twenty years ago, you can find a small street where Beethoven lived; but that is not so spectacular as it sounds, considering that Beethoven, a shy, deaf, impatient man who threatened many a robust landlady with nervous breakdowns, lived (I am told) in some twenty-six houses in Vienna and its outlying areas. What is loveliest about that little street near the University is the little townhouse called the Dreimaderlhaus, where three charming girls lived and where Schubert dwelt for a time in his short and complete life, where he enjoyed their company, and where, if I'm not mistaken, he wrote his immortal Octet for Strings. The little house always makes me think of you, and of the love for Schubert you carry in your affectionate heart.

But I don't want to suggest that Vienna is a city of monuments alone, however beloved and haunted such places may be. The genius of the city is in the contemporary life of its music.

I had to interrupt this letter for some two whole days, because the weather changed. After the soaking rain, October suddenly appeared. In America we call it Indian Summer, and in Italy and Austria it is called the summer of Saint Martin. Slightly to the north of the main city of Vienna there are some several little towns (Dorfe, as you know), and three of them are Grinzing (where the great Heuriger wine flows from the vineyards below Kahlenberg to the lovely gardens of the town itself), Nussdorf, where Beethoven lived in twenty-three different houses (according to the rumor which the Viennese still tell, after more than a century—apparently he didn't get along with landlords, etc.), and the one I suppose I love best, and which I think you would love too: Heiligenstädt [sic]. As you know, I am a professor, and years ago I rummaged among the journals and letters of Beethoven. Most of them are pedantic and commonplace. But he wrote a little prose piece called "Der Heilegenstädt Testament" [sic]. In it, he tried to explain to many people why he had seemed in his lifetime to be such a rude person. "The truth is," he said, "I like you very much. But, you see, I can't *hear* you. My ears hurt."

Dear, I would like to send you some message of happiness at this time. I have no special reason except the enduring one: you are my favorite niece and one of my most delightful friends. If you would like to please me also, why don't you get a recording of Beethoven's Symphony Number 6 (the Pastoral Symphony), and listen especially to the movement called "The Brook." We found that brook! In truth, I found it alone, some twenty years ago. It runs from the unspeakably beautiful beech-grove below Kahlenberg down through the Vienna Woods into the town of Nussdorf. I first found it a long time ago, before you were born, in a soaking rain, and it made me happy, because after all,

Beethoven wrote that exquisitely lovely music *after* learning that he would never be able to hear any sound again. He heard the music of that Nussdorf brook in his soul. He had something to sing to you and me, and he sang it. As Aunt Edie (my incomparable Annie) strolled down today through the long beech-grove, that natural cathedral almost as enriching as the greatest cathedral in Europe (Chartres), I thought again of you, how terrible life can be, and how much lovely people like Schubert, Beethoven, and you matter.

Love,
Uncle James

To Karin East

Rome
November 9, 1973

My dear Karin,

I've owed you a letter through a long slow summer and an autumn which is hard to understand in Italy, to me, because the warmth has lasted so long. You seem to me—rather, I should say, you have seemed to me—a perfect Parisienne, and yet I have now seen so many places in Italy where you belong, that now I begin to think you would love Italy best.

Adige is the name of the river. It runs around the fairly small town of Verona. I want to tell you about the color of the water. It is a slow and milky green, like the water that comes down from the Alps. The river is called the *Adige*, and it curls around the city very like the setting of a gem.

And the gem is the city itself. I have done a good deal of wandering in my lifetime, and Verona is like nothing I have ever seen. There is no place in this city that is not ravishingly beautiful. I won't even mention the great cathedral near the river, a miracle of architecture which contains underground, beneath its towering stone interior, another whole church of nearly the same size that contains only a few perfect stone pillars to balance and sustain the entire edifice; nor the tombs of the Scala family, which are surrounded by a wrought-iron fence of such incredible delicacy that one has to change his position merely by a few inches in order to see all the forms and figures change; nor the

Castelvècchio, an enormous fortified castle on the river, where one has to cross a teetering little bridge to find the smiling, delighted face on the equestrian statue of Can Grande della Scala I, the great Veronese nobleman who offered friendship and shelter to the poet Dante. These are merely the obvious glories of the city.

But what made me think of you there especially was the sweetness and loveliness of the people's faces and the gentleness of their manners.

We miss you very much.

Love,
James

To Franz Wright

Rome
November 27, 1973

My dear Franz,

You'll notice that above I'm using the Paris address, although actually at this time we're still in Rome. For the past couple of weeks Annie's sister Jane has been with us. We spent a few days in Florence, then rented a car, and wandered around Tuscany for a while. I think it would be folly for me to try to describe that place. In my lifetime I have stood on Fujiyama; I have drifted down the Seine in a boat while the summer rain turned gray; and at the Volksoper in Vienna I have looked down from the balcony and seen a trumpeter crouch over and hand a glass of wine to a violinist right in the middle of a performance of *Der Zigeunerbaron* by Johann Strauss; and I once spent an entire day talking with Pablo Neruda and looking at his face. But I have never anywhere and at any time seen anything so appallingly beautiful as Tuscany in late autumn. Darkness fell suddenly one evening as we descended from the fortress city of Volterra, which still broods suspiciously over the small valleys in every direction, like a paranoid dragon, or, except for the city's severe dark beauty, like Nixon keeping watch over the national security. We drove for a while, and even got lost, and found our way again at the tiny little bar-restaurant at the edge of a village, where an almost absurdly beautiful girl greeted us, gave us some coffee and grappa, spread out a huge map of Tuscany on the table, and sped us on our way. We finally found the sign pointing us to—San Gimignano. Then we drove up, and up, and around, and around, and up, and around, and up again, till we found ourselves picking our way in semi-darkness (the headlights in our rented Fiat were on the fritz) through very narrow medieval streets. At length, we emerged on a town square, not a very large one as piazzas go, and checked in at a ho-tel over in the corner. The town seemed pleasant enough, but we were road-weary and hungry; so, after stepping a few doors down the street to a trattoria for a small late meal, we went to bed.

The next morning Annie rose first, opened the curtained doors to bright sunlight, and went out on the balcony. I thought I heard her gasp. When she came into the room again, she looked a little pale, and said, "I don't believe it."

San Gimignano is poised hundreds of feet in the air. The city itself is comparatively small, and it is perfectly formed. We felt ourselves at the city glittering there in the lucid Tuscan morning, like a perfectly cut little brilliant sparkling on the pinnacle of a stalagmite. Far below us we could look almost straight down into vineyards and fields, where people—whole families, even small children—had evidently been at work for hours. In all directions below us were valleys whose villages were just beginning to appear out of the mist, a splinter of a church tower here, an olive grove there. The morning was more than beauti-ful. It was a life in itself.

I have to tell you that I'm somewhat disappointed to hear that you don't plan to go on with school this year. It is your life, of course, and I can't live it for you, nor do I want to. When you speak of drifting around Europe and subsisting on odd jobs, however, I have to wonder if you have been following the news of the world lately. Unemploy-ment is severe in Europe right now, and there is every indication that it, as well as inflation, will get worse. Furthermore, Europeans are not about to give a foreigner a job which could be filled by a native. I don't know much about economics, but friends in Austria, businessmen, fear a depression worldwide that will make the Great Depression of the '30s seem puny. I hate to harp on these unpleasant matters, but the state of the world right now gives me no choice. Nixon's the one, with-out a doubt.

Your new poems have seemed to me exquisitely fine, particularly the strange and powerful one about your Grandpa's death.

We'll be leaving Rome in a few days, and our next address will be in Paris. I'll try to keep in touch on the way. We think of you often and always with love.

Love,

Dad

Paris

December 17, 1973

Dear Franz,

On our last day in Italy, we were in Florence. On Saturday was the feast of the Immaculate Conception; and on Sunday, as on Saturday, nobody was allowed to drive a car. I know how hot Florence can be in the summer, caught and magically held as it is in the bowl of the Tuscan hills around the Arno; and I had been warned that it is caught there, too, in the winter, bitter and frozen.

But on that last day we spent there, all the motor traffic was gone, and some god must have taken Botticelli's *Primavera* seriously enough to breathe across the entire river valley. I can't remember a lovelier day in my lifetime, and I have lived through some lovely days. The great Florentines took advantage of the Feast of the Immaculate Conception and the absence of the automobiles to celebrate the coming of spring in the middle of winter. We walked over to one of the squares, and by God a parade began; we ran through back streets and met the town band of Bergamo at the Piazza Signoria, where we patriotically applauded and sang. Everywhere little Florentines were riding on their parents' shoulders and singing, conducting the musicians. The Florentines themselves seemed stunned at the incredible beauty of their city, which they could pause and contemplate without fear of being murdered in cold blood by fanatical traffic. The crowd remained, walking, strolling, singing; we walked up to the civic museum and saw *David*—Michelangelo's *David*. I will not try to describe it, or my feelings about it. I am reduced to the banality of abstraction: it is one of the precious few statements about what it means to be a human being on God's earth.

We've only been in Paris for a few days now, and we leave on January 15th. I hope you'll have time to write us here c/o American Express at least once. Today is Monday. On Saturday we took the train down to Chartres and made a reservation at a small nice hotel, where we plan to spend Christmas eve and Christmas day. After midnight mass, we return to the hotel for the *réveillon*—the dinner of awakening. Although it doesn't seem likely after all these years of fraudulence and folly, Chartres is still a small town, a hick town really, and the cathedral, which took hundreds of years to build, many humorous generations and anonymous lifetimes, still broods clearly on that little hilltop. The sun was so unseasonably brilliant that day, we walked inside and, for a wonder, found the church nearly empty. When we turned to see the great rose window, we saw something we hadn't seen before, something the architects must surely have planned—seen in a vision, I should say—: one whole wall of the cathedral inside, stippled with strange lengthening color poured through the window.

There are literally hundreds of small and large sculptures all over the cathedral there, inside and out. A man named Houvet has photographed them with great care and love. I found two of his photographs which I thought you would like. In fact, they made me think of you. I believe the little sculptures are to be found way high up on the north side of the cathedral. They were done in the thirteenth century. They both made me think of you, and I am enclosing the photographs. The single figure, with his head resting on his hand, is "God creating the day and the night." The other, exquisitely beautiful in stone and, even in its conception, hair-raisingly nutty in imagination, is called "God, while creating the birds, sees Adam in his thoughts." It sounds like the title of one of your poems.

Annie will add a note. We hope you are well, and that you have a good Christmas. I love you, my fine son.

Love,
Dad

To Donald Hall

Paris
January 4, 1974

Dear Don,

Tomorrow I'm going to start a long letter to Robert, and I am going to tell him that I wish to Christ he would sit down and think about the two forces in him which are wasting some of his best gift. They both have value. But I think they are now in conflict, and the result is waste. In the first place, he is fond of attacking the literary powers. They have needed attacking, and some people, including the literary powers, have learned and benefited from the attack. In the second place, Robert has shown in his best poems a power of reserve, of private attentiveness. You can even see this power at work on his farm, when in the middle of a literary discussion he will go outside and rescue a small animal. I think he is a very great man, and I think I know what this greatness consists of. It is a power of attention. I have been reading a startling book by Koestler, *The Ghost in the Machine*, in which he quotes L. L. Whyte: "I ask the reader to remember that what is most obvious may be most worth of analysis. Fertile vistas may open out when commonplace facts are examined from a fresh point of view." I have been thinking about Robert's last two books from this viewpoint, and I think it summarizes his best strength: the gentleness, the deep attentiveness. I have a letter from him in which he announces his intention to attack "three bullies: Howard, Hine, and Harold Bloom." I think such attacks have become a pain in the ass, a waste of time and poetry, and I want to write this to Robert. I wish we had a chance to meet together, and with Louis Simpson again, a man I respect as much as any.

This note sounds like an improvisation, but I don't care. I want to keep in touch.

How I wish Annie and I had been with you and Jane at the Michigan-OSU game! All right, it's Jan. 4, and OSU beat Southern Cal. My predictions were wrong. But I still believe that the Big Ten has collapsed, and I still think Michigan had the better team. I think the West Coast should drop its contract with the Big Ten and choose the best team (Oklahoma). We send love. We're leaving Paris on Jan. 15.

Love,
Jim

/ *403*

New York City
January 29, 1974

Dear Don,

I don't believe it. I accuse you of making it up. We just got back from Europe (England, our last six days), and I spent a couple of days looking at the *American Poetry Review*. You said that George MacBeth came out of 10 Downing Street and told the press "No Comment," while there was controversy about the selection of the new Poet Laureate. You know, I met Mr. MacBeth in New York a few years ago. He is too perfect. I don't believe it. I accuse you of making it up.

Did you get my letter from Paris? I had other thoughts about it, and so I quoted the entire letter in a further letter to Robert. I'm still hoping to hear from him, and I expect a fierce letter. But I wish he would write anyway.

Annie and I bought some four books in London. We went to the Chinese Exhibit. It seems that the army dug into some fantastic old tombs—some of them three thousand years old—and discovered some absolutely and exquisitely nutty things, and the most beautiful of all these are several bronze horses. There is one called The Flying Horse of Kung. This creature seemed so beautiful to the sculptor that he portrayed it in flight into the clouds. Its one hoof rests on the back of a swallow, that in turn is looking in astonishment over its shoulder. We saw these things at the Royal Academy of Arts and Sciences, and we got the book about them. We also found Vincent Cronin's *Napoleon*; his *Florentine Renaissance*; the poems of William Dunbar; and a little book by Gavin Ewart, a poet who seems minor but to me seems wonderful. He wrote the great poem "Miss Twye." Do you know it?

> Miss Twye was soaping her breasts in her bath,
> When she heard behind her a meaning laugh.
> And, to her amazement, she discovered
> A wicked man in the bathroom cupboard.

I don't know why, but I love that poem. It always makes me happy.

I'm writing this note to tell you we're home; to tell you that I, too, got that form letter from H. Loeb at Boston Univ. (I ignored it); that, in spite of my wrong prediction about the Rose Bowl, the Big Ten is still dead; and to send love, hoping for a letter from you and Jane. Please write, Don, and keep in touch.

Love,
Jim

To Morgan Epes

New York City
August 6, 1974

Dear Morgan,

I couldn't resist doing this after we last talked.

I DON'T WANT NO MORE CHARISMA
(A Song Composed After My Latest Conversation with Morgan Epes)

"It is un-American!
It is un-English!
It is French."
     —Mark Twain

I will be one puce-eyed son
Of my mother the three-headed bitch
That snarls in hell, if I can tell
Which Democrat is which.

If Ford and Jackson run,
We can live with either one.
But we've had already
Enough of Teddy:
We decline, like Imperial Rome.
Morgan, my friend, you bear with me
The grievance and tax and misery
Of our whole Republic's miasma
We'll pay for the days to come,
So sing with me, both lustily:
WE DON'T WANT NO MORE CHARISMA!
wejustwanttogohome (?)

Yours in friendship,
James Wright

To Bernetta Quinn

New York City
September 11, 1974

Dear Sister Bernetta,

One of the real mysteries of my life is my neglect of you in correspondence. Surely there must be something weirdly neurotic about it. You must remember years ago how I told you of my love for you; and you certainly remain one of the persons most beloved to me in all my life. Furthermore, though you may justifiably feel skeptical about what I say now, you would really be astonished at the number of times and places I've thought of you, with friendship, with affection, and always when I hear of you, or read your writings, or when I am in the presence of some grandeur, as in Italy or in the mountains of New York, or even when I am feeling sad about something—the last because I know that you would understand the sadness, even if no one else on earth did.

So, instead of going through a long apology (which can sometimes be neurotic in itself), I thought I would simply drop neuroses and apologies and not only write to you but, to make the effort stick, so to speak, send you copies of some of my new writings.

There are a million things to tell you, and I can't write them all at once. But I was reading some weeks ago in Italy from a little copy of *The Cloud of Unknowing* (which I often carry with me—as far as I know, its author is unknown; but, be that as it may, he certainly knows *me*), and noted the passage in which he advised the contemplative person who gets too tangled up in self-absorptions with his own sins simply to drop them, drop the past, cast them into the cloud of unknowing, and get on with living his life as well as he can. So I will tell you some news, and enclose the new writings.

I don't know whether Jerry Mazzaro told you or not, but one of the things I was struggling with was (please God) the final stages of abandoning alcohol altogether. I can't crow too soon. But I can say that I did stop, with the help of my two doctors; that I haven't tasted any alcohol at all for many months; that my weight has gone from 215 pounds to 179 (you would scarcely recognize me); and that my medical doctor says that my physical condition is like that of the very sturdy 18 year old soldier I once was. My physical health is excellent.

I was never better as a teacher when I taught in Buffalo this summer. Then Annie and I went to Italy for about three weeks, for my improving health and simply because we both love Italy so much. You know, I once climbed to the very hilltop of Assisi and found a snailshell there. I thought of the snail as a pilgrim, and I have a poem about it for you in one of my journals. I'll try to find it and send it to you in my next letter.

I'm afraid the critics are giving me a bit of a going over these days. I didn't see the review, but I'm told that while I was in Italy somebody took the hide off my last book in the *New York Times*, and did so rather brutally. It is puzzling to know how to deal in one's own mind with such reviews. In all my years of writing, of course, I've been attacked sometimes. I've got common sense enough to know that my writings have some value to others, certainly for their motive (which has always, however clumsily, been humane and even religious) and even, a few times, for their actual skill. Whenever I get sneered at by a reviewer, of course, it hurts; but the pain isn't so important. What concerns me more than that is what seems a total inability on my part to grasp the very real existence of such human emotions as Malice, envy, spite, and hatred. For example, the fact that Dante is a great poet in the sublime sense and that I am a minor poet doesn't make me feel envious; on the contrary, it makes me very happy to realize that in at least one part of my life I have genuinely aspired to practice an art that Dante glorified. To attempt to write poetry, however minor, seems to me a very fine, worthy thing indeed. Yet so many of our reviewers these days, especially in the *NYTimes*, seem actually bent on annihilating such attempts. It seems to me possible to criticize a book and reveal its errors and failures without sounding as if one wishes the poet were to be hanged. I find such a tone baffling, and even a little frightening—like the oddly disembodied spirit of malice that seems to float around in so much of American life these days.

You must write me again soon, even on a postcard. Your words always are precious to me, as is the very thought of you. And I faithfully promise to respond each time with at least one new piece that I've written. (It is amazing how new writing rushed out after I stopped drinking.) And *please* do send me your poems.

I trust that you'll accept the dedication of one of the prose pieces* (are they prose poems? I don't know) that I enclose.

I believe you'll forgive my neglect of you, my dear friend, without my asking; but I ask anyway.

Jim

To Elizabeth Kray

New York City
October 9, 1974

Dear Betty,

Your note to me is unspeakably lovely; and of course you know very well that there has never been any doubt about the affectionate devotion which we share and have shared for a good many years.

What I am doing is making a supreme attempt to face and contend with certain inner demons that emerged rather starkly after I stopped drinking. I think one drinks excessively in the first place to numb oneself against the problems that are most inwardly difficult; and yet, of course, numbing them doesn't solve them—in fact, it only makes it all the more difficult to solve them. I have taken the first step, though I found it hard at first; and now I am taking the second and far more important one.

I've received letters of similar affection from Jean Valentine and Jane Cooper and—rather wonderfully—from Connie Wilkinson, whom I really don't know very well, but who, it turns out, knows me much better than I had realized. I also just received some stark, brief, forceful new poems from David Ignatow, and he enclosed one by his daughter Yaedi, which seems to me marvelous in its talent and clear expressiveness. Certainly one's loving friends do rally round in one's illness, and it is a great reassuring help to be reminded of an affection which is so precious in our lives, all of us.

My efforts here proceed slowly; and yet I can't praise the staff of

---

*"For Dead Sons," published in *The American Poetry Review* and reprinted in *The Body Electric: America's Best Poetry from* The American Poetry Review, edited by Stephen Berg, David Bonanno, and Arthur Vogelsang (New York: W. W. Norton, 2000).

the hospital enough. They are all extremely well trained and sympathetic and understanding. However long it may take me, I feel that I have a good chance to come to terms with difficulties which have haunted and torn me since childhood.

Although the place is pretty busy—what with medical matters and activities of one kind or another—I have had a chance to do a little work each day. I have taken to writing prose poems, and I've completed a good many. Four of them will be in *The Ohio Review* in the Spring; and I've sent Steve Berg eleven more. These range in length from just a few lines to about three pages, single-spaced. I think you will find them interesting, sometimes slightly nutty, and at least one is unprintable (it is not obscene, though, just an insult to Rockefeller), which I'll show you later. Please keep in touch when you can. It is a great comfort and encouragement to hear from you.

Love,
Jim

To Stanley Kunitz

New York City
October 12, 1974

Dear Stanley,

That was a wonderfully heartening note you sent me, but it is just what I might have expected from a man whose nobility I've admired for so long.

I must tell you that I am still in the hospital, but that I seem to be making very good progress. I'm at Mt. Sinai, whose psychiatric unit is a marvel of sympathy and skill. What happened to me, briefly, is that last May I quit drinking cold turkey, and immediately thereafter took a hard job of summer teaching at Buffalo, where the struggle against booze (a successful struggle) and the work at teaching required an expenditure of energy that finally caught up with me about three weeks ago. Actually, I am glad I came to the hospital; for a heavy drinker like me drinks for reasons he won't face; and without booze to numb him, he has to face the reasons. I've been doing so; and they are interesting as well as frightening. In any case, my physical health is better than it's been for 25 years. I've lost thirty pounds, and I'm in the pink. As for my emotional problems, I am feeling much better. I haven't had to suffer anything like the terrors that good old Ted had to go through.

I am enclosing a poem that I've been working on and haven't been able to complete. This is the latest version, and there's still something wrong. If you can find time, would you be so good as to give me some of your typically severe and lucid help? I think the theme is important, but I haven't been able to get *inside* of it. E.g., if that poor weird guy who smashed the face of the *Pieta* thought he was Jesus Christ (and I believe he did), then—my God, he was smashing his own mother's face. I don't know yet what to do. And the rhythm is faulty. Will you help me, Stanley?

Annie and I both send love to you and Elise. You should write me c/o my home address.

Love,
Jim

To Robert Bly

New York City
October 23, 1974

Dear Robert,

It made me very happy to receive your beautiful letter, with the lovely essay by Montale on Char. I especially appreciated hearing from you because for the past month I've been in the hospital— Mount Sinai. The reason for my going into the hospital again is so extensively and deeply complicated that it would require a very long book to explain adequately. But I think I can briefly summarize what happened, and you know me well enough to understand how such things could be.

As I think I told you, last May I was home alone one Thursday morning. Annie was still in Ohio, where we had gone for me to receive an honorary degree at Kenyon. She had stayed on there, driving down to Zanesville to help my two brothers and their wives close up my parents' house. Both parents died last year, within a few months of each other. And there I was in New York, alone. I woke in the morning and it struck me like lightning: I had to stop drinking; and I had to have help in stopping. I suppose it was one of the supremely difficult efforts of my entire life, but I made it: I phoned my one doctor; he told me to come to his office immediately; when I got there, he phoned my medical doctor, who in turn instructed me to get to his office immediately; and when I got there, we had a three-way conversation by phone, the upshot of which was that I entered a hospital to "dry out" and begin taking a medication that would prevent me from drinking.

I must say that I haven't tasted any alcohol since that time, not even beer; though it was a hard struggle. There were the accursed academic cocktail parties and such at Buffalo, where I taught all summer, for example. But I held out, and I think booze is a thing of the past.

Nevertheless, one of the real curses of a man who has a so-called "drinking problem" is that the drinking isn't the problem. One drinks excessively in order to numb his mind and thus evade the problem, which is psychological. I had assumed that all I had to do was stop drinking and all would be well. What I found myself doing in Buffalo, however, was working about three times as intensely as I needed to do in order to prepare for classes, and, by the same token, limiting the enjoyment of the summer that Annie and I might easily have had. Even the three weeks we spent in Italy at the end of the summer were filled with compulsive nervousness, and it was hard to enjoy things, even Verona, which is a city (it is Dante's city preeminently) I love very much. When we returned to the United States, I had a difficult job to do even before I could begin teaching; and after two weeks of teaching, I got sick, dreadfully sick. On the urgent advice of both doctors, I entered the psychiatric ward at Mount Sinai hospital, and placed myself in the hands of the staff there.

They are beautifully sensitive, highly trained, intelligent people. Yesterday I was discharged, after spending a month, almost to the day, in that company.

It is difficult to explain further. I can say that I feel more whole and healthy inside myself—in my soul, really—than I can recall ever having felt before in my entire life. It sounds like an exaggeration, and I realize that I tend to go to extremes in attempting to describe a feeling; and yet I think truly that my description of my present state of mind is modest, if anything.

For drinking can bruise the soul as well as the body. And, as you know, for years I had been in the process of destroying myself. But

I thought I was just giving myself a physical beating. Nothing is that simple.

I'll write you further about this matter, if you like. But I think I am well. Not entirely, of course. The month I spent at Mount Sinai was intensely difficult, and I am somewhat tired. But I am refreshed. I feel a vast richness within me.

I have several new prose poems. All I'll enclose this time is my lament for Dizzy Dean,* the baseball player, who died last summer. *The New Yorker* turned it down because they "didn't know if it was a poem or not," and they weren't ready to publish "topical verse" and couldn't determine whether or not to consider the poem "light verse." (*Sic*).

I loved Dizzy Dean, and I believe he was a poetic genius.

Annie and I send our love to you and Carol and all the children. I've written a poem for them to sing together to the tune of "Lo, How a Rose E'er Blooming," and I'll send it soon. It's a Christmas song.

Please write.

Love,
Jim

*See Appendix, p. 594, for the poem "The Lesson of the Master: Ten Meditations on the Death of Jay Hanna Dean (1911–1974)."

Roots and Wings

1975–1977

At the University of Indiana, Bloomington, circa 1970

Annie and I have this peaceful new apartment now, in a comparatively quiet neighborhood . . . We like to see people just a few at a time. We had a splendid time with Galway and his two children when we brought them up one afternoon for a walk in the park and some ice cream cake afterwards.

—from a letter to Robert Bly
December 11, 1974

The year 1975 was a time of healing. By the summer of 1976 James had regained emotional stability and accepted a summer job in the English Department at the University of Hawaii. He enjoyed the slow-paced, friendly atmosphere at the University, the beauty of the islands, and the opportunity to spend time with W. S. Merwin, John Logan, and Isabella Gardner. James returned to Hunter and city life in New York with enthusiasm and renewed strength.

By this time in his life James had established a pleasing routine. He rose early in the morning, between five-thirty and six, made coffee, and spent several hours in quiet reflection sitting in his favorite orange upholstered chair. He'd put his coffee cup on a small table next to him and turn the radio softly to WQXR, the classical music station. The small pile of books stacked next to the radio would include whatever novels or poetry he needed for his classes. This was also the time James would work in his journal, a notebook small enough to slip into a jacket pocket, which was always on hand.

At eight o'clock sharp he would bring Anne a cup of coffee, then go into his study. There he might complete preparations for a class or type out a poem or prose piece to place into a black spring binder. Or he might begin a letter.

To Michael S. Harper

New York City
January 14, 1975

Dear Michael,

I just wanted to write you a note to tell you how much I value the new book *Nightmare Begins Responsibility*. I'm serious when I say that "Kin" is without doubt a great poem; and that there are many others throughout the book that sustain its special value. All of your work, it seems to me, is fairly drenched with love, but it is never an evasive love. You seem able to deal with so many harsh realities and, along with them, you include a tenderness that is as powerful as they are. That gives us something truly rare and original: a powerful tenderness. Very, very damned few human beings, in my experience, have had the strength of mind and feeling to balance and, finally, to fuse force and kindness into one new thing; very few human beings, and certainly fewer poets.

There is something in the sound of your language that I keep returning to with pleasure and curiosity. It is hard for me to describe. How on earth are you able to lend the single words and phrases such heaviness and at the same time keep them moving with such a variety of music. Maybe "heaviness" is the wrong word, because it might imply a language that sags till it becomes inert; and that's not what I mean. I think I mean "heaviness" in the sense that the language of Keats is often heavy, often gives the sense that one is dealing not with mere verbal symbols on a sheet of paper but rather with actual physical objects that one can reach out and touch—stroke the fur, whether sleek or rough; apply one's fingertips to the roundness; and even feel the movement from one word to the next, the way you can feel the wind, when you sense a physical body pressing on your own even though you know wind is not a thing but a movement.

Well, I can't figure it out; and, as an aesthetician, I. A. Richards has nothing to fear from me. Yet I wish I could describe the quality I mean. It is there, very real; and it is beautiful.

I hope all goes well with you and yours. I have to begin teaching again soon, after missing the semester because of illness, and, as usual, I'm frightened. But maybe things will be all right. Again, thanks for the superb new book.

Love,

Jim

To Janice Thurn

New York City

May 13, 1975

Dear Miss Thurn:

I trust you received that somewhat crumpled postcard that I sent you a couple of weeks ago from Cleveland. I promised you an adequate letter, and I'm afraid that this note will not be quite adequate. Nevertheless, it is important for friends to keep in touch, however briefly they may have to write.

In a way I am sorry that you told me that you are 17 years old, because now I am almost in the position of having to say that your two poems (both are untitled, but one begins with the line "wind that blew" and the other with the line "shadows on your black dress") are splendid poems, "even though they were written by a poet only 17 years old." And that is certainly what I don't mean to say. The fact is that they are splendid poems by any standards, and I am grateful to you for letting me read them. Anybody who can write the line "gravestoned on a cold sky" has a magnificent and unmistakable gift for poetry, I don't give a damn how old the poet is.

The note I am writing you right now will go no longer than a single page. I am a professor of literature at Hunter College; the semester is drawing to a close; and therefore it involves the hardest and most crucially important labor of the entire term. I am lecturing these last few days with a certain ferocity, an intensity, an effort to make things as clear as I can, with a special effort to relate every single thing I am saying to every book my classes and I have read together for the past fifteen weeks or so.

I love to teach, and that is why I work so hard at it.

Nevertheless, I have to say thank God the semester will be entirely over on May 30th, and, since I am not going to teach during the coming summer, as I usually do, I will be able to let up on myself and write in my notebook in the slow and leisurely way that I like best.

You made me happy by saying that you liked some of my poems. I am exactly thirty years older than you are, but there comes a point where age has nothing to do with poetry. John Keats died when he was 25 years old; but there is a profound sense in which he was older than I am and yet younger than you at the same time. I think your gift is true, and that you have already written beautiful poems. (I know—I sound stuffy, but I can't help it.) Will you please write to me again soon. Keep faith. You have good reason to keep faith.

Your friend,
James Wright

To Carolyn Bilderback

New York City
June 15, 1975

Dear Carolyn,

I have no excuse—I make no apology, really—for waiting so long to thank you for the stunning beauty of your dance recital. I didn't delay out of forgetfulness or neglect. On the contrary, hardly a day has passed but what I've found my imagination stunned and yet reawakened by the abiding image (I don't like to call it a memory) of the whole program, and most particularly "The Diamond Cutters."

I've told you before that I thought the first performance of it (which I saw—no, which I lived in) is your masterpiece. I can't remember in detail whether or not you technically revised the dance between that first performance and the one you danced the other night. All I am sure of is that "The Diamond Cutters" has changed. (Maybe that means that I myself have changed, but that's all right with me.) But,

leaving aside the matter of my change of understanding of your art—
I hope my change is a deepening—and leaving aside the technical
question, I can say that, for me, you and your company might very well
have performed exactly the same steps and made exactly the same
movements that you made when I saw the first performance, but even
this doesn't matter, to me, as much as the certain fact that this magnificent work of art has deepened. Before, it was stunningly beautiful.
Now—that is, in the recent performance—it is more than beautiful. It
is a beautiful and tragic statement about the meaning of being a human being on this earth, and this statement is made in the language
(dance) which is flawlessly appropriate to its meaning. I was delighted
by the first performance of "The Diamond Cutters." I was delighted
and shaken by the recent performance.

This mature version of the work has got to be filmed. As usual, I
speak out of entire technical ignorance and absolute artistic conviction.
Dance, like great singing, used to be lost. Modern technology has
made it possible to hear what Caruso and Heinrich Schlussnuss (yes, I
know, his name sounds funny, but you ought to hear his voice) sound
like. I didn't say sounded. I said sound. The same technology (which
has been used, so far in this century, to discover exquisite new ways for
human beings to kill one another with a maximum of pain, and to
send twelve clowns on the moon, where one of them hit a golf ball)
can also record what is in plain material fact the eternity of your art,
perfectly exemplified in "The Diamond Cutters."

I know. I ain't got no money. I know filming costs money.

But somebody has money, and somebody has got to understand
the absolute necessity of filming "The Diamond Cutters."

I am beginning to sound in this letter arrogant and authoritarian.

All I meant to say was that the recent concert you gave made me
feel the way I felt when I read Keats' "Ode to a Nightingale" for the
first time. I have never been the same person since I first read that
poem. I will never be the same person after living in the presence of
your concert.

Love,

Jim

To Ann Sanfedele

New York City
June 20, 1975

Dear Ann,

I could write you ten pages about Heine, and maybe sometime I will, but right now let me directly explain what I meant by saying that your poems at their best have the characteristic tone of Heine's at their best.

The poems share three things, at least: (1) a daring exposure of true feeling; (2) a purity of diction and an utter naturalness of syntax; and (3) an unmistakable ability to laugh at themselves. The third similarity is the most important and the most difficult to explain. Many of your poems, like Heine's, express the suffering of love. But you both have a sense of humor about yourselves. Don't ask me where this kind of humor comes from, because, if I know anything, I know I don't have it about myself. I have said many things to myself in secret—sometimes aloud, to my own face in the mirror—that were intended to be funny, but were in fact degrading and cruel. You and Heine don't feel that way about yourselves. I like to think of this ability you have to laugh at yourself as being really an ability to regard yourself with some kind of essential good will and kindness.

In Heine's case, sometimes this laughter comes wonderfully alive, as it does in your own poems. (It strikes me that, for all your alertness, you might not even be aware of this.) The three things I mentioned above have one major consequence for a grateful reader (i.e., me): you and Heine can write about true feeling without sentimentality or self pity.

When Heine was quite a young man, and got himself kicked out of the University of Göttingen (for reasons which themselves are very funny), he proceeded to take a long hike through the Harz Mountains. At this time, he began to put together his collection *Das Buch der Lieder* (*The Book of Songs*). It became a large book (I think there are about 200 poems), and yet each poem is very short, and each is about small things. That in itself is a gag, but never mind. In the first edition, Heine had a poem of only four lines. (He is difficult to translate, precisely because his language is so simple—people, I'm told, have had the same trouble with Pushkin—Vladimir Ussachevsky, whose genius I can

1975 / *421*

see and whose depth of feeling is beyond question—assures me that Pushkin in Russian is damned near the equal of Shakespeare. I have to accept Vladimir's word. But, in every English version I've seen, Pushkin sounds to me like a minor imitator of Longfellow.)

Now, about Heine's poem of four lines. Here is the way I translated it, for fun, years ago:

> I thought I could not bear it.
> My heart is healing now;
> And, as you see, I bore it,
> But do not ask me how.

When Heine was still in his twenties, he went to Paris, and there he made some friends. (By the way, to this very day the French will insist they don't know the German language, and the Germans will tell you they don't know the French language, and they are both liars, I can personally assure you.) In Paris, a French friend told Heine that he liked *The Book of Songs* very much, and Heine, congenial fellow that he was, replied that he was pleased, and also remarked that he still wasn't satisfied with the book, and asked if his friend could suggest improvements. The friend replied cordially that he liked the poem I've quoted (in my translation) above, but he couldn't understand what it literally was that the poet meant when he said "I could not bear it." What was "it"? All right, said Heine, what do you think "it" was. I don't know, said his friend, but surely it must have been something really heartbreaking—a lost love, perhaps? Heine replied thoughtfully as follows: One afternoon in Göttingen I realized my shoes were wearing out; I had a little extra money from home, so I entered a shoe store to get a new pair; there was a pair of shoes there so elegant that I was overwhelmed by their appropriateness; they fit my personality exactly. I bought them at once and proceeded to take a walk around the public square to show off my new shoes. But that night, at bedtime, I was in agony. I was so fascinated by the elegant appearance of the shoes, that I forgot to get the right size.

In the later edition of *Das Buch der Lieder*, Heine has another version of his four-line poem: he has added another stanza. Here is my translation of the entire final poem:

I thought I could not bear it.
    My heart is healing now;
And, as you see, I bore it,
    But do not ask me how.

Alack! I should have heeded
    My tortured toes themselves.
I cannot wear elevens.
    My feet are built for twelves.

* * *

What the hell got me on the subject of the strong wall I've built around myself, I wonder? Well, here is the more accurate description: I'm afraid of nearly everything and everybody, so I *try* to build a wall, but I don't succeed. So I live in fear. And yet—you know, I'm not afraid of you, even though you know my secret fears. I wonder why that is. I don't know.

Your poems will be in the next issue of *APR* (I'm told).

Love,
Jim

To a Reader

New York City
September 6, 1975

D. Groth,

Your kind letter made me happy. Poetry is a strange adventure: at crucial times it is—it *has* to be a search undertaken in absolute solitude. But when we emerge from the solitude, we so often find ourselves lost in loneliness—which is quite a different thing from solitude. America is so vast a country, and people who value the life of the spirit, and try their best to live such a life, certainly need times and places of uncluttered solitude all right. But after the journey into solitude—where so many funny and weird and sometimes startlingly beautiful things can happen, whether in language or—even more strangely—in the silences between words and even within words—we come out into crowds of people, and chances are that they also are desperately lonely. Sometimes it takes us years—years, years!—to convey to other lonely persons just what it was that we might have been blessed and lucky enough to discover in our solitude.

In the meantime, though, the loneliness of spirit can be real despair. A few years ago, when I lived in Saint Paul, Minn., I received unexpectedly a short note from a young poet* who was bitterly poverty-stricken in Chicago. He had never published anything; but it so happened that he had sent a few short poems to a close friend of mine, Robert Bly, who in turn showed them to me. I thought then, and I still think, that the young Chicago poet was an absolutely unmistakable genius. I am not using the word loosely. But when he wrote to me in Saint Paul, I did not know him personally. As I say, it was some years ago. I have long since mislaid or lost the short note to me, but I can still quote it, and I believe I will remember its words, its absolutely naked truth, until I die. He didn't even address me by name. Luckily, he did sign the note, and the envelope included his home address. Here is exactly what he said: "I am so lonely I can't stand it. Solitude is a richness of spirit. But loneliness rots the soul." I have made so many mistakes in my life, from the superficially silly to the downright stupid and destructive and self-destructive, but when I die and report to get my just deserts, I figure I ought to deserve at least six months or so in purgatory for my response to that young poet's short note. In the first place, I wrote him a reply without even rising from my desk. It so happened that his note had arrived on about a Sunday, the first day of Thanksgiving week. It also happened that I was living alone myself, and lived too far away from my home in Ohio to get home for Thanksgiving with my parents who were still alive at that time; and the kindly parents of one of my students had invited me to spend Thanksgiving day with them in the little town of Ogden, Iowa, which is within reasonable distance of Chicago. And so, without asking anybody's permission or making any plans whatsoever, I promptly wrote a reply to the young poet in Chicago, and within the hour I had posted my letter to him by air-mail special delivery. I had no more idea of what he looked like than Howard Hughes. Nevertheless, this is what I told him I was going to do: without even making the slightest reference to his remarks about

*Bill Knott.

424

his loneliness, I bluntly informed him that at approximately 2 p.m. on Friday, the day after Thanksgiving, I was going to arrive at his furnished room in Chicago (a very poor section of the city, by the way), and I informed him he could be absolutely certain that I would be accompanied by (1) two vivacious and pretty girls and (2) a large bag of fresh bananas.

And, by God, I did it!

The poet was waiting for us. He was very poor as I said above, and he worked a night-shift at a charity hospital in a skid row. Nevertheless, he had received my letter. His faith never faltered. There he sat on a broken three-legged chair at a rickety table in the center of his single room, and in the dead center of the table sat a gleaming unopened bottle of Jack Daniel's whiskey.

I suspect that anybody who ever really tries to write poetry secretly hopes that at least once he will be strucken by the Muse of inspiration in a way so unpredictably nutty that not even Shakespeare or Dafydd ap Gwyllam would have imagined such an inspiration even in his weirdest dreams. As for me, the thought of cheering up the lonely Chicago poet by visiting him with two pretty girls was merely conventional, though of course pleasant. But the bananas still fill me with such total delight that I sometimes mention them in my prayers. God knows how much second-rate bilge I have written in my many books. But a bag of bananas! Think of it on a tombstone: "He cheered up a lonely unhappy poet with two charming girls and a bag of bananas."

Yes, we need one another in deep, strange ways. Thank you for writing me your kind words. Now: will you do me a special favor? Will you send me a couple of your poems? And, by the way, will you please indicate whether or not you're a girl or a young man? "D. Groth" could be either, and left me off balance.

Yours,
James Wright

To Richard Hugo

New York City
September 7, 1975

Dear Dick,

Thanks for your note. Yes, you sent it to the right address [. . .]

I'd heard somewhere that you're married, and I am glad and relieved to hear it. The relation between men and women can be an extremely weird thing sometimes, but it is amazing how happy you can be. Annie and I have been married for eight years now, and our life has never been better. Come to think of it, we have always got along extremely well, except for one thing: booze. But about four months ago—a little longer than that—I joined AA, after trying just about everything else I could think of in order to quit. I really did try very seriously, even to the point of undertaking a program of cooperation with two doctors; but alcoholism, in my case at least, was so insidious (I should say *is* so insidious) that AA was the only help I had to turn to. Amazingly enough, it seems to be working. There's a great deal more to the program than mere abstinence. I'm making some fine friends at the meetings. As one woman pointed out one evening at a meeting, in reply to the question "Just who the hell *are* we in this room, anyway." "We are all those *really* interesting people who used to meet regularly in the neighborhood bar."

Anyway, I'm off the sauce, and within about the past year I've lost from forty to fifty pounds.

I'm glad you liked those prose poems, the one in the *Ohio Review* and the others in *APR*. You didn't mention the others, three of them, that were printed in the *Ohio Review*, so I'm enclosing an offprint of them with this note.

I'm very eager to receive your new book which, I saw somewhere, is called *What Thou Lovest Well Remains American*. It is going to be another year, at the very least, before I publish a book again. I have enough pieces to make a book, but I'm a long way from being satisfied with it. By the way, Dick, what is your opinion about including prose poems in a book that also contains straight poems. I would like to include some, but I don't know. What do you think? Although I didn't see the piece, I hear that somebody in the *Sewanee Review* wrote a review of my last book called "The Collapse of James Wright." I feel like Sugar Ray Robinson after his first fight with Randy Turpin . . . Ah, well: when you saw Jim Welch, did he remember to give you my secret-code message? I told him you would grasp the words in all their obscure simplicity. He was supposed to tell you: "Fuck Ed Bedford." Please write soon.

Love,

Jim

To Dave Smith

Dear Mr. Smith:

Over the years I have taken my share of bumps from critics, and they have nearly always made good sense to me. At the risk of sounding masochistic (which I am, though not, I think, in the present instance), I think one of the finest reviews ever written about my work was a full essay on the book *Saint Judas*. The author was Mr. David Galler, a brilliant critic and poet whom I admire and whom I have never met. Displaying his thorough grasp of the book, he condemned it. He had committed his whole imagination and his whole intelligence to the book. He didn't like it. He explained why. Of course, I wish he had liked the book. But I remember feeling that this was the way I would hope my books, such as they are, to be read and discussed. Flattery is nice; superficial contempt is distressing; to be ignored is frustrating. None of these has anything whatever to do with poetry and the criticism of poetry. (To me, the word "criticism" means a serious and attentive reading of a book.)

I have long been grateful to Mr. Galler because he read and discussed my book as seriously and intensely as I tried to write it. Of course, I wish he had liked it. But I would rather be closely read by David Galler than flightily praised by—oh, Rod McKuen (that's unfair; Mr. McKuen is not a poet; he is a Success; quite another thing).

Intelligent reviewers have often found my books wanting, and so have I. I do not want to get revenge on the universe because I am not Dante or Shakespeare. I do believe that the labors of a minor poet have value. For years I have tried to live by two noble sentences I found in an essay by James Baldwin: "I do not like people who like me because I am a Negro. I want to be an honest man and a good writer."

I think I have enough sense to understand as well as anyone else that my most recent book, *Two Citizens*, is so artistically flawed that I ought not to have allowed it to be published. At least one-third of the poems should have been deleted entirely, and nearly all the others should have been severely revised. I could recognize the justice of such a judgment by any reviewer.

But the book appeared three whole years ago. It is an artistic failure; and so many books are annually published, you would think that by this time *Two Citizens* would be forgotten as just one among many botched efforts.

But something very strange has happened. Certainly it is unique in my experience. In two or three cases (perhaps more, I don't know), certain reviewers responded to *Two Citizens* not by explaining in detail its artistic inadequacies. I could understand such a review. If a reviewer reads a book carefully and honestly judges it to be a failure, I believe he should say so, and explain his judgment. I wish *Two Citizens* HAD BEEN a good book. It is a bad book. I tried to do something serious, and I failed. I can cope with this indisputable fact. The world has not come to an end. I can face the failure of my book by attempting (as I am certainly attempting) to write a new book. It is perhaps a year or two away from completion; and certainly it will be different, in form and in feeling, from *Two Citizens*. What has troubled me—and troubles me still—is that some reviewers did not merely demonstrate that *Two Citizens* is an artistic failure. In at least three reviews that I've read, I was absolutely astounded to find an unmistakable expression of hatred. I know that my egotism in this case may amount to outright paranoia. But how else can I account for a title like "The Collapse of James Wright." And can that review (which I haven't read) actually have been written by Paul Ramsey, an old and cordial friend of mine whom I haven't seen for the past few years? Can he possibly be one of those people to whom the word "form" must literally be defined as verse written in strict rhymed iambics?

In the other two or three reviews I've seen, the sneers were so disturbed and disturbing, that I began to feel guilty. All I thought I had done was publish an inadequate book about a year and a half before it was really finished. A bad book is not one of the major joys of life, but it isn't a major calamity either. All a reviewer has to say is that "this book is an artistic failure, and I hope the author will do better next time." But evidently there is something about *Two Citizens* which inspired some reviewers with an impulse to murder. Some fellow (I've forgotten his name) in *The Hudson Review* sounded as if he were quivering all over like Lionel Barrymore. His review might have given him a hernia. What I wonder about is just what the hell in *Two Citizens*, a serious but commonplace failure, provoked such a hysterical reaction.

I've written this letter to thank you for the spirit of intelligent good will that pervaded your review of *Two Citizens*. Your essay gave me encouragement when I desperately needed it . . . I want to ask you something: are you by chance the David Smith who translated Vallejo's *Trilce?*

I'd just intended to write you a brief note of thanks but I see now that your essay has a value far beyond the success or failure of *Two Citizens.*

Gratefully yours,
James Wright

To M. L. Rosenthal

New York City
September 20, 1975

Dear Mr. Rosenthal:

I hope you won't mind a note from a personal stranger.

A few years ago I read Neruda's "Fable of the Mermaid and the Drunks" in Spanish, and it haunted me. You of all people know how you might discover a certain poem and you don't simply "memorize it"; it actually seems to become part of your personality, your very life. I never tried to translate the poem.

Then, about a year and a half ago, my wife and I were staying in the small Italian fishing village of Grado, on the Adriatic. A few foreigners visit the village in summer to swim; but mostly it is a laboring place; fishing is the main work; the men go out to sea long before daybreak and come back at twilight; there are people all over the place, wives and husbands and children sitting on their front steps after supper, mending nets. I remember being struck by the special strangeness of fishing as a way of making a living: how real fishermen are plain people, almost always poor, married to stocky and pleasant middle-

aged wives, surrounded by many children whose games often get inter-
mingled with the work shared, one way or another, by the whole family, in a way of life that, on shore, is just commonplace; and yet how the
men go far out to sea in the darkness and let down lines or nets, wondering surely just what weird creature they might draw into their boats
along with all the shrimp and piccolini and sardines and the rest of the
usual haul. I vividly remembered Neruda's poem. I didn't have the text
with me, and I didn't have the poem literally by heart. And so, just for
the fun of it, I wrote a poem on my own.* It isn't a translation. It's just
an attempt to write about an incident similar to the one in Neruda's
poem. You could call it an imitation, maybe; or a poem based on
something in Neruda. Well, it doesn't matter what you call it. It gave
me pleasure to write it. When I read your translation in the most recent
American Poetry Review, I was again struck by Neruda's ability to write a
poem of such truly enormous richness and depth, and yet do so in a
comparatively few lines. My own poem is a little more than twice as
long as Neruda's, and of course it doesn't contain anything even dis-
tantly approaching Neruda's great mastery.

I've written you this note to tell you that I am tremendously grateful to you for your translation. I think it is magnificent. Among the
many exciting problems involved in translation, one of the most important has to do with what the translator ought to try to accomplish.
Of course, he ought to be accurately faithful to the original text. And
yet many translations are accurate, and yet they're somehow poetically
thin and pale. I don't know Russian, but I have several personal acquaintances whose native language is Russian. They are all admirable,
cultivated, highly intelligent people whose taste and judgment I completely trust. They all assure me that Pushkin is an author quite as
great as Dostoevsky, Gogol, and Tolstoy. And I am willing to take their
word for it. Nevertheless, all the translations of Pushkin's poems that
I have ever seen make him resemble a tenth-rate imitator of Henry
Wadsworth Longfellow.

And yet a great poem *can* be translated, not only with linguistic accuracy but also with a thrilling poetic radiance. I think that your translation of the Neruda poem, read simply as a poem in the English

*See Appendix, pp. 597–601, for the poems "A Visit to the Earth" and "Neruda," published to-
gether in the spring of 1974.

language, is one of the most beautiful poems I have read in a long time.

I would like to add that, although for some reason I've never been lucky enough to meet you personally, your writings—including your poems, your translations, your anthology, and your longer critical studies—and they have been deeply helpful, instructive, and encouraging to me, in my reading as well as writing. I think that any period of poetry requires, basically, the presence of a literary criticism that is able to discuss poetry as a living art; the best critic of this kind must be intelligent, learned, capable of fine and true distinctions; he must be able to judge the value of the work he's discussing and to explain the reasons for his judgments. I think it is possible—in fact, I think it is necessary—for a critic to do and be all these things and at the same time be motivated by a true and deep love for the art of poetry. Certainly you are such a critic. I think one of our troubles these days is that you are quite possibly the only writer who possesses all of these major talents at once. In the same recent issue of the *APR*, you are quoted as saying that *APR* is the magazine "most likely to take over the role once played by *Poetry: A Magazine of Verse*." It's true that the old *Poetry* was once the single major American poetry magazine where all viewpoints could be discussed and poems of all kinds could be printed. I scarcely know what to say about the *Poetry* of today. I will say that I have wished, very strongly and more than once, that the editor of *Poetry: A Magazine of Verse* were M. L. Rosenthal. That's just my own opinion; but I'll bet it is an opinion very widely shared. Well, thank you again.

With admiration,
James Wright

To Merrill Leffler

New York City
November 2, 1975

Dear Mr. Leffler:

I have a sick tendency toward inflated language, and I hate it, so I will try to keep it in control here. I am trying to say that I am overwhelmed by your letter. My devotion to Dryad Press and all its works is something more than aesthetic pleasure in the beauty of its design and the excellence of its authors. It is a devotion that might almost be called a sense of relief. I see appearing all around me so many splendid writers; and yet I know that most of them would never appear at all through large commercial publishers. We are coming back where we belong in America in one realm of life, at any rate: the publication of real poetry by small independent presses. Dryad is very beautiful. (By the way, before I forget in the press of other things I want to say, will you please put me on the subscription list for the new volume called, I think, *Jewish Poems*, which I saw described on a flyer? I lost the flyer, but I think you are charging $3. Do you require the check immediately? I would write it for you now, but my checkbook isn't accessible at the moment. Anyway, I want the volume. The poems quoted on it are very fine. I would never even have heard of it if a friend equally an admirer of your press, hadn't shown me the flyer.)

After that pompous opening paragraph, let me try to say why I am overwhelmed. You see, I don't want to publish a full volume yet. My own publisher (Farrar, Straus & Giroux) would be willing, I'm sure, to publish an entire volume of prose poems if I wanted them to; but I don't want them to. I have a book going that will involve poems in verse and prose, and it won't be done for—oh, how do I know? All I know is that I am rewriting and severely revising all the new poems I have since my last book—there are about 50 of them. What I want to do first is to publish a chapbook. I have never had a chapbook in all my years of writing, for a reason that may strike you as weird: it is that I never till now felt ready for one. It seems to me, in the raging hell and waste of America (why am I sounding like Thomas Wolfe? is it because I've been reading Jane Austen all last night and for hours this morning?), an exquisitely spacious form of publication for poetry. I flop all over the place, and it takes me years to hone everything down into a book; it even sometimes takes me years to finish a single poem; maybe what I mean will be clearer if I point out that I had the same odd weakness of mine in mind when I published a *Collected Poems* before I tried to publish a *Selected*.

In response to your beautiful invitation (beautiful for its generosity and for its happy arrival at just the right time, for me), let me ask if you would be willing to consider publishing a chapbook of, say, 15 prose poems, all of them written in (or about) certain places in Italy. These are the prose poems that are closest to being finished—that is, ready to appear in a collection. They are also the ones which had been occupying my mind at the time I received your letter. Many of them have already been printed in magazines (the *American Poetry Review*, *The Ohio Review*, *The Paris Review*, chiefly); but I am still learning about this kind of poem, so thrillingly new to me even though I can now see it has been sleeping in me for a long time. Of course, my sending the poems to you would not mean that you would automatically publish them. The judgment would be yours, obviously. Moreover (I think I'm stating this correctly) my contract with my own publisher would allow me to grant you only non-exclusive rights to the poems. I may have got this statement mangled, but surely you will grasp what I'm trying to say. Finally, if you would like to see the manuscript I have in mind, I could send it to you by about the middle or end of the coming Spring. I suspect you are not in any great hurry; and I'm certainly not. I have given up hurrying as far as publication is concerned. The hell with it.

If you are interested in my idea, it would be worked out in detail something like this: I would like to open the book with a small poem in verse, a lovely poem about a small carving in a church in Lucca, a little marble boy playing with a fish in what looks to be a baptismal font (what a nutty idea! the new-born baby instantly begins to play with the fish in the font). The poem was written by my wife. It would be followed in the chapbook by about 15 prose poems of varying length, but none of them terribly long (the longest took up slightly more than 2 pages in an issue of the *Ohio Review*; I suspect you would want to use larger print than they use). The final prose poem in the chapbook would be called "The Fruits of the Season," and I think I'll enclose an offprint of it to give you a notion of the flavor of the prose poems I have in mind. They are varied in perspective and in length. One of them, called "Saying Dante Aloud," is a single sentence long in its entirety: "You can feel the veins rippling in widening and rising circles, like a bird in flight under your tongue." Finally, do you think it would be possible to include some illustrations?

I have further ideas about the project, if it appeals to you . . . By the way, I saw Mr. Spender's article, and also the correspondence that followed. I've always been grateful to you for your letter, though I really don't think Spender was all that hard on me. I have more to say about this, but I'll wait for your reply. Please be assured of my gratitude.

Yours,
James Wright

To Louis Simpson

New York City
November 30, 1975

Dear Louis,

I tried to phone you this evening, and I did have the pleasure of talking with Dorothy for a few moments, but I missed you.

It seems to me that your new poems are startling. You won't believe this, maybe, but my old love of E. A. Robinson turns out to be right after all. The language of prose is the most intense and musical language. "Searching for the Ox" is one of the nuttiest poems I have read. So is "How Annandale Went Out." They are indirect and therefore true.

On late Sunday evening, Nov. 16, I got a frightening pain in my insides, and went to the emergency ward of Mt. Sinai. After three days without food and water (literally), I was dismissed. I have to go through one more test to see if my stomach is all right. But now I am well.

Once you wrote me a very personal letter about my own physical welfare. I think it will matter to you to know that I have joined AA and am sober.

In the spring I am going to publish a little book of prose sketches about Italy. I have decided that the term "prose poem" is idiotically confused, so what I am going to publish are just prose sketches.

Your willingness to read my poems aloud at the YMHA when I was sick means so much to me that I do not want to talk about it.

The Groucho Marx song which I couldn't sing to Dorothy over the phone goes as follows:

> There's a little town called Omaha, Nebraska,
> And you'll find it in the hills of Tennessee.
> My sweetheart told me that
> One day she'd meet me at
> The corner of Delancey Street
> And Avenue B.
> From the rockbound coast of Maine
> To the California shore,
> We'll settle down in Washington, D.C.,
> In a little town called Omaha, Nebraska,

In the foothills
of Tennessee.

Porca la luce,
Jim

To Robert Bly

New York City
December 5, 1975

Dear Robert,

That was a lovely letter you sent me in November. It was just the kind of letter I meant when I took my latest turn at reminding both of us how important it is to restore our correspondence. Of course, I turned out to be the negligent one. It's silly to apologize or make excuses. Here is my response.

Your description of reading Irish fairy stories to the children was charming and light-hearted and entertaining—all nice qualities in themselves. But I also found myself deeply stirred in a strange way, not only by your summary of the one story itself, but also—maybe even especially—by the thought of your sitting there in the farmhouse, probably reading aloud to the children for the sheer joy of it without being particularly conscious of any serious purpose—that would have been too pedantic, and the kids would have sensed the absurdity of an adult's attempt to read aloud to them the old stories whose very nature has been always to awaken delight in children and yet to insist that the children pay serious attention. (I suspect that helps to explain why children are bored by some schoolteachers who are stuffy and boring: children are intelligent enough to see quite clearly the idiotic contradiction between the joyous spirit of the great fairy stories and the grim joylessness of the teacher.) Your account of the evening just shone with the pleasure you felt and shared with the children.

But I think I was so strangely moved for still another reason. I had no clear notion of the reason till today, when I read a really marvelous new essay by Bruno Bettelheim (Carol will be specially interested to know about this essay, I'm sure). It appears in (of all things!) *The New Yorker*, the issue dated December 8, 1975. The title of Bettelheim's essay is "Reflections on Fairy Tales." His general purpose is to distinguish between the "overwhelming majority" of contemporary stories written for children and, on the other hand, the old and very traditional and enduring fairy stories and folk tales, such as the stories collected by the Grimm brothers. In arguing that the old stories are superior, Bettelheim isn't just being an inflexible mossback reactionary. What he does is, first, to explain the function of story-telling as a way of educating what he calls the "inner life" of the child, a function traditionally performed by parents (who somehow can do this most beautifully); and, second, to offer an extraordinarily clear and beautiful explanation of the real world of the imagination which is embodied so fascinatingly and so truly in the great old fairy tales, which are of course really poems—and very great and vital poems, at that. Really, Robert, even as I write this note to you, I can still feel myself glowing with pleasure I found in reading Bettelheim's wonderful piece. To give just one example of ideas that excited me: I found a striking similarity between Bettelheim's conception of the truly healthy imagination and your own argument about the nature of truly effective meditation; and also, along the same lines of thought, between Bettelheim's reason for calling contemporary, commercially commissioned and published "children's books" (that is, such books—or most of them—implicitly deny the very existence of the true imagination by replacing it with a pre-calculated, entirely artificial story of plastically "perfect" characters whose effect (I wouldn't be surprised if it were a *deliberate* effect) on children is to promote in their own imaginations—which are by nature *active* and consequently most deeply delighted and most healthily educated by the experiences of characters who seek to live *adventurous* lives, lives which require them to grow in curiosity, creativeness, courage, risk, as opposed to most characters in contemporary commercial "children's" books, who seek to live lives whose main feature is an attitude of passive adjustment). Your own ideas—too extensive and rich to summarize briefly—that your word "daydream" indicates came vividly to my mind as I read Bettelheim's essay. And I think—more and more—that your set of ideas concerning "daydream" are among the most illuminating and also the most *helpful* that you've ever conceived and developed—for me, anyway.

I haven't written yet to Don Hall about his poem "The Falling Leaves," which astonished me. It is incomparably the best poem of his that I have ever read. In all the years of our friendship, I have been puzzled by the difference between most (not all) of his poems, which are always soundly written and intelligent and even courageous and yet somehow lacking in—in something, I don't know what to call it, but something absolutely essential to the most thrilling poetry, and on the other hand his life, his nature as a human being. Don is undoubtedly one of the most intelligent, clear-minded, generous, truly good-hearted people I have ever known. Like everybody else, he has made his mistakes and acted silly sometimes, but these things don't matter; what does matter is that, in his real nature, he is absolutely authentic. I've always wondered why all that richness and beauty and depth of feeling never quite made its way into his poems. Well, I don't know. Something happened. I wouldn't know how to explain it even if I knew what it was. But I don't care. "The Falling Leaves" gave me the joy that only the truest poetry can give. I am very glad . . . I've revised that "prose poem" which I read aloud to you when you were last here. It's a little longer now, but you said you liked it all right when I read it to you. You said, briefly, that you thought the last version successful because at the end of it I just let the woman leave the park and not return. In the enclosed version I tried to fulfill the poem.*

Love,
Jim

To Marshall Wright

New York City
January 11, 1976

Dear Marshall,

Here it is getting on toward the middle of January. It will take me at least six months to get used to writing the correct number of the new year. But, then, it might as well be any year right at this moment. As I write these words to you, the air outside my window is all blossoming with new snow flurries. It always makes me feel strange when I hear natives of New York groaning about a snowfall. The snow here is really a small hindrance to people; and at least for a little while, it is very beau-

*"The Secret of Light," included in *Above the River*, p. 302.

tiful. There is something healing about a new snow, especially when it falls on a city, a large city as battered and scarred as New York sometimes seems. It is now about the middle of Sunday afternoon. I have been working on my students' final examination papers for the past few hours, and Annie has been doing all kinds of chores around the house. Soon we are going to put on our warm coats and scarves and our boots and go outside to enjoy the snow while it is still new.

We received, first, your marvelous gift of the California wine-jellies, and then, a little later, the magnificent owl made out of rope. Did you make it yourself? I was given several new owl-things over the holidays, and once again the whole house seems aflutter with beautiful, silent wings.

During the entire Christmas and New Year time, we didn't leave the city. One evening we gave ourselves a small treat by staying at a nice hotel downtown, going to a movie to see something special, and having dinner at a very nice Korean restaurant. But most of the time we were right here at home. The weather has been pretty cold, even for this time of year, but our apartment has been warm enough. I want to mention the movie that we saw about a week ago. It was called "Bugs Bunny Superstar." It contained several old movie-cartoons, starring Bugs Bunny and other great geniuses like Elmer Fudd, Daffy Duck, and the immortal canary-bird Tweetie-pie with his frustrated friend Sylvester the red-nosed cat. It was a wonderful movie, so funny that it made us think of you. We think of you always with love, and wish we would hear from you. Your Christmas presents were beautiful. I love you, Marsh. Thinking of you reminds me of Paris . . . and Hawaii.

Love,
Dad

To Helen McNeely Sheriff

New York City
January 12, 1976

Dear Miss Sheriff:

I am so happy to have your splendid greeting. You may well wonder why I haven't written you for so long. I could list many things that have happened—illnesses, labors at teaching and writing, travels, and so forth—but these would all be beside the point. The truth is that I can't even offer the excuse of sloth; for I have not been indifferent and idle. Moreover, I have thought about you, and spoken about you with Annie and with a few close friends, so many times and in relation to so many places and ideas that it is not even enough to say that you have often come into my mind. It is more accurate, I believe, to tell you that in recent times I have become ever more clearly aware of how deeply you are actually and literally a part of my mind itself: how you truly live in that part of my character which is clearly intelligent and imaginative and faithful. (Of course, there are many other parts of my character that are anything but these.)

But if I've been aware of you so often, then why haven't I written? Well, I have no excuse and no explanation. Still, you will learn in a moment that in another sense I really *have* written to you. But first I want to tell you some news.

After some slightly confused negotiations, the City of Martins Ferry (whose mayor, Mr. John Laslo, sounds like a good, responsible person) has invited Annie and me to be guest of the town on the weekend of the coming June 25th (I think that's a Friday) through June 27th. Dr. Hollis Sommers, a distinguished author and professor from Ohio University at Athens, Ohio, will also be in Martins Ferry that weekend. We haven't been sent specific details yet, but I gather that there will be a program that involves some panel discussions and lectures open to the public. Whether or not they'll ask me to speak alone in public I don't know. (I would rather give a formal lecture than read aloud from my writings.) In any case, Annie and I, either before or after the weekend, plan to visit with my brother Ted (whom you remember) and his wife Helen, who now reside in Zanesville. If you and Nancy and her family could get to Martins Ferry for the occasion, it would be fine. But if for any reason you can't, then I will make arrangements to stop and see you in Cadiz. Annie has already written to Mr. Russell J. Woolman and told him; I still think it's important that you receive a formal invitation. For a little while, I had mixed feelings about returning to Martins Ferry. I haven't been there for just about twenty years. I'm sure the place must have changed drastically, just as so much else has changed in America during recent decades. And I myself have gone through so much since I left my home town for good: life in the army, hard work at Kenyon and just barely making it through my junior year on the G.I. Bill and, almost completely out of money, wondering how I could finish college and almost at that very moment being informed that I had made Phi Beta Kappa and was being granted a full scholarship, enough to get me through my final year; then winning the Fulbright scholarship to Vienna; and teaching while I took the M.A. and the Ph.D. at the University of Washington in Seattle; publishing my first book the very next day after I completed those long and punishing exams for the doctorate; living unhappily and mostly alone in Minneapolis and St. Paul for 8 years; getting a Guggenheim Fellowship grant and coming to New York (which I still care about) in an effort to finish a book and somehow make a desperate attempt to pull my life together; and discovering my magnificent Annie who (we've been happily married for nearly nine years!) never fails to be a revelation to me; and being honored wildly for a while and then provoking strange and violent critical controversy (with many wide-ranging attacks and defenses) with my last book; and, these days, living and teaching in New York while the city is in financial crisis and life has become in important ways so uncertain and yet, through all this, still struggling, still aspiring to be true to the great classical standard of language and teaching and writing, still (as the wonderful Welsh writer Alun Lewis wrote to his wife from Burma where he was killed in 1945) "striving, and seeking, and not finding, and *still seeking*" with "a robustness in the core of sadness." I have taken my wounds from the world, and no doubt I have foolishly wounded myself; I have changed in so many ways, and yet in some deeply important ways I have tried to be constant in devotion. All this: and also, after all, I have written some things about Martins Ferry that aren't very complimentary. Still, I perceive that the place, for all its physical ugliness and spiritual desperation, nevertheless had its noble spirits who were—and who are—good to me, who disregarded my family's poverty and my own ignorance and who saw what was worthy in me and required of me only that I be true to it. I am still trying. So, after all these years, I am taking Annie and going back to visit my home town.

In the Spring a distinguished small press called the Dryad Press is going to publish a book which I have just this week completed. It is entirely in prose, and it will be called *Moments of the Italian Summer*. It consists of about 18 prose sketches in and about Italy. I am in no hurry to publish things these days (I published my last book too soon; I failed to follow Horace's wise advice about laboring faithfully and being patient; but I won't make that mistake again). Nevertheless, as I was organizing the manuscript of the new little book I just mentioned, I realized that it is an abridgement of one major section of the larger book toward which I have been groping my way for more than three years. Once I discovered the proper order in which the 18 prose pieces must be presented, I was startled to realize that I had also discovered the artistically unifying principle of the entire large book. A couple of months ago I had occasion to make a list of all my publications since my last book in 1973, and I was really quite amazed to see how long the list was. I hadn't strained toward any deadline; I had written slowly and naturally and patiently; I hadn't published everything I'd written, not by a good deal. And yet there they were: about thirty new poems and about thirty prose pieces. And now I have a very clear idea about how these writings can naturally arrange themselves in the large book. My major publisher is Farrar, Straus & Giroux, which is, I should say, one of the most distinguished publishing houses in New York. I plan to take the entire manuscript, and all my notes on its organization, with me to Honolulu this summer (Annie and I will spend most of the summer in Hawaii, where I am going to teach a session in the graduate school of the university there). I plan to organize the manuscript in detail. Then, when we return to New York at the end of the summer, I think I will be able to turn the book over to Michael di Capua, my editor at Farrar, Straus & Giroux. Although, as I say, I have tried to free myself from the panic and consequent erratic judgment that accompany a frantic ambition and arrogance and impatience of any kind, but especially in one's spiritual life (and the attempt to write a book truly and well is certainly a spiritual effort); nevertheless, there does come a moment when I must face the fact that I have fought a good fight, kept the faith within my ability to do so, and finished my task. That is, once the book is as finished as I can make it, I must have enough courage to let it go, to let it be printed. Sometime next week I am going to describe to my editor everything I've described to you here, and show him a detailed outline of the large book. It will be in three sections, of which the smaller book I'm publishing this Spring is an abridgment of the second. Michael di Capua is a gentle, generous, highly intelligent young man: a good editor. We'll talk at length about my outline. He'll make suggestions. Perhaps we'll correspond about it. Anyway, I'm pretty sure I'll be able to give him the completed manuscript at the beginning of next Fall, and the book will probably appear during the following Spring.

The title I've so far decided on is the result of a great deal of pondering, and it may seem a little obscure all by itself, but I feel sure that it will become quite simple and clear once a reader sees it in relation to the book itself. I think I will call it *Redwings and the Secret of Light*.

And, by way of closing this long letter, I want to make a request of you, Miss Sheriff. Would you be so kind as to grant me permission to dedicate the large book to you? The dedication would signify even more than my abiding devotion and affection toward you, great and true as these are. You see, in a very special way your name and your influence serve to bring to a focus everything I have labored to write in the book itself. What I want to do is to name you on the dedicatory page, and, right beneath your name, I want to quote the last three lines of Goethe's great poem "Natur und Kunst." "Whoever wants to be great must restrain himself," Goethe writes; "It is in his (self)-limitations that the master is revealed, / And only law can give us freedom." I have carried those lines in the back of my mind since I first found them 20 years ago. I think Goethe's sublime words almost perfectly express the nobility of his spirit, and of yours. Here are the lines in German:

Wer Grosses will, muss sich zusammenraffen.
In der Beschränkung zeigt sich erst der Meister,
Und das Gesetz nur kann uns Freiheit geben.

I hope you will accept the dedication. It would mean something to me so fine that it is beyond my power to express it.

We hope you'll give our greetings to Nancy and her family (I wonder if she remembers me). And Annie especially wants to be remembered fondly to you.

I've written a long letter this time. But it would be silly to apologize. I had a lot on my mind.

With love,
Jim

Dear Miss Sheriff:

We're so happy to have your recent letter. I am utterly delighted that you approve of my planned dedication. It signifies a public and formal gesture of respect; but of course it has a much deeper and more complex meaning than that to me. Though I won a Pulitzer Prize (a nice but transient distinction), I still know that I am an apprentice in the art of poetry. I still would like my writings to be judged—whether praised or condemned—finally by the truest and best spirits I know of; and these, the best people and the best minds, include many persons who are not impressed by minor skill in language, nor by public recognition alone, not even by the official recognition of Martins Ferry. Among such abiding and noble spirits I include the great Horace, and Dr. Samuel Johnson, and Goethe (whether as a great poet, a great playwright, a great novelist, a great travel-writer, a great scientist, a great statesman, a great friend—he was all of these and more), and— it is God's truth—yourself. To dedicate my new large book to you means that I am more dedicated than ever to every excellence which you embody in your life: your courtesy, your seriousness, your positively Horatian sense of balance and good humor, your intellectual standards, your total refusal to compromise with any shoddiness at all, whether literary, intellectual, or moral. The dedication also means that, of all my books so far—there are about 11—I think I can consider my new one the best. Of course I live in the hope that some day I will write better; I just mean that this new book gives me a more authentically happy sense of accomplishment than any of the others.

I have some news for you, some pleasant and then some perhaps not so pleasant, according to one's point of view. First, let me tell you that Annie and I are *definitely* coming to visit Ted and his wife in Zanesville for a few days in the latter part of June; and that, during that visit, there will be ample time for a leisurely visit to your house in Cadiz where it will give me such joy to see you again and, especially, to present you and my wonderful Annie to each other.

Second, I have just written to Martins Ferry and informed the officials there of my decision *not* to visit Martins Ferry this June for their series of programs. I simply and decisively told Mr. Russell J. Woolman, of the Martins Ferry Division of Development, that, in view of the many problems involved, I had decided not to participate in the nine (!) public ceremonies within a mere two days that he had planned. I added that, though my decision would cause him inconvenience, I nevertheless had not been previously informed that he had any such extensive scheme in mind; that attendance, and performance, at so many functions would make a casual walk with Annie around Martins Ferry impossible; that his programs actually made me feel dubious and strained, for some of these programs are transparently political, and I have neither desire nor intention of entering local political discussions, which are none of my business; and that, finally, I could offer little to his ceremonies because they are all so remorselessly public, and I am an entirely private person. I closed my letter by asking him to greet the teachers and friends who are still in Martins Ferry and whom I always think of with affection and gratitude.

Miss Sheriff, it is true. Although I am a professor, I am not even the kind of person who has a taste for political or cultural or other "public" events. Consider how William Dean Howells would have been a perfect public guest of today's Martins Ferry. Howells was born there, of course; he went on to become a truly important person in American history and, indirectly, in American literature. As editor of Boston's *Atlantic Monthly* in its earliest and greatest days, he became socially prominent; he became a powerful and vitalizing influence on a new development of realism in American fiction; he was personal friends with both Henry James and Mark Twain, those two immortal Americans so totally different in background, in education, and in literary practice— and Howells needed something close to genius to mediate between these two authors, and to explain them to each other. How fine for Martins Ferry on this occasion if Howells were alive! I believe he would have accepted; he would have dazzled everybody during all nine ceremonies and then some; he would have been affable, genial, brilliant, socially gracious and yet personally commanding. But I am not William Dean Howells. I would say that, for all my respect for his distinguished memory, I have only three things in common with him: we both belong to the human race; we both wrote books in English; and we were both born in Martins Ferry, Ohio. I sometimes admire persons who have the gift of public presence, but I am not one of them. I don't even want to be one. I am just myself. My devotions and values, even when I fail them (as most often I do) are all private and personal. The very thought of standing up and saying something—even a grammatically complete sentence—to the Martins Ferry Kiwanis Club, or the Chamber of Commerce, gives me an absolutely real sense of vertigo. I would feel more at home back in the kitchen of the Public Hall, washing the guests' dishes or, during brief rests, pondering my Latin grammar or my geometry text or the poems of Keats—exactly the kind of thing I so often did when I was a boy in Martins Ferry.

I have written you all this at such length because I did not feel it was appropriate to explain myself thus to Mr. Woolman or to Mayor Laslo or to any other official. If Annie and I had been invited to, say, a single banquet, attended by my teachers and former classmates and so on, I think it would have been quite proper, for the town and for me. But they have been trying to persuade me to return there for at least the past three years. It is by now quite clear that they would be satisfied with nothing less than a packed schedule more appropriate to the visit of a candidate during a political campaign than to a visit by a lesser American author who grew up in Martins Ferry and has written about the place and its people sometimes in his books.

It is simply not for me.

The main reason why I've written to you all the things I thought to write to Mr. Woolman is my feeling that you will understand my decision and what I mean by it.

We will certainly be in touch with you concerning the exact dates of our visit to Ohio on the way to Honolulu this summer.

We both send our love.

> Always,
> Jim

To Franz Wright

> New York City
> May 2, 1976

My dear Franz,

It is hard to describe my feelings about your pure and beautiful letter, which you wrote to me on April 24th at the end of a long day of labor and search with your journal. I know well that you were writing not out of exhaustion but rather out of exultation. It is true that I must have written you "Welcome to Hell" when you first sent me a poem. Perhaps that was a kind of melodramatic thing to write to you. Certainly I was taking you seriously, and I still do, and will always. But now you know that I ought to have written something more precise. Perhaps I would have written more truly if I had bid you welcome to yourself, which as you well know contains hell all right, but a good deal more than hell, too. It is interesting—and I think deeply significant—that both of us should care so much about Rilke's "Christi Höllenfahrt."* The harrowing of hell has always moved me very much, perhaps even more than the story of the resurrection. There are many medieval poems about it—about what Christ did on Saturday night. (By the way, did you ever catch that overtone—I believe it is intentional—in Hemingway's "The Killers"? "This is a hot town . . . what do they do here on Saturday night?" "They eat the dinner. They all come here and eat the big dinner.")

I've read your exquisite rendering of *The Life of Mary* many times, and it seems to me masterful, an amazing orchestration of Rilke's language, and the music of his language, into English. Moreover, you show such a tender grasp of the many scenes which he imagines, and recreates out of the old traditions which, he knew, were "formed in still, deep places," that your translation made me more than ever look forward to the time when we can visit the great villages and towns in Italy where such events as the Annunciation are recreated with such miraculous variety and humanity by the medieval and Renaissance masters. For example, we must go to see Leonardo da Vinci's Annunciation—I think it is in Florence. Everything I've ever heard about Leonardo suggests that he must have been one of the strangest people who ever lived. Anyway, his Mary in the Annunciation is startling. She is like a ghost, a real ghost.

I love you, my fine Franz. Your letter makes me very happy . . . By the way, William Heyen's *American Poets in 1976* is now published (by Bobbs-Merrill). It contains my letters to you. The book is interesting, though a little disappointing, as a whole . . . Tom Lux sent me his new book, which I admire very much . . . Please write soon.

Love,
Dad

*For Wright's own 1960 translation of this poem, see Appendix, p. 588.

To Janice Thurn

New York City
May 4, 1976

Dear Janice,

We live near Carl Schurz Park, at the east end of the Manhattan neighborhood called Yorkville. Half a block away from us the park, one of the loveliest and oldest small parks in this strange city, lies like a kind of petal above the water, and the water roars under it silently, and the FDR Parkway roars so help me God right under the petal, so this New York City which I love is very like Rome after all, and I don't mean Rome in decay, but Rome in its troughs and petals of roar and silence. One of the pleasant possibilities in my mind is a slow walk with Annie and you and our son Franz, a slow and ambling progress, all the way from the loud corner in Rome where the newspaper *Il Messagero* squats among the scrambling Fiats and glumly accepts ears from J. Paul Getty III, breastbones from the Colosseum, fire-warnings from Crassus, snide poems from Martial, skeletons of some poor marmoset inlaid with hendecasyllabics from Carthage, anti-Communist Crusades from Dr. Hargis in Oklahoma, world without end—all the way to the Garden of the Vestal Virgins in the Forum, where there is a nice girl with a flawed face, still, still.

Another walk I take in my mind is at the edge of Spanish Harlem up on 111th Street, where Annie and I went just this last Sunday afternoon. There is a condemned hospital there, ratty now among the abiding greenery. You find the island, Ward's Island, by walking through a fierce slum to a green bridge over the Harlem River. The currents of the Harlem River, the East River, and the Atlantic Ocean meet just below Ward's Island, and where they meet is a shifting placed called, and I am not making this up, Hell Gate.

Annie was feeling kind of low on Sunday, what with the unsteady Spring, the looming of work before we can the both of us get the hell out of town to the mountains north of us before we leave (late in June) for Hawaii where I am to teach this summer. She is lovely, lovely, and I didn't want her face so darkened on such a strangely beautiful day. So we walked out of the roar and silence and roar, all the way across the river and around the island. And I'll be damned if she didn't find the most fantastic bed of violets I have seen in years, right in the heart of this city . . . Then I received your letter today, and it is like a good city in the heart of a violet. I am so happy that you wrote to me. Yes, I know you felt down when you wrote. But I knew also that you could write me and, I pray, feel better . . . I wrote you this note because you make me happy, dear.

Love,
Jim

P.S. I know how detestable "advice" can be, so I will just say that, from what I sense about you, you will continue with school. I think it is something—and some people, like your botanist—you can cling to and find silent roots in . . .

To Donald Hall

Lake Minnewaska
New Paltz, New York
June 7, 1976

Dear Don,

Actually, we're not in NYC at the moment. We left town on Saturday morning, and at the moment we're sitting in the very old—and old-fashioned—library of a kind of rickety hotel. A little beyond and below us a morning fog has settled over Lake Minnewaska. Somewhere on the other side of the water the fog is comfortable, I hope, for the lovely, sleek raccoon we saw yesterday, trotting along a path below a cliff.

It's not really an accident that I should think of that mysterious and fastidious animal as I begin this letter to you. Your new poems seem to be gathering all sorts of wild creatures into them—or maybe the poems are opening up and revealing the creatures that have always been moving about in them, like that silken and quiet raccoon up on the mountain side. I am thinking, for example, of that astonishing suckling pig ("Eating the Pig") and the curious wolves in "Captain Hoyt." I want to take these new poems with me to Hawaii this summer (we're supposed to leave NYC on June 25, by the way) and read them to my students. (I trust you don't mind.) In the course I'm giving, I want to deal with Lawrence and Hardy, both of whom have this odd power to move and move very prosaically and quietly into a poem and then, without any fuss to speak of, let the wild creatures appear whole and on their own terms. You've been revealing this power, I say, in so many of the new poems you've shown me, and I've been wondering if it has something to do with the rhythm of the language, and with its precision. The poems are sometimes long, as poems go—but the language moves forward with great ease, with a natural speed. Then, when the intense revelations come, they can sing and shine, because they have grown right up out of a solid, deep language.

You sent me these new writings on April 16. About a month and a half has passed. But I don't feel like "apologizing" for being—rather, seeming to be—unresponsive. Things have been tough in New York, what with the budget crisis, the closing of the City University, and the political haggling, which seems somehow even more stupid this year than usual. Yet I have been working at school as realistically—and healthily—as I've ever worked in my life. And I almost have a book manuscript to send you.

Is it all right, Don? The manuscript is in prose and verse. (I think prose is prose.) I don't want to try to publish a new big book until you and Robert and Galway read it and comment on it. Galway has already agreed. I know that all three of you will be as critical as necessary, and that Robert is likely to be fierce. But, then, Robert is Robert, and his ferocity is salutary as well as (I must admit) frightening sometimes. Well—is it okay if I send the mss. to you before we leave for Hawaii on the 25th?

Sometime in September, Dryad Press is going to publish a chapbook of my prose pieces about Italy.

Don, with your bundle of new writings you included a postcard on which you wrote, "I hope you can forgive the churlish letter I wrote you out of a bad mood last fall. We love you." I think you must have written this note because you were uncertain about the meaning of my silence. Don, I love you, too. I have simply been a dreadfully irresponsible friend this past year. It is really a matter of life and death to keep in touch with you and Robert and Galway. To give an example of my dangerous negligence: Galway and his family have been living only a few blocks from us, and yet I've seen him only four or five times the whole year. So we had a good long lunch last Thursday, with plenty of conversation. I really have got to snap out of my tendency to withdraw—it's unhealthy.

* * *

I was going to put this letter aside and finish it later. Then it suddenly occurred to me that to do so would be just one more instance of the withdrawal I mentioned above. So I will send the letter now, even though I've barely begun to comment on the acute essays and the poems—the beautiful new poems—which I have lying around me right now on the table. I have no doubt that these poems—"Eating the Pig," "Captain Hoyt," "Photographs of China," "O Cheese," (what a weird poem!) are like "The Falling Leaves"—an emergence of a new imaginative world in its own new rhythm.

I think of you all the time. Annie sends love. Love to Jane.

Love,
Jim

To Robert Bly

Honolulu
July 4, 1976

Dear Robert,

I'm sitting by a window on the 19th floor of Dick Foster's apartment here in Honolulu, and as you can well see, I'm having a slightly dizzy time getting control of this electric typewriter. But never mind. Today is Independence Day. The huge lawn below me, between the building and the canal, sounds like a battlefield. Fireworks are evidently not outlawed in Hawaii, and the whole town sounds like all the city dumps and railroad ties and viaducts in Martins Ferry, Ohio, long years ago. But now, of course, we're in the huge land of things like the Chinese New Year. John Logan says that, during that festival, people throw firecrackers out of the windows of the big Honolulu-Hilton Hotel all night long.

John is still here. He's been teaching at the University here for the past year and a half. The place seems to agree with him. For that matter, it's hard to imagine how the place could fail to agree with anybody at all. Still, John has a special feeling for particular places, what seems a touch of holiness, a gift for communing with the spirit of a place. You remember those three remarkable poems he wrote about Hawaii. He's even written a rather long poem about the city of Paris, and I think it is beautiful in the same general way—for example, he goes around in the poem translating the names of the streets in Paris, like the street of "the cat that goes fishing." And John, as always, is moved by the fantastic beauty of human faces here. I must say I know how he feels. A couple of days ago Annie and I set out to go swimming at Waikiki, took the wrong bus, and rode to a far side of the city where we found two huge open markets, for fish and produce. We spent a long time wandering around in the stalls and enjoying the Hawaiian faces—Filipino, Chinese, Japanese, Hawaiian. It is a lovely, lovely place.

I want to close this note so that I can get it into the mail. We think of you and Carol and the children all the time, and I would say that we wish we were with you on the farm right this instant if the gorgeousness of sunlight and greenery and flowers outside the window didn't make me wish even more strongly that you were all of you—all of you indeed—right here with us, walking around comfortably dressed and getting ready to ride over to the sands beneath Diamond Head.

Please write, Robert, even if it's only a note. It turns out that one of the worst of my troubles has been isolation—a common and severe affliction among us alkies—so correspondence, serious and friendly, is a healing thing.

Annie and I tried to find that book for Carol just before we left New York, but the first edition was all sold out. We'll get it as soon as we can.

Love,
Jim

Honolulu
July 21, 1976

Dear Robert,

What a joy it is to have your letter! Your suggestions for cutting the poems about the saguaro cactus and about the moor-hen seem to me entirely accurate. The moor-hen doesn't need a great deal in the way of deletion. It's rather a matter of replacing a word here and there in the light of your general remark about it. But the saguaro is a different thing entirely. You know, I had hesitated a good deal about even including that poem in the manuscript I sent you. I felt there was a real poem in it somewhere, but it was so cluttered with deadwood that I couldn't find it. But the cuts that you've indicated not only get rid of such deadwood. By their very nature, these cuts indicate what kind of deadwood it is. Sure enough, it turns out to be of two sorts: irrelevant and actually obstructing intrusions from my personal past; and—this is a hard one—self-pity, and the strange and quite horrible way the language turns to dead mush when self-pity starts to control it.

Anyway, I have been reading and reading the saguaro poem and reliving it, and when the new version is finished, I'll send it to you.

Your whole comment in your letter is in fact very encouraging. What you say—that you'll send "a list of poems that should be dropped out," and that "so far—in the American section—the book is lively and fresh, with not too much deadwood"—suggests that I did send the manuscript to you at the best time. For one thing, you have the time and opportunity to read it and think about it in total freedom and at leisure. For another, I succeeded in working on it myself up to the point where I was more or less able to spare you the necessity of just working through the whole thing and then sending it back with the exhausted suggestion that the entire book is ill-conceived and that, if I want to write a good book, I would have to start all over again. Of course, I *have* started all over again—several times—but, from what you say, I seem to have got the manuscript to the point where you can work on it profitably.

We're happy to have Mary's summer address. Annie is writing her a wild Hawaiian postcard this morning, I think, and I am going to write her a note directly. It is marvelous to think of her at the National *Music* Camp, and touching to realize that she is away from home for the first time. Since she is in Michigan, I presume that she—and you—will be seeing Don Hall sometime during the summer. He and I have been exchanging good letters, and he mentioned that he would be back in Ann Arbor for a while, before he undertakes to go back to New Hampshire and make a living as a writer. In general, I have the feeling that Don is happier than he's been in all the years I've known him, and that he has earned a kind of tough wisdom that is bringing into focus his great goodness of heart. I must say that I like his new poems more than I like anything he's ever written before. There is a clarity of *feeling* that comes into something like his poem on the black-faced sheep that, I think, hasn't shown itself in his previous poems nearly so well as it's

452

shown itself in his prose. I still think that *String Too Short to Be Saved* reveals the best and truest Don Hall, and he's written some stories that are just like it. Now it seems to be coming alive in his poems.

Annie and I are having a lovely time here in Hawaii. In spite of real-estate developments, etc., in Honolulu, the place still retains its sense of nature's immediacy, and that nature that it reveals is fantastically beautiful. And the people we've met are very sweet. I love my students. Bill Merwin is here, with a stunning and charming Hawaiian girl. He seems more relaxed and happier than I've ever seen him.

This evening I'm going to read poems here at the university. I really don't like to read in public very much, but I feel a little different here in Hawaii, maybe more at home somehow.

I found a marvelous book the other day—I haven't bought it yet—it's a paperback edition of one of those anthropological studies done by the U.S. Bureau of Ethnology, and it includes translations of many poems which are supposed to accompany the performance of the many different kind of *hula*—of all things. If I can find it, I'll get a copy for you.

We got John Logan sent off to San Francisco all right. He was very tired, but he seemed well, except for being troublingly overweight.

It is nice to think of you sitting in the mornings in the cabin under the pine trees. I remember the white sand up there. We haven't been yet to the beach on this island where the sand is black, or to the one where the sand is green. But we will go. Last week we went swimming at night in a bay where I carefully wriggled my way in the dark among some coral reefs where moray eels were sleeping. I'm told that they don't care to be disturbed, and I must have succeeded in leaving them alone, because I wasn't attacked. They aren't deadly, but people hereabouts say that the moray eels can raise merry hell if you go out of your way to bother them. That is all right with me. I don't blame them for feeling that way. And I certainly have no intention of bothering them. I just want them to go on living, and I hope to see them swimming one of these days.

Please write soon. Give our love to Carol and the children.

Love,
Jim

To Galway Kinnell

Dear Galway,

Yesterday afternoon I received the copy of my manuscript with your wonderful long letter and your careful comments on the individual poems. I had already heard from Robert about the same matter, and I still have to receive Don Hall's detailed remarks. I am fascinated by many things: the attention that both you and Robert gave to the manuscript, and the hard work; but mainly the suggestions about revisions and poems to delete. Your suggestions are more often identical than not. Robert's list of deletions is longer: he wants me to drop 17 poems. So far, I have thought of dropping about 12. But many of the others have to be worked on further.

In general, I feel that I have a fair group of about thirty poems or so, maybe a couple more; that these amount to at least the solid beginning of a real book; and that (I can't quite explain this) the book ought to have at least 40 poems in it.

At any rate, it pleases me to realize that I am letting the book grow into its own life, and that I have shown it at the right time to the right people. What I require is the help of sympathetic and entirely honest intelligence. Encouragement is necessary, but flattery is deadly. I feel all right about the manuscript, and I know that it isn't done yet.

I have to go to class in a couple of minutes. I'm sorry to have to cut this short. One thing I have to tell you—and Annie will elaborate in a forthcoming letter—is that, unhappily, we won't be able to come to Vermont on the Labor Day weekend. Classes start at Hunter almost immediately thereafter, and I have a lot of preparation to do.

I'll be in touch again soon, Galway, and thank you for commenting so carefully and helpfully on the manuscript.

Love to you all.

Love,
Jim

To Donald Hall

Dear Don,

We got back to NYC early in September, and I received your long fine letter. But almost immediately thereafter we stashed our luggage here in the city and moved to the mountains in upstate. We always do this when we return from travelling in the summer. It is our odd way of coming to terms with work in the city.

I had taken your long letter with me up to the mountains. I had half-intended to reply to it up there; but instead I just re-read it, and re-studied it several times. I see that it was necessary for me to do that, for my sake. Because what I want to do with this book is write it as well as I truly can. I can't write any book well without offering the manuscript—at a certain point, the point where I have temporarily done as much as I can with it—to the three friends or so whose intelligence, honesty, and devotion I can completely trust. After I offer a manuscript to such friends, and get their replies, I can study it again, with the replies. (My last book, *Two Citizens*, was bad, but certainly it wouldn't have been so bad if I had asked you and Robert and Galway—and, probably, Louis Simpson—to read it before I let it be published. I don't know if you have this problem or not, but I have an editor, Michael di Capua, who is a nice and generous and encouraging fellow, but the trouble is that he would publish anything I sent him, even my laundry list, and I don't want to publish my laundry list.)

So you can understand why I haven't written a detailed reply to your great letter. But I should have written you a postcard, for friendship's sake.

And friendship is everything. I think I finally understand: intelligent friendship is everything. It may not be entirely why we write our poems. But it is certainly why we have the courage to give those poems to each other. As far as poetry is concerned, I think this past summer has been the greatest summer of my lifetime. I speak only for myself, but I don't think that's nothing. I didn't write very much that was new during the summer, but I did offer some fifty or so poems to my intelligent friends, and I have now at the front of my manuscript about five fantastic letters. I have your long, detailed one. I have one good general one from Galway, including his whole copy of my manuscript with remarkable marginal comments; and I have three amazing letters from Robert.

If writing a book of poetry isn't that, then it isn't anything, as far as I'm concerned.

Now I want to respond in a little detail:

Robert urged that I delete 17 poems out of the 50 or so. I agree with him in most cases, but there are exceptions: I am trying to save, with revisions, a few such as the following:

Written on a Big Cheap Postcard
Under the Canals
The City of Evenings
With a Sliver of Marble from Carrara
The Lambs on the Boulder

Before I would include these in a manuscript to be published, I wonder if you would mind my sending you the revisions? Your comments, with Robert's, about what went wrong with the prose pieces, and about the differences between prose and poetry, seem to me sound and true.

Galway's letter was fine and pointed. His best comments came on the manuscript itself, which I am slowly revising, often according to his suggestions.

I figure there are about 35 poems that I can imagine being willing to put in, and that is not enough [. . .] Don, I wish you would send me a list of the poems out of my manuscript you think I could save. Maybe that will give me something yet more solid I can work on.

This hasn't turned out to be much of a letter, but I'm going to send it off anyway. I hope your moving chore is over, and that you and Jane are happily getting settled.

I had a phone conversation with De Snodgrass a few days ago— the first time I'd talked with him in years—and we spoke warmly of you.

Love,
Jim

To Jack Wright

New York City
September 25, 1976

Dear Jack,

Thanks for your good long letter. I don't want to give you heart failure, but here I am, trying to come alive again in a reply. Classes have begun at Hunter again, and at NYU also, so Annie and I are pretty much into the thick of things here on the ramparts. But I will try to keep in touch, as I ought and want to do.

Of course, after we left you and Elizabeth, we flew right back to New York. But we simply stashed our bags here and, within a few days, were up in the mountains north of here. The place where we go has become necessary to us. It is comfortable enough, and it is naturally wild. I suppose it is a kind of spring for us, a resource where we can go and drink (water) and gather strength for a return to the struggle of the city.

But now—my God, I guess it has been two whole weeks already—I have been fighting the fight at Hunter. The size of the teaching staff has diminished. According to rumors and newspaper reports (is there really any difference between a rumor and a newspaper report?) the number of students has diminished also. Yet classes are larger. Something strange is going on. But maybe not so strange. Like so many others, teachers are becoming the reserve army of the unemployed.

I can say that, whatever else is happening, I have been having a wonderful time with at least three of my four classes. In one, we have been reading Sir Thomas Wyatt, whose greatness increases for me all the time. In another, we have been reading *Don Quixote*; and in yet another, *Huck Finn*. What a joy that book is! At one point, Huck has been living for a while with the Grangerford family, a nice pleasant Southern family who have been having a murderous feud with the Shepherdsons. Both families go to church one Sunday. They don't shoot at one another there, but Huck has a hard time with the sermon. After the service they all go home, and this is the way Huck proceeds:

> I went up to our room, and judged I would take a nap myself.
> I found that sweet Miss Sophia standing in her door, which
> was next to ours, and she took me in her room and shut the
> door very soft, and asked me if I liked her, and I said I did; and

she asked me if I would do something for her, and not tell any-body, and I said I would. Then she said she'd forgot her Testa-ment, and left it in the seat at church, between two other books, and would I slip out quiet and go there and fetch it to her, and not say nothing to nobody. I said I would. So I slid out and slipped off up the road, and there warn't anybody at the church, except maybe a hog or two, for there warn't any lock on the door, and hogs like a puncheon floor in summer-time because it's cool. If you notice, most folks don't go to church only when they've got to; but a hog is different.*

It is a great pleasure to relish things like these with the students, when I can get them to pay attention. But there are so many of them that I expect I'll be worn down to a nub before it's over.

By the way, what is a nub?

I don't think you should hesitate to take that writing course if you really want to write the novel. The strange truth is that some people, some good people, have actually got good work done in such courses. I think the best thing the instructor can do, if he is a decent instructor, is to give you the *occasion* to write. It's then that you discover how many things were just waiting to come out but had never been summoned, so to speak.

Speaking of which, I don't have my own book done yet. And yes-terday I got a note from my editor in which he pleasantly and casually told me he was expecting the finished manuscript by the end of this month. (I just wrote him and advised him not to hold his breath.)

I am going to send this note now, so that at least I'll have started. We had a wonderful time with you and Elizabeth. Please give her our love. And for God's sake let's keep this correspondence going, so I won't sink into the quicksand.

Love,

Jim

*From chapter 18 of *The Adventures of Huckleberry Finn*.

To Janice Thurn

New York City
September 25, 1976

Dear Janice,

I received another letter from you today, a beautiful one, containing your startling real maple leaf (you seem always to send me one, so that I sort of expect it, but it is still startling, as if your letter had just fallen down into my hands out of a tree). And you sent me your good poem about the Northern Lights.

Reading your new letter made me realize that I must have heard from you at least three times without my replying. I don't know why I was silent. It's not that I was "busy." Everybody is busy. I suppose it's just that the correspondence we have is a pretty natural one, and that we write when we most feel like it. Anyway, I always *feel* that correspondence is still going on, even at moments when we're not writing letters. That sounds strange; even impossible. Well, it is strange, all right; but not impossible. I don't know why.

Between the last days of June and the first of September, we were in Hawaii, where, among other things, I was teaching at the University during the second summer session. I wish I knew how to give you a sense of that entire place, but I am afraid I will get confused or confusing if I try too much. Still, I want to suggest what it was like. Let me try one thing:

Now, you must understand that, after classes ended, we had a few more days before we were scheduled to return to the mainland. So we left Honolulu entirely, and flew a plane to the island of Maui. Maui is (or seems to me) as near to being unspoiled as any beautiful place is likely to be in our modern world.

Here is a story, an old, old Hawaiian legend: Maui is the name of a demi-god (his mother was human). His mother complained to him one day that she and the other Polynesians, though they were quite willing to work all day for long hours tending and reaping and pounding taro-roots into poi, simply did not have enough daylight left in the evening for singing and dancing. So Maui went to a mountain in the dark of night, and waited there. When the sun came out; Maui flung his net into the sky and caught it. All day the sun wriggled in the net, begging to be set free. Maui agreed on one condition: the sun must give human beings enough light for singing and dancing in the evening.

Annie my wife and I stood at the very tip-top of Haleakala, the mountain where all this is said to have taken place. Maui freed the sun, and the sun remains in a long, long twilight in Hawaii. We stood on Haleakala, ten thousand feet high, and saw the fantastic sun hovering for a long time on the far side of the great peaks and, below them, the great bays of the Pacific Ocean still gleaming, more than thirty miles away from us.

It's curious about that word "thirty." It was almost exactly thirty years ago that I was last in Hawaii. It was just at the end of the war. Our troop ship was on the way to Japan; we were to spend just about three hours refueling in Honolulu. But, as we moved into the harbor, the ship's engines broke down! We stayed there for ten days, swimming, laughing, loving the place. I have always felt that the engines were disrupted by some god or other, one of the gods who are on the side of human beings. Maybe it was Maui.

I am teaching again—it's hard this year in New York.

Where is Greaney? I've been around in Minnesota, but never there.

Love,
Jim

To Hayden Carruth

New York City
October 25, 1976

Dear Hayden,

Since we all met up at the Kinnells' place, I've been wanting to write you for several reasons. With my usual flair, I neglected to ask for your home address in Vermont. So I tried to get it from Galway and even from Fred Morgan; but every time I phone, they're somewhere else. (I don't blame them. I hate telephones.)

So I'm writing you in care of the *Hudson Review*, and I trust they'll forward my note.

I think the most important thing I want to say is to tell you how much it meant to Annie and me to meet you and Rose Marie and spend that long evening with you and all the Kinnells. A good while ago Annie and I talked over the matter of social gatherings, and we found that each of us had a secret horror of parties. Especially literary cocktail parties, and not only in New York. There is something sinister about such gatherings. They are a kind of satanic parody of a utopian commune. Nobody gets a chance to care about anybody else. Nobody gets a chance to say anything. Nobody gets a chance to listen to what somebody else is saying. Everybody gets sick drunk in despair. It is weird.

Yet Annie and I both care very much about friendship. So we agreed that we would try to meet friends only when we all could number about six or eight people at most. That long Sunday evening we all shared in Vermont was very beautiful.

I also felt a special pleasure in meeting you after admiring your poems for all these years. Also, I looked forward to hearing you talk about poetry and people because your critical ideas—so pluralistic and clear and just—are ideas that I can trust. But this is by the way.

I have a couple of other things on my mind. In the first place, I must have read *From Snow and Rock, from Chaos* as thoroughly as a book can be read within two weeks. I've read it from start to finish, from finish to start, from the middle to the end, from the middle to the beginning, upside down and (practically) inside out. Whether out of private petulance or out of some dim remembrance of some standards I used to carry more immediately in my mind when I cherished Herrick's *Hesperides* as a guide to excellence, I've become personally pitiless in reading books of poetry. (No doubt I'm unjust most of the time, but I don't care. It's my soul that I'm trying to save.) In the light of these thoughts and feelings, I have to tell you that if poetry means anything to me (and it does), *From Snow and Rock, from Chaos* is one of the books of poetry I care about most, in my lifetime or any other. There isn't a single phrase in it which isn't alive with an unmistakable music.

There is something else about the book that is important to me. For more than three years now I have been trying to put together a new book of my own. I have labored at it so harshly that I've reached the point of worrying it might end up too skinny and small. But I could see at once that *From Snow and Rock*, in spite of its brevity, is in reality a large book. It's just 57 pages long. Yet I can open it anywhere and find a fully realized poem. Now, I don't know how to explain the fact, but it is a fact: a fully realized poem somehow exists quite outside of the usual measurements of space. The little four-liner "O Western Wind" is in reality fuller (and in some nutty way it is actually *larger*) than . . . than . . . oh, for heaven's sake, too many examples occur to list here.

So the size of the book, any book, has nothing to do with the number of pages, or even the number of poems, it contains. This may seem obvious. But it hadn't been obvious to me during the past three years, and it is an enormous relief (and encouragement) to know it.

I want to bring this note to a close, so I will mention one more thing, a request: on February 14, that nice person Grace Schulman has asked me to speak at the Poetry Center (with a couple of other writers) on what she calls a "Valentine's Day Program." The idea is to read love poems. Now, it so happens that some of my favorite poems, which are also love poems, are to be found in *From Snow and Rock, from Chaos*. Among a few other poems that I want to read, I would like very much to read some of yours. May I have your permission? During recent years I've just about retired from public readings of poetry, but this one program seems to me especially worthwhile and interesting. I hope you won't mind my reading some of your poems. It would give me great pleasure. Would you mind?

I hope you'll give our delighted affection to Rose Marie.

Best,

Jim

To Wendy Gordon

New York City
November 3, 1976

Dear Miss Gordon:

I'm sorry I couldn't meet with you today to talk about your poems. One thing leads to another, as you well know.

But I want to tell you two things: first, I think you have an exquisite sense of poetry from the inside of the language. You quickly grasp the idea of a fixed form in poetry. That is an abstract idea, and it is as difficult to grasp as an idea in mathematics.

Second, there is a radiance in your life which your poems reveal. I don't quite know what to say about that inner radiance, except to tell you that it pleases me very much that you are alive and that you are yourself.

In an effort to say this to you in a way that would make entire human sense, I thought of some things that have mattered to me in my own life. One of the best is a book called *Briefe an einen jungen Dichter*, by the great poet Rainer Maria Rilke.

When I was quite a young man (not so young as you are now, but still quite young—I had just got out of the army, and I was still alive), I took a course in German literature from a man I still think was a great man. He was a Russian with a German name, and just before I got out of the army and went to college, he had just got out of a concentration camp in west Germany and come to Ohio.

He taught a course in Goethe, who I do dearly believe is the greatest lyric poet who ever lived. When I showed some of my own stumbling verses to my teacher Dr. Hanfman, he quietly placed in my hands Rilke's great book of letters. The copy he gave me was in German. I gave that copy to another poet years ago. Now it has been translated into English, and I would like to pass it on to you.

Why? Because we live in a horrible century, and poets have been able to keep one another alive. How? I don't know how. I do know this much: when I moved into Japan thirty years ago with a bayonet on my shoulder, another eighteen-year-old boy named Toshitada Iketani was waiting for the invasion with a bayonet on *his* shoulder. Somehow— don't ask me how—he and I didn't kill each other. Three years ago he translated one of my books into Japanese. In our correspondence, it turned out that he too had carried Rilke's *Letters to a Young Poet* with him in combat. Please accept the book from me.

James Wright

To J. D. McClatchy

New York City
November 3, 1976

Dear Mr. McClatchy:

I don't know why I have failed to reply to your two good letters, so we will have to put it down to sheer laziness.

I have to tell you that I cannot promise you an essay about Anne Sexton's poetry. I am so hounded by my own work at the moment that I have given up making promises.

But I will tell you this much: I believe from the bottom of my soul (shallow bottom of rot though it be) that her death, her suicide, is a totally meaningless pain in the ass. The way to write about her and her work is to remark her personal heroism and the genius of her poetry. Yes, she was ill, and you know it, and I know it. The hell with her illness and her death. The thing to concentrate on is the poetry itself.

If I were to write something about her work, I would concentrate on a couple of poems that to this day seem to me masterful and enduring: the first section of "The Double Image," and the short poem "Her Kind." In the first, she seems to me to equal the metrical genius of Wyatt. In the second, Hardy.

Your book of essays about her work can be important, and I sweetly and sincerely pray in the name of sweet leaping Jesus H. Chryste III that you will love her poetry and leave her alone.

Try to forgive this letter; I loved her, too.

Sincerely,
James Wright

November 4, 1976

Dear Mr. McClatchy:

Today while I was at school I had misgivings about the letter which I wrote to you last evening. I hadn't yet sent it. Unfortunately, I had left it on a small table by the front door, and my wife has apparently mailed it to you.

I've just reread my copy of the letter, and it seems to me that my words to you have an inexcusably rude and even insulting tone. Certainly there was no reason for me to write you in that way, for your two letters to me are friendly and well-disposed, and they reveal your devotion to Anne Sexton and her poems, a devotion which I share.

I wish you every success with your important book about her, and I hope you will try to excuse my bad manners.

Sincerely,
James Wright

To Michael Cuddihy

New York City
November 14, 1976

Dear Michael,

Thank you for your beautiful and detailed letter of November 1.

In general, I would actually prefer that you choose critics of my work on your own. By this time it is obvious that there are some readers who like my writings and others who distinctly don't (to put it mildly). I could easily send you a list of critics who could be counted on to say something flattering or at least friendly. Of course, I love to be flattered. Who doesn't? The trouble is that flattery by friends and acquaintances, though pleasant, is really kind of empty when it appears in print. I think there are plenty of intelligent, judicious, independent people who, if they wanted to write something for you about my work at all, could say something clearly and justly. As for critics in the past, I suppose the two who at least *know* my writings as well as anyone—that is, people who have actually studied my books and written about them—are Peter Stitt, who teaches in the Department of English at Middlebury College, Middlebury, Vermont; and Mr. Dave Smith, who is now in the Department of English at Utah State University, Salt Lake City, Utah. These two writers are friendly, all right, but they are not sentimental or sycophantic.

As for others, I don't know whether or not you'd like to bring in an out-of-town gun, so to speak: a critic who is sure to attack my books with all the weapons possible, from intelligent criticism to mockery to the exquisite sneer. If you think such an essay would contribute to your general plan for your special issue—and it might, who knows?—I feel sure you'd have no trouble finding eager candidates for the job. In fact, Robert Bly a few years ago recommended more than one such critic for a special issue on his own work. They had a fine time, spluttering and fuming . . . For the rest, you can be sure that I'll be sending you a handful of new poems when I'm more or less satisfied with them.

Say hello to our friends in Tucson: the Sheltons, and others [. . .]

Love,
Jim

To Hayden Carruth

New York City
December 5, 1976

Dear Hayden,

For all I know you may be home again in Vermont even while I'm writing this letter. I never did get it straight in my mind just how long people stay at Yaddo. In any case, it was a pleasure to learn that you're working well, and I'm looking forward to the "Paragraphs."

For some reason, I have never felt like going to Yaddo or MacDowell or any such place. I'm not sure why. Maybe in some way I'm afraid of it. My own ways of working have always been kind of erratic, and for some reason I kind of need the press of other kinds of work to get me down to writing. I also sometimes wonder if I really have the strength of character to cope with all the solitude.

On the other hand, I might some time go to Yaddo and find that things work out very well. I don't know. Certainly at the moment I'm feeling pressure, too much of it. The teaching load at Hunter has been increased, as I think I mentioned when we last met. Also, semesters in the City University of New York seem awfully spun out. For example, this year our last day of class meetings will be December 23rd. Then we have just a week for vacation, and then a final-exam period. It seems to me a silly and wasteful schedule. A friend at Brandeis tells me that classes will end there next Friday, December 10th. They have their exams the following week. And then they're finished till the Spring. I can't imagine that people—students and teachers alike—get any less work done at Brandeis than we do at Hunter.

I finally received my copies of the chapbook from Dryad. It's called *Moments of the Italian Summer*, and I think it looks very nice (physically). I've never had a book with drawings before, and there are five in this one. We'll send it to you and Rose Marie soon, as soon as we can get some envelopes, which we're always running out of.

Speaking of Rose Marie, it was a good idea you mentioned: I mean revising and correcting the Hesse translations. Certainly I'm not affronted. I've always been aware of awkwardnesses and inaccuracies all over that little book, and one of these days I want very much to correct them. Also the book should be expanded. The main problem right now is the academic pressure I've mentioned above, and then there's the book I'm working on. If it keeps growing as it's been doing, it ought to be finished some time in the spring.

We saw the Kinnells two nights ago. They came to us for dinner, and we had a splendid evening. Sometimes I worry about Galway's somewhat harried life. I don't mean his health, for he's a wonderfully robust man. I mean the erratic way he's forced to make a living— teaching here and there, and all the public readings. I think he's on the road again right now, reading about four different places within the next week. Then, in the Spring, he's going to teach for a semester at the University of Hawaii. We were there last summer, you know, and we love the place. I think Galway will, too, and I trust he'll be able to get some rest and some work done there.

This note isn't as long as it should be, but I'm going to send it now anyway. It's Sunday afternoon, and I'm getting ready for tomorrow's long day of teaching.

Annie just got home from church, and she sends her best.

Best,
Jim

To Janice Thurn

New York City
February 6, 1977

Dear Janice,

It's Sunday afternoon. I'd received your letter only on Friday, I think it was; and, since it was postmarked January 31, the mail seems more or less improving.

Your words about Japan fill me with all kinds of vivid memories and renewals. A few years ago I received a letter from a man named Toshitada Iketani, from the city of Nagoya, which I never visited. We exchanged letters several times; and, after his fulfillment of all sorts of courtesies, he revealed that he had translated an entire book of my poems, which he had had published. You can imagine how delighted I am to have this book. I can't read it, but I can admire its appearance. It turns out that he and I were soldiers at exactly the same time, though by some slight confusion of fate we were in opposing armies.

The forests up in the mountains of Japan are full of tall pines. One afternoon in 1946 I rode in a weapons-carrier (a half-ton truck) with some friends more than halfway up Fujiyama, and the trees were splendid. I remember that on that particular afternoon we got lost at the foot of the mountain and had to ask directions of a shinto monk who, thoroughly amused, gave us all a snort of *sake* and sent us on our way; how the fan-belt broke in the truck; and how we repaired it with the belt of Sgt. Clifford Bucey, whose khaki trousers promptly unravelled, till the ass fell out of them. It was a long, slow drive up that mountain, which became dazzling as one rose. It makes me think of how the peak floated above the clouds, above the ocean, disembodied from the planet itself as we had approached Japan in the troopship.

You speak of the almost unspeakable cold in Minnesota. Remember: I lived there for eight years. Recently I have been thinking of telling you to get into bed and stay there till Spring.

I don't know what my new book is to be called. The chapbook I just published is called *Moments of the Italian Summer*. I'll send it to you soon.

Be good to yourself, and try to keep warm.

Love,
Jim

To J. D. McClatchy

New York City
February 12, 1977

Dear Mr. McClatchy:

I trust your book of essays about the life and poetry of Mrs. Sexton will be published. She seems to me one of the two or three people in my lifetime who knew that poetry is an act of intelligence.

I have written part of my essay about her and Wyatt and Hardy in one of my notebooks and I am certainly not going to allow anyone to publish it while I live.

But I do have something to say about Mrs. Sexton, her life, and her poetry. Some fifteen years ago she and I exchanged long letters about this noble and difficult art. Thereby, we became friends. After I got lost and got found again and got lost again and got found again, we kept in touch when I came to live in New York City. Then she got sick again, as she had been sick many times, and she committed suicide.

Of course, I am sorry that she killed herself, because I share her mental and physical suffering. She was a fine friend, one of the best and most kindly normal persons I ever knew. She also happens to be a very great poet, but I don't see what her genius has to do with her suicide. The fine poor woman was mentally ill. To grieve for her poetry because she was mentally ill is like grieving for the poetry of John Keats because he had tuberculosis [. . .]

I continue to love Anne's "Her Kind," and I continue to love Wyatt's "You that in love have luck and abundance."

Good luck with your book.

Yours,
James Wright

To Hayden Carruth

New York City
February 21, 1977

Dear Hayden,

I hope you'll excuse this ratty paper. I'm running out of that white stuff that I like to use in my notebook—I have only a few pages left— and I'm using it to keep a carbon, which I like to do in the case of certain letters. I once had an enormous correspondence with Anne Sexton, both sides of it, and it all got destroyed in a fire. She kept it also, but I don't know where hers is. Probably in a library somewhere, waiting to be liberated.

At the moment I have the laundry going through its first phase around the corner, so this note will be interrupted in a few minutes. I'm afraid it isn't going to be a proper letter this time. In fact, my laxness in writing has been the result partly of the clutter of teaching and other things. But I am determined to maintain the current of correspondence with some crucial friends, however few—and I suppose a person can't, in the nature of things, have very many.

We have been thinking of you and Rose Marie, up there in Vermont. I reckon you must be accustomed by this time to the savage winter that has suddenly struck in other parts. We know many people in Buffalo, and were there once in mid-winter. It was wild enough, but this time—dear God.

I want mainly to tell you about our reading in celebration of Valentine's Day at the Poetry Center last Monday evening. Three of us read: Carolyn Kizer, Stanley Kunitz, and myself. I think the reading sounded very nice, and we had a good time. I read: "Dedication in These Days," "I Could Take," "For RM, 26 December," "If It Were Not for You," "Concerning Necessity," and "Moon." These are extraordinary poems, a joy to say aloud. Grace Schulman mentioned sending you a tape of the reading . . . I have to get the laundry now. Please write, and tell me more about the "Paragraphs." I'm happy you like my chapbook.

Best,
Jim

To Elizabeth Kray

New York City
April 26, 1977

Dear Betty,

We have been friends for nearly twenty years. Now that we have concluded the conference on Chinese poetry and America, I want to tell you how much your friendship has meant to me and to the other best friends I have.

It is a dreadful clutter, isn't it? And yet—Gary Snyder wrote a poem right before my eyes on Friday morning. David Ignatow wrote a new poem inspired by our conversations. On Monday evening I finished my new book, which I am to give to the messenger from Farrar, Straus and Giroux tomorrow.

The conference, which came after all out of your own imagination, is the finest discussion of poetry I have ever attended. I am sorry you didn't hear the tribute I paid to you at the very end of our reading on Saturday afternoon, a tribute which Stanley [Kunitz] and Gary and Robert [Bly] moved me to announce; and yet it is typical of you to be absent at such a time.

As I tried to tell you on the phone, your conference meant what I personally mean by the word *poetry*, and I know that I am not alone in saying this.

You are one of the noblest people alive, and your friendship makes me feel that it is a fine thing to live and be at my best.

Love,
Jim

To Liberty Kovacs

New York City
April 27, 1977

Dear Lib,

This evening I am sitting here alone for a little while before I go to my AA meeting, and I want to be in touch with you and let you know how we are going to proceed this summer. On June 13 Annie and I are leaving for Paris, and after a brief sojourn through Burgundy and Northern Italy we are going to meet her niece*—a very nice little girl whose father, a doctor, died of a disease in Vietnam—in Paris.

It is going to be a relief to get out of New York for a while. I know that things are tough all over, but there is something about this city—in some ways it has been a great city—which makes the general inflation and recession specially acute. At Hunter, which is part of the City University, we find ourselves fighting for our students against the Administration, the City government, and the State. Personally, I don't find this fight depressing, because I know, as you also know, the meaning of an education, especially its meaning for poor people. Still, the fight has been exhausting.

One odd thing that has been happening to me is the way I have assumed responsibility for work on several serious committees. I really did not know I have that sort of willingness in me; but the probable reason I didn't know is that I used to be drunk all the time.

Today I was able to send my new book to the publisher. It is to be called *To a Blossoming Pear Tree*, and it will appear in the Fall.

I am hoping that you and Mike and Andy are going to get some relief from what must have been the general pressure of the past year.

---

*Lisa Kayan Turner, actually a second cousin and godchild.

Soon I will be sending you some new publications of mine, and I hope you'll remember to send me yours, as you promised.

Since I don't know Marsh's address, I'm enclosing a note to him. I trust we'll be seeing you at Oberlin on the weekend of May 28.

Best,
Jim

To Marshall Wright

New York City
May 6, 1977

My dear Marshall,

Today is Friday. Yesterday afternoon I received your long and welcome letter. I was very happy to have that letter. I know how difficult it can be sometimes, just to complete a letter, and I am proud of you for writing it and sending it. What I want to do right now is to reply at once, however briefly. I think that one of the most important things you and I can do for a while is to keep in touch.

This morning I talked with my own doctor for an hour. Because I have been forced to do a great deal of work lately, it was a relief to see Dr. [Irving] Silver and to talk things over with him. He is a kind and understanding man. He never tries to tell me what to do or what to think. His main purpose seems to be to assure me that I have it in me to be a strong and good person, and that if I can only trust in my own strength, I will be able to cope with the problems of the world and live my life all right.

It is my opinion, Marsh, that a good doctor could help you find your way to your own self-assurance, your belief in yourself.

Whatever you decide to do, I want you to remember that I love you and believe in you. I believe now, as I have always believed, that you are a rare, marvelous human being, and that you will find your true way and be a fine man.

By this time you will have received an earlier letter from me. It deals in part with the trip which Annie and I plan to take to Europe this summer. It occurs to me that you will want to know exactly where we are at any given time, so that you can write. At the moment, I can tell you that from about the first of August till the end of August you can write to us c/o American Express, Paris, France. Before that time, we'll be in various places in Italy. Between now and June 13, when we depart, I'll ask Annie to send you our itinerary.

Please do keep in touch, now that we're writing to each other.

I love you very much.

Love,
Dad

To William Matthews

New York City
June 1, 1977

Dear Bill,

But of course we all like to be praised, and of course we get depressed when we're damned. It is a hell of a note that we are going to live our lives all the way through to the end, and that is why I love Edwin Arlington Robinson so much.

You know this pain as well as I do.

Nevertheless, you also know that there is something that reaches beyond praise or blame, and it is what matters most. It is a thorough reading by a poet whose beauty one loves, whose intelligence one entirely loves and respects.

I have to tell you that I had scarcely hoped anybody would read my books as truly as you've read mine.

I don't know why Robert Bly has insisted that I changed from one person to another. I love Robert, I mean I truly love him. He is my brother, if a brother is anything, and it is. But I don't understand his theories, not entirely. I sense that he is inspired by the idea of resurrection, and he has the genius, sometimes, to convey this genius.

I wish you would write to me. The best address I can tell you is c/o American Express, Paris, France, between August 1 and September 1.

My own secret feeling—and I am afraid it is kind of lonely—is that there is a great blossoming in American poetry right now. It does not belong to Robert and Louis Simpson and me, but it does belong to a lyrical and critical intelligence that somebody had to insist on.

I think we were right. Your poems, and those of Simic and some others, are superb—they are clear, enduring, because they are intelligent.

Annie sends, with me,

Love,

Jim

To Austin Warren

Paris
August 4, 1977

Dear Mr. Warren:

A few days ago, just before my wife Annie and I departed from Italy, I received your beautiful letter, which was forwarded to me from New York. You can well imagine the huge delight it gave me to read your recollections of the 1948 School of English at Kenyon. At that time I was just a Freshman with one semester behind me. I had been accepted at Kenyon while I was still in the army (I was stationed in Japan), and I became a student during the Spring semester of 1948. I was not able to attend the School of English, partly because only out-standing Seniors were accepted and partly because I spent my sum-mers working as a spectacularly unskilled laborer in some factories.

Of course Mr. Ransom and Dr. Timberlake were both teachers of mine, and you can certainly understand how I remain devoted to these noble men. I also carry with me constantly the inspiration of Dr. Charles Coffin, who I believe was the first director of the Kenyon School of English, and of Dr. Denham Sutcliffe. During one entire year I managed to get permission from the Dean to live off-campus, and I inhabited the attic-room of Dr. Timberlake's magnificent and rickety old house at the edge of Gambier. Our evenings—late evenings, indeed—in the old-fashioned living room of that wonderful house are unforgettable to me and, I'm sure, to such friends as Myron Bloy (now an Episcopalian minister in Michigan), Tony Stoneburner (a Methodist minister who is now a part-time professor at Denison), and others. Dr. Charles Coolidge, the historian, had somehow got hold of a more-or-less primitive wire-recorder. Heaven knows what has become of our macabre performances of scenes from *Henry IV, The Spanish Curate*, and *Wilhelm Tell* (in ghastly German).

Yes, David Wagoner is my friend. He was an instructor at Washington when I was a graduate student. In 1958 I completed my dissertation on Dickens. And, of course, I cherish the friendship of Jeff Mitchell, that fine man. Annie and I both send you greetings from exquisite Paris.

Sincerely,
James Wright

To Roger Hecht

Paris
August 8, 1977

Dear Roger,

We've heard from you quite well at the two places where we've picked up mail, and I hope you've been receiving the string of postcards I've sent you from various places in central Italy. I also hope you got the one I sent you from the divinely lovely Burgundian town of Avallon earlier in the summer. It was the card that showed the forlorn hog standing with his front tootsies in the slops of the trough and yearningly protesting, "Je ne suis pas cochon . . . je suis sentimental."

We wondered about the blackout, which according to the press (the *Herald Tribune* is an excellent paper, I think) was horrendous. It is a relief to hear that you're all right. It is also a relief to be in Paris. I am sitting in the study of Dr. Robert William Higgins, an excellently thorough Parisian whose taint of Irish blood suddenly broke out this summer and impelled him to leave Paris and take his family to Ireland (sic). Our lovely niece Lisa Kayan, whom you met I believe, just arrived a couple of days ago for her first visit to Paris. Seventeen, beginning to shed her adolescent plumpness, just finished high school and eager to begin college, she is utterly charming, even more delightful in Paris than she has been in New York.

Two notes on barbarism: earlier in the summer, some liberated spirit wrote unseemly words (in French, for God's sake) on a beautiful sculpture of Henry Moore's at the Orangerie, which is now being guarded by cops; and some developer razed the old windmill over at Montmartre. The latter is supposed to be rebuilt, though.

I'm glad to hear that Paul Ramsey is reviewing *A Parade of Ghosts*.

He is an intelligent man and I respect him. We used to be good friends, but I haven't been in touch with him for some time.

Speaking of prose, I have been discovering V. S. Naipaul, who is, I think, superb.

Annie sends love.

Best,
Jim

To Richard Hugo

Paris
August 20, 1977

Dear Dick,

> LAMENT: FISHING WITH RICHARD HUGO
> If John Updike had been
> Ed Bedford, his wife
> Zetta would have called
> Goose Prairie something high-toned.
> Swan Meadow? The Ironic
> Byronic Paradox in two
> Eleatic heuristic footnotes?
> Ed's dank tavern might have become
> The Puce Nook, featuring
> A menu illuminated by Doris Day,
> With Updike composing the prose
> Of Howard Johnson, accompanying himself
> On an oboe, singing of tender
> Succulent golden
> French fries.
>
> But now, though the hills around Goose Prairie
> Are full of voices, nobody echoes
> The rasping hinge of Zetta's quick cackle
> Nor the slow sighs of Ed Bedford
> Breaking the wind at dusk.
> And I miss the unhorned

Elk that drifted across
The other side of Goose Prairie
Into pines that evening so long ago:
When Ed Bedford charged double for beer,
The pink flesh of trout from the Bumping River
Turned into you, and Howard's prose
Rendered into fish fat
And drifted, drifted
Over white water.

* * *

I wrote the above when we were back in Arezzo, about the time I sent you the postcard of the obese Florentine on the turtle. Oddly, I sent it to Michael Cuddihy, who told me he doesn't yet know if he likes it. Your poem about the rivers moved me to tears. My poem isn't supposed to move you to tears, though. It's supposed to be funny. (Dear God, what a kiss of death, to say a thing like that.)*

Will you please tell me where and when I can get your two new books that I heard about? We'll be back in NYC on Aug. 30. If you have time on your way to Scotland, and you feel like it, phone me, even from the airport. I'm happy to have your Scotland address; we'll keep in touch. Love to your family.

Love,

Jim

P.S. We really must keep in touch. Did you see that little prose book of mine? I wish—one of these days—you'd send me some pictures of your family.

We are well here, but a little glum about returning. I wish we could get a year off to spend in Italy. Really, your rivers poem is extraordinary.

---

*Richard Hugo's "The Towns We Know and Leave Behind, the Rivers We Carry with Us" is dedicated to James Wright. "Lament: Fishing with Richard Hugo" is included in *Above the River*, p. 353.

To C. K. Williams

Dear Charlie,

Thanks for your note. You really mustn't feel depressed about my teaching Freshman English. We're all doing it at Hunter, off and on. It has to do with the city's bankruptcy, the overpopulation of students, the underpopulation of teachers, etc. I do have a job, which is more than I can say for a lot of my friends. Since Annie and I have been back in New York (we'd spent the summer in Italy and France), I've started to fall into the New York rhythm, which includes perpetual bitching about this, that, and the other. To coin a phrase, it is sovereign to take New York bitching with a witch's tit, and throw Wallace Stevens over your shoulder.

Your book arrived yesterday, and it seems important to me to write you something about it. I don't feel like discussing its technique, for God's sake. You know, I think Robert Bly is right when he says that American writers are threatened always by a kind of curse, by which they have a hard time talking about writing without getting bogged down in technical details. Let me just tell you that I sat up half the night reading and rereading *With Ignorance*, and I'm going back to it this afternoon. I can assure you, so help me God, that it is a very long time since I've felt that way about a new book of poetry. I think your book is totally alive and true, totally convincing.

I'm getting a little work done, mainly in my notebook, which I kept faithfully all through Europe, and which I think saves my life some times.

I, too, hope we'll meet again soon, and certainly keep in touch. Thanks for *With Ignorance*, Charlie. It is a beautiful book. I can't think of anything else like it.

Best,
Jim

To Roger Hecht

New York City
October 19, 1977

Dear Frank,*

Kenneth Rexroth is a writer I admire. His prose always delights and instructs me. I fondle his epigrams, and I learn of books I did not know existed. He always pleases me with his poetry. A curiously self-taught American from Illinois, he belongs more to the French tradition in American literature than to the English. His mastery of Italian literature is, I suppose, what moves me most; and his two poems about Vincenza belong, in their minor lyric mode, to the larger lyricism of Dante, who, clearly, had other fish to fry, and nobler, but who included in his intelligence a genius for the poetry of place. Rexroth understands the nature of such poetry, and he has written fine versions of it. I admire him.

So I am not trying to depredate (I learned that word on the door of the men's room just outside the railroad station in Chantilly, just north of Paris, this past Summer: "Parce que des depredations repetées, les toilettes sont fermées." It is a wonderful word. This can is closed because you frogs been depredating all over it.) Mr. Rexroth. I merely wished to offer you an explanatory note in loo of the following announcement:

According to an issue of *The Westigan Review* which I just received and enjoyed, "Kenneth Rexroth's translations in this issue will be part of a new anthology titled *The Burning Heart, The Women Poets of Japan.*" I hope to read this book. Mr. Rexroth's translations are very beautiful: precise, clear, cold.

His co-translator, as God is my witness, is Atsumi Ikuko Continuum-Seabury.

If you think I made this up, I am prepared to show you the printed text.

I am tangled deep in a new poem, and I need help. It is as formal as I can make it, and it is about the closing of the revival of *Hair.* Let's have lunch.

Bless,
Jim

---

*A nickname from their years at Kenyon College.

To Hayden Carruth

Dear Hayden,

I just want to write you a note to keep in touch. It's actually been a long time since I last wrote you—I think it was in Paris—or was I still in Italy? Wherever it was, you've been in my thoughts a good deal, and I'm thinking of you again today. After some weeks of soaking, gloomy, neurotic weather here, what I sometimes think of as Viennese weather, because in the Viennese rain the big Franz-Josef buildings look like the secrets of Freud's wealthier patients, the sun has come out. To my surprise, the New York autumn has assumed its richest color in years. Though we've both been locked up in work most of the time, during the past week Annie managed to get out and walk in Central Park, which is this city's best blessing.

I know how cold it can get in Vermont, but the weather so far at this time of year must be spectacular. Winters in Minneapolis, too, back in the old days, could be fierce; but the autumns were almost unbearably beautiful.

Last Monday evening I read from my new book at the YMHA. I shared the program with Richard Eberhart, whom I like very much. The reading went all right. I spoke for about 35–40 minutes. During my reading, something went wrong with the microphone; and, to my amazement when I thought about it afterwards, I simply ignored it. In the old days, somewhat boozed, I would either have gone to pieces or else made some stupid "witty" remark to the audience. I simply went on reading, and it was really all right. I mention this because in an earlier letter you asked me how it was to read in public while sober. Hayden, I can't say that I loved it. In fact, one thing I've discovered is that I just don't like very much to read in public. But it didn't upset me, either. It was all right.

Speaking of new books, somebody told me recently (I think it was Bob Mezey, who stopped by on his way to Europe) that your new book is going to be published all right. Who is going to do it? I remember you wrote me last summer that you were still working on it and having a hell of a time. By the way, the next time that happens, may I offer my help? I am a ragged, not very useful critic; but certainly people like Galway have given me a lot of help in this respect. My own new book, for example, now has thirty-five pieces in it. When I began the final, long struggle with it about a year ago, it contained about sixty. You said some very helpful things to me in yet an earlier letter about the manuscript, mainly about keeping in it the things I was sure of. This is, I guess, the final secret—or one of the final secrets—about this strange difficult art. It isn't the length alone—a book can be two hundred pages long, or it can be twenty-five. That's all right. But every single page has got to ring true, the words have got to be shaped, *formed*. What depressed me about my last book of verse (I just call my verse verse, and my prose prose) was that more than half of it wasn't formed. It was just sort of spewed. I think that a fallacy pervades American verse these days, worse than a fallacy, a real curse; and it might be stated thus: I am a poet; and therefore anything which I happen to write is a poem. The only way out of this bog that I can see is through a clear criticism (not personal attack, which is just another evasion) and through hard solitary work. I mean that the work has to begin in solitude; then one can get help from one's honest friends.

Well, enough moralizing. My book will be out next month, and I'll send it to you as soon as I get copies. I wish you'd let me know about yours. We haven't seen the Kinnells since we got back from Europe, but we hope to soon. You know, they live just a few blocks from here. But, as usual, Galway's running around to several jobs at once. Annie and I both send our affection to you and Rose Marie.

Best,

Jim

To Michael Cuddihy

New York City
November 14, 1977

Dear Michael,

Many years ago my grandmother used to say some little poems to me, and here is one:

> The eskimo sleeps in his white bear skin,
>   And sleeps very well, I'm told.
> Last night I slept in my bare white skin
>   And caught a hell of a cold.

I caught one my own self over the weekend, and I'm just now beginning to recover from it.

The copies of the issue have arrived, and I am thanking you, for me and Annie, for such a beautiful piece of work. I've already heard from Peter Stitt, who says the same. It is the most serious and extended work anybody has ever done on my books, and the most truly presented. What means most to me was that, as you intended, it was not just a job of puffery. For some reason, in spite of my idiotic attacks of vanity, unqualified praise is even more depressing than fanatical condemnation (which, to my real astonishment, I have received a couple of times).

It was a superb job, Michael, and I am grateful.

My new book is supposed to be in print by now, but I haven't yet received a copy of it.

This evening we're supposed to attend a gathering at the Riverside Church, where Hardie St. Martin is going to receive an award for his book of translations from the Spanish, *Roots and Wings*. There will also be a reading of poems from Spain and South America, in the original and in English. I am supposed to take part in it. It is all right with me, but the truth is that such programs always make me feel uneasy. As sure as God made little apples, the program, which begins at 8 o'clock, will go on until hell freezes over; and I have reached the point where late literary evenings make me shudder. A lot of things make me shudder these days; so I've decided to teach next Fall (1978) for a semester at the University of Delaware; and then Annie and I are going to take the rest of the year off and spend it in Italy and France.

I wonder if you would send a copy of the *Ironwood* to my older son Franz. Annie and I both send you

love,
Jim

To Laurence Green

New York City
November 27, 1977

Dear Mr. Green:

It seems a long time since I received your beautiful note at Hunter College, where I teach. I wanted to write you something appropriate and thoughtful; but it seems that the longer I wait, the more pompous I sound to myself. Maybe the best thing would be to take your questions as simply as I can.

You ask, "What inspires you to write poetry?" A subject like that is always obscure, and maybe it ought to be. But I can tell you how a poem begins, at least as far as I'm concerned. I was born and grew up in southern Ohio, a place which remains amazingly rich in the sound of its language: a mixture of hillbilly with all kinds of accents and intonations spoken by my friends who had backgrounds from so many different countries: Italy, Greece, Hungary, Wales, Ireland. Furthermore, the language of those people was very strongly *non*-literary: all the people I knew came from poor and working-class families. I don't want to sound gross, but I can't help it: if you ask a southern Ohioan where another person has disappeared to, and he doesn't know, then as like as not he'll answer—not "I don't know"; but "Oh, he went to shit and the hogs eat him." I don't know where that fusion of the violently physical and the exquisitely witty comes from, but in a strange way I think it is beautiful, and it has been ringing somewhere in my head all my life. I suppose what I'm saying is that a person—like your young poets—should not be afraid to pour into his poetry all the phrases and sayings and rhythms that in truth mean the most to him, the sounds that he can hear outside of himself—because, if he listens, he'll hear them inside of himself, too. Everybody surely hears some kind of song inside of himself. How amazing if he could only be brave enough to sing it out loud. If he does, often he gets back from other people something like an echo—an echo changed and transfigured by the secret songs of the very people who have heard him sing in the first place. The old Sioux Indians understood this matter very well; and each person among them had many inner songs. For example, everybody had his own "death song," and he kept it secret till the time when he faced death. Then he would sing it, and leave it to the living, and take his leave.

Then you ask, "What to look for in reading a poem?" My answer to that question would be related to what I just wrote above: I would listen first, and then look. I think people can enjoy poetry most by reading it aloud to one another and—most rarely—to themselves.

I think what gives a poem "lasting" importance is the truth by which a poet struggles to achieve the integrity—the wholeness—of his own soul. Since we really do have souls after all, everybody is constantly struggling to be true to his own. If a poet struggles hard enough and truly enough through his own words, others—they may live a thousand years after he's dead—will hear the sound of that struggle, and take heart from it—as I myself have heard, and taken heart from, the struggles of Shakespeare, and Catullus, and Dante, though they lived and died long before I was born.

I want to tell your students that I am well aware of what a huge and in many ways hellish country we live in, but that we are not totally alone in it, and that we have a chance to find one another, before we die, through the truth of our language.

I have had troubles of my own—not drug addiction, but a couple of things nearly as difficult—and I can understand how your students feel: it is a ferocious battle to try to make sense out of one's own life; but it is everything—everything.

Thank you for your kindness in writing to me.

Sincerely,
James Wright

The Last Journey

1978–1979

In Verona, Italy, 1979

I can scarcely believe this day, the sky clear, the sun of early spring beginning to warm the honey stones of the bell tower of tall Saint Sulpice, and Annie and I taking the train to Moret-sur-Loing, the country town that makes us happy.

(Paris, March 6, 1979)

The churches of Verona, their elegant towers rise into the green spring light like anemones under water.   (Verona, March 23, 1979)

Whatever else is happening this year, I have never failed to take pleasure in my notebook. Winter or spring, long entry or short, it makes me feel I am touching whatever reality I am able to touch. I think it is because my mind is clear these days.   (Rome, April 5, 1979)

We have only three more days in Paris, but it is, finally, foolish to count the days, here or anywhere else. Forget them—forget their names, at least—just as a stranger to the Seine might forget the names of the sycamores and poplars, as long as he can remember the name of the girl who walks with him on a September afternoon.   (Paris, September 1, 1979)

—from *A Secret Field: Selections from the Final Journals of James Wright*

          . . . The secret
        Of this journey is to let the wind
        Blow its dust all over your body,
        To let it go on blowing, to step lightly, lightly
        All the way through your ruins, and not to lose
        Any sleep over the dead, who surely
        Will bury their own, don't worry.

                                    —from "The Journey"

In the fall of 1977 James and Anne devised a plan for another long trip to Europe. James applied for and received a grant from the Guggenheim Foundation. This left him free to take a leave of absence from Hunter College and accept an invitation to serve as Distinguished Guest Professor at the University of Delaware in Newark for the fall semester of 1978.

This last journey actually commenced in the early summer of 1978, with time spent at Lake Minnewaska in the Shawangunk Mountains, and then a month in Misquamicut, Rhode Island. After Labor Day, they were met by Gibbons Ruark, who drove them, with a few of their possessions, to Delaware. They enjoyed a change from life in New York, as well as the companionship of Gib and Kay Ruark. James wrote, read, studied, and even baked bread, his new interest.

The Wrights arrived in Paris for Christmas. They took a series of short trips, first to Nice, where they saw Galway Kinnell and his family, then to London and Cheltenham, England; Amsterdam; and Brussels. After a few weeks in Nîmes and Albi they made their way to Italy, where they spent most of this journey. In August, Anne's sister Jane met them in Venice and drove them through the Tuscan countryside on little-used back roads. The sojourn ended in Paris, where they rented an apartment, shopped at a nearby open market, and enjoyed the splendors of the city they loved.

Anne and James returned to New York in early September, back to city life and the work of teaching and writing.

While in Paris, James had developed what he thought was a persistent sore throat. However, it was far more serious. When a biopsy was done at the end of November, a malignant tumor was discovered and diagnosed as cancer of the tongue.

James was able to stay at his home on Eighty-fifth Street until early January. He entered Mount Sinai Hospital a few days after he and Anne attended a tribute to American poetry and poets held by President and Mrs. Carter at the White House. James died at Calvary Hospital in the Bronx on March 25, 1980.

To Janice Thurn

New York City
January 2, 1978

Dear Janice,

I'm writing today to tell you that I'm still alive and, generally, flourishing. Sometimes in recent months I've come within an ace of writing you, and now and then I've felt guilty about the neglect, because you've written me about three times or so without getting a reply. But, really, the hell with considerations of that kind. I take it that we both write when we can and when we need to.

The new year's just begun. Tomorrow I've got to return to school for a pretty intense grind of exams during the coming week. Then I'll get a little time off. Annie has to be back at work (at NYU) tomorrow, and then next week, and then she'll get a few days free. What I've decided to do is to accept an appointment as Visiting Professor at the University of Delaware next Fall and then take the rest of next year off. I have a new book stirring around in my notebooks, and by next January it ought to have grown enough to accept some clearer cultivation. One of the things I want to do is take Annie up to the town of Husum in Schleswig-Holstein (in northeast Germany, just next to Denmark) and visit the home of Theodor Storm, one of whose books I translated some years ago. I really don't know yet what shape my new book will take, but right now I am having too hard a time with it in my notebook, and I know it is going to need room and time to grow and find its own shape.

It is cold in New York today. A bleak snow is on the ground and the roofs of cars. It was lovely last evening late: luminous and soft. But I would just as soon stay home today. If Minneapolis is holding true to the form I remember, it must be peachy-keen at this time of year. Well, blow, blow, thou winter wind! Thou art not so unkind As man's ingratitude. I just closed my eyes and could well feel the warm sand of Sirmione on Lake Garda, where we lay last summer all through the afternoons, nearly naked, with a towel covered with talleggio and figs and shrimp and prosciutto. No wonder so many northerners end up in Italy.

I hope all goes well with you these days.

Jim

To Donald Hall

New York City
January 2, 1978

Dear Don,

Thanks for your nice note and for the letter which was returned to you from Italy. Your remark that Poste Restante sounds like a nice place is like that old gag that Ring Lardner used in one of his weird one-act plays. The curtain rises and two milch-cows are discovered at a table in a restaurant. The younger begins to weep, and the older asks what's wrong. The younger: "I was born out of wedlock." The elder: "Don't cry, honey. They got some mighty pretty country out there."

How I neglected to reply to your letter, that contained "Flies," I don't know. One thing led to another. We were in Paris, and our 18-year-old god-daughter was with us. It was her first trip abroad, and she was enthusiastic about everything. But I did study through "Flies" with great joy, and I still think it is powerful and complete.

We finagled an apartment in Paris for the whole month of August, and each morning I rose quite early (you know, Don, maybe it has something to do with total abstinence from booze—our bodies *want* to wake up, just as flowers want to open in the morning, but alcohol won't let them). We were on the ninth floor over at Denfert-Rochereau, and I could stand on the terrace and see the rooftops all over hell's half-acre. I had my coffee, my Perrier, and my notebook, and my God I was happy. I felt like Thoreau and e e cummings rolled into one fat Ohioan.

Yes, my book is finally done, thanks God, and I am looking forward happily to *Kicking the Leaves*, whose title poem I have in my notebook.

I don't know when or how we will get up to New Hampshire. The coming semester is going to be very tight. I can understand why you wanted to escape from teaching. Anyway, next Fall I'm going to teach at the University of Delaware (where Galway is this Spring, by the way), and then Annie and I are going back to Europe for the rest of the year . . . I want to get this off. Please give love to Jane. Annie sends hers.

Love,
Jim

To Laura Lee

New York City
January 25, 1978

My dear Laura,

It gave me such delight to hear your voice over the phone at Christmastime, that you must wonder how it is I've taken just about a month to write. It hasn't been forgetfulness, dear; just an accumulation of work of one kind or another, most of it at school, some of it in my own notebooks. My own habits of work—at writing—are a little strange, I suppose, and they are hard to explain: I keep a small notebook, easy to carry around, and then I move from that to a larger notebook and then to a larger folder. Meanwhile, time passes and passes and passes, and so do I. From place to place. I just completed (I think) two pieces that I began in Hawaii two summers ago. I sometimes think that writing—writing of any kind, as long as it is done for its own sake—is a matter of joining the seasons and following their movements. For they don't move through time only. They move, as we move, from place to place. As we move, we carry them, and they carry us—I think of that odd and very beautiful word "bear"—the seasons bear us from one place to another. And how many seeds of how many plants we have inside us. Sometimes when I sit down beside the Adige, the river I love so much in Verona, where the rainfall changes the color of the water into a bewildering freshness, I feel as if I were about to emerge at the end of an Italian pine branch and blossom beside a Hawaiian plumeria.

Before I get lost in my own prose and drift away through the ceiling, I want you to note down the following names and address: Mr. and Mrs. Henry Esterly [. . .] These are old and dear friends who live near Foothills College. They are marvelous people, who know a good deal about education in California—indeed, about a great many things— and I am sure they would be happy if you were to get in touch with them to say hello. Henry is a scientist; Elizabeth is so many things, and she is one of the most amazing teachers I ever had. If you call them, please give them my love.

We had a nice time over Christmas in Lititz with your mother, who seemed to us pretty well. She certainly was happy to hear your voice, as we all were. We didn't do a great deal, but our visit was pleasant. We walked around the lovely town of Lititz, and visited the museum, and ate and ate and ate. I had the most interesting time with Brenton that I've ever had. He is becoming a fine boy [. . .]

Our own plans for the next year include a Fall semester at the University of Delaware, where I have been invited as Visiting Professor; and then another journey to Europe, probably from January through August.

Meanwhile, we will be here at home, certainly till the end of the coming Spring, and I hope you'll write soon. I think of you always with the fondest pride and affection.

Love,
Uncle James

To Debra Thomas and Sheri Akamine

New York City
March 12, 1978

My dear Debra and Sheri,

I hope and trust that you won't object to my writing to both of you in the same note. As I write, I can glance through the apartment window into the Spring sunlight, and it is remarkable to me how clearly I can call up both faces, and the plumeria blossoms tucked in your hair. In my new book (it's called *To a Blossoming Pear Tree*) there's a short prose piece called "How Spring Arrives." It is one of two, called "Moments in Rome," and indeed it is a description of a Spring day, early Spring, among the dead branches and gray winter grass up on the cliffs of the Borghesi Gardens where you can sit and look out over the exquisite sky and the rooftops of that strangely beautiful city. I had been sitting there, some time ago, and I'd seen three girls come up the path, brush some dead oleander branches lightly aside, take off their sweaters, shake out their black hair, and sit side by side on a bench. They made me think—I wrote it down in my notebook—of that amazing passage in Horace's poem about Spring, "Diffugere Nives" ("The snows are scattered"), in which he describes the three graces appearing in the woods and "putting off their fear" (as if they were taking off their winter sweaters) and playing among the trees. Of course, Horace's poem must surely have been lying just out of sight beneath the surface of my mind somewhere; but the odd thing is that the three Italian girls were actually there, no less vivacious and no less themselves for being, all unknowing, that lovely old Roman poet's dream come true again.

Your vividness is like that [. . .]

Sheri, it was lovely of you to send me that sheaf of poems. They are all as clear and fresh in detail as the ones you showed me toward the end of our class in Honolulu two summers ago. I must say that I am pleased by your learning to clarify these detailed images by placing them naturally into a larger context. One of the most difficult things to do in constructing a poem is to make unmistakably clear just who is addressing whom and on what occasion. You are learning to do this [. . .]

I want to say how interested I am in the prose that you've both been writing. It is an excellent discipline in the craft of writing, just because it can teach the larger structure of things—even of your poems—to you in a natural way. I wish you would both find a little book by E. M. Forster called *Aspects of the Novel*. What he has to say about "story and plot" is one of the most useful things I've ever heard or read about writing.

Annie and I are both grateful for the drawing and for the article about Okinawa.

It is Sunday and, in spite of the fair weather, we are both working today. One of the many fine things we have in our life is our understanding of each other in the matter of the work we do often at home. Right at this moment it's almost noon, and we'll be at our desks till five or six o'clock. But I don't want to sound stuffy. Yesterday we walked for a while along the East River—New York City is at its best in Spring.

Both of your letters are lovely. Annie joins me in sending

Love,

Jim

To Gibbons Ruark

New York City

March 12, 1978

Dear Gib,

If ever (it strikes me that I should write *when*ever) I fail to respond at once to your letters, you must understand that I almost always fail to respond immediately, unless somebody nudges me from the outside. But in truth I have been recently nudged from the outside in other directions—schollork, mainly—and so I've taken, once again, to writing letters in spasms.

(Look how I spelled "schoolwork." Of course it's a typo, but where did that particular one come from? My students have been having a lovely time reading Chaucer. Maybe if I type long enough, and make enough mistakes, I'll end up typing in Middle English.)

Given the occasion of the poem, and your grief for your friend; given especially the very meaning of the poem's grave style, which, I take it, is a total refusal to falsify that grief through the elaborate caterwauling which is the very native tongue of fraudulence; given these, it may be inappropriate to call the poem masterful. But the word will have to do. I'm aware that to use the word alone sounds like laziness; but I am not using it alone. I mean the justness of its diction, and especially the grave precision of its music, the lucid relation of one line to the others. These chords and arrangements, so to speak, become clearer to me with each reading, and I have read the poem many times, silently and aloud. Consider, for example, these lines:

> The year we were for Italy, you were for France,
> Their local wines so distant, yet the two countries
> Closer in the end than our South and your North.

The syntax here is naturally that of prose; yet consider the strange evocativeness in the parallel phrases "we were for" and "you were for." You know, Gib, it sometimes occurs to me that, bad as our time may be, we have our lucky chances. One of these is the neglect of T. S. Eliot. There is no longer, thank God, any political–academic–New York profit to be gained by dropping Eliot's name. Even Harold Bloom has publicly declared (I'm not making this up; it was in *Esquire*) that Eliot was an over-rated bad writer, and that consequently we need not pay him any mind. In fact, this current vogue gives us the marvelous chance to re-read Eliot, and to learn from his work. He wrote, for example, that the poetry of many masters is at its greatest and most memorable precisely at those points where it most resembles the language—the structure, the diction—of their prose. (Consequently, we need not be bullied by shaggy surrealists, nor by the sentence-structure of the structuralists.)

"Listening to Fats Waller in Late Light" is a very beautiful poem, wholly fulfilled and moving.

The weather in New York today is lovely—this city is at its best in Spring. Though the snow is still rotting on all sides, the sunlight continues its odd blessing of this place. We aren't going out, though—Annie and I are working at our desks till this evening, when the Kinnells and the Mosses are coming to dinner. I hope you've got to know Galway better, though from what I can see he seems to be moving about a good deal. He's a fine man, and we are good friends.

I have a vision of you and Kay and Jenny and Emmie today, out on a picnic or something.

Love,
Jim

To Robert Hass

New York City
March 18, 1978

Dear Mr. Hass:

Our mutual friend John Logan was in New York recently. He stayed with Annie and me over a long weekend, and then read his new poems at the YMHA. It was lovely to have this wonderful man with us again, and we talked at length about many things.

He spoke warmly of you, of course; and he sent me back to that long essay that you wrote about my own work and published in *Iron-wood*. Since John returned to Buffalo, and I returned to teaching, I've studied the essay again.

For some time I've thought of writing to you about it, and this seems a reasonably good occasion. Over the years my writings have come in for a good deal of discussion, some of it pleasant enough and much of it angry, snotty, and even vicious. So help me God, both kinds of discussion have seemed odd to me. Evidently there is something in my writing that tends to drive a certain kind of mind to extreme reactions.

Anyway, I want to tell you that your own essay is certainly, to my mind, the soundest and truest thing anyone has ever, to my knowledge, written about my books. You didn't flinch from facing whatever is flawed in my work, and a good deal of it is flawed all right, sometimes terribly, both in spirit and in language. Your honest intelligence always worked in the essay with a general spirit of serious good will. I am more grateful for this than I know how to say. I hope that someone will have similar intelligence, imagination, and plain sense to deal with your own beautiful poems in a similar way. By the way, I think you've published one book; and I'm sorry to say that I don't have it. Can you tell me where I could get a copy?

You'll be glad to hear that John L., though still overweight, got a good rest here in New York, and he was in fine condition. He spoke at the Y with Diane Wakoski, and they both read splendidly.

Thank you, again, for your own work.

Yours,
James Wright

To Diane Wakoski

New York City
March 20, 1978

Dear Diane,

In the dog-days of August, 1943, I had just got to the point of struggling with Virgil in Latin on my own, and in desperation for lack of money I got a job on a farm near Colrain, Ohio. So many of the young men were gone to war at that time, that I had a choice of jobs. I could have worked as minor assistant to the old guy who was sexton at the Weeks Cemetery, Colrain, Ohio, where my grandmother was already buried. I took the farm job instead. At the end of August I got sick and had to spend six weeks in the hospital. When I emerged, it was too late to return to high school; and so, in the middle of October, I took a long walk down the Ohio River, which was even beautiful at that time of year, and then went, grim-toothed, over to Wheeling, and by God I got a job. I spent that whole year working with people who had to work (well, *I* had to work, too), and that year has always seemed to me a time when I began to rise from the dead.

I don't think you are going to believe what I will tell you now. You may even think that I am trying to be funny. But I swear to God that this is the truth: that job that brought me back to life was in Receiving at Sears. Yes, Sears. In Wheeling, West Virginia.

I don't have to tell you how happy the fact makes me now, though who on God's green earth could have known. Life and poetry are lovely sometimes.

In a way, it would be silly to tell you that *The Man Who Shook Hands* is your best book, simply because your work has always seemed to me to be entirely whole and beautiful. But I want to tell you that the book is exquisitely beautiful, and it is certainly the best book of poetry I have read in a very long time. An added pleasure: I'd just received the book in the mail the day or so before I heard you give your totally clear and true reading at the Y with John Logan. Since that reading, I've surely read *The Man Who Shook Hands* five times, and it reveals itself more beautifully each time.

I want to conclude by asking you a question which I suspect will upset you a little; but I ask it because it is important to me, and, I think, to you. In the opening essay on music and poetry, you write the following: "Well, I did not write this essay to appease Marjorie Perloff and other critics who are looking for cases to add validity to their already final condemnation of my poetry." Now, I want to ask: who on earth is Marjorie Perloff? I think I can answer my own question, and I want to share my answer with you.

I have never read any of her work, but I have seen her name. One of the strange and interesting things about recent American literature is that it has seen the appearance of a new school of critics. They do not write poetry—or if they do, it is so bad that they cannot bear it—and, barren themselves, they have begun to form in English Departments everywhere a Subject which they call Modern Literature. They hate living poets with a fanaticism so intense as to be almost like love, and so they are close to being Vampires. Yet they cannot admit such hatred publicly, or they would not get tenure. So they must present themselves as the defenders of POETRY against living people who are writing poetry. Invariably they attack this or that living poet in the name of the Great Poets of the Past: George Herbert, Pound, even Wallace Stevens. Such persons were identified in a couplet by Theodore Roethke, who wrote an epigram about one of them:

> He heaps few honors on a living head.
> He loves himself and the Illustrious Dead.

God knows I would like my own work to receive the severest criticism before I publish it; and I ask for such criticism; but I resent having it tossed aside for the sake of some savagely ambitious ex-English-Major lusting for a Professorship.

Well, I have carried on too long. I hope I haven't upset you by bringing up something that you mentioned in your own essay.

I love *The Man Who Shook Hands*, and I guess I have to be true and say that I love you, too.

Love,

Jim

To Mark Strand

New York City

April 11, 1978

Dear Mark,

This will just be a note. I'd hoped to write you a fuller letter, and I will directly. Right now, on Tuesday evening, it occurs to me that in the midst of end-of-semester work I want to tell you a couple of things about your poems.

Ironically enough, I'd been waiting for the appearance of *The Late Hour* before writing you and telling you that I've had the poem called "Poem after Leopardi" on the wall right in front of my desk for weeks. It is there now, and there it will remain. It is a great poem, and I was disappointed not to see it in the book. But then I remembered that your wrote it since the book was completed.

May you always have problems of this kind.

I want to say that I'm slightly distracted by the word "after" in the title of the poem. It sounds as if the poem were going to be a mere imitation, and it is certainly not that. It is a poem in its own right, a fantastic leap of imagination and intelligence, totally yours. I wonder what it would be like to call the poem simply "Leopardi."* Doesn't that single name sound the main evocative theme? I'm thinking of a poem by August Graf von Platen called "Tristan," which Thomas Mann discusses in his *Essays of Three Decades*. It is another great poem, one of the true masterpieces of the entire 19th century, to my mind; and it is just about love and death, no mention of Tristan in it. But the plain name in the plain title suddenly transports the poem into a deep large world.

Well, I think the "Poem after Leopardi" is masterful.

The Late Hour is a radiant book, as I knew it would be. It arrived last Saturday morning, and I must have read it five times since then. I put it aside and go about my business, and I can still *hear* the book. Its clarity and depth are amazing.

I have to get back to work now. Thanks immensely for the poems, which are beautiful and encouraging.

Annie and I will be here in town till mid-June. Next year we'll be in Delaware (Fall) and then in Europe. But I'll give details later. Tonight I just want to send you this note.

Love,
Jim

---

*The concluding poem in Mark Strand's *Selected Poems* (New York: Atheneum, 1980) is titled "Leopardi."

To John Storck

New York City
May 6, 1978

Dear Mr. Storck:

I'm sorry to be so late in replying to your gracious letter of April 12. As you may know, I'm a professor at Hunter College, and as I'm sure you've heard, New York City has been having its financial difficulties, which affect the City University of which Hunter is a part, so that our faculty have had to assume even greater burdens than usual. I don't mean to complain, for I love teaching, the finest of the arts; I just want to explain my failure to respond at once to your kindness.

It pleases me that you enjoyed my new book, and I must say it relieves me also. I never appear in print but what I feel a slight apprehension that somebody in Martins Ferry might happen across one of my books and take umbrage at something I've written. This has happened from time to time over the years, and it's always made me feel sad to think that I might have offended somebody in the town where so many fine people live and where so many were good to me during my younger days. I never wished to attack Martins Ferry, but, on the contrary, only to aspire to write clearly and well about what mattered most to me.

It's good of you to ask about contributing manuscripts to a collection at the library. But I have decided for the time being that my own manuscripts—those I'm able to make sense of, among an accumulation of many years—are best kept at hand so that I can use them. It's odd how work of this sort proceeds, at least my own work: one short poem in my *Collected Poems* took me nearly fifteen years to complete.

I haven't returned to Martins Ferry for an awfully long time. I would like to, just for a private visit; and if I do, I will certainly visit you.

Thank you.

Sincerely,
James Wright

To Janice Thurn

Lake Minnewaska
New Paltz, New York
June 7, 1978

Dear Janice,

We arrived up here in the mountains day before yesterday. We both love to live in New York City, and we are tough and quick enough to fight the daily fight there. But as the school year came to its end, we realized that we had something like battle-fatigue.

We've been coming to this still and serene place for a decade now. The hotel where we stay is about a hundred years old. It is corny, and getting ramshackle more and more all the time. There's an overgrown lawn within a carriage-drive behind a cliff on the other side of the lake where another old turn-of-the-century hotel used to stand—it caught fire and burned down last winter in the middle of a snow-storm—and sometimes in the summer evening on that lawn you can see the ghosts playing croquet, with Henry James sitting on a wicker bench and murmuring long sentences to the sunset. I suppose we love this place so much because its rate of breathing is so natural and slow.

I think your essay on Coleridge's poem "This lime-tree bower my prison," is very intelligent, very beautiful. There's a remarkable, extremely odd and original essay about Coleridge by one of my own favorite writers—E. M. Forster—I think it's in his book of essays called *Abinger Harvest*, a book you ought to know. (You would also like his book *Two Cheers for Democracy*, especially his noble, true essay "What I Believe.")

You asked about our plans and addresses. On about June 11, we'll return to NYC, and our address will be the same there till the beginning of August. Then we'll go to Rhode Island for a month. (I don't know the address yet, but mail will be forwarded.)

Thereafter: perhaps I've told you already, but maybe not. Anyway, during the Fall semester I'm to be a Visiting Professor at the University of Delaware (Newark, Delaware). Then, next January, we're going to Europe again, this time for eight months: Holland, Northeast Germany, Belgium, then slowly south through France, then on to Naples, Italy, and on and on all the way to Apulia (which is the heel of the Italian boot). I think we're even going to Greece for a couple of weeks. Then in June we're meeting Annie's sister in Venice—finally we'll return to France. As soon as we've written out our itinerary, I'll send you a copy of it, so you'll know the various places where I can pick up our mail. It'll really be less frantic than I'm making it appear. I'm working slowly (as always) on a new book, and it will be lovely to start bringing it together in Paris.

I'll mail this now.

Love,
Jim

To Robert Bly

Lake Minnewaska
New Paltz, New York
June 7, 1978

Dear Robert,

Yesterday as we were returning from a twelve-mile walk across the mountain here, we startled a doe. But instead of running away, she turned on us and snorted ferociously. It was startling. Then sure enough, just around the corner of the mountain path, we found her fawn, lying damp and bright brown and puzzled on a big flat stone right at the edge of the cliff. It couldn't have been more than a day old. We just gazed at it for a few moments and then walked on as quietly as we could.

Robert, I've been thinking about you. I'm afraid that last telephone conversation we had wasn't very satisfactory. All I meant to say was that your divorce distresses me very much—I've known *both* you and Carol for nearly 20 years, and have felt very close to you both. For all I know, a divorce may be for the best. I don't want to nag you about a matter that can't help but cause you pain. Well—what I think I'll do when we get back to NYC is to send you a couple of new poems and see what you think. Please *do* keep in touch, even if you can write only a note.

It's wildly beautiful here in the mountains—everything is so incredibly green.

Love,
James

To Philip Levine

New York City
July 3, 1978

Dear Phil,

I want to write you a note about two things. One makes me feel awful, the other happy. Here goes:

Annie and I got to see you and Fran a couple of times this past year, thank God. We kept wanting to ask you to our house; and we finally did, when there was about a week left in the school year. Then we got lost in an avalanche of schoolwork, visiting relatives, and general desperation. We looked up one horrible day and faced the fact that we hadn't fulfilled our invitation to you. I'm writing now to beg your pardon. My God, I realize how stuffy that sounds; but I can't think of any other way to put it. You've both been so lovely to me, especially when I was wandering drunk out in California years ago; now that I have a decent home of my own, I wanted to welcome you to it. I blew it.

Anyway, I remain one of the exquisite Fran Levine's leading fans. (That photograph in the recent *Antaeus* killed me.)

The second thing I want to do is to thank you for writing the poem "The Face," which I now have on the wall just in front of me as I write. It's been in my mind almost constantly since I found it about a week ago. I've been wondering just what it was that reached so deep into me, what it was that happened in the poem. I am not exaggerating when I say that it is the best poem about a father and son I have ever read except David's poem in the second book of Kings. The weird thing is that the poem is even more than that. Now that I've read your letter to Wendell Berry (in *Antaeus*), I think I can begin to see what happened—happens, I mean—in your poem. What you say about "the landscape seemed me, seemed like a projection of my own inner being"—a gigantic leap of imagination—holds true in "The Face," which includes also the face of your father, and your own face. I am trying to say that the poem is magnificent and true. Thank God you wrote it.

I'm saying all this very poorly, I'm afraid.

We both send our love to you and Fran.

Jim

To Betsy Fogelman

Misquamicut, Rhode Island
August 2, 1978

Dear Bets,

Somewhere in the vastness of Thomas Hardy there's a poem that says in the last line, "The salt fog mops me." Fair enough. I'm sitting on a nice little front porch, surrounded on three sides by the salt mist of the Atlantic Ocean. I don't find it gloomy, though. It tastes just fine. I am hoping that by noon the sun will have reached through. If it does, we'll be here to greet it, by God. Well, we'll probably go swimming anyway, as we did yesterday afternoon, the ocean being just about a half-mile away.

We arrived just a couple of days ago, and there were some other matters to take care of, but now I can sit here in the early morning and write to you with the ease and pleasure I always feel in your company.

We'd been here before at Misquamicut, just a village by the ocean; and, last Spring sometime, I wrote the following* and sent it to David Ignatow, who's going to print it (with another piece about the edge of water) in a series of broadsides he's editing.

> AT PEACE WITH THE OCEAN OFF MISQUAMICUT
> A million rootlets
> Shifting their dunes
> Quiver a little on the deep
> Clavicles of some body,
> Down there, a while.
> It is still asleep, it is the Atlantic,
> A sting-ray drowsing his fill of sunlight, a moulting angel
> Breathing the grateful water,
> Praying face downward to a god I am afraid
> To imagine.
> What will I do when the sting-ray
> And the angel
> Wake?
> Whose mercy am I going to throw
> Myself upon?

*Published in *This Journey* (1982) and included in *Above the River*, p. 351.

When even the Atlantic Ocean
Is nothing more than
My brother the sting-ray.

* * *

I liked the prose piece (I prefer that phrase to "prose poem") that you sent me—very much indeed. Are you trying more of them?

We'll be here through the month of August and a little longer, dear Bets, and I hope you'll write to me soon. The summer in New York was all a-clutter with visitors and commitments of one kind or another. We did get away to see some friends in Buffalo for a week, and guess what I did? Well, a couple of men I know there were baking bread, and all at once I was seized with the inspiration. So I returned to NYC and tried it. My first batch was more or less okay. It was edible. But the second! It was marvelous. The second time, I even cut a slight line along the top of the loaves before I put them in the oven for the next-to-last phase, and sure enough, the tops of the loaves just opened up and breathed. I've begun to accumulate a small library of books about bread. Tomorrow, I believe I'll try out the oven here in this cottage. I'll follow the conventional, old-fashioned plan one more time; and, if it works again, then for my following batch I believe I'll try something a little more baroque: some kind of the so-called quick-bread. You can make it with bananas, a fairly popular cross between bread and cake. But I want honest-to-God bread, and one of my books suggests something with nuts, or water-cress, or even squash. This is a new world to me. During both of my bakings, I had a lovely, lovely time. There is something about it—intimate, graceful, light-hearted, and transcendently strong—a surrender and a kind of attentive strength, indistinguishable from each other. It's hard to say what I mean; but it is lovely.

There are two books which I wish you would find, if you don't know them already. Your words about Nietzsche made me think, in some deep way though not immediately obvious, of the wonderful book by José Ortega y Gasset, *The Revolt of the Masses*. It is stunning and deep, and has meant a great deal to me over the years. I return to it all the time; I must have read it fifty times. The other is just a novel, a comic novel, but I am thoroughly happy that it is in print again (a Penguin Books paperback): *Cold Comfort Farm*, by Stella Gibbons. Come to think of it, dear Betsy, you ought to read the latter at once. It is cheering, no end . . . Mist is still gray outside, but it's not raining. We're going soon to an immense farm-market, for corn, squash, sausage, and all those things that force me to confess what a startlingly sensuous person I am. I can't help it. (Gently sensuous, I hope.) Please write to me soon, dear.

Love,
Jim

To Carol Bly

Misquamicut, Rhode Island
August 5, 1978

Dear Carol,

It just occurred to me that I don't really have an address for you, but I trust that this note will be forwarded.

For some time now I've wanted to write to you, and several times it seemed to me that I didn't have anything to say that would make sense. Now I have something.

Yesterday, I baked bread. Yes, bread. A few weeks ago Annie and I were visiting friends in Buffalo, and two of them (both men) occasionally drifted out to the kitchen to check their loaves. Up to the last minute of the visit, their behavior seemed to me merely pleasant and mildly amusing. But just before I left, I asked for instructions. Then in New York, just two weeks ago, I got up in the morning, arranged my ingredients and utensils, and began the long, pleasing process. My first batch burned slightly, but was edible. The second, which I did last week, was splendid, and I kept taking slices of bread to people all over town. Finally, yesterday here in Misquamicut, I tried again. This new batch is about half-way between the first and the second: that is, it isn't burned, but it is a trifle soggy. Maybe the humidity, the misty air here near the ocean, has something to do with it.

Nevertheless, this baking has given me some simple, old-fashioned joy, and it's made me think of you. Years ago I was sitting glumly in my room in St. Paul, reading a note you had written me about something or other, and you said that you were yourself in the process of making bread. You remarked that it would be nice to have me on the farm at that moment because, as you so beautifully wrote, I understand bread.

It seemed a minor thing for you to write, but it wasn't minor to me. Somehow it gave me a moment of joy and sanity in the midst of the sick chaos in which I was trying to stay alive. Baking bread on my own, after all this time, made me think of you, and I am writing this note to assure you, as far as anything is sure, of my abiding gratitude and friendship.

We will be here at the present address till September 4th. Then we go back to NYC and travel on to Newark, Delaware. This Fall I am to be a visiting professor at the University of Delaware. As soon as the Fall term ends, we've decided to fly immediately to Paris and to spend Christmas in Chartres. We did that once before, and this will be a rare opportunity to spend the holiday in Chartres again, where they have a large choir downstairs and a children's choir way, way up in a very high loft, and also some locals playing ancient country musical instruments.

After Paris, we'll go on to Holland and Belgium, thence to England for a couple of weeks, and then—this took a good deal of discussion and planning—we're going on to Vienna for a little while. That, of course, is my old home town, so to speak, where I fall right in with the populace. We all scamper around trying to look busy in our schlamperisch business-suits, and we all know the general secret: that our shabby briefcases are all full of sausages, cheese, and hard rolls, and we're all on our way to hear music somewhere.

Then we'll go back to Paris, and, from there, drift south, till we get all the way to Apulia, which is the heel of the Italian boot. There are other details and plans, but this is enough to indicate the kind of thing we'll be doing during the eight months. I got a Guggenheim to help us, and Annie and I were both able to take a year's leave of absence.

I haven't mentioned the separation between you and Robert, but I can't not mention it either. All I can say is that it gives me real grief, that I know well how it grieves you, and that I think of you always with a brother's affection. I hope very much that you'll write to us here, to keep in touch. That seems to me awfully important. Meanwhile, please accept our love and hug the children for us.

Love,
Jim

To Leslie Marmon Silko

Newark, Delaware
October 12, 1978

Dear Leslie,

Some years ago—I forget how many—a friend wrote me a note from Chicago. I call him my friend, though at the time I hadn't met him. His note was simple: "I'm so lonely I can't stand it. I don't mean solitude. I need solitude. But loneliness rots the soul." It sounds as if I were just making this up, but I swear that's what he wrote to me, and all he wrote to me. My response will sound improbable and "literary" too, I'm afraid. Nevertheless, it is the simple truth: I immediately wrote to him that I was going to find him in Chicago on the day after Thanksgiving (I wonder what year it was) and that, furthermore, I was going to bring with me two pretty girls and a bunch of bananas.

I did it too. I forget how I did it, but I did it. We spent a long weekend, talking and shooting pool. Then I went back to St. Paul, Minnesota, where I was living at the time.

I've been thinking about his remarks about loneliness and solitude, because I am closer to finding the proper ceremony for my life now. I hope you'll forgive me for appropriating that word "ceremony" but it is a true word, and I need it. My ceremony is to rise early. It is in the early hours that I feel most at home with myself. My wife Annie doesn't rise so early, and I sit for a couple of hours pondering things. During the past week . . . the past four days, I should say . . . I've been spending those hours with your stories and poems. It's curious that I've thought about them throughout the day, and felt eager to return to them the next morning. I've had the poems with me in my briefcase, and even now, when I'm in my office and pondering what I'm going to say to my students this afternoon and how I'm going to try to listen to them, I've just gone through *Laguna Woman* yet again. It is curious how such a brief book has such enormous space in it, a space full of echoes and voices.

Of course your long letter gave me the same sense of something inexhaustible and refreshing. It made me happy, not only because of the story about the rooster, but because the very prose of the letter embodied, with its clarity and speed and force, that same spirit that moved with such ease and great strength through *Ceremony*, the novel. I think the word I am looking for is "abundance." You are abundant. I don't mean cluttered or overgrown. Abundant, rather, as the seasons themselves are abundant. Again, I may be sounding "literary" and that would be a pity, because I am trying to find words here for something that is very real for me. I am extremely glad, and, in a way, *relieved*, that you exist.

I once endured a divorce. I mention this, not to tell you the story of my life, which is commonplace and boring, but only to suggest that I can understand how bruised, even shattered, you have felt. And the poems make it clear how deep and painful the bruises are. Well, as you say, we must persist, and take heart. As you wrote with something like absolute finality in "Storyteller," it is essential that the story be told, and that someone go on telling it. I don't think it's mere flattery to tell you that no living writer known to me so deeply grasps that truth, and its significance, as you do. I know I need that truth, and your clarification of it, and I am very far from being the only one.

It makes me feel slightly formal to tell you that I am from Ohio. My family goes very far and very deep back into Ohio and West Virginia.

Let me tell you what is up here. I am here at Delaware as a visiting professor for the Fall semester. Annie and I hope to be in Paris before Christmas, and we want to spend that holiday in Chartres. Then we will be in Europe for eight months, much of the time in beloved Italy, in Apulia. As soon as we type up our itinerary, I'll send it to you, and I hope we can continue to keep in touch, even during the wanderings.

Please write when you can, even briefly.

When you refer in your poems to "Mei" is she by chance the Chinese-American girl who was also out in Michigan? If so, I've met her again, at Galway Kinnell's house. She is a fine person indeed, and also a beautiful poet.

You've sent me back to my own notebook, and I had a slow and lovely time this morning with a short poem. It takes me forever to get anything done, but sometimes I do.

With friendship always,
Jim

To Marshall Wright

Newark, Delaware
October 23, 1978

Dear Marshall,

Since your telephone call last Friday evening, I have done a great deal of thinking. I decided to write you this note. I want to ask you something very simple. It means very much to me, as you do.

I want to ask if you will simply write me a note, so that we can be in touch with each other again. Your words on the telephone made it clear that you are trying very hard to make sense out of your own life. I now realize that you are trying your best, and that you are *not* trying to suffocate anybody.

But you must remember that I had not heard from you, either by telephone or by letter, for more than *a year and a half.* During all that long time I had not forgotten you. Far from it. I thought about you constantly, and I always asked your mother for news of you.

There is a lot of confusion and misunderstanding between us, and I am asking you please to help me remove these things. Whether you believe it or not, I do know that you are desperately unhappy and are struggling to do your best. On the phone, you said that you found it difficult to make anyone understand and help you. I want to try. Will you let me. The world is a very confusing and painful place sometimes, I know. But maybe we can help each other in some way. No matter what has happened or what is happening now, you remain my son, and I love you.

I pray that you will write. Annie and I are going back to Europe in late December, and we are flying straight to Paris, our old happy haunting ground.

Annie sends her love, as always.

Love,
Dad

To Roger Jones

Newark, Delaware
November 6, 1978

Dear Mr. Jones,

Thank you for writing to me. I'm sorry to be late in replying. Your letter had to be forwarded to me here, where I am a visiting professor this semester. Also, I just returned from a trip of several days in Philadelphia.

I would like to help you in your work, but I am afraid that I am nearly as much at a loss as you seem to be. I have been hearing the phrase about "Deep Imagery" for years now, and I still do not have the faintest notion what it means. The poet Robert Kelly, who still teaches at Bard College I believe, has written extensively about this matter. As for "surrealism," I suggest that you might best deal with it, or at least begin to deal with it, in historical terms. For this purpose, you might consult the excellent, moving book *Exile's Return* by Malcolm Cowley; and the paperback volume *Poet in New York*, by Federico García Lorca, translated by Ben Belitt and published, I think, by Grove Press.

As for my own work, I am almost certain that what some critics have called "deep imagery" and "surrealism" in it is actually just the confusion that results from bad writing. My intention has always been to be as direct and clear as possible. For example, in the poem which you mention, "Written on a Bus in Central Ohio," you say that the poem "seems a very good piece for the conveying of sensory impression, but is somewhat confusing beyond that." No wonder. There *is* nothing "beyond that."

I would like to recommend to you an essay by Robert Hass on my work. It appeared in the magazine *Ironwood*, edited by Michael Cuddihy in Tucson, Arizona, in the Fall of 1977, I think. Mr. Hass's essay is, in my opinion, far and away the most just and intelligent thing anybody has ever written about my writings, with the exception of Mr. Peter Stitt, who, by the way, is in the English Department at the University of Houston. Good luck to you.

Cordially,
James Wright

To Michael di Capua

Newark, Delaware
November 8, 1978

Dear Michael,

I think the jacket copy is fine except for one little thing. Although Peter Stitt's comments are nice, they sound somehow almost comic to me. When I read the line, "have we any right to this new one?" my impulse is to snicker. And consider his remark, "The conclusion is inescapable." I can easily imagine a snotty reviewer commenting, "I find the conclusion escapable." I know of reviewers who would give their lives (sic) for such an opportunity. But you must do as you think best.

Life goes all right here. Last Saturday evening I spoke at the Walt Whitman International Poetry Center. By the way, on Tuesday evening, November 28, at 7:30 p.m., I am going to speak at the Guggenheim Museum in New York, and I am fairly well decided to read all new work. I hope you can come.

Michael, I've been thinking, among other things, about possibly putting together a little book of my occasional essays. You and I have discussed this once or twice. I could work on the idea while Annie and I are in Europe, but it wouldn't take too much time to put a manuscript together after we return in the Fall of 1979. I have fairly long pieces on Whitman, Hardy, Dickens, Storm; some shorter pieces about Hugo, Ignatow, Trakl, and Vallejo; a substantial piece about the poetry of David Schubert, which I gave as a lecture here at Delaware on October 17th, and which is now being typed for me; and a sermon; and about forty pages of various prose pieces which were published in William Heyen's anthology, *American Poets in 1976*. There are some other things, too. All of these, or some of them, might make a book. Then, they might not. What do you think?

Annie sends her best, as always.

Love,
Jim

To Robert Bly

Dear Robert,

It's early in the morning on the last day of the year. Chill rain is falling all over Paris, where I'm sitting on the ninth floor of an apartment building way over from the river, on the other side of the Luxembourg Gardens (by the way, in those gardens Rilke found the little carousel, and wrote the poem about it: "Und dann und wann ein weisser Elephant"). We're going to stay in this apartment for a few days yet, before we go south to Nice, to visit for a little while with the Kinnells. This Paris apartment belongs to Dr. Robert Higgins and his wife (he's thoroughly Parisian, though his distant family background is Irish). We hadn't really expected to stay here, and were fairly comfortable at a new (to us) hotel called the Recamier, a nice place to keep in mind: it's a small place, reasonable, right in one corner of Place Saint Sulpice. But when we got in touch with the Higginses, they and their three daughters were just about to leave the city for a small vacation, and they invited us to stay for a week at their apartment . . . We came to see them not only to greet them but also to deliver to Dr. Higgins a large bag full of books which he needed and hadn't been able to find in France. It's the matter of books that prompts me to write you this morning. While I was teaching at the University of Delaware this last Fall, I learned that Arthur's wonderful *Life of Po Chü-i* is in print again, after many years. In fact, one of my students at Delaware brought it to me. Now, my friend Herman Chessid in New York has a small concern in which he distributes books published in Ireland, and is alert to new things in print. When I told him of the Waley book, he agreed to find it for me. It had only just arrived a day or so before Annie and I left New York on Dec. 22nd. So Herman and his wife suggested that they send the book on to you in my name, and I trust they've done so. It's a Christmas present . . . I think it is distressing that you and I have sort of lost touch with each other. I've kept in touch with your work: I read the two magnificent new poems of yours in *The Georgia Review,* and another of my Delaware students brought me a copy of the *East/ West* magazine, that had the interview and article about you, and the lovely photograph of you and Noah. I hope you are well, and I wish very much you would write to me c/o Poste Restante, Toulouse, France.

Love,
Jim

To Betsy Fogelman

Cheltenham, England
February 13, 1979

My dear Bets,

I am sitting at the top of the stairs on the third floor of a tall house. Through the large window at my left, rising out of the hedges still remarkably green, a great bare sycamore is just visible—no, it nearly vanishes sometimes and then a moment later, as now, it emerges— among the thick snow flurries that actually seem trying to enclose the entire town of Cheltenham, here in the midlands of England. I want to be with you for a little while. And then we are going to walk out, in spite of the snow, to explore this lovely place a little more deeply than we could do yesterday.

Cheltenham is a little to the northwest of London, and yet it is already in the so-called midlands. It took us less than three hours to come here by bus from London two days ago. You have been in London, haven't you? If so, you know it is a great city, and to me, at any rate, it is menacing in its hysteria that fills the faces of the punk-rockers who seem to reproduce brutally by setting their eggs among the sweltering crevices of the city—there is to me something sweltering about London, something pallid and extravagantly fleshy and sagging and perspiring, even in the bleakest dryness and cold, like the back of Richard M. Nixon's neck by night in a desert, tossing his moon-shadows like spittle to the mutant crocodiles of the sand. And yet London is a solid city, in spite of the broken images it evokes in the mind of a wanderer like myself. There is a grandeur there, an impersonal power of endurance that is somehow comforting beneath the rot, the power that consoles me sometimes in those great layers of rock-spur you can find jutting up from the glades in Central Park in NYC.

But the countryside of the midlands is also comforting and, though immensely old, somehow to me always old, older than Italy even, graceful. The snow is gracefully enclosing us here. But we will walk through it in a little while.

Dear, I've written the Paris address on the outside of this envelope, although we will be in Holland next Monday. After our ten days or so in Holland and Belgium, we will take a train back to Paris, stay there for a week to care for some business, and then travel by train all the way to Italy, to Verona the beloved city, my holy city, the city of all cities that finally I love the best [. . .]

We are staying with Annie's old (best) friend Mrs. Sheila Ráshed.

Please write.

Jim

Amsterdam

February 25, 1979

My dear Bets,

I'd been thinking of sending you a postcard today. There is one in particular I want you to see. But I am sitting alone in our room at the excellent Hotel Hestia, and Annie has gone for a walk. She has the cards in her purse.

The postcard contains a photograph of a sculpture by the modern Dutch artist Pieter D'Hoont. I have seen some other work by him, and they are so exquisite in their craftsmanship that I will want to see more. But this particular one is more than beautiful. It is the form of a girl—thin, narrow-shouldered, a little gangly, her slender hands held just a little in front of her, her face somewhat bony and yet amazingly clear (you know, dear, not many faces, not many human faces, are clear, the way, say, a fox's face is clear, or the face of a mallard duck, or a chick-adee at that moment of its most irresistible curiosity). The girl in the statue seems the very spiritual essence of defenselessness, of vulnerability. And yet, there is something about her, something simple and direct, something that is really not very interested in the force of bullies and guns and treacherous people, something—call it just something else. I hesitate to name it, but it has been sort of humming in me all day. Just a little while ago I took a short nap, and I dreamed about it.

The statue is the memorial to Anne Frank.

Her house is over on the other side of the city from us, near the great West Church. It is along a canal. You enter and mount stairs that are even steeper than the Dutch stairs usually are, and halfway up these you open a little door to a young man who tells you where to go. You mount further, turn right, go through a small hallway and room, and you come to the sturdy bookcase, the famous bookcase that served as a concealed door leading on up and into the back of the house, to the rooms where for years Anne and her parents and sister and Mr. Daan the dentist and his wife sat still, very still, all day, and were able to move about a little in silence during the night.

One of the rooms is devoted to a startlingly detailed account, in text and photographs, of the entire Nazi party, its history, its invasions, its . . . oh, dear. It is truly appalling to read, but one can't force himself away from it. And, the mind full of horror, one walks then through the little room where Anne slept with Mr. and Mrs. Daan, and where she pasted all sorts of 14-year-old's fancies on the wall: newspaper cutouts of Deanna Durbin, Ginger Rogers, and the like. I'm running out of space.

Love,
Jim

To George Lynes*

Brussels
March 2, 1979

Dear George,

Toward the end of the 16th century, some nut tried to blow up—or set on fire—the town hall in Brussels, and some bareassed little bastard pissed on the wick and so saved the building. The community were so delighted, they erected this bronze statue to their fellow citizen.

That's the claim here, anyway; and I'll believe it till a better lie comes along.

Love,
James Wright

*This note is on the back of a postcard featuring the *Manneken-Pis*.

To Roger Hecht

Paris

March 7, 1979

Dear Roger,

We just arrived in Paris a couple of days ago and learned, through the mail, of your mother's death. You know very well how much Annie and I liked her, and I don't have to go into detail about the friendship that both of your parents showed me so unfailingly through the years.

I take it that you yourself are all right. (I.e., are you?) Bizarre as it may sound at this distance, if you need anything that we can possibly supply, please let us know.

In addition to those four paintings by Vermeer that I mentioned to you in the postcard from Amsterdam, I think the most remarkable thing that I personally saw in the city was the old house where Rembrandt lived. Of course he is famous for his oil paintings, etc., etc., but personally I am most struck by his drawings, the prints and the ink sketches. The number and range of these displayed beautifully in the Rembrandt House is almost appalling. I wonder if any other human being has ever seen things and places and people quite so clearly and drawn them with such accuracy. He has a little drawing of a professional rat-catcher dickering for a possible job with a rather dubious householder, and as you look at the drawing you start to feel that you can nearly smell them, all of them. And the whole thing is done with the purest simplicity.

By the way, speaking of simplicity and purity, did you get that earlier postcard in which I told you that the 100 meter dash in the Asian Games this year was won by a certain Sichart Jaessuraparp? His name sounds like a 40's tune played by a provincial dance-band in a novel by Kingsley Amis.

Among other things, I have been reading some stories by a new man named Raymond Chandler. He is fine. His hoodlums are always telling policemen to go climb their thumbs. I am charmed by the prospect.

Nobody we've talked to in England and France seems to have any idea about whether or not Carter has any idea. Neither do we. Do you?

On Monday we will be in Verona; and then we'll stop in Florence on the way to Rome. Annie sends her love.

Best always,

Jim

To Donald Hall

Dear Don,

I am sitting at a small wooden table in the corner of our tiny and yet curiously comfortable room at the Hôtel Recamier. It is truly a jewel of a hotel, in its physical arrangements, its management, and its location. The address here is 3/bis Place Saint Sulpice; and if and when you and Jane come to Paris, I recommend that you write them a card and try to stay here. The hotel is tucked charmingly and quietly into one corner of the great square in front of Saint Sulpice, an immense, awkward, twin-towered church, whose stones are the color of pure bees' honey in the spring sunlight. Just inside the front entrance, to the right, there are two huge frescoes by Delacroix, and to me the great one is the picture of Jacob wrestling with the angel. The church as I say seems somehow awkward, but it must have been constructed with some care, because the acoustics are totally marvelous. Marcel Dupré was the organist there for some years. Most wonderful of all, Mozart came there when he was six or seven years old and played the organ. And for Marie Antoinette, for heaven's sake.

Your fine letter was here when we returned from our fairly brief journey to Holland and Belgium, places that Annie had visited some time ago but that were new to me. Surely you must have been some time in Amsterdam, where the houses, strangely and delicately beautiful in their clean variety, reach up floor after floor, very skinny (is there an adverb for "skinny"? "Skinnily" sounds funny.), and the winding stairways of all buildings coil up very steeply, like ways clinging to the bulkheads of ships. I was astonished to realize the originality, the enormous intelligence, the wit and genuine stylishness of the Dutch. It makes me feel like a fool to realize that I had always imagined them, without thinking about it, as running around in wooden shoes, dusting everything in sight, and being dumb. They are probably the brightest single group of people I've ever met. We found the little square of alms houses in Amsterdam where the English pilgrims were welcomed during their long flight to America. How strange. The place took me startlingly back to my childhood and the shocking realization that some of that childhood was beautiful . . . I was very happy to hear the news about Robert. We go to Verona next and then Rome. Please write.

Love,

Jim

To Leslie Marmon Silko

Verona

March 14, 1979

Dear Leslie,

The small city of Bruges in Belgium is off by itself, away from Brussels, still some miles from the sea. Centuries ago, Bruges was a seaport. But remember that Belgium is one of the low countries, the Netherlands, and the sea has long since been silted up and over and back, till now there are only long winding canals. We arrived at the station in Bruges on a rainy afternoon a couple of weeks ago. It was strange to walk away from the station toward the town, for a heavy mist involved everything, and only a dim tower or two would reveal part of itself from time to time as the mist parted. We turned a corner at the end of a long street where the old low houses began to recede into the mist, and we came to a small bridge with a huge canal beneath it. It was still winter, but the warmth was beginning to stir things up. On a big slab of ice that was melting about halfway across the canal, a large flock of birds—mallards, moorhens or something that looked like them, and two swans—were in conversation.

The mist rose a little while after we were settled at the hotel in the town square. And so I found Bruges, a revelation. Among the low houses, with the delicacy of their roofs and gables, there are an astonishing number of towers, some of churches, others of municipal buildings. And everywhere there are bells, from the deep-throated bell of the church of St. Salvator to the carillons of the great tower of the city hall. You must imagine what it would sound like, the one hundred and thirty-five small bells of the great carillon all ringing out together, the musicians inside providing intricate patterns like those of a fine organist improvising, and the notes filling the air of the entire town.

As we strolled slowly, as we always do, morning and afternoon and very late evening through the narrow and exquisitely beautiful streets, we found some shops where lace was for sale. Among several places in northern Europe where the weaving of lace is still practiced as an old traditional art, Bruges is one of the finest. Sometimes I wonder about things like lace, things that human beings make with their own hands, things that aren't much help as shelter from the elements or against war and other kinds of brutality. Lace was obviously no help to the Belgians during two horrifying invasions in this century. Nevertheless, the art continues to survive, the craftsmen weaving away with the finest precision over their woofs and spools.

I found some nice examples of this lace and I have one for you. It is enclosed. Happy birthday from Annie and me.

Though most of this letter is about Bruges, we are right now in Verona, Italy, where a couple of days ago I received your beautiful— and very sad—letter. Of course I never saw your rooster, and he never had a chance to jump me, but I can share your feelings for him, and for the small white hens. What you wrote about the improbability of loving this fierce little creature struck me very deep, because your words are so close to a passage in Spinoza's *Ethics*. The passage has given me some pain, but finally it is heartening and bracing, because it is, in my own view, the clearest statement of the plain truth that I know. Spinoza says that the human being is a miraculous creature, and his miracle consists in his capacity for love. He can love anything, from an atom all the way to God. But it is just here, says Spinoza, that the tragic difficulty arises. For man must realize that his capacity for love gives him no right to de- mand that anyone love him in return. Not anyone. Not even God. I have found that a hard thing to face, but there is something in it that goes beyond pain. Frost wrote, "it must be I want life to go on living."

I'm happy that you'll be in Seattle for a little while. Up there in the English Department you might say hello for me to old friends I made when I studied there: David Wagoner, Jack Leahy, David Fowler, Wayne Burns, William Matchett . . . any number of fine people.

Leslie, we'll be in Verona for a couple of weeks yet, and then we go to Florence for a week (where, if you have time, you might write me c/o Poste Restante). But you sound busy, and Rome will probably be best. Take care of yourself, and have good journeys.

Love,
Jim

To Hayden Carruth

Rome
April 3, 1979

Dear Hayden,

A couple of weeks ago, when we were still in Verona, I wrote and told you that I'd probably send you a couple of new poems when we got to Florence. But somehow I never got down to it there, the city was so beautiful and, somehow, unwieldy.

Rome is another matter. When I first came to Rome years ago, it shocked and angered me at first, mainly because of its occasional horrible noise and the madness of its traffic. But even during that first visit I came to like the city, because of the discovery I made about it and that certainly a great many people have made before: that, in spite of its summer noise, one is forever stumbling on weirdly silent places, some of them so old as to be beyond the counting of years and even centuries. Yet these quiet places are, some of them, abruptly close in distance to the noise. The garden of the vestal virgins, down in the Forum, can't be more than a few hundred yards from the wide street curves of the Piazza Venezia, that big grandiose place just at the foot of the Capitoline, where Mussiloni used to step out on his balcony and put his lower lip out to the shuddering stars, and where once—so help me God, I am not making this up—I got goosed by some psychotic Roman driver in a Fiat. (It was a discreet and gentle goose, as gooses go, but it still startles me. I felt as though Roosevelt Grier or Bronko Nagurski had just stepped in my face on a football field and then came over and given me a big wet smacking kiss.) But the odd placing of silences and noise in Rome gives me now the sense of very ancient time in immediate touch with the present, and that sense is a relief to me, because, as you know, I really don't like the present age very much, to put it mildly.

Right now, Rome is in full blossom for Spring, the city's best season. In spite of everything, it is an amazingly youthful place . . . I was so pleased to hear that your medicine is working and that, as I said in that note I sent from Verona, your reading in New York went so well. The poems of yours that I read, out of *From Snow and Rock, from Chaos*, do go extremely well when read aloud.

Today is the third of April, and I hope that Spring is decently arriving in Vermont.

The two poems I'm enclosing: one, you see, is about being up at the Kinnells' in the morning dark; and the other is about Ohio. May I ask what you think of them? And, if you are still working at *Harper's*, may I submit these poems to you? Of course, you will judge them as harshly as necessary. That is why I'm sending them to you, in addition to wanting just to share them.

Mail being what it is, it probably wouldn't do much good to write me in Rome. So will you please write to me c/o Fermo Posta, Taranto, Italy?

By the way, I forgot to tell you that we didn't get to Uzes, but we heard a lot about it and are determined to go there some day. We both loved Nîmes and Arles, which we did visit and have stayed in before.

Annie sends her best.

Love,
Jim

To Roland Flint

Rome
April 4, 1979

Dear Roland,

We just arrived in Rome a couple of days ago, and your new book and letter of joy were waiting for us at American Express.

And Morning was certainly a fine book. The convention of publishing a first book in one's early twenties is a recent and, I suspect and hope, a brief one, having more to do with the occasional economics of academic and journalistic ambition than with poetry. Jacob Korg long ago observed that, however we may publicly deride and ignore and falsify it in America, poetry is so essential a fact of nature that it remains at the heart of all the great religions. It appears in the voices of Roman children (even the most bewildering and ferocious of them) in exactly the same way and for exactly the same reasons that the violets force their way in March through the walls of Can Grande della Scala's medieval fortifications when neither the Germans nor the Americans could, and as the wild dill plants, with their yellow heads swaying at the tips of long stems like Carthaginian ostriches turned loose in the city, are clambering at this very moment all over the crowns of the ancient arches in the Palatine Hill, not two miles from where I sit. A book of poetry like *And Morning* is in the patient and rewarded tradition of Whitman, Frost, Stevens, and Hardy, who were all in their forties when they let their first books come through.

And now, *Say It* is even better. I had heard and read some of the poems before, and found them memorable. Now I am in a good position to see and hear them as they compose a book; and they so compose a book. The purity of your feeling is beyond question; what matters here is that it is a purity fulfilled in the writing. You have dared to do things in this book that made my hair stand on end. "A Poem Called George, Sometimes" is a thoroughly realized work of art. It's just one of many.

I hope to Christ I haven't made all this sound too stuffy.

Annie and I are both deeply pleased about your marriage to the surpassing Rosalind. We are sorry we couldn't have attended . . . Roland, will you write to us c/o Fermo Posta, Taranto, Italy? We'll be there next, after Naples. Finally, as your senior in age and wintry experience, I must advise you to wear your scarf and galoshes and overcoat, and so forth. Love to Rosalind and the kids.

Jim

To Franz Wright

Rome
April 6, 1979

My dear Franz,

Today I was very happy to receive your excellent letter here in Rome. By the way, your letter was posted in Cleveland on March 28, and that means it took only ten days to get here. I very much hope you'll follow the itinerary that I sent you, and write at our various stops.

You sound pretty cheerful and strong. No, you can't hang yourself if your manuscript is rejected, but it is annoying. The main thing is to get yourself finally in a position where you do not have to think about its publication. This means having a decent publisher and a good editor there with whom you can work.

I look forward to reading the manuscript at leisure, and also the Rilke.

Rome! When first I visited it years ago, I was offended by noise and traffic at first; and when Annie first came here as a girl, she fainted with the sun down at the foot of the Palatine Hill. But we've both discovered the peculiar nature of Rome, its curious juxtaposition of loud noises and silences, which come to stand for the occasional modishness (it is still very much an international city and, as such, a honey-pot that draws the international creepery) and also the extraordinary accumulation of living remnants, fragments still alive from many pasts, not merely the great ancient one. All lovely things are fragile, I guess, and yet Rome reveals some unexpected ways that loveliness sometimes manages to survive. For example, the tortoise fountain. Many people have felt this to be the loveliest fountain in the entire city. It stands in a tiny square at the center of narrow streets and tall buildings, difficult to reach except by walking. Out of its lower basin several exquisitely formed young fauns step upward and balance on their toes, as their slender arms reach up and up until you fear they might fall over; and at the ends of their fingertips you see that they are gently and perilously helping to nudge several small tortoises further up so they can drink the water that spills clearly into the upper basin. Now, just after World War II, a friend of ours saw the figures of this fountain dismantled and scattered on a floor. They were undamaged. And guess who had been in the process of stealing them. Why, it was Goering! Yes, the porcine aesthete fancied shapely young boys, like the fauns, who outlived him.

Love,
Dad

To John Storck

Taranto, Italy
April 25, 1979

Dear Mr. Storck:

Thank you for your letter of March 16. I'm sorry to be late in replying. My wife and I are spending this year in Europe. At the moment, we are in the town of Taranto, in Apulia, and our mail was just forwarded to us here.

We won't be back in New York till the beginning of September, so I'm afraid I won't be able to visit you in Martins Ferry this year.

I want to congratulate you on the ten-year anniversary of your library. The old library meant so much to me when I was a boy. It was there one evening that Miss Katherine Pugh, who taught in the high school in the old days, loaned me her college text of Latin poetry, and I used to sit through many evenings wrestling with the gorgeous and difficult language of Catullus. It haunts me to reflect, for the thousandth time, that I will be spending an entire month at Sirmione (above address), the peninsula on Lake Garda where Catullus used to visit during the summers of his brief life, and where he wrote one of his most beautiful poems: "Paene insularum, Sirmio, insularumque ocelle . . ."

Thank you again for writing to me.

Sincerely,
James Wright

To Elizabeth Willerton Esterly

Taranto
April 27, 1979

Dear Elizabeth,

In the province of Apulia, or Puglia, the small seaport town of Taranto is set in the boot's instep. The old city, the citta vecchia, rests entirely on a tiny island, between two peninsulas. On the one side of the old city flows the bay of Taranto, which is still popularly called the Ionian Sea; and, on the other, a lovely inland water which the Italians call the piccolo mare, the little sea. Just over the little sea I am sitting next to a balcony, and I can lift my eyes and see for miles over the water and across the countryside, where the late afternoon sun is touching with rose the walls and roofs of several towns, some of them level with the plain and others beginning to rise with the rising mountains. From here, the cities in sunlight nearly all look pure white. But the people who live there, most of them, are sure to be dark, and very poor. It is strange that most of the world's southern areas are so struck by poverty. Certainly the poverty of southern Italy is legendary. I have never seen Calabria or Sicily, but Annie has been there, and she tells me that the poverty there is savage. Yet these southern people are themselves surpassingly gentle, and they are being lovely to us during our little while among them.

Not too many miles to the west of us is a small village called Eboli, and rising all around it are the highest and most difficult mountains in Italy, if not all Europe. We paused there for a moment on our train from Naples a few days ago. I mention it because of a book which I pray you will read. It is called *Christ Stopped at Eboli*, by Carlo Levi, and for a long time I have felt that it is one of the four or five greatest books written by anyone in this century. And now a superb movie has been made from it. In Italian it is *Cristo si è fermato a Eboli*, and it stars the great Gian Maria Volonte. We have seen it twice in Italian. You and Henry must see it when it comes to America. And you must certainly read the book.

I am sitting alone in our hotel room for a while. Annie is out walking and shopping. I usually spend a couple of hours at the desk in the afternoons, after an hour or so in the morning. I am getting some work done toward my new book. I must have written 300 pages.

Please write.

Love,
Jim

To Richard Hugo

Taranto
April 27, 1979

Dear Dick,

[. . .] We are in the seaport town of Taranto, on the instep of the Italian boot, in Apulia. It is not as grubby as Hayden Carruth told me it was in 1942 (he says they tried to land at Bari, and missed). It is still poor, though. I don't object to a little grubbiness now and then, however. This brings me to Naples.

At first, of course, the place startled me. Come to think of it, it still does. But after a few days there, something happened that pushed me over the line, and you can now consider me a bona fide lover of Naples. I had gone to our hotel, the Albergo Belvedere—in Vomero, by the way, just near the Hotel Sant' Elmo, where you stayed—in an attempt to take a little nap to gather my resources for our attempt once again to enter the great wild city below us; and somebody upstairs was playing a radio loud with rock music. I lay there a while, cursing my fate at being born a contemporary of Bob Dylan, Bruce Springsteen, The Rhythm Method, The Motherfuckers, and Meat Loaf, when suddenly I heard something so loud that it required a complete reorientation of my nervous system. Maybe it's the way Vesuvius sounded back in the good old days when the whole top half of the mountain blew off.

It turned out to be a wedding party who were having a reception in the restaurant upstairs. They brought their own orchestra with them, including an electric organ. Dear God, I heard speeches, community renderings of old Neapolitan songs, raucous laughter, and what sounded like Wilt Chamberlain dribbling Truman Capote's head downcourt for a dunk-shot.

But I did not hear rock music. The Neapolitan wedding party had destroyed it. You won't believe this, but I swear it's true: I went to sleep. Any town whose inhabitants can drown out rock music can put its shoes under my eardrums any time. I also wrote a poem. Please write to me. How are you?

Love,
Jim

To Jack Wright

Taranto
April 29, 1979

Dear Jack,

We are now in Taranto. We arrived a couple of days ago, and found your splendid card. After Ben Jonson died, he was buried in Westminster Abbey, and I suppose some suitably florid epitaph was contrived for his stone by one of the famous, earth-shaking, muck-a-muck hacks of the day. But some anonymous person snuck in and scrawled on his stone one of the most beautiful phrases of the world: "O rare Ben Jonson." I like to think that some other inspired lover of the arts will do the same in marble for the rare Miss Piggy. For my part, I think she is not only a great artist but also a great moral guide. Consider how graciously she bears her fame. She once observed to Raquel Welch, "Raquel, it is indeed a grave responsibility to be an international sex goddess, and I know you must feel that way, too."

By the way, Miss Piggy is making her way famously, and she has taken Paris by storm. That is only to be expected, of course. There is something French about her. But Annie and I have been unable to understand why we haven't seen any references to her in Italy. I suppose it has something to do with the notorious way the Italians have of catching on to movements of real significance long after everybody else is in the know. For example, in Arezzo a couple of years ago, we heard a great deal of rock-and-roll from the fifties, and the soldiers were trying to sing in English (sic) several old numbers by Johnnie Ray, including "Your Eyes Are the Eyes of a Woman in Love." But once the Italians grasp the deeper currents of history, they become devoted. Miss Piggy will yet give an outdoor dance performance on the hillside of Forte Belvedere in Florence, greet the paparazzi on the steps of the Capitoline in Rome, and distribute free salamis to the worthy orphans in Torri del Benaco.

Taranto is a small seaport town in Apulia. Around the sixth century before Christ, the Spartans from Greece got involved in a war that lasted seventeen years. Somehow, an entire generation of children got themselves born while the Spartans were gone, by some mysterious process known only to the ancients (I have reference to the Acheans). We are here in their city. Please write.

Love,
Jim

To Franz Wright

Lecce, Italy
May 4, 1979

Dear Franz,

I am feeling lazy this late afternoon in Lecce, the city in the south of Italy, here in the center of the Italian boot, where the sandstone walls and roofs of the buildings are more gold than gold, soft as they were in the earth, and damp and dark, and now so full of the years of this sunlight that the city itself seems built out of the sunlight. I have no call to be lazy, though. The weather has been as balmy and mild as anyone could hope for in spring. A critic in England recently (in England, of all places) in a friendly discussion of my books remarked how many English and American writers, heartsick among the ruins of our century and the last, came to Italy looking for the ruins of the past and instead discovered that the natural world is still alive. Last week we took a train to the tiny seaside town of Metaponto, once a wealthy metropolis of some 300,000 colonizing Greeks (they were originally the bastards who had appeared in Sparta after most Spartan men had been gone at war for seventeen years). In search of the Temple of Apollo, and the school of philosophy near it, where Pythagoras taught, we walked for miles through unbelievable masses of wildflowers: scarlet poppies so thick they concealed the green of their own leaves; wild brilliant yellow camomila flowers that look like daisies with aristocratic jaundice; and too many other varieties to count, much less name. It was healing to see and feel the creation still being created there. In the old city of Taranto there is a ragged statue of Leonardo da Vinci (who, by the way, has always struck me as some kind of nut) gazing out to sea; and right out of a hole that the years had worn through his cold face came a lizard, slender and alert and greener than the leaves around him. I was so delighted at the appearance of this lizard at such a time and place, that I wrote a new poem about him.*

At the moment we are in Lecce, and tomorrow we are going even further south, to Otranto, at the tip of the boot's heel, and then over to Gallipoli. Gallipoli: this is still our human century. A while ago in Venice, we met a middle-aged woman whose beloved was shot out of the sky by the Germans. She returns every year, and offers grapes. She offered us some, too. Annie sends love. Will you please write to me in Sirmione?

Love,
Dad

---

*"Wherever Home Is," included in *Above the River*, p. 326.

To Betsy Fogelman

Fano, Italy
May 23, 1979

Dear Bets,

I think I last wrote to you from Taranto, down on the Ionian Sea, about three weeks ago. Since that time we've gone deeper into Apulia, all the way down and over to Otranto. We visited a remarkably large number of cities and towns—Lecce, Otranto, Gallipoli, Maglie, Bari, Barletta, Alberobello, Trani, and Molfetta—and now, as we have a few days left before May 25th, we have decided to come northward a bit early. Right now I am sitting by a window that looks out over the exquisitely pure blue of the Adriatic. The sand is turning rosy and soft as the afternoon slows down. The town is called Fano. We had been here for a couple of days seven years ago, and we are especially grateful to be here again. In what seems to me a world so spiritually battered, so greedy for its own ruin, Fano has somehow so far kept itself alive, kept alive its own sane wish to preserve itself alive. Nature is almost unspoiled here. The sea is as pure as modern seas can go. In a little while we will watch the fishermen put off in the evening, and their lights will be visible again very deep into the horizon. They bring back nearly everything imaginable; and there are little shell creatures, including marvelously whorled snails, alive still on the beach. Very slightly below us to the South are the hills of the Abruzzi, where Horace was born, son of a father who was a freed slave. Here in Fano, and here from behind Fano, the pastures of the farmers run nearly down to the edge of the sea. The hills, very small slopes, are full of poppies, wild chives, and strange pink little bells, and reeds by the small waters where yesterday we saw and heard some frogs singing. As for the town, it is old, old, old as sunlight. The young Caesar Augustus came here and laid road. He was the most intelligent of all the Roman emperors, I think, the most constructive. He built roads and saved, by imperial decree, the manuscript of the *Aeneid*. It is pleasant to think of him visiting Fano, loving the Adriatic as he must have loved it, watching the evening begin as I am watching it now. In a church here there's Guercino's painting of *The Guardian Angel*, that Browning wrote about. It is awful. But there are also three great pieces by Perugino. Please write.

Love,
Jim

To Jack Wright

Sirmione, Italy

June 1, 1979

Dear Jack,

Today is the beginning of June. To my amazement, we have three more months to spend in Europe. I'm happy to have your card, which was waiting for us when we arrived in Sirmione a few days ago.

The old place is unchanged. Really, there's not much room for change. I think I may have sent you a postcard with an aerial photograph of Sirmione, but just in case I'll try to find another one today and send it. It is exactly what Catullus said it was: *paene insularum*, almost an island. It is quite narrow at the place where it joins the mainland via the small town of Colombare, and it goes on widening throughout the length of its skinniness till, at the very end sticking out into the lake, it is quite expansive and wide. Other configurations are curious, and weirdly beautiful. As the land reaches into the lake, it gradually rises. By the time you come to the point, you are high up over the water, on cliffs filled with an olive grove that has been here forever. The grove shares all space up there with the huge villa that Catullus evidently visited during the summer, to rest up from his evidently scarifying hell-raising in Rome. The villa is remarkably preserved. It must have been a pleasant dwelling, with its large baths, its living rooms, its halls under the arches still beautifully raised and standing and opening so you can look out from the cliff side and see the modest towns, whole, along the far shore. Last evening the light on all sides was hazy and darkening. The lake had shaken itself (I hadn't heard that expression before; it's Italian) and released, very quietly, whole masses and clouds of algae and strange plants from the deep places. The water was still, the air unmoving, so that even the swallows had difficulty staying aloft when they came out in the twilight to catch midges and then (D. H. Lawrence's phrase) to change the guard with the bats. But suddenly a tremendous gust came from the mountains and churned up the lake into whitecaps. It shook our building and even chased the swallows back to their nests. After dinner we walked over to the other side of the peninsula, not more than two hundred yards away, and I'll be damned! The water and air over there were still perfectly calm, unmoving. We could hear the mountain wind still blowing behind us, and in front of us everything was calm. It didn't even rain. But this morning the water is pure blue. The lake cleansed itself, and the wind cleaned up after it.

I'm glad you heard from Franz, and I wish he'd write to me. Please write again soon. Best to Elizabeth from Annie and me.

Love,
Jim

To Gibbons and Kay Ruark

Sirmione
June 6, 1979

Dear Kay and Gib,

Of all things, Sirmione has turned gray this morning. Ordinarily legendary in its sunlight, the entire lake cleared itself of haze last evening. It rained like hell, several days after the great wind from the Alto Adige blew across the water and cleared away the algae that the lake had been releasing. The result is strange. The air is clearer on the gray day than it was when the sun was shining.

I'm happy to hear about the good poetry readings. I'm sorry to have missed hearing X. J. Kennedy. I have a complicated admiration for him. He seems to me not only a superb poet but also a sane man. One evening in New York a few years ago I heard him and Keith Waldrup and their wives present (at the YMHA) An Evening of Bad Verse. Among other things, they sang some very ripe 19th Century temperance songs, in four-part harmony. "The Filthy Old Beer Bucket" in particular clings to the mind. One fine touch came in the printed program itself. X. J. Kennedy wrote his own blurb. It said, "A subtle, odious and, I daresay, beautiful performance." I got to say hello to him briefly during the reception afterwards. Unfortunately, that's the only time I've ever met him in person. Once I had asked the people at the YMHA if Kennedy would join me in a reading there. But on the day in question, I got seriously ill, so I missed him. I still hope to talk with him some time. I have some songs for his delectation.

I am in a lull for the moment here in Sirmione. But for the past ten days or so I have been surveying my thick notebooks and rewriting some things. I have been mainly working more recently on prose, and that is what I hope to resume shortly.

I hate to tell you this, but we were unsuccessfully mugged in Bari. All of Apulia was beautiful and gentle except that city, which is uglier and more menacing than New York and Chicago combined. One evening as we were going to eat, a vicious little son of a bitch darted out from behind a car, knocked Annie down, tried and failed to snatch her purse, leaped on the back of another bastard's motorcycle, and escaped. If a malign fate ever takes me to Bari again, I will go armed.

Love,
Jim

P.S. I'm sorry to end on a morbid note. We're having a lovely time everywhere else. Please write. —J.

To Robert Bly

Sirmione
June 8, 1979

Dear Robert,

[. . .] Don Hall just sent me your address, and I have been sitting here for a long time this morning, thinking about you. "Here" is actually the small town of Sirmione, the green peninsula way out in the lake of Garda where Catullus used to come in the summer [. . .]

Two old friends, teachers from New Zealand, have come here to spend a few days with us before they go back around the world. Annie has taken a long walk with them down along the water, and I have a chance to be alone for several hours. I mention this because I've come to realize how truly terrified I was of solitude, though I needed it so badly. But now it's been a long, long time since I've had even a hint of alcohol inside my body. I don't want to over-analyze my own feelings about sobriety to a fare-thee-well. Many people in AA have tried to help me to understand that such nervous self-analysis, for a drunk, will lead him back to drinking. I suppose one reason for this is that an authentic drunk has a truly frightening capacity to find an excuse for a drink. But the nervous self-analysis is like picking a scab, I guess. The thing to do is to learn how to trust life to live, and, when it is wounded, to let it heal itself. But the soberer I become, the easier it is to sit for hours in solitude, and I find myself less and less afraid. All sorts of forces come and reveal themselves, and they are lovely, peaceful ones sometimes. Come to think of it, maybe those were the ones I was afraid of.

I was thinking of you this morning, understanding once again that you have always had the great gift of solitude. So I wrote something for you, called "A True Voice." I think I will send it to you with this letter, with another piece that I wrote down in Otranto. Otranto is way down in the area of Italy called Apulia, or Puglia, which is the heel of the Italian boot. Otranto is a tiny white sea town built at about the place where the boot would have a spur on it. The town is strange. All the buildings are white, or near white, and they seem to keep the sunlight even late at night. The shores there are very wild. This is where the poet Parotti believes Virgil wanted Aeneas and his shipmates to land in Italy. Well, I'm sending you the piece about the limpet, also.*

Don also told me that you are putting together a book of your prose pieces. What will this consist of? Will it be essays, or interviews, or both? Don says he himself is trying to put together a book of interviews and essays by various people about poetry, and he asked me if I had anything. I don't know. I've only given two interviews of any length, and one of them, the one in the *Paris Review*, is a ridiculous mess. It was a long time ago. I talked with Peter Stitt for two days or more, and, needless to say, I was drunk the whole time. I looked at that interview after I'd been in AA for a while, and it amazed me that somebody didn't try to get me into a drying-out hospital immediately. Anyway, that interview is worthless. But I did one other that might do. Last Fall we went down to New Orleans where I spoke at Loyola University for a nice man, a former student of mine named Bruce Henricksen. I hadn't anticipated an interview, but he taped several remarks of a conversation, and now it is supposed to appear in print in their school magazine. The transcript didn't look half bad, to tell the truth. At least I was sober, and my mind was clear. In that interview I also got to say something about things besides the "technique of poetry" (for heaven's sake!). I talked about the books of Ortega y Gasset and about the educational ideas of the Reverend Jesse Jackson.

Speaking of interviews, did you ever get straightened out that interview you did for the *New York Quarterly*, the one that the editor mangled and ruptured without your permission? I remember your saying

---

*"A True Voice" and "The Limpet in Otranto" are included in *Above the River*, pp. 334 and 332.

that you worked very hard on it and succeeded in saying what you wanted to say, but that he spoiled it and that then for some reason you couldn't print your own version. What happened? Are you going to put it in your book?

It is lovely here now. Catullus says that the lake here can laugh aloud. And the Italians still say that the lake can *work itself*. One afternoon it released algae from the bottom and the water was covered. Then in the evening a big wind came from the mountains, and blew all the algae away, leaving the lake clear. It is a strange place. Please write to me.

Love,
Jim

To Janice Thurn

Sirmione
June 8, 1979

Dear Janice,

[. . .] We are still in Sirmione. This peninsula is full of song-birds who, after all these thousands of years, seem scarcely able to believe their good luck in their home. They can't get over it. Even the most irrepressible musicians among birds in other places seem to have their appropriate times for singing, like the robins and the thrushes in central Ohio that fairly explode just at the moment of daybreak. But the birds in Sirmione sing all the time. You can walk all the way up to the big olive grove on the cliff at the tip of the peninsula when everybody in his right mind, like the lizards, is taking a siesta, and the finches and swallows and sparrows go right on singing, intricate and recognizable tunes that even manage some counterpoint. They sing together and they sing alone. I've never heard anything quite like it. They even sing indecently in their sleep. It's possible, of course, that they're drunk. Or maybe it's because they're Italian. In Sicily there's a folk song in which a shark is singing. Some fishermen have caught his mate, and his song is very Sicilian, a curse joined with a heartbroken lament. I do not want some damned Germanic musicologist telling me that the shark is just a figure of speech. I believe the shark actually sang, and some illiterate Sicilian plagiarized the song before it hit the ground. (I mean the water.)

I think I told you on a postcard that I finally received, here in

Sirmione, the letter that you sent earlier to Rome. It was forwarded here. I admire the poem "And All That Surrounds It" that you enclosed. I've meant to ask you, Janice: do you keep a daily notebook? It is fun, and it's a relief. I write at least a single complete sentence in mine every single day. It is amazing how they grow by themselves. My European notebook for this year (since January) now has exactly 325 pages in it.

I'm thinking this morning of you, and your story-children, and your summer. I hope you are well and happy. Please write.

Love,
Jim

To Dr. Thomas Hodge

Sirmione
June 8, 1979

Dear Tom,

At the moment, this early evening, I'm sitting by the window of an old hotel, looking out over Lake Garda. The building is located about halfway out the long green peninsula called Sirmione. I wonder if you remember a little poem printed toward the back of Miss Sheriff's old beginner's text in Latin. It begins, *"Paene insularum, Sirmio, insularumque / Ocelle . . ."* (Almost an island, Sirmio, eye of islands). The lines are by the ancient Roman Catullus. He used to come to this place in the summer, to visit friends at the villa whose ruins lie in an olive grove on a cliff way up at the tip of the peninsula, to rest there, no doubt (if his other poems are to be believed) from a strenuous life in Rome.

On May 29, 1974, you posted an envelope that contained a beautiful poem you'd written about the old days in Ohio. I've carried it with me all over the place—oh, many places, all over the world, really—for five years. I've just been sitting here and reading it for the hundredth time, wondering why and how I've never yet written to you. But never mind. The years are awfully heavy, but this evening I feel like shaking them off. I hope you'll receive this note and write to me.

I am here in Europe for the year, with my wife, Annie, a marvelous woman whom you would like. You may know that Liberty (Kardules) and I were divorced in 1962. She's also in California, in Sacramento, remarried, and doing well as a psychiatric nurse. She and I retain the mutual respect of old friendship, and we exchange letters fairly often. Just about a month ago I wrote also to Elizabeth (Willerton) Esterly, from whom I hadn't heard in a very long time. I haven't heard from her yet, and I hope she is all right. I went back to Ohio and visited Miss Sheriff two years ago, just before she died at the age of 90. She was able to see that I dedicated my latest book to her, thank God.

From time to time I've heard about you, about your work as a doctor. I trust that you'll forgive my neglect, and that you'll reply, so that we can keep in touch. I have a lot to tell you.

Love,
Jim

To Sander Zulauf

Sirmione
June 12, 1979

Dear Sandy,

> Here they are at last, burned harsh into color,
> In the city of Pisanello and Stefano
> Who lightly touched the Madonna's hair into wings.
> I can buy this romantical junk for fifty lire
> (not any more, by the way)
> And send vulgarity home. Romeo, Giulietta,
> How do you survive?*

[From Anne Wright:] We are surviving very well ourselves. We've seen wonderful places—Bruges, Nîmes, Amsterdam, the province of Apulia. Now we are on familiar territory at Lake Garda—a stone's throw away from Verona.

We swim, have picnics in the olive grove by Catullus's villa, and James keeps on working. A happy and rewarding time.

Reality looms ahead in September. Ugh.

Love,
Annie and James

*"Written on a Big Cheap Postcard from Verona" is included in *Above the River*, p. 304.

To Leslie Marmon Silko

Sirmione

June 15, 1979

Dear Leslie,

We are still in Sirmione. We leave for Venice in ten days.

Not a morning has passed here without my working steadily, and I hope steadfastly, at this table for several hours. I have been trying to make sense out of this year's European notebook, which has gone way past three hundred pages. I am somewhat taken aback to realize that I have made more or less workable versions of exactly thirty new pieces. At least, I have revised them and copied them into a larger notebook. Now they will have to lie there by themselves for a while until they change. They almost always do. A poem is a very odd duck. It goes through changes—in form and color—when you leave it alone patiently, just as surely as a plant does, or an animal, or any other creature. Have you ever read a book by someone which you *know* has been written too quickly and impatiently and then published too soon? Such books always remind me of tomatoes or oranges that have been picked still green and then squirted full of artificial colors. They look nice on the supermarket shelves, and they taste awful. I remember reading such books and feeling the glands under my chin begin to ache. They made me feel as though I were getting the mumps.

Well, this new work of mine will change in time. Some of it is naturally ripening already. Before long I will send you three new little prose pieces, and see what you think.

The weather here on Lake Garda has been behaving strangely. Early in the morning the mountains around the lake reveal themselves with dreadfully powerful clarity in the air, but then, as often as not, a heat haze obscures them by the afternoon. But last evening—I swear it was nine o'clock and after—we saw a storm, a rain storm, crawl up over and down the side of Monte Baldo, totally cover the town of Bardolino across the lake, and then, right in the midst of the gray rain, reveal a rainbow. A brilliant one, in the rain, right after the sun had long gone down. It is a strange place.

Please write, dear friend. I hope you are well.

Love,

Jim

To Donald Hall

Venice

June 27, 1979

Dear Don,

When I last wrote to you, we were still in Sirmione, Catullus's almost-an-island, but we are in Venice now.

I have spent a while writing in my notebook this morning, trying to say something about this city. Mary McCarthy, in her excellent book, says that D. H. Lawrence did not like Venice, but his entire poem, from which she quotes just a phrase or two, shows a far more complicated response to the city than mere dislike. He calls it a green and slippery city, though there isn't all that much green, unless you consider the slime of algae on those little boat-stairs. I find it exquisitely beautiful, and yet I feel I am getting caught in some kind of conspiracy in which time, the sea, the (surely) unprecedented human brutality of the twentieth century, and human weakness and defeat and failure, and a strange guilefulness all have their share. Venice is in decay, and it has been decaying for a very long time. But what is decaying here is so vital and intelligent that even the processes of decay have a kind of vigor [. . .] The decay of Venice is somehow lovely, a relief, the falling of a city whose place, I can always hope, will be resumed by the sea.

I've met Robert Giroux several times, and I find him a fine person. He also is deeply devoted to literature, and I think this is unusual these days.

As soon as we get back to America, I'll get a copy of the Bruce Henricksen interview for you.

I want to tell you that, to my great pleasure and relief, I just received a superb long letter from Louis Simpson. His wit, his good humor, and his seriousness are as fine as ever. I haven't heard from Robert, though.

Annie and I have been talking about getting up to New Hampshire to visit you in the Fall. When is best for the leaves? We went once to see the Kinnells on Columbus Day weekend, and it was bleak and cold. Love to Jane, and you,

Jim

To Leslie Marmon Silko

Paris
July 29, 1979

Dear Leslie,

Your extraordinarily beautiful letter was waiting when we arrived in Paris on July 22nd, just a week ago today. I haven't been able to attempt a proper answer till now. We arrived to learn that we were five days early. Dr. Higgins had sent us a message in Venice which we never received. However, all has gone well anyway. We quickly changed plans and took a train to Moret-sur-Loing.

It is a small medieval village just south of Paris. The Loing is a little river that runs along limpidly and gently past Moret for some miles down to the town of St. Mammes, where in a sudden strange confluence it joins both the Seine and the Marne at once. The very great and enduring impressionist painter Alfred Sisley lived and worked in Moret for twenty-two years, and the citizens of the town and countryside love their earthly place so much that they have kept it thrillingly alive in its old form. We spent a whole day walking along the canal and the river Loing all the way from Moret to St. Mammes and beyond. Sisley painted the light and color here with such precise love that we could feel his angelic luminous spirit everywhere.

Tell me, Leslie: do you know Sisley and his work? Your writings have such a startling power of light and clarity that you remind me of him. That is, one side of your work reminds me of him. You also have something that he does express so strongly: a sense of darkness and human entanglement.

Though I haven't seen your photographs, I am convinced that you have done precisely the right thing in including them with the stories. What you've done is to create, into a single form, a new thing that grows naturally out of two other forms of experience and expression. You say in your letter, "there were always many stories that accompanied the evenings we spent with the tall Hopi basket full of photographs." Surely this is the heart of the book you've described to me, the imaginative heart of it.

In your final paragraph—about the lizards, the birds and the cactus fruit—I do declare, Leslie, something happens to you when you write with your characteristic warmth: you can sing like a bird. Whatever has happened to disrupt your life and feelings, you sound whole and beautiful.

Love,
Jim

To Ann Sanfedele

Paris
August 4, 1979

Dear Ann,

I received your wonderful letter about your visit to Canada and the musical computer while we were still in Venice. The delay in replying is a long story. I did send you that postcard of the Florentine dwarf again, however. I don't know why I should choose that particular card to send you all the time as a sign of affection, but there it is. It may be that I look exactly like the dwarf, except that his beard is a little fuller and that I have all my fingers—at least I did when I counted them a minute ago. Or maybe I secretly fancy the thought of sitting, nude and elite, on the back of a turtle, comfortably assured that I am one of Cosimo di Medici's favorite cronies. Do you know anything about Cosimo, by the way? He was a remarkable old bastard. He owned a string of banks that stretched all the way from Florence to England and from hell to breakfast and beyond. He invited the theologians from the Eastern Church to Florence so that they could debate about the true church with the Florentines, who insisted, with Cosimo's blessing, that the arguments be carried on in Greek. Cosimo also snared Fra Lippo Lippi from a monastery and trapped him in a room on a high floor to keep him painting and prevent him from getting out and raising cain after curfew on the streets (Lippi got out, though).

The Florentines are still pretty arrogant, but I found out a marvelous fact about them in the past: in 1369 they excommunicated the Pope. Talk about chutzpah.

Our plans got mildly snarled when we arrived in Paris on July 22. We couldn't move into the Higgins's apartment yet, so we managed to take a train to Moret-sur-Loing, an idyllically beautiful town just to the south, where the great impressionist painter Alfred Sisley, whom I love, lived for twenty-two years. We came back to Paris on the 27th, and now we're entertaining some friends from England. You won't believe this, but a couple of evenings ago we carried on a conversation in English, French, Italian, German, and (so help me) Persian. I am practically illiterate in 3 of these. Please write.

Love,
Jim

To Michael Cuddihy

New York City
September 5, 1979

Dear Michael,

Your letter was the first one I opened last evening after Annie and I had arrived by plane from Paris and had something to eat.

I'm enclosing the proofs. I decided not to phone you, because there is only one small error: the sixth line from the end of "Apollo" should have "moon" in lower case. You probably have caught this.

Did you ever find a typo or a printing error to be evocative—or comical—in such a way as to make you want, for just a moment, to keep it as it is? I have a favorite along this line: in the separate printing of the book *Shall We Gather at the River*, the word "whorehouse" appears in one of the poems (I think it's "In Terror of Hospital Bills"). Only the printer for Wesleyan somehow changed it to the gorgeous word "whorsehouse." It made me sad to change it back to the commonplace word I'd written in the first place, but change it I did, because a man would have to be James Joyce to get away with "whorsehouse." A man might stumble on dark magic, but he had better leave it alone unless he is an authentic magician. I sometimes think that the Beats, and other would-be wild men, got it all wrong. They wanted to be lofty and eldritch and magical, so they just threw the language around everywhich-way. Whereas the one thing a real magician has to do is to be very reverent and careful with words. They can be too much for a careless man. I quit while I was breaking even. "Whorsehouse," indeed. I felt like the sorcerer's apprentice the morning after.

I believe I wrote you earlier about the beautiful Italian movie *Christ Stopped at Eboli*, and Annie and I have been waiting for our chance to see *The Tree of Wooden Clogs*. I, too, have heard people object that both of these movies move too slowly, but I believe such an opinion is possibly a reflection of our own general impatience these days. One of the creepiest things I ever saw was a passage in a film where the camera got speeded up to show a flower opening. Of course it goes on, and it's beautiful, but somehow one ought not to look at it directly.

My God, classes begin on the 14th, and we are both far from ready. Keep in touch. Love to you both from Annie and me,

Jim

New York City
September 15, 1979

Dear Michael,

I received your good letter late yesterday afternoon. Now it's Saturday morning, and I'm trying to draw some things together—thoughts, correspondence, some work in my notebook. I'm enthusiastic about your plan to devote an issue to translations by H. R. Hays and to some comment about his work. At the same time, I think it would be wise for me to tell you, however regretfully, that I had better not undertake to write a piece about his work as a translator. One reason is that I am not a linguist as he is, by any means. The range of his work is very wise. But the more important reason for my declining the task is the personal one. My schedule of teaching is going to absorb nearly all of my attention for a good while, especially because we just got back from Europe. I like to teach, but I have been away from it for a long time, and I have got to concentrate on it. The problems in New York City are physical as well as intellectual.

I first came to Hays's work through the influence of Robert Bly, who has always seemed to know just how and where the really original and vital work was and is being done. When Bly showed me Hays's *Twelve Spanish American Poets*, I had never even heard of Vallejo and had scarcely seen anything by Neruda.* Since those days, about twenty years ago, both great poets have virtually become household words in the literary community (sic) of the United States, and yet you still

---

*It was, in fact, Wright who recommended Hays's translations of Neruda and Vallejo to Robert Bly in the letter to Bly dated August 6, 1958.

rarely see even a reference to Hays himself, without whose lonely and pioneering work most people would have gone to our graves without realizing that Vallejo and Neruda belong to our age, and to us, and that they prove how, even in our ghastly century (a peculiar age, characterized by sudden alternations of violence and apathy, even enervation) it is possible for human beings, through stubbornness and imagination and (most of all) courage to face the real world and transform it into its spiritual truth. I call Hays a pioneer, but my remark is misleading, seeming to imply that the significance of his translations is historical only, and to be supplanted by the more elegant or forceful work of the translators who followed him. But what made Hays important in the first place, and what will keep him important, is the fact that he is himself a poet, an artist whose own deepest imaginative impulses have often been wakened by a power of intellect that is at once critical and poetic, the critical enabling him to perceive the greatness of the South American poets and the poetic enabling him to create translations that are at once accurate renderings and also themselves original poems in the American language. Neruda's "Walking Around" is a noble poem in Spanish, and for me Hays's translation of it is equally great in our language.* I have no copy of it, but for years I have had it by heart. Robert Bly also has a translation of this same poem, and it is illuminating to compare his work with that of Hays. Both translations are admirable poems in English. Bly's reveals a delicacy, a close sensitivity to the world that characterizes his own genius in his original work, particularly his poems about nature. Hays's is distinguished by the forcefulness of its rhythm. Perhaps Bly would never have found Neruda's poem if Hays had not pointed it out to him. But Hays did point it out to him, and the result is two superb translations of a single piece. As a good poet, Hays has been able to present accurate translations which are also imaginatively awakening and fertilizing.

Of course, quite beyond the accuracy of his translations and their poetic force in English, Hays has simply drawn our attention to such men as Neruda and Vallejo. To do so is a moral act as well as an artistic one. It is a way of forcing American readers and writers to consider that there is a difficult nobility in poetry which commands, or ought to

---

*"Walking Around" by Pablo Neruda, as translated by H. R. Hays, is included in the Appendix, p. 572.

command, our whole spiritual attention, and that this nobility, by its very existence, is a rebuke to the triviality, the nit-picking, the politicking, and the giggling pseudo-surrealism that threaten to waste and destroy our hope for a serious life. The power of conveying the fact of human nobility through his translations: this power is alone enough to identify Hays as a serious, important man.

Michael, having gone on in this way, I regret my inability to write the essay you ask for.

I must have written to someone else, probably Hayden Carruth, about the film of *Christ Stopped at Eboli*. I hope you can see it.

We did indeed feel strange returning home—we haven't lived in our apartment for more than a year—and we're slowly getting accustomed to the spirit of the place again. I must get on to other work now.

Love,
Jim

To J. R. Salamanca

New York City
November 2, 1979

Dear Professor Salamanca:

It wasn't until yesterday afternoon at Hunter College that I received your kind letter with the copy of Mr. Rod Jellema's new book, *The Lost Faces*.

It is a pleasure to tell you that I find the book a superb piece of work, even finer than *Something Tugging at the Line*, two or three of whose poems are included in the new collection. Somewhat like the master Theodore Roethke, Jellema deals with a central theme, a conditional theme embodied exquisitely in a line from Plotinus: "If only we could see for a moment the holy light we pursue . . ." Jellema proceeds to give glimpses of this light through a set of poems entirely remarkable for the physical pungency of their language, their muscular and sensitive rhythms, their power of creating a particular world in its real time and place. Some of the poems in the new book are positively harrowing in their effectiveness, the truth and depth of their feeling, which, of course, can only be revealed by the most careful, intelligent craftsmanship. Such a poem as "The Work of Our Hands," an attempt to grasp the life of the poet's great-grandfather, can only be called beautiful, a quality as rare in the poetry of our day as in any other.

I want to say a word about Jellema's abilities as a teacher and critic of literature. A few years ago at the University of Maryland, I heard him speak at some length on a fine but very difficult poem by the excellent Richard Wilbur. It was called "Still, Citizen Sparrow." In his exposition of this poem by Wilbur—who, incidentally, must surely possess more sheer brains than any other American author now drawing breath—Jellema revealed himself as a scholar and critic of astonishing lucidity and force. Myself an aging and somewhat battered professor, I want to express my admiration of this poet's powers as critic and teacher.

He is in fact a superb teacher as well as an excellent writer. I recommend him to you most warmly and without reservation.

I honestly appreciate your letting me know about your deadline of November 9. The harassment of time seems the enduring curse of our profession. And at my back I always hear Time's winged classroom hurrying near. I do, however, want to make sure that you receive my present letter in time for it to help you, so I will send it to you by special delivery airmail and hope for the best.

Thank you for giving me the chance to say something about Rod Jellema's fine new book.

Sincerely,
James Wright

To Mary Oliver

New York City
November 5, 1979

Dear Mary,

Please excuse this pompous and official-looking stationery. I'm down at Hunter today, and so you might say I've put on my clucking robes.

I'm writing this note to keep in touch, mainly, and to tell you what you already knew: that I'm happy you listed my name on that Guggenheim form, and that I'm sure I can and will write a strong letter.

I want to tell you how I specially value the *Twelve Moons*. At a glance it looks like free verse, but it sounds like authentic poetry (of course, there's no such thing as free verse—there's just verse and prose). It is, on the whole, your best book. The others are fine, too, but this one is immediate, clear, and positively soaked with life, real life. "Aunt Leaf" has become one of my favorite poems, period.

My wife Annie is also delighted with the book, and has mentioned writing to you about it.

We spent eight months in Europe, and returned to New York early in September. Now, we are both hard at work teaching, and I am still working on something I started in Europe.

I sometimes idly wonder if and when you and I will ever actually meet—though, in a way, we seem to have known each other since childhood.

Please write me when you can.

Love,
Jim

To Robert Mezey

New York City
November 19, 1979

Dear Bob,

Thanks for your card, and the stunning picture of San Gimignano. Hell will probably freeze over before you receive this reply, because you neglected to tell me your zip-code number. For that matter, I don't even have your home address. Will you send it to me? Even if we write each other just short notes, I think it is very bad for us to be out of touch.

How are you?

Annie and I both got sucked into the whirlpool of New York (or is it all of America?) as soon as we got back to the States on September 4th. From that time to this, we've both been working frantically at school and at home—much more desperately than we can remember having ever done before. And most people we know feel the same terrifying harassment from the world these days. It's a strange atmosphere to live in. I have been trying to keep my head by writing each day in my notebook, which has always (when I've kept faith with it) helped me in time of need. Annie and I have together written a little book of prose pieces about our times in France and Italy. Now that that project is about done, I'm working further on a larger prose book of my own, to contain some essays, notes, and probably even some letters (having to do with travel).

I really do admire *Small Song* enormously. In a time when it seems there are at least 500,000 people in the United States writing "verse" (and it's been a long, long, long time since it was socially safe to speak of verse with respect) and each one seems to be publishing at least two books per year, *Small Song* (taken with *Couplets,* which I've been rereading with *Small Song*) has a remarkable depth and wholeness.

The *Hudson Review* is going to publish some new work of mine. Two of the poems are sonnets, and one is a ballade. I feel as if I were about to expose myself to the massed secretariat of the United Nations.

I hear indirectly that Galway is not terribly happy in Hawaii, because he and Ines wanted anyway to be around New York. As for Hawaii itself, I wish I could accept an invitation there for next year, but I can't. It is a lovely place, peaceful, peaceful.

Please write.

Love,
Jim

To Robert Bly

New York City
December 18, 1979

Dear Robert,

I appreciate the lovely note you sent me on the fifteenth of November, and I only wish I were able to reply in the same tone. But we are as close as family, just about, and I have to tell you difficult news.

I have learned that I have cancer. The doctors have explained clearly that it is quite serious but not hopeless. Early in January, Dr. Blaugrund will perform radical surgery on my throat, and he is a good, highly capable man. He is sure that he can save my life. It will take me the entire Spring semester to recuperate. My powers of speech will be affected somewhat, and they think they can save enough to allow me to continue to teach.

Annie and I are otherwise all right, except for being under the strain. We have been telling most people who ask that I am just seriously ill and need an operation.

I haven't yet let Don Hall know, and if you are writing to him soon, would you please tell him?

I'll be glad when the operation's done, because I seem to feel weaker every day. Love to the children, and please do write.

Love,
Jim

To Galway Kinnell

New York City
December 31, 1979

Dear Galway,

I wasn't surprised to get your note, and I think my earlier reluctance to write to you was, of all things, a certain shyness. I had been writing about you in my notebook, about your new poems (the proofs of which I now have, your best and most serious book, I think), and about something I think you and I have always shared, something so deep as to be terribly difficult to welcome into words. How am I ever going to be able to say this? For the truth is there is something terrible, almost unspeakably terrible, in our lives, and it demands respect, and, for some reason that seems to me quite insane, it doesn't hate us. There, you see? Every time I try to write it down it comes out gibberish.

Well, here are my facts: I have a malignant tumor at the base of my tongue. I am having a series of twenty radiation treatments which are to prepare me for surgery toward the end of January. I have been in some pain (of a complex and interesting kind) and nausea, but my various doctors—all of them remarkable men—are tending to me pretty well. The recovery from the operation will be slow and painful and pretty long, but it will not be any worse than what I feel now.

I've been reading Etheridge [Knight]'s new manuscript, and it strikes me with great pleasure that he is such an extraordinarily sophisticated artist. Nobody else going seems to have so much sheer fun with the sound of words in the language.

Please write to me, Galway. We weren't able to come to Hawaii even next Spring because of our complicated professional commitments here. It is a hell of a note, and we will certainly miss being there.

I've been working hard on something, and if it turns out all right, I'll send it to you. Love to Ines and the children and to you from both of us.

Jim

P.S. I haven't yet written to Hayden about my bad news, but I'll try to tomorrow.

Take leave of the sun, and of the wheat, for me.
—Miguel Hernández

Appendix

Including a selection of uncollected poems, translations, and early versions of published work by James Wright referenced in *A Wild Perfection*.

—*Compiled by Jonathan Blunk*

To Keats

Dim eyes, be warm in calm and careful speed,
   And bend your light face softly south, and wave
   Your curly hair in the dissolving lane
Of lessening wind. My ecstasy will bleed,
Will faint and follow, falling down the freed
   Tunnel of sleep of those who found the grave
   A gentle bed which only dreamers have,
A lipless song which only poets read.

I do not want to live forever. I know
   No golden cities shimmering on the wan
   Horizon; but I draw deep breath, and throw
   My arms around white clouds, and chant the slow
Sweet elegy of beauty and pain. The drawn
Pure face I love, that you loved years ago.

Unpublished. See letter to Susan Lamb dated August 7, 1946.

Sonnet—Peace

Paul, wait a moment. I shall not be long,
    Loitering here upon this tuft of grass.
There are not many words left in my song;
    I cannot live on love that never was;
And, anyway, my lips are crumbling,
    My lungs are fading out and turning grey,
And the white strength of flight I thought to fling
    Forever was only a breath, and gasps away.

Paul, you were wiser. Both we loved the sad
    Melancholy of our lives. Yet you chose
        The soft and acheless sleep, and I the birth.
Be patient. I am coming in a glad
    Descent, rapidly as my eyes can close.
        Move over; refuse me not my peace in the earth.

Unpublished. See letter to Susan Lamb dated December 2, 1946.

Ode to Lesbia's Pet Sparrow

—Catullus, 15

Sparrow of my Love's delight,
   Feathered soul of airiest flight
Whom she has blest against her breast
   In warmth, who felt her fingers prest
Surely upon your soft light wing—:

When she will listen as I sing
   The barbèd pain of my desire,
And laugh, as though love's aching fire
   Could never touch her, make her wear
Gem-like one single feminine tear;

Then she will jest as easily
With you as, in my torment, I
Attempt to salve in sleep the smart
Of bruised longing in my heart.

Unpublished. See letter to Elizabeth Willerton dated January 6, 1947.

The Ghost with the Silver Lyre

[After Rainer Maria Rilke, *Frühe Gedichte*]

A child, I sat inside the manor wall,
　　Listening to the call
Of May-bird murmuring of the distant fall.
　　May-blooms turned petals up to garden light,
Like moth tongues licking fire;
　　When far away and strumming out of sight,
I heard feet tapping, and a throbbing lyre.

There was a minstrel bore the lyre to me,
　　And touched the strings with free
Lift of sad fingers trembling audibly.
　　I looked up quickly in a shy surprise:
O mother, let me turn
　　My ears up to his hurting melodies,
The way these petals in the sunlight burn.

But strings inside my breast broke far apart,
　　And could not bear the dart
Of lightning music fired into the heart.
　　I knew as soon as music rose again
My blood would shiver to air;
　　My vein rivers would rush past dams of pain,
And change to vapor in the garden there.

Minstrel, you strike my chords of joy and pain,
　　And break my heart, and then
Sing me my manhood's destiny too soon.
　　I fear the incisive music coming clearly
May well uproot my tendrils,
　　Give my white blooms their furious growth too early,
And chant my death to melancholy timbrels.

And yet he sang. Song and footbeat went fading
   Off into distance, wading
Into the lakes of sunlight westward gliding.
   Only his ghost remained to pluck the strings
Of a remembered lyre
   That sought the caves of my imaginings,
And lit the core of my own ghost with fire.

The pain I never suffered, the distress
   I knew not, happiness
Unreached—all thrummed away from me to peace.
   The ghost of many dead men took my hand,
And off we walked together,
   Leaving spirituous footprints on the land;
The path led through a mist: I knew not wither.

Unpublished. See letter to Susan Lamb dated January 4, 1950.

A Dream of Charles Coffin's Voice

The trees accumulate my darkness now,
As I come back to see the summer stand,
The mounds of his imperfect lawn below,
The slow trees mourning him on either hand.
The moon rides lightly in the hollow sky,
The owls are calm. I cannot hear them cry,
Though other drifters quiver in their fear
Under the grass for whispers they can hear.

If I came in, no one would know me now.
Drowsed in the doorway, struggling to stand,
The husband of the house would look below
My unfamiliar eyes to shake my hand;
The windows gleam beneath the hollow sky,
Puzzled to rattle at my knock; and I,
Careful to offer friendliness, not fear,
Would listen for the voice I cannot hear.

I cannot hear it, though I hearken now,
Lonely among the shadows where I stand.
Earth lies the same as ever, and below
He turns with all beloved change, my hand
Loses his hand beneath the hollow sky.
Shall I speak out to love the stars? Shall I
Ascend his stairs before they disappear?
His voice recalls me, yet I cannot hear.

His mouth of laughter speaks for summer now.
His tall shoulders uplift the vines, or stand
Proud underneath the trees, and, far below
The spires of other vanished roofs, his hand
Points to the new moon in the hollow sky.
He fades, a dream of music now, so I

Walk to his patient trees, absolved of fear
That he might speak and I should fail to hear.

He molds his measure to the silence now.
He joins the movement of the dead who stand
Upright and sing below the earth, below
Visible dark where, fallen out of hand,
Wings of the moon loom in the hollow sky.
We heard him long ago, my friends and I,
Reading aloud of paradise, for fear
We should forget or we should never hear.

Dreaming or wide awake, I listen now:
He chants among the surge and fall and stand
Of Milton groping earthward and below,
Shaping a bitter grandeur with his hand,
Or hurling wings out of the hollow sky.
The proud man with the gentle face and I
Together sang that Fall of outraged fear.
The golden hinges of his voice I hear.

—James A. Wright, '52

As published in the *Kenyon Alumni Bulletin*, Autumn 1956. See letter to Philip Timberlake dated
August 25, 1956.

American Twilights, 1957

1

The buckles glitter, billies lean
Supple and cold as men on walls.
The trusties' faces, yawling green,
Summon up heart, as someone calls
For light, for light! and evening falls.

Checking the cells, the warden piles
Shadow on shadow where he goes
Beyond the catwalk, down the files,
Sneering at one who thumbs his nose.
One weeps, as stupid as a rose.

Tear and tormented snicker and fart
Chime in the vague romantic shade;
Clean locks together mesh and part,
And lonely lifers, foot and head,
Huddle against the bed they made.

2

Lie dark, beloved country, now.
Trouble no dream, so still you lie.
Citizens drawl their dreams away;
Stupored they hid their agony
Deep in the rock; but men must die.

Tall on the earth I would have sung
Heroes of hell, could I have learned
Their names to marvel on my tongue;
The land is dark where they have turned,
And lo their very names are burned.

But buried under trestled rock
The broken thief and killer quake;
Tower by tower and clock by clock
Citizens wind the towns asleep.
God, God have pity when they wake.

Haunted by gallows, peering in dark,
I conjure prisons out of wet
And strangling pillows where I mark
The misery many must not forget
Though I have found no prison yet.

Lo now, the desolation man
Has tossed away like a gnawed bone
Will hunt him where the sea began,
Summon him out of tree and stone,
Damn him, before his dream be gone:—

Seek him behind his bars, to crack
Out the dried kernel of his heart.
God, God have pity when we wake,
Mercy on man who dreamed apart.
God, God have pity on man apart.

Unpublished draft. A revised version appears in *Saint Judas*, 1959. See letter to Donald Hall
dated March 31, 1957.

At the Executed Murderer's Grave

To Kathryn Pratt

What shall we say who have knowledge
Carried to the heart? Shall we take the act
To the grave? Shall we, more hopeful, set up the grave
In the house? The ravenous grave?
                                    —Allen Tate

Bewildering calm, you tangle blade and bone,
Fang, fist, and skull that huddle down alone.
Sparrows above him, gay as young police,
Line-up the lawn, the hedge, the fearful trees.
The fierce blood of the dead lies smitten dumb
Under the vengeance of a lily's bloom,
And I have come to pacify this grave—
Too late: while I and all man's killers live,
Night shall electrocute that fugitive
My mind, who damned the living to the dead
Like one of those forlorn, bewildered mad
Yanked, staring, to the dark, murmuring their lullabies.
The dusk beams down. I cannot lift my eyes.
My shadow flees me over mattocked stone,
And cannot abide me. Father and citizen,
Myself, I killed this man:
For the blind Judges in my heart cried *Stone,*
Stone the murderer down!
So the blind murderer in my heart bowed down;
I flung my stone, and now myself turn stone.
My fear, my justice bleed away, and fade.
The moulting flocks of sunbeam round my head
Mother a brood of dusk, and I am dark.
I peer between the granites for his mark:
Surely the kind earth will console his name,
Cluster his grave with ivy and gentle briar,
The slow forgiving growth
That knows not man, to trouble why man came,
Crested and poised and mournful, out of slime

Slinging his quicklime fire into the eyes
Of his damned, of his dead.
I woo the grass to rise and be the veil
For a man's defeat and shame.
But this grave's festered gash I cannot heal
Till the last day, when my own face turns pale,
Uplifted, on the bone-diamonded shore
Where Nineveh's spendthrift sailors sigh for the bale
Unloosed and ravelling, out of reach, on the swell
Of the last sea, when graves are emptied forth
And the princes of the sea come down
To lay away their robes, to judge the earth
And its dead, and we dead stand undefended everywhere,
And all my bodies—father and child and criminal—
Blanch with the livid scars
Of my poor crimes, under God's pitying stars.
Staring and staring, they will not mark my face
From his, the killer buried in this place
Where the light sparrows flock and laugh in trees.
How can they tell, the stars or sparrows tell,
How, in God's name, that killer's face from mine?
Have we not hallowed life by naming life,
Not shaped the vacant air with the stars' names,
Lucifer, Venus, out of our savage grief,
Out of our stupid shames?
Are we not one with valley, with lawn? are we not vineyard, and hill?
And all the great hills shall melt on the last day,
And lose their wine,
And the hooded stars demand to learn of me
Which of my bodies has not trod the dark
With sneering angels and the innocent snake.
All, all of me must die, whichever fiend I take.
Our lonesome, gutted graves the sea must fill.
We shall stand up to pray for love at last.
One man, one mercy-naked man we are,
One judge, one murderer, one victim there,
Lipless and crying for the heart's release
Till the wind soothes our hands, our burning face.

Killers of killers, we shall be healed at last,
The stars relieve our pitiless wounds at last:

But my grammatical cries provide small time,
Small hope for naked victims dropped in lime.
Far hastier surgeons sewed this pious wound,
This grave of man, and stitches scar the ground.
Doty, the rapist and the murderer,
Rots in a ditch of fire, and cannot hear.
And where, through earth or hell's unholy peace,
The dying flesh goes free, God knows, not I,
Or those gay sparrows laughing through the trees
Or the local stars I cannot even trace
By name or body, as I leave this ground.
But I will weep, by God, before I die,
Into my bitter dungeons without sound,
Though here the county's quicklime tears are dry.

As published in *Poetry* 92, no. 5 (August 1958). A poem with this same title, extensively revised, appears in *Saint Judas* (1959), and is dedicated to James Dickey. See letter to Wayne Burns dated June 19, 1958.

To Wayne Burns: On the Appearance of a New Edition of Swift's Poems

Curse and obscenity I leave
For other men to speak about:
The faint worm on a lady's sleeve,
An enemy's disgusting snout,
The snarl at other enemies,
Amazement at the idiocies
Of sub-animalistic man
Who desolate in the dirt began.

Pedant and fool will still confess
Swift hated us for grubbing swine.
Yet, I observe what loveliness
Of face and footfall, line by line,
He laid away for none to read
Long after Stella's eyes were dead
And crumbling slippers sluffed no more
Over his bumpy sickroom-floor.

But, more reviving still, I found,
Upon his stark and barren page,
Bits of the world that live beyond
His low delight and grieving rage:
The London schoolboys' lagging feet,
Old vendors, singing in the street,
Riddles and mockings, lures and lies,
And turning back to damn your eyes.

Cobbles and dirty mops can free
The angry, straining eyes awhile.
The quick brain wilts in agony
At pride and idiocy and guile;
Yet always, past the towering fools
Who rule the earth, the swollen pools

Of water burst the dammed-up Fleet,
And ditches overflow the street:

Suddenly, freed of love and hate,
This poet sees the fragments, swirled
Beyond his curse, to celebrate
The sheer bulk of the living world.
Shedding his deep and ancient grief
He sings, to my involved relief,
Girls under awnings, soaked and driven,
And smirking thieves still unforgiven.

Therefore, another man may mourn
His lacerated heart for me;
His duns and turnkeys are not torn;
His fops and trollops hardly die.
Beyond both just and merciless
Divisions of this wilderness,
The housemaid and the crook endure;
And, therefore, I lament no more.

Unpublished. See letter to Wayne Burns dated June 19, 1958.

The Trees in Minnesota

to R. L.

I had not seen her before,
In a lifetime of stones and winters.
But I see her now, out of the trees
Her face beckons down to me.
I lift up to her a garland of her leaves,
And I love her.
I am blessed for nothing among the rootlets
Of this darkness.

At Fort Lewis, Washington,
Twelve years ago, when I was eighteen,
We fired all day long at practice targets
And wounded one of our own men.
When I ran to help him,
I saw a whole gray earth
Opening in a vein of his cry:
From full green to emptiness,
A mile's field of dead fir stumps
High as the level of adolescent waists,
Low as a man's knees.
We had mown a grove down.
I was one of the State's gardeners.

Autumn of Minneapolis,
You plough my grass, and my roof
You sow into holiness, a faint snowing of seeds,
As the sea elsewhere with its dark
Leaves and green resins of beginning
Enriches the scant acres of mollusk
With an autumn of drowned girls.
I am blessed for nothing.
When I was a young man,
Unclear of my strength and my heart

A blind granite face,
I killed trees.
Now I do not ask pity of the tall oak.
Today I saw the frail woman of the maples
Walking alive to me, and I do not need to pray
For the pity of her leaves.
They love me.
Her roots grow mine.

As published in *Botteghe Oscure* 25 (1960). See letter to Robert and Carol Bly dated September 4, 1958.

My Father's Lullabies to Me in 1932

By night, in the breadlines my father
Prowls, I cannot feed him. So
Far, now: 1,500 miles or
So away, and yet I can hardly
Sleep.

Long ago,
In a blue rag the old man gimped to
My bed on a blind dobbin
Of gentleness.
He sang me stammering
Jokes of Italy and a goose girl.

Then, whole evenings away,
His hard face wept a man's tears
Down the worn stair well
Of my mother's hands.

He lives still.
But, in the jungles of Ohio,
How shall I sing Mother Goose to
My father?

Unpublished draft of November 7, 1958. See letter to Robert and Carol Bly dated September 4, 1958.

Walking Around

[From the Spanish of Pablo Neruda, translated by H. R. Hays]

It so happens I am tired of being a man.
It so happens, going into tailorshops and movies,
I am withered, impervious, like a swan of felt
Navigating a water of beginnings and ashes.

The smell of barbershops makes me weep aloud.
All I want is a rest from stones or wool,
all I want is to see no establishments or gardens,
no merchandise or goggles or elevators.

It so happens I am tired of my feet and my nails
and my hair and my shadow.
It so happens I am tired of being a man.

Yet it would be delicious
to frighten a notary with a cut lily
or do a nun to death with a box on the ear.
It would be fine
to go through the streets with a green knife,
letting out yells until I died of cold.

I do not want to go on being a root in the darkness,
vacillating, spread out, shivering with sleep,
downwards, in the drenched guts of the earth,
absorbing and thinking, eating every day.

I do not want so many afflictions,
I do not want to go on being root and tomb,
being alone underground, being a vault for dead men,
numb with cold, dying of anguish.

That is why Monday blazes like petroleum
when it sees me coming with my jailbird face,

and it howls like a wounded wheel as it passes,
and takes hot-blooded steps towards night.

And it shoves me into certain corners, certain damp houses,
into hospitals where bones fly out of the window,
into certain shoeshops with a stench of vinegar,
into streets as frightful as chasms.

There are sulphur-coloured birds and horrible intestines
hanging from the doors of the houses that I hate,
there are false teeth forgotten in a coffeepot,
there are mirrors
that ought to have wept for shame and fear,
there are umbrellas all over, and poisons, and navels.

I walk with composure, with eyes, with shoes on,
with fury, with forgetfulness,
I pass, I cross by offices and orthopedic shoeshops
and patios with the washing hanging from wires:
underdrawers, towels and shirts that weep
slow filthy tears.

Included in Hubert Creekmore, ed., *A Little Treasury of World Poetry: Translations from the Great Poets of Other Languages, 2600 B.C. to 1950 A.D.* (New York: Charles Scribner's Sons, 1952). See letters to James Dickey dated September 28, 1958, and February 13, 1960. See also letter to Michael Cuddihy dated September 15, 1979.

A Bus Ride

Stones hunched up,
Hills of sawdust,
All-night movies turned out,
Houses panhandling
In a grove of chickenhawks,
Aircraft carriers pushing their shoulders
Through disused culverts,
Information desks of the Milwaukee Road
Drifting between U-boats and galleons,
Junior executives walking around platforms,
Pricing the tall Negro
Who governs the sea.

Unpublished. See letter to James Dickey dated February 13, 1960.

The Doors

When the rain goes on,
I know small sparrows
Are shivering in the gullies
Of wet clouds.

What is the beginning of water?
It is the blood of a man,
Whole armies of it, walking
In a dark city.

Doors are opening
In the snow.

Unpublished. See letter to James Dickey dated February 13, 1960.

Morning Song

When I walk toward myself
My feet drag into nothing
But dark leaves.
It must be that early snow
Is falling outside.
There are lakes galloping
Under the trees.
But no one else sees them.
And all kinds of people—
Students hurrying slowly to class,
Policemen waving their arms,
And old women taking their morning walks
In the lost summer of their clothes—
All of these are beaten
Into the pastures of wet snow,
Ploughed back into the earth
By the concrete hooves of wind,
The horses stumbling backward
From the sea.

Unpublished. See letter to James Dickey dated February 13, 1960.

Bells

Under the railway trestle
A girl has fallen
Asleep.

Streamliners, on the horizon,
Hulk like great birds.

I touch one eyelid, and
Suddenly the scared girl's voice
Rings three bells into the hall of
Rain.

My God, why can't she keep still?
I am getting out of here, I am
Hiding under the river before
The watchmen come.

Unpublished. See letter to James Dickey dated February 13, 1960.

At the Great Northern

In the men's wash room,
Rivers of lysol wash over
The dry shadows
Of drunks aspiring to the middle class.

Inner tubes float down
The veins of traveling librarians,
To the tunnels of dark girls.
Stained on the walls,
Animals flail, struck down
Between the eyes.

I long for the dignity
Of clear snow.
Under the earth,
The night crawls, soundless,
Inland.

Unpublished. See letter to James Dickey dated February 13, 1960.

The Empty Mill Field at Aetnaville, Ohio

The pyramid of lumber
Is the tomb of tall women
And their slaves from Greece.

Janitors
Limp down from the moon
To sweep sand.

The secondhand Chevrolet
Still grazes, happy.

Ghost of defeat crying among the charred trees,
A boxcar is a cold home.

Hoboes still blunder into each other's fires
Under the Ohio river.

Unpublished. See letter to James Dickey dated February 13, 1960.

The Night Clerk in Pennsylvania

She hears hysterical salesmen overhead
Galloping over the lumpy mattresses
On wild mares.

I said to her:
Yes ma'am, I've lost my suitcase,
Never mind, I don't care,
No, no, stay there, I can make it
To my room by myself.

Is that the men's room?
Yes sir, three doors down.

She is sixty-seven years old.
She sits between dark plants and the slag heaps
Of strange men. Under the sea
There are tall mountains, chasms more terrible than jails.

She guards keys.

Unpublished. See letter to James Dickey dated February 13, 1960.

The Vain Season

Once I hoped the landscape
Would comfort me. When
I was young I found
Abstractions of sorrow,
Hatred, loneliness,
In the stinkweeds where
Hoboes never appeared
In the broad day. Only
Now, when the night falls
In Minneapolis,
I stare at the railroad
Ties, and the
Tusk of a rhinoceros touches canned-heat boxes
Through gray cinders.
Out of the bombed city
Of the sky, angels
Follow the foxes of thunder
Hallooing the names of dead women
Into the darkness.
Wolves creep upward from buried forests
To get back their own.

Unpublished. See letter to James Dickey dated February 13, 1960.

Year Changes in the City

I see nothing before me
But the dark wing
Of a policeman,
And I hear nothing
But a violet
Dragging its chains.

It is only underground that I hear
The muffled cry of a tree,
A vixen laboring to bear
Ghosts in her sleep.

Unpublished. See letter to James Dickey dated February 13, 1960.

Prayer for Several Kind Women

In the new snow,
A sparrow.

Electric lights walking with subdued wolves
Into the black trees
Of the sky.

Now, wherever your slow hands are,
Now, now,
Moon.

Unpublished. See letter to James Dickey dated February 13, 1960.

To a Girl Heavy with Child

What tender force has driven me to find you
Wringing your nervous fingers tight,
Letting the cold beam of the noonday blind you;
When you, of all, should understand that night
Will bury you from sight?

My heavy love, you stood beside a tree
One day and shook a blossom with your hand:
An amsel from the waters flew away,
Your body slender as a tree would stand
And sow the laden land.

But now the trees unveil, you must lie under
A slide of pebbles; then the larger stone
Of the rough dark will roll away from your womb
And resurrect miraculous flesh and bone
Whose voice will ring a shadow down.

Silenced, human Jesus fought the cover
Of skin, sacked in wet shadow for three days,
And when the long and rainy week was over,
He blinked and rose; but knew before he rose
Ancient immediate agonies.

And, knowing how the earth labored with God,
I would touch you, love, and sow you with soft grass,
And mold my hand against your shaking side,
And kiss your falling face as shadows kiss
The spinning earth to solace.

How shall the earth tender a man forgiveness
For burying his love in her, and sleeping?
When the dark land lies down in quietness

I am not fooled, for I can hear her weeping
And reaching for my hands.

You are a grave to man, will roll and sicken
With storm as when the temple tore in twain,
The gauzy blankets of your bed will thicken
And fall like forests under dropping stone.
The lake will drag your lilies down.

And I, pacing an age beyond your room,
Will I feel nothing but the fall of wind
Flicking about my face, about your tomb,
And hear no more than angels groping blind
And stars that drop like sand?

After the burial, will you rise to reckon
With men, with me? what is my human share
In seeing your body, as my body, slacken,
Shudder, and pray beneath the burning air
Till the long dawn rinses your skin like rain?
Love is the child I bear, and love is pain.

As published in *The New Orleans Poetry Journal* 2 (July 1956). See letter to Liberty Wright dated August 12, 1960.

Afternoon

[From the Spanish of Federico García Lorca]

Was my Lucia standing
with her feet in the river?

Three immense poplars
And one star.

The silence, nibbled
By the frogs, resembles
A painted gauze
With small green blemishes.

In the river,
A dry tree
Has shed blossoms,
Widening in circles.

Sounding over the waters
To the tawny girls of Granada.

As published in *The Sixties*, no. 4 (Fall 1960). See letters to Robert Bly dated February 18, 1960, and September 7, 1960.

Grodek

[From the German of Georg Trakl]

At evening the woods of autumn are full of the sound
Of the weapons of death, golden fields
And blue lakes, over which the darkening sun
Rolls down; night gathers in
Dying recruits, the animal cries
Of their burst mouths.
Yet a red cloud, in which a furious god,
The spilled blood itself, has its home, silently
Gathers, a moonlike coolness in the willow bottoms;
All the roads spread out into the black mold.
Under the gold branches of the night and stars
The sister's shadow falters through the diminishing grove,
To greet the ghosts of the heroes, bleeding heads;
And from the reeds the sound of the dark flutes of autumn rises.
O prouder grief! you bronze altars,
The hot flame of the spirit is fed today by a more monstrous pain,
The unborn grandchildren.

Translated by James Wright and Robert Bly, from *Twenty Poems of Georg Trakl* (Madison, Minn.: Sixties Press, 1961). See letter to Robert Bly dated September 7, 1960.

Christ's Descent into Hell

[From the German of Rainer Maria Rilke]

Seduced at last, he escaped from that hideous
Body of suffering. Upwards. Left it.
And the darkness, alone, was frightened
And flung bats at the pale body,—
In the evening, dread still fluttered
In their wings, that flinched from the shock
Of that agony, grown cold. Dark nervous air
Was disheartened by the corpse; and the strong, alert
Animals of the night felt stupor and revulsion.
Perhaps his released spirit intended to stay
In the landscape, doing nothing. For the event of his suffering
Was still enough. The night-time
Presences of things seemed gentle to him,
And like a grieving room he reached out to enclose them.
But the earth, parched by his thirsting wounds,
The earth cracked open, and someone cried out in the abyss.
He, who knew of tortures, heard hell
Howling out, aching for the completion
Of his pain, in the faint hope of ending
Its agony with his, even while pain still frightened it.
And he plunged down, the spirit, with the full weight
Of his exhaustion: he walked like a hurried man
Through the surprised glances of the grazing shadows,
He lifted his gaze to Adam, hurriedly,
And ran downwards, vanished, came into view, and disappeared in
                                   the ruins
Of wilder depths. Suddenly (higher, higher) out over the midst
Of cries washing up, he climbed forth
To the long tower of his endurance: without breathing,
He stood there, without a handrail, landlord of anguish. Silent.

Unpublished draft dated September 27, 1960. See letter to Eugene Pugatch dated October 7, 1960. See also letter to Franz Wright dated May 2, 1976.

A Whisper to the Ghost Who Woke Me

Once more, the moon.
Why do I grieve for your shadow?
The scarred splotch on your face, alive,
Always made me ashamed
Of loving the snow.

Shall I kiss you, face?
But it is too late,
And the towers and supermarkets of the dead
Cast wrinkles all over me,
As you move in my trees,
Distributing baskets of gray snow.

When you were alive,
I loved you, one time
In the dim streets
At the end of your voice.
Now I am awake,
You are nothing but a curtain of flimsy rain
Between me and the sea's arms.

It is almost the end of winter
In the Minneapolis of graves.
I am growing old, as
The botched faces of the dead
Are combed under playgrounds.

Once more, the moon
Dies, and shall I kiss you,
Face? Oh, very well,
I still love you.
Let me alone now, go back
To your own grave.

As published in *Big Table* 1, no. 3 (Autumn–Winter 1959). See letter to W. D. Snodgrass dated December 14, 1960.

In a Warm Chicken House

Gerard de Nerval,
Locked in prison in 1832,
Under a liberal regime,
Prayed for some green thing
In the winter.
He spoke, aloud, to a bird dividing space
Into breezes and horizons.

This afternoon, in 1960, I sit, all alone,
At the end of the Eisenhower Administration,
Counting the blades of gold outside the window
Of a warm chicken house, near the border
Of South Dakota.

Gerard de Nerval was still young, his eyes nested
In green moss.
He felt ivy gracefully entering his soul
Through the bars of the prison window.
I am so delighted with his season of rare plants.
I have just paused in my own poem,
To step outside and fetch one of those blades of golden grass
To mark a page in his book,
One of those precious things I had forgotten to love.

As published in *The New York Times*, September 19, 1961. See letter to James Dickey dated December 18, 1960.

Heritage

Brooming the streets, sick drunk he hated life.
Winter after winter, his whining wife
Forgave him about midnight, and then she prayed,
John, 3-16. Pure slag-heap, smoldering his bed.
One winter afternoon of snow and smoke,
Fuddled by horses, traffic lights, and drink,
He tripped on old horse manure, and sprawled
Along the curb, favoring his broken back,
Chuckling through rot-gut fumes.
Pink graduates from morticians' colleges
Scuttered like roaches out of septic tanks
And offered bids. They haled him out of sight.
Three days, he harrowed the white funeral home.
They priced his molars, calculated sums,
Giggled together if they cracked his thumbs,
Threaded the cat-gut, and sewed up his gums.

He loved his brother, Christ alone knows why.
Christ and his family know he never told.
One evening, when his time had come to die,
My father said since I was four years old
I might as well get used to something now:
I had the old man's brother's name, and so
The dead drunk, wallowing in death, loved me.

I have nothing to live for but my death:
Alone, last of a crowd of solitudes,
Half-wondering where I am and how I came
To carry a beloved dead man's name.
Lashed to the wall by pain, half stupefied
By dreams of liquor, my grandfather died
Hoping to hang his fearsome love on me.

All right, he did so; now I let him be.
And, though I know the comfort of a lie,
I pray to keep my mouth shut when I die.

As published in *The Paris Review* 31 (Winter/Spring 1964). See letter to a reader dated March 16, 1964.

The Lesson of the Master: Ten Meditations on the Death of Jay Hanna Dean (1911–1974)

1. *PRAYER*

Heroic dream of my childhood, dream of my boy's laughter and delight again and again, dream of happiness in my childhood, be with me now as I mourn, and mourn, and mourn.

2. *THE LESSON OF THE MASTER*

He died last week. I loved him. To the sports journalist Grantland Rice, another noble man worthy of my America once, Dizzy Dean, weary after a baseball game, said:

"Sure, Granny, things ain't what they used to be. But, hell, what is?"

3. *THE SHY POET IN PUBLIC PRAYER*

When Dizzy Dean was inducted into the Baseball Hall of Fame, he accepted the honor, and was asked to say a few words. Out of a little silence, he finally said to all the wondering faces:

"I want to thank the Good Lord for givin' me a good right arm, a strong back, and a weak mind."

I believe in my heart that God himself must have smiled with happiness.

4. *THE CHILD OF LIGHT*

Now Jay Hanna Dean is one of the children of light.

I'll lay 8 to 5 all the angels are happy this evening, speaking his lovely words, truly happy.

5. *DIZZY DEAN AND THE SQUIRRELS*

He said that a baseball scout signed him after seeing him throw rocks at squirrels with his left arm.

Dizzy Dean, as the Boston Braves of old times will know as long as they live, was a right-hander. Oh, my, he surely was.

But why was he throwing rocks at squirrels with his left hand?

Dizzy answered:

"I throw so hard with my right arm that I squash up the squirrels somethin' turrible and they ain't fit eatin'."

6. *THE LINGUIST*

He created the word "SPART" for television, he said. "The spart is pretty much like fight or gumption. Like the Spart of St. Louis, that plane Lindbergh flowed to Europe."

God bless the fallen poet. God bless the Risen Poet.

God have mercy on me. Mercy me alive.

7. *IN DEFENSE OF POETRY*

When a wealthy radio executive tried to persuade him to become a disk-jockey, to comment on classical music, Dizzy Dean defended himself by saying:

"Me pronounce them composers' names? I can't even pronounce the Cleveland Indians' infield."

8. *A PRAYER FOR MYSELF IN MY LOSS*

Lord, for the love of sunlight, let me sleep with Frost and Quintus Horatius Flaccus, and waken on Sunday to the laughter of gentleness, the satirist who knows, and laughs, and is sad, and knows so much about our darkness that he smiles with us and at us all our short lives long. And don't forget to make sure that my poor friend Ell stops drinking and goes home and gets some sleep. He doesn't know to laugh yet.

Lord help him too.

9. *ANOTHER*

Lord, I mourn for the lonely child I was, for the good man I wanted to be, and never was yet. Dizzy Dean is gone, Lord.

He's gone.

10. *DIZZY DEAN IS ENTERING FOR HIS REST*
    "The players have now returned to their respectable bases."
    And where is Dizzy Dean gone, Lord?
    He slud home.

Unpublished. See letter to Robert Bly dated October 23, 1974.

A Visit to the Earth

On the Adriatic, the silver peacock,
Where I had been lounging all afternoon
Praying to the sun in the dark eye
Of the plume,

Brutal time
Plummeted down quickly
And I scampered for home where my love was,
While rain came scarring.

No more golden lollygagging for me
In that long water along the sides
Of the fishing hulks whose fishermen were gone,
Their sky blackened.

I know so little of the language
In the places where the old men and the young men
Scuttle and mutter together near the cold water
And nurse wine, frightened of women, frightened
Of the raining sea.

Soaked so badly,
I hunched into the place.
I know how to say wine.
I cowered alone.

Too many men there, too blinded by the sea
To know each other, the morose faces
That know the sea gives up
Only its dead.

Then the kitchen door opened.
A kid, not more than fifteen,

His pants dirty with the barnacles, yelled
Hey, look what I got!

Everyone fell suddenly still.
The kid disappeared, and came back
With an enormous silver tail wriggling
Over his shoulder.

God help me he slopped down
The whole thing on a table.
We all jumped back as he flipped her
To face us at last.

She had a small bruise at the corner of her mouth.
He must have struck her
To keep her stunned, knowing little else to do,
Fifteen, and frightened.

But he laughed, Catch!
And tossed her onto another table.
Everyone laughed, and I will see till I die
Her drenched face, cold as Maine stone,
Wondering.

They threw her from table to arm to hand,
Rolled her down in the sawdust,
Smeared wine on some of her body, though no one
Dared touch her breasts.

One by one
We tried to creep out,
But the door stuck.
We all broke it at once.

Solemn in shame the boy
Gathered her into his arms,
Turned once to look back, and left us
Drunk in a half-darkness.

What did she make of us,
Strange creatures of sand who sometimes walk on sand?
Are we frightened of the great delicate spaces
Under the waters,
Women and the miraculous shadows
Of some few men who touch bottom?
Frightened of the sea?

(September 1973)

As published in *Modern Poetry Studies* 5 (Spring 1974), together with an earlier version of the poem "Neruda." See letter to M. L. Rosenthal dated September 20, 1975.

Neruda

It was one evening
In an autumn
When bells hung in a vast
And yet most intricate design
From the webs of araucaria,
Trees that are not trees easily,
The little leaves
That are trees in secret.

Under one bough,
One vein of one leaf,
One side of the sea
Sang for a thousand inches
Uphill, as though
The tree in the leaf in the sea
Were sorry for being human
And wanted to run back
Across a river
In the center of America
Into the arms of an old beard,
Butterfly of ashes,
Architect of spiders
Climbing up the long
Slag heap to gain
The crumbling pinnacle and spin
One strand of his body to join
The earth to one star anyway,
And maybe save it.

The leaves of the little
Secret trees are fallen,
And where the earth goes on spinning
I don't know.

(September 1973)

As published in *Modern Poetry Studies* 5 (Spring 1974), together with "A Visit to the Earth." See letter to M. L. Rosenthal dated September 20, 1975.

Correspondents

John F. Adams (b. 1930)   American educator and scholar. Adams taught at the University of Denver from 1960 to 1964. In 1961 he wrote to Wright, inviting him to teach there—an arrangement that did not come to fruition.

Sheri Akamine   A student of Wright's when Wright was a visiting professor at the University of Hawaii in the summer of 1976.

Ghazi Al-Gailani   Poet, and a former graduate student at the University of Minnesota.

A. R. Ammons (1926–2001)   American poet and editor who taught at Cornell University from 1964 until his retirement in 1998. Ammons and Wright met in 1970 when Wright and Robert Bly gave a reading at Cornell University for Poets Against the Vietnam War.

Willis Barnstone (b. 1927)   American poet, scholar, and translator. He and Wright met in New York City in 1960; they exchanged translations of Spanish poets.

Ben Belitt (b. 1911)   American poet, editor, and translator, best known for his translations of Pablo Neruda, Rafael Alberti, Jorge Luis Borges, and other Romance language poets. He and Wright met at Bennington College, where Belitt was a professor, when Wright gave a reading there in 1958.

Carolyn Bilderback (b. 1915)   American dancer and choreographer. Wright met Bilderback through his wife Anne, who had worked with Bilderback at the School of Creative Arts in Manhattan.

Miriam Black   A student of Wright's in Minnesota.

Carol Bly (b. 1930)   American poet, essayist, and fiction writer. Wright met Carol Bly when he went to visit the Blys' farm after corresponding with her then husband, Robert Bly. Carol Bly and Wright remained good friends for Wright's entire life.

Robert Bly (b. 1926)   American poet, translator, and editor of the influential magazine *The Fifties*, which eventually became *The Sixties*, *The Seventies*, etc. In July 1958 Wright wrote Bly a long letter in response to the first issue of *The Fifties*, initiating a lifelong friendship. Wright frequently visited the Blys on their farm in Madison, Minnesota, and the two collaborated on translations and commented on each other's work.

Louise Bogan (1897–1970)   American poet and critic. Wright met her at the University of Washington in Seattle in 1956, and wrote to her in 1968 to express his admiration of her book of poetry *The Blue Estuaries*.

Wayne Burns (b. 1918)   American critic and scholar. An English professor at the University of Washington in Seattle, Burns was Wright's adviser for his doctoral work on Charles Dickens.

Paul Carroll (1927–1996)   American poet and editor. Carroll was the editor of the Big Table publishing company as well as founder and editor of *Big Table* magazine, in which Wright's work appeared. Carroll was known for his support of an eclectic group of young writers, including Bill Knott, Robert Hass, Anne Waldman, and Louise Glück.

Hayden Carruth (b. 1921)   American poet, critic, editor, and essayist. He is the author or editor of nearly forty volumes, including the anthology *The Voice That Is Great Within Us*. He was an editor at *The Hudson Review* and *Poetry*, and the poetry editor of *Harper's*. Wright and Carruth probably first corresponded when Carruth was an editor at *Hudson*, and they met in person through mutual friends in New York in the 1960s.

William Claire (b. 1935)   American poet and essayist. The founding editor of the literary magazine *Voyages*, he asked Wright to contribute a piece on Roger Hecht, published in vol. 1, no. 1 (1976).

Michael Cuddihy (b. 1932)   American poet, translator, and editor of *Ironwood*, an influential biannual poetry journal (1972–1988). Cuddihy devoted the entire Fall 1977 issue to Wright; it contained essays on Wright's work, memoirs about him, and a selection of new poems.

Madeline DeFrees (Sister Mary Gilbert) (b. 1919)   American poet and teacher. Although a nun for nearly forty years, DeFrees spent a great deal of that time outside the religious community, teaching at the University of Montana and at schools in Oregon and Washington State. She sent Wright her book *Springs of Silence*, and they shared a mutual friend, John Logan.

Michael di Capua   Editor at Farrar, Straus and Giroux, where he worked on Wright's translation of Herman Hesse's *Poems* (1970) and Wright's poetry collections *Two Citizens* (1972) and *To a Blossoming Pear Tree* (1977).

James Dickey (1923–1997) American poet, critic, and novelist. Wright first wrote to him in July 1958 with a sharp rebuke of a review Dickey had written for *The Sewanee Review*. They grew to respect one another and became friends, corresponding until Wright's death.

E. L. Doctorow (b. 1931) American novelist and playwright. Doctorow was a classmate of Wright's at Kenyon College, where they studied with John Crowe Ransom. As editor of the New American Library, Doctorow published Wright's translation of Theodor Storm's *The Rider on the White Horse* in 1964.

Karin East (Marvin) (b. 1957) Anne Wright's niece. She visited with the Wrights in Montreal in 1971 and traveled with them in France in 1972.

Richard Eberhart (b. 1904) American poet and playwright. Wright initiated their correspondence because he admired Eberhart's work.

Morgan Epes (b. 1926) Epes met Wright through Anne Wright, who had attended Wheelock College with Epes's wife, Carolyn. The Wrights were frequent guests at the Epeses' home in Buffalo, New York.

Elizabeth Willerton Esterly (1903?–1980) Wright's English teacher at Martins Ferry High School. She encouraged his writing and continued to correspond with him throughout his life. He often visited her and her husband, Henry, in Cupertino, California.

Olive Faries An English teacher at Martins Ferry High School; she also taught Wright.

Roland Flint (1934–2001) American poet. Flint was a graduate student at the University of Minnesota while Wright was teaching there and remained a close friend.

Betsy Fogelman (Tighe) A friend of Wright's whom he met when he was teaching at the University of Delaware in 1978.

Jack Furniss Wright's bunkmate in the peacetime army in Japan. After being accepted to Kenyon College, Furniss encouraged Wright to apply. They studied there together, giving each other the nicknames Harry (Furniss) and Adam (Wright). Wright frequently visited Furniss and his parents during his undergraduate breaks.

Isabella Gardner (1915–1981) American actor and poet. After leaving the stage, she was an associate editor at *Poetry* and wrote four volumes of verse. Wright was also a friend of her husband Allen Tate, to whom she was married from 1959 to 1966.

Susan Gardner   A student of Wright's at the University of Minnesota.

Wendy Gordon   A student of Wright's at Hunter College.

Laurence Green   A teacher who worked with teenagers in Harlem, Green wrote to Wright in 1977, asking him questions on behalf of his students.

Donald Hall (b. 1928)   American poet and editor. Hall served as the poetry editor of *The Paris Review*, as well as poetry consultant for Wesleyan University Press and Harper and Row. In 1954 Hall solicited poetry from Wright for *The Paris Review*, and they remained close friends until Wright's death. Wright regularly visited Hall and his first wife, Kirby, in Ann Arbor, Michigan.

Michael Hamburger (b. 1924)   German-born English poet, translator, and critic. Wright was aware of Hamburger's work because they both translated German poetry, and the two began corresponding in the early 1960s when Hamburger, then an editor in England, expressed interest in publishing Wright's work.

Michael S. Harper (b. 1938)   American poet and editor. In 1975, after a brief correspondence, Harper invited Wright to Brown University, where Harper still teaches, for a reading; they continued to correspond.

Robert Hass (b. 1941)   American poet, translator, and former poet laureate of the United States. Wright initiated a correspondence with Hass in 1978 to thank him for a piece he wrote on Wright in *Ironwood*.

Roger Hecht (1926–1990)   American poet; Wright's classmate and friend at Kenyon College. The two remained close throughout Wright's life, and Hecht served as Wright's best man at Wright's wedding to Anne in 1967.

Fred Hein   A friend of Wright's from Minneapolis.

Albert Herzing   A classmate of Wright's at Kenyon College and the editor of the student literary magazine *Hika*, which published Wright's undergraduate poetry.

Thomas Hodge   A childhood friend of Wright's from Martins Ferry.

Richard Howard (b. 1929)   American poet, translator, and critic. Wright met Howard shortly after moving to New York City.

Richard Hugo (1923–1982)   American poet, essayist, and novelist. Hugo and Wright met at the University of Washington and became friends as well as fishing partners.

Roger Jones (b. 1954)   American poet, educator, and scholar.

Jane Kenyon (1947–1995)   American poet and translator and the second wife of Donald Hall.

Galway Kinnell (b. 1927)   American poet and translator. Wright met Kinnell at a reading in 1966 at Hunter College in New York and the two became close friends.

Liberty Kovacs (Wright) (b. 1929)   Wright's first wife, whom he married in 1952. She had been a classmate at Martins Ferry High School. After their divorce in 1962, she moved to California and continued her nursing career.

Elizabeth Kray (1916–1987)   American arts administrator. Director of the 92nd Street Y in New York from 1954 to 1963, she left to become the director of the Academy of American Poets until 1981. In 1985 she founded Poets House with Stanley Kunitz. Kray befriended Wright in 1958 when he came to New York on a reading tour, and was instrumental in helping him with subsequent reading tours throughout his life.

Stanley Kunitz (b. 1905)   American poet. Wright studied with Kunitz at the University of Washington in 1955 when Kunitz was the visiting poet-in-residence.

Susan Lamb (Graham) (b. 1929)   Lamb and Wright were classmates at Martins Ferry High School, where they edited the yearbook together. Wright corresponded with her while he was in the peacetime army in Japan.

Elizabeth Lawrence   American editor. When Wright sent the manuscript of *St. Judas* to Russell Lynes at Harper & Brothers in 1958, Lynes passed it along to Elizabeth Lawrence, then an assistant editor. The book was utlimately published by Wesleyan University Press.

Laura Lee (DeCinque) (b. 1957)   Anne Wright's niece. She traveled with the Wrights in France in 1972.

Merrill Leffler (b. 1941)   American poet, scholar, and editor; cofounder and editor of Dryad Press, which published Wright's chapbook *Moments of the Italian Summer* in 1976.

Denise Levertov (1923–1997)   English-born American poet and essayist. Wright and Levertov's work appeared together in magazines in the late 1950s, and Wright, who greatly admired her poems, often copied them out and memorized them. They met in 1964 when Wright came to New York to give a reading.

Philip Levine (b. 1928)   American poet. He hosted Wright at California State University in Fresno in 1965.

John Logan (1923–1987)   American poet. Former poetry editor of *The Nation* and *Critic*, as well as the founder and coeditor of the literary magazine *Choice*. Wright met Logan in New York in 1959, and they became close friends.

Robert Lowell (1917–1977)   American poet. Wright attended a seminar at Boston University to which Lowell had invited him in 1959, and they corresponded briefly afterward.

George Lynes (b. 1937)   Wright's neighbor in New York from 1974 until Wright's death. He is the son of Russell Lynes, with whom Wright had corresponded years earlier.

Russell Lynes (1910–1991)   American art critic and editor. Lynes was an editor at Harper and Row when Wright submitted the manuscript of *Saint Judas*, which was ultimately published by Wesleyan University Press.

Freya Manfred (b. 1944)   American poet, daughter of the novelist Frederick Manfred. She was a student of Wright's when he was a visiting professor at Macalaster College from 1963 to 1965.

William Matthews (1942–1997)   American poet and professor at Cornell University in 1970, when Wright and Bly came to the campus for a Poets Against the Vietnam War reading.

Jerome Mazzaro (b. 1934)   American scholar, poet, and editor of the literary journals *Fresco* and *Modern Poetry Studies*. He became a good friend of Wright's when the two taught at the State University of New York at Buffalo.

J. D. McClatchy (b. 1945)   American poet and editor. McClatchy asked Wright to contribute to his 1978 book *Anne Sexton: The Artist and Her Critics*, but Wright declined.

James L. McCreight (1885–1983)   American educator. Wright met McCreight through Elizabeth Willerton Esterly; McCreight was a Latin professor at Muskingum College when Esterly was a student there.

Robert Mezey (b. 1935)   American poet and critic. Mezey and Wright were classmates at Kenyon College and remained close friends throughout Wright's life.

Jack Myers (b. 1941)   American poet and critic. He wrote to Wright in 1971, asking him to contribute to *A Trout in the Milk: A Composite Portrait of Richard Hugo* (Confluence Press, 1982). Wright provided a commentary, "On Minding One's Own Business," as well as a short essay, "Explorations, Astonishments."

Mary Oliver (b. 1935)   American poet. Fellow Ohioans, Wright and Oliver admired one another's work; they corresponded, but never met.

Gege and Lloyd Parks   Fellow graduate students of Wright's at the University of Washington.

Mary Philo   A resident of Martins Ferry; she wrote to Wright in 1973, asking him about his poetry.

Eugene Pugatch (b. 1932)   American neurologist. Pugatch and Wright met as classmates at Kenyon College and continued a close friendship and correspondence.

Sister Mary Bernetta Quinn (1915–2003)   American critic, poet, and scholar.

Henry Rago (1915–1969)   American poet and editor; editor of *Poetry* from 1955 to 1969.

John Crowe Ransom (1888–1974)   American poet and critic. A founder, with Allen Tate, of the New Criticism, and part of the Agrarian movement in Southern literature. Editor of *The Kenyon Review*. Ransom was Wright's professor at Kenyon and a lifelong friend and mentor.

Kenneth Rexroth (1905–1982)   American poet. Wright met Rexroth in San Francisco in 1960, while Wright was on a West Coast reading tour.

Harvey Rice (b. 1907)   American educator; president of Macalester College from 1958 to 1968.

Theodore Roethke (1908–1963)   American poet. He taught Wright at the University of Washington and was a lasting influence and lifelong friend.

Beatrice Roethke   Wife of Theodore, after whose death she remained close to Wright. His poem "To a Hostess Saying Good Night" is about her.

M. L. Rosenthal (1917–1996)   American poet and critic. Poetry editor of *The Nation* from 1970 to 1978.

Gibbons Ruark (b. 1941)   American poet. In 1969, as a new faculty member at the University of Delaware, he invited Wright to read there and they became friends. He and his wife, Kay, hosted the Wrights in the fall of 1978, when Wright was a visting professor at the university.

Kay Ruark (b. 1941)   Wife of Gibbons Ruark.

Edith Anne Runk (Anne Wright) (b. 1929) Wright's second wife, whom he married in the spring of 1967.

J. R. Salamanca (b. 1922) American novelist. When he was a professor at the University of Maryland, Salamanca invited Wright to participate in the Poets Against the Vietnam War reading series.

Ann Sanfedele (b. 1936) American photographer and poet.

Anne Sexton (1928–1974) American poet. Wright met Sexton at a seminar given by Robert Lowell at Boston University in 1959. She wrote to him shortly thereafter, and they continued to correspond.

Helen McNeely Sheriff (1887–1978) Wright's Latin teacher at Martins Ferry High School. She introduced him to some of the poets who were important to him throughout his lifetime, including Catullus. Wright dedicated *To a Blossoming Pear Tree* to her and John Logan.

Leslie Marmon Silko (b. 1948) Native American novelist, poet, and essayist. Wright and Silko met in 1975 at a writers' conference in Michigan. In 1978 Wright renewed their acquaintance when he wrote to her about her novel *Ceremony*. Their correspondence has been collected in *The Delicacy and Strength of Lace*, edited by Anne Wright.

Dorothy Simpson (b. 1933?) Former wife of Louis Simpson. The two were married from 1955 to 1979.

Louis Simpson (b. 1923) Jamaican-born American poet. Wright met Simpson through the Blys, and the two developed a close friendship.

Dave Smith (b. 1942) American poet. Smith founded the poetry magazine *Back Door* in 1969 and served as coeditor of *The Southern Review* from 1990 to 2005.

W. D. Snodgrass (b. 1926) American poet. Wright met Snodgrass in 1959 at Wayne State University, where Snodgrass taught, and wrote him to express his admiration for *Heart's Needle*.

Arnold Stein (b. 1915) American scholar and educator. Stein was a colleague of Wright's at the University of Washington.

John Stork (b. 1947) Director of the Martins Ferry Public Library from 1976 to 2000. He wrote to Wright in 1978 and 1979 to express his admiration for his work. Stork established a small collection of Wright material at the library and is a cofounder of the James Wright Festival, held annually in Martins Ferry.

Mark Strand (b. 1934)   Canadian-born American poet. Strand met Wright in 1964 at the University of Iowa, where Strand was teaching, when Wright came to give a reading. At one of Wright's last readings, at the Academy of American Poets in 1978, Strand introduced him.

Allen Tate (1899–1979)   American poet, critic, novelist, and biographer. A founder, with John Crowe Ransom, of the New Criticism, and part of the Agrarian movement in Southern literature. Tate and Wright shared an office when Wright first began teaching at the University of Minnesota in 1957, and Tate and Isabella Gardner, his wife, occasionally hosted Wright in their home.

Debra Thomas   A student of Wright's when Wright was a visiting professor at the University of Hawaii in the summer of 1976.

Janice Thurn (b. 1958)   Thurn wrote a fan letter to Wright in 1975, when she was seventeen years old. Their friendship grew during a four-year correspondence.

Philip Walcott Timberlake (1895–1957)   American scholar and educator. Timberlake taught Wright at Kenyon College and remained his mentor. Wright learned of Timberlake's death in 1957, when he was asked to write an obituary for him. Wright also wrote an elegy for Timberlake, "A Winter Day in Ohio."

Tomas Tranströmer (b. 1931)   Swedish poet and psychologist who was translated by Robert Bly. Tranströmer had translated Wright's poems into Swedish and wrote to Wright in 1964. Wright responded warmly and sent him more poetry.

David Wagoner (b. 1926)   American poet, novelist, and essayist. Wagoner, who studied with Theodore Roethke at the University of Washington, met Wright through Roethke, and the two became good friends.

Diane Wakoski (b. 1937)   American poet and essayist. In 1968 Wakowski, who knew of Wright through mutual acquaintances, sent him her book *Inside the Blood Factory*, which he admired.

Austin Warren (1899–1986?)   Teaching fellow at Kenyon College in the summers of 1948 through 1950. He wrote to Wright in 1977 to reminisce about the 1948 Kenyon English department, which included Philip Timberlake and John Crowe Ransom.

Elizabeth Willerton   *See* Elizabeth Willerton Esterly.

C. K. Williams (b. 1936)   American poet. Wright and Williams met in New York City after Wright moved there.

Oscar Williams (1900–1964) American poet and editor. Wright contributed an essay on Robert Frost to a collection edited by Williams called *Master Poems*, published in 1967.

Dudley Wright (1893–1973) James Wright's father.

Franz Wright (b. 1953) American poet. First son of Wright and Liberty Kovacs.

Jack Wright (b. 1934) James Wright's younger brother.

Jessie Lyons Wright (1897–1974) James Wright's mother.

Marshall John Wright (b. 1958) Second son of Wright and Liberty Kovacs.

Theodore Wright (1925–2000) James Wright's older brother.

Sander Zulauf (b. 1946) American poet. Zulauf asked Wright to read at the County College of Morris, New Jersey, in 1974 and 1976.

Index

"Abendländisches Lied" (Trakl), 236
Abinger Harvest (Forster), 501
Academy of American Poets, xxx, 345, 374, 389
Adams, J. Donald, 80, 81
Adams, John F., 271–72
Adventures of Huckleberry Finn, The (Twain), 457–58
Aeneid (Virgil), 530, 534
"Afternoon" (Lorca), 251–52, 586
Akamine, Sheri, xiv, 492–94
"Alarm, The" (Wright), 202
Al-Gailani, Ghazi, 329–30
Algren, Nelson, 347
Allen, Frederick Lewis, 307–8
"All the Beautiful Are Blameless" (Wright), 75
Ambrose, Saint, 213
Amenities of Stone (Wright), xxix
American Academy of Arts and Letters, xxx–xxxi
American Poetry Review (APR), 390, 404, 423, 426, 430, 431, 433
American Poets in 1976 (Heyen, editor), xxxi, 446, 512
"American Twilights" (Wright), 562–63
Amis, Kingsley, 143, 517
Ammons, A. R., 380–81
"And All That Surrounds It" (Thurn), 536
Anderson, Sherwood, 16
And Morning (Flint), 522, 523
"Animals, The" (Wright), 192

Anonymous Lover, The (Logan), 393
Antaeus, 503
Apollinaire, Guillaume, 390
"Apples" (Swift), 97
Aristophanes, xxi, 116
Aristotle, 93
Arnold, Matthew, 46, 178
Arrivistes, The (Simpson), 300
Art of Poetry, The (Valéry), 174–75
Ashman, Richard, 120n, 247, 368
Aspects of the Novel (Forster), 493
At the End of the Open Road (Simpson), 300–302
"At the Executed Murderer's Grave" (Wright), 91, 98, 150, 152, 199, 205, 564–67
"At the Great Northern" (Wright), 578
Atlantic Monthly, 361, 444
"At Peace with the Ocean Off Misquamicut" (Wright), 504–5
"At the Slackening of the Tide" (Wright), 90
Auden, W. H., xxviii, 62–63, 182, 254
Audience, 127, 190, 204
Augustus Caesar, 530
"Aunt Leaf" (Oliver), 547
Austen, Jane, 432
"Autumn" (Rilke), 29–31
"Autumnal" (Wright), 127
Avon Book of Modern Writing, 58

Babel, Isaac, 348
Bagehot, Walter, 136

Baines, Jocelyn, 274

Baldwin, James, 115, 427

"Ballad of John Cable and Three Gentlemen, The" (Merwin), 62

Barbieri, Giovanni Francesco (Il Guercino), 530

Bard College, 511

Barnaby Rudge (Dickens), 153

Barnstone, Willis, 219, 243–45

Bashō, 18

Baudelaire, Charles, 63–64, 108, 127, 253

Bedford, Ed, 368, 427, 476–77

Bedford, Zetta, 368, 476

Beethoven, Ludwig van, 29, 51, 392, 396–98

"Before the Cashier's Window in a Department Store" (Wright), 329

Belitt, Ben, 146, 153, 177, 241–42, 511

"Bells" (Wright), 577

Benn, Gottfried, 165, 166, 219

Bentham, Jeremy, 82

Beowulf, xxi, 33

Berg, Steve, 409

Berry, Wendell, 503

Berryman, John, xxix, 67, 84, 124, 130, 160, 229, 260, 371

Bettelheim, Bruno, 435–36

Bezat, Barbara, xiv

Bhagavad Gita, The, 322

Bickerstaff Papers (Swift), 251

Bilderback, Carolyn, 419–20

Bishop, John Peale, 93

Black, Miriam, 354–56

Blake, Patricia, 348

Blake, William, 128

Blanchot, Maurice, 146

Blaugrund, Dr., 548

"Blind Beggar-Musician of Anatolia, A" (Barnstone), 243

Bloom, Harold, 403, 495

Bloy, Myron, 474

Blue Estuaries, The (Bogan), 363–64

Blum, Morgan, 70, 94, 229, 230

Bly, Biddy, 306, 347–48

Bly, Carol, 183, 185n, 188, 213, 225, 235–43, 270, 382, 383, 435, 451, 453; divorce of, 502; in England, 306; letters to, 165–67, 169–71, 174–78, 223–24, 226–31, 236–43, 256, 340–42, 347–49, 370–71, 506–7; in New York, 240, 266; Wright's visits to farm of, xxix, 103, 220–21, 261–62, 267–68, 272, 273, 281, 282, 300, 335–38, 351, 375–76

Bly, Jim, 370

Bly, Kathryn, 370, 371

Bly, Mary, 337, 347–48, 382, 452

Bly, Noah, 513

Bly, Orrin, 370, 371

Bly, Robert, xi, xxix, xxx, xxxii, 103, 168, 184–90, 192, 203n, 206, 215, 225, 249, 256, 260, 262–64, 277, 293, 301, 316, 317, 334, 340–42, 356, 403, 404, 424, 449, 454–56, 465, 470, 473, 519, 539, 543, 544; divorce of, 502, 507; in England, 306, 309; Guggenheim Fellowship of, 305–6; letters to, xiv, xv, xxiv, 111–23, 140–47, 155–57, 163–67, 169–71, 174–83, 213, 223–24, 226–31, 233–38, 242–45, 251–53, 347–49, 370–71, 381–84, 410–12, 435–37, 450–53, 502, 513–14, 533–35, 548–49; in New York, 197, 240, 266, 332–33, 389; poetry magazine edited by, 128, 130, 132, 136, 140–41, 144–45, 162–63, 193, 214, 219, 222, 257, 265, 330; Wright's visits to farm of, xxix, 103, 220–21, 261–62, 267–68, 272, 273, 281, 282, 300, 335–38, 351, 375–76

Bly farm, 103, 155, 163, 165, 220–21, 223, 242, 244–45, 256, 261–62, 267–68, 272, 273, 280, 281, 282, 333, 336, 337, 341–42, 347, 375–76

Boehme, Jacob, 285

Bogan, Louise, xxi, 62–63, 363–64

Bonnefoy, Yves, 230, 231

Booth, Philip, 67–68, 106, 137, 160–62, 187, 189
Borges, Jorge Luis, xxii
Boston University, 204, 404
Botteghe Oscure, 63, 118, 236, 270
Botticelli, Sandro, 401
Bounoure, Gabriel, 146
Bowers, Edgar, 129
Branch Will Not Break, The (Wright), xxi, xxix, 287, 317, 318
Brandeis Award, 374
Brandeis College, 466
Bridges, Robert, 105, 142, 145, 160
Briefe an einen jungen Dichter (Rilke), *see Letters to a Young Poet*
Bright, Lorrie, 47
Brontë, Emily, 372
Brooke, Rupert, 12
Brooks, Van Wyck, 46
Brothers Karamazov, The (Dostoevsky), 26, 42
"Brother to Dragons" (Warren), 94
Brown, Dee, 383–84
Brown, Malcolm, 96, 97
Browning, Elizabeth Barrett, 9, 32
Browning, Robert, 32, 530
Bucey, Clifford, 468
Buch der Lieder, Das (Heine), 421–23
Büchner, Georg, 166
Bueno, J. R. de la Torre, 274, 275
Burke, Edmund, 87
Burning Heart, The (Rexroth), 479
Burns, Joan, 81
Burns, Wayne, xiv, xxii, xxviii, 55, 71–76, 78–81, 95–99, 151–53, 520
Bury My Heart at Wounded Knee (Brown), 383–84
"Bus Ride, A" (Wright), 574
"But Only Mine" (Wright), 202
Butt, John, 72, 79
By Love Possessed (Cozzens), 78
Byron, Lord, xxvii, 12

Caesar, Julius, 12
Caetani, Princess Marguerite, 146, 236

Campbell, Roy, 63
Campion, Thomas, 363
Camus, Albert, 146
Candlin, Clara M., 269
"Captain Hoyt" (Hall), 448, 450
"Carentan" (Simpson), 302
Carleton College, 309
Carossa, Hans, 113
Carpaccio, Vittore, 116
Carroll, Paul, 330–33
Carruth, Hayden, xxxii, 460–62, 466–67, 469–70, 480–81, 521–22, 526, 545, 550
Carruth, Rose Marie, 460, 466, 469
Carter, Jimmy, xxxii, 488, 517
Carter, Rosalynn, xxxii, 488
Caruso, Enrico, 420
Cather, Willa, xxi
Catullus, xxi, 3, 5–7, 10–11, 14, 15, 85, 237, 363, 484, 525, 531, 533, 535, 536, 539
Ceremony (Silko), 508
Cervantes, Miguel de, 73, 98
Chandler, Raymond, 517
Chanter, 329
Char, René, xxviii, 63, 88–89, 114, 118, 138, 146–47, 156, 161, 165, 219, 410
Chatterton, Thomas, 9–10
Chaucer, Geoffrey, 184, 494
Chelsea Review, 240, 245
Chessid, Herman, 513
Chicago, University of, 242
"Child in Armor, The" (Dickey), 150
Choice, 293
Chopin, Frédéric, 5
"Christi Hölenfahrt" (Rilke), 256, 446
"Christmas Is Coming" (Hecht), 81
"Christ's Descent into Hell" (Rilke), 588
Christ Stopped at Eboli (Levi), 526, 542, 545
"City of Evenings, The" (Wright), 456
City University of New York, 449, 466, 471, 500

Civilization and Its Discontents (Freud), 177, 178

Claire, William, 353–54

Clark, Ethelwyn, 24

Clark, Jim, 29

Cleveland, John, 60

Cloud of Unknowing, The (anonymous), 406

Coffin, Charles, xxii, xxviii, 45, 49, 52, 66–67, 474

Cold Comfort Farm (Gibbons), 505

Coleridge, Samuel Taylor, 143, 152, 501

Collected Poems (Wright), 374, 432, 500

Collins, Wilkie, 78

Colossus of Maroussi (Miller), 171

Columbia University, 219, 377; English Institute, 272

"Complaint" (Wright), 90

Connecticut, University of, 96

Connor, Rod, 272

Coolidge, Charles, 474

Cooper, Jane, 349–50, 408

Coraddi, 49, 50, 58

Couplets (Mezey), 548

"Court Martial" (Warren), 94, 95

Cowley, Abraham, 60

Cowley, Malcolm, 511

Cozzens, James Gould, 78

Crane, Hart, 32, 123, 206

Crane, R. S., 93

Crassus, 447

Crime and Punishment (Dostoevsky), 229

Crome, Nicholas, xiv, xxi, 49

Cronin, Vincent, 404

Crusack, Cyril, 331

Cuddihy, Michael, xxxi, 465, 477, 481–82, 511, 542–45

Cummings, E. E., 490

Cunningham, J. V., 64, 374

Curran, Keelin, xii

Dante, 106, 277, 376, 399, 407, 411, 427, 479, 484

Darker (Strand), 373

Dark Houses, The (Hall), 184

Davies, Sarah, 25

Davies, W. H., 84

Dean, Dizzy, 412

DeFrees, Madeline, 257, 264–66

Delacroix, Eugène, 518

de la Mare, Walter, 246–47

Delaware, University of, xxxi, 482, 487, 489, 491, 492, 499, 501, 507, 509, 512, 513

Democratic Party, 35

Dempsey, Jack, 249

Denver, University of, 271–72

D'Hoont, Pieter, 515

"Dialogue of Self and Soul, A" (Yeats), 316

"Diamond Cutters, The" (Bilderback), 420

Diario de Poeta y Mar (Jiménez), 203

di Capua, Michael, 360, 393–94, 441, 512

Dickens, Charles, xxi, 69, 72, 73, 76, 79, 82, 95, 98, 99, 127, 136, 152–53, 155, 156, 169, 190, 201, 203, 219, 229, 233–34, 357, 475, 512

Dickensian, The, 72, 79

Dickey, James, xxix, 103, 134–37, 143–45, 154, 164, 311–12, 361, 381; letters to, xiv, xv, 105–10, 124–31, 147–51, 159–63, 171–73, 197, 199–200, 205–7, 209–12, 220–26, 231–33, 249–51, 261–64, 272–74, 276–77, 335–36

Dickey, Maxine, 335

Dickey, William, 80

Dickinson, Emily, 93

di Giovanni, Norman, 219, 232, 241

"Disappearance" (Barnstone), 243

Doctorow, E. L., xxviii, xxx, 4, 34, 51, 287–90, 303, 318

Doheny, John, xiv

Don Quixote (Cervantes), 72–73, 274, 457

Donne, John, 60, 295, 297

"Doors, The" (Wright), 575

Dostoevsky, Feodor, xxi, 14, 30, 42–44

Doty, George, 57–58, 205, 385

"Double Image, The" (Sexton), 464
"Dover: Believing in Kings" (Dickey),
    148, 150, 199, 206
Drapier's Letters, The (Swift), 251
"Dream of Charles Coffin's Voice, A"
    (Wright), 560–61
Dream of Governors, A (Simpson), 300,
    306
"Dream of the American Frontier,
    The" (Wright), 215
Dreiser, Theodore, 92
Dryad Press, xxxi, 431–32, 440, 449,
    466
Dryden, John, 60
Duffy, William, xxix, 103, 122, 144,
    175, 188, 190, 230, 236, 253
Dunbar, William, 404
Dupré, Marcel, 518
Durrell, Lawrence, 124
"Dusk Near a Mental Hospital"
    (Mezey), 61
Dylan, Bob, 527

"Earth: a True Romance, The"
    (Wright), 46, 49
East, Karin, 370, 398–99
East-West, 513
"Eating the Pig" (Hall), 448, 450
Eberhart, Richard, 105, 124, 127, 156,
    311–15, 480
Eckhart, Meister, 216, 253
Eclogues (Virgil), 32
Egan, Pierce, 79
Ekelof, Gunnar, 138
"Elegies" (Wright), 5, 7
"Elegy for Jane" (Roethke), 84
"Elegy for My Father" (Strand), 374
Eliot, T. S., 16, 31–32, 60, 167, 168,
    254, 495
Emerson, Ralph Waldo, 16
"Empty Mill Field at Aetnaville, Ohio,
    The" (Wright), 579
Enscoe, Jerry, 80, 154, 178, 238
Epes, Morgan, 405
Epoch, 73, 80

"Espergesia" (Vallejo), 228, 251n
Esquire, 495
Essays of Three Decades (Mann), 499
Esterly, Elizabeth Willerton, xiv, xxii,
    xxii–xxiii, xxvii, xxx, 3, 6–9, 11,
    14–17, 27–33, 41–47, 217–20,
    282, 334–35, 375, 385, 492, 525–
    26, 537
Esterly, Henry, 16, 28, 30, 32, 33, 41–
    45, 217, 282, 375, 492, 526
Ethics (Spinoza), 520
Ewart, Gavin, 404
Ewing, Chatham, xiv
Exile's Return (Cowley), 511
Exiles and Marriages (Hall), 164
Eyman, Hubie, 26

"Fable of the Mermaid and the
    Drunks" (Neruda), 429
"Face, The" (Levine), 503
"Falling Leaves, The" (Hall), 436–37,
    450
Faries, Olive, 379
"Farmer, The" (Wright), 201
Farrar, Straus and Giroux, xxx, xxxi,
    360, 432, 441, 470
"Father" (Wright), xxviii, 59–60
Fauchereau, Serge, 390
Faust (Goethe), 43
Fifties, The, xxiv, 111, 114, 117, 118,
    120n, 128–30, 132, 136, 140, 141,
    144, 145, 162, 165, 187, 188, 190,
    193, 214, 218–19, 228, 235, 240,
    257
Finnigans Wake (Joyce), 331
"Fire of Despair Has Been Our Sav-
    iour" (Bly), 164, 170
"First Lesson" (Booth), 106
"First Morning of Cancer, The"
    (Dickey), 150
"Fit Against the Country, A" (Wright),
    127
Flannery, Nina, 347
"Flat One, A" (Snodgrass), 260
Flint, Roland, xiv, xxx, 522–23

Flint, Rosalind, 523
Florentine Renaissance, The (Cronin), 404
Fogelman, Betsy, 504–6, 514–16, 530
Foley, Martha, 34
Foothills College, 492
Ford, Ford Madox, 79
Forster, E. M., 79, 493, 501
Foster, Dick, 450
"Foundations of American Industry, The" (Hall), 133, 164
Fountainhead, The (Rand), 33
Fowler, David, 96, 97, 520
"France: An Ode" (Coleridge), 152
Frank, Anne, 515–16
Franklin and Marshall College, 377
Fresco, 178, 192, 193, 257, 368
Freud, Sigmund, 39, 146, 169, 177, 178, 395, 480
From Snow and Rock, from Chaos (Carruth), 461–62, 521
Froment, Edith Hoyt, 380
Frost, Robert, 49, 126, 228, 238, 315, 520, 523
Fulbright Scholarship, xxviii, 4, 47, 49, 112, 440
Furniss, Jack, xiv, xxviii, 3, 26–27, 35–41

Galassi, Jonathan, xxiii
Galler, David, 427
Gallimard, 89
Gandhi, Mohandas K., 350
Gardner, Isabella, 331, 339–40, 365–66, 415
Gardner, Susan, 328–29
Gattuccio, Nicholas, xii
Gellens, Jay, 49, 66
Genitron Press, xiv
Georgia Review, The, 513
Getty, J. Paul, III, 447
"Ghost, The" (Wright), 202
Ghost in the Machine, The (Koestler), 403
"Ghost with the Silver Lyre, The" (Wright), 558–59

Gibbons, Stella, 505
Gibson, Richard, 35, 49, 231
Gielgud, John, 186
Ginsberg, Allen, 73, 80, 117, 130, 132, 133
"Girl Walking into a Shadow, A" (Wright), 88, 91, 201, 202
Giroux, Robert, 539
Gissing, George, 72
Gitanjali (Tagore), 350–51
Goering, Hermann, 524
Goethe, Johann Wolfgang von, xxi, xxviii, 42–43, 372, 442, 443, 463
Gogol, Nikolai, 430
Goldhurst, Richard, 51
Goldhurst, William, 51
Goodbody, Roland, xiv
Good News of Death (Simpson), 300
Gordon, Wendy, 462–63
Gorky, Maxim, 73
Göttingen, University of, 421
Graham, Billy, 73, 133
Graham, Susan Lamb, xiii, xiv, xxiii, xxv, 3, 9–15, 17–25, 33, 196n
Graham, W. S., 136, 149, 277
Graves, Robert, 228, 231
Graywolf Press, xiii
Green, Laurence, 482–84
"Green Leaf, A" (Storm), 289
Green Wall, The (Wright), xxviii, 68, 83, 87, 112, 152, 183, 184, 187, 217, 247, 248, 275, 318
Grimm brothers, 436
"Grodek" (Trakl), 587
Gross, Harvey, 272
Groth, D., 423–25
Grove Press, 173
Guardian Angel, The (Il Guercino), 530
Guard of Honor (Cozzens), 78
Guercino, Il, 530
Guest, Edgar A., 127
Guggenheim Fellowships, xxx, xxxi, 281, 305, 337, 339, 354, 356, 359, 375, 440, 487, 507, 546
Guggenheim Museum, 512

Guillén, Jorge, xxi, 219, 220, 232, 245
"Guilty Man, The" (Kunitz), 128
Gullans, Charles, 64, 84
Gulliver's Travels (Swift), 205
Gunn, Thom, 63, 129, 212, 250, 264
Gwyllam, Dafydd ap, 425

Haislip, John, 67
Hall, Andrew, 183, 188, 190, 203, 270
Hall, Donald, xxviii, xxxii, 55, 103,
    115, 145, 164, 178, 192, 199, 222,
    341, 436–37, 452–54, 533, 534,
    549; anthology edited by, 120, 141;
    at Bly's farm, xxix, 272, 273; in
    England, 212, 221, 306, 309; letters
    to, xiv–xv, xxiv–xxv, 57–65, 67–68,
    131–37, 153–55, 167–68, 173–74,
    183–90, 197, 201–3, 214–17, 267–
    71, 281, 349–50, 388–92, 394–96,
    403–5, 448–50, 455–56, 490–91,
    518–19, 539
Hall, Jane, *see* Kenyon, Jane
Hall, Joe, 325
Hall, Kirby, 173–74, 183, 188, 190,
    203, 217, 268, 270, 273, 306, 309,
    341, 350
Hamburger, Michael, 166, 176n, 274–
    75, 357
Handbook for Boys, 108
Hanfman, Andre, xxii, 4, 31, 44,
    463
Hanson, Ken, 368
Harding, Warren G., 308
Hardy, Thomas, xxi, xxviii, 45, 55,
    84, 85, 94, 146, 204, 309, 313–14,
    345, 372, 389, 448, 464, 504, 512,
    523
Hargis, Dr., 447
Harper, Michael S., 417–18
Harper & Brothers, 86–91
Harper and Row, 350
Harper's Magazine, 91, 522
Harrison, John, 6
Harvard University, xxxii, 45, 205
Harvey, Edward, xiv

Hass, Robert, 495–96, 511
Hass, Willie, 34
"Hatred of Men with Black Hair"
    (Bly), 348
Hauptmann, Gerhard, 213
Hawaii, University of, xxxi, 415, 441,
    450
Hawthorne, Nathaniel, 378
Hays, H. R., 147, 172, 219, 232n,
    543–45, 572–73
Heart's Needle (Snodgrass), 238, 260
Hecht, Anthony, 81, 93, 137, 230, 234,
    349
Hecht, Roger, xxviii, xxx, 4, 48, 49,
    63, 66, 184, 282, 311, 349, 353–54,
    475–76, 479, 517
Heilman, Robert, xxviii, 74, 82, 208
Hein, Fred, 358–59
Heine, Heinrich, xxi, xxviii, 46, 166,
    226, 421–23
Hemingway, Ernest, 26, 446
Henricksen, Bruce, 539
"Her Becoming" (Roethke), 138, 139,
    159
Herbert, George, 498
"Herbst" (Rilke), 29–31
"Heritage" (Wright), 290, 592–93
"Her Kind" (Sexton), 464, 469
Hernández, Miguel, 240, 243–44,
    245, 267, 349, 551
Herrick, Robert, xxi, 42, 133, 461
Herzing, Albert, 4, 34–35, 47–50
Hesperides (Herrick), 461
Hesse, Hermann, xxviii, xxx, xxxi,
    360, 366, 375, 466
Heyen, William, 446, 512
Heym, Georg, 166
Higgins, Robert William, 475, 513,
    540, 541
Hika, 34, 35, 46, 312
Hill, Geoffrey, 168, 190, 200, 212,
    221–22, 254–56, 270, 276, 395
Hine, William Daryl, 403
"His Farewell to Poetry" (Wright), 136,
    145
Hispanic Institute, 228, 240

"His Prayer to the True Muse" (Wright), 164

History as a System (Ortega y Gasset), 307

History of English Literature (Taine), 120

Hitchcock, Alfred, 78

Hitler, Adolf, 167

Hobbes, Thomas, 70

Hodge, Thomas, 536–37

Hölderlin, Friedrich, 113, 166, 357

Holms, John, 264

Holton, W. Milne, xxv–xxvi

"Homage to Mistress Bradstreet" (Berryman), 67

Homer, 106

Hopkins, Gerald Manley, 9, 190

Hopwood, 390

Horace, xxi, 5, 12, 32, 377, 380, 441, 493, 530

Hornberger, Theodore, 69, 70, 79

Horrell, Joseph, 96

Housman, A. E., 7, 167

Houston, University of, 511

Houvet, Étienne, 402

"How Annandale Went Out" (Robinson), 434

Howard, Richard, 367

Howard, Willie, 186

Howe, Irving, 78

Howells, William Dean, 444

"How Spring Arrives" (Wright), 492

Hudson Review, The, 120, 143, 190, 206, 229, 234, 269, 380, 429, 460, 548

Huff, Robert, 139

Hughes, Mary Margaret, 25

Hugo, Richard, xxviii, 117–19, 156, 179, 206, 209, 215–16, 222, 276, 367, 426–27, 476–77, 512, 526–27

Hugo, Victor, 142

Hunter College, xxii, xxx, xxxiii, 282, 346, 348, 353, 354, 356–57, 359, 362, 364, 371, 376, 415, 418, 454, 457, 466, 471, 478, 482, 500, 545, 546

Huxley, Aldous, 322

Hyman, Stanley Edgar, 66

Hypnos Waking (Char), 63, 118, 146, 161

"I Am Freed" (Vallejo), 245n

Ibsen, Henrik, 116

"Idiot Boy, The" (Wordsworth), 7

Ignatow, David, xxiv, 240, 256, 276, 408, 470, 504, 512

Ignatow, Yaedi, 408

Iketani, Toshitada, 463, 467

"Illiterate, The" (Kunitz), 201

"In a Warm Chicken House" (Wright), 591

"In Fear of Harvests" (Wright), 176

Ingram Merrill Foundation, xxx

"In Response to a Rumor That the Oldest Whorehouse in Wheeling, West Virginia, Has Been Condemned" (Wright), 385

"In Shame and Humiliation" (Wright), 202

Inside the Blood Factory (Wakoski), 364

"In Terror of Hospital Bills" (Wright), 542

"In the Environs of the Funeral Home" (Mezey), 50

"In the Hard Sun" (Wright), 219

Into the Stone (Dickey), 263, 264

Ironwood, xxxi, 482, 496, 511

Isherwood, Christopher, 322

"I Wish to Go Out but Encounter Rain" (Lu Yu), 270–71

Jackson, Jesse, 534

Jaessuraparp, Sichart, 517

James, Henry, 378, 444, 501

James, Stuart, 272

James, William, 249

Jarrell, Randall, 82–83, 148, 309

Jellema, Rod, 545–6

Jenyns, Soame, 169

Jiménez, Juan Ramón, 202–3, 219, 242, 259, 263, 269

Joan of Arc, 387
Johnson, Andrew, 35
Johnson, Dave, 225
Johnson, Samuel, 60, 443
Jones, Roger, 511
Jonson, Ben, 85, 204, 295, 296, 527
Joyce, James, 35*n*, 218, 542
Jung, Carl, 146, 169

Kafka, Franz, 147
Kappus, Franz, 28, 115
Kardules, Liberty, *see* Kovacs, Liberty
  Kardules Wright
Keats, John, xxii, 9–10, 31, 306, 338,
  417, 419, 420, 445, 469, 555
Kelly, Robert, 511
Kennedy, X. J., 532
Kenyon, Jane, 389, 390, 391, 396, 403,
  405, 450, 491, 518, 539
Kenyon College, xii, xiii, xxi, xxii,
  xxviii, xxix, xxxi, 3–4, 16, 27, 45,
  47–49, 51, 58, 59, 61, 66, 76, 84,
  184, 311, 312, 325, 410, 439–40,
  474; *Alumni Bulletin*, 66, 184; Robert
  Frost Poetry Prize, xxviii, 49
Kenyon Review, The, xxviii, 46, 58, 59,
  62, 88, 138, 177, 234; Poetry Fel-
  lowship, 76, 99, 127, 144
Kessler, Jascha, 323
Kicking the Leaves (Hall), 490
"Killers, The" (Hemingway), 446
"Kin" (Harper), 417
Kinnell, Galway, xxx–xxxii, 395, 449,
  454–56, 460, 467, 480, 481, 487,
  491, 495, 509, 513, 522, 539, 548–
  50
Kinnell, Ines, 548
Kirkup, James, 263
Kizer, Carolyn, xxviii, 215, 217, 248,
  470
"Klage" (Trakl), 170
Kleist, Bernd Heinrich Wilhelm von,
  166
Knight, Etheridge, 549
Knoepfle, John, xxix, 103, 345

Knopf, Alfred A., 139
Knott, Bill, 293, 294, 381, 424–25,
  508
Knudsen, Dan, 254
Koestler, Arthur, 8, 403
Korg, Jacob, 522
Kovacs, Liberty Kardules Wright (first
  wife), 25, 27–28, 45, 48, 49, 55, 62,
  69–71, 75, 78, 83, 92, 124–25, 127,
  154, 158, 159, 173–74, 178, 183,
  186, 201, 211, 217, 241, 242, 244–
  45, 274, 276, 299, 300, 327–28,
  387, 510; birth of children of, xxviii,
  xxix, 4, 51, 95, 103, 137–38, 153;
  conflicts with, 223, 228–30, 236–
  37, 268; divorce from, xxix, 281,
  375, 536; letters to, 247–49, 302–6,
  318–21, 471–72; marriage to,
  xxviii, 47; nervous breakdown of,
  216; remarriage of, 375, 536
Kovacs, Miklos, 375, 471
Kray, Elizabeth, xxxi, 240, 260, 304–
  5, 332, 345, 408–9, 470–71
Kreuzer Sonata, The (Tolstoy), 261
Krieger, Murray, 92
Kunitz, Stanley, xxviii, 128, 138, 150–
  51, 156, 168, 201, 264, 409–10,
  470

La Fountaine, Jean de, 19
Laguna Woman (Silko), 508
"Lambs on the Boulder, The"
  (Wright), 456
"Lament: Fishing with Richard Hugo"
  (Wright), 476–77
"Lament for My Brother on a
  Hayrake" (Wright), 127
Lamartine, Alphonse de, 142
Lamentation of Saint Judas, The (Wright),
  see Saint Judas
Lamb, Susan, *see* Graham, Susan
  Lamb
Landor, Walter Savage, 295, 297
Lane, Charlotte, 29
Lannum, Pete, 25, 33

Lardner, Ring, 490
Laski, Harold, 37
Laslo, John, 439, 445
Late Hour, The (Mark), 499
Lathrop, Alan, xiv
Lawrence, D. H., 149, 392, 448, 531, 539
Lawrence, Elizabeth, 86–91, 99–100
Lawrence, Larry, 74
Leahy, Jack, 520
Lee, Jane, *see* Runk, Jane
Lee, Laura, 396–98, 491–92
Leeds, University of, 254
LeFever, Frank, 326
Leffler, Merrill, 431–33
"Legend of My Child's Awakening, A" (Wright), 51
Leggett, Glenn, 74
Lehmann College, 376
Leonardo da Vinci, 446, 529
"Lesson of the Master, The" (Wright), 594–96
Letters to a Young Poet (Rilke), 28, 64, 115, 463
Levertov, Denise, 169, 177, 361
Levi, Carlo, 526
Levine, Fran, 503
Levine, Philip, 503
Lewis, Alun, 153, 440
Lewis, C. Day, 389
Lewis, Sinclair, 27, 38
Library of Congress, 83
Life of Po Chü-i (Waley), 513
"Limpet in Otranto, The" (Wright), 534
Lincoln, Abraham, 35
Lindenberger, Herbert, 177
Lion's Tail and Eyes, The (Wright, Bly, and Duffy), xxix
Lippi, Fra Lippo, 541
"Listening to Fats Waller in Late Night" (Ruark), 495
"Litanies" (Strand), 373–74
Livingston, Ray, 213, 304
Lockwood, Willard, 173, 193, 201, 218, 223, 269, 275
Loeb, H., 404

Logan, John, xxiv, xxix, xxxi, 103, 257, 293, 381, 392–93, 415, 450–51, 453, 495–97
London, 63
Longfellow, Henry Wadsworth, 130, 422, 430
Longmans Publishers, 274
Longview Foundation, 216
Look Homeward, Angel (Wolfe), 7
"Looking Back on the Spanish War" (Orwell), 140
Lorca, Federico García, 114, 118, 122, 125, 142, 146, 148, 152, 153, 177, 233, 251–52, 348, 511, 586
Lord, George deF., 363
Lord Weary's Castle (Lowell), 267
Lost Faces, The (Jellema), 545
Louis, Joe, 41
Love in the Western World (Rougement), 334
Lowell, Robert, 67, 122, 189, 203–5, 239, 349, 363
Loyola University, 534
Luce, Henry, 117
Lux, Tom, 446
Lu Yu, 269–71
Lynes, George, 516
Lynes, Russell, 86–88
Lyons, Elizabeth, xxvii

Macalester College, xxix, xxx, 242, 281, 285–86, 303–5, 311, 318, 329, 341, 375
MacBeth, George, 404
MacDiarmid, Hugh, 309
MacDonald, Dwight, 253
Machado, Antonio, 243, 259, 265–66
Macmillan Publishers, 214
Mailer, Norman, 26–27
Mallarmé, Stéphane, 142
Man Who Shook Hands, The (Wakoski), 497, 498
Mandelbaum, Alan, xxx, 376, 377n
Manfred, Fred, xxix, 348, 384
Manfred, Freya, 369–70

Mann, Thomas, 16, 288, 499
Marie Antoinette, Queen of France, 518
Martial, 447
Martin Chuzzlewit (Dickens), 79, 153, 233–34
Marvell, Andrew, 89–90, 208, 363
Marx, Groucho, 434
Marx, Karl, 39
Matchett, William, 58, 68, 372, 520
Maryland, University of, 546
Mathews, Jackson, 63–64, 118, 146, 161, 175, 230
Mathiessen, F. O., 187
Matthews, William, 473–74
Maud, Ralph, 190
Mazzaro, Jerome, 178–79, 191–92, 257, 265, 345, 368, 372, 406
McCarthy, Joseph, 65
McCarthy, Mary, 539
McClatchy, J. D., 463–64, 468–69
McClelland, Sherry, 330
McCreight, James L., 3, 5–7
McKenna, Siobhan, 331
McKuen, Rod, 374, 427
Medici, Cosimo di, 541
Meistersinger, Die (Wagner), 51
Melville, Herman, 27, 354
Melville Cane Award, xxxi
Ménard, René, 146
Mencken, H. L., 358
"Men's Room in the College Chapel, The" (Snodgrass), 116, 121
Mercian Hymns (Hill), 395
Meredith, William, 201
Merwin, W. S., xxxi, 62, 415, 453
"Mexico: Avenue of San Juan" (Barnstone), 243
Mezey, Robert, xv, xxviii, xxxii, 4, 48–52, 61, 64, 93, 322–26, 352, 480, 547–48
Michaux, Henri, 114, 118
Michelangelo, 401
Michigan, University of, 212, 221–22, 341
Middlebury College, 465
"Midnight Sassafras" (Wright), 201

Miller, Henry, 171–72
Miller, Vassar, 120, 156, 214, 263–64
Milton, John, 6, 67, 94, 167
"Milton by Firelight" (Snyder), 117
Minnesota, University of, xxii, xxix, 55, 67, 77, 99, 172, 281, 309, 316, 319, 357, 371, 375; Elmer L. Andersen Library, xiv, 72, 341; Press, 83, 118, 222
Minnesota Review, 371, 372
"Mission to Linz" (Hugo), 222
Miss Lonelyhearts (West), 258, 307–8
"Miss Twye" (Ewart), 404
Mitchell, Jeff, 475
Modern Poetry Studies, 372
"Moments in Rome" (Wright), 492
Moments of the Italian Summer (Wright), xxii, xxxi, 346, 440, 466, 468
Montag, Alma, 385
Montale, Eugenio, 410
Moore, Henry, 391, 396, 475
Moore, Julia A., 77
Moore, Marianne, 231
Moorhead State College, xxix, 318
Morgan, Fred, 460
Morgan, J. P., 187
Morley, Christopher, 7
"Morning Hymn to a Dark Girl" (Wright), 127
"Morning Song" (Wright), 576
Mounin, Georges, 146
Mozart, Wolfgang Amadeus, 67, 518
Muir, Edwin, 124
Muse's Library, 96
Musset, Alfred de, 142
Mussolini, Benito, 521
Myers, Jack, 367–68
"My Father's Lullabies to Me in 1932" (Wright), 166, 571

Naipaul, V. S., 476
Naked and the Dead, The (Mailer), 26–27
"Name and Nature of Poetry, The" (Housman), 167
Napoleon (Cronin), 404

Narcissus (Zweig), 334
Nation, The, 204, 240, 241, 247, 348
National Book Awards, 390
National Institute of Arts and Letters, xxix, 212, 216
Natural Numbers (Rexroth), 294
"Natur und Kunst" (Goethe), 442
Nemerov, Howard, 126
Neruda, Pablo, xxxi, 114, 134, 138, 149, 152, 165, 169, 182, 185, 186, 219, 399, 429–30; translations of, xxx, 147, 213, 241, 543–44, 572–73
"Neruda" (Wright), 600–601
Nerval, Gerard de, 262, 267
New American Library, xxix–xxx
New and Selected Poems (Wagoner), 372
New Anthology of the Great Poems in the English Language, 315
New Directions, 63, 171
New Hampshire, University of, Library, xiv
New Orleans Poetry Journal, The, 120, 187, 247, 368
New Poems (Wright), 273–75
New Poets of England and America (Hall, Pack, and Simpson), 120, 128, 131, 134, 139, 141, 159, 163
New Republic, The, 204, 380
New World Writing, 63
New York, State University of, at Buffalo, xxx, xxxi, 345, 346, 368, 372, 378, 406, 409, 411
New Yorker, The, 113, 125, 127, 136, 251, 329, 330, 331, 412, 435
New York Quarterly, 534
New York Times, The, 264, 407; *Book Review*, 132, 183
New York University, 224, 228, 457, 489
Nicholas Nickleby (Dickens), 153
Nietzsche, Friedrich, xxi, 39, 139, 297, 505
"Night Clerk in Pennsylvania, The" (Wright), 580
Nightfishing, The (Graham), 146

Nightmare Begins Responsibility (Harper), 417
Nims, John Frederick, 263, 264
Nixon, Richard, 399, 400, 514
Nobel Prize, 350
Nonesuch, 79
"Note Left in Jimmy Leonard's Shack, A" (Wright), 90
Novalis, 166
Nugent, Robert, 16

Oberlin College, 375, 379, 386, 472
"O Cheese" (Hall), 450
O'Connor, William Van, 69, 84
"Ode on a Grecian Urn, The" (Keats), 143
"Ode to a Nightingale" (Keats), 420
"Ode to Lesbia's Pet Sparrow" (Wright), 557
"Ode to Walt Whitman" (Lorca), 122, 125, 153, 348
"Offenbarung und Untergang" (Trakl), 227
Of Time and the River (Wolfe), 40
O'Hara, John, 14
Ohio Review, The, xxxi, 409, 426, 433
Ohio University, 439
Old Curiosity Shop, The (Dickens), 153
Oliver, Mary, 333–34, 336–37, 546–47
Oliver Twist (Dickens), 153, 208
Olson, Elder, 93
One Hundred Poems from the Chinese (Rexroth), 293
"One Word More" (Browning), 32
Only Yesterday (Allen), 307
"On Minding One's Own Business" (Wright), 91, 368
"On the Skeleton of a Hound" (Wright), 127
Open House (Roethke), 85
"Opening of the Wm. Dinsmore Briggs Reading Room, The" (Winters), 160
Ord & Bild, 317

Ortega y Gasset, José, xxi, 23, 307, 355, 505, 534

Orwell, George, xxi, 46, 140

"Our Daily Bread" (Vallejo), 210–11

"Out of Childhood" (Rilke), 176n

Ovid, xxiii, 13

"O Western Wind" (Carruth), 461–62

Oxford Book of German Verse, 31

Oxford University, 254, 255

Pack, Robert, 120, 141, 206

Palmer, John, 70, 138

Palmer, Mary, 89

Parade of Ghosts, A (Hecht), 475

"Paragraphs" (Carruth), 466, 470

Paris Review, The, xxxi, 164, 433, 534

Parks, Gege, 77–78

Parks, Howard, 78

Parks, Lloyd, 19, 77–78

Parotti, Philip, 534

Partisan Review, 80, 204, 243

Pasternak, Boris, 372

Perloff, Marjorie, 497

Personae (Pound), 166–67

Perugino, 530

Philo, Mary, 385

"Photographs of China" (Hall), 450

Pickwick Papers, The (Dickens), 79, 152, 153

Picon, Gaetan, 146

"Pilgrimage" (Vallejo), 232–33

Platen, August Graf von, 499

Plato, xxi, 24, 116

Plotinus, 545

Poe, Edgar Allan, 5

"Poem after Leopardi" (Strand), 499

"Poema para ser leído y cantado" (Vallejo), 237

"Poem Called George, Sometimes" (Flint), 523

"Poem to Commemorate General Eisenhower's Visit to Generalissimo Franco in December, 1959" (Wright), 240

Poet in New York, The (Lorca), 146, 152, 153, 177, 511

Poetry, 48, 58, 63, 69, 92, 95, 98, 125, 129, 137, 148, 149, 152, 165, 177, 199–200, 226, 264, 270, 275, 293, 431

Poetry Center, 462, 470

Poetry Northwest, 372

Poetry Society of America (PSA), xxxi, 223, 225, 228; Melville Cane citation, 374

Poetry of Vision, The (Zweig), 334

Poetry Workshop of Iowa, 48

Poets Against the War in Vietnam, xxx

Pollack, Felix, 368

"Politics" (Nerval), 262

"Politics and the English Language" (Orwell), 140

Pope, Alexander, 77, 354

Portland State University, 179

Pound, Ezra, 166–67, 295, 352, 498

Prabhavananda, Swami, 322

"Prayer for Several Kind Women" (Wright), 583

"Problems of Poetry" (Valéry), 141–42

Pugatch, Eugene, xiv, xxviii, 4, 51, 253–56, 360

Pugh, Katherine, 525

Pulitzer Prize, xxx, 300, 306, 374, 443

Pushkin, Alexander, 421–22, 430

Pythagoras, 529

Quarterly Review of Literature, 206, 270, 372

Quasimodo, Salvatore, 241

Quinn, Bernetta, 287, 366–67, 406–8

Rago, Henry, 69, 168, 226, 230, 263

Ramakrishna, Sri, 321–22, 355

"Rampart of Twigs, The" (Char), 88

Ramsey, Paul, 428, 475–76

Random House, 63, 146, 161

Ransom, John Crowe ("Pappy"), xxii, xxviii, 4, 16, 19, 49, 50, 52, 59, 76, 88, 92–95, 204–5, 219, 220, 295, 356, 356–58, 363, 474
Ráshed, Sheila, 515
Ray, David, xxx
Ray, Johnny, 528
Read, Herbert, 73, 149, 364
Reason and Energy: Studies in German Literature (Hamburger), 166
"Red Bow, The" (Dickey), 150
Redwings and the Secret of Light (Wright), 442
Reed College, 207
Rembrandt van Rijn, 517
Reminiscences of Tolstoy (Gorky), 73
Republican Party, 35
Revolt of the Masses, The (Ortega y Gasset), 505
Rexroth, Kenneth, 80, 81, 116–17, 240, 292–94, 298, 479
Reynolds, Tim, 293, 294
Rice, Harvey, 285–86
Rice, Philip Blair, xxii, xxviii, 204, 304
Richards, I. A., 418
Richer, Miss, 290–92
Rider on the White Horse, The (Storm), xxx, 281, 288
Rilke, Rainer Maria, xxi, 28–31, 33, 60, 113, 115, 147, 166, 355, 446, 463, 513, 523; translations of works of, xxviii, xxix, 176, 256, 446, 558, 588
Rimbaud, Arthur, 142, 177
"Rime of the Ancient Mariner, The" (Coleridge), 143
Ripon College, 338
Rizzardi, Alfredo, 165, 202
Robbin, Harvey, 51
"Robert Burns of Ayreshire" (Mezey), 323
Robinson, Edwin Arlington, xxi, xxiv, 126, 131, 181, 182, 185, 186, 220, 260, 265, 267, 298, 304, 434, 473
Robinson, Sugar Ray, 426

Rockefeller Foundation, xxx
Rodin, Auguste, 29
Roethke, Beatrice, 69, 76–77, 83, 86, 137–39, 159, 361
Roethke, Theodore, xxi, xxii, xxxi, 64, 124, 147, 160, 168, 216, 265, 295–97, 361, 498, 545; letters to, xiv, 68–71, 76–77, 81–86, 137–39, 157–59, 207–8; studies with, xxviii, 55, 248
Romantics, 143
Roof of Tiger Lilies, A (Hall), 338
Roosevelt, Franklin D., 34
Roots and Wings (St. Martin), 482
"Rosebushes" (Jiménez), 203
Rosenberg, Harold, 216
Rosenthal, M. L., 429–31
Rothberg, Winterset, 138
Rougemont, Denis de, 334
Rousseau, Jean-Jacques, 70
Royal Academy of Arts and Sciences, 404
Ruark, Gibbons, xiv, xvi, xxxi, 379–80, 487, 494–95, 532–33
Ruark, Kay, 379–80, 487, 532–33
Runk, Edith Anne, *see* Wright, Anne
Runk, Jane, 395, 399, 487, 501

Sainte-Beuve, Charles-Augustin, 120
Saint Judas (Wright), xxix, 83, 86, 87, 152, 168, 173n, 183, 201, 204, 218, 219, 222–23, 248, 269, 274, 275, 318, 368, 427
"Saint Judas" (Wright), 89
St. Martin, Hardie, 482
St. Scholastic, College of, 298
Salamanca, J. R., 545–46
Sanfedele, Ann, xiv, 421–22, 541–42
Sanity of Art, The (Shaw), 116
Santayana, George, 133
Sappho, xxi
Sarah Lawrence College, 341
Sarton, May, 124
"Schlaf, Der" (Trakl), 165, 170

Schlussnuss, Heinrich, 420
Schmitt, John, 51
Schneider, Barbara, 327
Schneider, Franz, 257, 266
Schubert, David, 512
Schubert, Franz, 397
Schulman, Grace, 462, 470
Scribner's Publishers, 222
"Searching for the Ox" (Simpson),
    434
Secker & Warburg, 81, 83
"Secret of Light, The" (Wright), 437
Seeing Is Believing (Tomlinson), 168
Seferis, Georgios, 172
Self and Other, The (Ortega y Gasset),
    253
Sewanee Review, 58, 63, 93, 95, 105,
    107, 120n, 124, 127, 128, 130, 138,
    143, 145, 150, 156, 159–62, 177,
    210, 250, 262, 263, 426
Sexton, Anne, 204n, 239, 246–47,
    266–67, 464–65, 468–69
Shakespeare, William, 31, 42, 43, 64,
    66, 72, 84, 89, 106, 116, 158, 181,
    184, 213, 250, 274, 277, 296, 377,
    422, 425, 427, 484
Shall We Gather at the River (Wright), xxi,
    xxx, 359, 360, 367, 376, 377, 542
Shapiro, Karl, 122
Shaw, Dick, 293–94, 298
Shaw, George Bernard, 72, 116, 254,
    362
Shelley, Percy Bysshe, 18
Sheriff, Helen McNeely, xxii, xxvii,
    374–78, 385, 438–45, 536, 537
Sidney, Philip, 296
Silkin, Jon, 146
Silko, Leslie Marmon, xiii, xiv, xxxi,
    508–9, 519–20, 538, 540–41
Silver, Dr. Irving, 472
Simon, John, 127
Simpson, Annie, 310
Simpson, Dorothy, 266, 272, 273,
    300–302, 306, 308, 434
Simpson, Louis, xxix, 63, 103, 140,
    145, 180–81, 202, 229, 234, 251,

253, 266–68, 276, 348, 389, 455,
    473, 539; anthology edited by, 120,
    141, 143; at Bly's farm, xxix, 272,
    273; letters to, 300–302, 306–10,
    434–35
Sir George Williams University, 378
Sisley, Alfred, 540–42
Sixties, The, 120n, 257, 265, 330
Sixties Press, xxix, xxx
Sleepers Joining Hands (Bly), 381–83
Small Song (Mezey), 548
Smith, Dave, 427–29, 465
Smith, H. Allen, 239
Smith, William, 124
"Snow" (Quasimodo), 241
Snodgrass, W. D., 116, 121, 132, 136,
    139, 145, 228, 231, 238–39, 258–
    61, 456
Snyder, Gary, 116, 117, 267, 276,
    470
Socrates, 43n, 143
"Sole Arabian Bird, The" (Wilmot),
    324–25
Solomon, Richard, 44
Something Tugging at the Line (Jellema),
    545
Sommers, Hollis, 439
Song of God, The (Prabhavananda and
    Isherwood), 322
"Song of Myself" (Whitman), 364
"Sonnet—Peace" (Wright), 556
Sonnets from the Portuguese (Browning),
    9
Sophocles, 30, 250
Southern Review, 389
Spears, Monroe, 92, 105, 107, 138,
    159
Spender, Stephen, 70, 433
Spillane, Mickey, 160
Spinoza, Baruch, 520
Springs of Silence (DeFrees), 257
Springsteen, Bruce, 527
"Springtime Salvation" (Guillén),
    241
Stafford, William, 179, 276
Stange, Bob, 76, 82

Stein, Arnold, 67, 68, 295–97
Sterne, Laurence, xxi, 72, 73
Stevens, Cat, 387
Stevens, Wallace, 220, 478, 498, 523
Stevenson, Adlai, 65
Stevenson, David, 377
"Still, Citizen Sparrow" (Wilbur), 546
Stitt, Peter, 465, 482, 511, 512, 534
Stoneburner, Tony, 474
"Stopping by Woods on a Snowy
  Evening" (Frost), 315
Storck, John, 500, 524–25
Storm, Emil, 288
Storm, Theodor, xxviii, xxx, 51, 281,
  288–90, 294, 303, 318, 371, 489,
  512
"Storyteller" (Silko), 509
Strand, Mark, 373, 498–99
Strauss, Johann, 399
Strindberg, August, 33
String Too Short to Be Saved (Hall), 391,
  396, 453
Summoning of Stones, A (Hecht), 81
"Supermarket in California, A" (Gins-
  berg), 73, 80
Surtees, Robert Smith, 79
Susini, Professor, 112
Suspect in Poetry, The (Dickey), 262
Sutcliffe, Denham, 45, 474
Swift, Jonathan, 96–97, 99, 205, 251
Swinburne, Algernon, 31

Tagore, Rabindranath, 350–51
Taine, Hippolyte, 120
Tanks, Annie, 385
"Tarde" (Lorca), 251–52, 586
Tate, Allen, xxix, 67, 69–71, 73, 76,
  82, 84–86, 93, 126, 138, 219, 222,
  229, 255, 331, 341, 357, 362–63,
  564
Tate, Helen, 363
Taylor, Elizabeth, 331
Teapot Dome Scandal, 308
Teasdale, Sara, 127
Tenney, Tom, 48

Tennyson, Alfred, Lord, 150
This Journey (Wright), xxii, xxxii
Thomas, Debra, xiv, 492–94
Thomas, Dylan, 108, 118, 206–7
Thomas, Edward, xxi, 246–47
Thoreau, Henry David, 68, 91, 490
Thorpe, Jim, 173
"Three Husbands" (Wright), 127
Thurn, Janice, xi–xii, xiv, 418–19,
  447–48, 459–60, 467–68, 489–90,
  501–2, 535–36
Tillotson, Kathleen, 72, 79
Timberlake, Philip, xxii, xxviii, 4, 34,
  49, 52, 65–67, 83–84, 184, 185n,
  186, 192, 474
Time, 78, 117
Tintoretto, 393
To a Blossoming Pear Tree (Wright), xxii,
  xxiv, xxxi, 346, 492
"To a Girl Heavy with Child"
  (Wright), 248–49, 584–85
"To Build a Sonnet" (Wright), 325
"To Evan" (Eberhart), 160
"To Flood Stage Again" (Wright), 367
"To Keats" (Wright), 555
Tolstoy, Leo, xxi, 26–27, 29, 72, 73,
  186, 261, 430
Tomlinson, Charles, 168
"To My Infant Daughter" (Winters),
  160
Torres, Ines Delgado de, 288, 289
"To the Snake" (Levertov), 177
"To Wayne Burns: On the Appear-
  ance of a New Edition of Swift's
  Poems" (Wright), 567–68
"Toy Bone, The" (Hall), 391
Trakl, Georg, xxi, xxiv, xxviii, 113,
  114, 166, 176n, 177, 181, 219, 237,
  245, 317–18, 512; translations of
  works of, xxix, 165, 169, 170, 221,
  226–27, 231, 236, 240, 252–53,
  273, 587
Tranströmer, Tomas, 316–18
Treasure Island (Stevenson), 139
Tree of Wooden Clogs, The (movie),
  543

"Trees in Minnesota, The" (Wright), 166, 569–70
Trilce (Vallejo), 429
"Tristan" (Platen), 499
Tristram Shandy (Sterne), 73, 129, 239
"Triumph of Life, The" (Shelley), 143
"Troubador Removed, A" (Hugo), 117–19
Truesdale, C. W. "Bill," xxx, 281–82, 372
"True Voice, A" (Wright), 534
"True Weather for Women, The" (Simpson), 302
Truman, Harry S., 34, 35
Tufts University, 96
Tu Fu, 293, 340
Turner, Lisa Kayan, 471, 475
Turpin, Randy, 426
Twain, Mark, 405, 444
Twelve Moons (Oliver), 546
Twelve Spanish American Poets (Hays), 543
Twenty-Seven Poems (Hecht), 353
Two Cheers for Democracy (Forster), 501
Two Citizens (Wright), xxi–xxii, xxxi, 428–29, 455

Ulysses (Joyce), 35n, 218
"Unborn Child" (Hall), 63
"Und dann und wann ein weisser Elephant" (Rilke), 513
"Under a Streetlight" (Wright), 201
"Under the Canals" (Wright), 456
University of Kansas City Review, 63
Urseth, Sonjia, 75–76
Ussachevsky, Vladimir, 345, 421–22
Utah State University, 465

"Vain Season, The" (Wright), 581
Valentine, Jean, 408
Valéry, Paul, 63, 118, 141–44, 156, 165, 174–75

Vallejo, César, xxi, xxix, 138, 147, 210–11, 219, 228, 232–33, 237, 245, 251, 258–59, 266–67, 371, 429, 512, 543–44
"Verdict" (Vallejo), 251
Verlaine, Paul, 142
Vermeer, Jan, 517
Victor, Tom, 367
Vienna, University of, xxviii, 4, 49, 58, 112, 376, 396, 440
Viereck, Peter, 70
Villon, François, 108
Virgil, 5, 32, 376, 496, 534
Virginia Quarterly, 241
"Visit to the Earth, A" (Wright), 597–99
Volonte, Gian Maria, 526

Wagner, Richard, 51
Wagoner, David, xxviii, 139, 168, 207, 208, 216, 371–72, 475, 520
Wagoner, Patt, 372
Wahlverwandschaten, Die (Goethe), 372
"Waking, The" (Roethke), 70, 85
Wakoski, Diane, 364, 496–98
Waldrup, Keith, 532
Waley, Arthur, 169, 513
Walker Art Center (Minneapolis), 70, 82, 85
"Walking Around" (Neruda), 172n, 232n, 544, 572–73
Walt Whitman International Poetry Center, 512
Wandering (Hesse), xxxi, 375
War and Peace (Tolstoy), 26–27
Warren, Austin, 474–75
Warren, Robert Penn, 94–95, 124, 138, 372
Washington, University of, xii, xiv, xxii, xxviii, xxix, 55, 58, 63, 74, 75, 82, 117, 172, 219, 440, 475, 520
Washington University, Department of Special Collections, xiv

"Way to Death, The" (Hall), 133
Wayne State University, 93
Weiss, Theodore, 372
Weissman, Sy, 51
Welch, Jim, 427
Welch, Raquel, 527
"Wendung" (Rilke), 166
Wesleyan University Press, xxix, xxx,
    192–93, 199, 204, 218, 222, 223,
    232, 273–75, 317, 355, 357, 359,
    360, 366, 368, 375, 542
West, Nathanael, 258
West, Ray B., Jr., 77
Western Review, 58, 95
West of Childhood (Gardner), 340
Westigan Review, The, 479
"What a Man Can Stand" (Wright), *see*
    "Winter Day in Ohio, A"
What Thou Lovest Well Remains American
    (Hugo), 426
Wheelock, John Hall, 222
Wheelock College, 378
Where Is My Wandering Boy Tonight?
    (Wagoner), 372
"Wherever Home Is" (Wright), 229
"Whisper to the Ghost Who Woke
    Me, A" (Wright), 260, 589–90
"White Buildings" (Crane), 32
Whitman, Walt, xxi, xxiv, 16, 29, 87,
    112, 113, 114, 122, 131, 147, 149,
    181, 184–86, 219, 220, 235, 246,
    253, 267, 364, 512, 523
Whittemore, Reed, 93, 187
Whyte, L. L., 403
Wilbur, Richard, 51, 137, 189, 546
Wilde, Oscar, 132
Wilderness Stair (Belitt), 241
Wilkinson, Connie, 408
Willerton, Elizabeth, *see* Esterly, Eliza-
    beth Willerton
Williams, C. K., 478
Williams, Oscar, 240, 315–16
Williams, William Carlos, 232, 352,
    361
Wilmot, John, Earl of Rochester, 324–
    25

Wilson, Woodrow, 353
"Winter Day in Ohio, A" (Wright),
    83*n*, 182, 185*n*, 186, 189, 191–92
"Winter Night" (Trakl), 226–27
Winters, Jonathan, 336
Winters, Yvor, 130, 160, 184–85, 218–
    19, 235, 295–96
Wisconsin, University of: Library,
    Marvin Sukov Little Magazine Col-
    lection, 368; at Milwaukee, 345,
    351, 357, 378
"Witches Waken the Natural World in
    Spring" (Wright), 247–48
"With a Sliver of Marble from Car-
    rara" (Wright), 456
With Ignorance (Williams), 478
Wolfe, Thomas, xxi, 7, 12, 14, 16, 27,
    37, 39–40, 432
Woman in White, The (Collins), 78
"Woman Too Well Remembered, A"
    (Simpson), 301–2
Wood, Frank, 240
Woodlanders, The (Hardy), 313–14
Woods, John, 139, 179, 188
Woolman, Russell J., 439, 443, 445
Words for the Wind (Roethke), 81, 138
Wordsworth, William, 7, 29
"Work of Art, The" (Dickey), 150, 206
"Work of Our Hands, The" (Jellema),
    545–46
Wormwood Review, 233
Wozzeck (Berg), 51
Wright, Anne (second wife), 353, 355,
    358, 360, 363, 367, 370–75, 382,
    385, 387, 389, 403, 410, 411, 415,
    438, 439, 443–45, 454, 457, 460–
    61, 480, 482, 488, 489, 493, 495,
    503, 506, 508, 539, 542, 547, 548;
    European travels of, xxx, xxxi, 345,
    383, 388, 391, 392, 394, 396, 398–
    400, 404, 407, 447, 471–74, 478,
    487, 491, 499, 501, 507, 509, 510,
    512, 513, 515, 517, 518, 524–26,
    528, 533, 536, 537; in Hawaii, 441,
    451–53, 460; letters to, 350–51,
    365; marriage to, xxx, 345, 357,

359, 362, 377–78, 380, 390, 426,
440
Wright, Dianna (Theodore Jr.'s wife),
386
Wright, Dudley (father), xv, xxvii, xxxi,
3, 8, 326–27, 346, 351, 382, 386,
400, 410
Wright, Franz (son), xxix, xxxi, 52, 55,
69, 138, 174, 230, 267, 270, 299,
319–21, 357, 447, 482, 532; birth
of, xxviii, 4, 51; in Europe, 370–71;
letters to, 283, 327–28, 399–402,
445–46, 523–24, 528–29; at Oberlin College, 375, 379, 386
Wright, Helen (sister-in-law), xiv, 439,
443
Wright, Jack (brother), xxvii, 8, 310–
11, 327, 329, 335, 356, 385, 386,
410, 457–58, 527–28, 531–32
Wright, James: Army service of, xxiii,
xxvii–xxviii, 3, 6, 8–10, 18–20,
112; awards and honors of, xxx–
xxxi, 300, 374, 443; birth of, xxvii,
318; birth of sons of, xxviii, xxix, 4,
51, 103, 137–38, 147–48, 151, 153,
155, 163; Bly farm visits of, 103,
155, 163, 165, 220–21, 223, 244–
45, 256, 261–62, 267–68, 273, 281,
282, 300, 334, 335, 338, 347, 375–
76; breakup of first marriage, xxviii,
223, 228–30, 236–37, 268, 281,
375, 536, 509; childhood and ado-
lescence in Martins Ferry, Ohio,
xxiii, xxvii, 75, 112, 250, 379, 497;
doctoral dissertation of, 69, 72, 76,
79, 82, 98, 99, 127, 136, 152–53,
155–56, 169, 190, 201, 203, 207,
208, 219, 229; emotional illnesses of,
xxvii, 75, 181, 183, 197, 209–10,
216–17, 230, 236, 247–49, 276,
323–24, 327, 346, 356, 358, 371,
408–12, 472, 497; European travels
of, xxx, xxxi, 345–46, 387–404,
407, 472–77, 480, 486, 487, 490,
492, 501–3, 507, 509, 510, 513–42,
547; final illness and death of, xii,

xxxii, 487–88, 548–50; Fulbright
Scholarship to Vienna of, xxviii, 4,
47, 49–51, 112–13; graduate studies and teaching at University of
Washington, xxviii, xxix, 55, 63,
65–68, 74, 75; Guggenheim Fellowships of, xxx, xxxi, 281, 305, 337,
339, 354, 356, 359, 375, 440, 487,
507; at Kenyon College, xxi, xxviii,
3–4, 16, 44–50, 58, 61, 66, 463;
Macalester College guest professorship of, xxix, xxx, 242, 281, 285–
86, 303–5, 311; marries Anne, xi,
xxx, 345, 351, 377–78; marries Liberty, xxviii, 4, 47; New York City life
and teaching of, xi, 282, 344–47,
349, 353–57, 359, 360, 362, 376–
78, 414, 415, 419, 438, 447, 457–
58, 466, 467, 471, 478, 480, 482,
487, 489, 493–96, 500, 501, 547;
and parents' deaths, xxxi, 346, 410;
on University of Minnesota faculty,
xxix, 55, 69–73, 77, 81, 84–85, 99,
206, 216, 230, 233, 237, 241, 274,
281
Wright, Jessie Lyons (mother), xxvii,
xxxi, 3, 8, 9, 346, 351, 386, 410
Wright, Liberty Kardules, see Kovacs,
Liberty Kardules Wright
Wright, Marge (sister), xxvii, 8
Wright, Marshall (son), xxix, 173–74,
183, 327, 328, 346, 357, 375, 379;
birth of, xxix, 103, 137–38, 153; letters to, 299–300, 321–22, 387–88,
437–38, 472–73, 510; on trip to
Europe, 345
Wright, Richard, 14
Wright, Theodore (brother), xxvii,
351, 356, 386, 410, 439, 443
Wright, Theodore, Jr. (nephew), 386
"Written on a Big Cheap Postcard
from Verona" (Wright), 456
"Written on a Bus in Central Ohio"
(Wright), 511
Wyatt, Thomas, 301, 457, 464, 468,
469

Yaddo Artists' Colony, 82, 466
Yale Review, The, 70, 92, 95, 138, 207
Yale University Press, xxviii, 62, 65,
  68, 83, 87, 126, 275
"Year Changes in the City" (Wright), 582
Yeats, William Butler, 84, 94, 254, 297,
  316

You Can't Go Home Again (Wolfe), 14
Youngblood, Sarah, xxix, 316

Zea, Carlo de Francisco, 242
Zulauf, Sander, 537
Zweig, Paul, 334, 338